INTERNATIONAL
BUSINESS

3E

Les R. Dlabay

James Calvert Scott

THOMSON

SOUTH-WESTERN

Australia · Canada · Mexico · Singapore · Spain · United Kingdom · United States

THOMSON

SOUTH-WESTERN

International Business 3e

Les R. Dlabay and James Calvert Scott

VP/Editorial Director
Jack W. Calhoun

VP/Editor-in-Chief
Karen Schmohe

Executive Editor
Eve Lewis

Project Manager
Enid Nagel

Production Manager
Patricia Matthews Boies

Production Editor
Colleen A. Farmer

VP/Director of Marketing
Carol Volz

Senior Marketing Manager
Nancy Long

Marketing Coordinator
Angela A. Russo

Editorial Assistant
Linda Keith

Manufacturing Coordinator
Kevin Kluck

Art Director
Stacy Jenkins Shirley

Cover Illustrator
© Kevin Ghiglione/i2iart.com

Cover and Internal Designer
Joseph Pagliaro Graphic Design

Compositor
Electro-Publishing

Printer
Courier, Kendallville

ASIA (including India)
Thomson Learning
5 Shenton Way
#01-01 UIC Building
Singapore 068808

CANADA
Thomson Nelson
1120 Birchmount Road
Toronto, Ontario
Canada M1K 5G4

AUSTRALIA/NEW ZEALAND
Thomson Learning Australia
102 Dodds Street
Southbank, Victoria 3006
Australia

UK/EUROPE/MIDDLE
EAST/AFRICA
Thomson Learning
High Holborn House
50-51 Bedford Road
London WC1R 4LR
United Kingdom

LATIN AMERICA
Thomson Learning
Seneca, 53
Colonia Polanco
11560 Mexico
D.F.Mexico

SPAIN (includes Portugal)
Thomson Paraninfo
Calle Magallanes, 25
28015 Madrid, Spain

Don't Settle for the Status Quo!

Marketing Yourself

Knowing how to sell yourself is critical to success in any field. **Marketing Yourself** utilizes a marketing framework to develop a self-marketing plan and portfolio. The self-marketing plan is based on the analysis of student marketable skills and abilities. Every student text includes a Portfolio CD.

Text/Portfolio CD Package 0-538-43640-9

Entrepreneurship: Ideas in Action 3E

Take students step-by-step through the entire process of owning and managing a business. Focus their attention on the real skills required of entrepreneurs – start with meeting a market need and work through planning, financing, incorporating technology, hiring, managing, and avoiding legal problems. Students learn by doing using the innovative, activity-based **Build a Business Plan** in every chapter. **Winning Edge** gets students prepared for **BPA, DECA,** and **FBLA** competition.

Text 0-538-44122-4

Workbook 0-538-44124-0

Law for Business and Personal Use 17E

Give your students the most comprehensive coverage of cyberlaw, contracts, ethics, employment law, banking, bankruptcy, and personal law available in one book. Maintain your fundamental emphasis on business law, while presenting topics such as criminal law, marriage law, and wills. Expand your classroom by using the free Xtra! Web Site, which contains a wealth of online learning tools. **Winning Edge** gets students prepared for **BPA** and **FBLA** competition.

Text 0-538-44051-1

Activities and Study Guide 0-538-44065-1

E-Commerce Marketing

Prepare students to plan and market electronic products and services online. Explore electronically linked distribution systems, international e-commerce, digital media design, e-tailing, online customer behavior, data mining and warehousing, and security/privacy issues. **DECA Prep** Case Studies and Event Prep included in every chapter.

Text 0-538-43808-8

Module (ExamView CD, Instructor's Resource CD, Video, and Annotated Instructor's Edition) 0-538-43810-X

Investing in Your Future 2E

Start students on the path to dollars and sense. Use NAIC's respected Stock Selection Guide process to teach smart saving, investing, and planning. Students learn how to analyze the value of stocks and mutual funds. Company Profiles introduce every chapter and the lesson-plan approach makes material easy to comprehend.

Text 0-538-43881-9

Module (ExamView CD, Instructor's Resource CD, Video, and Annotated Instructor's Edition) 0-538-43885-1

THOMSON
SOUTH-WESTERN

Instructor Support and Other Materials Available
Join us on the Internet at www.swlearning.com

HOW TO USE THIS BOOK
ENGAGE STUDENT INTEREST

IF YOU WERE THERE Describes the life of an ordinary person living in the highlighted region.

REGIONAL PROFILE
Discusses the general historical, cultural, social, and economic conditions in the various regions around the world.

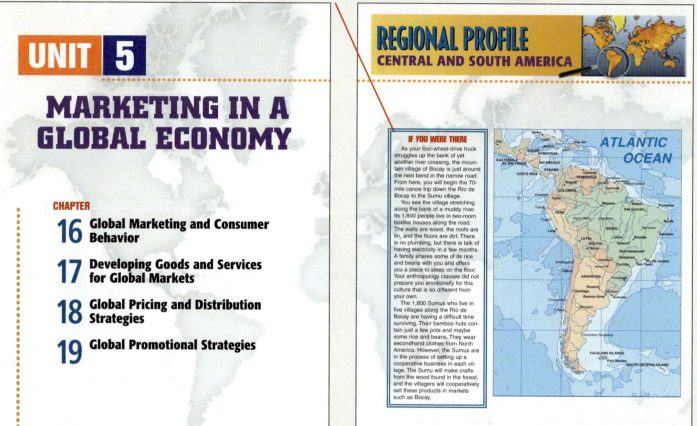

UNIT 5

MARKETING IN A GLOBAL ECONOMY

CHAPTER

16 Global Marketing and Consumer Behavior

17 Developing Goods and Services for Global Markets

18 Global Pricing and Distribution Strategies

19 Global Promotional Strategies

REGIONAL PROFILE
CENTRAL AND SOUTH AMERICA

ATLANTIC OCEAN

IF YOU WERE THERE

As your four-wheel-drive truck struggles up the bank of yet another river crossing, the mountain village of Bocay is just around the next bend in the narrow road. From here, you will begin the 70-mile canoe trip down the Río de Bocay to the Sumu village.

You see the village stretching along the bank of a muddy river. Its 1,800 people live in two-room boxlike houses along the road. The walls are wood, the roofs are tin, and the floors are dirt. There is no plumbing, but there is talk of having electricity in a few months. A family shares some of its rice and beans with you and offers you a place to sleep on the floor. Your anthropology classes did not prepare you emotionally for this culture that is so different from your own.

The 1,800 Sumus who live in five villages along the Río de Bocay are having a difficult time surviving. Their bamboo huts contain just a few pots and maybe some rice and beans. They wear secondhand clothes from North America. However, the Sumus are in the process of setting up a cooperative business in each village. The Sumu will make crafts from the wood found in the forest, and the villagers will cooperatively sell these products in markets such as Bocay.

COUNTRY PROFILE
Presents key economic and social data about each country in the region.

REGIONAL PROFILE/CENTRAL AND SOUTH AMERICA

COUNTRY PROFILE/CENTRAL AND SOUTH AMERICA

Country	Population (thousands)	Population growth rate %	GDP $billions	GDP $ per capita	Exports $billions	Imports $billions	Monetary Unit	Inflation percent	Unemployment percent	Life Expectancy years	Literacy Rate percent
Antigua and Barbuda	72	0.69	0.67	10,000	0.4	0.46	East Caribbean Dollar	0.4	11	71.31	89
Argentina	38,428	1.17	392	10,200	26.7	20.3	Peso	41	21.5	75.48	97.1
Bahamas, The	295	1.13	5	16,800	0.61	1.77	Bahamian Dollar	1.8	6.9	65.71	95.6
Barbados	270	0.35	4	14,500	0.29	1.03	Barbadian Dollar	-0.6	10	71.84	97.4
Belize	256	2.06	0.83	3,250	0.21	0.4	Belizean Dollar	1.9	9.1	67.36	94.1
Bolivia	8,808	1.89	21.4	2,600	1.29	1.49	Boliviano	2	7.6	64.78	87.2
Brazil	178,470	1.24	1,340	7,400	58.2	57.7	Real	8.3	6.4	71.13	86.4
Chile	15,805	1.23	153	10,000	18.5	16.4	Chilean Peso	2.5	9.2	76.35	96.2
Colombia	44,222	1.59	255	6,300	12.8	12.3	Colombian Peso	6.2	17.4	71.14	92.5
Costa Rica	4,173	1.93	31.9	8,500	4.91	6.12	Costa Rican Colon	9.1	6.3	76.43	96
Cuba	11,300	0.27	25.9	2,300	1.8	4.8	Cuban Peso	7.1	4.1	76.8	97
Dominica	70	0.29	0.26	3,700	0.5	0.13	East Caribbean Dollar	1	23	74.12	94
Dominican Republic	8,745	1.49	50	5,800	5.33	8.78	Dominican Peso	5.3	14.5	67.96	84.7
Ecuador	13,003	1.49	39.6	3,000	4.86	5.33	U.S. Dollar	12.5	7.7	71.89	92.5
El Salvador	6,515	1.55	28.4	4,600	2.9	4.81	U.S. Dollar	3.8	10	70.62	80.2
Grenada	89	-0.26	0.42	4,750	0.85	0.22	East Caribbean Dollar	2.8	12.5	64.52	98
Guatemala	12,347	2.55	48.3	3,700	2.87	5.14	Quetzal	8.1	7.5	65.23	70.6
Guyana	765	0.24	2.5	3,600	0.5	0.54	Guyanese Dollar	4.7	9.1	63.09	98.8
Haiti	8,326	1.32	12	1,700	0.3	0.64	Gourde	11.9	NA	51.61	52.9
Honduras	6,941	2.34	17	2,600	1.93	2.81	Lempira	7.7	28	66.65	76.2
Jamaica	2,651	0.92	9.8	3,700	1.6	3.1	Jamaican Dollar	7	15.4	75.85	87.9
Nicaragua	5,466	2.43	12.3	2,500	0.6	1.63	Gold Cordoba	3.7	24	69.68	67.5
Panama	3,120	1.84	16.9	5,900	5.88	6.71	Balboa	1.1	16	72.32	92.6
Paraguay	5,878	2.37	26.2	4,600	2.41	2.95	Guarani	10.5	18.2	74.4	94
Peru	27,167	1.5	132	4,800	7.11	7.2	Nuevo Sol	0.2	9.4	70.88	90.9
Saint Kitts and Nevis	39	-0.3	0.34	8,700	0.06	0.17	East Caribbean Dollar	1.7	4.5	71.57	97
Saint Lucia	149	0.78	0.7	4,400	0.06	0.31	East Caribbean Dollar	3	16.5	73.08	67
Saint Vincent and the Grenadines	116	0.58	0.34	2,900	0.05	0.14	East Caribbean Dollar	-0.4	22	73.08	96
São Tomé and Príncipe	155	0.8	1.5	3,500	0.01	0.02	Dobra	9	N/A	66.28	79.3
Suriname	436	0.71	1.48	3,500	0.44	0.3	Surinamese Guilder	17	17	69.23	93
Trinidad and Tobago	1,303	0.34	10.6	9,000	2.26	3	Trinidad and Tobago Dollar	4.3	10.8	69.59	98.6

©Paul Hilton/ EPA/ Landov

● **Chapter 17**

DEVELOPING GOODS AND SERVICES FOR GLOBAL MARKETS

17-1 Global Product Planning

17-2 Developing and Researching Products

17-3 An International Product Strategy

GLOBAL FOCUS Introduces real-world examples of companies engaged in international business activities.

445

CHECKPOINT Short questions within lesson to assist with reading and to assure students are grasping concepts.

WORK AS A GROUP Stimulates group discussion and cooperative learning.

17-1 | GLOBAL PRODUCT PLANNING

GOALS

- Describe sources of product opportunities for international marketing.
- Identify categories of consumer products and the importance of product lines.
- Explain how services are marketed.

©Getty Images/PhotoDisc

GOALS Begin each lesson and offer an overview.

INTERNATIONAL PRODUCT OPPORTUNITIES

Every day you see advertisements for clothing, food, motor vehicles, financial services, Internet sites, and other consumer goods and services. It sometimes seems as though everyone has something to sell. When you apply for a job, you also are selling your talents and abilities. The product offerings of global companies are the foundation of international business and foreign trade.

A *product* is a marketplace offering (good or service) that satisfies a need or want. Marketing's major goal is to satisfy needs that have not been met. This can be accomplished in one of four ways: a new product, an improved product, an existing product with a new use, or an existing product sold in a new market.

New Product An organization's marketing activities may start with a marketplace offering that did not previously exist. For example, Federal Express pioneered overnight delivery services. Now, several companies are involved in this industry.

Improved Product Sometimes a product is on the market for several years, but it may no longer be as popular with consumers. When this happens, a company may introduce variations, such as new flavors of a food product. Also, technology may result in improved versions of an item.

Existing Product with a New Use When a company wants to expand its sales, it may attempt to find new uses for a product that has been on the market for years. Various kitchen storage containers have been adapted to store tools and supplies for a home workshop or office.

Existing Product Sold in a New Market In the late 1970s and early 1980s, when fewer babies were born in the U.S., Johnson Baby Shampoo was advertised as being mild for adults who wanted to shampoo every day. Selling existing products in new markets is a significant part of international business. Soft drinks, fast foods, and hundreds of other products that originated in one country are now sold in the global marketplace.

✓ CheckPoint
What are four ways a company can satisfy the consumer's needs that have not been met?

MARKETING PRODUCTS AROUND THE WORLD

Each day people around the world buy and use thousands of different products. A student in Brazil buys a home computer, while a person in Egypt purchases a bottled soft drink.

CONSUMER PRODUCT CATEGORIES
The many items sold in the global market can be classified as convenience goods, shopping goods, or specialty goods, as shown in Figure 17-1.

Convenience Goods You probably buy low-cost items on a regular basis without thinking much about them. **Convenience goods** are inexpensive items that require little shopping effort. Examples include snacks, soft drinks, personal care products, and school supplies. Marketing for convenience goods involves offering an item in many locations. For example, candy bars are sold in food stores, movie theaters, gas stations, and vending machines.

Shopping Goods Some products (such as clothing, furniture, cameras, televisions, and home appliances) are purchased only after consumers take

WORK AS A GROUP

Suggest ways to use an existing product in different ways.

Figure 17-1 The items bought by people around the world can be classified as convenience goods, shopping goods, or specialty goods.

TYPES OF CONSUMER PRODUCTS

Convenience Goods

Shopping Goods

Specialty Goods

SPECIAL FEATURES ENHANCE LEARNING

E-COMMERCE IN ACTION

Japanese Convenience Stores Go Online

While Japan trailed other countries in the use of the Internet, consumers in that country were making use of e-commerce through convenience stores. Online shoppers are able to buy a late-night snack of seaweed-covered rice balls with mayonnaise or chocolate chip *mochi* (rice cakes) from their local *combini*—the Japanese name for convenience store.

7-Eleven Japan had an agreement with a software company and other companies to sell programs, videos, books, and other products over the Internet. Japanese consumers can choose from one of the more than 10,000 7-Eleven stores in Japan and have the merchandise delivered to their home.

Think Critically
1. Why might customers buy online?
2. What are the benefits of selling online for convenience stores?
3. Find web sites that allow consumers to buy food online.

E-COMMERCE IN ACTION Analyzes the technological needs and concerns of businesses in a global context.

Communication Across Borders

THE EVAPORATING E-MAIL MESSAGE

Jason Pierson was frustrated. He had waited impatiently for 72 hours—three full working days—for a reply to his urgent request for information from the Nairobi, Kenya, office. At midnight local time, he telephoned his Kenyan counterpart.

"Why haven't you responded to my e-mail message? I sent it three days ago. I need the information now."

"What e-mail message are you talking about, sir? I haven't received any e-mails for four days. The last one I got from you was about two weeks ago."

"But I sent it three days ago. It's urgent."

"Mr. Pierson, you've got to realize that Kenya is a developing country. Yes, we have e-mail, but it doesn't always work. The connections to the Internet aren't very good, I'm afraid. Sometimes our power goes out. We have no backup power system. When that happens, we lose everything."

Think Critically
1. Why did Jason Pierson place his call to Nairobi at midnight his time?
2. Why did Jason Pierson expect a prompt response to his e-mail message?
3. What did Jason Pierson fail to understand about the use of e-mail in developing countries?

A Question of Ethics

SELLING LUXURY ITEMS IN LESS DEVELOPED ECONOMIES

When a company enters a new market in a developing economy, consumers are attracted to the new products. However, many people in these new markets may not be able to afford the items sold by the multinational company.

A fast-food company or cosmetic distributor may start selling its products in a country with a very low income per household. The availability of these new products can create very high demand. People have been known to wait in line for hours to buy a fast-food meal or another item that costs several days' pay. They are willing to make this sacrifice to obtain an item not previously available.

Think Critically
1. What are potential benefits and drawbacks of selling products in countries with very low levels of income?
2. Use the three guidelines for ethical analysis to examine the above situation.

A QUESTION OF ETHICS Challenges students to analyze the ethical implications of certain global business scenarios.

COMMUNICATION ACROSS BORDERS Explains the importance of communication as tool for conducting international business.

REGIONAL PERSPECTIVE

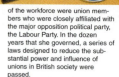

HISTORY: UNIONS IN THE UNITED KINGDOM

In the United Kingdom in 1979, the Conservative Party formed a new government under the leadership of Prime Minister Margaret Thatcher. Mrs. Thatcher believed in a free market economy with as little government intervention or involvement as possible. She also thought that labor unions were preventing the United Kingdom from achieving economic success.

When Prime Minister Margaret Thatcher took office, more than half of the workforce were union members who were closely affiliated with the major opposition political party, the Labour Party. In the dozen years that she governed, a series of laws designed to reduce the substantial power and influence of unions in British society were passed.

Many elements of the new laws in Britain were borrowed from the United States, where labor laws are much less open to abuse. Various types of strikes were outlawed, the role of union leaders was reduced, and workers were given the opportunity to stop having a union represent them or to change unions. As a result, union membership in the United Kingdom has fallen dramatically, and strikes, which were relatively commonplace, occur much less frequently now than in the past.

©Peter Turnley/CORBIS

Think Critically
1. Why did Margaret Thatcher oppose the unions in the United Kingdom?
2. Why was Margaret Thatcher able to radically change the labor laws in the United Kingdom?
3. How do you think the changes in the labor laws benefited the British economy?

REGIONAL PERSPECTIVE Provides in-depth analysis of cultural, social, or historical conditions in the various regions around the world.

GLOBAL BUSINESS EXAMPLE Provides case studies related to international business concepts as they are presented in the lessons.

GLOBAL BUSINESS EXAMPLE

THE TECHIMAN WOMEN'S MARKET CREDIT UNION

Most days for the market women of Techiman begin at sunup and continue until after sundown. The women sell multicolored fabrics and produce dried cassava (a starchy root), soup, furniture, and clothing. As many as 10,000 customers come to the Techiman market in Ghana on a Thursday or Friday.

The vendors in this market need money for stall fees, supplies, school fees, and day care. Before the creation of the Techiman Women's Market Credit Union, moneylenders were the main source of borrowed funds and charged as much as 50–60 percent interest. Now the more than 200 credit union members can borrow at 18 percent interest.

Think Critically
1. What services are commonly offered by credit unions?
2. Go to the web site of the World Council of Credit Unions to obtain current information about this organization. Write a summary of your findings.

TEAM PROJECT Provides an opportunity for students to work as a team to better understand cross-cultural business activities.

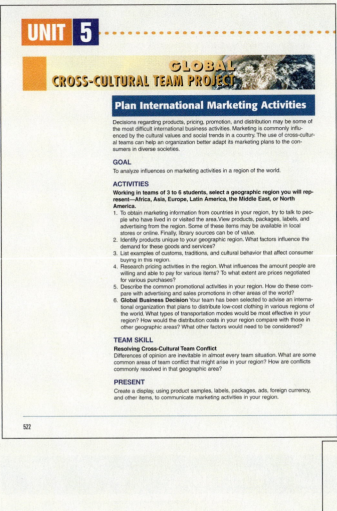

NET BOOKMARK Provides online activities for students on the Xtra! Web Site.

WINNING EDGE Helps students prepare for DECA, BPA, and FBLA competitive events.

ASSESSMENT AND REVIEW

Chapter 17 ASSESSMENT

XTRA! QUIZ PREP Provides an online chapter review with immediate feedback.

CHAPTER SUMMARY

17-1 GLOBAL PRODUCT PLANNING

A The sources of product opportunities for international marketing are new products, improved products, new uses for existing products, and existing products in new markets.

B The categories of consumer products are convenience goods, shopping goods, and specialty goods. A product line provides an assortment of items available for sale to varied target markets.

C Services are marketed with an emphasis on personalization, as they are usually produced as they are consumed.

17-2 DEVELOPING AND RESEARCHING PRODUCTS

A The steps in the new product development process are (1) generating product ideas, (2) evaluating product ideas, (3) researching product ideas, and (4) marketing product ideas. The steps in the marketing research process are (1) identify problem, (2) collect data, (3) analyze data, and (4) report results.

B Data collection methods used in international marketing research include secondary data and primary data (surveys, observations, and experiments).

17-3 AN INTERNATIONAL PRODUCT STRATEGY

A Brands used by companies are names, symbols, or designs that identify a product or service. Packaging is used to protect the product, to capture the attention of customers, and to make the product easy to use.

B A global product strategy involves decisions about whether to offer a standardized version or an adapted version of a good or service.

GLOBAL REFOCUS

Read the Global Focus at the beginning of this chapter, and answer the following questions.

1. In what ways does Mattel use both a global product approach and an international product approach?

2. How might Mattel use technology and joint ventures for continued success of its international operations?

REVIEW GLOBAL BUSINESS TERMS

Match the terms listed with the definitions.

1. Data collected by watching and recording shopping behaviors.

2. Large-scale surveys used to collect numeric data that are often used to study consumers.

3. Products purchased after consumers compare brands and stores.

4. A standardized item that is offered in the same form in all countries in which it is sold.

5. An assortment of closely related products designed to meet the varied needs of target customers.

6. A directed discussion with 8 to 12 people.

7. The stages a good or service goes through from the time it is introduced until it is taken off the market.

8. Inexpensive items that require little shopping effort.

9. A customized product adapted to the culture, tastes, and social trends of a country.

10. The type of data collection that involves a statistical comparison of two or more very similar situations.

11. Open-ended interview questions that allow researchers to obtain comments from consumers about their attitudes and behaviors.

12. The name, symbol, or design that identifies a product.

13. Unique products that consumers make a special effort to obtain.

14. An experimental research study that measures the likely success of a new product or service.

15. The orderly collection and analysis of data that is used to obtain specific marketing information.

- **a.** brand
- **b.** convenience goods
- **c.** experiment
- **d.** focus group
- **e.** global product
- **f.** international product
- **g.** marketing research
- **h.** observational research
- **i.** product life cycle (PLC)
- **j.** product line
- **k.** qualitative research
- **l.** quantitative research
- **m.** shopping goods
- **n.** speciality goods
- **o.** test market

MAKE GLOBAL BUSINESS DECISIONS

16. Why do stores and online retailers have larger product lines than in the past?

17. Name some services that have increased in importance for our economy in recent years.

CHAPTER ASSESSMENT Contains Chapter Summary, Global Refocus, Review Global Business Terms, Make Global Business Decisions, and Global Connections.

Chapter 17 ASSESSMENT

18. List some ideas that could be the basis for new products in our society.

19. Create some examples of topics for international marketing research studies that would be interesting to investigate.

20. When may qualitative research be preferred to quantitative research for a marketing research study?

21. What makes certain brands popular and easy to remember?

22. Does packaging cost too much for certain products? Find examples of products with packaging that could be made less expensive.

23. Why do some items go through the stages of the product life cycle faster than others?

24. Create a list of products that may be sold anywhere in the world without major changes being made. What determines whether an item is a global product or an international product?

GLOBAL CONNECTIONS

25. GEOGRAPHY Describe geographic factors that might influence whether a company could sell its product as it is in other countries or if they would have to adapt it.

26. COMMUNICATIONS Conduct a survey of the products people buy without extensive comparison shopping. How important is place of purchase, price, and brand for these items?

27. HISTORY Talk to older people about products that are no longer on the market. What factors might have influenced the decline of these items?

28. CULTURAL STUDIES Collect advertisements, labels, and packages from products made in other countries. How would you describe the marketing approach for these items?

29. RESEARCH Find examples of secondary data in the library and on the Internet that could help a company with its international marketing activities. Describe how the information could be of value for preparing a global marketing plan.

30. VISUAL ART Prepare a poster or bulletin board display with examples of products or services in the various stages of the product life cycle. Suggest marketing activities that would be appropriate for one item in each stage of the cycle.

31. CAREER PLANNING Select a good or service. Describe the jobs that would be required to make the product available to consumers in another country.

32. TECHNOLOGY Use the Internet to locate online resources for data collection and analysis. Prepare a description of each of the resources you find.

IS INTEGRAL AND ONGOING

17-3 AN INTERNATIONAL PRODUCT STRATEGY

REVIEW GLOBAL BUSINESS TERMS

Define each of the following terms.

1. brand
2. product life cycle (PLC)
3. global product
4. international product

intlbizxtra.swlearning.com

REVIEW GLOBAL BUSINESS CONCEPTS

5. What purpose does packaging serve?
6. What are the stages of the product life cycle?
7. How does a global product differ from an international product?

SOLVE GLOBAL BUSINESS PROBLEMS

Most packaged products sold in the United States and almost all products in other countries use the metric system for weights and liquid measurements. The following is an approximate reference for converting to metric measurements.

When you know:	Multiply by:	To find:
ounces (oz)	28.35	grams (g)
pounds (lb)	0.45	kilograms (kg)
pints (pt)	0.47	liters (l)
quarts (qt)	0.95	liters (l)
gallons (gal)	3.79	liters (l)

8. A 14-ounce package of spaghetti would weigh about _____ grams.
9. Six pounds of cheese would weigh about _____ kilograms.
10. Eight pints of fruit juice is equal to about _____ liters.
11. Three quart bottles of soft drinks contain about _____ liters.
12. Estimate how many gallons are equal to 12 liters. Then check your answer with a calculator. How accurate was your estimate?

THINK CRITICALLY

13. Locate examples of famous brands not associated with packaged products.
14. Explain why different advertising would be needed in different stages of the product life cycle.
15. Why do companies often take legal action against others who try to use the same brand name?

MAKE CONNECTIONS

16. **TECHNOLOGY** What types of technology have improved packaging for consumers and the environment?
17. **CULTURAL STUDIES** How might a nation's customs or traditions affect the brand names used in a country?

465

XTRA! STUDY TOOLS Provides an interactive review of every lesson with games such as Beat the Clock, First Things First, Labeler, Scenario, Sort it Out, and Test Your Knowledge.

END-OF-LESSON ACTIVITIES

Review Global Business Terms Assess knowledge of key lesson terms.

Review Global Business Concepts Review comprehension of important lesson concepts.

Think Critically Provides opportunity to apply concepts.

Make Connections Provides connections to other disciplines.

THE GLOBAL ENTREPRENEUR

Presents students with an ongoing project that emphasizes data collection and analysis in the creation of an international business plan.

THE GLOBAL ENTREPRENEUR
CREATING AN INTERNATIONAL BUSINESS PLAN

PRODUCT PLANNING FOR INTERNATIONAL MARKETING

Develop a marketing strategy based on the company and country you have been using in this continuing project, or create a new idea for your business in the same or a different country. Make use of previously collected information, and do additional research. This phase of your business plan should include the following components.

1. A description of the product (good or service), including characteristics and benefits of the item.
2. A description of the target market. Who would be the main buyers and users of the product? What are their demographic characteristics? What are their social attitudes and cultural behaviors?
3. A description of how the product might need to be adapted to accommodate social, cultural, or legal differences.
4. A description of what research activities could the company do to better understand its potential customers and the marketplace.
5. A description of branding and packaging ideas that could be used for this item.

Prepare a written summary or present a short oral report (two or three minutes) to communicate your main findings.

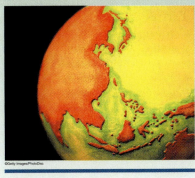

©Getty Images/PhotoDisc

469

TABLE OF CONTENTS

TABLE OF CONTENTS

TABLE OF CONTENTS

TABLE OF CONTENTS

UNIT 4

INFORMATION AND PRODUCTION SYSTEMS FOR GLOBAL BUSINESS   364

UNIT 5

MARKETING IN A GLOBAL ECONOMY — 412

TABLE OF CONTENTS

TABLE OF CONTENTS

REVIEWERS

Monica Caillouet
Instructor
East Ascension High School
Gonzales, LA

Susan Cowart
Teacher, Business and Technology
Centennial High School
Roswell, GA

Lyn Dominguez
Finance/Social Studies Teacher
High School of Economics and Finance
New York, NY

Arlene Gibson
Assistant Director, Instructional Support and
Accountability
Detroit Public Schools
Detroit, MI

Brian S. Horwitz
International Brand Manager
Unilever
London, England

Gretchen Horwitz
Senior Manager
Deloitte & Touche LLP
London, England

Georgia Klautzer
Curriculum Chair Business and Vocational Ed
Business Marketing Teacher
Ft. Zumwalt School District
St. Peters, MO

Carol Kontchogulian
Business Teacher
Williamsville North High School
Williamsville, NY

Rhonda Matthews
Teacher, Business Department
East Ascension High School
Gonzales, LA

Sherry J. Roberts
Assistant Professor
University of Central Arkansas
Conway, AR

Daniel L. Smith
International Business/Economics Teacher
Sandy Creek High School
Tyrone, GA

ABOUT THE AUTHORS

Les R. Dlabay, Ed.D., is a Professor of Business in the Department of Economics and Business at Lake Forest College in Illinois. The courses he teaches include Cultural Perspectives of International Business, Global Marketing, Latin American Global Business, and Asia Business Culture and Trade Relations. Dr. Dlabay has presented teacher workshops and seminars in over 20 states, and has taught more than 30 different courses in high school, community college, university, teacher preparation, and adult education programs. He has also served as International Business editor for *Business Education Forum*, published by the National Business Education Association, and helped develop the National Curriculum Standards for International Business. Dr. Dlabay's "hobbies" include a cereal package collection (from over 100 countries) and paper currency from 200 countries, which are used to teach about economic, cultural, and political aspects of foreign business environments.

James Calvert Scott, Ph.D., is a professor in the Department of Business Information Systems at Utah State University. He three times served as a visiting professor at the Bristol Business School, University of the West of England, Bristol. He earned his B.A. from Boise State University and his Ed.M. and Ph.D. from Oregon State University. He completed postdoctoral work in international business at the University of South Carolina at Columbia. An award-winning researcher, he has authored more than 175 publications. Active in business education-related organizations, he has served as editor for *The Delta Pi Epsilon Journal* and for two National Business Education Association yearbooks.

UNIT 1

THE WORLD OF INTERNATIONAL BUSINESS

The year is 1392, 100 years before the arrival of Columbus. You are a sixteen-year-old Aztec woman, and it is your wedding day. Your city has a population of 100,000 and sits on the site of present-day Mexico City. Your father is a merchant. Your mother cares for the house and the younger children. Your older brother recently finished school and is training for a military career.

The homes in your neighborhood are adobe, and each has a courtyard containing a sauna that is surrounded by beautiful flowers. The man whom you are about to marry designs streets, canals, and irrigation systems for the city. This evening, burning pine branches will light the way as an older woman carries you on her back to your groom's house. While you sit before the hearth, your partner's tunic will be tied to your blouse as a symbol of the union.

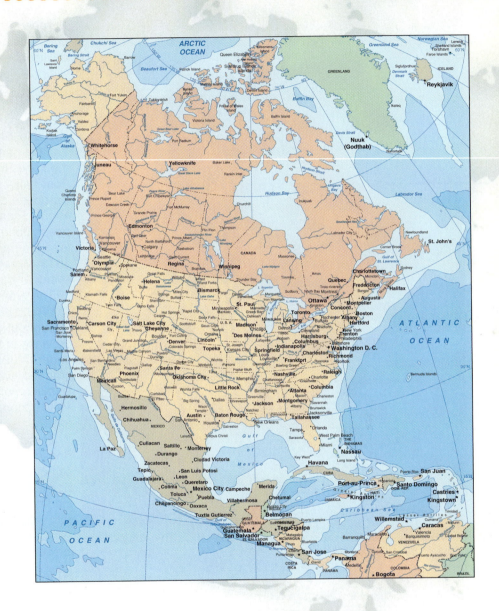

The First North Americans

The vast land that we now call North America was discovered and settled by people who probably migrated to Alaska from Asia. Over a period of 30,000 years, more groups arrived and gradually built a variety of civilizations in this Western Hemisphere. The Aztec example above is just one Native American culture in which you could have been born. You also could have lived among the Leni-Lenape of the eastern woodlands or on the plains with the Arapaho. You might have raised a family in the great complexes built by the Anasazi in cliffs near the Grand Canyon. Hundreds of cultural groups were spread throughout the continent—each with its own unique language, religion, government, and customs.

The Norwegians explored North America in the tenth and eleventh centuries, but they had little effect on the native cultures. Explorers and settlers from Spain, Britain, France, Holland, and Sweden arrived in great numbers during the sixteenth and seventeenth centuries, bringing with them cultures that conflicted with those they met. The native population decreased quickly as a result of battles and the diseases carried by the newcomers. And so began a great cultural transformation—a destructive and creative process that continues today. Soldiers, farmers, trappers, artisans, and merchants came from Europe to help build colonies for their mother countries. Some came to escape religious and political persecution, while others came to share their religion.

©Getty Images/PhotoDisc

Struggles for Independence

Wars were fought to establish control over these valuable lands that held great resources. In 1810, a priest named Miguel Hidalgo y Costilla set off the Mexican War of Independence from Spain. Poor natives and mestizos (of mixed native and European ancestry) fought the war. Although Miguel Hidalgo y Costilla soon died, another priest, José María Morelos y Pavón, continued to lead the movement that led to independence in 1813. Morelos was captured and shot, but Mexico eventually formed a republic in 1824.

The French lost control of Canada to the British in 1763, but the French heritage is still evident throughout Canada and most especially in the province of Quebec. Over the next 100 years under the British Crown, the Canadian assemblies gradually won power without a war. In 1867, the Dominion of Canada was established, and in 1931, Canada became a completely independent nation.

The United States won its independence from Britain through a treaty signed in 1783. Immigrants came to the new country from all over the world. Some stayed in the eastern cities and worked in the textile mills, while many others headed west with wagon trains hoping to build a new life in Kentucky, Ohio, California, and all the territories in between.

Slavery

The economies of the West Indies and the southern United States depended on labor that was supplied by the violent importation of Africans to be used as slaves.

Olaudah, an Ibo man, describes his trip to North America in 1756: "The shrieks of the women and the groans of the dying rendered it a scene of horror almost inconceivable. . . I began to hope that death would soon put an end to my miseries."

Colonial America thrived on this slave labor. By 1860, the South was producing three-quarters of the world's supply of cotton.

Immigrants Build the Economy

After the Civil War, Chinese, Japanese, Mexican, Irish, German, and Italian immigrants joined former slaves and Union and Confederate veterans to work in factories and fields. Together they created the world's most powerful industrial economy.

Canada's earliest immigrants came from France, England, Ireland, and Scotland. In the twentieth century, Russians, Ukrainians, and Germans were attracted to the western prairies. As in the United States, more recent immigrants to Canada are Asian and Latin American.

North America Today

Canada's 3.8 million square miles of territory is second in size only to Russia. The majority of the country's 31 million people are concentrated near its southern border with the United States. The cold northlands hold exquisite natural environments but few inhabitants. Canada's abundance of natural resources and manufacturing industries have produced a high standard of living for most of its people. Its service industries create most new jobs. Mexico is the largest Spanish-speaking country in the world. Its population is growing by about 2 percent each year. Since 1950, land reform and a growing manufacturing base have increased incomes for a large number of Mexicans. Many, however, still live in extreme poverty. And it is these people who often attempt to cross illegally into the United States with the hope of finding work.

Mexico's economic growth has centered on its silver, industrial minerals, and petroleum. The country's white beaches and Aztec ruins attract tourists from all over the world.

All of the nations of continental North America and the West Indies have developed unique cultures that combine the diverse richness of Native Americans, Europeans, Africans, and Asians. Although conflicts still exist, the future of these societies depends upon the mutual appreciation of this diversity.

Think Critically

1. Which Native Americans once had communities where you live?
2. Why do you think Columbus receives most of the credit for "discovering" North America?
3. How do you think the geographic features of the United States influenced the settlement of the West?
4. How do you think Canada has influenced the culture of the United States and vice versa?

COUNTRY PROFILE/NORTH AMERICA

Country	Population		GDP		Exports	Imports	Monetary Unit	Inflation	Unemploy-ment	Life Expectancy	Literacy Rate
	thousands	growth rate	$billions	$ per capita	$billions			percent	percent	years	percent
Canada	31,510	0.77%	923.0	29,400	268.0	226.5	dollar	2.2	7.6	79.8	97.0
Mexico	103,457	2.10%	920.0	9,000	158.4	168.4	peso	6.4	3.0	72.3	92.2
United States	294,043	1.03%	10,082.0	36,300	722.0	1150.0	dollar	1.6	5.8	77.1	97.0

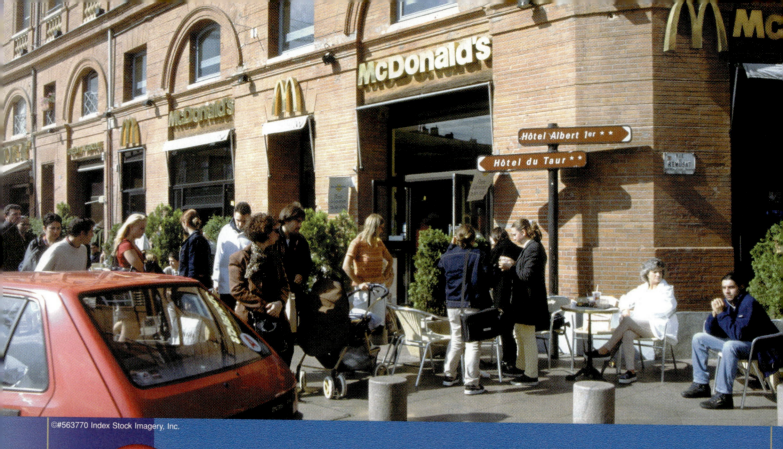

Chapter 1

WE LIVE IN A GLOBAL ECONOMY

1-1 The Foundation of International Business

1-2 International Business Basics

GLOBAL FOCUS

Global Golden Arches

If you have ever thought about having *saimin* for breakfast or a *Bolshoi Mac* for lunch, you were probably at a McDonald's restaurant in another country. Each day, millions of people eat at one of the 28,000 McDonald's restaurants around the world.

When McDonald's started in 1955 with a limited menu (hamburgers, french fries, milkshakes, and soft drinks), few people would have imagined that the company would be serving meals in 120 countries.

In 1967, McDonald's opened its first restaurants outside the United States—in Canada and Puerto Rico. These restaurants were followed by openings in other nations. McDonald's, however, did not venture into Mexico until 1985 because the company couldn't obtain the same quality meat used at its other restaurants.

During the first 20 years of international expansion, McDonald's averaged two new countries per year. During the next ten years, the company doubled the number of countries in which it operated. McDonald's opened restaurants in 12 new markets in 1996 alone. McDonald's menu has been adapted to the tastes of various countries. For example, mixed spaghetti is served in the Philippines, and corn soup is available to customers in Japan.

The company's success has not been without difficulties. In the late 1970s, political trouble in Iran forced McDonald's to close its restaurants there. In early 1992, after being open only a few months in Taiwan, McDonald's shut down its 57 restaurants there due to bomb explosions in or near some of its business locations. In 2002, the company stopped doing business in Bolivia and seven other countries due to poor profits. Bolivia is the poorest country in South America. As McDonald's and other companies have discovered, doing business in other countries can have rewards and risks.

Think Critically

1. Why do companies frequently expand their business operations into other countries?
2. What are the benefits and drawbacks of doing business in other countries?
3. Go to the McDonald's web site (www.mcdonalds.com) to find additional information about the company's international operations. Prepare a report of your findings.

1-1

GOALS

- Distinguish between domestic business and international business.
- Discuss the reasons why international business is important.
- Understand that international trade is not just a recent event.

THE FOUNDATION OF INTERNATIONAL BUSINESS

©Getty Images/PhotoDisc

WHAT IS INTERNATIONAL BUSINESS?

In the early days of the United States, most families grew the food they ate and made the clothes they wore. Then the population increased. Production and distribution methods improved. People began to depend on others for goods and services. That dependence grew as more people specialized in the work they did. Today, the United States has a complex business system. That system is based on peoples' specialties and makes a wide variety of items available for use.

In many countries, people still work on their own to provide for their daily needs. Most nations do not have the extensive production and distribution facilities that the United States, Canada, Japan, and the western European nations have. Although these countries have some level of economic independence, they are still dependent on other countries. For example, most of the coffee used in the United States comes from Brazil. Japan depends on other countries for much of its oil.

Most business activities take place inside a country's own borders. Making, buying, and selling goods and services within a country is called **domestic business**. If you purchase a soft drink made in your own country, you have conducted domestic business.

In contrast, if you purchase a shirt made in Thailand, you are now participating in the global economy. Even if you buy the shirt from a U.S. store, it was made by a foreign manufacturer. **International business** includes all business activities needed to create, ship, and sell goods and services across national borders. International business may also be called *global business, international trade,* and *foreign trade.*

✔ CheckPoint

List examples of domestic business and international business.

WHY IS INTERNATIONAL BUSINESS IMPORTANT?

International business allows you to purchase popular items made in other countries, such as televisions, shoes, and clothing. Without global business, your life would probably be different. People around the world would not have the opportunity to enjoy goods and services made in other countries.

International business is important for many reasons. It provides a source of raw materials and parts and demand for foreign products. Global business allows for new market and investment opportunities. It can even help improve political relations.

MATERIALS, PARTS, AND DEMAND

Products made in the United States often include materials from around the world. Each year, American companies buy oil and steel from other nations to use in factories. Nearly every U.S.-built car has parts that were manufactured in Japan, Mexico, France, Korea, England, and many other countries.

A **global dependency** exists when items that consumers need and want are created in other countries. For example, recently the African country of Zimbabwe had very little rain. Crops failed and farm animals died. As a result, the nation had to buy 90 percent of its food from other countries.

GLOBAL OPPORTUNITIES

Companies such as McDonald's sell to customers in other countries to expand business opportunities. Many businesses, large and small, increase sales and profits with foreign trade. These companies are involved in the global economy.

Many people invest in businesses to earn money for themselves. As companies

GLOBAL BUSINESS EXAMPLE

THE NORTH AMERICAN FREE TRADE AGREEMENT

After intense debate, the United States Congress passed the North American Free Trade Agreement (NAFTA) in 1993. This pact unifies the United States with two of its major trading partners, Canada and Mexico. NAFTA eliminates taxes on goods traded among the three countries. It also eases the movement of goods between these countries.

NAFTA benefits consumers by increasing product variety and lowering prices. Increased demand could create new employment opportunities.

After NAFTA went into effect, Mexican exports expanded. Manufactured goods made up almost 90 percent of these exports. Mexico previously depended on oil as its biggest export.

NAFTA creates a trading bloc like those in other regions of the world. This economic link can help Canada, Mexico, and the United States compete effectively in the world marketplace.

Think Critically

1. Why do countries create trade agreements such as NAFTA?
2. Use Internet sites such as www.nafta-sec-alena.org to find additional information about NAFTA. What are the advantages and disadvantages of the agreement?

WORK AS A GROUP

Suggest ways in which your community benefits from international business.

expand into other countries, they create new investment opportunities. Investors also provide funds to foreign companies that are either just getting started or are growing enterprises.

IMPROVED POLITICAL RELATIONS

An old saying warns "countries that trade with one another are less likely to have wars with each other." International business activities can help to improve mutual understanding, communication, and the level of respect among people in different nations.

We are all affected by international business. Even if business owners do not deal directly with companies in other countries, they are still affected. Every business competes against companies that are either foreign-owned or that sell foreign-made products. As a result, even when you may not realize it, international business is affecting your life.

✔ CheckPoint

List ways that international business is important to companies and countries.

WHEN DID INTERNATIONAL BUSINESS START?

International business is not a new idea. Evidence suggests that countries such as China, India, and Japan were trading products throughout the world 15,000 years ago. There is also evidence that Africans traded with South Americans several thousand years ago.

In the fifth century B.C., Greek and Middle Eastern merchants were involved in foreign trade. Later, the Roman Empire dominated international business for more than 600 years.

©Getty Images/PhotoDisc

NETBookmark

China's acceptance into the World Trade Organization in 2001 led to an increased pace in the development of franchises there. Access intlbizxtra.swlearning.com and click on the link for Chapter 1. Read the article entitled "Chinese Market Offers Franchise Challenges" on the Wall Street Journal's Center for Entrepreneurs web site. What marketing techniques did Kodak use to ensure a continuing market for its products? How has Kentucky Fried Chicken adapted its menu to Chinese tastes?

intlbizxtra.swlearning.com

The next few centuries had limited foreign trade activity. The Arab Empire brought together people from Portugal and Spain, northern Africa, the Middle East, and China. Charlemagne created the Holy Roman Empire out of most of Europe. Viking explorers reached Iceland and Greenland.

The eleventh century saw renewed interest in global commerce. European countries such as England, France, Spain, and Portugal were shipping products by water. By the fifteenth and sixteenth centuries, explorers such as Columbus and Magellan sought a shorter water route to India. Instead of sailing east around Africa, they ventured west.

From about 1500 to 1900, many European countries established colonies in Africa, Asia, and North and South America. These colonies provided European businesses with low-cost raw materials and new markets for selling products. However, these colonies were often created at the expense of the native inhabitants.

Most European countries maintained strong economic and political control over their colonies for years. However, these colonies eventually achieved independence. The United States declared independence from the United Kingdom in 1776. The African country of Mozambique gained independence from Portugal in 1975. For more information about colonial heritage, see Figure 1-1.

Various inventions created between 1769 and 1915 expanded interest in and opportunities for international business. These discoveries included the cotton gin, the steam engine, and the telephone. The inventions from this period improved communication, distribution, and production. They also helped create new global industries.

Recent world events continue to highlight the importance of international business. Expanded trade among companies in different countries increases interdependence. A number of wars in the twentieth century demonstrated

SELECTED COUNTRIES AND THEIR COLONIAL HERITAGE

Country	Colonized By	Date of Independence
Australia	United Kingdom	1901
Brazil	Portugal	1822
Cambodia	France	1953
Canada	France, United Kingdom	1867
Chad	France	1960
Chile	Spain	1818
Cyprus	Turkey, United Kingdom	1960
El Salvador	Spain	1821
Iceland	Norway, Denmark	1944
Mexico	Spain	1821
Mozambique	Portugal	1975
Namibia	Germany, South Africa	1990
South Africa	United Kingdom, Netherlands	1910
United States	United Kingdom, France, Spain, Russia	1776
Vietnam	France	1955

Figure 1-1 Many countries did not achieve independence until the last half of the twentieth century. Some countries are still struggling for independence.

E-COMMERCE IN ACTION

Global E-Commerce Opportunities

"In how many countries does your company do business?" This question is heard often among global managers. Today, the answer is likely to be "Wherever there is Internet access."

Technology allows firms to buy, sell, and exchange information around the world. The Internet, automated production methods, and video conferencing are changing the way people do business. These technologies are creating global e-commerce opportunities. The scope of global e-commerce includes many activities.

- Companies sell goods and services to anyone with Internet access.
- Businesses buy online from suppliers in other countries.
- Firms meet customers' geographic and cultural needs.
- People process information and distribute data worldwide.
- Marketers research global customers and markets online.

Think Critically

1. What types of international business activities are faster and easier because of technology?
2. Find an Internet site that buys or sells online. How does the site handle international customers?

the need for political cooperation. These military conflicts limited global business activities. World peace is important if countries want to achieve economic benefits from international trade.

The creation of the European Union, started in the 1950s, is changing the way most countries do business with one another. Political freedom among former communist countries has created new global business opportunities in these emerging economies. The international business marketplace is expanding daily.

✓ CheckPoint

How has history been important in the development of international business?

©Getty Images/PhotoDisc

REVIEW GLOBAL BUSINESS TERMS

Define each of the following terms.

1. domestic business
2. international business
3. global dependency

REVIEW GLOBAL BUSINESS CONCEPTS

4. How does domestic business differ from international business?
5. Why is international business important?
6. What are some examples of international business activities that occurred before 1800?

SOLVE GLOBAL BUSINESS PROBLEMS

In Dodgeville, Wisconsin (population 4,220), telephone and online orders come in for pants, sport shirts, and other clothing from customers around the world. The Lands' End Company has distribution facilities in the United Kingdom, Germany, and Japan. The North American operations also serve customers in Canada and Mexico. The company sells a full line of clothing by mail, with shipments usually going out within 24 hours.

7. Why did Lands' End get involved in international business?
8. What technology made it possible for the company to serve customers around the world?
9. What problems might the company encounter as a result of its international business activities?
10. Visit the Lands' End web site (www.landsend.com). How does the company serve the needs of customers in other countries?

THINK CRITICALLY

11. How are you affected by international business?
12. What factors affect a country's decision to trade goods and services with another country?

MAKE CONNECTIONS

13. **TECHNOLOGY** How are the Internet and other technologies expanding international trade and global business activities?
14. **MATHEMATICS** Find information about the main products and services created in your state. Create a graph displaying the top five items in dollar value produced in your state.
15. **HISTORY** Describe an event from world history. Explain how that event might encourage or deter trade among countries.

1-2

INTERNATIONAL BUSINESS BASICS

GOALS

- Describe basic international business activities.
- Explain the components of the international business environment.
- Name important skills for international business and describe the importance of international business for workers, consumers, and citizens.

©Getty Images/PhotoDisc

THE FUNDAMENTALS OF INTERNATIONAL TRADE

Have you ever had a lot of one item, such as sports trading cards? Perhaps you had a friend who had something you wanted, such as some comic books. The two of you might have decided to trade. You could give up some of what you had to get something else you wanted. That's what happens when companies in different countries trade goods or services.

These foreign trades usually are not an exchange of items for items. Instead, cash payments are usually made for the items bought or sold. For example, a manufacturing company in Korea can sell radios to an electronics store in the United States. Also, a computer company in the United States might sell its products to a retailer in Russia.

These trade activities can be viewed from two sides—the buyer and the seller. For the buyer, products bought from businesses in other countries are called **imports**. In the previous example, the United States is importing radios. Russia is importing computers.

For the seller, **exports** are products sold in other countries. Using the same example, Korea is exporting radios. The United States is exporting computers. Figure 1-2 shows the flow of imports and exports for a country.

IMPORTS AND EXPORTS OF THE UNITED STATES

Figure 1-2

Although the process sounds simple, obstacles can arise. These obstacles are called trade barriers. **Trade barriers** are restrictions that reduce free trade among countries. These barriers could appear in several forms.

- Import taxes increase the cost of foreign products.
- Quotas restrict the number of imports.
- Laws prevent certain products from coming into a country.

U.S. COMPANIES FACE TRADE BARRIERS

In the past, Japan did not allow foreign accounting firms to use their international names in advertising. Several nations continue to impose high import taxes on products from other countries. These are some examples of trade barriers from the annual report of the U.S. Office of the Trade Representative. This federal government agency encourages other nations to reduce or eliminate trade barriers for U.S. exports. In exchange, restric- tions on imports to the United States are lowered or removed. This ongoing discussion is aimed at creating a worldwide free trade environment.

Think Critically

1. Go to the web site of the U.S Government Export Portal (www.export.gov) to obtain information about exporting.
2. Why do governments sometimes create trade barriers to discourage imports from other countries?
3. What are some examples of trade barriers that are not created by government actions?

How do imports differ from exports?

THE INTERNATIONAL BUSINESS ENVIRONMENT

Buying and selling goods and services is similar in most parts of the world. Consumers try to satisfy their needs and wants at a fair price. Businesses try to sell products at a price that covers costs and provides a fair profit. So, why is international business any different from local business?

INTERNATIONAL BUSINESS ENVIRONMENT FACTORS

In many parts of Iran, the exchange of goods and services takes place in an open-air market rather than in an air-conditioned store. Consumers in Japan buy meals that non-Asians might not enjoy, such as raw fish. In Cuba, office workers have been required to work several weeks in the fields to increase the food supply.

These are examples of factors that make up the international business operating environment. Look at Figure 1-3. It shows the four major categories of the international business environment. They are geographic conditions, cultural and social factors, political and legal factors, and economic conditions.

THE INTERNATIONAL BUSINESS ENVIRONMENT

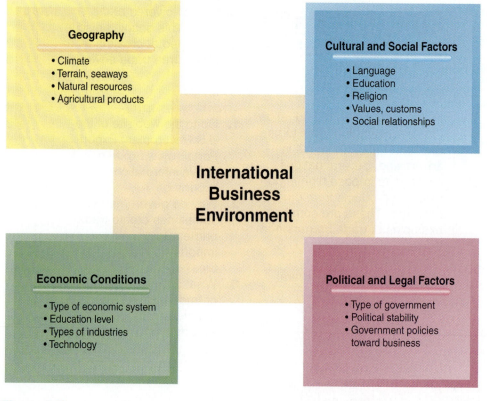

Geography
- Climate
- Terrain, seaways
- Natural resources
- Agricultural products

Cultural and Social Factors
- Language
- Education
- Religion
- Values, customs
- Social relationships

International Business Environment

Economic Conditions
- Type of economic system
- Education level
- Types of industries
- Technology

Political and Legal Factors
- Type of government
- Political stability
- Government policies toward business

Figure 1-3

Geographic Conditions The climate, terrain, seaports, and natural resources of a country will influence its business activities. Very hot weather will limit the types of crops that can be grown. It also will restrict the types of businesses that can operate in that climate. A nation with many rivers or seaports is able to easily ship products for foreign trade. Countries with few natural resources must depend on imports.

©Getty Images/PhotoDisc

Cultural and Social Factors In some societies, hugging is an appropriate business greeting. In other societies, a handshake is the custom. These differences represent different cultures. **Culture** is the accepted behaviors, customs, and values of a society. A society's culture has a strong influence on business activities. For example, many businesses were traditionally closed in the afternoon in Mexico while people enjoyed lunch and a rest period known as a *siesta*.

The main cultural and social factors that affect international business are language, education, religion, values, customs, and social relationships. These relationships include interactions among families, labor unions, and other organizations.

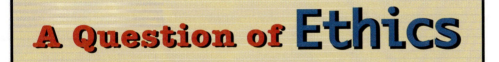

A Question of Ethics

In some countries, people expect family members to be given jobs in a company before others. In other countries, payments or gifts are expected before a company does business.

These cultural differences can create ethical problems. Ethics are principles of right and wrong guiding personal and business decisions. When considering the ethics of business situations, you should follow three guidelines.

Is the action legal? Laws vary among countries. Most companies base international decisions on the statutes in their home country. When a conflict occurs, managers usually consider such other factors as professional standards and the effect of the action on society.

*Does the action violate profes-*sional or company standards? Professional or company standards will frequently exceed the law. This helps to ensure that decisions will be in the best interest of both the company and the country in which it operates.

Who is affected by the action and how? Although an action may be legal and within professional or company standards, decision makers should also consider possible effects on employees, consumers, competitors, and the environment.

Think Critically
1. How do cultural differences create problems when business is done in different countries?
2. What actions can global managers take to avoid ethical problems?

WORK AS A GROUP

Prepare a list of examples for the four components of the international business environment.

Political and Legal Factors Each day, we encounter examples of government influence on business. Regulation of fair advertising, enforcement of contracts, and safety inspections of foods and medications are a few examples. In general, however, people in the United States have a great deal of freedom when it comes to business activities. However, not all countries are like the United States. In many places, government restricts the activities of consumers and business operators. The most common political and legal factors that affect international business activities include the type of government, the stability of the government, and government policies toward business.

Economic Conditions Everyone faces the problem of limited resources to satisfy numerous needs and wants. This basic economic problem is present for all of us. We continually make decisions about the use of our time, money, and energy. Similarly, every country plans the use of its land, natural resources, workers, and wealth to best serve the needs of its people.

Factors that influence the economic situation of a country include the type of economic system, the availability of natural resources, and the general education level of the country's population. Other economic factors include the types of industries and jobs in the country and the stability of the country's money supply. The level of technology available for producing and distributing goods and services influences a nation's economic situation.

✓ CheckPoint

What are the four components of the international business environment?

©Getty Images/PhotoDisc

THE GLOBAL BUSINESS WORLD

International business is an important field of study. Certain basic skills and knowledge are needed in our global economy. There are also a number of obligations and responsibilities that the global economy requires of people.

INTERNATIONAL BUSINESS SKILLS

Certain skills are needed in every type of job. For example, you must be able to read work manuals, do calculations, and write reports. These abilities will continue to be important as business activities among countries increase. There are also a number of other subject areas that are important for global business.

- **History** Your awareness of the past can help you better understand today's international business relations.
- **Geography** Geography is more than names on a map. Knowledge of geography will help you understand how the climate and terrain of a country can affect transportation, housing, and other business activities.
- **Foreign language** As countries increasingly participate in foreign trade activities, your ability to communicate effectively with people from other societies increases in importance.
- **Cultural awareness** Understanding that cultures vary from nation to nation allows people to be more sensitive to customs and traditions of all societies.
- **Study skills** Asking questions, taking notes, and doing research are the tools necessary to keep up to date on changes in international business.

©Getty Images/PhotoDisc

THE GLOBAL CITIZEN, WORKER, AND CONSUMER

Working, voting, and shopping represent three common roles of people in a society. Workers, citizens, and consumers participate in many business activities. These roles expand as a country becomes more involved in international business.

As consumer choices increase, the selection of goods and services is no longer limited to items produced in one country. For workers, career opportunities expand because of international business. International trade affects business owners when competitors import or export products.

Finally, as citizens, international business activities make it necessary to have an increased awareness of the world. The decisions you make are likely to affect many people in your community, state, country, and world.

✓ CheckPoint

Other than business skills, what knowledge is important for working in international business? What are the three roles that every person takes on in a society?

REGIONAL PERSPECTIVE

GEOGRAPHY: CANADA'S VAST NATURAL RESOURCES

Canada occupies more than 3.8 million square miles (9.8 million square kilometers), making it the second largest country in the world. With fewer than seven people per square mile, compared to 68 people per square mile in the United States, Canada is an immense haven of forests, lakes, rivers, and farmland. The country's economy is dependent on these abundant natural resources.

Canada's 1.3 million square miles (3.4 million square kilometers) of forests are a major source of wealth. More than 150 species of trees are native to Canada. Forestry-related products, such as paper, wood pulp, and timber, account for about 15 percent of the country's exports.

Commercial fishing has been a part of Canada's economy for 500 years. The Atlantic and Pacific Oceans and the most extensive bodies of freshwater in the world make fishing an important industry. Common commercial species caught include cod, haddock, herring, salmon, lobster, scallops, and halibut.

Canada's fast-flowing rivers are also an important source of energy. The country is the world's second leading producer of hydroelectricity. Its coasts provide natural seaports in cities such as Vancouver, Halifax, and St. John. Water access through the St. Lawrence River earns Montreal, Toronto, and Quebec City recognition as vital shipping ports.

Wheat—grown in the western prairie provinces of Alberta, Manitoba, and Saskatchewan—is Canada's primary farm product. Other agricultural commodities include barley, potatoes, corn, soybeans, and oats. Livestock such as beef cattle, poultry, dairy cows, hogs, sheep, and egg-laying hens are also major exports.

As a result of its natural beauty, over 40 million tourists visit Canada each year. Many of these travelers go to the cities; however, fishing, hunting, camping, and other outdoor activities are also major tourist attractions. Spending by visitors brings in over $3 billion a year to the Canadian economy.

Think Critically

1. What advantages in the global economy are created by Canada's natural resources?
2. How should Canada use its natural resources to expand its international business activities?
3. Conduct an Internet search for additional information about Canada's economy and international trade activities.

©Getty Images/PhotoDisc

REVIEW GLOBAL BUSINESS TERMS

Define each of the following terms.

1. imports **2.** exports **3.** trade barriers **4.** culture

REVIEW GLOBAL BUSINESS CONCEPTS

5. What are the four parts of the international business environment?

6. What cultural factors affect international business activities?

7. Name four factors that influence a country's economic conditions.

8. What skills are important for success in an international business?

9. How does international business affect you as
   a. a consumer

   b. a worker

   c. a citizen

SOLVE GLOBAL BUSINESS PROBLEMS

A company making small engines plans to sell its products in an eastern European country. This country recently changed from a government-controlled economy to a free market. The country also has become more democratic. Based on this information, answer the following.

10. What geographic factors might influence the company's international business activities?

11. How might economic conditions affect business decisions?

12. What social and cultural influences could affect this business?

13. How could politics and laws affect the company's exporting activity?

THINK CRITICALLY

14. What actions might a country take to encourage other countries to buy its goods and services?

15. How could geography create international business opportunities?

16. What responsibilities do you believe people have as citizens in our global economy?

MAKE CONNECTIONS

17. **GEOGRAPHY** Describe how the terrain, climate, and waterways of a country might influence international trade activities.

18. **LAW** Describe some laws in foreign countries that are different from those in the United States.

CHAPTER SUMMARY

1-1 THE FOUNDATION OF INTERNATIONAL BUSINESS

A International business includes all the business activities needed to create, ship, and sell goods and services across national borders. International business is also referred to as *global business, international trade,* and *foreign trade.*

B International business is important as a source of raw material and a supplier of foreign products. It allows for new market and investment opportunities, and paths to improved political relations.

C Trading products throughout the world started more than 15,000 years ago. The Roman Empire dominated international business for more than 600 years. The eleventh century saw renewed interest in global commercialism. From 1500 to 1900, several European countries established colonies in Africa, Asia, North America, and South America.

1-2 INTERNATIONAL BUSINESS BASICS

A Trade activities are viewed from two sides—the buyer and the seller. Products bought from businesses in other countries are called imports. Products sold in other countries are exports.

B The four major categories of the international business environment are geographic conditions, cultural and social factors, political and legal factors, and economic conditions.

C Success in learning about international business requires knowledge of history, geography, foreign language, culture, and study skills.

D As a worker, you have new career opportunities created by international business. As a consumer, you have more buying choices. As a citizen, you must have an increased awareness of the world.

GLOBAL REFOCUS

Reread the Global Focus at the beginning of this chapter, and answer the following questions.

1. What factors prompted McDonald's to open restaurants outside the United States?

2. How have social and cultural factors affected the company's international business activities?

3. What risks has the company faced when opening restaurants in other countries?

4. What actions would you suggest for McDonald's to continue to be successful in international business?

REVIEW GLOBAL BUSINESS TERMS

Match the terms listed with the definitions. Some terms may not be used.

1. Products sold in other countries.

2. People need and want goods and services produced in other countries.

3. The activities necessary for creating, shipping, and selling goods and services across national borders.

4. Making, buying, and selling goods and services within a country.

5. Products bought from businesses in other countries.

6. The accepted behaviors, customs, and values of a society.

7. Restrictions that reduce free trade among countries.

a. culture
b. domestic business
c. exports
d. global dependency
e. imports
f. international business
g. trade barriers

MAKE GLOBAL BUSINESS DECISIONS

8. Explain how both domestic and international business activities create jobs.

9. What are some examples of our global dependency on other countries?

10. How do investments by a company in a foreign country help the economies of both nations?

11. What actions might a country take to encourage exporting of goods and services?

12. Why might a country use trade barriers?

13. How might religious beliefs affect international business activities?

14. How could a country's type of government affect its business activities?

15. Why would a country with many natural resources have the potential for a strong economy?

16. What actions could you take to improve your history, geography, foreign language, cultural awareness, and study skills?

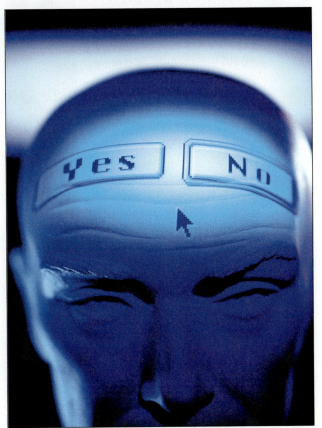
©Getty Images/PhotoDisc

GLOBAL CONNECTIONS

17. **GEOGRAPHY** Use the library or Internet to prepare a map poster that shows locations of American trade with other countries.

18. **COMMUNICATIONS** Survey students and other people about their knowledge of international business. Prepare a list of eight or ten questions on the geography, culture, and economies of different countries. Ask ten people to answer the questions. Determine the topics on which people are most informed and least informed, and write a one-page summary of your findings.

19. **HISTORY** Write a one- to two-page paper about how a historic event has affected international business. Consider topics such as early Chinese trade with other areas of the world, European colonization, the Industrial Revolution, the creation of the European Community, and the political freedom of eastern European countries.

20. **CULTURAL STUDIES** Interview a person who has lived or worked in another country. Ask him or her about the cultural and business differences of that country compared to the United States (or compared to your native country). Prepare a report of your findings.

21. **SCIENCE** Find an article from a newspaper, magazine, or the Internet with information about current scientific or technological developments. Prepare a short written or oral summary of the information in the article. Explain how this information might expand trade among countries.

©Getty Images/PhotoDisc

22. **MATHEMATICS** Select a country other than the United States. Research the major imports and exports of that nation for a recent year. Calculate the difference between the country's total exports and imports and the percentage change in exports and imports from the previous year.

23. **CAREER PLANNING** Based on current articles, advertisements, product packages, and an Internet search, prepare a list of international business job opportunities. What types of skills are needed for an international business career?

THE GLOBAL ENTREPRENEUR
CREATING AN INTERNATIONAL BUSINESS PLAN

CREATING AN INTERNATIONAL BUSINESS RESOURCE FILE

To help you learn about international business relationships, you will need to create an international business plan. This instructional experience will allow you to build your knowledge and skills. The first activity involves creating an international business resource file that you will use for future assignments.

Start a file of articles and information on a country and a company involved in international business. Obtain information related to the geography, history, culture, government, and economy of the country. For the international company file, include a list of products sold in different countries, examples of ways the company adapted to different societies, and other information about its foreign business activities.

©Getty Images/PhotoDisc

Sources of information to create your file may include any of the following.

- reference books such as encyclopedias, almanacs, and atlases
- current newspaper articles from the news, business, and travel sections
- current news and business magazine articles, including news stories, company profiles, and advertisements
- web site searches for country and company information
- materials from companies, airlines, travel bureaus, government agencies, and other organizations involved in international business
- interviews with people who have lived in, work in, or traveled to the country

Prepare a written summary or present a short oral report (two or three minutes) about your country and company. Give an example or situation involving international business. Plan to add to your file throughout the course, as these materials will be used for other chapter projects.

Chapter 2

OUR GLOBAL ECONOMY

GLOBAL FOCUS

An Economic Plan for Mexico

In the early 1980s, Mexico had several economic difficulties. The country's governmental policies created barriers to international trade. These decisions meant fewer foreign companies wanted to do business in Mexico. Therefore, fewer jobs were available.

The government created programs to help those without jobs. The Mexican government had to borrow money to pay for this state assistance program. Soon, the government was using more and more of its money to pay back the loans. Little money was left to spend on public services.

One problem led to another until the country decided to take a new course of action. Mexico then took several steps toward economic reform. The Mexican government

- Allowed more foreign businesses to produce and sell goods and services in Mexico
- Reduced government spending and created programs that served only the neediest people in the country
- Sold several unprofitable government-owned businesses that were costing the taxpayers money
- Worked out a new plan to reduce government debt

The Mexican government chose actions to help the country compete in the global marketplace while also improving the economic situation of its citizens. In recent years, Mexico has seen improved economic conditions. The prices of goods in the country have not increased as quickly as in the past. Global business activities helped to create more jobs and higher incomes for Mexican workers.

Think Critically

1. Obtain current information on the Internet about doing business in Mexico. Prepare a one-page summary of your findings.
2. What factors created economic difficulties for Mexico?

2-1

GOALS

- Describe the basic economic problem.
- List the steps of the decision-making process.

ECONOMICS AND DECISION MAKING

©Getty Images/PhotoDisc

THE BASIC ECONOMIC PROBLEM

Each day people throughout the world make economic decisions. For example, selecting what groceries to buy is an economic choice. Choosing whether to buy a shirt or a compact disc is an economic choice. As you make choices, you probably are not able to obtain everything you want. These choices are the basis of economics.

You are limited by the amount of time and money you have available to acquire the things you want. Countries and individuals have limited resources available. As a result, decisions are necessary to make the best use of resources.

Scarcity refers to the limited resources available to satisfy the unlimited needs and wants of people. All people and all nations face scarcity every day. A country must decide whether to grow its own food or to import agricultural products so its workers can produce other items. Many factors affect the choices made by an individual, a company, or a country. The study of how people choose to use limited resources to satisfy their unlimited needs and wants is called **economics**.

Economics can be an exciting topic to study. Knowledge of economics helps people understand why some earn more than others and why certain items cost more at different times of the year. Economic principles can explain why business managers make one choice over another.

What is economics?

MAKING ECONOMIC DECISIONS

People and countries cope with scarcity by making decisions. Every time you decide how to use your time, money, and energy, you are making an economic decision. Companies and nations also have to make choices.

THE DECISION-MAKING PROCESS

One way to help make economic choices is to use the decision-making process. Using the steps shown in Figure 2-1 can help people make wiser decisions and get the best use of resources. This process can help consumers make faster and better choices. Saving time and money when making a purchase is something most people want.

There are six steps in the decision-making process.

Step 1 **Define the problem** What do I need or want?

Step 2 **Identify the alternatives** What are the different ways my problem can be solved?

Step 3 **Evaluate the alternatives** What are the advantages and disadvantages of each of the choices available?

Step 4 **Make a choice** Based on the advantages and disadvantages, which would be my best choice? Can I live with the consequences of that choice?

Step 5 **Take action on the choice** What needs to be done to put the decision into action?

Step 6 **Review the decision** Did your decision solve the problem? As time goes by, what different actions might be necessary? Were there consequences you did not predict when you evaluated the alternatives?

WORK AS A GROUP

Discuss an important decision that you might have to make in life, such as buying a car or going to college. Work through the six steps of the decision-making process to help you make your decision.

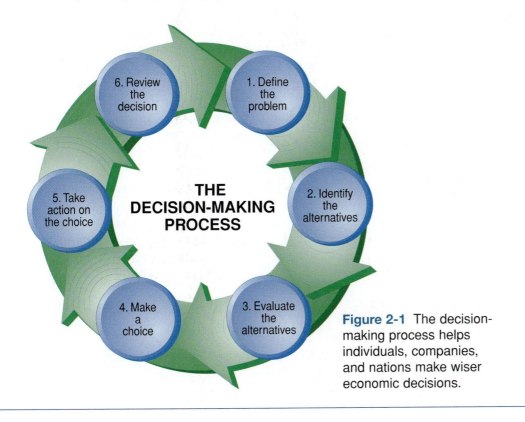

6. Review the decision

1. Define the problem

THE DECISION-MAKING PROCESS

2. Identify the alternatives

3. Evaluate the alternatives

4. Make a choice

5. Take action on the choice

Figure 2-1 The decision-making process helps individuals, companies, and nations make wiser economic decisions.

DECISION MAKING IN ACTION

How do companies use the decision-making process? An example of economic decision making for international business could involve a company in the United States that wants to increase the sales of its product.

©Getty Images/PhotoDisc

Step 1 **Define the problem** The problem might be "How can the Benson Electric Company continue to increase its sales over the next five years?" Right now, the company only sells home audio and electronic products in the United States.

Step 2 **Identify the alternatives** Solutions include

- Increasing advertising to attract new customers
- Reducing prices to attract more customers
- Selling products over the Internet and mailing information to customers in other countries
- Shipping products to sell in other countries
- Producing and selling products in other countries

Step 3 **Evaluate the alternatives** Each of these choices has costs and benefits. The process of evaluating these options involves comparing the risks and costs of each alternative. Benson Electric must consider the expected increase in sales from each alternative. For example, reducing prices may increase the number of customers but could reduce total dollar sales. The cost of producing products in another country could be greater than the money earned from additional sales.

Step 4 **Make a choice** Every time a choice is made, something else is given up. So, once Benson Electric selects a course of action, it probably will not be able to choose other alternatives. **Opportunity cost** is the most attractive alternative given up when a choice is made. In your own life, a decision to go to college, for example, could mean you would not be able to use your time to earn money in a job right now. Generally, the benefits of a decision should be more valuable to you than the opportunity cost. So, the decision to continue your education is likely to benefit you throughout your life with higher earnings.

Step 5 **Take action on the choice** Finally, the Benson Company must put its choice into action.

Step 6 **Review the decision** Over the weeks, months, and years that follow, the company should review this decision to determine whether it needs to be changed or if other decisions need to be made. Remember that decision making is an ongoing process in your life.

✓ **CheckPoint**

List the six steps of the decision-making process. Give an example of each step from a recent decision you have made.

REVIEW GLOBAL BUSINESS TERMS

Define each of the following terms.

1. scarcity

2. economics

3. opportunity cost

REVIEW GLOBAL BUSINESS CONCEPTS

4. What is the basic economic problem?

5. Describe the six steps of the decision-making model.

6. Why does every decision have an opportunity cost?

SOLVE GLOBAL BUSINESS PROBLEMS

For each of the following international business situations, describe the problem and list two or three alternatives that the company could take to solve the problem.

7. A food company is having trouble selling its frozen products in other countries because it is very expensive to transport frozen foods.

8. A computer store is losing business to a competitor. The competitor is selling imported software at a very low price.

9. Buyers of a tool exported to Bermuda are not following the safety directions, and users are being injured.

THINK CRITICALLY

10. Explain how scarcity affects you and your family, school, and community.

11. What are some examples of situations in which you make decisions without thinking about every step of the decision-making process?

12. Think of three choices you have made recently. What were the opportunity costs of those choices?

MAKE CONNECTIONS

13. **COMMUNICATION** Talk to a person who works in the business world. Obtain an example of a business decision that the person has made.

14. **TECHNOLOGY** Explain how new computer systems have improved decision making for companies involved in international business.

15. **MATHEMATICS** A cloth manufacturer has the opportunity to purchase new machinery for its factory for $1 million. The machinery will require five equal annual payments while the equipment is being installed. How much will the company have to pay each year for the machinery? During installation, the company can expect profits to rise by $100,000 per year. After that, they can expect profits to rise by $250,000 per year. How long will it be before the increase in profit pays for the machinery entirely?

2-2

Basics Of Economics

GOALS

- Describe how the market sets prices.
- Explain the causes of inflation.

©Getty Images/PhotoDisc

PRICE-SETTING ACTIVITIES

Price is one of the most visible economic factors you encounter every day. The amount paid for goods and services results from economic decisions made by consumers, businesses, and governments. Daily economic decisions affect you in many ways. For example, if people rent many videos, more stores will make DVDs available. In addition, more jobs will be available for people working in video stores. If consumers no longer want to purchase a certain video, the availability or price of that video will decrease.

Have you ever noticed that when something has limited availability and many people want to buy it, the price increases? If many people want to buy tickets for a hockey game or a concert, for example, ticket prices are likely to go up. When freezing temperatures destroy the fruit blossoms and reduce the number of oranges available, prices go up.

The opposite is also true. If a musical group is no longer popular, the prices of its posters, CDs, and T-shirts are likely to go down. The price system is a method of balancing unlimited needs and wants with limited resources.

Determining prices involves two main elements—supply and demand. **Supply** is the relationship between the amount of a good or service that businesses are willing and able to make available and the price. The amount of an item supplied tends to go up when producers see an opportunity to make money. For example, many years ago only a couple of companies made baseball and other sports cards for collecting. As these cards became more popular, other companies got involved in the sports card business.

Supply also works the other way. If companies can no longer make money producing an item, they will get out of that business. As video replaced film, most companies that made film projectors for schools and libraries went into other types of businesses. The number of film projectors available declined.

On the buyer's side is **demand**, which is the relationship between the amount of a good or service that consumers are willing and able to purchase and the price. In general, as the amount of a good or service that people want increases, the price of that item goes higher. If more people want tickets to a sports event or concert, the price of admission can be set higher for those events. If fewer people want tickets, the price will likely be lower. For example, near the end of the summer, swimsuits are usually at their lowest prices.

The downward sloping line marked D in Figure 2-2 shows that as price declines, demand increases. This is called the *law of demand*. For example, at a price of $12, ten videos are demanded, but if the price is $2, sixty videos are demanded. On the supply side (the S line), higher prices mean a greater amount supplied since businesses can make a larger profit. At a price of $2, twenty videos are offered for sale, while at $8, fifty videos are available.

The point at which supply and demand cross is called the **market price**. Look at Figure 2-2. At a price of $6 sellers are willing to offer 40 videos and consumers are willing to buy 40 videos. The market price, therefore, is $6. This point is also known as the *equilibrium price*. While supply and demand in the real world do not work as neatly as the graph shows, market forces do cause prices to rise and fall.

WORK AS A GROUP

Explain how new technology and bad weather could affect the supply (or demand) for products and how prices might change.

MARKET PRICE IS SET BY SUPPLY AND DEMAND

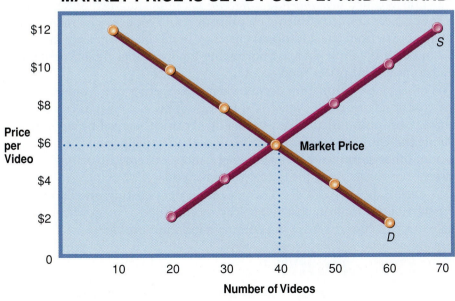

Figure 2-2 The point where supply equals demand is known as the market price.

Communication Across Borders

DISAPPEARING LANGUAGES

Language experts predict that in the next 50 years, almost half of the world's 6,000 languages will disappear. The native languages of people are becoming extinct twice as fast as endangered mammals. This trend could mean a world in the future dominated by only a dozen languages.

Of the 250 languages once spoken in Australia, 150 are extinct and 70 are endangered. Some language loss is natural and predictable. For a language to remain healthy, it must be passed on to the next generation.

Fewer languages may seem better for business. However, fewer languages may also mean fewer diverse thoughts. Language diversity reflects the music, history, literature, and culture of a society.

Think Critically
1. What causes languages to become extinct?
2. Why is language diversity important?

✔ CheckPoint

How do supply and demand determine the market price?

CHANGING PRICES

Prices constantly change. The price of a gallon of gasoline over the past 30 years has gone from less than fifty cents to more than two dollars, depending on supply and demand. When the supply of oil (used to make gasoline) was threatened during various Middle East crises, gasoline prices went up. As hostilities lessened, prices dropped.

A common economic concern is continually rising prices. An increase in the average prices of goods and services in a country is known as **inflation**. Inflation allows people to buy fewer goods and services. Inflation is an indication of the buying power of a country's monetary unit (such as the U.S. dollar, the British pound, or the Japanese yen).

Inflation has two basic causes. First, when demand exceeds supply, prices go up. This is called *demand-pull inflation*. It can occur when a government tries to solve economic problems by printing more money. The increased demand comes from the additional currency in circulation. A similar situation can occur if people increase borrowing for spending. Again, demand exceeds supply, and prices tend to rise.

The other cause of inflation occurs when the expenses of a business (such as the cost of salaries or raw materials) increase. This is known as *cost-push inflation*. Cost-push inflation results in a higher price charged by a company.

While the United States and Canada have had some periods of high inflation, other countries have experienced more extreme situations. Consumer prices in Peru, for example, increased by 400 percent in one month during the early 1990s. This meant an item costing one Peruvian sol at the start of the month, cost five sol by month's end. The government had to take drastic action to solve the country's inflation problem.

✔ CheckPoint

Why might higher operating costs for a business result in inflation?

REVIEW GLOBAL BUSINESS TERMS

Define each of the following terms.

1. supply   **2.** demand   **3.** market price   **4.** inflation

REVIEW GLOBAL BUSINESS CONCEPTS

5. What factors affect the supply of a good or service?

6. How does consumer demand create inflation?

7. How can the price of raw materials affect inflation?

SOLVE GLOBAL BUSINESS PROBLEMS

Identify the type of inflation that will result from each of the following situations.

8. The price of silicon used to make computer chips increases.

9. The government prints more money to pay its expenses.

10. Consumers borrow more to buy additional goods and services.

11. Labor unions make employers increase workers' pay.

THINK CRITICALLY

12. Sometimes demand goes up even if prices go up. Describe an example when that might occur.

13. Describe three situations in which inflation has affected you, your family, or your friends. What were the possible causes of that inflation?

MAKE CONNECTIONS

14. **MATHEMATICS** Figure 2-3 is a graph of the supply and demand for sweaters at a local clothing store. Use the graph to identify the market price. How many sweaters will be bought and sold at that price?

15. **HISTORY** Research a period in history when a country experienced a period of extremely high inflation. Where and when did this period of inflation occur? What were the causes of the inflation? What measures were taken to end the period of extreme inflation? Did that country later experience another period of extreme inflation?

Figure 2-3

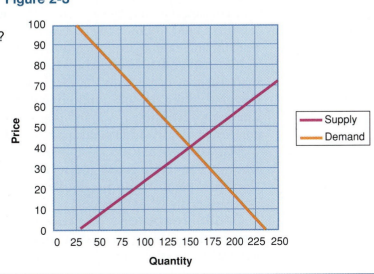

2-3 ECONOMIC SYSTEMS

GOALS

- Name the three main factors of production.
- Understand how different countries make economic decisions.

©Getty Images/PhotoDisc

ECONOMIC RESOURCES SATISFY NEEDS

Every country makes economic decisions. These decisions provide a basis for solving the basic economic problem—unlimited needs and wants with limited resources. The production of goods and services is a primary activity to satisfy the needs and wants of consumers.

To start a company that makes a product requires several elements. These elements are the **factors of production**, which are the three types of resources used to produce goods and services. These resources are natural, human, and capital, as shown in Figure 2-4.

Natural resources Also known as *land*, these resources are the raw materials that come from the earth, from the water, and from the air. Iron ore, gold, silver agricultural products, rivers, and oxygen are examples of natural resources. These items are used in the production of goods and services consumed by individuals, businesses, and governments.

Human resources Also known as *labor*, these resources are the people who work to create goods and services. While technology has changed or eliminated certain tasks previously performed by people, new types of work are continually being created.

Capital resources Also called *capital*, these resources include buildings, money, equipment, and factories used in the production process. These items are expensive and are used over several years by business organizations.

FACTORS OF PRODUCTION

Natural Resources

Human Resources

Capital Resources

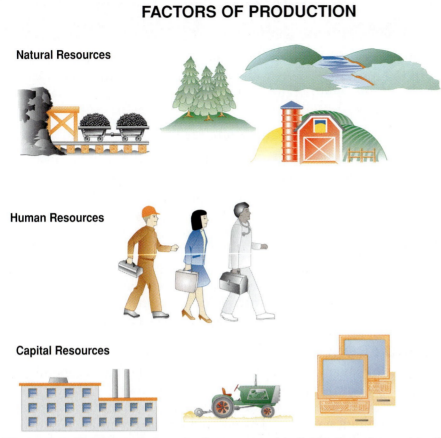

Figure 2-4 The factors of production are used individually or in combination to produce the goods and services in any economy.

GLOBAL BUSINESS EXAMPLE

FACTORS OF PRODUCTION FOR FAST-FOOD COMPANIES

McDonald's and KFC were joined by Burger King, Arby's, and Wendy's in selling their products to the consumers of Mexico. Each of the companies combined money, buildings, and equipment (capital resources) with beef, chicken, and wheat (natural resources) and hired local workers (human resources) to provide meals at their restaurants. Some of the most popular locations for the fast-food restaurants are Acapulco, Cancun, Tijuana, and suburban Mexico City.

Think Critically

1. Go to the web site of one of these fast-food companies to obtain additional information about its business operations in different countries. Prepare a one-page summary of your findings.
2. What might cause problems in obtaining factors of production to do business in another country?

✓ CheckPoint

Name the three factors of production, and give an example of each.

TYPES OF ECONOMIC SYSTEMS

Every nation decides how to use its factors of production to create goods and services for its people. The way in which these resources are used differs from country to country. The economic choices of a country relate to three basic questions.

- What goods and services are to be produced?
- How should the goods and services be produced?
- For whom should the goods and services be produced?

Every country must decide how to use its productive resources to answer these three basic economic questions. An **economic system** is the method a country uses to answer the basic economic questions. Nations organize for production and distribution of goods and services based on customs, political factors, and religious beliefs.

Economic systems can be categorized based on ownership of resources and government involvement in business activities. The three common types of economic systems are command, market, and mixed economies.

COMMAND ECONOMIES

Throughout history, many nations decided to answer the basic economic questions by using central planning. In a **command economy**, the government or a central-planning committee regulates the amount, distribution, and price of everything produced. The government also owns the productive resources of the country. Any income from these resources is used to help fund government activities. At the start of the 21st century, Cuba is one of the few countries using a command system of economic decision making. The political and economic environment where the government owns all of the productive resources of the economy and a single party controls the government is called *communism.*

In some command economies, consumers have very few choices of products to buy. A government agency could even decide what job a person will have.

MARKET ECONOMIES

In contrast to command economies, where all of the decisions are made by the government, market economies are based on the forces of supply and demand. **Market economies** are those in which individual companies and consumers make the decisions about what, how, and for whom items will be produced. The economic and political environment where a market economy exists is called *capitalism.* It has three main characteristics.

- **Private property** Individuals have the right to buy and sell productive resources and to own business enterprises.

©Getty Images/PhotoDisc

- **Profit motive** Individuals are inspired by the opportunity to be rewarded for taking business risks and for working hard.
- **Free, competitive marketplace** Consumers have the power to use their choices to determine what is to be produced and to influence the prices to be charged.

Since market economies have minimal government involvement with business, they are commonly called *free enterprise systems or private enterprise economies.* Since every country has some governmental regulations affecting business activities, no perfect market economies exist. The United States, although not a pure market economy, is one of the best examples of this type of economic system. Despite strong government involvement in business activities, the Japanese, Australian, and Canadian economies are also usually labeled as market economies.

MIXED ECONOMIES

Many economies are a blend between government involvement in business and private ownership. This is known as a **mixed economy**. For example, some countries have publicly owned transportation companies, communication networks, and major industries. The income from these enterprises is used to help fund government activities.

Socialism refers to a political and economic system with most basic industries owned and operated by government with the government controlled by the people as a whole. In socialism, individuals are usually free to engage in other business opportunities and free to make buying choices. In recent years, examples of socialist countries include Sweden and France.

In changing from a command economy to a market economy, a country may sell government-owned industries to private companies. This process of changing an industry from publicly to privately owned is called **privatization**. In recent years, local governments in the United States have hired private companies to provide services such as trash collection, landscaping, road repairs, and fire protection.

GLOBAL BUSINESS EXAMPLE

PUBLIC SERVICES GOING PRIVATE

In recent years, many countries have decided to let private companies buy and operate various government-owned businesses. For example, the Mexican government sold control of the country's telephone company, airlines, and banks to private companies. This action helped to save the country tax dollars. The businesses also became more profitable. Privatization was also very popular in the countries of eastern Europe in the 1990s as they changed from command to market economies.

Think Critically

1. What are some examples of privatization in your school or community?
2. What problems might be associated with privatization?

✓ CheckPoint

What are the three types of economic systems?

REVIEW GLOBAL BUSINESS TERMS

Define each of the following terms.

1. factors of production
2. economic system
3. command economy
4. market economy
5. mixed economy
6. privatization

REVIEW GLOBAL BUSINESS CONCEPTS

7. List examples of the three factors of production.
8. What are the basic economic questions?
9. What are the three characteristics of capitalism?

SOLVE GLOBAL BUSINESS PROBLEMS

Indicate whether each of the following situations describes a command economy, market economy, or mixed economy.

10. The government tells you what type of job you will have.
11. The government owns the mill that supplies steel to private construction firms.
12. Private investors own a mine that supplies gold to a family jewelry maker.
13. You are free to choose when and where you will buy a new CD for your friend.
14. A privately owned clothing store buys electricity from a government-owned power company.

THINK CRITICALLY

15. Is one of the three factors of production more important than the others? Explain your answer.
16. If you could choose to live in communism, capitalism, or socialism, which one would you choose? Why?

MAKE CONNECTIONS

17. **HISTORY** Conduct research to find examples of countries that have changed from a command economy to a market economy. What kind of changes did the country need to make?
18. **SCIENCE** Describe how scientific developments have changed the skills needed for labor.

ACHIEVING ECONOMIC DEVELOPMENT

2-4

GOALS

- Describe the factors that affect economic development.
- Identify the different levels of economic development.

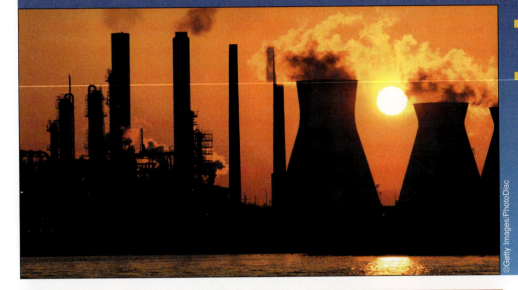

©Getty Images/PhotoDisc

DEVELOPMENT FACTORS

In some countries, people travel on a high-speed bullet train to manage a computer network in a high-rise building. In other countries, people go by ox cart to a grass hut to operate a hand loom to make cloth for family members and other people in their village. These differences in living and work environments reflect the level of economic development. The main influences on a country's economic development are literacy level, technology, and agricultural dependency.

- **Literacy level** Countries with better education systems usually provide more goods and services that are of higher quality for their citizens.
- **Technology** Automated production, distribution, and communications systems allow companies to create and deliver goods, services, and ideas quickly.
- **Agricultural dependency** An economy that is largely involved in agriculture does not have the manufacturing base to provide citizens with a large number of high quality products.

CheckPoint

What factors influence a country's economic development?

TYPES OF DEVELOPMENT

The level of economic development of a country can be categorized in three different ways. A country can be industrialized, less developed, or developing. Each of the different levels has unique characteristics.

INDUSTRIALIZED COUNTRIES

The nations with the greatest economic power are usually those with many large companies. An **industrialized country** is a country with strong business activity that is usually the result of advanced technology and a highly educated population. Such countries have attained high levels of industrialization with high standards of living for their residents. Population tends to be centered in large cities and suburbs rather than in rural areas.

Another factor that supports international trade in industrialized countries is infrastructure. **Infrastructure** refers to a nation's transportation, communication, and utility systems. A country such as Germany—with its efficient rail system, high-speed highways, and computers—is better prepared for international business activities than many other nations with weaker infrastructures.

Industrialized countries are actively involved in international business and foreign trade. A portion of the wealth of these nations is the result of successful business activities conducted throughout the world. Countries commonly described as industrialized include Canada, the United Kingdom, France, Germany, Italy, Japan, and the United States.

GLOBAL BUSINESS EXAMPLE

TYPES OF INFRASTRUCTURE

The infrastructure of a country usually refers to the transportation, communication, and utility systems that facilitate business activities. These may be referred to as the *physical infrastructure.*

Countries also have a *natural infrastructure.* This includes climate, waterways, farmland, and other natural resources that contribute to a nation's economic development.

Business activities are also affected by a nation's *social infrastructure.* This involves family relationships, labor unions, the church, educational institutions, and other social organizations.

Finally, the *managerial or entrepreneurial infrastructure* involves the ability of people to organize and implement business activities. For example, when McDonald's first opened a restaurant in Russia, company representatives worked with local businesspeople to teach managerial skills. They taught them how to obtain, coordinate, and use the food products, workers, buildings, and equipment necessary to operate a fast-food restaurant.

Think Critically

1. Explain why "infrastructure" refers to more than just the transportation, communication, and utility systems.
2. How do the various types of infrastructure affect the economic development of a country?

LESS-DEVELOPED COUNTRIES

Many countries of the world have a very low standard of living. A **less-developed country** (LDC) is a country with little economic wealth and an emphasis on agriculture or mining. Sometimes these countries have abundant resources but no technology to make use of them. Most LDCs have an average annual income per person of less than $3,000. This compares to the United States' average annual income per person of more than $30,000.

As a result of low incomes in less-developed countries, citizens often have problems such as inadequate housing, starvation, and poor health care. This situation results in a high death rate among infants, a shorter life expectancy, and the potential for political instability. Examples of LDCs include countries such as Bangladesh, Bulgaria, Chad, Ecuador, Ethiopia, Hungary, Kenya, Liberia, Nepal, Nigeria, Pakistan, Peru, and the Philippines.

Future economic development for less-developed countries presents a challenge for all nations. Industrialized countries tend to assist LDCs with the problems of poor health care, limited natural resources, low literacy rates, low levels of employment skills, shortage of investment capital, and uncertain political environments. As these obstacles are overcome, all countries will benefit.

DEVELOPING COUNTRIES

Between the extremes of economic development are the **developing countries** that are evolving from less developed to industrialized. These nations are characterized by improving educational systems, increasing technology, and expanding industries. These factors result in an increasing national income. Examples of developing countries include Brazil, India, Singapore, South Korea, Taiwan, and Thailand. Figure 2-5 summarizes the factors that affect a country's level of economic development.

LEVELS OF ECONOMIC DEVELOPMENT

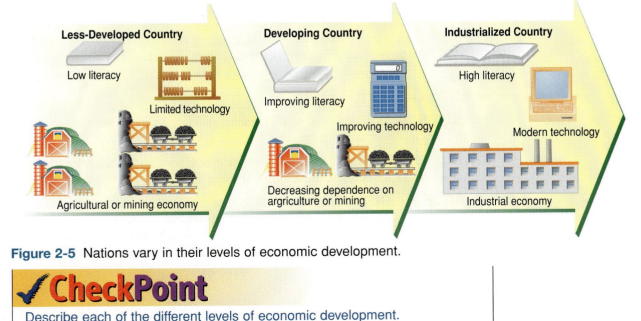

Less-Developed Country
Low literacy
Limited technology
Agricultural or mining economy

Developing Country
Improving literacy
Improving technology
Decreasing dependence on agriculture or mining

Industrialized Country
High literacy
Modern technology
Industrial economy

Figure 2-5 Nations vary in their levels of economic development.

✓CheckPoint

Describe each of the different levels of economic development.

REVIEW GLOBAL BUSINESS TERMS

Define each of the following terms.

1. industrialized country
2. infrastructure
3. less-developed country (LDC)
4. developing country

REVIEW GLOBAL BUSINESS CONCEPTS

5. What are the main influences on a country's economic development?
6. Why is infrastructure important to the economic development of a country?
7. What types of business are commonly found in developing countries?

SOLVE GLOBAL BUSINESS PROBLEMS

For each of the following factors, indicate if the item would usually result in an *improving* or *declining* level of economic development for a country.

8. Increased spending on schools and education.
9. Government tax reductions to attract businesses that build new factories.
10. Use of manual labor instead of automated machinery to harvest crops.
11. Reduced government spending for literacy programs.
12. Expanded use of computers for record keeping by business organizations.

THINK CRITICALLY

13. Why would a modern infrastructure give a country an advantage over other countries?
14. What actions can improve a country's education level?
15. Use the Internet to research ways that industrialized countries are working with less-developed and developing countries to create economic growth.

MAKE CONNECTIONS

16. **SCIENCE** Describe how new scientific discoveries might improve the economic development of a country.
17. **CULTURAL STUDIES** Describe how a country's customs and traditions can influence economic development.
18. **TECHNOLOGY** Use the Internet to research ways a developing country is trying to improve the quality of life for its people.

RESOURCES SATISFY NEEDS | 2-5

GOALS

■ Discuss economic principles that explain the need for international trade.

■ Identify various measures of economic progress and development.

©Getty Images/PhotoDisc

THE ECONOMICS OF FOREIGN TRADE

In the past, economies were viewed solely in terms of national borders. With international trade expanding every day, these boundaries are no longer completely valid in defining economies. Countries are interdependent with each other and so are their economies. Consumers have come to expect goods and services from around the world, not just from suppliers in their own country.

Buying and selling among companies in different countries is based on two economic principles. **Absolute advantage** exists when a country can produce a good or service at a lower cost than other countries. This situation usually occurs as a result of the natural resources or raw materials of a country. For example, South American countries have an absolute advantage in coffee production, Canada in lumber sales, and Saudi Arabia in oil production.

A country may have an absolute advantage in more than one area. If so, it must decide how to maximize its economic wealth. For example, a country may be able to produce both computers and clothing better than other countries. The world market for computers, however, might be stronger. This means the country would better serve its own interests by producing computers and buying clothing from other countries. This is an example of the second economic principle, **comparative advantage**. In this situation, a country specializes in the production of a good or service at which it is relatively more efficient.

Describe an absolute advantage a country may have as a result of natural resources.

MEASURING ECONOMIC PROGRESS

The World Cup, the World Series, and the Olympics are sports events that involve scorekeeping. As with sports, international business also keeps score. Various economic measures are used to evaluate and analyze the economic conditions of a country.

MEASURE OF PRODUCTION

Gross domestic product (GDP) measures the output of goods that a country produces within its borders. It includes items produced with foreign resources. For example, the GDP of the United States would include automobiles manufactured in the United States by foreign-owned companies.

Gross national product (GNP) measures the total value of all goods and services produced by the resources of a country. GNP is like GDP but also includes production in other countries using resources of the country whose GNP is being measured.

Since all nations have different populations, comparing total GDP or GNP is not always meaningful. To help compare the economic progress of countries, businesspeople use a *per capita* comparison, which refers to an amount per person. The per capita GDP of the United States is total GDP divided by the number of people in the country. Figure 2-6 shows per capita GDP in U.S. dollars for selected countries.

INTERNATIONAL TRADE ACTIVITY

An important measure of a country's international business activity is its balance of trade. **Balance of trade** is the difference between a country's exports and imports. When a country exports (sells) more than it imports (buys), it

E-COMMERCE IN ACTION

International Domain Names

The location of a business or another organization on the Internet is defined by a URL (uniform resource locator), such as www.swep.com or www.congress.gov. The last section of a URL is the domain name that indicates the type of organization and the country location.

The United States, which has the most web sites in the world, uses the domain names below, as well as others.

    .com for commercial organizations
    .org for nonprofit organizations
    .gov for government agencies
    .edu for educational institutions
    .mil for military institutions
    .net for networking organizations

When conducting international business, you will encounter domain names that indicate other countries. Some examples include:

.ca for Canada	.mx for Mexico
.br for Brazil	.jp for Japan
.de for Germany	.ng for Nigeria
.uk for United Kingdom	.za for South Africa

Think Critically

1. How can a domain name help an organization communicate its purpose or location?
2. Locate a web site based in another country. What differences of format, language, and other features are present?

PER CAPITA GDP FOR SELECTED COUNTRIES

Country	Per Capita GDP in U.S. Dollars
United States	$36,300
Canada	29,400
Japan	28,000
Iceland	27,100
France	25,700
Sweden	25,400
Italy	25,000
New Zealand	19,500
Greece	19,000
Israel	19,000
South Africa	9,400
Mexico	9,000
Brazil	7,400
Thailand	6,600
China	4,600
India	2,540
Ethiopia	700
Tanzania	610

Source: *Time Almanac 2004*, Pearson Education Company, Needham, MA, 2004.

Figure 2-6 Per capita GDP can be used to compare economic output among nations.

has a favorable balance of trade. This is also called a *trade surplus*. However, if a country imports more than it exports, the nation has an unfavorable balance of trade, or a *trade deficit*. Figure 2-7 shows a comparison of the balance of trade for Canada and the United Kingdom.

In the process of doing international business, payments must be made among businesses in different countries. Since different nations have different monetary units, a comparison of the value of currencies is required. The **foreign exchange rate** is the value of one country's money in relation to the value of the money of another country. Each day in the business section of newspapers or online at various web sites, you can see the changing value of currencies for different countries.

©Getty Images/PhotoDisc

BALANCE OF TRADE FOR CANADA AND UNITED KINGDOM

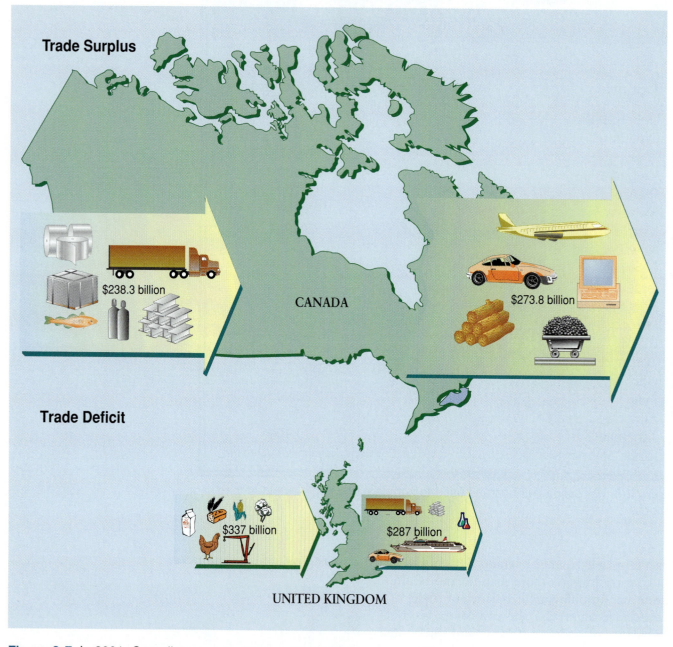

Figure 2-7 In 2001, Canadian exports were greater than imports, and the country enjoyed a favorable balance of trade (surplus). The United Kingdom, however, experienced an unfavorable balance of trade (deficit) because it imported more than it exported.

When you buy more than your current income allows, you go into debt. In the same way, when a country continually has an unfavorable balance of trade, it owes money to others. **Foreign debt** is the amount a country owes to other countries. While owing money to others will affect a country in several ways, the largest effect on the economy is that the nation must use future income to pay for current and past spending. This limits the funds available for improving a country's infrastructure and for providing services for its citizens in the future.

REGIONAL PERSPECTIVE

THE FOUNDER OF BLACK HISTORY MONTH

Each February, the United States celebrates the contributions of African Americans. Black History Month was the idea of Dr. Carter Godwin Woodson, the son of former slaves, who was born in 1875 in New Canton, Virginia. As a young boy, Woodson was only able to attend school a few months of each year. The rest of the year he worked in the coal fields of West Virginia. Despite this hardship, Woodson earned a bachelor's degree from Berea College and went on to earn a Ph.D. from Harvard.

Woodson's many contributions to education include serving as supervisor of a school in the Philippines; serving as a dean at Howard University and West Virginia State College; and teaching French, Spanish, English, and history in the District of Columbia schools. Despite this success, Woodson gave up his educational career in 1922 to devote his energies to developing materials and programs focusing on the experiences of African Americans. This effort resulted in the publication of 20 books—including *The Negro in Our History, The Negro Church,* and *The Miseducation of the Negro.* In 1926, Woodson started Negro History Week, which was later expanded and renamed Black History Month.

Dr. Carter G. Woodson made sure everyone would know about the important role that Africans and African Americans have played in the history of the United States and in the history of the world.

©Getty Images/PhotoDisc

Think Critically

1. Conduct Internet research about local and national activities for Black History Month. Prepare a one-page report of your findings.
2. How did Dr. Woodson's efforts improve the educational and economic opportunities for African Americans?

WORK AS A GROUP

Describe situations in which a person or country would have an absolute or comparative advantage.

OTHER ECONOMIC MEASUREMENTS

Inflation refers to general increases in prices in a country. In the United States, inflation is measured by the **consumer price index (CPI)**. The CPI is a federal government report published by the Bureau of Labor Statistics. Each month, data are provided on price levels for various products and services in different regions of the country. This information can help consumers and business managers make buying decisions. Inflation rates for other countries are available on the Internet or in reference books.

A final indicator of a country's economic situation is the *unemployment rate*. When people are not earning an income, they cannot purchase needed goods and services. This causes other people to lose their jobs. The result is a weaker economy. For any country to operate efficiently, a constant flow of money must be in circulation. When this monetary flow slows down, the economic potential of a nation is not realized.

✔ CheckPoint

What are common economic measurements of production and international trade activity?

©Getty Images/PhotoDisc

NETBookmark

The United States, Germany, and Japan are considered developed countries. However, they still suffer from many of the issues that plague underdeveloped countries, such as hunger and homelessness. Access intlbizxtra.swlearning.com and click on the link for Chapter 2. Read the Thinkquest Library article entitled "Development and Underdevelopment: The Dynamics of Economic Progress." Study the information and write a paragraph detailing some reasons for differences in development levels.

intlbizxtra.swlearning.com

REVIEW GLOBAL BUSINESS TERMS

Define each of the following terms.

1. absolute advantage
2. comparative advantage
3. gross domestic product (GDP)
4. gross national product (GNP)

5. balance of trade
6. foreign exchange rate
7. foreign debt
8. consumer price index (CPI)

Xtra!
Study Tools
intlbizxtra.swlearning.com

REVIEW GLOBAL BUSINESS CONCEPTS

9. What is the difference between absolute advantage and comparative advantage?

10. What does gross domestic product (GDP) measure?

11. How does a country's balance of trade affect its foreign debt?

SOLVE GLOBAL BUSINESS PROBLEMS

Using the data in the Regional Profile at the beginning of this unit, answer the following questions.

12. Which country has the highest per capita GDP? Which has the lowest?

13. Which countries have a trade surplus?

14. Which country had the highest inflation rate of those listed?

THINK CRITICALLY

15. How can a nation create an absolute advantage through its investment activities?

16. How would a high inflation rate affect a country's economic image in the world?

MAKE CONNECTIONS

17. **GEOGRAPHY** Locate examples of natural resources that would give a country an absolute advantage.

18. **MATHEMATICS** A country has exports of $4.2 billion and imports of $4.6 billion. (a) What is the country's balance of trade? (b) Is this amount a trade surplus or a trade deficit?

19. **VISUAL ART** Select one or more economic statistics for several countries. Prepare a graph comparing these data.

CHAPTER SUMMARY

2-1 ECONOMICS AND DECISION MAKING

A The basic economic problem involves scarcity—balancing limited resources with unlimited needs and wants.

B The steps of the decision-making process are (1) define the problem, (2) identify the alternatives, (3) evaluate the alternatives, (4) make a choice, (5) take action, and (6) review the decision.

2-2 BASICS OF ECONOMICS

A The main factors that affect prices are supply and demand.

B Inflation occurs when demand exceeds supply or when business operating costs increase. There are two basic causes for inflation: demand-pull inflation and cost-push inflation.

2-3 ECONOMIC SYSTEMS

A The three main factors of production are natural resources (land), human resources (labor), and capital resources (money and equipment).

B Countries make economic decisions using command economies, market economies, and mixed economies.

2-4 ACHIEVING ECONOMIC DEVELOPMENT

A The main influences on a country's economic development are literacy level, technology, and agricultural dependency.

B The three levels of economic development are industrialized countries, less-developed countries, and developing countries.

2-5 RESOURCES SATISFY NEEDS

A Absolute and comparative advantages are economic principles that explain buying and selling among companies in different countries.

B Measures of economic progress and development include gross domestic product, gross national product, balance of trade, foreign exchange rate, foreign debt, and consumer price index.

Read the Global Focus at the beginning of this chapter, and answer the following questions.

1. After taking various corrective actions, what future economic problems might occur in Mexico?

2. How has NAFTA (the North American Free Trade Agreement) contributed to Mexico's economic development?

3. Conduct an Internet search to obtain current information about the Mexican economy.

REVIEW GLOBAL BUSINESS TERMS

Match the terms listed with the definitions. Some terms may not be used.

1. The difference between a country's exports and imports.

2. A situation that exists when a country specializes in the production of a good or service at which it is relatively more efficient.

3. The study of how people choose to use limited resources to satisfy their unlimited needs and wants.

4. The amount of a good or service that businesses are willing and able to make available at a certain price.

5. The process of changing an industry from public to private ownership.

6. The limited resources available to satisfy the unlimited needs and wants of people.

7. The amount of a good or service that consumers are willing and able to purchase at a certain price.

8. The method a country uses to answer the basic questions of what to produce, how to produce it, and for whom to produce it.

9. A measure of the productive output of a country within its borders, including items produced with foreign resources.

10. The monthly United States federal government report on inflation.

11. The amount a country owes to other countries.

12. A measure of the total value of all goods and services produced by the resources of a country.

13. A nation's transportation, communication, and utility systems.

14. The three types of resources used to produce goods and services.

15. A country's ability to produce a good or service at a lower cost than other countries.

a. absolute advantage
b. balance of trade
c. command economy
d. comparative advantage
e. consumer price index (CPI)
f. demand
g. developing country
h. economics
i. economic system
j. factors of production
k. foreign debt
l. foreign exchange rate
m. gross domestic product (GDP)
n. gross national product (GNP)
o. industrialized country
p. inflation
q. infrastructure
r. less-developed country (LDC)
s. market economy
t. market price
u. mixed economy
v. opportunity cost
w. privatization
x. scarcity
y. supply

MAKE GLOBAL BUSINESS DECISIONS

16. Describe situations of people, companies, and nations facing the basic economic problem of scarcity.

17. Explain how a person goes through the decision-making process many times a day, usually without thinking about the specific steps.

18. If the demand for a product in our society is high, what are some things that happen to reduce that demand?

19. Give examples of capital resources that are used by business organizations to produce goods and services.

20. If you were creating an economic system for a country, what traits would you want it to have? Explain your answer.

21. What problems may arise when a government decides to sell government-owned businesses to private companies?

22. How are people in all countries affected by poor economic conditions in less-developed countries?

23. Name a famous person who is able to do something better than anyone else. This is an absolute advantage. Now, for an example of comparative advantage, describe a person who does several things well but selects only one of these talents to make a living.

24. What actions could a country take to improve its balance of trade?

25. What factors could affect the value of a country's currency compared to that of another country?

GLOBAL CONNECTIONS

26. COMMUNICATIONS Find an article about changes in prices. Prepare a one-minute oral explanation about how supply and demand influence these prices.

27. SCIENCE Prepare a poster or display that shows how the factors of production are used to create a specific product.

28. GEOGRAPHY Prepare a research report on a less-developed country. Describe ways in which that nation could improve its economic development and the quality of life for its citizens.

29. HISTORY Conduct research on the historic factors of production previous to the Industrial Revolution. What types of factories existed in Europe and Asia before 1870?

30. CAREER PLANNING Find a recent news article that deals with a change in the economy as a result of international business. Describe how the events in the article could affect the supply and demand for certain international jobs.

THE GLOBAL
ENTREPRENEUR
CREATING AN INTERNATIONAL BUSINESS PLAN

ECONOMIC CONDITIONS AROUND THE WORLD

Obtain data on GDP, per capita income, balance of trade, and unemployment for six countries for three recent years. Choose two less-developed countries, two developing countries, and two industrialized countries. (Include the country you chose in Chapter 1.) Use library reference materials (such as *The World Almanac* or the *Statistical Abstract of the United States*) or an Internet search to obtain your data.

Find additional information about each country. Locate the countries on a world map or globe. Try to picture their climates, geography, and neighbors. What is it like to live in each of the countries? What natural resources are available? What type of economic system operates in each country: command, market, or mixed? What is the literacy rate in each country? Does most of the population live in an urban or a rural setting?

1. Prepare four graphs: one that compares GDP for the countries over the past three years, one that compares per capita income, one that compares balance of trade, and one that compares unemployment.

2. Prepare a written report that answers the following questions. Include your graphs as part of the report.

   - How has the level of economic development changed in recent years for less-developed countries? for developing countries? for industrialized countries?

   - What do these changes mean for countries involved in international business?

   - Are GDP, per capita income, balance of trade, and unemployment related to each other in any way? If so, how are they related?

   - How could a company involved in international business use this information to make better company decisions?

©Getty Images/PhotoDisc

©Getty Images/PhotoDisc

Chapter 3

CULTURAL INFLUENCES ON GLOBAL BUSINESS

GLOBAL FOCUS

Walt Disney Company Adjusts to France

Bridging cultures was a major goal when the Walt Disney Company developed its Euro Disneyland (now called Disneyland Paris) in France. Many of the French disliked the introduction of popular U.S. culture into their country. They believed that having such an icon of American culture would threaten French culture. Disney had not experienced this kind of opposition when it developed a theme park in Japan.

In response, Disney used a variety of strategies. It pointed out that Disney was of French descent. The original name of Disney's family was D'Isigny. The company agreed to use French as the primary written language for theme-park signs and designed several new attractions with French and other European cultural themes. Disney also slightly relaxed its strict dress code for cast members (employees). Although males still are not allowed beards, females were allowed to wear brighter red nail polish than in the United States.

To maintain its traditional U.S. family image, Euro Disneyland initially refrained from selling liquor in the theme park. However, after significant losses due to weak attendance, Euro Disneyland decided to sell champagne, beer, and wine at its upscale restaurants. These beverages are commonly sold at entertainment businesses throughout Europe, which has a different attitude about alcohol than the United States does.

Think Critically

1. What barriers did the Disney Company face when planning and operating Disneyland Paris?
2. Why do you think Disney emphasized that the name originally was D'Isigny?
3. Go to the web sites for the Disney Company and Disneyland Paris to obtain additional information about the international operations of the company. Prepare a report of your findings.

3-1 | CULTURE AROUND THE WORLD

GOALS

- Describe influences of culture on global business activities.
- Explain the role of subcultures.

©Getty Images/PhotoDisc

CULTURAL INFLUENCES IN INTERNATIONAL BUSINESS

Some people have their evening meal at five o'clock. Others eat at nine or ten in the evening. This is a simple but distinct example of differences in culture.

A **culture** is a system of learned, shared, unifying, and interrelated beliefs, values, and assumptions. Beliefs are statements about the nature of a person, thing, or concept. Values are the positive and negative ideals, customs, and institutions of a group. Assumptions are statements that are taken for granted as fact. Cultural beliefs, values, and assumptions are directly and indirectly acquired throughout a lifetime. They are accepted and valued by other members of the group. They cause group members to respond in similar and usually predictable ways. Put another way, culture is a mind-set, or a way of thinking that is acquired over time. To members of a particular culture, their ways are logical and reasonable. To outsiders, their ways sometimes seem different or even strange.

A culture is the sum of a group's way of life. Some, but not all, of the parts are discussed and recorded. Different aspects of culture are taught in different arenas. Some of those arenas include homes, schools, religious institutions, and work. Still other parts are learned indirectly through experiences. Members of cultural groups often do not share their cultures willingly with outsiders.

A culture can be compared to an iceberg. You can easily see the tip. Most of the beliefs, values, and assumptions of a culture are hidden beneath the

58

surface, just as most of the iceberg is hidden beneath the water. You can easily see such objects of a culture as clothes, foods, and vehicles. You can read a culture's literature and hear its music. You can also observe the behaviors of its members. However, these items alone do not make a culture. Hidden away are unseen but important parts of culture. These include the supporting expectations, attitudes, values, beliefs, and perceptions of its members.

THE SAME OR DIFFERENT?

When a company does business in another country, it must decide whether to use a standardized product or a customized product. While some products can be sold in basically the same form throughout the world (cameras, computers, motor vehicles), others must be adapted to a culture.

The McDonald's menu is revised in different parts of the world based on tastes, customs, and religious beliefs. In the Philippines and other countries, Tide detergent is sold in three forms—powder, liquid, and bar. The detergent bar is used for washing clothes by hand in areas that do not have washing machines.

Global companies must also decide whether to standardize or adapt other business activities. The advertising message that is successful in one country might be offensive in another country. Or a company may not be able to use the same hiring and firing process in all countries because of differences in customs, traditions, and family relationships.

Think Critically

1. Name some products that might be sold in the same form around the world.
2. What aspects of culture might require a company to adapt its product when selling in another country?
3. List other business decisions that must be customized to the culture of a nation.

✔ CheckPoint

How do members of a group learn its culture?

THE SUBCULTURES WITHIN A SOCIETY

A **subculture** is a subset or part of a larger culture. A subculture may have some values, beliefs, and assumptions that are different than the larger culture of which it is a part. You are a member of many different subcultures. You are a member of the general culture of your country, but you are also a member of some of its component groups. You are a member of the student subculture. You are also a member of the male or the female subculture. You are a member of an ethnic-based subculture. You might identify with various other subcultures as well. However, you are not a member of some subcultures because you don't meet the requirements. For example, high school students are not members of the senior-citizen subculture because of their age.

WORK AS A GROUP

Discuss the personal beliefs, values, and assumptions that make up your cultural baggage.

Subcultures often choose from the allowable behaviors within their respective general cultures. For example, music is part of the general U.S. culture. However, not all U.S. subcultures choose to listen to the same music. Young people may prefer heavy metal, alternative, R and B, techno, and hip-hop music. In contrast, the adult subculture might prefer contemporary, jazz, or classical music.

INFLUENCES OF CULTURES AND SUBCULTURES

Cultures and subcultures are important because they influence the actions of their members. **Cultural baggage** is the idea that you carry your beliefs, values, and assumptions with you at all times. Your cultural baggage influences how you respond to others. In business settings, your cultural baggage influences what you say and do as you conduct business.

Cultures and subcultures set the standards against which people judge behaviors. Consequently, people behave in ways that are acceptable to other

©Getty Images/PhotoDisc

members of their culture and subcultures. You have learned through experience that if you behave in unacceptable ways, members of your culture will let you know. If you are rude to your parents, for example, they may discipline you. If you insult your friends, they may not ask you to join them in future activities. If you steal a car, you may receive a jail sentence. The influences of cultures and subcultures on the behaviors of individuals are quite strong.

SUBCULTURE OF U.S. BUSINESS

The U.S. business subculture is composed of the business-related part of the general U.S. culture. This business subculture has certain beliefs, values, and assumptions that differentiate it from the general U.S. culture. With some exceptions, businesspeople share a core of common beliefs, values, and assumptions that shape their behaviors. These common behaviors allow U.S. business to be conducted in predictable ways.

Many of the important beliefs, values, and assumptions of the U.S. business subculture appear in common sayings. Cultural groups use such sayings to preserve and transmit important guiding principles to others. Figure 3-1 lists several of the sayings of the U.S. business subculture. Can you think of some other common sayings with business-related meanings?

SOME GUIDING PRINCIPLES OF U.S. BUSINESS

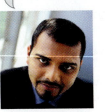
Where there is a will, there is a way.

Don't count your chickens before they are hatched.

Waste not, want not.

Time is money.

If at first you don't succeed, try, try again.

You can influence your own future.

You must not count on predictable outcomes.

You should use your resources carefully.

Time is a valuable resource that you should use wisely.

You should strive persistently toward your goals.

©Getty Images/PhotoDisc

Figure 3-1 These common sayings reflect some widely held beliefs, values, and assumptions of the U.S. business culture.

VARIATIONS IN BUSINESS SUBCULTURES WORLDWIDE

Just as the U.S. business subculture has its own set of beliefs, values, and assumptions, so do other business subcultures. Consequently, no two business subcultures share identical sets of beliefs, values, and assumptions. However, when two general cultures are similar, their business subcultures are apt to be similar as well.

For example, the United States trades extensively with Canada and the United Kingdom. One reason for these trade links is that the business subcultures of these countries are similar. These similarities cause U.S., Canadian, and British people to conduct business in somewhat similar ways. Less trade may occur between American and Chinese or Kenyan businesses because their business subcultures are much different.

People cannot escape from the influences of business subcultures around the world. These subcultures are powerful. They shape the personal and professional behaviors of businesspersons everywhere. Your behavior in the business world will be guided by the standards that are deemed permissible in your country's business subculture. Other business subcultures will operate with different sets of beliefs, values, and assumptions. Becoming aware of these cultural differences is the first step toward understanding them and their influence.

✔CheckPoint

How does the business subculture of a country affect which countries it is most likely to do business with?

intlbizxtra.swlearning.com

REVIEW GLOBAL BUSINESS TERMS

Define each of the following terms.

1. culture
2. subculture
3. cultural baggage

REVIEW GLOBAL BUSINESS CONCEPTS

4. How is a subculture different from a culture?
5. Why is it important to understand a country's business subculture?

SOLVE GLOBAL BUSINESS PROBLEMS

Which of the following statements are characteristic and uncharacteristic of the U.S. business subculture? Why?

6. Hard work is valued and rewarded.
7. Leisure is more important than work.
8. Intention is more important than accomplishment.

THINK CRITICALLY

9. Explain why cultural knowledge of a country is necessary for being successful in international business.
10. What actions must a person take when doing business in countries with strong family-work relationships?
11. What are some assumptions of the U.S. business culture?
12. What is one item that makes your culture different from other cultures?

MAKE CONNECTIONS

13. **TECHNOLOGY** How can the use of technology help to preserve and destroy cultures?
14. **COMMUNICATIONS** Interview a person who has visited or lived in another country. How is the culture of that nation different from that of the United States.?
15. **LAW** Every country has its own culturally sanctioned legal system. What are the fundamental characteristics of the common law system of the United States?
16. **CULTURAL STUDIES** Use the Internet to find examples of businesses that have had to adapt their business practices to local cultural conditions.

CULTURE AND SOCIAL ORGANIZATIONS

3-2

GOALS

- Describe how family relationships can affect culture.
- Explain the role of societal influences on culture.

©Getty Images/PhotoDisc

FAMILY RELATIONSHIPS

Cultures and subcultures influence the ways in which societies organize themselves. Social organization includes the relationships between both the family unit and society. These components affect not only the entire culture, but also many other institutions, including the business community.

FAMILY UNITS

Most societies are at least partially organized around family units. A **nuclear family** is a group that consists of a parent or parents and unmarried children living together. Most developed countries have societies organized around nuclear families. An **extended family** is a group that consists of the parents, children, and other relatives living together. Other relatives might include married children, grandchildren, the parents' parents, the brothers and sisters of the parents, and others. Many developing countries have societies organized around extended families.

FAMILY-WORK RELATIONSHIPS

Family ties to business are weak in some cultures and strong in others. In Canada, the United States, and most northern European countries, links between family and business are weak. Fairly often there is no connection at all. However, in most of the remainder of North and South America, much of southern Europe, most of Asia, northern Africa, and the Middle East, family ties to business are strong. Quite often employees of businesses in these areas are family members. It is difficult to separate family from business. Figure 3-2 identifies some countries that have weak ties between family and business and some that have strong ties.

TIES BETWEEN FAMILY AND BUSINESS

Figure 3-2 In certain parts of the world, ties between family and business tend to be weak, but in other parts of the world, the ties are very strong.

Countries with Weak Ties   Countries with Strong Ties

A Question of Ethics

BLOOD IS THICKER THAN WATER

Miguel Hernandez heads a small Mexican exporting firm that sells women's sandals in the United States. His brother Javier is the company salesperson who travels to Texas, New Mexico, Arizona, and California, selling the product line.

Lydia Martinez is the shoe buyer for a chain of stores throughout the southwestern United States. She likes the sandals she buys from the Mexican firm. They are stylish, sell well, and represent good value for her customers. They also are a significant source of profit for her employer. Nevertheless, Javier increasingly frustrates Lydia.

According to Lydia, Javier rarely calls on her in person, doesn't respond to her communications, and is unreliable in processing her large orders. Disgusted, Lydia telephoned Miguel to ask that he fire Javier. After listening to her complaints and empathizing with her frustrations, Miguel responds that Javier is his brother. He has to retain Javier as salesperson to keep peace in the family—even if his actions are not in the best interest of the Mexican firm.

Think Critically

1. Was it ethical for Lydia Martinez to ask Miguel Hernandez to fire Javier Hernandez?
2. Why do you think the Mexican company retained Javier Hernandez in spite of his poor work?
3. What are some cultural aspects of this situation that need to be considered?

✓ CheckPoint

How can family relationships affect the culture in a country?

SOCIETY'S INSTITUTIONS

The institutions of a society can be just as important to a culture as family relationships.

EDUCATION

The family unit provides the early education for its younger members. It instructs the young in the ways of its culture. In economically developed societies, the family often shares responsibilities with other cultural institutions for providing later education. Religious groups often provide moral and spiritual education. Schools provide formal education, which prepares people to function productively as members of society. Businesses sometimes provide specialized work-related education and training. This upgrades the job-related knowledge, skills, and attitudes of employees.

Families and their societies decide what types and amounts of education will be made available to members. In the United States, a person has many opportunities to receive different types and amounts of education. One reason for the global economic success of the United States is that its workers are well educated and trained.

GENDER ROLES

In most cultures, family members are assigned different roles to fulfill. Sometimes these roles are assigned based upon gender. In some cultures, only males or females are allowed to fill certain roles. In some societies, females are the primary workers outside the household. In others, males are

WORK AS A GROUP

Suggest ways in which technology might affect the culture of a nation.

©Getty Images/PhotoDisc

NETBookmark

Every country, no matter how developed, has a class system. Access intlbizxtra.swlearning.com and click on the link for Chapter 3. Read the web article describing the caste system in modern India. After reading the article, write a brief paragraph describing how the caste system differs from the class system of the United Kingdom as described on page 66.

intlbizxtra.swlearning.com

the primary workers away from home. In still other societies, both males and females are employed outside the home.

Viewpoints vary worldwide about the roles males and females can fill in business. Some business subcultures may favor males over females in the workplace. In the United States, women increasingly participate in international business activities as equals with men.

In Japan, in the past, native women had very inferior workplace opportunities when compared to men. Japanese women traditionally participated in the international business activities of Japanese companies only as translators and interpreters. In Libya, women have very limited workplace opportunities. They do not typically participate in international business activities.

MOBILITY

Some cultures, such as the dominant one in the United States, have relatively little geographic attachment. In other words, the family members are not usually tied to their current location. They are mobile and willing to relocate for better employment opportunities. In some other cultures, the ties to birthplace or region are much stronger. Members of these cultures would almost never consider moving away.

People who would not consider leaving their region permanently are sometimes willing to move elsewhere temporarily for better work opportunities. For example, guest workers from Turkey are a significant portion of the population of Germany. Guest workers bring their native culture with them. They also maintain strong ties with their home country. Sometimes their culture conflicts with that of the host country. Some host cultures do not make adjustments for guest workers. Other host cultures try to ensure that guest workers are treated similarly to native workers.

CLASS SYSTEM

Cultures also organize their members beyond the family unit. A **class system** is a means of dividing the members of a cultural group into various levels. The levels can be based upon such factors as education, occupation, heritage, conferred or inherited status (nobility), and income. In some cultures, you can move from one class to another. This is true to a great extent in the United States, where the class system is weak.

Sometimes the levels are based upon your lineage. When this occurs, you can become locked into your class. It is very difficult or impossible for you to change classes. In the United Kingdom, to a significant degree, your bloodline still influences your class and occupational choices. If you are born into the British aristocracy, you belong to the highest class. If you work, you might oversee your family's property and fortune. However, you probably would not engage in trade. That would be considered beneath your privileged position. For the remainder of British society, nobility is not a factor. Some people do shift class levels. However, it is more difficult to change class level in the United Kingdom than it is in the United States.

What types of social organization are commonly found in most cultures?

REVIEW GLOBAL BUSINESS TERMS

Define each of the following terms.

1. nuclear family

2. extended family

3. class system

intlbizxtra.swlearning.com

REVIEW GLOBAL BUSINESS CONCEPTS

4. How does social organization influence general cultures?

SOLVE GLOBAL BUSINESS PROBLEMS

Historically, the United Kingdom has had a rigid class system in which members of the aristocracy have enjoyed special privileges. In contrast, the United States has a flexible class system that allows individuals to shift from one class to another.

5. Why doesn't the United States have a reigning king or queen like the United Kingdom?

6. What fundamental principle in the United States requires that the class system be flexible, at least theoretically?

7. Why do you think there are attempts in the United Kingdom to break down some of the barriers of its class system?

THINK CRITICALLY

8. Why do nuclear families often have a higher living standard than extended families?

9. Why are countries with well-educated and trained citizens likely to be economically successful?

10. How does high geographic attachment handicap workers in a global economy?

MAKE CONNECTIONS

11. **HISTORY** What are some countries that have monarchs?

12. **CULTURAL STUDIES** What role is traditionally given to women in the Islamic Middle East?

13. **GEOGRAPHY** Why are there more extended families in Mexico than in Canada and the United States?

14. **CULTURAL STUDIES** Use the Internet to research countries or cultures that have rigid class systems.

3-3 COMMUNICATION ACROSS CULTURES

GOALS

- Understand the importance of knowing another language for global business sucess.
- Compare direct and indirect communication.
- Describe the influence of nonverbal communication.

和平、進步
迎接新世紀

PEACE PROGRESS FOR A BETTER WORLD

©Getty Images/PhotoDisc

LANGUAGE DIFFERENCES

All cultures and subcultures use language to communicate with other societies. Language facilitates international business transactions. Without language, conducting business would be very difficult.

Many languages are used for business purposes. However, English is widely considered to be the language of international business. More people use English to conduct international business than any other language. More people speak Mandarin Chinese than any other language. However, English is understood in almost every country around the world. Figure 3-3 shows the numbers of native speakers of major world languages.

As a language for conducting business, English has some advantages over other languages. It contains many words drawn from other languages, and ideas can be expressed in many ways. It also has a large number of business-related words. Further, English can be concise and precise. Often it takes fewer words to send the same message in English than to send it in other major languages. For example, the French version of a message may be 20 percent longer than the English version. The Spanish version may be 30 to 40 percent longer and the Russian version may be 35 to 50 percent longer than the English version.

MAJOR WORLD LANGUAGES

Language	Number of Speakers	Where It Is Used
Chinese, Mandarin	874,000,000	China
Hindi	366,000,000	India
English	341,000,000	United Kingdom, United States, Canada, Ireland, Australia, India, numerous African and Asian countries
Spanish	322,000,000	Spain, Mexico, most Central and South American countries
Bengali	207,000,000	India, Bangladesh
Portuguese	176,000,000	Portugal, Brazil
Russian	167,000,000	Russia, former republics of the Soviet Union
Japanese	125,000,000	Japan
German	100,000,000	Germany, Austria, Switzerland, numerous European countries
Korean	78,000,000	Korea
French	77,000,000	France, Canada, numerous European and African countries
Chinese, Wu	77,000,000	China

Source: *The World Almanac and Book of Facts, 2004*

Figure 3-3 Most of the world's citizens are not native speakers of English, which is the generally accepted language of international business.

LEARNING A SECOND LANGUAGE

Being a native speaker of English is both an advantage and a disadvantage. It is an advantage because you already know the major language of international business. It is a disadvantage because you may decide wrongly that there is little need to learn another language. Since people often prefer to transact business in their native language, you could also learn a second language.

You may be wondering which foreign language is most useful for business purposes. The answer is not easy; all languages have use in some business situations. Figure 3-4 shows the languages

Figure 3-4 The languages most frequently spoken are not the same as those recommended for business purposes to U.S. native English speakers.

BUSINESS LANGUAGES USEFUL TO LEARN

Rank	Language
1	Japanese
2-3 (tie)	French and Spanish
4	German
5	Chinese
6	Russian
7	Arabic
8	Portuguese
9-10 (tie)	Italian and Korean

Discuss which language besides English you would choose to learn in order to get ahead in international business.

most frequently recommended to native U.S. English speakers by respondents from the 100 largest U.S. businesses.

Note that Japanese is the most frequently recommended language for Americans to learn. It is the language of one of the dominant trading nations. On the other hand, French, German, and Spanish, as well as most of the other languages, are used by several important trading nations.

Learning any language will help you to understand the culture of those who speak it. Some people say that a language represents the highest form of a group's culture. As you learn the language, you learn how things are done where that language is spoken. You learn the beliefs, values, and assumptions of that society.

Over time, you may learn to think and communicate like a native. This helps you conduct business like a member of that society. Being fluent in a second language for business purposes is a competitive advantage. It will help you succeed in the world of international business.

✓CheckPoint

What are some benefits of knowing a second language?

DIRECT AND INDIRECT COMMUNICATION

One important feature of communication is that it can be direct or indirect. **Contexting** refers to how direct or indirect communication is. A

SAYING "NO" THE JAPANESE WAY

Carl Byrd, a U.S. businessperson, asked his Japanese trading partner, Masahiro Watanabe, for a lower price on the Japanese product he was purchasing. Mr. Watanabe smiled and replied, "I will do my best." Two weeks later Mr. Byrd discovered that the product was invoiced at the original price. Mr. Byrd appealed to Mr. Watanabe, asking that the price be decreased because of the size of the order. Mr. Watanabe replied, "That will be very difficult." Two weeks later Mr. Byrd received another invoice, and it showed the original price. Mr.

Byrd felt let down by Mr. Watanabe since he had not said "no" directly.

Several weeks later, in an international business seminar, Mr. Byrd learned that the Japanese culture is a high-context culture. Suddenly, things made sense to Mr. Byrd. Mr. Watanabe was not being deceptive after all; he was being very polite and indirect. Both "I will do my best" and "That will be very difficult" suggest an unlikely outcome. Mr. Watanabae had been consistently saying "no" in the correct Japanese manner, but Mr. Byrd was prepared to understand "no" only in the direct manner of U.S. businesspersons.

Think Critically
1. Why do different cultures have different ways of saying "no"?
2. What are some other countries that say "no" indirectly?

low-context culture is one that communicates very directly. These cultures value words and interpret them literally. The general and business subcultures of both Germany and the United States are relatively low context. Members of these groups convey information directly.

A high-context culture is one that communicates indirectly. These cultures attach little value to the literal meanings of words and interpret them figuratively. The general and business subcultures of both Japan and Iraq are relatively high context. Members of these groups convey information indirectly.

The concept of *face-saving* or minimizing personal embarrassment is directly related to contexting. In low-context cultures, people are not too concerned about being personally embarrassed. In high-context cultures,

©Getty Images/PhotoDisc

however, personal embarrassment must be avoided at all costs. If you cause a Japanese business partner to lose face, you have blundered badly. You have jeopardized your personal and business relationship with that person.

Many international communication problems can be better understood if you know about contexting and face-saving. For example, Saddam Hussein criticized the United States regarding the Gulf War and the later invasion of Iraq. The question is whether he really meant what he said. He could not deliver on all of his threats. However, since the Iraqi culture is high context, Saddam Hussein's words shouldn't have been taken too literally. They should be interpreted figuratively. In Iraqi culture, intention is much more important than what is actually done. He lashed out at the United States to save face. During the conflicts involving Iraq, Saddam Hussein endured considerable personal embarrassment. He was humiliated publicly. Consequently, he struck back verbally at the United States since he could not do so militarily in any large-scale way.

 **CheckPoint**

How does a high-context culture communicate differently than a low-context culture?

WORK AS A GROUP

Convey an idea using only nonverbal communication techniques.

NONVERBAL COMMUNICATION

Not all communication takes place with language. **Nonverbal communication** is communication that does not involve the use of words. You have probably heard the saying that actions speak louder than words. Actions are an example of nonverbal communication.

Body Language One type of nonverbal communication is called body language. **Body language** refers to the meaning conveyed by facial expressions, upper and lower body movements, and gestures. All cultures and subcultures use body language. However, they do not always attach the same meanings to body language. The meaning of body language is not universal. For example, in Japan, you should cross your legs only at the knees and ankles. You should not rest your foot on your knee. The Japanese feel this position is offensive. They believe the bottom of a foot is unclean and should not be exposed to view.

Appearance In the international business world, your appearance counts. Your clothing has no voice, but it can communicate. Although people dress differently in various parts of the world, they dress similarly when

©Getty Images/PhotoDisc

conducting international business. For such purposes, you should dress in a conservative manner. You might, for instance, wear dark-colored suits and white shirts or blouses. As a male, you would choose color-coordinated ties that are not too bright. As a female, you might choose simple jewelry to complement your outfit. Of course, your clothing should be clean and well pressed. Your hair should be carefully groomed, too. Your business associates will be favorably impressed if you always dress and behave in a professional manner. If you care about your appearance, you are likely to care about business matters, too.

Eye Contact Eye movements vary from culture to culture. They are another means of nonverbal communication. In the United States, you should have direct eye contact with the person to whom you are speaking. That is not the case, however, in South Korea. There you show respect for the person speaking by looking away from the eyes of the speaker. This is also true in many other Asian cultures.

Touching Touching is another part of nonverbal communication. What kind of touches are acceptable varies worldwide. In Arab countries, business associates hug and kiss each other when they meet. They may also hold hands as they discuss business matters. Such behaviors may be considered inappropriate for business in many other regions of the world.

Personal Space Different cultural groups use space differently for communication purposes. Jordanians confer very close to each other with only a few inches separating them. People in the United States require more distance. They often confer with each other at arm's length. Japanese prefer even more distance between speakers than do people in the United States. When businesspersons with different space requirements interact, they must remember to respect the space needs of others. If they don't, they may find themselves dancing around the room because as one person moves forward, the other steps back.

Color Other forms of nonverbal communication exist. Color is one. For example, the U.S. culture values dental products that produce white teeth. However, in Southeast Asia, teeth blackened by chewing betel nuts are valued. This value could pose a problem for a U.S. company trying to sell its toothpaste in that area of the world.

Numbers Numbers also communicate. In the United Kingdom and continental Europe, the first floor is the floor above the ground floor. The first floor in a building in the United States is customarily the ground floor. Numbers can confuse businesspersons since numbers sometimes carry different meanings in different cultures and subcultures. For example, in many Western countries, the number 13 is considered unlucky. In parts of Asia, the number 11 is a favorable sign.

©Getty Images/PhotoDisc

Emblems Emblems or other symbols communicate. A Canadian could wear a cross-shaped necklace in many countries. However, in a country that doesn't practice Christianity, doing so would be culturally insensitive. In fact, it is illegal to display non-Islamic religious symbols in Saudi Arabia.

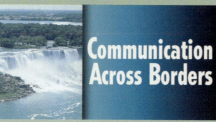

Communication Across Borders

THE CANADIAN HANDSHAKING CODE

Canadian businesspersons customarily shake hands when meeting others. For a Canadian not to shake an associate's hand would be considered impolite and rude.

A brief cursory handshake with only one limp pump suggests little warmth in the relationship. A handshake with several pumps suggests a neutral relationship. An extended handshake with a number of firm pumps suggests a warm and friendly relationship. Such a handshake is usually reserved for close colleagues. Thus, Canadian businesspersons send subtle messages about their relationships with others as they shake hands. In many cases, foreigners are not aware of the cultural meanings Canadian businesspersons attach to their handshakes and miss the intended messages.

Think Critically

1. Why do you think that information about the Canadian handshaking code is not widely known outside of Canada?
2. Locate a web site that provides more information about the cultural practices of Canadians. What surprising information did you uncover?

Smells Smells are another means of nonverbal communication. Natural body odors are considered unacceptable in the United States. Selling such products as deodorants and colognes, therefore, is big business. In most African and Middle Eastern countries, body odors are accepted as being natural and distinctive. People there do not try to hide them. Consequently, the market for deodorants and colognes in those regions is much smaller.

©Getty Images/PhotoDisc

✓ CheckPoint

What are some common methods of nonverbal communication?

REVIEW GLOBAL BUSINESS TERMS

Define each of the following terms.

1. contexting

2. nonverbal communication

3. body language

REVIEW GLOBAL BUSINESS CONCEPTS

4. What languages are the most useful ones for international business purposes? Why?

5. How is nonverbal communication different from other forms of communication?

SOLVE GLOBAL BUSINESS PROBLEMS

You and a friend are discussing which foreign language to study for business purposes. You think you might study Spanish. Your friend is leaning towards French. Both languages are highly recommended for business. Both are widely available throughout the United States.

6. Which language will allow you to talk with more potential customers?

7. Which language is useful in more countries?

8. What are some reasons why it might be sensible to learn the other language anyway?

THINK CRITICALLY

9. Describe ways in which knowing a different language could benefit you in both personally and professionally.

10. How long do you think it would take you to learn to communicate in a foreign language like a native speaker does?

MAKE CONNECTIONS

11. **TECHNOLOGY** How might technology help you learn a foreign language?

12. **MATHEMATICS** Using the data in Figure 3-3, what is the approximate ratio of Spanish speakers to Russian speakers?

13. **CULTURE STUDIES** Why do you think that the Korean culture is likely to be a high-context culture?

14. **GEOGRAPHY** What is a region where many high-context cultures are found?

15. **COMMUNICATION** Use the Internet to research methods of nonverbal communication and their uses in business situations around the world.

3-4

VALUES AROUND THE WORLD

GOALS

- Identify and explain five major types of values that vary from culture to culture.
- Describe the two major reactions to cultural differences.

©Getty Images/PhotoDisc

VALUES VARY AMONG CULTURES

Values are ideas that people cherish and believe to be important. They tend to vary from culture to culture, often creating major differences among cultures. Some of the more important fundamental values involve individualism versus collectivism, technology, leadership, religion, and time.

INDIVIDUALISM AND COLLECTIVISM

Individualism is the belief in the individual and her or his ability to function relatively independently. Self-reliance, independence, and freedom are closely related to individualism in the United States. However, many other cultures see individualism as undesirable. They do not approve of the negative aspects of self-centeredness and selfishness. Instead, they prefer **collectivism**, the belief that the group is more important than the individual.

The Japanese culture has a strong collective orientation. It has a saying that translates "The nail that stands out is soon pounded down." This saying means that individuals should not stand out from the group. If they do, the group will force these individuals to conform to the expectations of the group. Japanese businesspersons tend to function collectively. Consequently, they do not make decisions without getting consensus, or group agreement. Group harmony is more important to them than individual gain. In contrast, U.S. businesspersons tend to function individually. They often make decisions without consulting fellow employees. Individual gain is more important to them than group harmony.

No culture is based entirely on individualism or collectivism. All cultures have both, but most cultures lean toward one or the other. Cultures that lean toward individualism are apt to value the entrepreneurial spirit. That means people are willing to accept some risk for possible personal gain.

TECHNOLOGY

Fundamental beliefs about technology also vary from culture to culture. Some cultures embrace technology as a means of providing more and better material objects. Most developed countries have business subcultures that view improvements positively. Often less-developed countries have business subcultures that resist improvements in technology. Some countries view technology negatively for cultural or religious reasons. For example, attitudes toward technological change are generally positive in France. In India, they are mixed. India tries to balance the use of technology so that it doesn't intrude on important spiritual beliefs and displace people from menial tasks. Technological change is viewed at best as neutral and often as negative in some countries. Technology is sometimes seen as a threat to fundamental Iranian ways.

LEADERSHIP, POWER, AND AUTHORITY

Different cultures have different values relating to leadership, power, and authority. These three are shared among a number of different people and institutions in democratic societies. For example, in the United States, the power to govern is divided among the legislative, judicial, and executive branches of the government. That way no one individual or group has too much power.

In authoritarian societies, leadership, power, and authority are granted to a few. Much of the power in these societies seems to be in a chosen person and not in the institution. In the People's Republic of China, the leadership, power, and authority are concentrated in the hands of a few older leaders, who govern without question. They make all of the major decisions, which are carried out by middle-aged bureaucrats. The younger generation has essentially no power. Their protests for more freedom are viewed as threatening the time-honored Chinese tradition of respect for the wisdom of age, which is a major cultural value.

RELIGION

Religious beliefs also regulate the behaviors of members of many cultural groups, including business organizations. Such beliefs influence how people view the world. Some cultural groups are dominated by one religion. This is the case in Iran, for example, which is strongly influenced by Islam. Businesspersons there must follow Islamic practices. Some countries, such as the United States, have several major religions. Businesspersons in those countries must respect the value choices of various religious practices. In some countries, such as the United Kingdom, religion is not a major social force. The relationship between religions and business is controversial. Good arguments can be raised that various religions both encourage and discourage business activity.

GLOBAL BUSINESS EXAMPLE

SAUDI ARABIA PROTECTS ITS OWN CULTURAL VALUES

To work in Saudi Arabia, guest workers and their families must agree to respect and adapt to the Saudi culture. For example, they must live a lifestyle that is acceptable to Saudis. They must wear modest clothes that cover most parts of their bodies. They must not drink alcoholic beverages. Women may not drive and must have written permission from their husbands to travel beyond their neighborhoods. Then male chaperones must accompany them.

To reduce the influences of foreign cultures on Saudi culture, guest workers and their families typically live in certain locations. These are called compounds. Most of the goods and services needed by guest workers are available in or near their compounds. Consequently, they have little need to interact with most Saudis and have little opportunity to influence Saudi culture.

Think Critically

1. Why would a country such as Saudi Arabia want to protect its culture?
2. What are other ways that countries might limit the influence of foreigners on their cultures?

TIME

Time is another factor to which different cultural groups attach different meanings. In most developed countries, time is often viewed by the clock or in the mechanical sense. Time is seen as a scarce resource that must be carefully spent. It is viewed this way in both Canada and the United States. In most less-developed countries, time is often viewed in a natural or fluid sense. Time relates to the unending cycles of day and night and the seasons. Time is viewed this way in many underdeveloped parts of Latin America.

✓ CheckPoint

Name five major types of values that can vary from culture to culture.

ADJUSTING TO CULTURAL DIFFERENCES

Individuals and businesses must make cultural adjustments. In other words, they must adapt to different cultural values. To show respect for other cultural groups, you may need to make adjustments when dealing with them. These changes will help to minimize the differences that separate the cultural groups. Businesses that operate in other countries also make cultural adjustments.

ETHNOCENTRISM

Ethnocentrism is the belief that one's culture is better than other cultures. Ethnocentrism is a major obstacle to conducting successful international business. Cultures and subcultures are different worldwide. However, different does not mean that one is better than the other. Different simply means that the cultures are not alike.

REGIONAL PERSPECTIVE

CULTURE: FRENCH CUISINE

Every country has foods for which it is well known. But which country has the most appealing foods overall? Perhaps the answer most often heard around the world is "France." The foods of France are recognized and highly regarded wherever you go. What makes French food so special? France is well known for the high-quality ingredients, the proven culinary techniques, and the recognition that time is an important factor in the preparation of outstanding food.

What might you eat at a simple, traditional French meal? For breakfast, you might have a *café complet* of yeast rolls, croissants, *brioche* (cake-like buns of yeast dough), or other fresh breads with *confiture* (jam) or *marmelade*. You might drink hot chocolate or *café au lait* (hot coffee with hot milk in equal parts).

At lunch, which is sometimes the main meal of the day, you might eat *hors d'oeuvres* (side dishes or starters) of thinly sliced smoked meats and assorted vegetables marinated in oil, radishes with butter, and crusty bread. This would be followed by a main course of fish, meat, or poultry or even an omelet with a side of potatoes. Next, you might have a separate vegetable course. It could be asparagus with *hollandaise* (a rich sauce made from egg yolks, butter, and lemon juice). The next course, designed to cleanse your palate, would be a salad with vinegar-and-oil dressing that is mixed at the table. For dessert, you could eat a baked good or fresh fruit and cheese with *cremè gâteau* (cake).

For dinner, the menu is similar to that for lunches, except that the *hors d'oeuvres* are replaced by soup. A fish and a meat course are both served. The dinner dessert course will likely be more elaborate than the one served at lunch. Dessert possibilities include *mousse* (a sweetened mixture with a whipped-cream base sometimes stabilized with gelatin) or a sweet *soufflé* (a baked food made fluffy with beaten egg whites, egg yolks, and a thickening sauce).

The French enjoy leisurely meals with good talk accompanied by wine, beer, or cider. Black coffee, once the traditional finishing touch for a French meal, is often dispensed with today. After-dinner drinks, *liqueurs*, are often served.

©Getty Images/PhotoDisc

Think Critically

1. Conduct an Internet search for additional information about the culture of France. How are French meals like and unlike the meals you typically eat?
2. Why do you think the food culture of Canada's Quebec province shares a number of similarities with the food culture of France?

WORK AS A GROUP

Prepare a list of ethnocentric statements U.S. citizens make.

When you engage in international business, you will frequently have to deal with other cultures. Interacting with a person from another culture is called a cross-cultural experience. As an international businessperson, you will have many cross-cultural experiences. With patience and practice, you can learn how to adapt to other cultures.

REACTIONS TO CULTURAL DIFFERENCES

When you enter another culture or subculture, you will experience culture shock. **Culture shock** is a normal reaction to all the differences of another culture. When you experience culture shock, your reactions change from happiness to frustration to adaptation to acceptance. When you complete the culture shock adjustment process, you accept the new culture for what it is and enjoy it.

When you return to your native culture after having been gone for a while, you will experience reverse culture shock. *Reverse culture shock* is your reaction to becoming reacquainted with your own culture after having accepted another culture. Reverse culture shock is a normal reaction to the cultural readjustment process. The intensity of reverse culture shock is determined by the length of time spent in another culture and the degree of isolation from your native culture.

If you return to the United States after a long stay in England, you may notice the excesses of the U.S. culture. For example, room temperatures are carefully controlled. Most areas are brightly lit. People speak in harsher and louder tones. You may be initially overwhelmed by all of the choices. For instance, the grocery store has 50 different cereals from which to choose. You become depressed. Later, you may realize that you are homesick for the other culture. As you readjust to life at home, the symptoms of reverse culture shock decrease. Usually they disappear within a year after a long stay abroad.

©Getty Images/PhotoDisc

To be a successful participant in the global economy, you must be culturally sensitive. You must understand the major role that culture plays in shaping human behavior. You must understand not only your own general culture and its business subculture, but also that of your international business partners. You must consider all the various components of culture and how they affect your international business communication. You must be willing to make accommodations because of differences in your own and your international partners' cultures. Developing cultural sensitivity is one key for success in the global economy.

✔ CheckPoint

What are two ways people react to different cultures?

REVIEW GLOBAL BUSINESS TERMS

Define each of the following terms.

1. individualism

2. collectivism

3. ethnocentrism

4. culture shock

REVIEW GLOBAL BUSINESS CONCEPTS

5. What are five important value categories that differ from culture to culture?

6. Why do people and businesses need to make adjustments for cultural differences?

SOLVE GLOBAL BUSINESS PROBLEMS

A potential business partner from Shanghai, Wang Jian-Jun, will meet with you next Monday to discuss an opportunity for trading clothes for machinery. Mr. Wang has never traveled to the United States before, and you have never traveled to China. Nonetheless, you know that your cultures are much different. How might you bridge the following cultural differences?

©Getty Images/PhotoDisc

7. Mr. Wang may nod politely or bow slightly when he greets you.

8. Mr. Wang understands some spoken English but communicates primarily in the Wu (Shanghai) dialect of Chinese, which you do not understand.

9. Mr. Wang eats with chopsticks; you eat with a knife, fork, and spoon.

THINK CRITICALLY

10. Why do many people think their native culture is best?

11. Why might it take a year or more of living abroad to get to the point where you enjoy the local culture?

MAKE CONNECTIONS

12. **TECHNOLOGY** Why might advanced technology be negatively viewed in a developing country with a large, uneducated workforce?

13. **HISTORY** Why did the culture of Iran change considerably after the Shah was removed?

14. **GEOGRAPHY** Why might countries near the equator tend to perceive time in a fluid sense?

15. **LAW** In what countries, besides Iran, is Islamic law found?

Xtra! Quiz Prep

intlbizxtra.swlearning.com

CHAPTER SUMMARY

3-1 CULTURE AROUND THE WORLD

A Culture influences global business by shaping the personal and professional behaviors of businesspersons around the world.

B Subcultures are parts of larger cultures that may vary in some aspects from the larger cultures from which they developed.

3-2 CULTURE AND SOCIAL ORGANIZATIONS

A Most societies are at least partially organized around family units. There are both nuclear and extended families.

B Societies are comprised of many institutions. Some of these institutions are schools, religious groups, and professional groups. Gender roles and the degree of mobility differ greatly between cultures.

3-3 COMMUNICATION ACROSS CULTURES

A Although many languages can be used for international business purposes, English is often considered the language of international business.

B Knowing another language is important for global business success because it allows you to transact business much like a native speaker of that language does.

C Direct communication attaches considerable value to words and interprets them literally; indirect communication attaches much less value to words and interprets them figuratively.

D Nonverbal communication influences business activities through such non-word means as body language, appearance, eye contact, touching, personal space, color, numbers, emblems, and smells.

3-4 VALUES AROUND THE WORLD

A Five major types of values that vary from culture to culture involve individualism versus collectivism; technology; leadership, power, and authority; religion; and time.

B Two major reactions to cultural differences are culture shock and reverse culture shock.

GLOBAL REFOCUS

Read the Global Focus at the beginning of this chapter, and answer the following questions.

1. Where besides France and the United States does the Walt Disney Company have theme parks?

2. Why did many French people oppose Euro Disneyland?

3. What adaptations did the Walt Disney Company make to French culture?

4. Why do you think the Walt Disney Company initially chose not to sell alcoholic beverages in the theme park?

REVIEW GLOBAL BUSINESS TERMS

Match the terms listed with the definitions. Some terms may not be used.

1. A system of learned, shared, unifying, and interrelated beliefs, values, and assumptions.

2. A type of nonverbal communication where facial expressions, upper and lower body movements, and gestures convey what is meant.

3. A group that consists of parents, children, and other relatives living together.

4. Communication that does not involve the use of words.

5. The belief that the group is more important than the individual.

6. A group that consists of a parent or parents and unmarried children living together.

7. The belief in the individual and her or his ability to function relatively independently.

8. The belief that one's culture is better than other cultures.

9. A subset or part of a larger culture.

10. A means of dividing the members of a cultural group into various levels.

11. A normal reaction to all the differences of another culture.

12. The idea that you carry your beliefs, values, and assumptions with you at all times.

a. body language
b. class system
c. collectivism
d. contexting
e. cultural baggage
f. culture
g. culture shock
h. ethnocentrism
i. extended family
j. individualism
k. nonverbal communicaton
l. nuclear family
m. subculture

MAKE GLOBAL BUSINESS DECISIONS

13. How is culture like the programming in a computer?

14. What evidence suggests that geographic attachment is weak in the general U.S. culture and in its subcultures?

15. Swahili is the Bantu language of the Swahili people in eastern Africa. It is also a trade and governmental language among speakers of other languages in Tanzania, Kenya, and parts of Zaire. Do you think this language has significant potential for international business purposes? Why or why not?

16. What do you think is the cultural relationship between the personal space business communicators prefer and touching behaviors?

17. What are some other countries besides the People's Republic of China where leadership, power, and authority are concentrated in the hands of a few people?

18. A good friend recently said that she wouldn't even think of living temporarily in another country. Is her statement ethnocentric? How do you know?

GLOBAL CONNECTIONS

19. GEOGRAPHY Using library sources and the Web, investigate how the people of the French-speaking province of Quebec are trying to protect their French cultural heritage. What effects are their actions having on the people in other parts of Canada, who are primarily speakers of English? Do you think these differences will eventually lead to the breakup of Canada? Why or why not? Debate this matter with your classmates.

20. COMMUNICATIONS After interviewing a local businessperson, create a poster that depicts his or her cultural baggage.

21. HISTORY Find out about the caste system in India, which is a highly structured class system, by interviewing a native of the country or by using library resources. Write a paper that explains the caste system and what the Indian government has done in an attempt to eliminate this system.

22. CULTURAL STUDIES Select one primary color (red, yellow, or blue) and one secondary color (orange, green, or purple). Find out what these two colors represent in an eastern and western culture of your choice.

23. CAREER PLANNING Interview someone who has worked in another country. What similarities and/or differences did he or she find in the job application process in the other country?

24. TECHNOLOGY What are some ways in which technology might be used to benefit learners of a culture?

25. LANGUAGE Using library sources and the Internet, investigate one of the accents of the English language. How is the researched accent like and unlike the accent you have?

©Getty Images/PhotoDisc

THE GLOBAL
ENTREPRENEUR
CREATING AN INTERNATIONAL BUSINESS PLAN

CULTURAL ANALYSIS OF A FOREIGN MARKET

Select a country to research. Prepare a business cultural file with the following information about that nation's culture.

- history that influences current business activities
- languages and verbal and nonverbal communication customs
- education systems and literacy rates
- role of social institutions, such as family, religion, labor unions, and place of employment
- shopping practices and commonly eaten foods unique to the country
- major holidays and customs
- business practices related to place of employment, types of businesses, length of workday, and hiring practices

There are several sources of information for researching culture.

- reference books such as encyclopedias, almanacs, atlases, and current newspaper articles
- web search
- materials from companies, airlines, travel bureaus, government agencies, and other organizations involved in international business
- interviews with people who have lived in, worked in, or traveled to the country

©Getty Images/PhotoDisc

Prepare a written summary or a short oral report. Your report should last about two or three minutes. Present the main findings about the country's culture.

©Getty Images/PhotoDisc

Chapter **4**

GOVERNMENT AND GLOBAL BUSINESS

4-1 Politics and Global Business

4-2 How Government Discourages Global Business

4-3 How Government Encourages Global Business

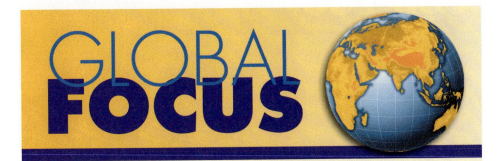

GLOBAL FOCUS

U.S. Department of Agriculture Promotes the Food Exports

The United States exports many products. These include agricultural goods such as popcorn, apples, poultry, seafood, and even frozen convenience dinners. The Foreign Agricultural Service (FAS), an agency of the U.S. Department of Agriculture (USDA), assists farmers in exporting their products. Several other state and federal government agencies also promote and assist with exporting. The FAS is responsible for U.S. agricultural, livestock, and processed food products and commodities worldwide.

The FAS provides various export marketing services for U.S. companies. The agency conducts international market research to find the best foreign markets for U.S. food products. In addition, it maintains a database on more than 20,000 foreign buyers of food and agricultural products. The agency also distributes foreign trade leads to U.S. suppliers and promotes U.S. food and agricultural products at trade shows in Europe, Asia, the Middle East, and Latin America.

This agency of the USDA also guarantees payment to U.S. banks that make loans to foreign governments wanting to purchase U.S. agricultural products such as wheat, soybeans, and corn. The USDA has trade offices in more than 80 countries, all of which are major foreign markets for U.S. agricultural and food products.

Think Critically

1. Why do you think the U.S. government spends tax dollars to promote the export of U.S. agricultural and food products?
2. How might foreign countries benefit by the actions of the Foreign Agricultural Service?
3. Go to the Foreign Agricultural Service web site (www.fas.usda.gov) to obtain current information about agricultural products and foreign markets for U.S. food producers. Describe your results.

4-1

POLITICS AND GLOBAL BUSINESS

GOALS

- Discuss various political systems around the world.
- Explain the political environment for a company's host and home countries.

©Getty Images/PhotoDisc

TYPES OF POLITICAL SYSTEMS

A country's economy usually reflects its political system. A **political system** is the means by which people in a society make the rules by which they live. Political systems vary around the world, ranging from democracy to totalitarianism.

DEMOCRACY

In a **democracy**, all citizens take part in making the rules that govern them. A democracy emphasizes the importance of the individual's needs and interests. In this political system, the people have equal rights, including the right to vote for political leaders. They also have many freedoms, including freedom of speech and freedom of religion.

A democracy's emphasis on individual rights and freedoms extends to its economy. In a democratic society, people have the freedom to own and operate private businesses. Democratic societies, therefore, usually have a market economy. In a country with a market economy, there is little or no government ownership or central planning of business and industry. Individuals or groups of individuals run most businesses. Companies, therefore, either succeed or fail based on their owners' abilities to compete effectively in a market. The United States is basically a market economy.

TOTALITARIANISM

In a **totalitarian system**, most people are excluded from making the rules by which they live. In this system, political control is held by either one person

©Getty Images/PhotoDisc

or a small group of people. There are different kinds of totalitarian systems. For example, in a military dictatorship, a member of the armed forces makes all the decisions. In a pure monarchy, the right to absolute rule for life is based on heredity. In another totalitarian system, one political party holds all the power and prohibits others from participating. In a totalitarian system, people's rights and freedoms are restricted. People may not be allowed to travel freely outside the country or to practice the religion they choose.

Totalitarian systems tend not to have market economies, but command economies. In a command economy, the national government owns and controls almost all businesses. Individuals may be allowed to own a small one-employee business—using a somewhat mixed-economy approach. But the government owns all larger businesses, industries, farms, utilities, transportation, and mining operations. Traditional communist countries, such as Cuba, are basically command economies.

MIXED SYSTEMS

In reality, there is no pure form of either a democracy or a totalitarian system. Most political systems are considered mixed. That means they have characteristics of both systems and fall somewhere in between. In the same way, economic systems of most countries are considered mixed systems. In most countries, the majority of businesses are privately owned, and some key industries are owned and run by the government. Key industries include steel production, mining, national airlines, and telephone and public utilities. Many European countries are mixed economies.

GLOBAL BUSINESS EXAMPLE

THE VIEW FROM CHINA

International businesspeople must be cautious when classifying the political system of a country. They must do their own research because the classification claimed by the country itself can be misleading. For example, China's full name is The People's Republic of China. However, the people of China have very little representation in the actual governing body, and the government is not responsible to elected representatives. In that sense, China is not a republic.

Think Critically

From the description above, would China be considered a democracy or a totalitarian system?

WORK AS A GROUP

Discuss how key industries are owned in your country. Discuss the advantages and disadvantages of this type of ownership for the industries and the citizens.

✔CheckPoint

How does a democracy differ from a totalitarian system?

REGIONAL PERSPECTIVE

HISTORY: TEOTIHUACAN

Imagine a city of 200,000 people with a well-planned road system, production facilities, beautiful art, and ball courts for sports. This sounds like a modern city of today. However, the city of Teotihuacan, located about 40 kilometers (25 miles) northeast of Mexico City, declined into ruins over 1,300 years ago.

The civilization of Teotihuacan began about 200 B.C. and flourished until about 650 A.D. During this period, the city was an influential commercial and religious center. The people of Teotihuacan developed many art forms into a high degree of elegance, including sculpture, ceramics, stone masks, and murals. In addition, major monuments were constructed, including the Pyramid of the Moon and the Pyramid of the Sun—one of the largest structures built by Native Americans.

The people of Teotihuacan had close contact with the Mayan culture in the Yucatan area of Mexico and Guatemala. They were also a strong influence on later Mexican cultures, such as the Aztecs.

Today Teotihuacan is an archaeological site. It contains the remains of the largest pre-Columbian city in the Western Hemisphere. The Avenue of the Dead, the city's main roadway, can still be seen passing through the ruins of temples and other structures.

Think Critically

1. Conduct an Internet search for Teotihuacan to obtain information about the commercial activities in this ancient city. Prepare a one-page report of your findings.
2. How did Teotihuacan influence our culture of today?

©Getty Images/PhotoDisc

POLITICAL RELATIONSHIPS IN BUSINESS

International business can be affected dramatically by political developments that take place in our rapidly changing world. Businesses have different perceptions of their responsibilities to the countries in which they operate.

GLOBAL COMPANIES OPERATING IN HOST COUNTRIES

A **host country** is the country in which a multinational enterprise is a guest. Multinational enterprises fulfill a number of positive roles in host countries while operating within the existing economic, social, and legal constraints.

Multinational enterprises stimulate economic activity. Whenever feasible, they purchase land, goods, and services locally. They provide employment for citizens of the host country. Often they introduce more advanced technologies that help the economic development of the host country.

Host countries expect multinational enterprises to comply with societal expectations and standards. Social responsibility is key to the success or failure of a multinational enterprise. **Social responsibility** is the process whereby people function as good citizens and are sensitive to their surroundings. For example, a multinational enterprise that pollutes the host country's environment is not operating in a socially responsible manner. It is failing to meet the set standards regarding the environment. The multinational enterprise is harming the environment and its inhabitants.

To have the right to operate within a host country, a multinational enterprise must substantially benefit the host country. The company must be able to document that it operates in full compliance with the local social and legal standards. If a multinational enterprise does not meet these conditions, then the host country may restrict or deny its right to conduct business. In rare cases where the offensive actions are long-standing and serious, the government of the host country might seize the assets of the multinational enterprise.

GLOBAL COMPANIES' RELATIONSHIPS WITH HOME COUNTRIES

A **home country** is the country in which a multinational enterprise is headquartered. As a domestic corporation in its home country, a multinational enterprise is expected to comply with the home country's social, economic, and legal mandates.

The home country expects multinational enterprises based within its borders to demonstrate social responsibility. They must comply with societal expectations and standards and meet both the spirit and the letter of the laws of the home country.

Improper actions could jeopardize the right of the multinational enterprise to exist and to be headquartered in the country. If the offensive actions are long-standing and serious, the home country could restrict or deny the multinational enterprise the right to engage in business and to be headquartered within the country.

✓ **CheckPoint**

What is social responsibility, and why is it important?

REVIEW GLOBAL BUSINESS TERMS

Define each of the following terms.

1. political system
2. democracy
3. totalitarian system
4. host country
5. social responsibility
6. home country

REVIEW GLOBAL BUSINESS CONCEPTS

7. How are businesses owned in a democracy?
8. How are businesses owned in a totalitarian system?
9. What relationship does a global company have with a host country and its home country?

SOLVE GLOBAL BUSINESS PROBLEMS

For each of the following descriptions, determine whether the country is a democracy, totalitarian system, or mixed system.

10. Farmers must produce a required quantity of crops to meet government requirements.
11. Citizens are free to start and operate any kind of business.
12. Government owns most businesses.
13. Government regulates some large businesses in the essential industries, but the businesses are mostly privately owned.

THINK CRITICALLY

14. Would a totalitarian system of government encourage or discourage trade with other countries?
15. Explain how a host country might put political pressure on a global company operating within its borders.

MAKE CONNECTIONS

16. **HISTORY** Obtain information about changes in the past ten years to the political systems operating in various eastern European countries.
17. **CULTURAL STUDIES** Describe the incentives workers have to achieve high standards of production in a totalitarian system.

HOW GOVERNMENT DISCOURAGES GLOBAL BUSINESS

4-2

GOALS

- Describe laws and trade barriers that can discourage global business.
- Explain how political risks can disrupt global business activities.
- Identify the major types of taxes that governments impose around the world.

©Getty Images/PhotoDisc

GOVERNMENT ACTIVITIES INFLUENCE BUSINESS

Have you ever heard of "government red tape?" For centuries, business-people have complained about government reports, licenses, permits, and forms they must obtain or complete. Every day businesses throughout the world must comply with thousands of government laws and regulations. These laws directly affect how businesses operate.

LAWS THAT PROTECT WORKERS AND CONSUMERS

Why do governments regulate businesses? Often it is to protect the health and safety of workers. Many countries establish occupational protection laws to protect workers from dangerous conditions on the job. For example, in many countries, the law requires factory workers to wear safety equipment such as protective eye goggles, hard hats, and earplugs. Other worker protection laws prohibit employing children as farm or factory workers. Today there is growing interest in establishing new safety requirements for office employees who use computers all day.

In addition to occupational protection laws, governments establish consumer protection laws to ensure that products are safe to use. For example, most developed countries require that all food ingredients be listed on product labels. And most developed countries have electrical safety standards to protect consumers from purchasing faulty electrical appliances, such as hair dryers and toasters. Laws also exist to protect consumers from deceptive or false advertising practices, such as claiming a particular medicine can cure the common cold.

Complying with worker and consumer protection laws usually increases the cost of doing business for companies. These increased costs may make a product less competitive with products manufactured in countries that do not have such laws. In general, occupational and consumer protection laws are not as strict in poor developing countries as they are in major industrialized countries. A product made in Canada will probably cost more than a similar product made in Mexico, even if both are marketed in Ireland.

TRADE BARRIERS

Specific actions by governments can directly discourage or prevent the growth of international business. To protect local businesses from foreign competition, governments may establish trade barriers. *Trade barriers* are government actions or policies that make it difficult to trade across borders. Governments that establish such trade barriers are enforcing protectionism. **Protectionism** is a government policy of protecting local or domestic industries from foreign competition. Several ways are used by governments that may restrict foreign competition.

- Establishing tariffs or customs duties to increase the price of imported products
- Placing quotas on the importing of certain products
- Requiring domestic companies to boycott particular countries
- Enacting restrictive licensing requirements for importers

Tariffs A government can place a tariff, or duty, on imported products. A tariff, or **duty**, is a tax placed on products that are traded internationally. Duties raise the cost of the product to the importer, which discourages consumers from buying the imported product. Duties are the most common trade barriers.

GLOBAL BUSINESS EXAMPLE

CONSUMER PROTECTION LAWS AROUND THE WORLD

In recent years, the following laws existed in various countries.

- In Canada, the packages and labels of all consumer products must be printed in both French and English.
- In Venezuela, the price of every retail product must be clearly marked, together with the date on which the price was marked.

- In Belgium, laws limit how loud a lawn mower engine can be.
- In Australia, children's nightclothes must be labeled to indicate the degree of fire hazard or flammability.
- In Greece, advertising toys on television is not allowed.

Think Critically

1. Conduct an Internet search to locate examples of laws in various countries that are designed to protect consumers. Present your findings to the class.
2. How might the consumer protection laws of a country affect international business activities?

In the past, exporting to Pakistan was very difficult. The country's import customs duties ranged from 20 to 90 percent. All imports were also subject to a 5 percent education tax, a 6 percent import license fee, a 12.5 percent sales tax, and a 10 percent import surcharge tax. A product costing $100 before entering Pakistan could cost the equivalent of $223.50 after clearing the Pakistani Customs Office.

Quotas Governments also may place quotas on certain imported products. A **quota** is a limit on the quantity, or monetary amount of a product that can be imported from a given country. Once the quota has been met, no more of that product can be imported for a certain period of time. The quota creates a limited supply of the imported good. This protects domestic products from too much foreign competition. Import quotas have been used to protect the textile, shoe, automobile, and steel industries in some countries.

Boycotts Sometimes a government issues an absolute restriction on the import of certain products from certain countries. This is called a **boycott**. For example, in India, the importation of many consumer goods is banned. This ban forces foreign companies that want to sell consumer goods in India to invest in India and manufacture the products locally. In Japan, the government maintains a nearly complete ban on the import of rice. This action protects Japanese rice farmers from foreign competition. Norway protects its apple and pear producers by allowing imports only after the domestic crop has been sold.

Licensing Requirements Some governments control imports by requiring that companies have a government import license. The license grants permission to import a product. This license can be withdrawn at any time.

©Getty Images/PhotoDisc

NETBookmark

Eliminating trade barriers can encourage global economic growth, and in some cases advance democracy. Access intlbizxtra.swlearning.com and click on the link for Chapter 4. Read the article entitled "Does Trade Promote Democracy?" According to the article, what are some specific ways that free trade can promote political freedom? How do the countries that are not open to free trade compare politically to countries that are more open?

intlbizxtra.swlearning.com

✓ CheckPoint

What are four trade barriers governments use to directly discourage international business?

POLITICAL RISKS IN INTERNATIONAL BUSINESS

Government actions or political policies can change at any time, thereby adversely affecting foreign companies. This is called *political risk*. Major political risks to international business include trade sanctions, expropriation, economic nationalism, and civil unrest or war. These risks are shown in Figure 4-1. All of these actions can temporarily or permanently disrupt global business activities.

TRADE SANCTIONS

Governments can impose trade restrictions against another country to protest that country's behavior. This use of trade barriers is usually the direct result of political disputes between countries. For example, in August 1993, the United States banned the sale of high-technology equipment to China. The United States was protesting China's apparent sale of missile technology to Pakistan, which violated an international arms-control agreement.

Trade sanctions range from tariffs to boycotts. A country can impose a **trade embargo** against another country and stop all import-export trade with that country. In recent years, the United States issued a trade embargo against several countries due to various political differences, one of those being acts of international terrorism. These embargoes banned the export of any goods, technology, or services from the United States to those countries.

EXPROPRIATION

In extreme cases, the host government of a company could confiscate, or expropriate, the subsidiary. **Expropriation** occurs when a government takes control and ownership of foreign-owned assets and companies. This happened in 1990 as a result of the breakup of the Soviet Union. Some cities in the new republics took over property and assets of the ruling communist party of the former Soviet Union.

ECONOMIC NATIONALISM

Economic nationalism is a political force that can also create political risk for companies conducting international trade. **Economic nationalism** refers to the trend of some countries to restrict foreign ownership of companies and to establish laws that protect against foreign imports. Economic nationalism is a form of protectionism. Protectionist governments may encourage their people to "buy domestic" instead of purchasing imported products.

TYPES OF INTERNATIONAL POLITICAL RISK

- **Trade sanctions due to foreign policy**
- **Expropriation**
- **Growth of economic nationalism**
- **Civil war, revolution, uprisings within the country**
- **War with other countries**

Figure 4-1 Business must be aware of the forms of international political risk.

CIVIL UNREST OR WAR

Evidence of the following factors signals the possibility of civil unrest in a country.

- social disorder
- extreme income unevenness, with a few very rich people and a massive number of poor people
- frequent changes in the structure and activity of political parties

Civil unrest interrupts production, sales, and other business activities. Transportation of goods may be hindered, and people may not be able to shop because of gunfire and riots. When unrest escalates to war, there is often massive destruction of property and goods.

GLOBAL BUSINESS EXAMPLE

POLITICAL RISKS AND PERSONAL DANGER

While companies face risk when doing business in other countries, individuals may also be in danger. Workers and travelers can encounter robberies, attacks, and abductions while living in or visiting another nation. In recent years, total attacks against U.S. citizens and U.S. facilities in other countries averaged about 100 a year.

The U.S. State Department issues travel warnings to reduce the chance of danger for people involved in international activities. These public notices list countries to which Americans are advised not to travel.

Think Critically

1. Go to the web site of the U.S. State Department, www.state.gov, to find current examples of travel warnings. What are some common warnings?
2. What factors create potential dangers for people working and living in other countries?

✓ CheckPoint

Name four political risks that can seriously affect global business.

INTERNATIONAL TAXES

Second to complaints about government "red tape," businesses worldwide complain that their governments tax them too much. Governments collect revenues to pay for welfare programs, to build roads and bridges, to provide health care insurance, and to support military forces, among many other things. Revenue to pay for these programs comes from many types of taxes. There are taxes on purchases, property, income, and wealth.

CUSTOMS DUTY

A *customs duty*, or import tax, is a tax assessed on imported products. While sometimes used by governments as an import trade barrier, customs duties are also collected specifically to raise revenue to pay for government programs.

SALES TAX

A *sales tax* is a tax on the sale of products. The consumer pays it at the time of purchase. Sales taxes are considered *regressive* taxes because the same rate of tax is charged to all consumers, no matter what their income level. Some countries, such as Singapore and Canada, have taxes similar to sales taxes called consumption taxes or goods and services taxes (GST).

EXCISE TAX

An *excise tax* is a tax levied on the sale or consumption of specific products or commodities—such as alcoholic beverages, tobacco, telephone service, airline tickets, gasoline, and motor vehicles. For example, the United States collects gasoline excise taxes for highway construction and repair. These taxes are often based on the "benefits received" principle, meaning that only automobile drivers, who would receive the most benefit from well-maintained highways, are assessed the tax.

PAYROLL-RELATED TAX

Payroll-related taxes are those taxes that are automatically deducted from an employee's pay. Typical payroll taxes in the United States include taxes to pay for Social Security, Medicare, and unemployment insurance—all matched by the employer.

VALUE-ADDED TAX (VAT)

A *value-added tax* (VAT) is a tax assessed on the increase in value of goods from each stage of production to final consumption. The tax on each stage is levied on the value that has been added before moving the product to the next stage. Value-added taxes are used in most European countries. VAT is similar to a national sales tax.

INCOME TAXES

A tax on the amount of income a person or corporation earns, minus allowable deductions and credits, is called an *income tax*. Income tax is usually a *progressive* tax because the percentage a person pays increases, or progresses, the more income a person makes. This tax is based on the "ability to pay" principle—the more income a person has, the more tax that person is able to pay.

Corporations also pay income tax, which is based on corporate annual income, minus allowable business deductions and tax credits. Governments may give companies various tax credits to enable them to purchase new equipment, invest in research and development, and employ new people.

A corporate income tax is viewed as an *indirect* business tax on consumers. Corporations pass along the cost of the tax indirectly to the consumer by charging a higher price for the goods or services sold or produced by the company.

WORK AS A GROUP

Describe the characteristics of what most people would consider a "fair" tax.

✔ **CheckPoint**

What are the common types of taxes paid by consumers and businesses?

REVIEW GLOBAL BUSINESS TERMS

Define each of the following terms.

1. protectionism
2. duty
3. quota
4. boycott

5. trade embargo
6. expropriation
7. economic nationalism

REVIEW GLOBAL BUSINESS CONCEPTS

8. Why do governments establish trade barriers to discourage international business?

9. What political risks could companies encounter when doing business in other countries?

10. What is the "ability to pay" principle of taxation?

SOLVE GLOBAL BUSINESS PROBLEMS

Decide if the following situations would increase or decrease the political risk faced by companies involved in international business.

11. A country reduces custom duties on imports.

12. A trade embargo has been created by a nation against several of its major trading partners.

13. The ruling party in a country has changed three times in the past five years.

14. A host country expands its use of expropriation.

15. The government of a country eliminates import quotas.

THINK CRITICALLY

16. What problems might an international company have when trying to do business in a country that is fighting a civil war?

17. How can taxes be used by the government to encourage or discourage the use of a certain good or service?

MAKE CONNECTIONS

18. **HISTORY** Find examples of war or civil unrest that resulted in a company having buildings taken away or destroyed.

19. **CULTURAL STUDIES** Go to the web site for Transparency International and Transparency USA to obtain information about the political risks in other countries.

20. **LAW** Go to the web site of the Internal Revenue Service (www.irs.gov) to obtain information about current tax rates for U.S. taxpayers.

4-3

GOALS

- Explain government actions that can encourage global business activities.
- Discuss U.S. government agencies that can help reduce international risk.
- Describe how tax incentives encourage global business.

HOW GOVERNMENT ENCOURAGES GLOBAL BUSINESS

©Getty Images/PhotoDisc

ENCOURAGING INTERNATIONAL BUSINESS

Specific actions by governments also can directly encourage and promote international business. Governments around the world encourage domestic industries to export by providing export counseling and training, export insurance, and export subsidies and tax credits. Governments view exporting as an effective way to create jobs and foster economic prosperity. Governments encourage business through a number of techniques.

- Establishing free-trade zones
- Granting most-favored-nation status
- Establishing free-trade agreements
- Providing export insurance to exporters to guarantee against foreign commercial and political risks
- Providing free or subsidized export marketing assistance to exporters to help research foreign markets, promote their products overseas, and find foreign buyers
- Providing tax incentives for foreign companies to invest and to locate manufacturing plants in their countries
- Reducing or eliminating trade barriers such as tariffs, import licenses, and quotas

Free-Trade Zones To promote international business, governments often create free-trade zones in their countries. A **free-trade zone** is a designated area, usually around a seaport or airport, where products can be imported duty-free and then stored, assembled, and used in manufacturing. Only when the product leaves the zone does the importer pay duty.

Most Favored Nation A government can also encourage international trade by granting most-favored-nation status to other countries. **Most-favored-nation (MFN) status** allows a country to export into the granting country under the lowest customs duty rates. Products imported from countries without MFN status are charged a higher rate.

Free-Trade Agreements A growing trend throughout the world is for countries to establish free-trade agreements with each other. Under a **free-trade agreement**, member countries agree to eliminate duties and trade barriers on products traded among members. This results in increased trade between the members. For example, the United States and Canada formed a free-trade agreement in January 1989. During the phase-in period of this agreement, duties on U.S. and Canadian products were eliminated between the two countries.

Another example of a free-trade agreement is the Latin American Integration Association (LAIA). Its members include Argentina, Bolivia, Brazil, Chile, Colombia, Ecuador, Mexico, Paraguay, Peru, Uruguay, and Venezuela. The goal of LAIA is to further trade between member states and promote regional economic integration. The member countries of LAIA are shown in Figure 4-2.

Common Markets Some countries join together in a common market to promote more trade among members. In a **common market**, members eliminate duties and other trade barriers, allow companies to invest freely in each member's country, and allow workers to move freely across borders. Common-market members also have a common external duty on products being imported from non-member countries. Examples of common markets include the European Union (EU) and the Southern Cone Common Market (Mercosur) consisting of Argentina, Brazil, Paraguay, and Uruguay.

MEMBERS OF LAIA

Figure 4-2 The Latin American Integration Association took over from the Latin American Free Trade Association in 1981.

What are four ways governments can encourage global business?

WORK AS A GROUP

Suggest ways in which a government can encourage exporting and international trade activities.

GOVERNMENT PROTECTION FROM INTERNATIONAL RISK

How can a company protect itself from international political risk? U.S. companies can protect their international sales and assets by using the services of two U.S. government agencies—the Export-Import Bank of the United States (EXIM) and the Overseas Private Investment Corporation (OPIC).

EXIM is the U.S. government agency that helps to finance the export sales of U.S. products. It provides export loans, export loan guarantees, and export credit insurance. An exporting company can purchase an export credit insurance policy from EXIM that will provide 100 percent protection from political risk for international sales. This includes protection from foreign governments that refuse to convert local currency to dollars. It also covers damage or destruction of a shipment caused by wars, revolutions, and civil disorders. If these political actions occur, the exporter can then file a claim with EXIM for 100 percent reimbursement of all export sales losses.

The Overseas Private Investment Corporation (OPIC) provides investment insurance to U.S. companies that establish operations in developing countries. A U.S. company can protect its overseas investment by purchasing OPIC insurance. This shields the company from several types of political risk—including expropriation and damage or destruction caused by war, revolution, terrorism, and sabotage. If any of these political actions occur, the U.S. company can file a claim with OPIC to recover its losses.

✓ CheckPoint

For what types of political risks does the Overseas Private Investment Corporation provide protection?

©Bob Witkowski/CORBIS

TAX INCENTIVES

A basic practice of companies is to treat all business taxes as regular business costs. Companies recover those costs by increasing the price of the products they sell. The actual burden of tax payment, therefore, is usually shifted to the consumer in the form of higher prices.

In conducting international business, U.S. companies want to avoid being taxed twice on income they earn from their foreign operations. The U.S. government allows companies a corporate tax deduction on income earned by their foreign subsidiaries.

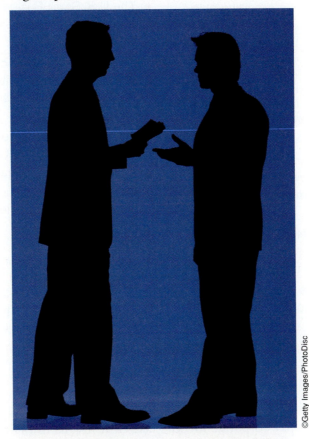

©Getty Images/PhotoDisc

In addition, the U.S. government has double-taxation avoidance treaties with some countries. This provides relief from double taxation of U.S. multinational corporations. This is a tax incentive that foreign governments use to attract U.S. companies to invest in their countries and create local jobs. U.S. companies are more likely to invest in countries with a favorable tax environment.

A Question of Ethics

PAYING FOR SPECIAL FAVORS

Aggressive companies in some regions of the world commonly use payoffs to gain access to new markets. Some countries consider bribes to be tax-deductible business expenses. However, U.S. companies can face hefty fines and prison sentences when U.S. laws are violated.

Sometimes companies cave in to local customs. A U.S. computer company offered Chinese journalists the equivalent of $12 to attend its news conferences. The company said the money was for taxi fares; however, the amount was equal to a week's pay for some journalists.

Think Critically

According to the guidelines for ethical analysis, are the payments to Chinese journalists ethical?

E-COMMERCE IN ACTION

Online Exporting Assistance

"What are the best countries for exporting electronics components?"

"How can I contact distributors in Asia to sell packaged food products?"

These and many other questions can be easily answered online. Various government agencies and other organizations offer extensive information related to planning how to export and on international business activities.

- The International Trade Administration of the U.S. Department of Commerce at www.trade.gov offers information on exporting, trade missions, and trade statistics.

- Information about exporting, foreign markets, trade shows, and other global business may be obtained at usatc.doc.gov and at www.export.gov.

- The U.S. Customs Service offers importing and exporting information at www.customs.gov.

- The U.S. Small Business Administration provides assistance in starting an export business at www.sba.gov/oit/.

- Information about exporting food products may be obtained at the web site of the Foreign Agricultural Service (www.fas.usda.gov).

- Many global business sources may be accessed at the web sites of the Federation of International Trade Associations and the Global Edge.

- The World Trade Centers Association web site (www.wtca.org) provides access to World Centers in more than 100 countries.

Think Critically

1. Using one or more of the web sites above, obtain specific information that would be useful to a company involved in exporting or in international trade.
2. How do these web sites benefit businesses, consumers, and society?

As a further tax incentive, many foreign governments provide a foreign company with a tax holiday. A **tax holiday** means the corporation does not pay corporate income taxes if it invests in their country. These tax holidays may last for as long as ten years.

✓CheckPoint

How does the U.S. government protect U.S. companies from double taxation?

©Getty Images/PhotoDisc

REVIEW GLOBAL BUSINESS TERMS

Define each of the following terms.

1. free-trade zone
2. most-favored-nation (MFN) status
3. free-trade agreement
4. common market
5. tax holiday

intlbizxtra.swlearning.com

REVIEW GLOBAL BUSINESS CONCEPTS

6. Why do countries join in free-trade agreements?

7. How do U.S. government agencies help reduce political risks for companies involved in international business?

8. Why do governments give tax incentives to foreign companies to invest in their countries?

SOLVE GLOBAL BUSINESS PROBLEMS

For the following situations, name the type of action being taken to encourage international business among countries.

9. Countries in Africa decide to join together to eliminate tariffs and other trade barriers.

10. A country in eastern Europe attempts to attract foreign investors by eliminating their taxes for the next seven years.

11. The U.S. agrees to allow imports from selected countries at the lowest customs duty rates.

12. Mexico and Israel agree to eliminate certain tariffs and trade barriers on products sold between the two countries.

13. A Middle Eastern country designates an area for manufacturing with no import duties.

THINK CRITICALLY

14. What actions might a government take to attract foreign companies to do business in its country?

15. How does a common-market agreement benefit citizens of a member country?

MAKE CONNECTIONS

16. **GEOGRAPHY** How might the natural resources in a region encourage countries to join together to create a common market?

17. **TECHNOLOGY** Locate a web site for your state department of commerce or other state government agency that promotes international trade by companies in your state. Find out what tax and financial incentives are available to attract foreign companies to invest in your state.

CHAPTER SUMMARY

4-1 POLITICS AND GLOBAL BUSINESS

A The main political systems operating in the world are democracies, totalitarian systems, and mixed systems.

B A multinational company must operate within existing economic, social, and legal constraints of a host country. In addition, the company is expected to comply with the social, economic, and legal mandates of its home country.

4-2 HOW GOVERNMENT DISCOURAGES GLOBAL BUSINESS

A A government can discourage international trade with protectionism policies, tariffs, quotas, boycotts, and licensing requirements.

B Political risks can disrupt global business activities through trade sanctions (such as embargoes), expropriation, economic nationalism, and civil unrest or war.

C The main taxes governments impose are customs duties, sales taxes, excise taxes, payroll-related taxes, value-added taxes, and income taxes.

4-3 HOW GOVERNMENT ENCOURAGES GLOBAL BUSINESS

A A government can encourage international business with free-trade zones, most-favored-nation status, and free-trade agreements.

B The Export-Import Bank of the United States (EXIM) provides export loans, export loan guarantees, and export credit insurance. The Overseas Private Investment Corporation (OPIC) provides investment insurance to U.S. companies that establish operations in developing countries.

C A government can encourage international business with tax incentives such as tax credits on foreign income, double-taxation avoidance treaties, and tax holidays.

GLOBAL REFOCUS

Read the Global Focus at the beginning of this chapter, and answer the following questions.

1. You are the manufacturer of Grandma's Original Jams and Jellies. In what ways could the USDA help you develop export markets for your products?

2. Why would the USDA guarantee payment to U.S. banks that make loans to foreign governments wanting to buy U.S. agricultural commodities?

3. The USDA also provides export subsidies, or grants, to U.S. farmers who export. How could this be viewed as an obstacle for a foreign farmer who doesn't receive export subsidies from his or her own government but is trying to export?

REVIEW GLOBAL BUSINESS TERMS

Match the terms listed with the definitions that follow.

1. A government system in which political control is held by one person or a small group of people.

2. A tax on imported products.

3. A limit on the amount of a product that can be imported from a given country.

4. Government policy used to protect local, or domestic, industries from foreign competition.

5. The country in which a multinational enterprise is headquartered.

6. Designated area where products can be imported duty-free.

7. Designation given to certain countries that allows their products to be imported into the granting country under the lowest customs duty rates.

8. An arrangement between countries that eliminates duties and trade barriers on products traded among members.

9. A policy of restricting foreign ownership of local companies and hindering foreign imports.

10. The process whereby people function as good citizens and are sensitive to their surroundings.

11. Complete ban on any trade with a particular country.

12. A political system in which all people take part in making the rules that govern them.

13. A country in which a multinational enterprise is a guest.

14. Member countries eliminate trade barriers, encourage investment, and allow workers to move freely across borders.

15. Means by which people in a society make the rules by which they live.

16. Government takeover of a foreign-owned business.

17. Absolute restriction on the import of certain products from certain countries.

18. Tax incentive used by governments to attract foreign investment where a corporation does not pay income taxes for a time after investing.

a. boycott

b. common market

c. democracy

d. duty

e. economic nationalism

f. expropriation

g. free-trade agreement

h. free-trade zone

i. home country

j. host country

k. most-favored-nation (MFN) status

l. political system

m. protectionism

n. quota

o. social responsibility

p. tax holiday

q. totalitarian system

r. trade embargo

MAKE GLOBAL BUSINESS DECISIONS

19. As a consumer, why might you object to your government creating import trade barriers, such as high customs duties or restrictive import quotas?

20. How could the study of international affairs and world current events help a company anticipate and evaluate potential political risks around the world?

21. How effective do you think trade embargoes are as a method of "punishing" another country for its actions?

22. What factors, other than tax incentives, should companies evaluate before deciding to invest in a particular country?

23. What services are provided by the U.S. government to help promote the export of nonagricultural products, such as manufactured products and consumer goods?

GLOBAL CONNECTIONS

24. **TECHNOLOGY** What types of laws might be needed to protect workers and consumers as a result of the expanded use of computers?

25. **GEOGRAPHY** Conduct research to obtain information about various free-trade agreements, such as the European Union, MERCOSUR, and ASEAN. Prepare a map that shows the countries involved in these organizations.

26. **COMMUNICATIONS** Interview a small business owner about the actions of government (local, state, and federal) that influence business activities. What ways has government made it more difficult to do business? What ways has government helped business?

27. **CULTURAL STUDIES** Talk to people who have lived in or visited other countries. How do political freedoms differ in those countries compared to the freedoms in the United States?

28. **LAW** Prepare arguments in favor of and in opposition to legislative actions for the creation of trade barriers, such as higher tariffs and import quotas.

29. **MATHEMATICS** One household has an annual income of $40,000 while another has an annual income of $80,000. Each household spends $10,000 a year on food. If the sales tax on food is 5 percent, show how this would be an example of a regressive tax.

30. **CAREER PLANNING** Conduct library research about another country's government regulations of wages, employment opportunities, and occupational safety.

31. **TECHNOLOGY** Use the Internet to find examples of trade barriers in use around the world today.

32. **TECHNOLOGY** Use the Internet to find a list of all the current members of a free-trade zone or a common market.

33. **POLITICAL SCIENCE** Create a list of ten countries. Using information collected on the Internet, classify each country's government as a democray, totalitarian system, or mixed.

THE GLOBAL ENTREPRENEUR
CREATING AN INTERNATIONAL BUSINESS PLAN

ASSESSING POLITICAL RISK AND LEGAL RESTRICTIONS

As a company considers doing business in another country, the political and legal environment must be assessed. To help evaluate the advantages and disadvantages, as well as the risks, of making such an expensive investment, companies collect specific information about the "investment climate" of the country. The more favorable the climate, the more likely the company will profit from the investment.

Using your international business file and research skills, gather information on the investment climate for a country. Prepare a written or short oral report with information on the following topics.

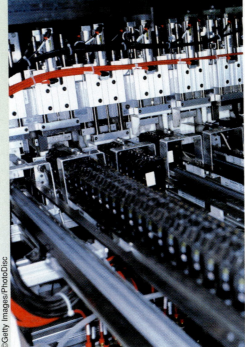

©Getty Images/PhotoDisc

1. Political stability of the country and possible civil disruptions.

2. Labor laws, labor costs, and occupational safety laws.

3. Trade barriers or investment restrictions.

4. Tax and other investment incentives to foreign companies.

5. Laws concerning establishing or restricting investment.

6. Other information you think is important to making an investment decision.

Compare the investment climate of your chosen country with those of other students. Which countries would be the best locations for manufacturing plants?

Sources of information to research the country may include the following.

- reference books such as encyclopedias, almanacs, and atlases
- current newspaper articles from the news, business, and travel sections
- current news and business magazine articles, including news stories, company profiles, and advertisements
- Internet search for country information
- interviews with people who have lived in, worked in, or traveled to the country

GLOBAL
CROSS-CULTURAL TEAM PROJECT

Compare International Business Environments

Each day, millions of people work in teams to plan and implement business activities. The activities of these teams range from creating new products for international markets to cross-cultural negotiations for a joint venture agreement. While many teams involve people from the same country or similar cultures, other work groups require interaction among people with different backgrounds.

GOAL

To compare similarities and differences among various regions of the world in relation to factors that affect business activities.

ACTIVITIES

Working in teams, select a geographic region you will represent—Africa, Asia, Europe, Latin America, Middle East, or North America.

1. Conduct research about the geography, culture, and business activities of several countries in your region. Obtain information on the Web, from library materials, and by talking to people who have lived in or visited that area.
2. Identify geographic factors that are unique to your region, such as climate, terrain, and natural resources. Describe how they might affect business activities.
3. List customs, traditions, and cultural behavior unique to your region. How might they effect business activities among people from different geographic regions? For example, how should business cards be exchanged? What types of gifts are considered appropriate to exchange with business partners?
4. Research the economic systems and conditions in the region. What economic influences on business in the region differ from those in other regions?
5. Describe political situations and business regulations in your region. How do these compare with the political and legal situations in other regions?
6. **Global Business Decision** An international organization plans to do business in various countries. What can it do to ensure success? What products or services might be most successful in your region?

TEAM SKILL   Benefits of Cross-Cultural Teams

Discuss with your team members the benefits of working on cross-cultural teams for both employees and business organizations. How might team activities and decision-making differ in your region from those in other regions?

PRESENT

- Prepare an individual report with a written summary of your regional findings and your experiences working on this simulated cross-cultural team.
- Create and present a team summary comparing the business environments in different regions using an in-class presentation, video, web site, newsletter, poster, photo display, slide presentation, or display of items (maps, clothing, food, music, packages, money) from the various geographic areas.

International Business Plan Event

DECA *WinningEdge*

International trade has opened new opportunities for increased business profits. Multinational companies realize the value of locating in more than one country. Some companies complete different phases of their business process in countries that are the most cost effective.

You will write an international business plan for conducting business in a country other than the United States. You will apply marketing skills in an international setting. This project requires you to research the demographics of the country where you will locate your business. You must also consider customs, political conditions, trade regulations, currency exchange, and other cultural factors that will influence your business in another country. Your international business plan must follow the guidelines outlined in the DECA Guide.

The competition consists of two parts: the written document and the oral presentation. The written document will account for 70 points and the oral presentation will account for 30 points.

PERFORMANCE INDICATORS EVALUATED

- Define the reasons for locating your business in a foreign country.
- Define the demographics of the country.
- Explain special considerations for locating a business in a foreign country.
- Explain the management function of your business.
- Describe the political, social, and economic factors to consider for your international business venture.
- Develop financial statements that project the financial results of your business.
- Describe how the workforce in the foreign country is suited for your business.
- Explain training, development, and management of your workforce.

For more detailed information about performance indicators, go to the DECA web site.

THINK CRITICALLY

1. Why do U.S. businesses move to other countries?
2. Why is more research required before deciding to locate a business in another country?
3. Why are demographics so important to consider for international business?
4. How will you satisfy U.S. workers concerned about jobs leaving the U.S?

www.deca.org/publications/HS_Guide/guidetoc.html

UNIT 2

ORGANIZING FOR INTERNATIONAL BUSINESS

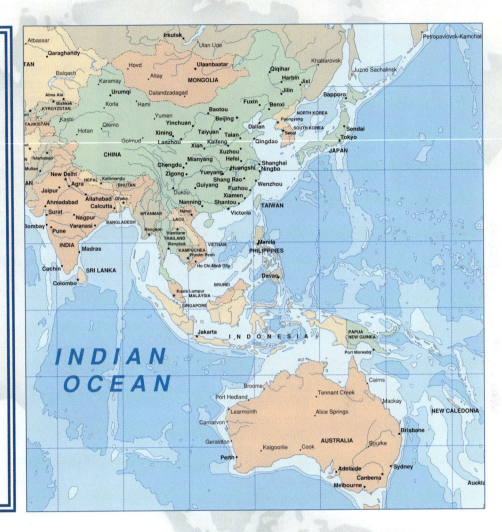

IF YOU WERE THERE

Suppose you were born in the late twentieth century in the city of Djakarta on the island of Java in Indonesia. Indonesia is a 13,677-island archipelago located south of the Asian mainland. It was once known as the East Indies. Over 8 million people live in your city, speaking languages ranging from Bahasa Indonesian to Javanese. Your relatives on Sumatra work on offshore oil rigs, and you sell food to tourists.

Perhaps you would rather have been born in Japan. There you might live in Toyota's company town, Toyota City, where you would attend a Toyota-owned school, live in a Toyota-built home, and eventually work in a Toyota facility. You would make an excellent salary, but you would live in a country that experiences 1,500 earthquakes per year.

Early Asian Civilizations

Archaeologists believe that one of the earliest Asian civilizations flourished from about 2500 to 1600 B.C. Its ruins lie in present-day Pakistan and India in the Indus River Valley. These ancient Asian cities included well-planned streets, large public buildings, and multistory houses with indoor bathrooms.

Our knowledge of early Chinese civilization comes from the discovery of oracle bones that were used instead of paper. Priests in the Shang Dynasty (1700 to 1000 B.C.) would scratch a question to their ancestors on an animal bone before firing the bone, forcing it to crack. The priest would interpret the pattern of cracks as an answer to the question.

China, Oldest Civilization in the World

China has the oldest continuous civilization in the world. Mountain barriers, the Gobi Desert, and large bodies of water have protected it from invasion and cultural influences for centuries. For added protection, The Great Wall in northern China was completed in about 200 B.C. By the 19th century A.D., a weak Chinese dynasty gave in to European demands for trading privileges, causing large sections of China to be claimed by Great Britain, France, Germany, Russia, and Japan. This control was the result of a series of unequal treaties that established the basic pattern for China's relations with the West for the next century. The communist government of the People's Republic of China (the ruling party since 1949) reacted to this western influence by isolating China. However, recent economic reforms have led to a more open policy.

©Getty Images/PhotoDisc

Japan, From Isolation to a Global Economy

The Japanese archipelago consists of four main islands and thousands of smaller ones. Together these islands make up the modern nation of Japan. Japan's history is rather brief when compared to that of India or China. By 500 A.D., it was ruled by emperors and powerful clans (noble families). The shoguns (great generals) took power in the twelfth century and created the shogunate (military government) that lasted until 1867.

Japan's cultural development had some influence from the Chinese. In the sixth century, Prince Shotoku encouraged the Japanese to accept the Chinese political philosophy that stressed the importance of an orderly society with obedience to authority. The Chinese also brought Buddhism to Japan. Siddhartha Gautama (563-483 B.C.), known as Buddha, or "enlightened one," founded Buddhism. The tradition teaches that you let go of desire by meditating and that, through this process of intense striving, you attain enlightenment.

Like the Chinese, the Japanese wanted to protect the purity of their culture by preventing trade with the West. However, in 1853, the United States sent Commodore Matthew Perry and four warships to Japan to force an end to Japan's isolation. Instead of war, the shogun signed trade treaties with Britain, France, the Netherlands, Russia, and the United States.

©Getty Images/PhotoDisc

By the twentieth century, Japan was competing actively in the global economy. With an expanding economy and population, Japan fought wars with Russia and China over control of Korea and Manchuria. By 1940, Japanese troops had taken the northern and eastern parts of China and Southeast Asia, where they gained access to rich deposits of oil, rubber, and other essential natural resources. The United States then cut off exports to Japan in response to its occupation of China. The Japanese navy attacked the U.S. naval base at Pearl Harbor in Hawaii on December 7, 1941. This pushed the United States into World War II.

The atomic bombs dropped on Hiroshima and Nagasaki in August of 1945 killed about 100,000 people. Many thousands more were injured, and Japan surrendered on September 2, 1945. Economic recovery began after the war, and the manufacture of products for export has helped to drive an economy that provides one of the highest standards of living in the world.

Southeast Asian Peninsula

The Southeast Asian peninsula juts out of the Asian continent south of China. Vietnam, a long narrow country, runs along the peninsula's east coast. Like other countries in the area, Vietnam contains lush tropical rain forests and fertile river valleys. Stronger countries have dominated Vietnam throughout history. China ruled Vietnam for about 1,000 years, and it was a French colony from the 1880s until it was lost to the Japanese in World War II.

The French returned when the Japanese were forced out. After the Vietnamese defeated the French in 1954, negotiations divided the country into North and South Vietnam. About 500,000 U.S. soldiers were sent to Vietnam during the Cold War to prevent the communist-ruled North from taking over the South. However, the U.S. troops were forced out in 1973, and a unified Communist Vietnam was formed in 1975. By the 1990s, Vietnam's per capita income was just $125 per year. The Vietnamese look forward to loans from the International Monetary Fund and closer relations with the United States to build their economy.

Other nations in Southeast Asia—such as Myanmar (formerly Burma), the Philippines, and Thailand—face continuing political unrest. Cambodia, Vietnam's neighbor, suffered through years of repression and civil war. A communist government known as the Khmer Rouge killed between 1 and 2 million people in the late 1970s. As civil war continued in 1993, 90 percent of the country's registered voters turned out for the first free elections in Cambodian history.

©Getty Images/PhotoDisc

Down Under

Australia and New Zealand constitute the continent of Australia in the Southern Hemisphere. Australia, about the size of the United States, was originally settled by the Aborigines who are thought to have migrated there from southeast Asia about 40,000 years ago. Great Britain used Australia as a penal colony from 1788 to 1839 and settled about 161,000 prisoners there. Other European settlers, attracted by gold mining and farming opportunities, settled the six colonies in Australia and gave the country its western traditions. Many of the prisoners also remained after their sentences had ended. Australia has vast deserts and mountain ranges, and its Great Barrier Reef extends over 1,200 miles on the northeast coast. New Zealand lies about 1,200 miles southeast of Australia. Maori people from other Polynesian islands first settled on New Zealand. Europeans, primarily from Great Britain, settled there in the eighteenth and nineteenth centuries. New Zealand is mountainous with fertile plains.

Both New Zealand and Australia are noted for liberal social policies. New Zealand was the first country in the world to allow women to vote.

©Getty Images/PhotoDisc

A Region of Contrasts

The Asia-Pacific Rim is a region of contrasts. People living in Australia, Japan, and New Zealand enjoy a stable economy, while political and economic instability has occurred in Pakistan, Bangladesh, and Laos. Food shortages and human suffering have been common for millions of people in these countries. The region is faced with various challenges. Indians seek relief from religious and ethnic violence. Young reformers battle political repression in China. Koreans struggle with reunification. Efforts to build modern industrial states compete with attempts to maintain cultural traditions and social customs.

Think Critically

1. Why do you think so many of the Asian countries resisted ties with Western countries?
2. How do the mountainous regions of Asia and Australia affect trade?
3. Research the history of China, and discover what inventions are attributed to it.

COUNTRY PROFILE/ASIA-PACIFIC RIM

Country	Population		GDP		Exports	Imports	Monetary Unit	Inflation	Unemployment	Life Expectancy	Literacy Rate
	thousands	growth rate	$billions	$ per capita	$billions			percent	percent	years	percent
Australia	19,731	0.96	528	27,000	63.7	61.8	Australian Dollar	2.8	6.3	80.13	100
Bangladesh	146,736	2.02	230	1,750	6.09	8.13	Taka	3.1	40	61.33	43.1
Bhutan	2,257	2.96	2.5	1,200	0.15	0.2	Ngultrum	3	N/A	53.58	42.2
Brunei	358	2.27	6.2	18,000	3	1.4	Bruneian Dollar	-2	10	74.3	91.8
Cambodia	14,144	2.4	18.7	1,500	1.38	1.73	New Riel	3.3	2.8	57.92	69.9
China	1,289,697	0.73	6,000	4,600	266	232	Yuan	-0.8	10 (urban)	72.22	86
East Timor	997	2.13	0.4	500	0.008	0.24	USD	N/A	50 (incl. underemp.)	65.2	48
Fiji	839	0.98	4.4	5,200	0.54	0.65	Fijian Dollar	2	7.6	68.88	93.7
Hong Kong	6,847,125	1.9	168.1	25,100	188.08	208.63	Hong Kong Dollar	3	7.5	79.93	94
India	1,065,462	1.51	2,660	2,540	43.1	55.3	Indian Rupee	5.4	8.8	63.62	59.5
Indonesia	219,883	1.26	687	3,000	57.4	34.7	Indonesian Rupiah	11.9	10.6	68.94	88.5
Japan	127,654	0.14	3,550	28,000	384	313	Yen	-0.9	5.4	80.93	99
Kiribati	96	1.41	0.08	840	0.006	0.027	Australian Dollar	2.5	2	60.93	N/A
Korea, North	22,664	0.54	22	1,000	0.83	1.87	North Korean Won	N/A	N/A	70.79	99
Korea, South	47,700	0.57	931	19,400	151.4	138	South Korean Won	2.8	3.1	75.36	98.1
Laos	5,657	2.29	9.2	1,630	0.31	0.53	New Kip	10	5.7	54.3	52.8
Malaysia	24,425	1.93	200	9,000	98.4	77.6	Ringgit	1.9	3.8	71.67	88.9
Maldives	318	2.98	1.2	3,870	0.11	0.35	Rufiyaa	1	Negl.	63.3	97.2
Micronesia, Federated States of	136	0.81	0.27	2,000	0.2	0.15	US Dollar	1	16	69.13	89
Mongolia	2,594	1.29	4.7	1,770	0.46	0.55	Tughrik	3	20	63.81	99.1
Myanmar (Burma)	42,281	1.28	63	1,500	2.3	2.56	Kyat	53.7	5.1	55.79	83.1
Nauru	12	2.29	0.6	5,000	NA	NA	Australian Dollar	-3.6	0	61.95	N/A
Nepal	25,164	2.23	35.6	1,400	0.72	1.49	Nepalese Rupee	2.8	47	59	45.2
New Zealand	3,875	0.77	75.4	19,500	13.9	12.5	New Zealand Dollar	2.7	5.3	78.32	99
Pakistan	153,578	2.44	299	2,100	9.13	9.74	Rupee	3.9	7.8	62.2	45.7
Palau	19	2.11	0.17	9,000	0.01	0.13	US Dollar	3.4	2.3	69.5	92
Papua New Guinea	5,711	2.22	12.2	2,400	1.81	0.93	Kina	9.8	N/A	64.19	66
Philippines	79,999	1.79	335	4,000	31.2	28.5	Philippine Peso	3.1	10.2	69.29	95.9
Samoa	177	0.97	0.62	3,500	0.02	0.12	Tala	4	N/A	70.11	99.7
Singapore	4,253	1.69	106.3	24,700	122.5	109.6	Singapore Dollar	-0.4	4.6	80.42	93.2
Sri Lanka	19,065	0.81	62.7	3,250	4.82	5.38	Sri Lankan Rupee	9.6	8	72.62	92.3
Taiwan	22,500	0.8	386	17,200	122	109	New Taiwan Dollar	-0.2	5.2	76.87	86
Thailand	62,833	1.01	410	6,600	63.2	54.6	Baht	0.6	2.9	71.24	96
Tonga	104	0.97	0.23	2,200	0.009	0.07	Pa'anga	8.4	13.3	68.88	98.5
Tuvalu	11	1.23	0.01	1,100	0.003	0.007	Tuvaluan Dollar	5	N/A	67.32	N/A
Uzbekistan	26,093	1.51	62	2,500	2.8	2.5	Som	26	10	64	99.3
Vanuatu	212	2.43	0.26	1,300	0.02	0.078	Vatu	3.2	N/A	61.71	53
Vietnam	81,377	1.35	168.1	2,100	14.5	14.1	New Dong	3.9	25	70.05	94

N/A—Data not available

©Digital Vision

Chapter 5

STRUCTURES OF INTERNATIONAL BUSINESS ORGANIZATIONS

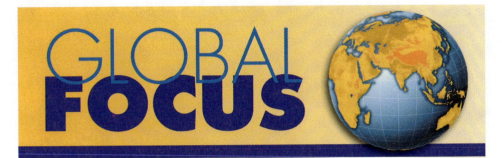

Mitsubishi: From Trading Company to Multinational Corporation

During the 20 years after it started as a trading company (sogoshosha) in 1870, Mitsubishi got involved in mining, banking, shipbuilding, and railroads. The company started as a zaibatsu (family-run conglomerate) and continued to expand into various types of business activities. In 1946, the organization divided into 139 separate entities. Twelve years later, Mitsubishi Trading established a division in the United States to export U.S. goods and to import raw materials to Japan.

As a result of growth and foreign investments, the company has expanded into many service areas and manufacturing. Today, Mitsubishi is involved in banking, insurance, real estate, glass production, cable television, clothing fibers, agricultural products, chemicals, steel, plastics, electrical equipment, paper mills, motor vehicles, mining, shipbuilding, energy, food, power plants, aircraft production, and information systems.

Based in Tokyo, the company has more than 48,000 employees serving customers through 35 offices in Japan and over 100 offices in other countries. In 1985, Chrysler and Mitsubishi formed a cooperative agreement to build automobiles in central Illinois. The company is also part owner in the world's highest-producing copper mine, located in Chile.

Think Critically

1. What economic and social factors contributed to the creation and expansion of Mitsubishi?
2. How might Mitsubishi expand its international business activities in the future?
3. Go to the Mitsubishi web site to obtain additional information about the company's structure and main business divisions.

5-1

METHODS OF BUSINESS OWNERSHIP

GOALS

- Describe the advantages and disadvantages of a sole proprietorship.
- Describe the advantages and disadvantages of a partnership.
- Explain the characteristics of a corporation.

©Getty Images/PhotoDisc

THE SOLE PROPRIETORSHIP

Have you ever wondered how a business gets organized? Almost every company you can think of started small with the efforts of one or two people. Both Texas Instruments and Apple Computer started with two people who had an idea for a new business opportunity. As a business grows in size, the company is likely to expand its operations and increase the number of owners. Every business organizes as one of three types: sole proprietorship, partnership, or corporation.

Most companies in the world are started and owned by one person. In the United States, over 70 percent of all businesses are sole proprietorships. A **sole proprietorship** is a business owned by one person. Many of the stores, companies, and other businesses you see each day have a single owner, even though they employ many people.

For a person to start a sole proprietorship, three major elements are needed. First, the new business owner must have a product or service to sell. Second, money for a building, equipment, and other start-up expenses will be required. Third, the owner must know how to manage the business activities of the company or hire someone else who knows how.

ADVANTAGES OF A SOLE PROPRIETORSHIP

Before you decide to organize your business as a sole proprietorship, you need to consider the advantages and disadvantages of this form of business organization.

Ease of Starting Obtaining a business license and meeting other minor legal requirements are usually the only steps needed to start a sole proprietorship. Your idea, funds, and willingness to accept the risk associated with running a business are all you need to get started. Throughout the world each day, thousands of people start companies that serve their customers and create employment opportunities.

Freedom to Make Business Decisions As a single proprietor, all company decisions are your own. As owner, you can run things yourself or hire others.

Owner Keeps All Profits The difference between money taken in and payments for expenses is called **net income** or **profit**. Since you are taking all of the risk, you receive all of the financial rewards.

Pride of Ownership As your own boss, you have the chance to see the results of your efforts. Many people like to have their own company so they do not have to work for someone else.

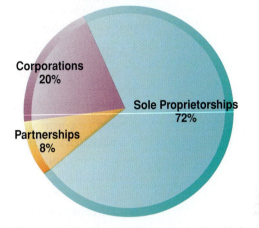

SOLE PROPRIETORSHIPS, PARTNERSHIPS, AND CORPORATIONS IN THE UNITED STATES

Corporations 20%

Sole Proprietorships 72%

Partnerships 8%

Figure 5-1 Most businesses in the United States are organized as sole proprietorships.

DISADVANTAGES OF A SOLE PROPRIETORSHIP

Even though there are advantages to running a business as a sole proprietorship, there are also disadvantages of this form of business organization.

Limited Sources of Funds The ability to raise money for a sole proprietorship is limited to the owner's contribution plus loans. As a new business owner, lenders may see you as a risky borrower. Even if you get a loan, it is likely to have a high rate of interest resulting in higher costs for the business.

Long Hours and Hard Work Since many new and small companies find it difficult to compete against established businesses, you will probably put in many long hours. When you own your own business, you cannot call in sick or take a vacation unless you have dedicated employees you trust.

Unlimited Risks In other forms of business organizations, several owners share the risks. As the sole owner, you are responsible for all aspects of the enterprise. The owner has unlimited liability. **Unlimited liability** means that the owner's personal assets can be used to pay for any debts of the business.

Limited Life of the Business If the owner dies or is unable to run the business, the enterprise will either cease to exist or be sold to someone else. When the business is sold, it becomes a different company with a new owner.

✓ **CheckPoint**

What is unlimited liability?

PARTNERSHIP

A **partnership** is a business that is owned by two or more people, but is not incorporated. A partnership may be organized when a company needs more money or the talents of additional people. Each owner, or partner, usually shares in both the decision making for the company and the profits.

Partnerships can be formed for any type of business. Stores, manufacturing companies, and restaurants can be organized as partnerships. Law firms and many professional sports teams use this type of ownership format.

ADVANTAGES OF A PARTNERSHIP

Like a sole proprietorship, a partnership also has a number of important advantages.

Ease of Creation A partnership is easy to start. A written agreement is created to communicate responsibilities and the division of profits.

Additional Sources of Funds With several owners, a partnership can raise more capital, expand business activities, and earn larger profits.

Availability of Different Talents Many partnerships can take advantage of the different skills of people. One partner may be responsible for selling, another takes care of company records, while a third supervises employees.

DISADVANTAGES OF A PARTNERSHIP

Even though there are advantages to running a business as a partnership, there are also disadvantages of this form of business organization.

Partners Are Liable As with the sole proprietorship, a partnership has *unlimited liability*. Any or all of the partners may be held personally responsible for the debts of the business.

Profits Are Shared among Several Owners The written partnership agreement determines the division of profits. Even if an uneven workload occurs, the net income is divided based on the agreement.

Potential for Disagreement among Owners Differences in opinions are likely to occur in every work situation. Two or more people who work closely together may have disagreements. Some people suggest that you avoid going into business with friends or relatives to prevent possible personal conflicts.

Business Can Dissolve Suddenly When one partner dies or cannot continue in the partnership, the business must stop. At this point, a new company and partnership agreement must be created. This may not be easy since some of the company assets may have to be sold to buy the departing partner's share of the business.

✔ CheckPoint

What is the purpose of a partnership agreement?

CORPORATION

WORK AS A GROUP

Suggest ways a person could obtain funds to start a new business.

While sole proprietorships are the most common type of business in the United States, corporations account for nearly 90 percent of the sales, as shown in Figure 5-2. A **corporation** is a business that operates as a legal entity separate from any of the owners.

SALES OF SOLE PROPRIETORSHIPS, PARTNERSHIPS, AND CORPORATIONS IN THE UNITED STATES

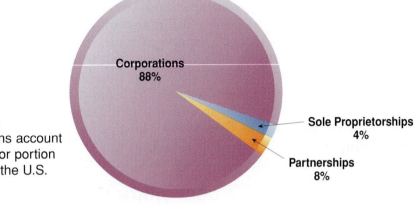

Corporations 88%

Sole Proprietorships 4%

Partnerships 8%

Figure 5-2 Corporations account for the major portion of sales in the U.S. economy.

A corporation raises money for business activities through the sale of stock to individuals and organizations that wish to be part owners of the corporation. A **stock certificate** is a document that represents ownership in a corporation. A stock certificate is shown in Figure 5-3.

The owners of a corporation are called **stockholders**, or **shareholders**. Stockholders usually have two main rights. The first is to earn dividends, and the second is to vote on company policies. Many people buy stock in corporations to earn **dividends**, which are a share of company profits.

Stockholders also indirectly control the management of the company. A stockholder typically has one vote for each share of stock owned. The stockholders vote to elect the board of directors of the company. The board of directors hires managers to run the company.

Unlike sole proprietorships and partnerships, in which individual owners are responsible for any actions of the business, corporations act as a legal "entity" on behalf of the owners.

Figure 5-3 A stock certificate certifies ownership in a corporation.

ADVANTAGES OF A CORPORATION

A corporation has several advantages when compared to partnerships and sole proprietorships.

More Sources of Funds As a result of having many people interested in being part owners, corporations have an easier time raising funds than a sole proprietorship or partnership. This capital can be used for a company to purchase expensive equipment or to build large factories.

Fixed Financial Liability of Owners The business risk of a corporation is spread among many owners. A company such as General Motors or McDonald's has thousands of stockholders. Each person who buys a share of stock has **limited liability**, which means stockholders are only responsible for the debts of the corporation up to the amount they invested. Unlike sole proprietors and partners, people who become part owners of a corporation can only lose the amount of money paid for the stock.

Specialized Management Most corporations can afford to hire the most skilled people to run the company. The board of directors of the corporation hires the president and other administrative employees.

Unlimited Life of the Company Unlike a sole proprietorship or partnership, a corporation is a continuing entity. When stockholders die or sell out, the company still exists. Ownership just transfers to other people.

DISADVANTAGES OF A CORPORATION

Even though there are advantages to running a business as a corporation, there are also disadvantages of this form of business organization.

Difficult Creation Process The organizers of a corporation must usually meet complex government requirements. A **charter** is the document granted by the state or federal government that allows a company to form a corporation.

Owners Have Limited Control Unless you own a large portion of the stock, you are unable to influence the operations of a corporation. Small or family-held corporations may have only a few stockholders, but most large corporations are owned by thousands of people.

Double Taxation Sole proprietors and partners pay individual income tax on their companies' earnings. However, a corporation pays corporate income taxes as a separate entity. Then stockholders pay personal income tax on the dividends they receive. Therefore, corporate earnings are taxed twice.

GLOBAL BUSINESS EXAMPLE

HOW DO YOU SPELL INC.?

In the United States, you can tell that a business is a corporation if the abbreviation *Inc.* (meaning incorporated) follows the company name. In Canada, Japan, and the United Kingdom, *Ltd.* (for limited) is used, referring to the limited liability of the owners. The notation for a corporate form of business in various other countries is listed below.

France, Belgium	Sarl
Germany, Switzerland	GmbH
Italy	Srl
Denmark	A/S
Spain, Mexico, Brazil	S.A.
Netherlands	N.V.

Think Critically

1. Conduct an Internet search to find some corporations based in other countries.
2. What cultural factors might influence different corporate notations?

CheckPoint

What are the rights of the owners of a corporation?

REVIEW GLOBAL BUSINESS TERMS

Define each of the following terms.

1. sole proprietorship
2. net income, or profit
3. unlimited liability
4. partnership
5. corporation
6. stock certificate
7. stockholders, or shareholders
8. dividends
9. limited liability
10. charter

REVIEW GLOBAL BUSINESS CONCEPTS

11. What are the advantages of a proprietorship?
12. What are the disadvantages of a partnership?
13. What are the disadvantages of a corporation?

SOLVE GLOBAL BUSINESS PROBLEMS

For each of the following situations, what type of business organization would you recommend?

14. A group of programmers in India plan to start a software company and sell stock to other investors.

15. A person in Italy who creates small home decorations as a hobby plans to start a business selling these items.

16. Three doctors in South Africa wish to share office space, staff, and equipment.

17. Three friends in Finland are opening a small store to sell sports equipment.

THINK CRITICALLY

18. "Because of the advantage of limited liability, every business should be organized as a corporation." Do you agree? Explain.

19. Is buying stock in a corporation a good investment?

MAKE CONNECTIONS

20. **BUSINESS** Name a sole proprietorship, a partnership, and a corporation in your community. Speculate about why each of these businesses chose its form of organization.

21. **LAW** Conduct an Internet search to obtain information on other forms of business organization, such as a limited partnership and an S corporation. Prepare a presentation of your findings for the class.

5-2

OPERATIONS OF GLOBAL BUSINESSES

GOALS

- Name other forms of business ownership.
- Describe the activities, characteristics, and concerns of multinational companies.

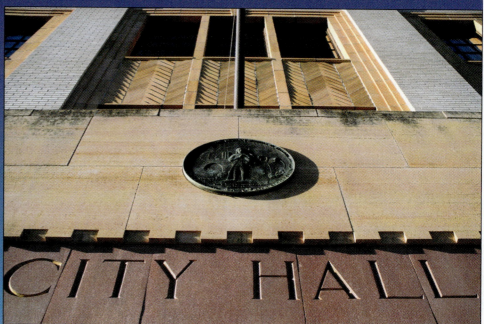

©Getty Images/PhotoDisc

OTHER FORMS OF BUSINESS ORGANIZATION

Most businesses are organized as sole proprietorships, partnerships, or corporations. However, other types of business organization exist for special situations. Increasingly, many of them also engage in international business activities.

A **municipal corporation** is an incorporated town or city organized to provide services for citizens rather than to make a profit. You might think that a city would only engage in local activities. However, many cities have partnerships with cities in other countries, import goods and services, and engage in cultural exchanges.

Nonprofit corporations are created to provide a service and are not concerned with making a profit. Included in this category are churches, synagogues, and mosques, some hospitals, private colleges and universities, many charities, the American Red Cross, Boy Scouts of America, and The Salvation Army. Nonprofits provide a significant portion of the jobs in the labor force in some countries. These organizations employ over 6 percent of the total workforce in the Netherlands, Ireland, Belgium, Israel, United States, Australia, and Britain. Many local nonprofit organizations are affiliated with international organizations.

Nonprofit organizations are also referred to as nongovernmental organizations, or NGOs. In recent years, NGOs such as labor unions, environmental groups, and public interest organizations have taken action on various social and economic issues. Labor groups are concerned about lost jobs and safe working conditions, while environmental organizations work to protect clean air and water.

A **cooperative** is a business owned by its members and operated for their benefit. Consumer cooperatives may be formed by a group of people in a community or at a place of worship. The group is organized to purchase food or other goods and services at a lower cost than usual. Any profits are returned to the cooperative members. A credit union is a cooperative created to provide savings and loan services to its members.

✔ CheckPoint

Discuss situations when municipal corporations, nonprofit corporations, and cooperatives would be the best business organization to implement.

MULTINATIONAL COMPANIES

In 1670, King Charles II of Britain granted a business charter to create a trading company named after English explorer Henry Hudson. The Hudson's Bay Company started as an international fur trading enterprise and today operates nearly 500 stores throughout Canada.

Just as the Hudson's Bay Company started as a global business, many firms today operate in several countries. A **multinational company or corporation (MNC)** is an organization that conducts business in several countries. MNCs are also called global companies, transnational companies, and worldwide companies. Figure 5-4 shows an example of the global business operations that a multinational company might have.

MULTINATIONAL COMPANIES CROSS BORDERS

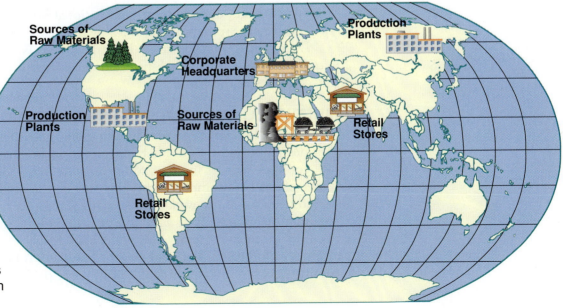

Figure 5-4 A multinational company has business operations in different countries.

KOMATSU ABANDONS JAPANESE FOR ENGLISH

When industrial giant Komatsu was founded in Japan, it marketed its products within the country. The Japanese language served Komatsu well as a means of communication. As Komatsu expanded and began to market its heavy equipment elsewhere in the region, it continued to rely primarily on Japanese. However, as Komatsu developed worldwide markets in direct competition with the likes of Caterpillar Tractor, the Japanese language proved to be a handicap. Its employees and customers increasingly were not fluent in Japanese, which created major communication problems. To better compete in the global marketplace, Komatsu decided that it needed to switch from Japanese to English. Now that transition is in process—even at the home office in Japan. To facilitate the conversion to English, Komatsu is providing its employees with English language lessons. Over time, Komatsu will reach its goal of being an English-speaking multinational organization.

Think Critically

1. Why did Japanese serve Komatsu reasonably well when it expanded into nearby countries?
2. What do you think would be some of the challenges for a business that abandons the language of the home country?
3. Why do you think Komatsu chose English to replace Japanese?

MNCs usually consist of a parent company in a *home country* and divisions or separate companies in one or more *host countries*. For example, Mitsubishi of Japan (home country) consists of 160 companies doing business in several countries (host countries). Whirlpool has manufacturing facilities in North America, South America, Europe, and Asia with products sold in more than 170 countries. Coca-Cola sells its products in about 200 countries.

Today, as a result of widespread international business activities, thousands of multinational corporations exist. Many of these companies are very large. Royal Dutch/Shell, Ford, Exxon, General Motors, Wal-Mart, General Electric, IBM, and Toyota each have annual sales that exceed the GDP of many countries in the world.

MULTINATIONAL COMPANIES IN OPERATION

Multinational companies get involved in global activities to take advantage of business opportunities in other geographic areas. The potential for MNCs to sell goods or services in other countries is the result of a competitive advantage held by a company. This edge can be the result of technology, lower costs, location, or availability of natural resources.

Another major activity of MNCs is adapting to different societies. Social and cultural influences along with political and legal concerns must be continually monitored. For example, if a company is not aware of changes in a country's tax law, the result could mean lower profits.

CHARACTERISTICS OF MULTINATIONAL COMPANIES

Multinational companies commonly have the following characteristics.

- **Worldwide Market View** They view the entire world as their potential market. Companies seek product ideas through foreign subsidiaries and obtain raw materials on a worldwide basis.
- **Standardized Product** Companies look for similarities among markets to offer a standardized product whenever possible.
- **Culturally-Sensitive Hiring** They use consistent hiring policies throughout the world but are also culturally sensitive to host countries. The companies recruit managers internationally rather than just from the organization's countries of operation.
- **International and Local Perspective** These businesses distribute, produce, price, and promote with both an international outlook and a local perspective.

Debate the benefits and potential problems of multinational companies.

CONCERNS ABOUT MULTINATIONAL COMPANIES

The presence of a multinational company can have many benefits for a host country—more jobs, products, services, and even improved roads created by the MNC. However, there are two main concerns about MNCs.

As a foreign company becomes a major business, the MNC's economic power can make a host country dependent. Workers will depend on the MNC for jobs. Consumers will depend on the company for needed goods and services. The MNC could become a country's main economic entity.

When this occurs the MNC could start to influence and even control the country's politics. The company may require certain tax laws or regulations that only benefit the powerful MNC. The regulation and control of global companies is likely to be an issue in years to come.

BUSINESSES EXPAND TO MALAYSIA

Since gaining independence in 1963, Malaysia has demonstrated a political stability that has made the country an attractive destination for many foreign investors. U.S. companies such as Colgate-Palmolive, Goodyear, and Texas Instruments have had a strong presence there. Malaysia's neighbors, however, are even larger investors. Taiwan and Japan have built and operate business facilities to produce manufacturing equipment, telecommunications equipment, and electronics products.

Think Critically

1. How does political stability encourage foreign investment?
2. Why have neighboring countries invested in Malaysia?

REGIONAL PERSPECTIVE

HISTORY: AUSTRALIA'S BEGINNING WITH CONVICTS

Economic development in a geographic area can result from unusual circumstances. Consider Australia in the late 1700s. At the start of the Industrial Revolution in Britain, food shortages, lost jobs, and strict laws contributed to an increase in crime and legal penalties. People were jailed for their inability to pay bills. (There was no bankruptcy protection in those days.) The British people wanted lawbreakers and debtors removed from their society. The newly independent United States no longer allowed British criminals to be sent there, so a new location was needed.

In 1787, Captain Arthur Philip of the Royal Fleet navigated 11 ships with 759 convicts to Port Jackson (now called Sydney) in Australia. One of the early governors of Australia was Captain William Bligh. who had gained notoriety when the crew of his ship, the H.M.S. *Bounty*, mutinied.

Australia continued to be used as a penal colony until 1840, when free settlers began to dominate the area. In total, about 160,000 convicts were sent to Australia over the years. The country gained its independence from Britain in 1901.

Think Critically
1. Conduct a web search for additional information about the history of Australia.
2. Explain how this situation resulted in economic development for Australia.

✔ CheckPoint

What are two concerns host countries have about multinational companies?

©Getty Images/PhotoDisc

REVIEW GLOBAL BUSINESS TERMS

Define each of the following terms.

1. municipal corporation
2. nonprofit corporation
3. cooperative
4. multinational company or corporation (MNC)

REVIEW GLOBAL BUSINESS CONCEPTS

5. Give an example of a municipal corporation, a nonprofit corporation, and a cooperative.

6. What is the relationship between a home country and a host country?

7. What kinds of competitive advantages can a multinational company have?

SOLVE GLOBAL BUSINESS PROBLEMS

For each of the following situations, decide whether the situation reflects a characteristic of a multinational company.

8. A product is designed to meet the strictest consumer protection laws so that it will be marketable in any country.

9. Advertising themes are the same in all countries, but the language is changed.

10. A company hires host country citizens as managers as often as possible.

11. Each country is considered a separate market, and a product is formulated to be sold in a single country.

12. Products are shipped to other countries only by mail.

THINK CRITICALLY

13. How do nonprofit organizations benefit society?

14. Is it likely that a well-managed multinational company could be successful in every country in the world? Explain.

15. Describe ways a global company could provide social and economic benefits to a host country.

MAKE CONNECTIONS

16. **CULTURAL STUDIES** Why are nonprofit organizations more popular in some countries than others?

17. **MATHEMATICS** Go to the web site of a multinational company. Determine the percentages of the company's sales for different regions of the world, such as Africa, the Middle East, and Asia.

5-3 STARTING GLOBAL BUSINESS ACTIVITIES

GOALS

- Identify five low-risk methods for getting involved in international business.
- Discuss higher-risk methods for getting involved in international business.

©Getty Images/PhotoDisc

LOW-RISK METHODS FOR GETTING INVOLVED IN INTERNATIONAL BUSINESS

Companies use eight main ways to get involved in international business, as shown in Figure 5-5. As you move up the steps, the firm has more control over its foreign business activities as well as more risk. For example, indirect exporting has less risk associated with it than a joint venture. However, a company has more direct control over its business dealings with a joint venture than with indirect exporting.

METHODS FOR GETTING INVOLVED IN INTERNATIONAL BUSINESS

Wholly-Owned Subsidiary

Foreign Direct Investment

Joint Venture

Franchising

Licensing

Management Contracting

Direct Exporting

Indirect Exporting

Figure 5-5 A company may choose from a variety of methods to get involved in international business.

INDIRECT EXPORTING

At first, a business organization may get involved with international business by finding a demand for its service or product without really trying. **Indirect exporting** occurs when a company sells its products in a foreign market without any special activity for that purpose.

During a sales meeting or another business encounter, for example, someone in a foreign company may show interest in your product. A buyer who represents several companies may tell a small manufacturing company about the need for its product in Southeast Asia. Since the company was not looking for foreign business opportunities, indirect exporting is sometimes called *casual* or *accidental* exporting. Indirect exporting makes use of agents and brokers who bring together sellers and buyers of products in different countries. This method of international business has minimum costs and risks. Many companies have started their foreign business activities using this method.

DIRECT EXPORTING

After sales increase and a company decides to get more involved in international business, the organization will probably create its own exporting department. **Direct exporting** occurs when a company actively seeks and conducts exporting. The company may still use agents or brokers from outside of the organization. However, a manager within the company plans, implements, and controls the exporting activities.

While direct exporting requires higher costs than indirect exporting, the company has more control over its foreign business activities. The risk is still relatively low because the firm does not have an extensive investment in the other country. The exporting process is discussed in greater detail in the next chapter.

MANAGEMENT CONTRACTING

Knowledge is a powerful tool in business. An ability to find business opportunities, coordinate resources, solve problems, and make productive decisions is a skill that will be in demand throughout your life. The abilities of managers to assist companies in developing countries are important exports for industrialized countries. A **management contract** is a situation in which a company sells only its management skills. This has a fairly low risk for a company since managers can usually leave a country quickly if the business environment becomes too risky. An example of management contracting may involve a hotel company that agrees to help hotel owners in other countries.

A variation of this type of agreement is *contract manufacturing*. This arrangement involves a company in one country producing an item for a company located in another country. This relationship allows a business to enter a foreign market without investing in production facilities. Contract manufacturing is usually considered as having low to moderate risk.

©Getty Images/PhotoDisc

LICENSING

To produce items in other countries without being actively involved, a company can allow a foreign company to use a procedure it owns. **Licensing** is selling the right to use some intangible property (production process, trademark, or brand name) for a fee or royalty. The Gerber Company started selling its baby food products in Japan using licensing. The use of television and movie characters or sports team emblems on hats, shirts, jackets, notebooks, luggage, and other products is also the result of licensing agreements.

A licensing agreement provides a fee or royalty to the company granting the license. This payment is in return for the right to use the process, brand name, or trademark. The Disney Company, for example, receives a royalty from the amusement park it licensed in Japan. Licensing has a low monetary investment, so the potential financial return is frequently low. However, the risk for the company is also low.

FRANCHISING

Another method commonly used to expand into other countries is the **franchise**, which is the right to use a company name or business process in a specific way. Organizations contract with people in other countries to set up a business that looks and operates like the parent company. The company obtaining the franchise will usually adapt various business elements. Marketing elements such as the taste of food products, packaging, and advertising messages must meet cultural sensitivities and meet legal requirements.

Franchising and licensing are similar. Both involve a royalty payment for the right to use a process or famous company name. Licensing, however, usually involves a manufacturing process, while franchising involves selling a product or service.

Franchise agreements are popular with fast-food companies. McDonald's, Burger King, Wendy's, KFC, Domino's Pizza, and Pizza Hut all have used franchising to expand into foreign markets.

✓ CheckPoint

What are five relatively low-risk methods of getting involved in international business?

HIGHER-RISK METHODS FOR GETTING INVOLVED IN INTERNATIONAL BUSINESS

It is often true that business activities with higher risks also return greater profits to justify taking those risks. Joint ventures and foreign direct investments also give companies more direct control over its business operations than most of the less risky methods.

JOINT VENTURES

A partnership can provide benefits to all owners. One type of international partnership is the **joint venture**, an agreement between two or more companies from different countries to share a business project. A joint venture is illustrated in Figure 5-6.

The main benefits of a joint venture are sharing raw materials, shipping facilities, management activities, and production facilities. Some drawbacks are sharing profits and having less control.

Joint venture arrangements can share costs, risks, and profits in any combination. One company may have only 10 percent ownership and the other 90 percent. It depends on the joint venture agreement.

Joint ventures, also called *strategic partnerships,* can be used for any type of business activity. This arrangement is especially popular for manufacturing. Joint ventures between Japanese and U.S. automobile manufacturers have been common. For example, the Ford Motor Company entered a joint venture with Mazda Motor Corporation. Ford used Mazda-produced parts for several cars. Mazda set up assembly plants for Ford motor vehicles.

FOREIGN DIRECT INVESTMENT

As a company gets more involved in international business, it may make a direct investment in a foreign country. A **foreign direct investment (FDI)** occurs when a company buys land or other resources in another country. Real estate and existing companies are common purchases under this method. Many British, Japanese, and German companies own office buildings, hotels, and shopping malls in the United States.

Another type of FDI is the

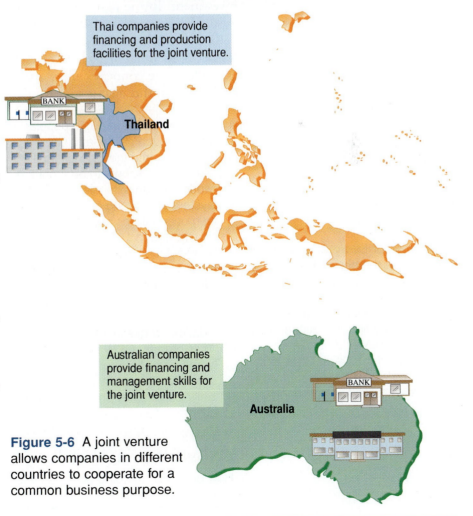

A JOINT VENTURE IN ACTION

Thai companies provide financing and production facilities for the joint venture.

BANK

Thailand

Australian companies provide financing and management skills for the joint venture.

BANK

Australia

Figure 5-6 A joint venture allows companies in different countries to cooperate for a common business purpose.

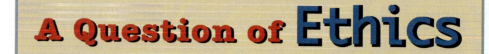

A Question of Ethics

STEALING SECRETS BY FOREIGN PARTNERS

Working relationships between foreign enterprises and companies in host countries can be strained by the loss of technology secrets. In a closed society (one with a centralized government), outside companies may be required to provide their local partners with computer hardware, software, and knowledge to operate these systems. However, often the technology is then borrowed and duplicated by the local company to start a new business.

Think Critically

According to the guidelines for ethical analysis, how will the actions of the government and companies in the host country affect the business and economy of the other partner?

wholly-owned subsidiary, which is an independent company owned by a parent company. Multinational companies frequently have wholly-owned subsidiaries in various countries that are the result of foreign direct investment. In the past, foreign companies have owned U.S.-based businesses such as Burger King, Pillsbury, and Green Giant.

To prevent economic control of one country by another, a nation may restrict how much of its land or factories may be sold to foreign owners. For example, some countries allow a foreign investor to own only 49 percent of companies in those countries.

GLOBAL BUSINESS EXAMPLE

CEREAL PARTNERS WORLDWIDE

Cheerios or Lucky Charms with Nestlé on the box instead of General Mills would seem strange to most consumers in the United States. However, in Latin America, Europe, the Middle East, and other areas of the world, this is a common sight. Cereal Partners Worldwide (CPW) is a joint venture between these two companies.

General Mills brought popular brands, such as Trix and Golden Grahams, into the partnership. Nestlé, well known throughout the world, has an extensive distribution system and strong brand presence in grocery stores and supermarkets.

Created in 1989, Cereal Partners Worldwide is now the second-largest cereal company outside of North America. CPW operates in more than 130 countries with more than 40 distinctive cereal brands. In addition to the well-known General Mills brands, CPW has created some cereal products for specific markets. The joint venture company sells Zucosos in Chile, Chocapic in Spain, and Snow Flakes in the Czech Republic. CPW makes it possible to buy Trix or Cheerios at a rural store in Chile as well as in a supermarket in Israel.

Think Critically

1. What factors influenced the creation of CPW?
2. What are some examples of products you use each day that might need to be adapted to other cultures?
3. Go to the web site of General Mills to obtain current information about the activities of CPW and other joint ventures of the company.

✔ CheckPoint

How does risk of doing business internationally differ for exporting and direct foreign investment?

REVIEW GLOBAL BUSINESS TERMS

Define each of the following terms.

1. indirect exporting
2. direct exporting
3. management contract
4. licensing
5. franchise
6. joint venture
7. foreign direct investment (FDI)
8. wholly-owned subsidiary

REVIEW GLOBAL BUSINESS CONCEPTS

9. Why is management contracting a safe method for getting involved in international business?

10. What is the difference between licensing and franchising?

SOLVE GLOBAL BUSINESS PROBLEMS

For each of the following situations, tell what method the company is using for its global business activities.

11. A Vietnamese company shares production costs and profits of a chemical manufacturing enterprise with an Israeli company.

12. A British toy company allows a Japanese company to create clothing and school supplies with one of the British company's doll characters on the products.

13. A company in Egypt has purchased 51 percent of the stock of a company in Peru.

14. A small food-packaging firm cannot afford to sell in other countries, so it asks an export agent to obtain orders for the company.

THINK CRITICALLY

15. What factors would affect how the parties in a joint venture divide future profits?

16. In what ways does a company making a direct foreign investment in a new factory have more control than a company engaged in direct exporting?

MAKE CONNECTIONS

17. **CULTURAL STUDIES** Visit a toy store, sporting goods store, or another kind of store that sells merchandise printed with logos or images belonging to other companies. List the items you see and any information on the tags or packaging that indicates a licensing agreement.

18. **TECHNOLOGY** Do an Internet search for "joint venture." Select a site that describes a joint venture involving two countries. Write a report on the companies and countries involved, the products, and other major details about the joint venture.

CHAPTER SUMMARY

5-1 METHODS OF BUSINESS OWNERSHIP

A The advantages of a sole proprietorship are ease of starting, individual business freedom, owner gets all profits, and pride of ownership. The disadvantages are limited funds, potential long hours, unlimited liability, and limited life of the business.

B The benefits of a partnership are ease of creation, additional sources of funds, and availability of different talents. The possible drawbacks are partners are each liable, profits are shared, potential for disagreement, and business can dissolve suddenly.

C Advantages of a corporation are more sources of funds, limited liability, management availability, and unlimited life. Disadvantages include difficult creation process, owners' limited control, and double taxation.

5-2 OPERATIONS OF GLOBAL BUSINESSES

A Other forms of business ownership include municipal corporations, nonprofit corporations, and cooperatives.

B Multinational companies take advantage of business opportunities in several geographic areas by adapting to cultural and economic influences in different societies. Multinational companies with a global perspective consider the entire world as their potential market. They look for similarities among markets in order to offer a standardized product whenever possible.

5-3 STARTING GLOBAL BUSINESS ACTIVITIES

A Low-risk methods used for getting involved in international business include indirect exporting, direct exporting, management contracting, licensing, and franchising.

B Higher-risk methods used for getting involved in international business are joint ventures, foreign direct investment, and wholly-owned subsidiaries.

Read the case at the beginning of this chapter, and answer the following questions.

1. What are the benefits and potential problems of a company being involved in many types of products and services?

2. Describe a joint venture that might be appropriate for Mitsubishi in the future.

REVIEW GLOBAL BUSINESS TERMS

Match the terms listed with the definitions. Some terms may not be used.

1. A business owned by its members and operated for their benefit.

2. The difference between money taken in and expenses.

3. The owners of a corporation.

4. Selling the right to use some intangible property for a fee or royalty.

5. The situation in which a business owner is only responsible for the debts of the business up to the amount invested.

6. The document granted by government allowing a company to organize as a corporation.

7. A document that represents ownership in a corporation.

8. The selling of a company's products in a foreign market without any special activity for that purpose.

9. An independent foreign company owned by a parent company.

10. The situation in which a business owner's personal assets can be used to pay any debts of the business.

11. A business that operates as a legal entity separate from any of the owners.

12. A situation in which a company sells only its management skills in another country.

13. A share of corporate earnings paid to stockholders.

14. The right to use a company name or business process in a specific way.

15. An agreement between two or more companies from different countries to share a business project.

16. A company actively seeking and conducting exporting.

17. The purchase of land or other resources in a foreign country.

18. An organization that conducts business in several countries.

a. charter
b. cooperative
c. corporation
d. direct exporting
e. dividends
f. foreign direct investment (FDI)
g. franchise
h. indirect exporting
i. joint venture
j. licensing
k. limited liability
l. management contract
m. multinational company or corporation (MNC)
n. municipal corporation
o. net income, or profit
p. nonprofit corporations
q. partnership
r. sole proprietorship
s. stock certificate
t. stockholders, or shareholders
u. unlimited liability
v. wholly-owned subsidiary

MAKE GLOBAL BUSINESS DECISIONS

19. List reasons why most companies in the world start out and remain sole proprietorships. How does being a sole proprietorship benefit or limit a company's ability to become involved in international business?

20. Describe a situation in which a partnership or sole proprietorship could raise capital to expand business activities more easily than a corporation.

21. Why do you think the government makes the creation of a corporation more difficult than the creation of other forms of business ownership?

22. Name goods and services that could be the basis for creating a consumer cooperative.

23. What are some ways a multinational company can have a competitive advantage over local businesses?

24. What types of restrictions might a foreign government put on a multinational corporation doing business in its country?

25. Describe actions a manager might take when (a) planning, (b) implementing, and (c) controlling a company's exporting activities.

26. What are some services companies could sell to other countries using management contracts?

27. How would a business that sells licenses and franchises control the image of the company name?

28. What are some concerns people might have about a company making many foreign investments in their country?

GLOBAL CONNECTIONS

29. **GEOGRAPHY** Locate examples of multinational companies in different countries. Create a map showing where the companies are based and the other nations in which the companies operate.

30. **COMMUNICATIONS** Interview a local business owner about the form of business organization used by his or her company. Ask the owner how the company got started, and ask for suggestions he or she could give to others who want to start a business.

31. **HISTORY** Conduct library research about a major foreign company and its home country. Obtain information on how the country's history may have influenced the development of the company.

32. **CULTURAL STUDIES** Describe how a multinational company might need to adapt its products to meet the traditions, customs, and cultural norms of various societies.

33. **SCIENCE** Collect advertisements, articles, and other information about multinational companies. Describe what natural resources and production processes would be necessary to create the products of these companies.

34. **MATHEMATICS** Conduct an opinion survey of students and others to determine their attitudes toward products and companies from other countries. Survey questions could include: (a) Which countries make the best products? (b) Do consumers benefits from being able to buy products from other countries? (c) Should our government restrict products from other countries? (d) Should foreign governments restrict U.S. products from entering their markets? Prepare a chart showing your results.

35. **CAREER PLANNING** Talk to someone who owns a business. Obtain information about the types of jobs the person had before becoming an entrepreneur.

THE GLOBAL
ENTREPRENEUR
CREATING AN INTERNATIONAL BUSINESS PLAN

PLANNING AND ORGANIZING GLOBAL BUSINESS OPERATIONS

Select a company to work with. Make use of previously collected materials, or do additional research to get the information you need.

1. Describe how your company might have started as a sole proprietorship or a partnership. Explain the factors that may have influenced the owners' decision to select this form of business organization.

2. If the company becomes a multinational corporation, what benefits and problems could result?

3. Describe appropriate international business opportunities for the company. What products and services would be most appropriate for different geographic regions? What economic, cultural, legal, or political influences must the company consider?

4. Which of the methods described in the final section of this chapter (see Figure 5-5) would be appropriate for the company to use for international business activities?

5. Explain the possible use of two or more of these methods for getting involved in international business.

6. Prepare a written report or present a short oral report (two or three minutes) that answers these questions. Or if instructed by your teacher, create a poster or scrapbook with pictures and information that answer these questions.

Chapter 6

IMPORTING, EXPORTING, AND TRADE RELATIONS

GLOBAL FOCUS

The Scoop on Ice Cream Exports

As U.S. producers of ice cream look for new international markets, they face a continuing problem. Refrigeration, or rather the lack of it, can greatly influence market potential. In the urban areas of China, for example, very few homeowners own freezers. As a result, most Chinese prefer their ice cream in the form of small snacks and consume them on the street.

During the late 1980s, annual exports of U.S. ice cream to Japan were only $200,000. This was due to a Japanese import quota for ice cream and frozen yogurt. With the elimination of that trade barrier, Japanese customers bought more ice cream from U.S. companies. After ice cream sales in Asia dropped in the late 1990s (due to poor economic conditions), demand then started to increase.

In Costa Rica and other Central American countries, there was little or no market for ice cream in the mid 1990s. Then Costa Rica honored its commitment to the World Trade Organization by reducing the 44 percent tariff and increasing the 500-ton import quota.

Another strong growth area for expanding ice cream exports is the Caribbean market. The hot climate and many tourists in that region create a strong demand for various frozen snacks and desserts.

Think Critically

1. What factors have increased the demand for ice cream from overseas customers?
2. What obstacles might an ice cream exporter encounter when doing business in other countries?
3. Go to the web site of the Foreign Agricultural Service of the U.S. Department of Agriculture (www.fas.usda.gov) to obtain current information about ice cream exports.

6-1 | IMPORTING PROCEDURES

GOALS

- Explain the importance of importing.
- Identify the four steps of importing.

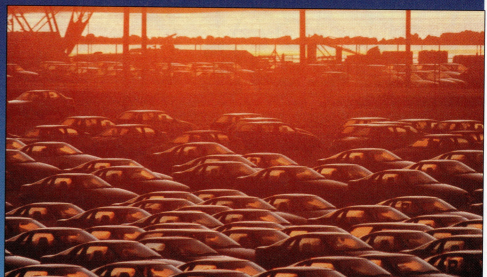

©Getty Images/PhotoDisc

THE IMPORTANCE OF IMPORTING

Imagine how life in the United States would be without international business. Most television sets, calculators, athletic shoes, and video recorders bought in the United States come from other countries. And these products are only a few of the imported products in use each day. Importing provides a wide variety of products and services for U.S. consumers. Exporting creates jobs and expands business opportunities. Importing and exporting are primary international business activities.

Imports are services or products bought by a company or government from businesses in other countries. Businesses can get involved in international trade by importing goods and services and selling them in their own country. The importing business can create new sales or expand sales with existing customers. A company usually gets involved in importing for one of three reasons. These reasons are consumer demand for products unique to foreign countries, lower costs of foreign-made products, or foreign-made parts used in domestic manufacturing.

Product Demand Customers who want a unique item or a certain quality may purchase a foreign-made product. Some goods and services may be available only from other countries. Almost all bananas, cocoa, and coffee consumed in the United States are imported.

Lower Costs The prices of goods and services are constantly changing. An item from one country may be less expensive than the same item from another country. Electronic products manufactured in Taiwan are frequently less expensive than similar items produced elsewhere.

Production Inputs Companies regularly purchase raw materials and component parts for processing or assembly from other countries. For example, the radios, engines, transmissions, and windshield washer systems for many cars assembled in the United States come from companies in Canada, Mexico, Brazil, Japan, Korea, and other countries.

✔ **CheckPoint**

What are the three main reasons companies import?

IMPORTING ACTIVITIES

What does a company have to do to become an importer? Importing usually involves four main activities or steps, as shown in Figure 6-1 on the next page.

STEP 1 DETERMINE DEMAND

The first activity is to determine whether consumers in this country will purchase imported products. As with any business venture, there are risks. Many companies import goods, only to have these items remain in a warehouse because no one wants them due to differences in buying habits.

STEP 2 CONTACT SUPPLIERS

The second importing activity is to contact foreign suppliers. Finding foreign companies that provide what you want when you want it may be difficult. By using the appropriate information sources, importers can identify the companies that will best serve their needs.

WORK AS A GROUP

Examine labels and other marks on clothing and other items students in the group own. Determine which items have been imported or manufactured in another country.

©Getty Images/PhotoDisc

IMPORTING ACTIVITIES

Identify potential
market demand

Contact potential
suppliers

Finalize the purchase
agreement

Receive goods and
make payment

Figure 6-1 Importers go through several steps to find and purchase products that are in demand.

STEP 3 FINALIZE PURCHASE

The third importing activity is to finalize the *purchase agreement.* The importing company must come to an agreement with the supplier on specific terms for the purchase. Who will pay for shipping? When will items be delivered? How will payment be made? Will payment be made in advance, during shipping, or after the receipt of the goods? These are just some of the details that need to be described in the purchase agreement.

STEP 4 RECEIVE GOODS

The fourth activity is to receive the goods and make payment. This includes checking the order for accuracy and damage, paying for the order, and paying any import duties. This tax can be based on either the value of goods or other factors, such as quantity or weight.

These duties are paid to customs officials. A **customs official** is a government employee authorized to collect the duties levied on imports. The term *customs* also refers to the procedures involved in the collection of duties. You may have heard a person traveling to another country say "I have to go through customs." This means travelers must report to customs officials the value of anything bought in the country they are leaving or anything they plan to sell in the country they are entering.

AN IMPORTING ERROR

Clear and complete communication for foreign suppliers is vital. A U.S. retail company contracted with a foreign shirtmaker to manufacture men's shirts. The contract stated that the shirts must be made of 60 percent cotton and 40 percent polyester. The manufacturer provided shirt labels to that effect. The shirtmaker manufactured shirts that were 35 percent cotton and 65 percent polyester. Without verifying the material content, the U.S. company accepted the shirts and sold them with the incorrect information on the label. The Federal Trade Commission fined the company for deceptive labeling.

Think Critically

How might this situation have been avoided?

IMPORT ASSISTANCE

Several U.S. government agencies are available to assist companies and individuals interested in importing. The Customs Department of the U.S. Treasury (www.customs.gov) provides current information on import regulations.

REGIONAL PERSPECTIVE

HISTORY: THE GREAT WALL OF CHINA

While nations frequently take actions to communicate with others, sometimes a country wants to seclude itself. Imagine a structure about 2,400 kilometers (1,500 miles) long that varies in height between 5.5 and 9.1 meters (18 and 30 feet). Then imagine that it is 4.6 to 9.1 meters (15 to 30 feet) wide at the base and tapers to about 3.7 meters (12 feet) wide at the top. The wall includes watchtowers about 12 meters (40 feet) high that are placed about every 180 meters (about 200 yards). Those are the dimensions of the Great Wall of China.

The Great Wall of China was built of earth and stone. The largest portion was constructed during the rule of Emperor Ch'in Shih Huang Ti, which ended about 204 BC. The Great Wall was designed to protect the Chinese people from nomadic invaders. It runs along the northern and northwestern frontiers of the country.

During the Ming dynasty (1368–1644), the wall was expanded to its current length and received extensive repairs. The Great Wall continues to be one of the most popular tourist attractions in China.

Think Critically
1. What historic factors may have influenced the building of the Great Wall?
2. What effects might the Great Wall have had on economic development?

✔ CheckPoint

What are the four steps involved in importing?

©Getty Images/PhotoDisc

REVIEW GLOBAL BUSINESS TERMS

Define the following term.

1. customs official

REVIEW GLOBAL BUSINESS CONCEPTS

2. What are the main reasons companies import goods?

3. What is the purpose of the customs department of a country's government?

SOLVE GLOBAL BUSINESS PROBLEMS

For each of the following situations, predict whether the imports will be successful in your country. Explain your reasons.

4. Imported in-line skates that are more expensive than those already on the market but that have the reputation of being the best in the world.

5. Ten thousand cases of shampoo in bottles with foreign-language labels that can be sold for a price matching the lowest-price shampoo on the market.

6. An imported soy-flavored dessert called *Zenzip*.

7. Imported automobiles that are small and can be sold for less than any domestic car but that are difficult to repair.

8. An imported packaged dinner entrée that is based on blue pasta.

THINK CRITICALLY

9. What types of imports should not be allowed to enter the United States?

10. Do imports threaten the jobs of people in the importing country?

MAKE CONNECTIONS

11. **STATISTICS** In the Asia-Pacific Rim Country Profile table on page 117, what is the average value of exports for South Korea, Singapore, and Taiwan?

12. **TECHNOLOGY** Find a web site for one of the larger countries in the Asia-Pacific Rim Country Regional Profile. List the country and its five largest imports.

13. **VISUAL ARTS** Prepare a flow chart or other visual representation of the importing process.

14. **CULTURAL STUDIES** Collect examples of unusual food products imported from other countries.

EXPORTING PROCEDURES

6-2

GOALS

- Discuss the steps of the exporting process.
- Describe the exporting of services.

THE EXPORTING PROCESS

Companies commonly export goods or services to companies in other countries. *Indirect exporting* occurs when a company sells its products in a foreign market without actively seeking out those opportunities. More often, however, a business will conduct *direct exporting* by actively seeking export opportunities.

Exporting activities are the other side of the importing transaction. As exporters, however, businesses face different decisions. The process of exporting involves five steps, as shown in Figure 6-2.

THE EXPORTING PROCESS

STEP 1	STEP 2	STEP 3	STEP 4	STEP 5
Find Potential Customers	Meet the Needs of Customers	Agree on Sales Terms	Provide Products or Services	Complete the Transaction

Figure 6-2 Successful exporting can help a nation expand its economic activities and create additional jobs.

E-COMMERCE IN ACTION

E-Tailing and Lower Barriers to Entry

Buying books, music CDs, videos, computer software, clothing, and even groceries without leaving home is nothing new. People have been able to do this for years with mail-order buying and television shopping channels. Today this buying process is even easier.

The Internet has reduced some barriers to entry for new companies. In the past, an entrepreneur had to rent a store, hire employees, obtain inventory, and advertise when starting a business. Now a person can begin operations with a computer. Contacting suppliers, promoting the company, and filling orders are all done online.

This ease of start-up has resulted in lower barriers to entry and increased competition. No longer must a company have a store, an office, or a factory. Instead, a book or clothing seller can serve customers with an online transaction, with the shipping company representative being the only one who has to leave home.

Think Critically

1. What types of enterprises are best suited for doing business online?
2. How will expanded online buying affect job opportunities and economic development in local communities?
3. Locate a web site that offers customers a variety of products online. How does the company attempt to attract customers?

STEP 1 FIND POTENTIAL CUSTOMERS

Before you sell anything, you have to find buyers. Who are the people who want to buy your goods and services? Where are these people located? Are the potential customers willing and able to purchase your products?

Answers to these questions may be found through an Internet search and library research. Businesses use many sources to find out about the buying habits of people in different countries. Also, businesspeople familiar with foreign markets have experience helping companies that want to sell in other countries.

The U.S. Department of Commerce and other agencies and organizations provide *trade leads*—lists for companies planning to do business overseas. You also can find information on potential customers in other countries at web sites such as www.buyUSA.gov, www.fas.usda.gov, and www.fita.org.

STEP 2 MEET THE NEEDS OF CUSTOMERS

Next, determine if people in other countries can use your product or service. Sending company representatives to possible markets around the world is one way to make sure your product can be sold there. If visits are not possible, companies can obtain reliable information from others as well.

Will your product be accepted by foreign customers exactly as it is, or will it be necessary to adapt it? Product adaptation may need to be in the form of smaller packages, different ingredients, or revised label information to meet geographic, social, cultural, and legal requirements.

Some products are *standardized* or sold the same around the world. Popular soft drinks, some clothing, and many technical products (such as cameras, computers, and stereo equipment) are frequently sold in various geographic areas with only minor changes. However, food products, personal care items, and laundry detergent usually need to be *adapted* to the tastes, customs, and culture of a society.

STEP 3 AGREE ON SALES TERMS

Every business transaction involves shipping and payment terms. These terms require businesses to answer a number of important questions. How will the product be shipped? Who will pay for shipping costs, the buyer or the seller? In what currency will the payment be made? What foreign exchange rate will be used? When is the payment due?

Shipping costs vary for different types of transportation. Airfreight is more costly than water transportation. However, it is also much quicker. Items in high demand or that are perishable products might require the quickest available method of delivery.

Transportation costs can be a major portion of the cost of exporting. It is important to consider which party will pay transportation costs. Sometimes the seller pays for shipping. In other situations, the buyer pays. Certain terms are used to describe the shipping and payment methods. **Free on board (FOB)** means the selling price of the product includes the cost of loading the exported goods onto transport vessels at the specified place.

FOB is just one way that buyers and sellers may agree to pay shipping costs. **Cost, insurance, and freight (CIF)** means that the cost of the goods, insurance, and freight are included in the price quoted. **Cost and freight (C&F)** indicates that the price includes the cost of the goods and freight, but the buyer must pay for insurance separately.

©Getty Images/PhotoDisc

Banks and other financial institutions are commonly involved in export transactions. A company may have to borrow funds to finance the cost of manufacturing and shipping a product for which payment will not be received until a later date. Besides loans, international financial institutions may also offer other exporting services.

STEP 4 PROVIDE PRODUCTS OR SERVICES

After agreement is reached on selling terms, the finished goods are shipped. If the exchange involves a service, the company must now perform the required tasks for its foreign customers.

Companies are available to help exporters with shipping. A **freight forwarder** is a company that arranges to ship goods to customers in other countries. Like a travel agent for cargo, these companies take care of the reservations needed to get an exporter's merchandise to the required destination.

GLOBAL BUSINESS EXAMPLE

EXPORTING CULTURE

The demand for U.S. clothing, soft drinks, fast food, candy, movies, music, television programs, and other entertainment is very strong in many parts of the world. Jeans, T-shirts, sports team hats, and athletic shoes are top sellers in many countries. People in some nations will wait in line for hours to pay for Coca-Cola or for a McDonald's hamburger.

Programs such as *The Simpsons, Wheel of Fortune,* and *Friends* are seen by hundreds of millions of television viewers each day. Movies such as *Titanic, Star Wars,* and *Lord of the Rings* earn movie studios millions of dollars in profits outside the United States. The songs of pop stars such as Britney Spears, *NSYNC, and the Backstreet Boys are played on radio stations, in stores, and in homes in over 150 countries.

Other countries are also known for their cultural exports. For example, Sweden, a country of about 9 million people is one of the world's largest exporters of music. Many Swedish musicians are popular through all of Europe, and some have become world famous. In the late 1970s and early 1980s, exports of music were Sweden's single largest export, beating out large Swedish industrial companies like carmakers Volvo and Saab and appliance maker Electrolux.

©Getty Images/PhotoDisc

Think Critically

1. What effect could exporting of U.S. culture have on the cultural environment of other countries?
2. What are the benefits associated with exporting culture?
3. Locate a web site with information about a country's cultural exports. What are the country's largest cultural exports? How does the volume of cultural exports compare with other exported goods and services?

Often a freight forwarder will accumulate several small export shipments and combine them into one large shipment to get lower freight rates. Since these companies are actively involved in international trade, freight forwarders are excellent sources of information about export regulations, shipping costs, and foreign import regulations.

Companies must prepare many export documents for shipping merchandise to other countries. A **bill of lading** is a document stating the agreement between the exporter and the transportation company. This document serves as a receipt for the exported items. A **certificate of origin** is a document that states the name of the country in which the shipped goods were produced. This document may be used to determine the amount of any import tax.

STEP 5 COMPLETE THE TRANSACTION

If payment has not been received, it would be due at this time. Many times, payment involves exchanging one country's currency for another's. Financial institutions convert currency and are usually involved in the payment step.

CheckPoint

What are the five steps of the exporting process?

OTHER EXPORTING ISSUES

In addition to the five steps of exporting, other issues must be considered when exporting. There are a number of hurdles that must be avoided when exporting. Also, there are special considerations when exporting services instead of goods.

AVOIDING EXPORTING HURDLES

The United States Department of Commerce estimates that thousands of small and medium-sized businesses could easily get involved in international business. However, there are several reasons companies may not export.

- No company representatives in foreign countries
- Products not appropriate for foreign consumers
- Insufficient production facilities to manufacture enough goods for exporting
- High costs of doing business in other countries
- Difficulty understanding foreign business procedures

©Getty Images/PhotoDisc

- Difficulty obtaining payment from foreign customers

Many of these barriers could be overcome if companies obtained assistance from agencies such as the U.S. Department of Commerce (www.export.gov), the U.S. Small Business Administration (www.sba.gov/oit), and the U.S. Trade Center (usatc.doc.gov).

EXPORTING SERVICES

Most people can relate to selling, packing, and shipping a tangible item. However, a major portion of U.S. exports involves the sale of *intangible* items—services. Service industries account for about 70 percent of GDP in the United States. International trade by service industries is significant. Services provided by U.S. companies are more than 20 percent of the world's total cross-border sales of services.

Companies export services with some of the same techniques they use to export products. These techniques include international consulting, direct exporting, licensing, franchising, and joint venture.

The most commonly exported services include hospitality (hotels and food service), entertainment (movies, television production, and amusement parks), and financial services (insurance and real estate). Other areas of expanding service exports involve health care, information processing, distribution services, and education and training services.

 ✔ **CheckPoint**

What services are most commonly exported by U.S. companies?

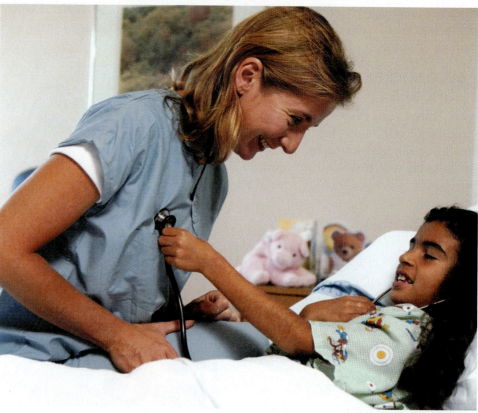

©Getty Images/PhotoDisc

REVIEW GLOBAL BUSINESS TERMS

Define each of the following terms.

1. free on board (FOB)
2. cost, insurance, and freight (CIF)
3. cost and freight (C&F)
4. freight forwarder
5. bill of lading
6. certificate of origin

REVIEW GLOBAL BUSINESS CONCEPTS

7. How can exporting companies determine if their products can be sold in other countries?
8. Why are banks often involved in export transactions?
9. What determines whether an exporter ships by air or water?

SOLVE GLOBAL BUSINESS PROBLEMS

For each of the following exporting situations, decide whether the company should sell the same product (standardize) as in other countries or adapt the product (customize) to local tastes, customs, and culture. Explain your reasons.

10. Exporting World Cup championship shirts and hats.
11. Exporting digital cameras for sale in major cities of Europe and North America.
12. Exporting electrical appliances to a country with a different voltage system.
13. Exporting plain, unflavored yogurt to a country in which the people do not usually eat yogurt.
14. Exporting forklift trucks for use in warehouses in Asia.

THINK CRITICALLY

15. How does the exporting of services differ from exporting goods?
16. Why are governments frequently interested in encouraging exports?

MAKE CONNECTIONS

17. **TECHNOLOGY** Visit the web site of The Bureau of Industry and Security (www.bxa.doc.gov) to obtain current information about the exporting regulations faced by U.S. companies.
18. **SCIENCE** Describe recent scientific developments that have improved the speed and efficiency of exporting.
19. **HISTORY** Research the effect of various inventions on the major exports of a country.
20. **TECHNOLOGY** Use the Internet to reseach local rules and regulations for exporting from various countries around the world.

6-3 | IMPORTANCE OF TRADE RELATIONS

GOALS

- Identify the economic effects of foreign trade.
- Describe the types of trade agreements between countries.

©Getty Images/PhotoDisc

THE ECONOMIC EFFECT OF FOREIGN TRADE

Every importing and exporting transaction has economic effects. The difference between a country's exports and imports is called its *balance of trade*. However, balance of trade does not include all international business transactions, just imports and exports. Another economic measure is needed to summarize the total economic effect of foreign trade.

Balance of payments, illustrated in Figure 6-3, measures the total flow of money coming into a country minus the total flow going out. Included in this economic measurement are exports, imports, investments, tourist spending, and financial assistance. For example, in recent years, tourism has helped the U.S. balance of payments because it has increased the flow of money entering the United States.

A country's balance of payments can either be positive or negative. A *positive*, or *favorable*, balance of payments occurs when a nation receives more money in a year than it pays out. A *negative* balance of payments is *unfavorable*. It is the result when a country sends more money out than it brings in.

Some countries continually buy more foreign goods than they sell. The result is a **trade deficit**, which is the total amount a country owes to other countries as a result of importing more goods and services than the country

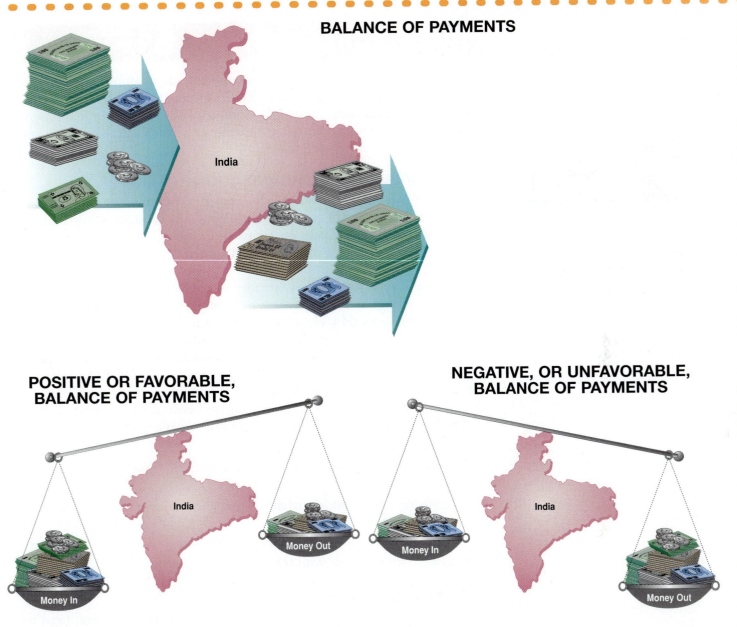

BALANCE OF PAYMENTS

POSITIVE OR FAVORABLE, BALANCE OF PAYMENTS

NEGATIVE, OR UNFAVORABLE, BALANCE OF PAYMENTS

Figure 6-3 Balance of payments is the total flow of money coming into a country minus the total flow of money going out of a country.

is exporting. The United States, despite being the largest exporter in the world, has had a trade deficit for many years. This situation can result in a country borrowing from other countries. Borrowing means the country must pay back money in the future, reducing the amount available for spending.

✓CheckPoint

How does a country create a trade deficit?

TRADE AGREEMENTS

How can a country improve its international trade situation? One answer is by negotiating trade agreements. Trade agreements can occur between countries to promote economic development on a worldwide basis or in a geographic region. Or individual nations and companies may reach agreements that encourage international business activities.

THE WORLD TRADE ORGANIZATION

After World War II, world leaders who wanted to promote peaceful international trade developed a set of ground rules to guide the conduct of international trade. The General Agreement on Tariffs and Trade (GATT) was negotiated in 1947 and began operating in January 1948 when 23 countries signed the treaty agreement.

This multicountry agreement intended to reduce trade barriers and to promote trade. The goals of GATT were to promote world trade through negotiation and to make world trade secure. Working toward these goals helped increase global economic growth and development.

In 1995, GATT was replaced by a new organization—the World Trade Organization (WTO). With over 140 member countries, WTO has many of the same goals as GATT. But in addition, WTO has the power to settle trade disputes and enforce the free-trade agreements between its members.

Based in Geneva, Switzerland, the WTO has several main goals.

- Lowering tariffs that discourage free trade
- Eliminating import quotas, subsidies, and unfair technical standards that reduce competition in the world market
- Recognizing protection for patents, copyrights, trademarks, and other intellectual properties, such as software
- Reducing barriers for banks, insurance companies, and other financial services
- Assisting poor countries with trade policies and economic growth

ECONOMIC COMMUNITIES

An **economic community** is an organization of countries that bond together to allow a free flow of products. The group acts as a single country for business activities with other regions of the world. An economic community is also called a *common market*. An economic community has several main benefits.

- Expanded trade with other regions of the world
- Reduced tariffs for the member countries
- Lower prices for consumers within the group
- Expanded employment and investment opportunities

WORK AS A GROUP

Prepare a list of benefits and concerns associated with economic communities and countertrade.

NET Bookmark

The World Trade Organization (WTO) is the only organization of its kind. It deals with the global rules of trade between nations and helps assure that trade flows smoothly and freely. To learn more about the history and functions of this organization, access intlbizxtra.swlearning.com and click on the link for Chapter 6. After navigating this web site and reading the information, make a list of ten benefits of the WTO trading system.

intlbizxtra.swlearning.com

GLOBAL BUSINESS EXAMPLE

EUROPEAN UNION

The European Union (EU) is an organization of a number of member nations across Europe. The agreement of this association allows over 400 million consumers to purchase products from any of the countries without paying import or export taxes.

The headquarters of the EU are located in Brussels, Belgium. The EU Commission has 20 commissioners who are responsible for areas such as labor, health, the environment, education, transportation, and trade. The policy-setting body is the Council of Ministers, consisting of the prime ministers from the member countries. Voters in each member country elect the European Parliament, 732 representatives and meets in Strasbourg, France.

This economic community works toward several goals.

- Eliminating tariffs and other trade barriers
- Creating a uniform tariff schedule
- Forming a common market for free movement of labor, capital, and business enterprises
- Establishing common agricultural and food safety policies
- Channeling capital from more advanced to less developed regions

In 1999, the EU introduced a common currency—the *euro*. During the transition to full use of this new monetary unit, prices in the stores of EU countries were stated in both euros and the previous national currencies such as the franc, lira, and deutsche mark.

In 2004, 10 other countries joined, bringing the total number of countries to 25: Cyprus, Czech Republic, Estonia, Hungary, Latvia, Lithuania, Malta, Poland, Slovakia, and Slovenia. Still others (Bulgaria, Romania, and Turkey) are being considered for future membership.

Think Critically

1. What are some concerns with a highly integrated economic community such as the European Union?
2. Go to the web site of the European Union to obtain current information about the activities of this economic community. Which countries are currently members of the EU? Which countries are seeking to gain membership to the EU?

Examples of this type of regional economic cooperation between countries include the European Union (EU), Latin American Free Trade Association (LAFTA), the Association of Southeast Asian Nations (ASEAN), the Economic Community of West African States (ECOWAS), and the North American Free Trade Agreement (NAFTA).

BARTER AGREEMENTS

Most people have traded one item for another at some time. The exchange of goods and services between two parties with no money involved is **direct barter**. A company may use this method for international business transactions.

Since trading items of equal value is difficult, a different barter method is used. **Countertrade** is the exchange of products or services between companies in different countries with the possibility of some currency exchange. For example, when PepsiCo owned Pizza Hut, it sold soft drinks in China in exchange for mushrooms used on pizzas. Countertrade can involve companies in several countries, as shown in Figure 6-4 on the next page.

Since countertrades are quite complex, they usually involve large companies. Smaller companies, however, can get involved in countertrade by working with large trading agents who bring together many buyers and sellers.

Companies use countertrade to avoid the risk of receiving payment in a monetary unit with limited value. Currencies from some nations are not in demand due to the weakness of those countries' economies. Countertrade

COUNTERTRADE IN ACTION

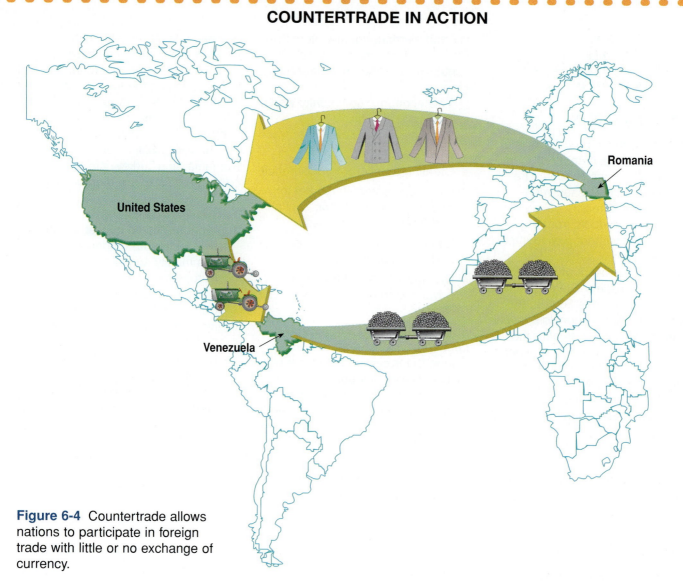

Figure 6-4 Countertrade allows nations to participate in foreign trade with little or no exchange of currency.

also occurs when the government of an importing country requires the selling company to purchase products in return. This helps the importing country to avoid a trade deficit while stimulating economic growth.

▌FREE-TRADE ZONES

A *free-trade zone* is an area designated by a government for duty-free entry of nonprohibited goods. Free-trade zones are commonly located at a point of entry into a nation, such as a harbor or an airport. Merchandise may be stored, displayed, or used without duties being paid. Duties (import taxes) are imposed on the goods only when the items pass from the free-trade zone into an area of the country subject to customs.

What are examples of trade agreements among countries?

REVIEW GLOBAL BUSINESS TERMS

Define each of the following terms.

1. balance of payments
2. trade deficit
3. economic community
4. direct barter
5. countertrade

Xtra!
Study Tools
intlbizxtra.swlearning.com

REVIEW GLOBAL BUSINESS CONCEPTS

6. How can a trade deficit affect a country's economy?

7. Why is countertrade used in international business?

SOLVE GLOBAL BUSINESS PROBLEMS

For the company or country mentioned in each of the following situations, decide whether the balance of payments or the trade balance is affected and whether the effect would be favorable or unfavorable.

8. A country in Europe receives foreign aid from the government of another country.

9. A six-month long World's Fair is held in the United States and attracts over a million tourists from other countries.

10. An Asian country imports oil that it will pay for later.

11. A multinational company in England pays cash for a factory in India.

12. A new advance in genetic testing is made in Argentina, and the technology is exported all over the world.

THINK CRITICALLY

13. What can a government do to improve a trade deficit?

14. What are possible concerns of labor unions, environmental groups, and public interest organizations regarding actions of the World Trade Organization?

MAKE CONNECTIONS

15. **MATH** Using the data in the Asia-Pacific Rim Country Profile, calculate the difference between the exports and imports for three countries. Which countries, if any, have a trade deficit?

16. **HISTORY** Research the start of the European Economic Community in the 1950s. What factors influenced the start of this common market?

17. **COMMUNICATIONS** Without using words, demonstrate a barter transaction between people from different cultures.

6-4 | THE NATURE OF COMPETITION

GOALS

- List factors that affect international business competition.
- Explain the types of competitive market situations.

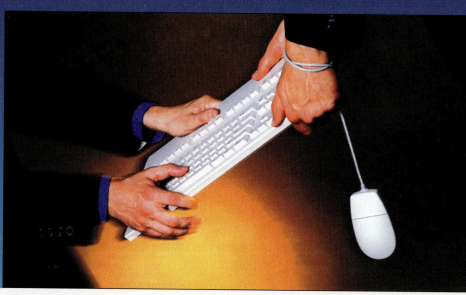

©Getty Images/PhotoDisc

INTERNATIONAL BUSINESS COMPETITION

It is likely that you have participated in a sport or an activity in which you attempted to do better than others or better than you had done previously. While winning may not always be the main goal, competition is an on-going activity for people, companies, and nations. In an effort to improve a country's economic situation, a strong competitive effort may be beneficial.

Companies compete in both domestic and international markets. The *domestic market* is made up of all the companies that sell similar products within the same country. In contrast, the *international market* is made up of companies that compete against companies in several countries. For example, major soft drink companies have competition in other countries with Crazy Cola in Russia and Thums Up Cola in India.

For companies or countries to gain a competitive advantage they need to do something better, faster, or cheaper than others do. While many people believe the best product is always successful, sometimes a company can also succeed through an effective delivery system. For example, Kodak film is available in almost every tourist location in the world. This distribution program creates a *competitive advantage* and makes it difficult for other film manufacturers to gain sales.

Companies can also compete by successfully doing one thing and doing it well. For example, Japanese airplane companies have not been able to make aircraft that are in demand as much as planes made in the United States. Japanese companies, however, have specialized in producing components used by U.S. aircraft manufacturers, such as fuselage parts, landing-gear doors, and on-board computers. Besides using successful planning and engineering methods, the airline parts companies are involved in hundreds of joint ventures and licensing agreements. These efforts increased Japanese aerospace exports by over 100 percent during the 1990s.

FACTORS AFFECTING COMPETITION

Three major factors affect the degree of competition among businesses. These factors are the number of companies, business costs, and product differences.

Number of Companies When many companies are selling the same product, there may appear to be a high degree of competition. However, if just a few large firms control the major portion of sales, then competition is limited.

Business Costs The cost of doing business often affects competition. Expensive equipment or having to compete against well-known brands prevent new companies from starting. These are commonly called *barriers to entry*. If a business needs large amounts of capital and equipment to start operations, only a few companies are likely to enter the market. Or if an existing company has an established brand name, it will be very costly for new companies to make their name known.

Product Differences The third factor that creates competition is product differences. Companies use advertising, brand names, packages, and ingredients to convince consumers that their products are different and better. The addition of flavoring to toothpaste and a pump on an athletic shoe are examples of attempts by companies to gain a competitive advantage. Companies use advertising messages to inform consumers about the benefits of their products and to persuade them to buy.

BENEFITS AND CONCERNS OF COMPETITION

Competition can improve the economic situation and living conditions of a nation. Individual and company efforts to create better goods and services in

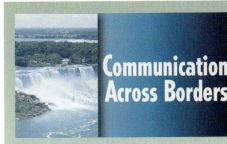

Communication Across Borders

UNDERSTANDING ASIAN NAMES

When communicating with Asians about trading opportunities, it is important to realize that their naming practices may be different from yours. Consider last names, for example. In the People's Republic of China, more than 100 million people, about 10 percent of the population, have the last name of Zhang. Fewer than 20 last names account for more than 60 percent of the population.

In Korea, four last names account for more than 50 percent of the population. Thus, the last names in some Asian countries aren't as distinctive an identifier as they are in the United States. Therefore, it is necessary to learn full names, titles, and divisions within the business in order to be able to communicate with the desired Asian business associates.

In many Asian countries the family name comes first, followed by the given names. Thus, in Korea Kim Yun is Mr. Kim, not Mr. Yun. The same name order is also followed in the Chinese and Japanese cultures.

Think Critically

1. What kind of an impression will you create if you reverse the order of the names of a potential Asian business partner?
2. What question should you ask to find out about the naming customs in another country?

less time have been a benefit for many nations. Some business competition, however, can result in major concerns. If a company becomes so large that it controls a geographic area or a portion of an economy, many people may suffer. Consumers will have to pay whatever the business charges. Workers will have to work for the amount the company wants to pay since other jobs may not be available. For these reasons, most countries have laws that limit the power of companies.

✓ CheckPoint

What are common barriers to entry for new competitors in an industry?

TYPES OF COMPETITIVE SITUATIONS

Have you ever wondered why there are so many breakfast cereals or why only a few stores sell a certain brand of shoes? These questions can be answered with an understanding of the competitive situations in an industry. An **industry** refers to companies in the same type of business. For example, Kellogg, General Mills, Kraft General Foods, and Quaker are the major companies in the breakfast cereal industry. Nike, Reebok, and Adidas are in the athletic shoe industry. The competitive situation among companies is also called the *market structure* of an industry. Four main competitive situations may be present in a country's economy, as shown in Figure 6-5.

Courtesy of Les Dlabay

PURE COMPETITION

Pure competition is a market situation with many sellers, each offering the same product. For example, when farmers sell their wheat or corn, there is little difference from one bushel to another. Supply and demand determines the price. Rivalry among businesses is most free when many companies offer identical or very similar products to buyers. Various factors in our economy and society, however, limit pure competition.

WORK AS A GROUP

Discuss the way you compete with other students in academics, athletics, and social relationships. Then discuss the advantages and disadvantages of such competition.

COMPETITIVE MARKET SITUATIONS

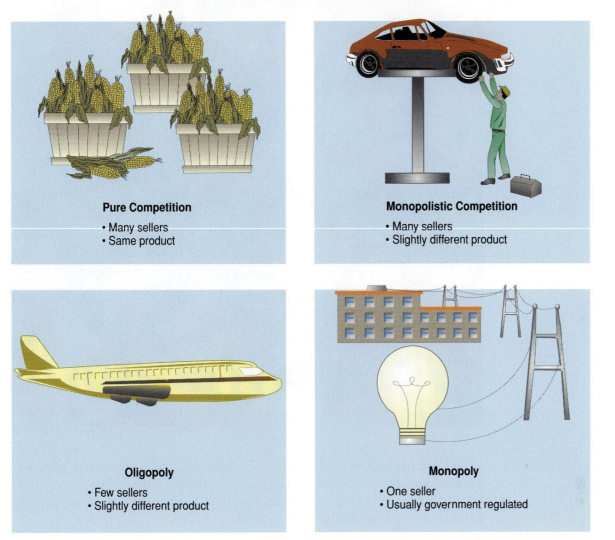

Pure Competition
- Many sellers
- Same product

Monopolistic Competition
- Many sellers
- Slightly different product

Oligopoly
- Few sellers
- Slightly different product

Monopoly
- One seller
- Usually government regulated

Figure 6-5 The number of businesses and differences in products affect the amount of competition in a market.

MONOPOLISTIC COMPETITION

In order for companies to attract customers, they make their products slightly different. One hamburger company offers a special sauce, another adds bacon and cheese, while another gives away a game or toy with the sandwich. **Monopolistic competition** refers to a market situation with many sellers, each with a slightly different product. The difference in products can be actual (such as ingredients) or implied (such as different advertisements, a brand name, or a package design).

OLIGOPOLY

When a few large companies control an industry, an **oligopoly** exists. In this market situation, the few sellers usually offer products that are slightly different. However, competition is mainly the result of large companies being able to advertise and sell their goods in many geographic areas. For example, only

©Getty Images/PhotoDisc

a few large companies make automobile tires. Therefore, these large manufacturers are able to control the market. Another example is that with only a few countries having oil as a natural resource, companies in these nations can influence the availability and price of oil.

MONOPOLY

When one company controls the total supply of a product or service, there is no competition. A **monopoly** is a situation in which one seller controls the entire market for a product or service. It is very unusual for this to happen without actions by government or other businesses. Like pure competition, few examples of true monopolies exist. Situations that are near monopolies include South Africa's diamond mines and a small village or town served by only one store. Monopolies that exist in the United States, such as cable television, local water service, and first-class mail delivery service, are government regulated.

✔ CheckPoint

What are the four types of competitive situations?

REVIEW GLOBAL BUSINESS TERMS

Define each of the following terms.

1. industry
2. pure competition
3. monopolistic competition
4. oligopoly
5. monopoly

REVIEW GLOBAL BUSINESS CONCEPTS

6. What are the main factors that affect the amount of business competition?
7. What are the advantages of competition?
8. What is the difference between actual and implied differences in monopolistic competition?

SOLVE GLOBAL BUSINESS PROBLEMS

For each of the follow situations, decide which competitive situation is present: pure competition, monopolistic competition, oligopoly, or monopoly.

9. A country in Asia allows only one company to manufacture a product.
10. In a European country, four companies control over 85 percent of sales in the supermarket industry.
11. In a region of western Africa, minerals are mined and sold by many extracting companies.
12. In an area of the Middle East, many small shops offer a variety of clothing styles.

THINK CRITICALLY

13. What actions could consumers and government take to promote competition?
14. What kind of competition exists in the microcomputer operating systems market today?

MAKE CONNECTIONS

15. **CULTURAL STUDIES** Select a product that you use frequently. Determine what appeals to you about the product, including how it is advertised. Consider whether the elements you have determined would appeal to people in most other countries. Write a summary of your findings.
16. **LAW** Research the start of antitrust legislation in the United States. What applications of those laws are in the news today?

CHAPTER SUMMARY

6-1 IMPORTING PROCEDURES

A Importing is important to business for meeting consumer demand, lowering operating costs, and obtaining production inputs.

B The four steps of importing are (1) determine demand, (2) contact suppliers, (3) finalize purchases, and (4) receive goods.

6-2 EXPORTING PROCEDURES

A The five steps of the exporting process are (1) find potential customers, (2) meet the needs of customers, (3) agree on sales terms, (4) provide products or services, and (5) complete the transaction.

B The exporting of services can be a significant percentage of a country's export activities.

6-3 IMPORTANCE OF TRADE RELATIONS

A A country's balance of payments measures the total flow of money coming into a country minus the total flow going out and may be positive or negative. A trade deficit is the total amount a country owes to other countries as a result of importing more goods and services than are exported.

B The main types of trade agreements are the World Trade Organization, economic communities, barter agreements, and free-trade zones.

6-4 THE NATURE OF COMPETITION

A The competitive situation in a country is affected by (1) the number of companies, (2) business costs, and (3) product differences.

B The four main types of competitive markets are pure competition, monopolistic competition, oligopoly, and monopoly.

GLOBAL REFOCUS

Read the Global Focus at the beginning of this chapter, and answer the following questions.

1. What actions might an ice cream company take to expand export activities?

2. How could foreign companies become more competitive in the global ice cream industry?

REVIEW GLOBAL BUSINESS TERMS

Match the terms listed with the definitions. Some terms may not be used.

1. Government employee who is authorized to collect the duties levied on imports.

2. A company that arranges to ship goods to customers in other countries.

3. The exchange of products or services between companies in different countries with the possibility of some currency exchange.

4. Control of an industry by a few large companies.

5. A document that states the agreement between the exporter and the transportation company.

6. The total flow of money coming into a country minus the total flow going out.

7. A market situation with many sellers, each with a slightly different product.

8. An organization of countries that bond together to allow a free flow of products.

9. Terms of sale that mean the selling price of the product includes the cost of loading the exported goods onto transport vessels at the specified place.

10. A situation in which one seller controls the entire market for a product or service.

11. The exchange of goods and services between two parties with no money involved.

12. A group of companies in the same type of business.

13. A document that states the name of the country in which the shipped goods were produced.

14. A market situation with many sellers, each offering the same product.

15. The total amount a country owes to other countries as a result of importing more goods and services than the country is exporting.

a. balance of payments

b. bill of lading

c. certificate of origin

d. cost and freight (C&F)

e. cost, insurance, and freight (CIF)

f. countertrade

g. customs official

h. direct barter

i. economic community

j. free on board (FOB)

k. freight forwarder

l. industry

m. monopolistic competition

n. monopoly

o. oligopoly

p. pure competition

q. trade deficit

MAKE GLOBAL BUSINESS DECISIONS

16. Name some examples of imported products that the people in the United States need and want.

17. Why are taxes imposed on products imported into various countries?

18. List some resources you could use to determine the buying habits in different countries.

19. What factors would affect whether the buyer or the seller pays for the shipping costs in an international business transaction?

20. Why might a country's balance of payments be a better measurement of its international business activities than its balance of trade?

21. What problems might arise when nations create an economic community for international trade?

22. Describe some examples of countertrade involving products from different countries with which you are familiar.

GLOBAL CONNECTIONS

23. **TECHNOLOGY** Go to the web site of the World Trade Organization (www.wto.org) to obtain additional information about the current activities of this global trade association.

24. **LAW** Investigate the duties and customs procedures of one of the following countries: Malaysia, Australia, Taiwan, China, India, South Korea, Singapore, or New Zealand.

25. **GEOGRAPHY** Find the location of the free-trade zone closest to your city. Draw a map that includes your state, the location of the free-trade zone, and all states in between. Then draw a line between your city and the free-trade zone. Mark the distance above the line. If the free-trade zone is in your city, draw a map of your city, and identify the location of the free-trade zone.

26. **COMMUNICATIONS** Talk to someone who has shipped goods to another country. Prepare a short oral report about the procedures for transporting merchandise to a foreign country.

27. **CULTURAL STUDIES** Collect advertisements, packages, and other information about products made in another country and sold in the United States. Ask five friends or relatives to identify the country of origin for the product.

28. **SCIENCE** Many products in our society compete on the basis of very minor differences. Collect information on five different brands of soap, toothpaste, breakfast cereal, or shampoo from advertisements, packages, and periodicals. Based on your analysis and comments from others, list the similarities and differences of the brands selected. *Consumer Reports* is a good source of information for this activity.

29. **CAREER PLANNING** Obtain information about the imports and exports of a country of your choice. What types of job opportunities would be created by these foreign business activities?

30. **TECHNOLOGY** Use the Internet to find examples of businesses that are involved in pure competition, monopolistic competition, oligopolies, and monopolies.

31. **ECONOMICS** Go to the web site of an economic community. Make a list of the members of that community and some of the activities in which it engages.

THE GLOBAL ENTREPRENEUR
CREATING AN INTERNATIONAL BUSINESS PLAN

DEVELOPING AN EXPORTING PLAN

Use a product or service that your chosen company is actively exporting or that you believe has potential for sales in other countries. Then select a country that would provide a market opportunity for that product or service. Use information collected for Chapters 1–5 and additional research to prepare an exporting plan. Include the following components.

1. Product description
   - Describe the product or service in detail, including specific features.
   - Describe any changes in the product or service that may be necessary before exporting.
2. Foreign business environment
   - List cultural and social factors that may affect the sale of the product.
   - Discuss the geography of the country to which you have chosen to export this product or service.
   - Describe economic conditions that may affect exporting this product.
   - Report any political or legal factors that could affect exporting activities.
3. Market potential
   - Describe the type of customer who is best suited for this product or service in the country you have chosen.
   - Identify methods that could be used to contact potential buyers in the country you have chosen.
   - Estimate sales for the product or service based on country size, market demand, and competition.
4. Export transaction details
   - Describe import taxes or other restrictions that may affect exporting costs.
   - Discuss the shipping and documentation requirements for the country you have selected.
   - Identify the amount of time the exporting plan will take to execute.

Sources of information for researching your exporting plan are listed below.
   - reference books such as encyclopedias, almanacs, and atlases
   - current news, business, and travel articles, including news stories, company profiles, and advertisements
   - web sites for exporting information (www.trade.gov, www.fas.usda.gov, www.sba.gov, and www.export.gov)
   - materials from companies, airlines, travel bureaus, government agencies, and other organizations involved in international business
   - interviews with people who have been to the country

Prepare a written summary or a short oral report (two or three minutes) of the key information in your exporting plan.

©Getty Images/PhotoDisc

Chapter 7

FOREIGN EXCHANGE AND INTERNATIONAL FINANCE

GLOBAL FOCUS

An Unexpected Currency for Ukraine

In the early 1990s, the formerly united Soviet Union divided into separate countries. When this occurred, the Russian ruble was no longer the monetary unit for these newly independent nations.

Ukraine was one of these nations. While the people of Ukraine were waiting to convert to a new currency, the need for money to be in circulation was critical. To prevent a financial crisis, the Ukrainian government issued coupons for use in buying the country's limited supplies of food and other products.

These coupons were not originally intended to be the new Ukrainian currency. However, as Ukraine's economy developed, these coupons became widely accepted as money. At first, Ukrainians were using both the coupons and the Russian ruble. As the new monetary system replaced the old one, rubles became less acceptable for making purchases. The acceptance of the ration coupons made them the unofficial currency of Ukraine.

Today Ukraine's currency is the *hryvnia*. In recent years, in an effort to expand the country's economic development, the World Bank has provided Ukraine with several major loans. Two of these were designed to improve agricultural productivity and to expand food product exports. Ukraine's rich soil is well suited to growing grains, sugar beets, vegetables, and other farm products.

Think Critically

1. What problems can occur in an economy that does not have enough money in circulation?
2. What made the ration coupons valuable in the Ukrainian economy?
3. What made the Russian ruble less acceptable among Ukrainians?

7-1 | MONEY SYSTEMS AROUND THE WORLD

GOALS

- Explain the role of money and currency systems in international business.
- Identify factors that affect the value of currency.

©Getty Images/PhotoDisc

MONEY AND CURRENCY SYSTEMS

Each day billions of people buy goods and services using something called *money*. Have you ever thought about what makes money valuable? The metal and paper that make up coins and currency have very little actual value. So why can you use these items to buy goods and services?

Most people take money for granted. If they have money and can buy what they need, they usually don't care how it works. However, an understanding of how money works can help you better understand international business transactions.

WHAT IS MONEY?

Money is anything people will accept for the exchange of goods and services. Throughout history, many different things have served as money, including corn, cattle, tobacco, shells, and salt. There are almost 200 slang terms for money in English. Many are related to food, such as bread, cabbage, clams, and dough. Colors are also commonly associated with money in slang terms—gold, green, greenbacks, greenies, and lean green. Other money descriptors include do-re-mi, folding stuff, scratch, mint sauce, and palm soap (especially when referring to a bribe). No matter what it's called, money has five main characteristics, as shown in Figure 7-1.

CHARACTERISTICS OF MONEY

Acceptable

Scarce

Durable   **Divisible**   **Portable**

Figure 7-1 For something to be used as money, it must have certain characteristics.

Acceptability The most important characteristic of money is that it is *acceptable*. In other words, people must be willing to take an item in exchange for what they are selling.

Scarcity For something to be used as money, it also must be *scarce*. If the item being used as money is very plentiful, it will not maintain its value. As items used for money become common, they lose their buying power.

Durability A problem with some items used as money in the past, such as farm products, was that they spoiled or got damaged easily. Items used as money should be *durable*. Gold and silver, commonly used as money because of durability, were first made into coins in the seventh century B.C. in Greece.

Divisibility For money to be useful, it should also be *divisible*. What would happen if someone wanted to buy an item using a cow as payment? The item to be purchased would have to be of equal value to the cow since livestock is not easy to divide into smaller monetary units. Most nations have

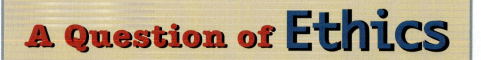

A Question of Ethics

PRINTING ADDITIONAL CURRENCY

In times of economic difficulties, a country might try to solve its problems by printing more money. As unemployment increases, the government would issue additional currency so people could buy needed goods and services. However, fewer items are being produced. Therefore, the increased demand would cause prices to rise, while the value of the currency declines. This higher inflation usually results in greater suffering among the people. In addition, the lower value of the currency hurts the country in the international trade marketplace.

Think Critically

According to the guidelines for ethical analysis in Chapter 1, how will the printing of additional money affect various groups in an economy?

different units of money. In the United States, for example, we have the five dollar bill, the ten dollar bill, quarters, dimes, nickels, and pennies. In Mexico, the peso is divided into 100 centavos. In India, the rupee is divided into 100 paise. And in Thailand, the baht is divided into 100 satang.

Portability Some objects used as money in the past could not be moved easily from one place to another. As people became more mobile, they demanded a money form that was *portable*. The earliest known paper currency was issued by banks in China in the eleventh century.

WHY IS MONEY USED?

Money serves three main purposes. It acts as a medium of exchange, a measure of value, and a store of value. Before the widespread acceptance of money, people would make exchanges through barter. *Barter* is the direct exchange of goods and services for other goods and services. However, you may not want what someone else is offering. Money allows you to put a value on something you have to sell and to use the money received to buy something else.

Medium of Exchange Money is useful only if people are willing to accept it in exchange for goods and services. As a medium of exchange, money makes business transactions easier. At a store, you know you can use coins, currency, or checks rather than having to trade a good or service.

©Getty Images/PhotoDisc

Measure of Value If you work for four hours, is your time worth a steak dinner or one pair of jeans? Without money, it would be difficult to put a value on such things as food and clothing. As a measure of value, money allows us to put a value on various goods and services. Money makes it possible to compare prices for different items so you can make the wisest spending decisions.

Store of Value You may not want to spend all of your money at the same time. As a store of value, money can be saved for future spending. However, the amount you can buy with your money in the future may be reduced because prices increase.

✓ CheckPoint

What are the three main purposes of money?

FOREIGN EXCHANGE

Would you be willing to pay 40 pesos for a hamburger? Or is 4,200,000 yen a good price for an automobile? Business transactions between companies in different countries create money problems. Japanese companies want to receive payment in yen, while Mexican businesses expect to pay in pesos.

Since countries have different currency systems, a method of determining the value of one nation's money in terms of another's is needed. As companies in different countries exchange goods and services, payment must be made. A company usually wants its payment in the currency of its home country. As a result, the money of one country must be changed into the currency of another country. **Foreign exchange** is the process of converting the currency of one country into the currency of another country.

The **exchange rate** is the amount of currency of one country that can be traded for one unit of the currency of another country. Each day these values change slightly depending on changing conditions and perceptions. Figure 7-2 shows the value of various currencies in relation to the U.S. dollar in early 2004. For example, one peso was worth 8.8 cents in U.S. money, and you could exchange 11.40 pesos for one U.S. dollar.

The value of a currency, like most things, is affected by supply and demand. If a country's money is believed to be a solid store of value, people will accept it as payment and its value will increase. However, if a country is having financial difficulties, its currency is likely to lose value compared to the money of other countries.

©Getty Images/PhotoDisc

EXCHANGE RATES FOR SELECTED CURRENCIES

Currency	Country	Symbol	Code	Value in U.S. Dollars	Units per U.S. Dollar
pound	Britain	£	GBP	$1.84	0.54 pound
dollar	Canada	$	CAD	0.76	1.31 Canadian dollars
euro	European Union	€	EUR	1.23	0.81 euro
rupee	India	Rs	INR	0.0216	46.34 rupees
yen	Japan	¥	JPY	0.00902	110.79 yen
peso	Mexico	Mex$	MXN	0.088	11.40 pesos
riyal	Saudi Arabia	SRls	SAR	0.267	3.75 riyals
rand	South Africa	R	ZAR	0.162	6.16 rand
real	Brazil	R$	BRL	0.33	3.022 real
bolívar	Venezuela	Bs	VEB	0.00052	1,919.0 bolívars
yuan	China	Y	CNY	0.12	8.28 yuan

Figure 7-2 Currencies from various nations have different values compared to the U.S. dollar.

CHANGING VALUE OF CURRENCY

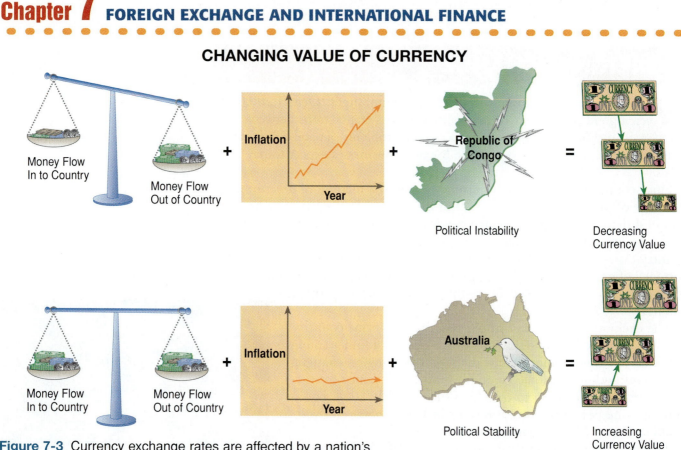

Figure 7-3 Currency exchange rates are affected by a nation's balance of payments, economic conditions, and political stability.

Currency exchange rates between countries are affected by three main factors. These factors are the country's balance of payments, its economic conditions, and its political stability, as shown in Figure 7-3.

BALANCE OF PAYMENTS

The *balance of payments* is a measure of the total flow of money coming into a country minus the total flow going out. When a country has a favorable balance of payments, the value of its currency is usually constant or rising. This situation arises when there is an increased demand for both the nation's products and for its currency.

However, when a nation has an unfavorable balance of payments, its currency usually declines in value. This decline results from lower demand for the monetary unit since fewer companies need to obtain the currency to make payments for goods and services purchased.

ECONOMIC CONDITIONS

Every nation faces the economic conditions of potential inflation and changing interest rates. When prices increase and the buying power of the country's money declines, its currency will not be as attractive. Inflation reduces the buying power of a currency. High inflation in Brazil, for example, would reduce the demand for the *real*.

The cost of borrowing money also affects the value of a currency. When individuals, businesses, and countries borrow money, they incur a cost. The **interest rate** is the cost of using someone else's money. Higher interest rates mean more expensive products and lower demand among consumers. This

©Getty Images/PhotoDisc

WORK AS A GROUP

Suggest actions that could be taken to lower interest rates in a country.

in turn reduces the demand for a nation's currency, causing a decline in its value.

Interest rates are affected by three main factors.

- **Money supply and demand** When more people want to borrow than to save money, interest rates increase. In contrast, if money is available but few are borrowing, interest rates decline.

- **Risk** The higher the risk associated with a loan, the higher the interest rate charged. The higher rates cover the business costs incurred when lenders try to collect on loans and when loans are not repaid.

- **Inflation** As prices rise, the buying power of money declines, so lenders charge higher interest rates on loans. Lenders need to collect more money for a loan when inflation is present so they can cover the lost buying power of the currency they receive in later payments from the borrowers.

To address concerns of an unstable currency and poor economic conditions, some countries use the currency of a more stable economy. For example, the U.S. dollar is the official currency of Ecuador, El Salvador, and Panama.

POLITICAL STABILITY

Companies and individuals want to avoid risk when doing business in different nations. If a government changes unexpectedly to create an unfriendly business environment, a company may lose its building, equipment, or money on deposit in banks. Political instability may also occur when new laws and regulations are enacted. These rules may not allow foreign businesses to operate as freely.

Uncertainty in a country reduces the confidence businesspeople have in its currency. In 1979, for example, when a revolution changed the government in Iran, many foreign companies were closed, and several U.S. officials were taken hostage.

CheckPoint

What three factors influence the value of a country's currency?

REVIEW GLOBAL BUSINESS TERMS

Define each of the following terms.

1. money
2. foreign exchange
3. exchange rate
4. interest rate

REVIEW GLOBAL BUSINESS CONCEPTS

5. What are the five characteristics of money?
6. How does a country's balance of payments affect the value of its currency?
7. How does risk affect interest rates?
8. How does political instability affect the value of a country's currency?

SOLVE GLOBAL BUSINESS PROBLEMS

Which of the characteristics of money would make each of the following items not practical to use as money, even if some people found them acceptable?

9. Shells
10. Works of art
11. Produce (fruit, vegetables, herbs, etc.)
12. Diamonds

THINK CRITICALLY

13. If a country had to create a money system other than coins and currency, what items might be used?
14. How would printing additional money affect the value of a country's currency?

MAKE CONNECTIONS

15. **TECHNOLOGY** What are the potential advantages and disadvantages with an electronic money system that uses plastic cards similar to credit cards?
16. **LAW** What problems would be created in a country if every business were allowed to create its own money system?
17. **CULTURAL STUDIES** Describe the types of events commonly portrayed on a country's coins and currency.
18. **ECONOMICS** Based on the data in the Country Profile, describe what influences the value of a country's currency.
19. **ECONOMICS** Use the Internet to find the current exchange rates for all the currencies in Figure 7-2 on page 177.

FOREIGN EXCHANGE AND CURRENCY CONTROLS

7-2

©Getty Images/PhotoDisc

GOALS

- Discuss foreign exchange activities.
- Describe the main activities of the World Bank and the International Monetary Fund.

FOREIGN EXCHANGE ACTIVITIES

The value of a country's currency is important for success in international business. If trading partners do not accept a country's currency, the country may have to make payment in another currency. A currency that is not easy to exchange for other currencies is called **soft currency**. While the currency is a medium of exchange in its home country, the monetary units have limited value in the world marketplace.

In contrast to soft currencies, money such as the Japanese yen, the euro, the Swiss franc, and the U.S. dollar are accepted for most global transactions. Companies in most nations of the world accept these monetary units. **Hard currency** is a monetary unit that is freely converted into other currencies.

CHANGING EXCHANGE RATES

In years past, the value of a country's currency was set in most countries by its government. More recently, most countries use a system of floating exchange rates. **Floating exchange rate** is a system in which currency values are based on supply and demand. When a country exports large amounts of goods and services, companies in that nation want payment in their own currency. To make these payments, buyers must purchase this monetary unit. As the demand for the currency increases, the value of that monetary unit also increases.

For most of the 1980s, Japan had a very favorable balance of payments as a result of high foreign demand for its automobiles, electronic products, and other goods. Since Japanese companies wanted payment in yen, importers in other countries had to buy yen in order to make their payments. This demand for Japanese currency resulted in its increased value. In recent years, the yen has varied in value compared to the U.S. dollar as a result of changing economic conditions in Japan, as shown in Figure 7-4.

JAPANESE YEN PER U.S. DOLLAR

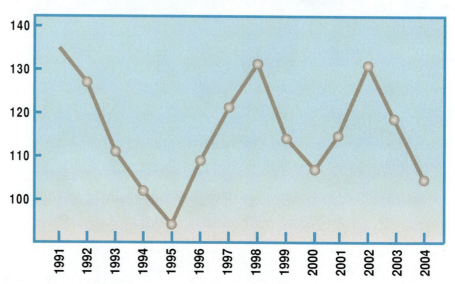

Figure 7-4 The value of the U.S. dollar compared to the Japanese yen has changed repeatedly in recent years.

GLOBAL BUSINESS EXAMPLE

FOREIGN EXCHANGE AND TOURISM

Travelers visiting other countries usually have a choice of making payments with cash, traveler's checks, or credit cards. You would think the payment method would not affect the cost of a purchase. However, due to changing exchange rates and other factors, one payment method can be more costly than another. The foreign exchange on credit card purchases is not calculated until the charges reach the credit card office. If a foreign currency is declining in value, you would be charged less than if you had paid cash.

As the value of the dollar in- creases in relation to other currencies, the cost of traveling to other countries decreases. For example, at one point in time, a hotel room in London that cost £100 required about $200. Two weeks later the hotel room still cost £100. However, the exchange rate had changed, and it cost $179.

Increased availability of cash machines makes it easier to obtain cash when traveling. But transaction fees and the exchange rate at ATMs in another country may be much higher than expected.

Think Critically

1. Conduct an Internet search to locate information about travel costs in other countries.
2. What factors influence the cost of different payment methods used when traveling to other countries?

THE FOREIGN EXCHANGE MARKET

The process of exchanging one currency for another occurs in the foreign exchange market. The **foreign exchange market** is the network of banks and other financial institutions that buy and sell different currencies. Most large banks are part of the foreign exchange market and may provide currency services for businesses and consumers. Before citizens travel outside of the United States, they can exchange dollars for the currencies of the countries they will visit. This exchange can be done at some large banks or companies that specialize in foreign currency services.

If a company knows it will need a certain currency in the future, it can enter into an agreement to buy that monetary unit later at a price agreed upon today. A **currency future** is a contract a person or company buys that allows the buyer the option to purchase a foreign currency sometime in the future at today's rate. For example, suppose an Australian company needs 20 million yen in two months to pay for imports from a Japanese company.

By buying a currency future contract, the importer will get the yen in two months at today's exchange rate. This protects the Australian importer from the possibility of having to buy the currency later at a higher price. However, if yen are less expensive in two months, the importer does not have to

GLOBAL BUSINESS EXAMPLE

CALCULATING FOREIGN EXCHANGE

Calculating foreign exchange can be a confusing process. However, there are some steps you can take to make the process less confusing.

First, foreign exchange rates are usually quoted as a certain amount of one currency per unit of another currency. For example, a recent exchange rate was listed as 1.27 U.S. dollars per euro. An exchange rate is considered a price for foreign currency. In the example, the price of one euro is $1.27.

To buy five notepads that are $1.27 per notepad, multiply the price by 5. The notepads would cost $6.35.

$5 \times 1.27 = 6.35$

So to buy 5 euros at 1.27 dollars per euro, it would cost $6.35.

Foreign exchange rates can work the other way as well. You can use an exchange rate to figure out how much of a foreign currency you can buy. For example, a recent exchange rate was listed as 1.88 U.S. dollars per British pound. For $1.88 you can buy £1. But how many pounds can you get for $1?

If gasoline is $1.88 per gallon and you have $10, to find out how many gallons you can buy, divide the amount you have by the price per gallon. You can buy 5.32 gallons of gasoline. ($10 \div 1.88 = 5.32$ to the nearest hundredth.)

So if you want to buy $10 worth of British pounds at 1.88 dollars per pound, you could buy £5.32.

Think Critically

1. How much would seven Brazilian reals cost you if the exchange rate is 0.34 U.S. dollars per real?
2. How many Saudi Arabian riyals could you buy with $25 if the exchange rate is 3.75 U.S. dollars per riyal?
3. Go to a web site that lists current exchange rates. Recalculate questions 1 and 2 with the current rates.

exercise the option to buy the yen at the contract price. Instead, the currency may be purchased at the going market price. The importer will allow the option in the contract to expire, without needing to take advantage of it. However, the buyer must still pay the fee to purchase the future contract.

FOREIGN EXCHANGE CONTROLS

To maintain the value of its currency, a nation may limit the flow of money out of the country. **Exchange controls** are government restrictions to regulate the amount and value of a nation's currency. These controls can be either a fixed exchange rate or a limit on the amount and cost of currency. One common exchange control limits the amount of local currency a person can take out of a country. In past years, Australia, Bangladesh, France, Italy, Japan, Portugal, South Africa, Spain, and Sweden placed restrictions on exporting local currency.

✓ CheckPoint

What is the purpose of the foreign exchange market?

INTERNATIONAL FINANCIAL AGENCIES

Exchange controls can help maintain the value of a nation's money by limiting the amount in the foreign exchange market. Two international agencies, the International Bank for Reconstruction and Development and the International Monetary Fund, work to maintain a stable system of foreign exchange.

THE WORLD BANK

The International Bank for Reconstruction and Development, commonly called the World Bank, was created in 1944 to provide loans for rebuilding after World War II. Today the **World Bank** is a bank whose major function is to provide economic assistance to less developed countries. Its funds build communications systems, transportation networks, and energy plants.

The World Bank, with over 180 member countries, has two main divisions. The International Development Association (IDA) makes funds available to help developing countries. These loans can be paid back over many years (up to 50) and have very low interest rates. The International Finance Corporation (IFC) provides capital and technical assistance to businesses in nations with limited resources. The IFC encourages joint ventures between foreign and local companies to encourage capital investment within the developing nation.

THE INTERNATIONAL MONETARY FUND (IMF)

The **International Monetary Fund (IMF)** is an agency that helps to promote economic cooperation by maintaining an orderly system of world trade and exchange rates. The

NETBookmark

The value of the dollar changes daily against other international currencies. To see today's exchange rate, access intlbizxtra.swlearning.com and click on the link for Chapter 7. Using the Universal Currency Converter, compare the value of the dollar to at least ten other currencies and make a graphic organizer to record your results. Against which currencies did you discover the dollar to be strongest and weakest?

intlbizxtra.swlearning.com

IMF was established in 1946, when the economic interdependence among nations was escalating at a greater pace than ever before in history.

Before the International Monetary Fund, a country could frequently change the value of its currency to attract more foreign customers. Then as other countries lost business, they would impose trade restrictions or lower the value of their currency. As one nation tried to outdo another, a trade war could have resulted. Today cooperation among IMF nations makes trade wars less likely.

The IMF, also with over 180 member nations, is a cooperative deposit bank that provides assistance to countries experiencing balance of payment difficulties. When a nation's debt continues to increase, its currency declines in value, resulting in more debt. High debt payments mean less money is available for the country to improve its economic development. To prevent this situation, the International Monetary Fund has three main duties.

- **Analyze economic situations** In an attempt to help countries avoid economic problems, the IMF will monitor a country's trade, borrowing, and government spending.

- **Suggest economic policies** After analyzing the economic factors of a nation, the IMF will suggest actions to improve the situation. If a country imposes restrictions that limit foreign trade, for example, the IMF may recommend changes to encourage global business.

- **Provide loans** When a country has a high foreign debt, the IMF lends money to help avoid major economic difficulties. These low-interest loans can keep a country from experiencing an escalating trade deficit and a declining currency value.

GLOBAL BUSINESS EXAMPLE

THE ECONOMIC AND TRADE PROBLEMS OF GHANA

Before taking a new course of action, Ghana, located on the west coast of Africa, had many economic problems. Inflation was 120 percent, exports had declined by 50 percent, and the nation had a crumbling infrastructure. An overvalued currency did not encourage extensive exporting of cocoa, Ghana's main export. Between 1983 and 1990, the *cedi* decreased in value from 2.75 per U.S. dollar to 350 per U.S. dollar.

Ghana obtained suggestions from the International Monetary Fund. To improve the trade situation, quotas, tariffs, and other import controls were used to limit products coming into the country. These actions, along with lower tax rates, helped to improve Ghana's balance of payments and stimulate economic growth for its economy.

Think Critically

1. Go to the web site of the International Monetary Fund (www.imf.org) to obtain current information about Ghana.
2. How did the suggestions from the IMF improve Ghana's economy?

✓ CheckPoint

How does the International Monetary Fund encourage economic development?

REVIEW GLOBAL BUSINESS TERMS

Define each of the following terms.

1. soft currency
2. hard currency
3. floating exchange rate
4. foreign exchange market
5. currency future
6. exchange controls
7. World Bank
8. International Monetary Fund (IMF)

REVIEW GLOBAL BUSINESS CONCEPTS

9. What purpose do exchange controls serve?
10. What is the World Bank?
11. What are the main activities of the International Monetary Fund?

SOLVE GLOBAL BUSINESS PROBLEMS

Calculate the following.

12. A hamburger at a restaurant in Tokyo costs 400 yen. If the exchange rate is 0.008 U.S. dollars per yen, how much would the hamburger cost in U.S. dollars?

13. A Thai company is buying a computer from a company in the United Kingdom. The computer costs 1,700 British pounds. If the exchange rate is 0.025 pounds per Thai baht, how much does the computer cost in baht?

14. A Philippine company has 83,000 pesos to purchase grain from a Canadian farmer. If the exchange rate is 40 pesos per Canadian dollar, how many dollars' worth of grain can the Philippine company purchase?

THINK CRITICALLY

15. How might currency exchange controls affect the trade situation of a country?

16. Suggest ways in which the World Bank and the International Monetary Fund might reduce economic difficulties in developing nations.

MAKE CONNECTIONS

17. **TECHNOLOGY** Go to the web site of the International Monetary Fund (www.imf.org), and determine the source of funds for money loaned to member countries.

18. **MATHEMATICS** Select a country other than the United States. Using newspapers that report exchange rates, find the exchange rate for the country's currency on the first day of the month for the last six months. Prepare a line graph of the rate.

CURRENCY TRANSACTIONS BETWEEN NATIONS

7-3

GOALS

- Discuss payment methods and financing sources for international business transactions.
- Explain other payment methods and financial documents used in international trade.

©Getty Images/PhotoDisc

INTERNATIONAL FINANCIAL TRANSACTIONS

When you go to a store to buy something, you must decide how to pay for the item. You can use cash. Other times, however, you might want to write a check or use a credit card. In a similar manner, global buyers must decide how to pay for an import purchase.

FOREIGN TRADE PAYMENT METHODS

Three types of payment methods are commonly used for international business transactions—cash in advance, letter of credit, and sale on account.

Cash in Advance Making payment before receiving goods can be risky for the buyer. After paying in advance, you might not receive the items, or you might have difficulty obtaining a refund for damaged or returned goods. Cash in advance is not often used. This method, however, is usually required for first-time customers, small orders, or customers in high-risk countries. Since the payment was made before shipping, goods will usually be sent without delay.

Letter of Credit A **letter of credit** is a financial document issued by a bank for an importer in which the bank guarantees payment. A letter of credit is a method of payment in which the importer pays for goods before they are received but after the goods are shipped. This agreement, issued by

WORK AS A GROUP

Create a list of reasons a company might present when attempting to borrow money to expand its global business operations.

the importer's bank, promises to pay the exporter a set amount when certain documents are presented.

The letter of credit communicates to the exporter that it will receive payment once the goods are shipped. Before the payment is made, certain documents—usually including a *bill of lading*—must be presented as proof that the goods have been shipped.

Sale on Account Almost every business buys or sells on credit at one time or another. A very common practice in the United States is to sell *on account*. This means regular customers have a certain time period to make payment, usually 30 or 60 days. **Credit terms** describe the time required for payment and other conditions of a sale on account.

When selling on account, a company wants to obtain its money as soon as possible. To encourage fast payment, a discount may be offered. In the United States, companies can sell on account with the following credit terms: 2/10, n/30. This means that customers can either take a 2 percent discount if they pay within 10 days or pay the net (full) amount in 30 days.

©Getty Images/PhotoDisc

Another example of the credit terms for a sale on account would be 1/15, n/EOM. This means a 1 percent discount may be taken if paid in 15 days. The net amount is due by the end of the month (EOM).

SOURCES OF INTERNATIONAL FINANCING

Buying and selling on credit means that one party (an individual or a company) uses the money of another party (an individual, a company, or a financial institution). This is commonly called *financing*. Financing can be either short-term (one year or less) or long-term (more than one year).

Short-Term Financing The major portion of transacting business involves credit. A company may allow customers 30 days to make their payments. The same company probably buys store supplies, raw materials, and other items from suppliers on credit. Buying or selling on account is called **trade credit**. Trade credit comes in two forms, accounts receivable and accounts payable.

An **account receivable** is an amount due from a customer to a company that sells on credit. Accounts receivable are the result of sales on account. A company that sells on credit allows its customers a certain time period to pay for purchases. An **account payable** is an amount owed to a supplier. Accounts payable are the result of purchases on account.

Accounts receivable and accounts payable may seem confusing. A helpful way to distinguish between them is that receivables are amounts to be received and payables are amounts to be paid.

Business loans, also called commercial loans, are another source of short-term financing. Business loans are commonly obtained from banks and other financial institutions.

Long-term financing Some business activities require financing for more than one year. Companies commonly need large sums of money for expensive business projects that will occur over several years. For example, a Japanese company may need funds to build an electronic manufacturing plant in the United States. Or a German company may buy a food company in Mexico. An expensive, long-term financial activity is a **capital project**. Examples of capital projects include the following.

- Introducing new products
- Buying an existing company
- Building a factory
- Buying new equipment
- Opening a new office in another country

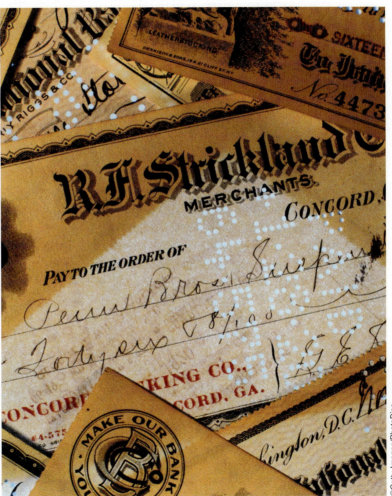
©Getty Images/PhotoDisc

Capital projects often require millions of dollars. To pay for capital projects, companies can do one of two things, borrow the necessary funds from a bank or another financial institution or issue bonds. A **bond** is a certificate representing money borrowed by a company over a long period of time, usually between 5 and 30 years. This document represents the company's promise to repay the money by a certain date with interest. Bonds are a type of financing commonly used by large companies.

✔ **CheckPoint**

Describe three common payment methods for international business transactions.

OTHER PAYMENT METHODS AND FINANCIAL DOCUMENTS

With hundreds of nations and millions of companies in the world, there are many ways of doing business. Besides the import-export documents and payment methods already mentioned, several other methods of payment are commonly used for global business.

Promissory Note A **promissory note** is a document that states a promise to pay a set amount by a certain date. Promissory notes are signed by buyers to confirm their intention to make payment. These documents communicate to both the buyer and the seller the amount of a purchase, the date by which payment must be paid, and any interest charges.

Bill of Exchange A **bill of exchange** is a written order by an exporter to an importer to make payment. The instructions to the importer include the amount, the due date, and the location of where to make the payment (usually a bank or another financial institution).

Electronic Funds Transfer Moving payments through banking computer systems is known as **electronic funds transfer (EFT)**. After an importer receives the ordered goods, a bank can be instructed to transfer the payment for the merchandise to the bank of the exporter. The main advantage of an EFT is prompt payment. Electronic funds transfer systems are commonly used by consumers to obtain cash, deposit money, and make payments.

Commercial Invoice A **commercial invoice**, prepared by the exporter, provides a description of the merchandise and the terms of the sale. This document includes details about the buyer, seller, merchandise, amounts, prices, shipping method, date of shipment, and terms of payment. A sample commercial invoice is shown in Figure 7-5.

Insurance Certificate Proof of insurance is usually a part of import-export transactions. An **insurance certificate** explains the amount of insurance coverage for fire, theft, water, or other damage that may occur to goods in shipment. This document also lists the name of the insurance company and the exporter.

E-COMMERCE IN ACTION

European E-Cash

The European Union did not start using actual euro bills and coins until 2002, even though the new currency became effective in 1999. During this conversion period, some Europeans used e-cash. The Proton card stored Belgian francs and currencies of other nations on a silicon chip for use when making small purchases. The company that developed the card encourages consumers to use it for newspapers, coffee, pastries, and other snacks. Today, the use of e-cash continues to expand in Europe and around the world.

Think Critically

1. Conduct an Internet search to obtain additional information on the use of "e-cash," "cyber-cash," and other forms of electronic money and online payments.
2. What problems might occur with this monetary system?

A COMMERCIAL INVOICE

ExIm EXPRESS
8612 Locust
Madeira, Ohio 45243
(513) 555-0835

SOLD TO:
Serendipity, Sarl
14 Siam
Bangkok, Thailand

SHIPPED TO:
Order of Shipper

CUSTOMER'S ORDER NUMBER AND DATE:
IMP 12
Jan. 1, 2006

INVOICE NUMBER AND DATE:
EI/SS/06/06
Jan. 10, 2006

DATE SHIPPED:
Jan. 15, 2006

VIA:
Ocean freight on CU WINGED SOUL

TERMS:
Sale: CIF Bangkok
Payment: Sight Draft

PACKAGE NO	QUANTITY	OUR NO.	DESCRIPTION	PRICE PER UNIT	AMOUNT
1-40	100	10	Fire Extinguishers	US$ 40	US$ 4000
			Total shipment EX WORKS MADEIRA		US$ 4000
			Plus: Inland Freight to Port		US$ 200
			Total Boston Port		US$ 4200
			Plus: Ocean Freight		US$ 75
			Plus: Insurance		US$ 23
			Total CIF Bangkok Thailand		US$ 4298

We certify that this invoice is true and correct and that the origin of these goods is the United States of America.

These goods licensed by the United States for ultimate destination Thailand. Diversion contrary to U.S. law prohibited. LIC. G-DEST.

Jennifer Hamm
Jennifer Hamm, Export Manager
ExIm Express

Figure 7-5 A commercial invoice gives the details of an international business transaction.

REGIONAL PERSPECTIVE

HISTORY:
VIETNAM: A NATION DIVIDED

Political differences split Vietnam into communist North Vietnam and democratic South Vietnam in 1954. For the next 21 years, military battles continued between the two areas. Between 1963 and 1975, 1.3 million Vietnamese, along with 56,000 U.S. soldiers, were killed. On April 30, 1975, the South surrendered and the country united.

Today Vietnam is divided in another way. One part of the economy consists of traditional open markets with fish, farm products, and handmade items. At stores just a few steps away, shoppers wearing NBA shirts are buying Coca-Cola, Huggies diapers, and Suave shampoo. Many Vietnamese live in single-room huts or on boats along one of the rivers that flows into the South China Sea, while others reside in modern apartments with various home entertainment electronics.

Vietnamese companies have established business relationships with enterprises in Japan, Germany, Canada, and the United States. As Vietnam expands its trading partners, hopes are that economic development will improve living standards for most of the nation's people. As of the late 1990s, the country had a trade deficit in its economic relationship with other countries.

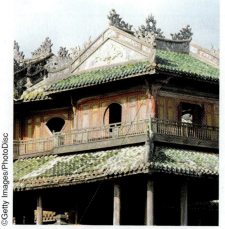

©Getty Images/PhotoDisc

Economic reform in Vietnam can also be viewed in other ways. In the late 1980s, the nation's currency, the *dong*, had an annual inflation rate of 700 percent. More recently, annual cost of living increases were less than 10 percent. A stock exchange in Hanoi was started to build on the dong-U.S. dollar foreign currency exchange activities that were already in operation.

Think Critically

1. What factors influenced the "divided" societies in Vietnam over the years?
2. What actions might be taken by the country to improve economic development?
3. Conduct a web search to obtain current information about the economic and cultural situation in Vietnam.

✔ CheckPoint

Name five different payment methods and financial documents.

REVIEW GLOBAL BUSINESS TERMS

Define each of the following terms.

1. letter of credit
2. credit terms
3. trade credit
4. account receivable
5. account payable
6. capital project
7. bond
8. promissory note
9. bill of exchange
10. electronic funds transfer (EFT)
11. commercial invoice
12. insurance certificate

REVIEW GLOBAL BUSINESS CONCEPTS

13. Why is cash not usually paid in advance of shipping?

14. Why do capital projects usually require a company to borrow money?

SOLVE GLOBAL BUSINESS PROBLEMS

Which type of financial document or payment method would be appropriate for the following situations?

15. A business in India needs to borrow money to build a factory that produces computers.

16. A company wants to delay payment for 60 days but is willing to pay interest on the amount owed during that time period.

17. A business in Costa Rica needs to make payment to a supplier in Thailand today.

18. A supplier in Canada requires that its customer in Singapore have a bank guarantee payment for a shipment of machine parts.

THINK CRITICALLY

19. Why do you think the letter of credit is the most popular payment method used for international business transactions?

20. What are the benefits for a company that offers a discount to customers who pay within 30 days?

MAKE CONNECTIONS

21. **TECHNOLOGY** How does technology result in new capital projects for companies expanding their business operations to other countries?

22. **MATHEMATICS** You receive an invoice from a company in India for 100,000 rupee with payment terms as 2/20, n/60. What would be the amount of the discount you could take if you pay within 20 days?

CHAPTER SUMMARY

7-1 MONEY SYSTEMS AROUND THE WORLD

A Money has five characteristics: acceptability, scarcity, durability, divisibility, and portability. The purpose of money is that it serves as a medium of exchange, a measure of value, and a store of value.

B A country's balance of payments, economic conditions, and political stability influence the value of money. Money supply and demand, inflation, and risk affect interest rates.

7-2 FOREIGN EXCHANGE AND CURRENCY CONTROLS

A Foreign exchange involves the process of exchanging one currency for another in the foreign exchange market. This market consists of banks and other financial institutions that buy and sell different currencies.

B The main activity of the World Bank is to provide economic assistance to less developed countries. The International Monetary Fund helps to promote economic cooperation among countries by maintaining an orderly system of world trade and exchange rates.

7-3 CURRENCY TRANSACTIONS BETWEEN NATIONS

A Cash in advance, a letter of credit, and sale on account are the main payment methods for international business. The main financing sources for international business transactions are trade credit, bank loans, and bonds.

B Common payment methods and financial documents used in international trade include the promissory note, bill of exchange, electronic funds transfer (EFT), commercial invoice, and insurance certificate.

GLOBAL REFOCUS

Read the Global Focus at the beginning of this chapter, and answer the following questions.

1. What actions can a government take to create and maintain an appropriate currency system?

2. Go to the web site of the World Bank (www.worldbank.org) or the web site of the International Monetary Fund (www.imf.org) to obtain current information on Ukraine and other developing economies in Eastern Europe.

REVIEW GLOBAL BUSINESS TERMS

Match the terms listed with the definitions.
Some terms may not be used.

1. The network of banks and other financial institutions that buy and sell different currencies.

2. The amount of currency of one country that can be traded for one unit of the currency of another country.

3. The cost of using someone else's money.

4. Anything people will accept for the exchange of goods and services.

5. A currency that is not easy to exchange for other currencies.

6. A certificate representing money borrowed by a company over a long period of time.

7. Buying or selling on account.

8. An expensive, long-term financial activity.

9. A contract a person or company buys that allows the buyer the option to purchase a foreign currency sometime in the future at today's rate.

10. A financial document issued by a bank for an importer in which the bank guarantees payment.

11. Government restrictions to regulate the amount and value of a nation's currency.

12. A monetary unit that is freely converted into other currencies.

13. A method of moving payments through banking computer systems.

14. A system in which currency values are based on supply and demand.

a. account payable

b. account receivable

c. bill of exchange

d. bond

e. capital project

f. commercial invoice

g. credit terms

h. currency future

i. electronic funds transfer (EFT)

j. exchange controls

k. exchange rate

l. floating exchange rate

m. foreign exchange

n. foreign exchange market

o. hard currency

p. insurance certificate

q. interest rate

r. International Monetary Fund (IMF)

s. letter of credit

t. money

u. promissory note

v. soft currency

w. trade credit

x. World Bank

MAKE GLOBAL BUSINESS DECISIONS

15. What actions could a country take to make its currency more widely accepted around the world?

16. Some people believe that interest rates are one of the most important economic indicators. How are people and businesses affected by interest rates?

17. Give some examples of capital projects in your community. How do capital projects benefit the people of a community?

18. What are some concerns people might have about electronic banking?

GLOBAL CONNECTIONS

19. GEOGRAPHY Research travel costs for three different countries in various regions of the world. Obtain information on the costs of hotels, meals, rental cars, and other travel expenses.

20. COMMUNICATIONS Interview a local business owner about buying and selling on credit. Ask the owner about the benefits and problems encountered when doing business on account.

21. VISUAL ARTS Prepare a poster, bulletin board, newsletter, web site, or another visual that displays the changing value of the dollar in relation to other major currencies of the world.

©Getty Images/PhotoDisc

22. HISTORY Conduct research on the history of money systems that have been used in other countries.

23. CULTURAL STUDIES Interview a person who has traveled to another country. Obtain information about how purchases were made and the exchange rate that was paid.

24. MATHEMATICS Calculate the following foreign exchange transactions.

a. A U.S. citizen is renting a hotel room in Paris for $184.92 a night. If one euro equals $1.20 in U.S. funds, how many francs will the tourist need for each night's stay?

b. A U.S. tourist receives a $5AUS traffic ticket in Australia. If each Australian dollar is equal to $0.74 in U.S. money, what is the cost of this driving violation in U.S. dollars?

c. A videotape made in the United States costs 115 kroner in Norway. If each krone is worth $0.15 in U.S. funds, what is the cost of the videotape in U.S. dollars?

25. CAREER PLANNING Obtain information about the value of a nation's currency. Explain how changes in a country's exchange rate might affect the jobs in that nation.

THE GLOBAL
ENTREPRENEUR
CREATING AN INTERNATIONAL BUSINESS PLAN

THE CHANGING VALUE OF CURRENCIES

Select a country, and research its currency. Obtain information to answer the following questions.

1. What is the main monetary unit used in the country? How is it divided into other units?

2. Over the past couple of years, what have been the economic conditions of the country (inflation, interest rates, unemployment)? How have these affected the value of the currency?

3. How has the country's balance of payments affected the value of its currency?

4. How have political factors affected the value of the currency?

5. Describe any exchange controls used by the country.

6. What factors might affect changes for this currency over the next few months?

7. Graph the recent value of the currency in relation to two other major currencies (e.g., U.S. dollar, Japanese yen, British pound, the euro, Swiss franc).

Prepare a written report with a summary of this information and your graphs. Indicate on the graph any events that have caused a major increase or decrease in the value of the currency.

Sources of information include the following.

- reference books such as encyclopedias and almanacs
- current newspaper articles from the news, business, and travel sections
- web sites such as www.xe.com, www.x-rates.com, and www.oanda.com can provide current information on foreign currency values.

©Getty Images/PhotoDisc

Chapter 8

LEGAL AGREEMENTS AROUND THE WORLD

GLOBAL FOCUS

Trademarks, Brand Names, and International Trade

Apple. Dove. Windows.
To some people, these are a fruit, a bird, and a part of a house. To others, these are a computer, a soap, and computer software.

Trademarks and brand names are an important part of a company's identity. These emblems and words allow customers to quickly know what they are buying and from whom. The process of registering a trademark or brand name requires an application with the U.S. Patent and Trademark Office (www.uspto.gov).

In 1999, the Trademark Law Treaty and Implementation Act (TLTIA) took effect. This law simplifies the process for obtaining a trademark. TLTIA also coordinates U.S. trademark laws with those of other countries participating in this agreement.

When doing business in other countries, trademarks may not be protected. A local company may use a well-known name to attract customers. In South America, Asia, and other regions, small business owners often use this practice. Some have been known to use names such as "Fantasyland," which is a part of Disney, and "Macdonalds" instead of "McDonald's".

The translation of brand names may also cause problems. Chevrolet once had a car called the Nova, which when translated into Spanish could mean "doesn't go," not necessarily an appropriate name for a car. Also, a brand name, when translated into another language, may have an inappropriate meaning.

Think Critically

1. Name some other examples of common words that have become trademarks or registered brand names.
2. What problems might be encountered when a company uses a brand name while doing business in other countries?
3. Conduct an Internet search to obtain information on trademarks and brand names used in different countries.

8-1

GOALS

- Identify and describe the legal systems upon which international law is based.
- Explain product liability.

INTERNATIONAL LEGAL SYSTEMS AND LIABILITY

©Getty Images/PhotoDisc

LEGAL SYSTEMS

Businesspeople of all nations must be familiar with the laws of their own countries. They must obey all laws affecting the ownership and operation of their companies. If they do not, they are subject to legal action, which could result in large losses to the companies.

When people conduct business in a country other than their own, they must observe the laws of the host country as well as the laws of their own country. They must first assess the internal political situation of the host country. Then they must decide whether profits will outweigh any risks. These risks include political instability, war, or hostilities between the business' native country and the host country. Once a country enters into business in or with a foreign country, business relationships are often guided by treaties and trade agreements.

People involved in international business are guided by the principles of international law as well as by trade agreements. Unlike the domestic laws of individual countries, there are few effective ways of enforcing international law. Nevertheless, there is a growing body of international law that many countries respect.

International law is largely based on the legal principles of western civilization. This is a result of the continuous dominance by the West in world affairs since the time of the Roman Empire. The main legal systems around the world are civil law, common law, and statutory law.

CIVIL LAW

Civil law, also called *code law*, is a complete set of rules enacted as a single written system or code. When a government enacts a civil code, it attempts to write down all of the laws and rights that govern every aspect of its society.

Hammurabi, a Babylonian king, enacted the first civil laws in the seventeenth century B.C. Modern civil law is based on the Justinian Code and the Napoleonic Code. Justinian was the leader of the Byzantine Empire, which had conquered almost the entire world known to the West. To maintain an orderly administration of this empire, in 529 A.D. Justinian codified the law in a complete system of rules to govern the empire's citizens. The Justinian Code was based on the traditions of the Roman Empire that had preceded the Byzantine Empire and described in detail the rights of Byzantine citizens, including rights to private property.

In 1804, Napoleon Bonaparte became emperor of France and established a civil code, also based on the Roman model. The Napoleonic Code established as law many of the changes that occurred in the aftermath of the French Revolution, including rights to a jury trial and civil equality. Currently, the majority of countries are governed by civil law, including many that were once a part of the Roman Empire, such as Italy, Spain, Germany, and France.

COMMON LAW

England is the only western European country that did not develop a comprehensive set of rules at one time. Instead, England approached the establishment of law on a case-by-case basis. This approach came to be known as **common law**, which is a legal system that relies on the accumulation of decisions made in prior cases.

English common laws grew out of the deterioration of the feudal system. In medieval times, feudal lords were the supreme rulers of their castles, lands, and the serfs who lived within their territory. Disputes between lords were settled mainly in battle, and serfs had very few rights. Thus, there were few laws.

As serfs began to attain some rights as tenant farmers, disputes between them needed to be resolved. At first, the feudal lords and later judges or magistrates would simply listen to both sides of the dispute and then make a judgment. Since there were no laws to guide these early magistrates in their decisions, they began to write down their decisions so they and others had something to refer to when similar cases arose.

After the conquest of England in 1066 by William the Conqueror, who was also the Duke of Normandy,

English kings established a legal system alongside the developing common law. In this system, the king was the highest legal authority. Because most kings were not knowledgeable about common law, they based their decisions on common sense and the principle of fairness, or equity. The king's courts were, therefore, referred to as the *equity courts*. Equity courts had exclusive jurisdiction over contracts. Gradually, the equity courts merged into the common law system.

England is still governed by common law, as is the United States. In modern common law, also referred to as *case law*, judges make their decisions guided by rulings in previous cases. The principle of equity, or fairness, is often cited. It retains particular influence in business law, where the concept of fairness is very important.

STATUTORY LAW

Statutes are those laws that have been enacted by a body of lawmakers. The German Reichstag, the British Parliament, the Chinese National People's Congress, and the United States Congress, for example, were all formed to pass laws to govern their citizens. Statutes are most often enacted to add to or change existing laws and to define laws for new situations that arise. Figure 8-1 highlights the differences among civil law, common law, and statutory law.

LEGAL SYSTEMS AROUND THE WORLD

Civil Law

An entire body of decisions is made, all at one time by a government for all of its citizens.

Figure 8-1 Civil law, common law, and statutory law are based on different sources.

Common Law

Individual decisions are made in various circumstances. As time goes on, the decision makers refer to the decisions from previous situations and apply those decisions to other similar situations. As new situations arise, new decisions are made. In time, a formal set of decisions, or rules, is developed to which decision makers refer.

Statutory Law

Laws are made by a set of decision makers whose specific purpose is to make laws. The decisions, or laws, made by this body often change or are added to previous decisions.

✓ CheckPoint

What are the main types of legal systems in operation around the world?

LIABILITY

Liability is a broad legal term referring to almost every kind of responsibility, duty, or obligation. In business law, these responsibilities can relate to debt, loss, or burden.

Liabilty for Debt, Loss, and Injury Liability for debt generally includes such claims against a company as wages owed to employees, dividends owed to stockholders, taxes owed to government, and loans owed to banks. Business owners are also responsible for the condition and contents of their facilities and must ensure that their work procedures are safe. Thus, if an employee experiences any loss or burden as a result of unsafe conditions, the company could be declared negligent and, therefore, liable for that loss or injury.

Product Liability The specific responsibility that both manufacturers and sellers have for the safety of their products is called **product liability**. A person can hold a company and its officers responsible for product defects that cause injury, damage, or death to buyers, users, or even bystanders. If a manufacturer does not use "due care" in designing and making a product, it may be guilty of either intentional or negligent harmful action.

Intent to cause harm by a manufacturer or seller is rarely proven. **Negligence**, which is the failure of a responsible party to follow standards of due care, can also be difficult to prove. Thus, modern law has developed the concept of strict liability to help consumers who have suffered a loss due to a defective product to prove the manufacturer's liability.

©Steve Chenn/CORBIS

WORK AS A GROUP

Select a product that has been in the news recently because of a claim that it harmed someone. Discuss how the product meets the six conditions for strict liability.

Strict liability imposes responsibility on a manufacturer or seller for intentionally or unintentionally causing injury to another. For a manufacturer to be held liable for damages under strict liability laws, all of the following six conditions must be met.

1. The product was sold in a defective condition.
2. The seller is in the business of routinely selling the product.
3. The product reached the user without having been substantially changed.
4. The product was unreasonably dangerous to the user.
5. The user of the product or a bystander suffered harm or injury by using the product.
6. The defect was the primary cause of the injury.

Product liability laws vary from country to country. Many countries, such as the United States and members of the European Union, enforce strict liability on manufacturers, sellers, and importers of defective products. International law recognizes the general principle that a responsible party owes just compensation to the injured party.

GLOBAL BUSINESS EXAMPLE

DIPLOMATIC IMMUNITY

Imagine being stopped for speeding when going 85 miles per hour in a 55 miles per hour zone. Then you are allowed to go without getting a ticket. Or what if you accidentally drove into another car, causing several thousand dollars' damage, and were not held liable for the damage?

These are examples of *diplomatic immunity*, which is an exemption from taxation and ordinary legal processes given to diplomatic personnel in a foreign country. Diplomatic personnel include ambassadors, consulate members, and others serving in an official capacity.

Some family members of diplomatic personnel may also be given this immunity.

Diplomacy refers to the practices and institutions by which nations conduct their relations with one another. The privilege of diplomatic immunity, with some freedom from arrest or legal action, is intended to help speed the legal process and to avoid causing political disputes between countries.

Think Critically

1. Why do countries with normal political relations provide immunity for diplomats?
2. When might diplomatic immunity not be appropriate?
3. Conduct an Internet search to obtain additional information about diplomatic immunity.

✓ CheckPoint

How are manufacturers and sellers legally responsible for the safety of their products?

REVIEW GLOBAL BUSINESS TERMS

Define each of the following terms.

1. civil law

2. common law

3. statutes

4. liability

5. product liability

6. negligence

7. strict liability

REVIEW GLOBAL BUSINESS CONCEPTS

8. The justice systems for most countries in the world are based on what kind of law?

9. How did common law develop?

10. Does negligence have to be proven in a successful strict liability case? Why or why not?

SOLVE GLOBAL BUSINESS PROBLEMS

For each of the following situations, explain why the manufacturer of the product can be held liable for damages under strict liability laws.

11. A driver is injured after the car's transmission fails on the highway; the driver had used motor oil instead of transmission fluid.

12. A baby chokes on a small piece of metal that broke off of a toy.

13. You are injured pushing a lawnmower up and down a steep hill.

14. You are hospitalized after eating a salad dressing that contains an ingredient, not listed on the label, to which you are allergic.

THINK CRITICALLY

15. Why might a country prefer code law to a common law system?

16. In the United States, new drugs require FDA (Food and Drug Administration) approval before they can be released. Do you think FDA approval should relieve the manufacturer of product liability?

MAKE CONNECTIONS

17. **COMMUNICATIONS** Select a consumer product that has extensive instructions and other text on or in the package. List the sentences you think attempt to protect the manufacturer from product liability lawsuits.

18. **LAW** Use the Internet or library to research a product liability case. Write a summary of the case, and give your opinion on the verdict.

19. **CULTURAL STUDIES** Use the Internet to research the legal system of a country.

Xtra! Study Tools

intlbizxtra.swlearning.com

8-2 PROPERTY AND CONTRACTS

GOALS

- Explain laws and international trade agreements that protect property rights.
- Describe when an agreement has all of the components of a contract.

©Getty Images/PhotoDisc

PROPERTY RIGHTS AND RESPONSIBILITIES

Property includes everything that can be owned. Property includes land, money, stocks and bonds, buildings, factories, and other goods. There are three main categories of property. Land and whatever is built on or attached to that land is *real property*. Property that is tangible but does not have a permanent location is *personal property*. Property based on ideas (such as patented inventions, trademarks, and copyrights for literary, musical, and artistic works) is *intellectual property*.

PROPERTY LAW

All democratic countries recognize the individual's right to private property. The law protects these rights. **Property rights** are the exclusive rights to possess and use property and its profits, to exclude everyone else from interfering with it, and to dispose of it in any legal way.

A number of international agreements protect the rights of individuals and businesses to own property. These agreements were designed to ensure that individuals and corporations living or located in foreign countries were not deprived of their property except under due process of law or when just compensation had been made. For example, the 1883 Paris Convention of Industrial Property, to which more than 95 countries are members, provides international protection for copyrights, patents, and trademarks.

At different times in history, some countries have rejected individuals' rights to own private property. For example, Communist countries, especially when they were newly formed, subjected both domestic- and foreign-owned property to controls that amounted to a complete loss of property.

Developing countries, particularly those that are former colonies, sometimes expropriate, or confiscate, the property of foreigners. Often this expropriation is made in the name of nationalism or for the developing countries' best interests. As these countries enter into the mainstream of international relations, however, they tend to submit to international laws that recognize the rights of both individuals and businesses to private property. For example, the People's Republic of China, a Communist country, adopted a new constitution in 1982 that included assurances to foreigners engaged in business relationships with China that agreements and contracts will be honored and that violations by Chinese businesses will not be allowed. This new constitution was a direct result of leader Deng Xiaoping's far-reaching changes to move China into the international marketplace.

INTELLECTUAL PROPERTY

Often the greatest asset of a business is its intellectual property. **Intellectual property** is the technical knowledge or creative work that an individual or company has developed. This type of situation is especially true for computer software companies, clothing designers, film companies, writers, inventors, and many others. When intellectual property rights are not protected, dishonest competitors can steal knowledge to make products similar to the original product and deceive consumers into buying them.

The World Intellectual Property Organization (WIPO) is part of the United Nations. This agency, with over 170 nations as members, coordinates various international treaties designed to protect patents, trademarks, copyrights, and other intellectual property. *Piracy*, the illegal use of intellectual property, is a great concern for the companies that first developed these products. As trade becomes more global, the protection of intellectual rights will be a major focus of international law.

Patents The grant of an exclusive right of an inventor to make, sell, and use a product or process is called a **patent**. To be protected, a product or process must be new and useful. Once a patent expires in the United States, it cannot be renewed unless a new improvement or design is incorporated into the idea or product.

Patent rights are only available for a limited time, ranging from five to twenty years in different countries. Patent rights granted in one country do not necessarily extend to other countries. To be protected, a company must apply for patent rights in each country in which it plans to do business. There are, however, international agreements that coordinate and streamline this process.

The Patent Cooperation Treaty also makes the international patent process simpler and more efficient. More than 40 countries—including the United States, Japan, Russia, and members of the European Union—are parties to this treaty. A company can file a single patent application in which it names the countries in which it seeks patent coverage. The application will then be filed in each of those countries.

WORK AS A GROUP

Suggest ways that international trade agencies could protect the intellectual properties of businesses.

Other regional treaties provide similar coordination of patent rights. The Inter-American Convention serves the United States and Latin American countries, and the European Patent Organization coordinates protection among European Union members. The United Nations also works to coordinate intellectual property agreements among countries.

Trademarks A distinctive name, symbol, word, picture, or combination of these that is used by a business to identify its services or products is called a **trademark**. Trademark protection was designed to protect the good reputation of businesses' services and goods. It prevents competitors from representing their products as being those of another business. Such misrepresentation deceives the public and unfairly takes business away from reputable companies.

The symbol ® indicates that a name is a registered trademark in the United States. Most labels of brand-name products include the symbol identifying the name as a registered trademark. To remain protected, a trademark must be in continual use and must continue to be identified with the original business. Once a term becomes accepted to mean all things of that kind, it is no longer protected. For example, T-shirt and aspirin were once trademarks, but they are no longer protected by trademark because they have become everyday terms.

Trademark protection is covered by several international agreements. The

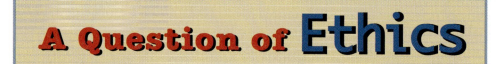

A Question of Ethics

COUNTERFEIT PRODUCTS

- "Mickey" and "Donald" characters not authorized by the Disney Company appearing in a local park
- NBA Championship T-shirts printed illegally
- A Seiko watch that doesn't look just right
- A music CD costing $5 on the street that costs about $15 in a shop

These are just a few of the many examples of counterfeit products and piracy occurring around the world. Each year it is estimated that financial losses from counterfeiting amount to 5 to 7 percent of world trade—over $300 billion.

Violations of trademarks and copyrights are very common in some countries, including Turkey, China, and Thailand. In Italy, vendors selling pirated products control 25 percent of the music CD market. At the same time, unlicensed software in the country accounts for over 40 percent of that market.

While these pirated products give consumers lower prices, sales income is taken away from lawful companies. Efforts to prevent production, distribution, and sales of counterfeit products must involve local and international agencies as well as consumers.

Think Critically

1. Use the three guidelines for ethical analysis presented in Chapter 1 to examine the above situation.
2. How do counterfeit products affect businesses and consumers?

poco più f

poco cresc.

©Getty Images/PhotoDisc

Paris Convention of Industrial Property covers trademarks as well as patents. The Madrid Agreement of 1891 concerning the International Registration of Marks enables member countries to submit a single application for protection in all of its member countries. The European Union has a trademark office that is responsible for the recognition and protection of trademarks used in all EU countries, including those belonging to companies based in countries outside of Europe.

Copyrights A legal right that protects the original works of authors, music composers, playwrights, artists, and publishers is called a **copyright**. A copyright gives the originator exclusive rights to publish, sell, and exhibit his or her creative work for his or her lifetime plus 70 years. For a copyright to be valid, the copyrighted item must be an original and fixed expression. For an item to be fixed, it must be set down in a permanent fashion in a way that others can understand—written words, standard computer codes, or blueprints. The copyright is only extended to the fixed original expression, not to the ideas behind it. The copyright notice © followed by the name of the copyright owner and the date of publication must be prominently displayed on the publication. Anyone who uses work protected by copyright without the creator's permission can be subject to legal action.

The Berne Convention of 1886 established the International Union for the Protection of Literary and Artistic Works. Today, more than 90 countries, including all members of the European Union, participate in this agreement. The Berne Union extends copyright protection in all member countries to its members as long as the first publication takes place in one of those countries. The International Copyright Convention of 1955 also provides international copyright protection based on the agreement that each member country will offer the same protection to foreign works that it does to domestic works.

CheckPoint

What do the Patent Cooperation Treaty, the Paris Convention of Industrial Property, and the International Copyright Convention protect?

CONTRACT LAW

A **contract** is a legally enforceable agreement between two or more persons either to do or not to do a certain thing or things. A contract encourages competent parties to abide by an agreed-upon set of items. Contracts are the basis for almost all business arrangements.

Contracts can be either implied or express. An *implied contract* is one that is not explicitly agreed to by the parties but is inferred either from the parties' conduct or from the law. An *express contract* is one whose terms are openly declared, either orally or in writing. Businesses nearly always enter into express contracts because it is wise for parties to agree to and set forth very clearly what is expected of everyone, However, both implied and express contracts are binding on both parties, and neither party can withdraw without the agreement of the other party.

COMPONENTS OF A CONTRACT

For a contract to be considered valid, it must contain the following four essential components.

1. **Capacity** All parties must be competent, of legal age, and mentally capable.
2. **Mutual agreement** One party offers valid terms and the other party accepts.
3. **Consideration** Something of value must be given by both parties.
4. **Legal purpose** The terms of the contract must be in agreement with the law.

For a contract to be enforceable, the contract must be valid—that is, it must meet all four of the conditions. Either party can enforce a valid contract. A contract that fails to meet one of those four requirements is unenforceable by either party.

Businesspeople in the international arena frequently enter into contracts with representatives of companies from other countries and with the governments of other countries. Such agreements are most often made according to the rules of international law.

TREATIES AND TRADE AGREEMENTS

Treaties and trade agreements between countries are examples of contracts that have a tremendous effect on global business activities. These agreements impose a degree of stability and uniformity for trade relations where members have different cultures and customs. Since contracts are the basis of business relationships, many trade agreements provide guidelines for the enforcement of contracts.

Some of the most far-reaching international trade agreements in force today include the following.

- The World Trade Organization with more than 140 member countries
- The European Union which allows the free flow of goods, services, labor, and capital between the member countries of the EU
- The North American Free Trade Agreement, designed to ensure open markets and fair competition between companies in Canada, Mexico, and the United States

Communication Across Borders

WHEN IS A CONTRACT NOT A CONTRACT?

When doing business in Japan, it is important to realize that the communication known as a contract may not have the same meaning to Japanese businesspersons as it does to U.S. businesspersons. The Japanese often aren't eager to sign contracts, although they will do so because they know most Western businesspersons require them. Because Japanese businesspersons consider agreements based on personal promises to be binding, they discount the importance of contracts, which are agreements based on written words that are flexible in meaning. As a result, Japanese businesspersons view signed contracts as a point from which to begin negotiations when circumstances change or disputes arise, not as the absolute rules for business transactions, as U.S. businesspersons view them.

Think Critically

1. Why do you think Japanese businesspersons consider written words and contracts to be flexible in meaning?
2. How do Japanese businesspersons benefit by valuing personal promises over written contracts?

©Getty Images/PhotoDisc

✓ CheckPoint

What is necessary for a trade agreement to be an enforceable contract?

REVIEW GLOBAL BUSINESS TERMS

Define each of the following terms.

1. property
2. property rights
3. intellectual property
4. patent
5. trademark
6. copyright
7. contract

REVIEW GLOBAL BUSINESS CONCEPTS

8. What are the three types of property?
9. What four elements must be present for a contract to be valid?

SOLVE GLOBAL BUSINESS PROBLEMS

For each of the following intellectual properties, decide if the item would be protected by a patent, trademark, or copyright.

10. The brand name of a packaged food product
11. A musical composition
12. A process for sending photos over the Internet
13. A logo for a sports team
14. This book

THINK CRITICALLY

15. What actions could be taken to protect intellectual property in a country?
16. Why are persons of a certain age not allowed to enter into a legally binding contract?

©Getty Images/PhotoDisc

MAKE CONNECTIONS

17. **TECHNOLOGY** How do the Internet and other technology make protection of patents, trademarks, and copyrights more difficult?

18. **GEOGRAPHY** How might the climate and terrain of a country affect contracts?

RESOLVING LEGAL DIFFERENCES

8-3

GOALS

- Identify several different ways to resolve international legal disputes.
- Explain the litigation process.
- Describe the role of the International Court of Justice in international business.

RESOLVING LEGAL DIFFERENCES WITHOUT COURT ACTION

Throughout the world, most legal disputes are resolved without the parties ever going to court. This is true of disputes between individuals, businesses, and nations.

There are many reasons why businesses, particularly those in the international arena, are willing to settle conflicts out of court. The time and expense involved in lawsuits, the need for a quick resolution, the concern about bad publicity, the uncertainty of outcomes, and the desire to maintain a good relationship with the other party all must be considered. Businesses also may fear that they will receive discriminatory treatment in a foreign court. Moreover, the complexity involved in determining which country's laws to use and the location of the trial contributes to companies' preference for dispute resolution outside of the courtroom. The two major means of alternate dispute settlement used by businesses in the international arena are mediation and arbitration.

MEDIATION

Mediation is a dispute resolution method that makes use of a neutral third party, or *mediator*. A mediator attempts to reconcile the viewpoints of the disputing parties. A mediator is involved with the substance of the dispute and makes suggestions and proposals. Therefore, the mediator is often an attorney or expert in the disputed matter. Mediators cannot make binding decisions. Only when the disputing parties voluntarily agree to a mediator's decision is a settlement reached. Thus, mediation is most successful when both parties are willing to compromise.

WORK AS A GROUP

Describe a trade difference that might occur between countries. Present both sides of the situation. Have a group member serve as a mediator or an arbitrator for the situation.

GLOBAL BUSINESS EXAMPLE

LEGAL DIFFERENCES IN OTHER SOCIETIES

The criminal procedures used in France are different from those used in the United States and Great Britain. For example, a person accused of a crime is not presumed innocent until proven guilty. Victims and their families may become part of the investigation. In addition, persons accused of crimes have no protection from self-incrimination.

In the People's Republic of China, two systems of contract law exist. One is for domestic transactions, and another is for foreign contracts. In 1981, the Economic Contract Law code was enacted for domestic business transactions. The Foreign Economic Contract Law, created in 1985, was designed to attract foreign buyers for Chinese products.

Think Critically
1. Conduct an Internet search to locate examples of different legal systems in other countries.
2. What factors might influence the different legal systems used in various countries?

Some cultures have a strong tradition of using mediation to settle disputes. In Japan, for example, it is a point of honor to settle disputes without having to go to court. In the People's Republic of China, approximately 90 percent of all civil disputes are settled by mediation. More than 800,000 Mediation Committees exist throughout China, each composed of a group of knowledgeable people on various topics.

ARBITRATION

Arbitration is a method of conflict resolution that uses a neutral third party to make a binding decision. Unlike a mediator, an *arbitrator's* decision is legal and binding on both parties. An arbitrator acts as a private judge at a location of the disputing parties' choice and establishes procedures and rules of evidence. The parties specify the issues to be decided by the arbitrator. In this way, they avoid receiving a decision based on legal technicalities or other reasons that are not central to the issue being decided.

Arbitration is particularly well suited to settling disputes involving international business. Such disputes normally do not involve serious or complicated legal issues. So most businesses prefer to resolve disputes in a speedy, economical, and private way. Most often a dispute comes to arbitration because a contract either requires it or allows a party to demand it. Such provisions are common in union contracts.

In the international business arena, a contract will frequently include a requirement of arbitration. An intermediary, a person both parties agree is impartial, also may be provided for in the original contract. A representative from the international business community is often chosen to be an arbitrator. A typical choice is an officer in a chamber of commerce or a trade association from a third country.

CheckPoint

Why would a company want to avoid court action to settle a dispute?

RESOLVING LEGAL DIFFERENCES USING COURT ACTION

Two parties may decide on litigation when they are unable or unwilling to resolve their differences through mediation or arbitration or through their own agreements or compromises.

LITIGATION

Litigation is a lawsuit brought about to enforce the rights of a person or an organization or to seek a remedy to the violation of their rights. Litigation involves many complex procedural rules. These rules vary widely from country to country and even among courts within a given country. Most countries have a federal or national court. Many also have state or provincial courts, as well as even more localized courts. Nearly all legal systems have separate rules for criminal and civil cases.

People living in or doing business in a foreign country are usually subject to the laws of that country. Thus, if a dispute arises between a business and someone in the host country, the matter must be settled in the host country's courts. When a conflict arises between two companies of different countries, the conflict may be settled either in the courts of the country in which the agreement was made or in the courts of the country in which the contract will be fulfilled. Figure 8-2 provides a brief outline of dispute settlement methods and options.

If a government violates the terms of a contract with a foreign company, the company is expected to pursue a remedy within that host country. If the company is unable to obtain a resolution, it may present its claim to its own government, which may then press an international claim against the foreign country on behalf of the company. However, many governments are unwilling to press such claims for two reasons. First, the company is presumed to have had a clear conception of the risks involved in entering into such an agreement. Second, pressing such a claim may interfere with the delicate political balance that might exist between the two countries.

©Getty Images/PhotoDisc

DISPUTE RESOLUTION ACROSS BORDERS

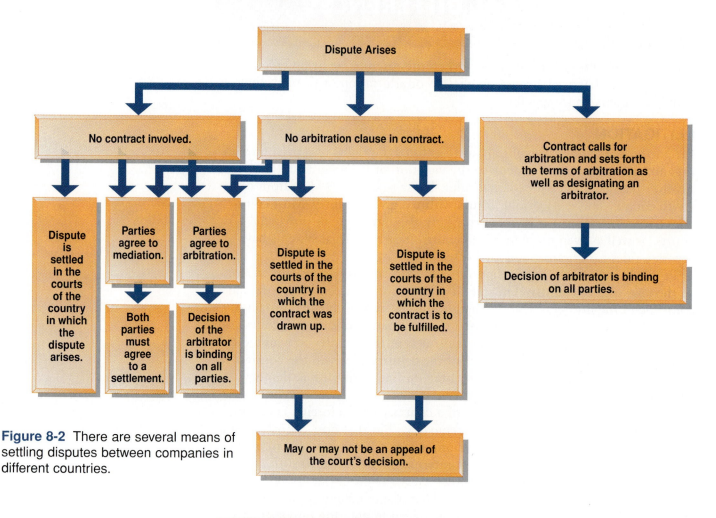

Figure 8-2 There are several means of settling disputes between companies in different countries.

✓ CheckPoint

When might litigation be appropriate?

THE INTERNATIONAL COURT OF JUSTICE

The International Court of Justice was established in 1946 by the Charter of the United Nations. It sits in The Hague in the Netherlands. The **International Court of Justice** is a court that settles disputes between nations when both nations request that it do so and also advises the United Nations on matters of international law. The decisions of the Court are binding for all parties.

Many of the procedures of the International Court of Justice are derived from Western civil law systems. For example, the International Court primarily uses documentary evidence to decide a case. It also has the power to request additional evidence as it wishes.

The International Court does not use procedures that are routine under common law. There is no jury, and for that reason, oral testimony is rarely heard. Evidence is rarely removed from the record, and false testimony and documents are simply ignored.

While Western principles of law are predominate in the International Court, some non-Western principles have been incorporated into international law. Islamic law has contributed to the division of law into primary and secondary sources. The *primary source* corresponds to the Islamic concept of certain, or definite, proof. The *secondary source* corresponds to the Islamic concept of reasoned proof. The great majority of international rules of war, as well as many rules regarding treaties, are also based on Islamic law. The reliance of the International Court on negotiation and mediation as means of dispute settlement are derived primarily from Asian customs.

Because of the dominance of Western principles, some newly developed states have found that international law is in conflict with their interests. Communist and developing nations, for example, do not accept many of the legal principles of the older developed states that form the basis of international law. Because of the past and continuing dominance of the West, the effect of these newer countries on international law has been slight.

Since law must change to adapt to emerging situations, some principles not in harmony with Western ideas have been integrated into international law. As the world becomes more interdependent, the needs of developing countries receive increased attention. As a result, these developing countries become more willing to abide by international law and offer new concepts to it.

Only nations can be parties before the International Court of Justice. Individuals and organizations, including businesses, are specifically excluded. Thus, very few commercial cases are heard by the Court. Such cases are heard only when a government presses an international claim on behalf of a company.

What then is the importance of the International Court of Justice to the world of international business? The answer is that it provides guidelines for acceptable ways of doing business around the world.

The continuation and expansion of world trade requires that businesses in foreign environments be treated in a consistent manner. Businesspeople in all countries want to engage in profitable relationships. As long as international principles of law are observed—particularly property rights and responsibilities and enforcement of contracts—international business will bring countries of the world closer together.

NETBookmark

The International Chamber of Commerce (ICC) is a global business organization that champions the global economy. It promotes economic growth, job creation, prosperity, and understanding between national economies. To check out the ICC web site, access intlbizxtra.swlearning.com and click on the link for Chapter 8. Read the article entitled "What Is the ICC?" Then write several paragraphs outlining the functions of the ICC.

intlbizxtra.swlearning.com

©Getty Images/PhotoDisc

REGIONAL PERSPECTIVE

HISTORY: TAIWAN

Taiwan, officially called the Republic of China, is an island nation off the southeast coast of mainland China between the East and South China Seas. Mountains form the backbone of the country, but the western slopes are fertile and well cultivated. Most of Taiwan's people live in the lowlands on the western side of the island.

Chinese immigrants came to the island in the seventeenth century. After a brief period of Dutch rule (1620–1662), Taiwan experienced about 160 years of Chinese control. Japan ruled from 1895–1945, using the island for farming and military operations. After World War II, civil war between the Nationalist and Communist factions broke out in China. The leader of the Chinese Nationalist party, Chiang Kai-shek, fled to Taiwan. He proclaimed Taipei the provisional capital of China, renamed Taiwan the Republic of China, and took control of the island. Both the People's Republic of China on the mainland and the Nationalist Chinese government in Taiwan continued to claim sovereignty over Taiwan.

The conflict regarding whether the Communist government, which was based on mainland China, or the Nationalist government, which was based in Taiwan, was the legitimate government of China was the source of bitterness, international tension, and armed clashes throughout the 1950s and 1960s. By the late 1980s, however, there had been a gradual decrease in the hostilities. In 1986, the mainland Chinese government announced that the principle of "one country, two systems" would be applied to Taiwan. This policy retains Taiwan's economic independence and army but submits it to China in matters of foreign policy.

After World War II, Taiwan enjoyed rapid industrial growth and now has one of the strongest economies in Asia. The country's strong educational system is one of the main influences on Taiwan's economic success. Taiwan is one of the most literate countries in the world, with a literacy rate of 94 percent. Most of its people work in industry or service jobs. Less than 15 percent work in agriculture. Taiwan particularly promotes high-tech industries, such as those that produce computers and electronic items. Taiwan's economy is largely based on exports, which account for more than half of its gross domestic product.

Think Critically

1. Conduct a web search for additional information about the current cultural, political, and economic situation of Taiwan.
2. What factors contributed to the economic development of Taiwan?

✓ CheckPoint

What is the purpose of the International Court of Justice?

REVIEW GLOBAL BUSINESS TERMS

Define each of the following terms.

1. mediation
2. arbitration

3. litigation
4. International Court of Justice

REVIEW GLOBAL BUSINESS CONCEPTS

5. What is the difference between mediation and arbitration?

6. What are some of the reasons why two businesses from different countries might prefer to resolve a dispute through mediation or arbitration rather than litigation?

7. What is the importance of international law to businesses engaged in international trade?

SOLVE GLOBAL BUSINESS PROBLEMS

For each of the following situations, decide if the dispute should be resolved using mediation, arbitration, or litigation.

8. After years of negotiation, a company is unable to collect for the value of property lost by a shipping company.

9. A company and a supplier in another country have slight differences about a recent business transaction.

10. Mediation between two companies has not been successful. The businesses want a third party to decide a legally binding settlement.

11. A labor union and management want a third party to recommend a possible settlement for the differences in their contract negotiations.

THINK CRITICALLY

12. Why is the International Court of Justice important to international business?

13. While not legally binding, why is the mediation process sometimes effective for settling disputes?

MAKE CONNECTIONS

14. **TECHNOLOGY** What are some international legal concerns that could result from increased use of technology in business?

15. **LAW** Write a contract to use when doing a job for a neighbor, such as taking care of pets, mowing a lawn, installing a computer, or babysitting.

16. **LAW** Use the Internet to research the International Court of Justice and some of its recent cases and decisions.

CHAPTER SUMMARY

8-1 INTERNATIONAL LEGAL SYSTEMS AND LIABILITY

A The main legal systems of the world are civil law, common law, and statutory law.

B Manufacturers and sellers are responsible for the safety of their products. Intent to cause harm and negligence are difficult to prove, so the principles of strict liability apply in product negligence in many countries.

8-2 PROPERTY AND CONTRACTS

A Property rights are protected through government actions such as patents, trademarks, and copyrights.

B Contracts are the basis for almost all business arrangements. A valid contract must have four components: capacity, mutual agreement, consideration, and legal purpose.

8-3 RESOLVING LEGAL DIFFERENCES

A International legal disputes may be resolved without court action through mediation or arbitration.

B Litigation is court action used to resolve global business disputes.

C The International Court of Justice settles legal disputes between nations when both nations request that it do so. This court also advises the United Nations on matters of international law.

GLOBAL REFOCUS

Read the Global Focus at the beginning of this chapter, and answer the following questions.

1. What actions might a company take to plan, implement, and protect its international brand names and trademarks?

2. How might a joint venture help a company protect its trademarks?

3. Go to the web site of the World Intellectual Property Organization (www.wipo.org) to obtain current information related to trademarks and brand names.

REVIEW GLOBAL BUSINESS TERMS

Match the terms listed with the definitions.
Some terms may not be used.

1. A legal system that relies on the accumulation of decisions made in prior cases.

2. A legal right that protects the original works of authors, music composers, playwrights, artists, and publishers.

3. A legally enforceable agreement between two or more persons either to do or not to do a certain thing or things.

4. Everything that can be owned.

5. A court that settles disputes between nations when both nations request that it do so and also advises the United Nations on matters of international law.

6. The specific responsibility that both manufacturers and sellers have for the safety of their products.

7. Those laws that have been enacted by a body of lawmakers.

8. The failure of a responsible party to follow standards of due care.

9. A distinctive name, symbol, word, picture, or combination of these that is used by a business to identify its services or products.

a. arbitration

b. civil law

c. common law

d. contract

e. copyright

f. intellectual property

g. International Court of Justice

h. liability

i. litigation

j. mediation

k. negligence

l. patent

m. product liability

n. property

o. property rights

p. statutes

q. strict liability

r. trademark

10. A dispute resolution method that makes use of a neutral third party.

11. The exclusive right of an inventor to make, sell, and use a product or process.

12. A method of conflict resolution that uses a neutral third party to make a binding decision.

MAKE GLOBAL BUSINESS DECISIONS

13. If you were creating the laws for a country, what would some examples of those laws be?

14. Describe a situation in which a person or an organization might be held negligent for injury or property damage.

15. Some people believe patents, copyrights, and trademarks create monopolies. Describe the advantages and disadvantages of protecting intellectual property.

16. List examples of contracts commonly entered into by individuals and companies.

17. Describe a situation in which a company might use mediation or arbitration in an international business situation.

18. Jean Claude Nallet, an eight-year-old French boy, received a model fire engine as a present. While playing with the toy, a sharp tip on the toy ladder punctured Jean Claude's finger, and he required medical treatment. Later the family found out that the fire engine was defective and had been recalled by the manufacturer.

  a. In your opinion, do Jean Claude's parents have a legitimate reason to file a product liability claim?

  b. Under the guidelines of strict liability, which elements apply to Jean Claude's case?

GLOBAL CONNECTIONS

19. **COMMUNICATIONS** Write a letter to a publishing company or a music video production company requesting permission to copy an artist's work. Save a copy of your letter, and summarize the response you receive in a short written report.

20. **VISUAL ART** Look for examples of trademarks on products sold around the world. Based on these examples, create a picture for a trademark and brand that might be used for international business.

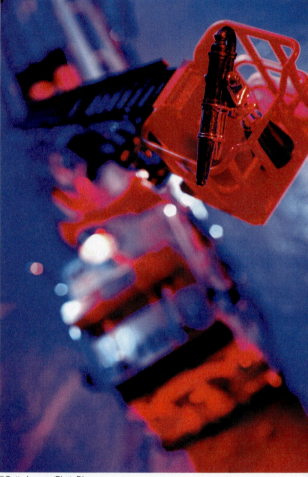
©Getty Images/PhotoDisc

21. **COMMUNICATIONS** Create a logo or package design for a product that could be used in many countries around the world.

22. **LAW** Create a legal system for a new country that just became independent from another country that had controlled its political and legal activities in the past.

23. **CULTURAL STUDIES** How might the culture of a country affect the format and conditions of a contract?

24. **SCIENCE** Research a patent on a product. Identify the inventor, the year the patent was granted, and the product's function. Prepare a summary report of your findings.

25. **CAREER PLANNING** Find out what types of legal agreements a person would encounter when applying for a job with and working for a multinational company.

THE GLOBAL ENTREPRENEUR

CREATING AN INTERNATIONAL BUSINESS PLAN

LAWS AROUND THE WORLD

Research the legal system of a foreign country. Focus your research on cultural issues and political influences on legal agreements and business regulations in that country. Obtain information for the following questions.

1. What are the basic components of the country's legal system?

2. How does the culture of the country affect its legal system?

3. What are the issues that affect legal agreements in the country?

4. What legal restrictions affect international trade with the country?

5. What sort of out-of-court resolution process might be used in the country to settle legal differences?

Sources of information for your research may include the following.

- reference books such as encyclopedia, almanacs, and atlases

- current newspaper and magazine articles

- web sites for the *CIA Factbook* and other country information

- materials from companies, airlines, travel bureaus, government agencies, and other organizations involved in international business

- interviews with people who have lived in, worked in, or traveled to the country

Prepare a written summary or present a short oral report (two or three minutes) of your findings.

©Getty Images/PhotoDisc

Chapter 9

GLOBAL ENTREPRENEURSHIP AND SMALL BUSINESS MANAGEMENT

GLOBAL FOCUS

A Real Chief Executive

For many years, the Mississippi Band of Choctaw Indians faced difficult economic conditions. In the 1960s, 90 percent of this Indian nation lived in poverty. Today, as a result of Chahta Enterprise and other businesses, things are different. Chahta is the first Native-American-owned company to expand into the global economy.

This diversified company is involved in various businesses. Recently Chahta Enterprise opened a production plant in Empalme, Mexico, about 300 miles south of Tucson, Arizona. This facility produces electric-wire harnesses for car switches used by Ford Motor Company. The company has plans to open a second factory in Mexico that will produce car-stereo components.

Company chief executive Phillip Martin is also chief of the Mississippi Band of Choctaw Indians. According to Chief Martin, the North American Free Trade Agreement brought about the company's move to Mexico in order to take advantage of lower labor costs. While the Choctaws were no longer making the electric-wire harnesses in Mississippi, the former employees were able to obtain work with other businesses on or near the reservation.

Over the past 25 years, the average annual household income on the Choctaw reservation has increased from $2,500 to over $26,000. At the same time, unemployment declined to less than 5 percent from a high of over 50 percent. The community now includes quality schools and day-care facilities and an excellent hospital.

Think Critically

1. What social and economic factors influenced the activities of Chahta Enterprise?
2. How did the community benefit from Chief Martin's business leadership?
3. Conduct an Internet search to obtain additional information about the Mississippi Band of Choctaw Indians.

9-1 | ENTREPRENEURIAL ENTERPRISES

GOALS

- Explain the importance of entrepreneurs in the development of an economy.
- Differentiate between the types of entrepreneurial businesses.
- Describe telecommuting and the effect of technology on home-based businesses.

©Getty Images/PhotoDisc

THE ECONOMIC IMPORTANCE OF ENTREPRENEURS

The world of business is constantly changing. No one knows this better than small business owners in the United States. More than 15 million people in the United States own their own small business. Each day foreign competition increases. A store down the street now acquires items from manufacturers in Asia and Europe. Businesses of every type and size are adapting to the global marketplace.

Nations do not start out highly industrialized with international airports, superhighways, and computer networks. In every country, people get ideas and take action to make products better, faster, and more available. This inventive effort is the basis for economic development and improved quality of life.

INNOVATION AND THE ENTREPRENEURIAL SPIRIT

An **entrepreneur** is a risk taker who operates a business. Every business combines land, labor, and capital to sell a product or service. An entrepreneur is the person who brings together those resources for a company to get started and operate successfully.

Entrepreneurs may be people with a creative vision, such as David Filo and Jerry Wang, who founded Yahoo!, or Lydia Moss Bradley, who made millions in real estate development and went on to found Bradley University. A common trait of entrepreneurs is that they don't listen to people who say

"It can't be done!" These business innovators have an idea they believe in and dedicate their time, money, and effort to its success.

ECONOMIC AND SOCIAL BENEFITS OF SMALL BUSINESS

Most entrepreneurs start small. Some have started in a basement or garage. Small companies are an important part of every economy. A **small business** is an independently owned and operated business that does not dominate an industry.

Small businesses are commonly categorized by number of employees. The U.S. Small Business Administration defines a small business as one with fewer than 100 employees. About 95 percent of all businesses in the United States have fewer than 50 employees. Of the 15 million businesses in the European Union, fewer than 10 percent have more than nine employees.

Entrepreneurial efforts provide a nation with three main economic and social benefits.

1. **Small businesses are major creators of new products.** Entrepreneurs are willing to take risks and try ideas that may be rejected by larger companies. Entrepreneurs have invented products such as personal computers, ballpoint pens, video games, and fiberglass snow skis.

2. **Small businesses are the major source of jobs.** In recent years, the 500 largest companies in the United States reduced their work forces by several million people, while small businesses hired over 20 million employees. Business organizations with fewer than 500 employees employ more than half of all U.S. workers and produce half of the country's GDP.

3. **Small businesses often provide personal service.** In that way, they compete successfully against larger companies to meet the individual needs of customers. A bank, for example, can grant loans to people in its community who may be denied funding by larger financial institutions. Small manufacturing companies can produce custom-made parts for foreign companies, an activity that large businesses might not find profitable.

Entrepreneurial businesses often turn to international business to expand their markets. Exporting is promoted by the U.S. Department of Commerce, Small Business Administration, World Trade Centers, and state departments of economic development. These agencies and organizations help entrepreneurs plan and execute international business activities.

Entrepreneurs may invent ways to adapt products and services to meet the economic, cultural, and legal needs of customers in other countries. The activities of small businesses in Europe and Asia have energized economic development. Thailand started as an agricultural society with a system of landlords and peasants. Chinese influence in the late 1800s helped change the economic emphasis of Thailand. By the 1970s, over 30 major companies were based in the country. Entrepreneurial activities stimulated economic development. Today Thailand is one of the largest and fastest-growing economies in the world.

©Getty Images/PhotoDisc

COMMON ENTREPRENEURIAL BUSINESS IN EUROPE AND ASIA

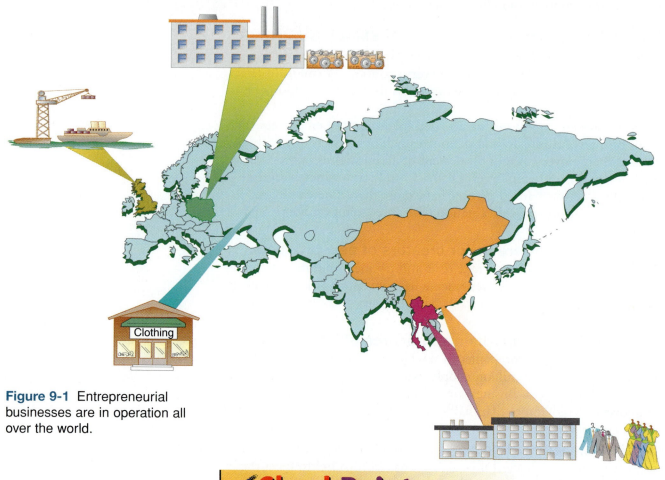

Figure 9-1 Entrepreneurial businesses are in operation all over the world.

✓ CheckPoint

What are the three main economic and social benefits small businesses provide?

TYPES OF ENTREPRENEURIAL BUSINESSES

Types of entrepreneurial enterprises are as varied as types of large corporations. Entrepreneurial businesses can be grouped into five major categories: extracting companies, manufacturing companies, wholesalers, retailers, and service companies.

Agricultural, Mining, and Extracting Companies Diamond-mining companies in South Africa, oil companies in Saudi Arabia, and flower growers in California are all examples of extractors. These enterprises grow products or take raw materials from nature. Extracting companies include businesses involved in agriculture, fishing, forestry, and mining.

Manufacturing Companies Manufacturing involves changing raw materials and parts into usable products. Entrepreneurs in this category range from computer manufacturers with many employees to basket weavers with just a few workers.

Wholesalers Products must get from producers to consumers. If clothing manufactured in Taiwan is not shipped to appropriate selling locations, the garments have little value. A wholesaler is a business that buys from a manufacturer and sells to other businesses. Wholesalers are commonly called *intermediaries* because they are links between producers and sellers of products.

Retailers A retailer is a business that sells directly to consumers. In a typical week, you probably go to several stores. You may also buy from mail-order companies or vending machines. These are examples of retailing businesses. Online retailers are retailers that operate over the Internet.

Service Companies How often does someone in your household have clothes cleaned, get the car washed, use a telephone, have film developed, or rent a video? These are all examples of services. Consumer services include businesses such as law offices, doctors' offices, dentists' offices, hair salons, daycare centers, Internet service providers, repair shops, travel agencies, and music schools.

Service companies also sell business services to other companies. Business services include advertising, information systems, custodial, security, and equipment rental. These companies are commonly called *business-to-business (B2B)* enterprises because they sell to other companies rather than to individual consumers.

E-COMMERCE IN ACTION

Internet Entrepreneurs

All you need is a computer, a modem, a phone line, a printer, a scanner, a credit card business account, and the delivery services of Federal Express or UPS. Then what do you have? You have an online business capable of competing with any major organization.

Online, big companies and small companies look alike. Take away the big buildings, fancy offices, and well-dressed employees, and what do you have left? A company image that is judged on the content and services provided by a web site.

When Amazon.com started, it began selling books without any experience in that industry. It started with technology and the idea to provide the latest bestsellers online. Next, the cyber-retailer expanded into music CDs, videos, software, toys, video games, tools, and other home improvement products. More recently, the company started selling clothing, furniture, small household appliances, digital cameras, and home entertainment

equipment. Today they have sales that exceed most traditional stores.

The company's international sales also continue to expand. The largest segment of foreign orders comes from the United Kingdom and Germany, with web sites also for Japan and France. These markets have minimal political risk and populations with a large percentage of Internet access.

Think Critically

1. What are the benefits of online businesses for employees and consumers?
2. What actions might be taken for Amazon.com to expand its international operations?
3. Locate a web site for an online business that is probably a small operation but is able to compete against larger companies.

WORK AS A GROUP

Discuss the advantages and disadvantages for the person who works from home.

FUTURE GROWTH FOR SMALL BUSINESS

In addition to over 15 million self-employed workers in the United States, there are another two million people who operate part-time businesses while working for someone else. Government agencies and business experts project that in the coming years, entrepreneurs involved in the following types of enterprises have the greatest potential for success.

- Health-care services
- Retailing and food service companies, especially those using the Internet and other technology to interact with customers
- Environmental businesses that recycle and offer environment-friendly goods and services
- Training and education enterprises to help workers adapt to a changing workplace
- Personal services such as childcare, financial planning, entertainment, and recreation
- Commercial services such as marketing, financial consultants, delivery, transportation, and information systems

These business opportunities will be available in both the United States and other countries.

✓ CheckPoint

How does a wholesaler differ from a retailer?

HOME-BASED BUSINESSES

Years ago most people worked from their homes as farmers, weavers, and toolmakers. These home-based businesses are still present in many countries, including the Philippines, Pakistan, Chad, Liberia, Kenya, and Peru.

In major population areas of industrialized countries, however, most work moved to factories, stores, and offices during the industrialization process. However, technology is currently providing the opportunity for many workers to return to their homes to work. Today over 5 million people in the United States and more than 2 million in Canada operate businesses from their homes.

Other types of common home businesses

©Getty Images/PhotoDisc

include real estate brokers, insurance agents, construction contractors, repair shops, hair stylists, pet groomers, childcare providers, accountants, and tax preparers. Also, home-based Internet businesses have expanded to include almost any type of business, such as retailers, auto parts suppliers, online greeting cards, grocery stores, and flower delivery services.

Telecommuting In addition to running their own businesses from home, many people also are working for another company by telecommuting. **Telecommuting** involves using a computer and other technology to work at home instead of in a company office or factory. Telecommuting is best suited to jobs that do not require regular in-person contact with others and may be done through computer networks and other telecommunications equipment. This employment arrangement is most common for writers, editors, researchers, economists, accounting clerks, information processing workers, database supervisors, and computer programmers.

Employers who use telecommuting report several benefits.

1. Businesses save money since they do not need as much office space.

2. Companies are able to keep talented employees who may not want to work in a structured environment.

3. Workers save time and energy since they do not travel to a place of employment.

Many home-based entrepreneurs and telecommuters select working at home so they can have more time with their families and save money on childcare.

People planning to work at home must consider the government regulations for these types of businesses. For example, in recent years in Toronto, operating a mail-order company from your home was considered illegal.

©Getty Images/PhotoDisc

NETBookmark

The Small Business Association (SBA) is an excellent source of information for anyone who needs help starting and running a small business. Access the Small Business Association's web site through intlbizxtra.swlearning.com. Click on the link for Chapter 9. Read the article, and then write a few paragraphs outlining the Equal Opportunity Loan program. Explain how the SBA works to increase the participation of women and minorities with this program.

intlbizxtra.swlearning.com

✔CheckPoint

What are the advantages of telecommuting to a company?

REVIEW GLOBAL BUSINESS TERMS

Define each of the following terms.

1. entrepreneur
2. small business
3. telecommuting

REVIEW GLOBAL BUSINESS CONCEPTS

4. Why do entrepreneurial businesses frequently turn to international business?

5. What are five common types of entrepreneurial businesses?

6. What kinds of jobs are best suited to telecommuting?

SOLVE GLOBAL BUSINESS PROBLEMS

Determine whether each of the following companies is primarily engaged in extracting, manufacturing, wholesaling, retailing, or providing a service.

7. Company that acquires kitchen appliances and sells them to construction companies.

8. Toy store.

9. Employment agency.

10. Airline.

11. Company that printed this textbook for the publishing company.

12. Person who traps lobsters and sells them to seafood stores and restaurants.

THINK CRITICALLY

13. What actions could a government take to encourage the start up of new businesses?

14. How would differences in cultures affect the operation of a small business in various countries?

15. When you work from home, you need to be especially well disciplined. You also may miss interacting with other people. How could you overcome these disadvantages of working at home?

MAKE CONNECTIONS

16. **GEOGRAPHY** Describe how a country's natural resources could encourage entrepreneurial activities

17. **LAW** What legal restrictions might a person face when starting a new business?

THE BUSINESS PLAN AND SELF-EMPLOYMENT

9-2

©Getty Images/PhotoDisc

GOALS

- Evaluate self-employment as a career option.
- Describe the first three sections of a business plan.

SELF-EMPLOYMENT AS A CAREER

When you own your own business, the good news is that you don't have to listen to a boss anymore—because you are the boss. The bad news is that you can't call in sick unless someone else can be trusted to keep things going.

ADVANTAGES OF SELF-EMPLOYMENT

The two main advantages of owning a business are independence and pride of ownership. A small business owner makes the company decisions and is at the center of action. Because of political and legal restrictions, however, this same independence may not be available to entrepreneurs in all countries.

As entrepreneurs achieve success, they usually gain a feeling of accomplishment. They gain confidence in their ability to organize resources, make decisions, and manage business activities. Serving customers, employing workers, and contributing to the economic growth of a community or nation can also provide a sense of satisfaction for entrepreneurs.

DISADVANTAGES OF SELF-EMPLOYMENT

Being an owner-operator of a company also has disadvantages. The drawbacks of self-employment are the time commitment, uncertain income, and possible loss of investment. Every small business owner can tell you about the time involved. More than half of all small business owners who sell their companies do so because of boredom or burnout.

As a business owner, income is uncertain. In the first few years of owning a business, it is possible that the owner will not earn enough to get a salary. Business experts recommend that money be set aside for personal living expenses before starting a new business. Even after the business has been operating for awhile, poor economic conditions can reduce sales and profits.

Each year more than 50,000 businesses fail in the United States, with owners and other investors losing millions of dollars. In that same time frame, however, more than 600,000 new businesses start in the United States. After three years, statistics show that three out of four new companies will still be operating. Business failure is commonly caused by limited cash, poor management decisions, and a weak economy.

GLOBAL BUSINESS EXAMPLE

STREET ENTREPRENEURS IN LATIN AMERICA

In Brazil, *feiras* provide a wide variety of healthy, fresh produce within walking distance of home. *Tianguis* are pushcarts that meet the personal service needs of consumers in Mexico. These local entrepreneurs have an ability to be where the customers are giving these informal retailers a competitive advantage over other types of stores.

Informal businesses and retailers are common in Latin America. These businesses include pushcarts, temporary street stands, and peddlers on foot, as well as unregistered offices, shops, and factories in homes and other locations. In Mexico, the number of street-vendor stalls is estimated at over 450,000. In Peru, an estimated 40 percent of the GDP occurs in the informal market. Throughout Latin America, this informal economy can represent between 40 and 60 percent of business activities.

While street vendors may post prices in writing, these informal retailers commonly "deal" with both regular customers and tourists. These negotiated prices can benefit the needs of low-income community members.

Think Critically

1. What economic and social factors cause a person to become a street entrepreneur?
2. What are the benefits and drawbacks of street entrepreneurs for a country?

©Getty Images/PhotoDisc

QUALITIES OF SUCCESSFUL ENTREPRENEURS

What are successful entrepreneurs like? Most entrepreneurs have a desire for adventure. They are risk takers who are willing to give up a secure job in exchange for the chance to own and operate a business. Global entrepreneurs must consider the added risk of potential cultural, social, political, and legal barriers.

©Getty Images/PhotoDisc

Is there some activity you participate in and perform well? Being self-confident is another quality of successful entrepreneurs. Successful entrepreneurs believe in themselves and believe they can get others to get things done. Remember that it may mean getting things done in different ways in foreign markets. People in different cultures have different attitudes and behaviors regarding work and business relationships.

Entrepreneurs spend almost all their time either on the job or thinking about their business. Hard-working people have the potential for being the most successful. Are you someone who is willing to put in extra time and effort for your business?

Someone once said that if you don't know where you are going, you might end up somewhere else and not even know it. A goal-oriented person has a clear direction for the company, stated in the business plan. Goals should be clear and realistic. Goals also should have a time limit for achievement and should be measurable in some numeric way. For example, a business goal may be to have ten new customers in Greece within the next three months.

A new product idea or an old idea presented in a new way can both be paths for entrepreneurial success. Creativity is a key to entrepreneurial success. Think about ways that existing products can be improved, or create a business that can make the lives of busy people a little easier.

Finally, knowing about the world of business is important for success as an entrepreneur. Business knowledge involves having an understanding of economics, organizational structure, decision making, selling, advertising, finance, and technology. Business knowledge for the global entrepreneur should include information about foreign cultures, exchange rates, shipping methods, product labeling, and more.

✓CheckPoint

What are the main characteristics of a successful entrepreneur?

CREATING A BUSINESS PLAN

Before you start any business, you should first develop a business plan. This document will guide you through the complex process of establishing, financing, and running a business.

THE BUSINESS PLAN

Every driver planning a trip, every team, and every company needs a plan to achieve its goal. A **business plan** is a guide used to start and operate a business. Every small business needs a plan to guide it to success. A business plan has two main uses. First, this document may be used to attract new investors or to convince a bank to lend money to the company. Second, the business plan provides a blueprint for company activities.

THE PARTS OF A BUSINESS PLAN

1. **Business description**
2. **Organizational structure**
3. **Marketing activities**
4. **Financial planning**
5. **Production activities**
6. **Human resource activities**
7. **Information needs**

Figure 9-2 A business plan is designed to help a manager organize business activities.

A business plan includes the seven main sections shown in Figure 9-2. The first three sections—the business description, the organizational structure, and the marketing activities—are all related to setting up a business.

Business Description The introductory section of a business plan covers three topics. First, the legal name and location of the company is identified. Second, a brief description of the background and experience of the owners and main employees is provided. Third, a description of the company's product or service, potential customers, and competition is presented.

Organizational Structure Most businesses are organized as sole proprietorships, partnerships, or corporations. A company's organizational structure, covered in the second section of the business plan, will be based on its size, number of owners, and method of financing. Companies involved in international trade and exporting would present information about their foreign business partners. This section would include an explanation of any joint ventures, licensing agreements, distributor contracts, and supplier relationships.

Marketing Activities Two vital activities for every business, communicating with and serving customers, are discussed in the third section of the business plan. **Marketing** includes the business activities necessary to get goods and services from the producer to the consumer. Marketing activities include product or service planning, risk management, marketing information management, promotion, pricing, financing, distribution, purchasing, and selling.

REGIONAL PERSPECTIVE

GEOGRAPHY:
AN UNCERTAIN FUTURE
FOR THE WILDLIFE OF INDIA

Their neighbors include crocodiles, leopards, rhinoceroses, tigers, and musk deer. The people in India share their land with more varieties of wildlife than any other nation. The country has over 400 national parks and sanctuaries to preserve these natural wonders. Despite protected areas, however, many species still face extinction.

©Getty Images/PhotoDisc

Hunting and killing for food, animal skins, horns, and tusks result in vanishing breeds. Cutting down trees for firewood and using natural vegetation to feed livestock also threaten these endangered animals. Many species of wildlife no longer have the habitat necessary for survival. In recent years, the country had 140 animals on its list of endangered species.

As the second most populous nation in the world, India's diminishing resources are already stretched to an extreme. Tree planting and other conservation activities may help. Only time will tell if these efforts will allow for the survival of such animals as the jackal, Asiatic lion, and a tiny bird known as the Himalayan monal.

Think Critically

1. Conduct an Internet search for current information about the wildlife of India.
2. How could the extinction of various animal species affect the economic environment of a country?

Many companies organize this phase of their business with a marketing plan. A **marketing plan** is a document that details the marketing activities of an organization. A marketing plan includes information about customer needs, social factors, competition, target markets, economic trends, the political environment, and the marketing mix. Global marketing for companies involved in exporting and other international business activities will also take into account the geography, history, culture, and trade barriers of other countries.

CheckPoint

What are the first three sections of a business plan?

REVIEW GLOBAL BUSINESS TERMS

Define each of the following terms.

1. business plan
2. marketing
3. marketing plan

REVIEW GLOBAL BUSINESS CONCEPTS

4. What are the advantages of owning your own business? What are the disadvantages?

5. What are the two main uses of a business plan?

6. What kinds of marketing activities should be included in a marketing plan?

SOLVE GLOBAL BUSINESS PROBLEMS

Answer the following questions. If you answer "yes" to most of the questions, you probably would enjoy being a small business owner.

7. Are you comfortable making decisions even when others might not agree?

8. Do you have leadership ability? Are you respected as a leader?

9. Do you complete tasks without becoming discouraged?

10. Are you able to assess situations from different viewpoints?

11. Can you clearly communicate your ideas both orally and in writing?

12. Are you able to start a project without encouragement from others?

13. Are there situations in which a failure helped you to learn and improve?

14. Are you willing to do tasks that are necessary but unpleasant?

THINK CRITICALLY

15. Describe hobbies and activities that might be useful when preparing to be an entrepreneur.

16. In what ways would an entrepreneur use a business plan?

MAKE CONNECTIONS

17. **TECHNOLOGY** Use the outline feature of a word processing software package to outline the first three sections of a business plan.

18. **STATISTICS** Use the *U.S. Statistical Abstract* or a similar publication from the library or an Internet search to explore data about the number of companies, their size, number of employees, form or organization, percentage of small businesses in particular industries, and other statistical data. Create a bar graph or pie chart for one type of data.

OPERATING AN ENTREPRENEURIAL ENTERPRISE

9-3 GOALS

- Outline the process of financing a small business.
- Identify the major business activities of a small business manager.

©Getty Images/PhotoDisc

FINANCING A SMALL BUSINESS

The most important part of the business plan may be the financial planning section. Money is needed for many purposes when starting and running a business. Funds are needed to buy advertising, to pay employees, to purchase supplies, and to acquire equipment. A **budget** is a financial tool that estimates a company's funds and its plan for spending those funds. One of the most common causes of business failure is lack of money to pay company expenses. Constantly changing exchange rates are an additional problem for small companies involved in international business. The process of financing a business starts with calculating operating costs and determining how to acquire the funds to pay those costs.

ANALYZING COSTS

One of the most difficult tasks when starting a new business is determining how much money will be needed to get started and continue operations. *Start-up costs* are those expenses that occur when a company is new. Start-up costs include equipment purchases, remodeling costs, legal fees, utility company deposits, and beginning inventory expenses.

Continuing expenses are business operating costs that occur on an on-going basis. Continuing expenses include rent, utilities, insurance, salaries, advertising costs, employee training costs, taxes, and interest on loans.

Variable costs are business expenses that change in proportion to the level of production. For example, the cost of materials and parts to make radios

WORK AS A GROUP

Select a type of business. Prepare a list of variable and fixed costs that would be necessary for this business to operate.

depends on the number of radios that are produced. If parts and materials cost $8 per radio, the variable costs for making 100 radios would be $800. The variable costs for making 10 radios would be $80.

Fixed costs are expenses that do not change as the level of production changes. For example, rent of $1,000 a month and a manager's salary of $3,200 a month will be the same whether the company makes 10 or 100 radios.

BREAKEVEN POINT

A comparison of variable and fixed costs with sales revenue will tell a company the amount of profit or loss. The **breakeven point** is the number of units a business must sell to make a profit of zero. Sales below the breakeven point will result in a loss for a business. Sales above the breakeven point will result in a profit for a business.

THE PARTS OF A BUSINESS PLAN

1. Business description
2. Organizational structure
3. Marketing activities
4. **Financial planning**
5. Production activities
6. Human resources activities
7. Information needs

Figure 9-3 The most important part of the business plan may be the financial planning section.

Calculating the breakeven point involves two steps. First, you must find the **gross profit** on each item you sell. The gross profit, or gross margin, is the difference between the cost of an item for a business and the price for which the business can sell that item. For example, a company can make a radio for $8 and then sell it for $12. So the gross profit on one radio is $4.

$$\text{Cost} \;-\; \text{Selling price} \;=\; \text{Gross profit per unit}$$
$$\$12 \;-\; \$8 \;=\; \$4$$

Next, you must calculate how many items you must sell to cover all the fixed costs for a business, the breakeven point. To do this, you divide the total fixed costs for a business by the gross profit per unit. In the example above, the manufacturer has fixed costs of $44,000. That company must then sell 11,000 units to cover all its fixed costs.

$$\text{Total fixed costs} \;\div\; \text{Profit per unit} \;=\; \text{Breakeven units}$$
$$\$44,000 \;\div\; \$4 \text{ per unit} \;=\; 11,000 \text{ units}$$

At the breakeven point of 11,000 units, costs are covered but no profit is earned.

SOURCES OF FUNDS

Where do companies get the money to finance the start-up costs and continuing expenses? This funding can be secured in one of two ways, either through equity or through debt. **Equity funds** are business funds obtained from the owners of the business. Equity is the money the owners of a business have invested from their personal accounts.

Debt funds are business funds obtained by borrowing. The amounts owed by a business are called the debts of the company. Loans from financial institutions also help to finance companies and are debt funds.

FINANCIAL RECORDS OF SMALL BUSINESSES

The financial records of a company are like the scoreboard for a sporting event. Financial record keeping helps a business keep track of its financial status, just like a scoreboard helps fans keep track of how the teams on the field are doing. A **balance sheet** is the document that reports a company's *assets* (items of value), *liabilities* (amounts owed to others), and *owner's equity* (net worth). Assets include cash and anything that could be sold for cash, such as equipment, land, and inventory. The relationship among the items on a balance sheet is

$$\text{Assets} - \text{Liabilities} = \text{Owner's equity}$$

For example, if a company has $4 million of assets and $1.5 million in liabilities, the owner's equity is $2.5 million.

$$\$4 \text{ million} - \$1.5 \text{ million} = \$2.5 \text{ million}$$

An **income statement** is a document that summarizes a company's revenue from sales and its expenses over a period of time, usually one year. On the income statement, a business will total all of the revenues it brings in as well as all of its expenses. It will then subtract the expenses from the revenues to find its profit or loss. For example, a company had sales revenue of $670,000 and $430,000 in operating expenses. Its profit would be $240,000.

$$\text{Sales revenue} - \text{Operating expenses} = \text{Profit}$$
$$\$670,000 - \$430,000 = \$240,000$$

The continuing costs of a business are usually paid for with current cash flows. **Cash flow** is the inflow and outflow of cash. The major sources of *cash inflows* are cash sales and money collected from customers that is owed on account. Occasionally, a company will require additional cash inflows due to slow sales or a need to buy expensive equipment. When this happens, the business will need to borrow or get additional investments from owners.

The main *cash outflows* of a business are for current operating expenses, new equipment, debt payments, and taxes. A *cash flow statement* reports the current sources and amounts of cash inflows and outflows. Weak cash inflows are a major cause of small business failure.

©Getty Images/PhotoDisc

✓ CheckPoint

How does a balance sheet differ from an income statement?

MANAGING THE SMALL BUSINESS

In a large company, a manager is usually responsible for only one area of the business, such as marketing or finance. In a small business, however, the owner may be responsible for several or all areas of management. The five major management areas of every business are shown in Figure 9-4. These areas, along with a description of the business and the organization of the business, are all covered in the business plan.

MAJOR ACTIVITIES OF EVERY BUSINESS

| Marketing | Finance | Production | Human Resources | Information Systems |

Figure 9-4 Every company has five major management areas.

PRODUCTION MANAGEMENT

The factors of production are combined to create goods and services. Every business must produce something to sell. That something may not always be too obvious. For example, what does a school produce? Or what does a retail store produce?

The production department of a company may involve a factory with machinery or an office with computers. In both situations, production takes place. Production methods are influenced by the cultural and economic situation of a nation. A country with few machines will use more manual activities than automated methods.

HUMAN RESOURCES MANAGEMENT

Labor is probably the most important factor of production. Without people, highly automated equipment could not be built, operated, or repaired. Every business owner and manager must recognize this fact. Human resources are

THE PARTS OF A BUSINESS PLAN

1. Business description
2. Organizational structure
3. Marketing activities
4. Financial planning
5. Production activities
6. Human resources activities
7. Information needs

Figure 9-5 The management areas of a business are all covered in the business plan.

GLOBAL BUSINESS EXAMPLE

FINANCING WOMEN ENTREPRENEURS IN NIGER

Guy Roget, a mother of nine, is a Muslim in Niger. According to religious and cultural tradition, she should not work outside the home. However, her family has very little income.

Niger, in Central Africa, has a population of about 10 million with desert covering two-thirds of the country. In recent years, Niger faced economic difficulties because of a decline in the world price for the country's main export, uranium. Political unrest also contributed to the economic instability. Niger has a per capita GDP of less than $850.

Guy Roget worked to improve economic conditions in her community. She helped start a women's organization. The group's members contribute to a fund from which they borrow to start small businesses.

Guy started her enterprise by selling seasonings on the street and eventually was able to save enough to acquire a tiny grocery store. Other women in the capital city of Niamey are involved in raising cattle, growing vegetables, collecting firewood, making pottery, and weaving brightly patterned traditional fabrics.

Think Critically

1. How do geographic and political factors influence business opportunities?
2. In what ways can community organizations encourage new business enterprises?

one of the most important components of every organization. Human resources management involves activities needed to obtain, train, and retain qualified employees.

First, a human resources manager must hire needed employees. A description that lists the qualifications for a job is advertised to prospective employees. Hiring involves screening applicants, interviewing candidates, and selecting the most qualified people for available positions.

A second major duty of human resources managers is training employees. Training does not occur only when a person starts a job. It is a continuous process. Technology, the economy, and legal rulings often have an effect on the job skills employees need in order to be productive. Continued training is important for all workers.

The final duty of human resources managers is to maintain employee satisfaction. Workers must be paid adequately so they do not become discouraged or leave the company. Most businesses also provide employee benefits such as paid holidays and vacations, medical insurance, retirement plans, and discounts for company products. Human resources managers also motivate employees with awards, bonuses, and prizes for productivity, customer service, safety, and ideas that save the company money.

©Getty Images/PhotoDisc

INFORMATION MANAGEMENT

Information is something companies have always needed but usually didn't think about too much. In recent years, computers and other technology have made information easier, faster, and cheaper to obtain. The main areas of information needed by every business include data about finances, production and inventory, marketing, and human resources.

A *management information system (MIS)* is an organized method of processing and reporting data for business decisions. An MIS involves a plan for all of the following.

1. Identifying a company's information needs

2. Obtaining the information

3. Organizing the information in a useful manner

4. Distributing reports to those who make decisions

5. Updating data files as needed

Management information systems have created many new career opportunities: computer operators, programmers, systems analysts, database managers, computer service technicians, and information systems managers.

©Getty Images/PhotoDisc

Communication Across Borders

CHOOSING A COMPANY LANGUAGE

Sooner or later every business must choose one or more designated company languages to facilitate communication among its employees, suppliers, customers, owners, and regulatory agencies. As the business grows domestically and internationally, the language choice becomes more critical.

A very small business in India could use any one of more than 700 local languages. If it operates within one region of India, it might choose one of 15 governmentally recognized regional languages. If it operates throughout India, it might choose one of the official languages of the country, Hindi or English, which are spoken by less than one-third of the population. As the business spreads beyond India, it will probably choose English as the designated company language if it hasn't already done so. Choosing English will allow international businesses to communicate in many countries around the world since most international businesspersons speak English as either a first or second language.

Think Critically

1. Why might choosing an official company language be more challenging for a very small business in rural India than for a very small business in rural United States?

2. Why would a business have two or more official languages?

✔ CheckPoint

What activities does human resources management involve?

REVIEW GLOBAL BUSINESS TERMS

Define each of the following terms.

1. budget
2. variable costs
3. fixed costs
4. breakeven point
5. gross profit
6. equity funds
7. debt funds
8. balance sheet
9. income statement
10. cash flow

REVIEW GLOBAL BUSINESS CONCEPTS

11. How do variable costs differ from fixed costs?
12. What are the three major activities of human resources management?
13. What is a management information system?

SOLVE GLOBAL BUSINESS PROBLEMS

Indicate whether each of the following business activities would be the responsibility of a marketing, finance, production, human resources, or information systems manager.

14. Checking quality control of finished goods.
15. Monitoring information records on salaries and vacation time.
16. Creating a system to provide data for decision making.
17. Recommending advertising activities for the company.
18. Coordinating parts and supplies for the assembly line.
19. Projecting the organization's cash inflows and outflows.

THINK CRITICALLY

20. When expanding into another country, should a business use equity funds or debt funds? Explain your choice.
21. How could the culture of a country affect the duties of a human resources manager?

MAKE CONNECTIONS

22. **TECHNOLOGY** Find the web site of a major corporation that presents career opportunities in the organization. Find a job that appeals to you, and write a brief description of the job responsibilities.
23. **MATHEMATICS** Calculate the net income (or loss) of a company with $168,000 of sales revenue and $145,000 of operating expenses.
24. **MATHEMATICS** Calculate the breakeven point for a product selling for $5 with variable costs per unit of $3. Fixed costs are $38,000.

CHAPTER SUMMARY

9-1 ENTREPRENEURIAL ENTERPRISES

A Entrepreneurs are important in the development of an economy because they create new products and services, create new jobs, and provide personal service.

B The main types of entrepreneurial businesses are extracting companies, manufacturing companies, wholesalers, retailers, and service companies.

C Telecommuting involves using a computer and other technology to work at home instead of in a company office or factory.

9-2 THE BUSINESS PLAN AND SELF-EMPLOYMENT

A The advantages of self-employment as a career option are independence and pride of ownership. The disadvantages are the time commitment, uncertain income, and possible loss of investment.

B The first three sections of a business plan are the business description, organizational structure, and marketing activities.

9-3 OPERATING AN ENTREPRENEURIAL ENTERPRISE

A Financing a small business involves determining variable and fixed costs while obtaining the use of equity and debt funds.

B The major business activities of a small business manager involve marketing, finance, production, human resources, and information systems.

Read the Global Focus at the beginning of this chapter, and answer the following questions.

1. What factors may influence the continued success of Chahta Enterprise in the future?

2. What actions would you suggest for Chahta Enterprise to expand in the global economy?

REVIEW GLOBAL BUSINESS TERMS

Match the terms listed with the definitions.

1. Business funds obtained by borrowing.

2. Business expenses that change in proportion to the level of production.

3. Business funds obtained from the owners of the business.

4. An independently owned and operated business that does not dominate an industry.

5. The business activities necessary to get goods and services from the producer to the consumer.

6. A financial tool that estimates a company's funds and its plan for spending those funds.

7. A guide used to start and operate a business.

8. The document that reports a company's assets, liabilities, and owner's equity.

9. Expenses that do not change as the level of production changes.

10. A risk taker who operates a business.

11. The production level at which profit is zero.

12. The inflow and outflow of cash in a business.

13. Using a computer and other technology to work at home instead of in a company office or factory.

14. A document that details the marketing activities of an organization.

15. The document that summarizes a company's revenue from sales and its expenses over a period of time.

16. The difference between the cost of an item for a business and the price for which the business can sell that item.

a. balance sheet
b. breakeven point
c. budget
d. business plan
e. cash flow
f. debt funds
g. entrepreneur
h. equity funds
i. fixed costs
j. gross profit
k. income statement
l. marketing
m. marketing plan
n. small business
o. telecommuting
p. variable costs

MAKE GLOBAL BUSINESS DECISIONS

17. What are some problems in the world that might be solved by new products or services created by entrepreneurs?

18. Name some ways small businesses can provide personal service better than larger companies.

19. Why are wholesaling companies important to the business environment of a country?

20. Why do people give up secure jobs and start their own businesses?

21. Explain how a budget helps a business.

22. As a manager, how would you decide if you should let some employees work from their homes?

GLOBAL CONNECTIONS

23. GEOGRAPHY Conduct library research about entrepreneurial activities in other countries. Locate articles and other information about new businesses, the types of products and services they offer, and the problems they encounter. Prepare a short written or oral report about the influence of geographic factors on the success of entrepreneurs in various countries.

©Getty Images/PhotoDisc

24. COMMUNICATIONS Interview the owner of a small local company about the influences of international business on the firm's activities. How has the company's competition changed due to global business? Are any local companies owned or controlled by foreign corporations?

25. VISUAL ART Create a poster or bulletin board display with variable and fixed costs for different types of businesses. Use magazine photos or create drawings to show examples of these two types of business operating expenses.

26. CULTURAL STUDIES Talk to someone who has lived in or worked in another country. Obtain information about the types of small businesses operated by entrepreneurs in that nation. Ask how the accounting procedures and record-keeping activities used in that country differ from those in other countries.

27. SCIENCE Research recent technology to obtain information about a scientific development that could create new opportunities for home-based businesses.

28. MATHEMATICS A company sells shirts for $15. Each shirt has a variable cost of $9. The company has fixed costs of $7,200. What is the breakeven point for this business?

29. CAREER PLANNING Interview the owner of a small business who exports or sells imported products. Ask the entrepreneur about the skills needed to be successful in that type of business. What should a person learn in school to prepare for a career as an entrepreneur?

THE GLOBAL ENTREPRENEUR
CREATING AN INTERNATIONAL BUSINESS PLAN

STARTING YOUR OWN BUSINESS

Develop a plan for starting your international business based on the company you have been using in this continuing project, or create a new idea for your business. Make use of previously collected information, and do additional research. This phase of your business plan should include the following components.

1. General description of the company—list the name, location, and major international business activities of the company.

2. Organizational structure—(a) explain what type of organization (sole proprietorship, partnership, or corporation) the company uses; and (b) list foreign business partners (joint ventures, licensing agreements, distributor contracts, and supplier relationships).

3. Marketing activities—describe the company's customers, distribution systems, and advertising methods.

4. Financing activities—(a) estimate start-up costs, and (b) estimate sources of cash inflows and operating expenses for the company's global business activities.

5. Production activities—explain how the company obtains the products or services it sells.

6. Human resources activities—list the main types of jobs in the company and the general qualifications needed for these positions.

7. Information needs—describe financial, production and inventory, marketing, and human resources information needed by managers to make appropriate international business decisions.

©Getty Images/PhotoDisc

GLOBAL CROSS-CULTURAL TEAM PROJECT

Organize International Business Activities

When international enterprises begin operations in other countries, decisions related to organizing their business activities are needed. To gain a wider perspective for these decisions, companies frequently use cross-cultural teams.

GOAL

To organize international business activities using information from various regions of the world.

ACTIVITIES

Working in teams, select a geographic region you will represent—Africa, Asia, Europe, Latin America, Middle East, or North America.

1. Obtain information related to the major imports, exports, regional trade agreements, major currencies, and common legal systems in your region. Library materials, web research, and personal interviews are recommended.
2. List major imports and exports of several countries in your region. Explain why these items are commonly bought and sold by people in the region.
3. Identify the major currencies in the region. Research factors that might affect the value of these currencies. If possible, conduct an interview with a person who has visited this region to obtain information about the monetary system and shopping activities. What economic and political factors influence currency values in the region? How do these differ from factors in other regions?
4. Locate examples of laws that affect business activities and international business trade in your region. How do these compare with business regulations in other areas of the world?
5. Small businesses are important for jobs and economic growth in every country. List the common types of businesses of small organizations (less than 10 employees) in your region. What difficulties are commonly faced when starting or operating a small business in your region?
6. **Global Business Decision** You and your team are planning to start a new business. What type might have the greatest success in most regions? If your team could only locate the company in one region, which one would you select?

TEAM SKILL

Characteristics of Productive Teams

The measurement of a productive cross-cultural team can be influenced by the history, traditions, and culture of a region. Create a list of characteristics of a productive team. What items on the list differ for different regions?

PRESENT

- Prepare a summary report of your regional information.
- Make a 1-2 minute presentation to report a couple of key findings from your research and your simulated cross-cultural team experience.

Extemporaneous Speaking

Success in the business world depends on strong communication skills and the ability to make decisions within a limited time frame. Extemporaneous speaking provides you with the opportunity to analyze a situation or topic for a short amount of time and then present a speech to actual business leaders who determine the effectiveness of the communication.

Public speaking is enhanced by the confidence gained from experience. International business has numerous issues for possible speech topics. Some examples of international topics include the North American Free Trade Agreement, technology jobs transferring to India from the United States, illegal immigrants working in the United States, and trade barriers.

When participating in extemporaneous speaking, you will improve your chance for success by reading current international events and watching the news. Taking an international topic from the news and outlining the main points to highlight in a speech can help you gain valuable experience.

Tips to prepare for extemporaneous speaking include:

- Watch the news and read newspapers to keep up-to-date on the latest international events.
- Outline news items and strategies to solve different problems.
- Record personal experiences involving customer service and how businesses could handle situations more effectively.
- Network with business leaders who provide practice extemporaneous speeches.
- Enter competitions on the local, district, state, and national levels to increase confidence.
- Dress professionally to feel confident.

PERFORMANCE INDICATORS EVALUATED

- Understand immigration laws in the United States.
- Explain why U.S. companies hire illegal immigrants.
- Discuss the reasons why United States should be concerned about illegal workers.

For more detailed information about performance indicators, go to the BPA web site.

THINK CRITICALLY

United States has numerous illegal immigrants from Mexico working in construction, landscaping, agriculture, manufacturing, and food processing.
1. What should the U.S. policy be for these illegal immigrants? Why?
2. How will the policy be maintained?

www.bpa.org/

251

UNIT 3

MANAGING IN A GLOBAL ENVIRONMENT

REGIONAL PROFILE
EUROPE

In 1962, the press was there to record Peter Fechter as he was shot and killed by East German border guards when he tried to climb the Berlin Wall to freedom. He was one of 191 East Germans who lost their lives trying to escape to the West. But at midnight on November 9, 1989, an extraordinary event happened. The gates opened, thousands of East Germans rushed around and over the Berlin Wall, and the guns remained silent. Border police, who had previously been ordered to shoot anyone who went near the Wall, now lifted small children so they could set foot on the other side. The Wall had stood for 28 years as a symbol of the Cold War that had divided Europe and simultaneously imprisoned eastern Europe under the rule of the Soviet Union. Berliners from both sides were overwhelmed.

East Germans proclaimed the following with glee, "I don't feel like a prisoner anymore!" "This is the most marvelous moment of my entire life." "Everything we ever really wanted suddenly came true." "Knock it down."

And so they did. Within days, souvenir pieces of the Wall were turning up all over the world.

The Roman Empire

The nearly half century of Soviet dominance over eastern Europe was relatively brief when compared to the Romans, who controlled western and southern Europe for more than five centuries. They were able to subdue their neighbors with superior military forces. The Roman Empire forced people of different cultures to live together. It established local governments that took orders from Rome and created an economy that depended on roads, bridges, and public buildings.

©Ali Meyer/CORBIS

The Roman Emperor Constantine gave Christians freedom of religion in the year A.D. 313. By 392, Christianity had become the official religion of the Roman Empire, and it continued to strengthen its influence in Europe by making alliances between popes and various kings who ruled the continent. On December 25, 800, Charlemagne—a Frankish king who had conquered nearly all the Germanic lands—was attending church services at St. Peter's Cathedral in Rome when Pope Leo III placed a gold crown upon his head. The Pope proclaimed him Charles Augustus, "Emperor of the Romans." Charlemagne pretended to be surprised, but some evidence suggests that he and the Pope had planned this coronation after Charlemagne's armies had rescued the Pope from his enemies.

The newly crowned emperor expanded his empire until it stretched from the Danube River to the Atlantic, from Rome to the Baltic Sea. Those living within the empire who were not already Christians or Jews were forced to accept Christianity. They were also forced to accept all laws made at Charlemagne's capital at Aix-la-Chapelle (present day Aachen, Germany). These were diverse people who lived great distances from one another and spoke many different languages.

The task of controlling the empire was too great for Charlemagne's successors. After his death, the empire began to dissolve as local nobles regained power. This set the stage for a return to the political and economic system known as feudalism, which had preceded Charlemagne's empire.

The Byzantine Empire

At the same time that Charlemagne was building his empire, the Byzantines in southeastern Europe were fighting to control land on both sides of the Mediterranean Sea. The Byzantine Empire was the eastern portion of the Roman Empire, which survived after the western provinces and Italy were lost to the Germans. The empire was centered in Constantinople (present day Istanbul, Turkey), which was built on a point of land above the Bosporus Straits that separates Europe and Asia. Throughout history, Persians, Arabs, Russians, Europeans, and Turks have fought over this strategic location because it links the trade routes between Europe, the Middle East, Asia, and Africa.

Other Attempts to Control Europe

Later attempts to control the European continent were short-lived. Napoleon I, like Charlemagne, wanted to be crowned emperor by the Pope, who at that time was Pius VII. Unlike Charlemagne, however, the French Emperor called the Pope to Paris, where he took the crown from the Pope and crowned himself. By 1812, Napoleon controlled most of Europe. Nevertheless, his dreams were soon destroyed when most of his empire rebelled against him after his disastrous invasion of Russia.

Hitler's attempt to control Europe started World War II. His country house at Obersalzberg offered him a view of the Untersberg, where, legend has it, Charlemagne sleeps and from where he will return in glory. Hitler said it was no accident that his residence sat opposite this great emperor. By 1941, Hitler's armies occupied most of Europe, threatened England, and marched into Russia. Hitler committed the same mistake as Napoleon: He stranded his troops in the harsh Russian winter, and Soviet counter thrusts stopped the German advance.

Conflicts between Ethnic Groups

The many ethnic groups of eastern and southeastern Europe have lived side by side within empires for centuries. Many conflicts have resulted from their nationalistic interests in self-determination. Bulgaria, Greece, Montenegro, and Serbia declared war on Turkey in 1912 to free members of their nationalities from Turkish rule. In 1914, a Serb assassinated the Austrian Archduke Franz Ferdinand in support of Bosnian nationalism. This event helped begin World War I. When they sought greater freedom, the Hungarians (in 1956) and the Czechs (in 1968) were violently crushed by the Soviets, who dominated the region after World War II.

As the might of the Communist systems in the Soviet Union and eastern Europe crumbled in the late 1980s and early 1990s, some nationalist forces peacefully formed new governments. Others, such as those in the former Yugoslavia, began killing each other over historical hatred or current jealousy.

Europe's Contributions to Civilization

Although the history of this continent is heavily marked by wars and political repression, its writers, explorers, philosophers, scientists, and artists have created a world that is known as Western Civilization. The entire planet has been enriched by the likes of Homer and Plato, Chaucer and

©Getty Images/PhotoDisc

Shakespeare, Michelangelo and Renoir, Pasteur and Einstein, and Bach and the Beatles.

Europeans have contributed many things to the world, including self-government; the abolition of slavery; the first microscopes and telescopes; vital antiseptics and vaccines; theories of evolution and psychoanalysis; and initial discoveries in molecular physics, electricity, radioactivity, relativity, and rocketry.

The European Union

While strong nationalistic values continue to separate Europeans, another attempt to unify the region is in progress. The key players this time are not emperors and dictators with swords and tanks. Rather, they are economists armed with arguments about competition from the United States and Japan. The European Union has eliminated trade barriers among the member countries with a European Central Bank and a common European currency. The Treaty of Maastricht provides for a common European citizenship and European passports.

©Getty Images/PhotoDisc

Think Critically

1. Use the Internet and the library to research any nations in existence today that base their authority on a particular religion. Which nations base their authority on a religion? Do they have anything in common?

2. Do you think that a powerful nation should force people of different cultures to live together peacefully as one nation?

3. Europe has many ocean port cities and inland waterways. A number of countries have excellent railroad systems and highways as well. How does this affect trade among nations in Europe? How does it affect different cultures in Europe?

4. What effect do you think the European Union will have on the individual cultures within the member nations?

COUNTRY PROFILE/EUROPE

Country	Population		GDP		Exports	Imports	Monetary Unit	Inflation	Unemploy-ment	Life Expectancy	Literacy Rate
	thousands	growth rate	$billions	$ per capita	$billions			percent	percent	years	percent
Albania	3,166	0.68	14	4,500	0.31	1.33	Lek	6	30.0	72.37	86.5
Andorra	68	2.59	1.3	19,000	1.077	0.5	French Franc	4.3	0.0	83.49	100
Austria	8,116	0.05	226	27,700	66.9	68.2	Euro	1.8	4.8	78.17	98
Belarus	9,895	-0.45	84.8	8,200	7.26	8.06	Belarusian Rubel	42.8	2.1	68.43	99.6
Belgium	10,318	0.21	296.6	29,000	163	159.3	Euro	1.7	7.2	78.29	98
Bosnia and Herzegovina	3,964	1.13	7	1,800	1.1	3.1	Convertible Marka	3.5	40.0	72.29	N/A
Bulgaria	7,897	-0.85	50.6	6,600	5.11	6.7	Lev	5.9	18.0	71.8	98.6
Croatia	4,428	-0.19	38.9	8,800	4.75	8.76	Croatian Kuna	2.2	21.7	74.37	98.5
Czech Republic	10,236	-0.1	155.9	15,300	33.4	36.5	Koruna	0.6	9.8	75.18	99.9
Denmark	5,364	0.24	155.5	29,000	50.9	44	Danish Krone	2.3	5.1	77.1	100
Estonia	1,323	-1.1	15.2	10,900	3.34	4.13	Estonian Kroon	3.7	12.4	70.31	99.8
Finland	5,207	0.18	136.2	26,200	43	30.2	Euro	1.9	8.5	77.92	100
France	60,144	0.47	1,540	25,700	291	289	Euro	1.8	9.1	79.28	99
Germany	82,476	0.07	2,184	26,600	570	481	Euro	1.3	9.8	78.42	99
Greece	10,976	0.14	201.1	19,000	10.6	29.7	Euro	3.6	10.3	78.89	97.5
Hungary	9,877	-0.46	134.7	13,300	28.1	30.1	Forint	5.3	5.8	72.17	99.4
Iceland	290	0.79	7.7	27,100	1.9	2.38	Icelandic Krona	5.2	2.8	79.8	99.9
Ireland	3,956	1.12	111.3	28,500	78.4	48.4	Euro	4.6	4.3	77.35	98
Italy	57,423	-0.1	1.438	25,000	242.4	226.6	Euro	2.4	9.1	79.4	98.6
Latvia	2,307	-0.93	20	8,300	2.22	3.57	Latvian Lat	2	7.6	69.31	99.8
Liechtenstein	33	0.85	0.73	23,000	2.47	0.92	Swiss Franc	1	1.3	79.25	100
Lithuania	3,444	-0.58	29.2	8,400	4.89	6	Lithuanian Litas	0.8	12.5	69.6	99.6
Luxembourg	453	1.32	20	44,000	9	11.4	Euro	1.6	4.1	77.66	100
Macedonia	2,055	0.51	10	5,000	1.15	1.58	Macedonian Denar	1.1	37.0	74.49	N/A
Malta	394	0.42	7	17,000	2	2.5	Maltese Lira	2.4	7.0	78.43	92.8
Moldova	4,267	-0.11	11	3,000	0.57	0.22	Moldovan Leu	5.5	8.0	64.88	99.1
Monaco	32	0.92	0.87	27,000	N/A	N/A	Euro	N/A	3.1	79.27	N/A
Netherlands, The	16,149	0.5	434	26,900	202.9	183.1	Euro	3.4	3.0	78.74	99
Norway	4,533	0.43	143	31,800	59.7	33.7	Norwegian Krone	1.3	3.9	79.09	100
Poland	38,587	-0.08	368.1	9,500	41.7	49.3	Zloty	1.9	18.1	73.91	99.8
Portugal	10,062	0.13	182	18,000	25.8	38.8	Euro	3.7	4.7	76.35	93.3
Romania	22,334	-0.23	152.7	6,800	11.4	14.4	Leu	22.5	8.3	70.62	98.4
Russia	143,246	-0.57	1,270	8,800	101.6	53.8	Ruble	15	7.9	67.66	99.6
San Marino	28	0.99	0.94	34,600	N/A	N/A	Italian Lira	3.3	2.6	81.43	96
Serbia and Montenegro	10,527	-0.08	25.3	2,370	2.2	5.3	Yugoslav New Dinar	19	32.0	73.97	93
Slovakia	5,402	0.08	66	12,200	11.9	12.8	Koruna	3.3	17.2	74.43	N/A
Slovenia	1,984	-0.11	36	18,000	9.34	9.96	Tolar	7.4	11.0	75.51	99.7
Spain	41,060	0.21	828	20,700	117.6	149.1	Euro	3	11.3	79.23	97.9
Sweden	8,876	0.09	227.4	25,400	76.2	62.4	Swedish Krona	2.2	4.0	79.97	99
Switzerland	7,169	-0.05	231	31,700	95.8	94.3	Swiss Franc	0.5	1.9	79.99	99
Ukraine	48,523	-0.78	205	4,200	17.1	16.9	Hryvna	-1.2	3.8	66.5	99.7
United Kingdom	59,251	0.31	1,520	25,300	276	324	British Pound	2.1	5.2	78.16	99
Vatican City	1,000	1.2	N/A	N/A	N/A	N/A	Vatican Lira	N/A	N/A	N/A	N/A

N/A = Data not available.

©Getty Images/PhotoDisc

Chapter 10

MANAGEMENT PRINCIPLES IN ACTION

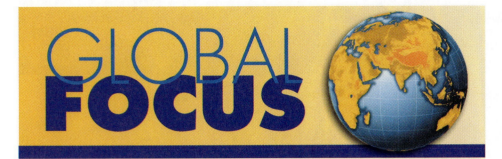

Virtual Corporations
Here Today and Gone Tomorrow

The virtual corporation offers some promising approaches to the tough facts of life in the global marketplace. Most companies can't react fast enough to take advantage of changing opportunities. By the time managers of giant companies get the necessary people and other resources ready, those opportunities have vanished. The managers of smaller companies often lack the influence and resources to respond to opportunities that are here today and gone tomorrow.

Managers who want to form virtual corporations must first identify what their company does best. Then they must form ties with other companies that represent "the best of the best." These fast-reacting, sharply focused, world-class competitors have the muscle and cutting-edge technology to pounce on short-term opportunities.

The U.S. film industry already functions in this way. Virtual corporations have replaced the old Hollywood studio system. Various industry talents temporarily link up for specific film projects before going their separate ways. Perhaps it's no small coincidence that the U.S. film industry has been very successful in the global marketplace. It is one of the biggest export successes for the country. Maybe Hollywood managers could teach other managers worldwide a lesson or two!

Think Critically

1. Why do virtual corporations exist?
2. What characteristic describes each component of a virtual corporation?
3. Go to the web site of MGM Motion Pictures, Paramount Motion Pictures, or Sony Pictures Entertainment to learn about the structure and management of the film company.

10-1 MANAGERS AND CULTURAL DIFFERENCES

GOALS

- Explain the characteristics of successful managers and how management styles vary.
- Understand the effects of cultural differences on a global workforce.

©Getty Images/PhotoDisc

MANAGERS IN ORGANIZATIONS

Managers are people in charge of organizations and their resources. They are men and women who assume responsibility for the administration of an organization. Managers work with and oversee employees to meet organizational goals in an ever-changing environment. They try to use the available resources for maximum gain, just as you try to use your time and money to derive the most desirable benefits.

Whether you realize it or not, you already have some managerial experience. You are in charge of and responsible for yourself. You are responsible for other people and things. You are also responsible for your textbooks, school supplies, and assigned homework. You may even be responsible for cleaning your own room or for maintaining your own car. Consequently, managing is not a totally foreign concept to you.

CHARACTERISTICS OF MANAGERS

Successful managers possess a wide variety of conceptual, technical, and interpersonal abilities. Supporting these abilities are certain skills and personal characteristics. One characteristic of managerial ability is leadership. Leadership is the ability to get others to follow. Another characteristic is the ability to communicate effectively. Managers must have strong writing, reading, listening, speaking, and presenting skills to be successful.

The ability to plan and organize is important. Managers must be able to use resources to achieve goals. They must be able to gather, analyze, and acquire information to solve problems. The ability to make decisions is also important.

©Getty Images/PhotoDisc

Managers must be able to take reasoned positions based on relevant information and to live with the consequences of the decisions.

Managers must be able to judge when they should be in charge and when they should delegate and allow others to be in charge. The ability to be objective is also useful. Managers need to know their strengths and weaknesses, as well as the strengths and weaknesses of others. Managers must be willing to lead others in new, untried directions and must be able to adapt to change. You might already possess a number of these important skills that influence managerial success.

STYLES OF MANAGERS

One way to examine managers is to look at how they use power or authority. There are three distinct types of management styles. These styles are *autocratic*, *participative*, and *free-rein*. These three styles can be placed along a continuum that represents managerial power or authority, as Figure 10-1 shows. Autocratic managers maximize their personal power or authority to control others. Free-rein managers minimize their personal power or authority to control others. Participative managers balance their personal power or authority to control others against the power people assume for themselves.

Autocratic Management Style Managers who centralize power and tell employees what to do are **autocratic managers**. They are authoritarian and rule with a heavy hand. The autocrat takes full authority and assumes full responsibility. If an autocratic manager uses power negatively, then the employees feel uninformed, insecure, and afraid. If an autocratic manager uses power positively, then rewards are distributed to those who comply. Sometimes the term "benevolent autocrat" is used to refer to an autocratic manager who uses power positively.

Most people do not work well under autocratic managers, especially negative ones. Autocratic management is considered an old-fashioned style of management and could be replaced by a more participative management style.

USE OF POWER OR AUTHORITY BY MANAGERS

Maximize — Power or Authority to Control Others → Minimize

| Autocratic Managers | Participative Managers | Free-Rein Managers |

Figure 10-1 Autocratic, participative, and free-rein managers use power or authority differently.

WORK AS A GROUP

Discuss how widespread beliefs, values, and assumptions within the culture of the United States influence the actions of managers in this country.

Participative Management Style Managers who decentralize power and share it with employees are **participative managers**. The manager and employees work together to achieve goals. Participative managers keep employees informed and encourage them to share ideas and suggestions. The participative manager uses group forces rather than power or authority to keep the unit operating effectively. For most managerial situations, the participative style is recommended.

Free-Rein Management Style Managers who avoid the use of power are **free-rein managers**. They let employees establish their own goals and monitor their own progress. Employees learn on their own and supply their own motivation. Managers exist primarily as contact persons for outsiders. Since free-rein management can lead to chaos in many situations, experts recommend that managers use it in circumstances where employees are self-disciplined and self-motivated and can make wise choices for themselves.

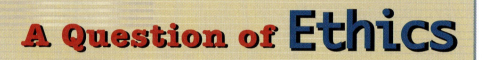

A Question of Ethics

SHARING CONFIDENTIAL INFORMATION

Geir Alver works for a Norwegian multinational corporation as a senior manager. His sister Gerd Grieg works for a competing company in a similar position. Since they work for rival organizations, they have mutually agreed never to discuss corporate business with each other. The two siblings enjoy a close personal relationship and see each other every two or three weeks.

Yesterday when Geir and his family were visiting Gerd and her family, their visit was interrupted by a long-distance telephone call from the New York headquarters of Gerd's employer. Although Gerd took the call in another room and closed the door behind her, the animated conversation spilled into the hallway and the nearby room where the others were finishing their desserts and beverages. As Geir walked down the hall to the kitchen with a stack of dishes a few minutes later, he over-

heard Gerd confirming privileged strategic information that would be very useful to his organization. Having that information could give his organization a competitive advantage over its American rival. Best of all, because his sister was not aware that he had overheard the information, she would never realize that she had inadvertently been the source of the leaked information. If he relayed the strategic information to top-level managers, Geir was certain that he would be rewarded with either money or a promotion—or maybe even both.

Think Critically

1. Since Geir and Gerd did not discuss the privileged information from the New York headquarters, did either of them engage in unethical behavior?
2. If you were Geir, what would you do with information you overheard from a rival corporation? Explain.

✓ CheckPoint

How do the styles of managers vary along a continuum?

INFLUENCES OF CULTURAL DIFFERENCES

Managers must remember that people's behaviors are shaped by their cultural backgrounds. Every culture and subculture has norms or standards for its members. However, certain members of cultural groups will deviate from those norms. People from different cultural backgrounds may not be alike even though they may appear to be similar on the surface. They may actually have very different beliefs, values, and assumptions. Consequently, managers must be very careful when managing people. Managers must be very sensitive to and respectful of cultural differences. They also must be aware that certain culturally based patterns of behavior exist and need to be considered.

Participation in Making Decisions For example, some cultural groups want subordinates to be actively involved in decision making. This is generally true for natives of the United States. In contrast, natives of Venezuela may prefer little or no role in decision making. They typically prefer to have managers tell them what to do.

Hiring Preferences Different cultural groups value different selection criteria for hiring employees. For example, natives of the United States tend to value job-related qualifications. Natives of Greece tend to value family membership or friendship above all other qualifications.

Permanence of Employment Attitudes about the permanence of employment vary among members of different cultural groups. Natives of the United States generally accept less employment security than natives of Japan. U.S. workers are frequently laid off during economic downturns and receive minimal company compensation. They also freely look for new opportunities with new companies. The Japanese are less mobile and until recently, expected lifetime employment from a company.

©Getty Images/PhotoDisc

Labor-Management Relationships U.S. laborers tend to have confrontational attitudes towards managers. They believe that confrontation brings about equitable work and rewarding relationships. By contrast, in Sweden many workers help to determine their work and rewarding relationships by serving on managerial boards. In general, U.S. managers are shaped by a culture and subcultures that value personal freedom, independence, and self-respect. Employees from other cultural groups—especially European and Asian—tend to view these values as selfish and insensitive. Such opposing cultural perspectives can lead to conflicts between managers and employees in the culturally diverse business world unless those differences are sensitively addressed.

NETBookmark

For a firsthand account of some of the issues facing cross-cultural workers, access the Indonesian Expatriate web site through intlbizxtra.swlearning.com. Click on the link for Chapter 10. Read the article entitled "Business Across Cultures" by George Whitfield. How can a multinational company avoid misunderstandings about what is acceptable behavior on the job? How could you, as a cross-cultural worker, avoid making an embarrassing mistake?

intlbizxtra.swlearning.com

While it is useful for managers to be aware of prevailing cultural preferences, they must realize that not all individuals fit their cultural molds. Consequently, managers must temper their understandings about cultural preferences. They must also consider the values, beliefs, and assumptions of the individuals involved. Managers who fail to consider individual differences and cultural norms will be less successful in the culturally diverse global business environment.

GLOBAL BUSINESS EXAMPLE

THE MANAGERS WHO REFUSED TO MAKE DECISIONS

As the new plant manager, Cynthia Hopkins, a U.S. citizen, was shocked during her first encounters with her local Panamanian managers. Guillermo, Maria, and Diego refused to participate in decision making, politely deferring to Cynthia's judgments instead. When Cynthia finally made decisions on her own for the managers, she noticed that they made good-faith efforts to implement those decisions. Cynthia was puzzled by their reactions involving decision making. Was there something wrong with her managerial style? Did the Panamanian managers resent being supervised by a foreigner?

When Cynthia mentioned her uncooperative decision makers to another Panamanian plant manager, she was surprised by the explanation she received. Most Panamanians, like many Latin Americans, come from cultural backgrounds that place little value on acting independently or as a consultant. A superior who seeks employees' opinions or encourages employees' decision making causes the employees to question the superior's decision-making abilities. When faced with the culturally unacceptable task of making decisions that they believed the plant manager should make, the Panamanian managers did not cooperate. To them, their participation in decision making undermined the role of the new plant manager.

Cynthia learned her lesson quickly. She tried to manage in a more culturally sensitive way. Rather than relying on participative U.S.-style management, she started making the decisions for her Panamanian supervisors. The employees were quite comfortable being told what to do. They carefully carried out Cynthia's decisions, and soon their working relationships with Cynthia became "muy simpático"—very congenial.

Think Critically

1. Why was Cynthia Hopkins unaware of Panamanian perspectives about the roles of managers?
2. Why did Guillermo, Maria, and Diego fail to make managerial decisions on their own?
3. What managerial style did Cynthia use that was effective with the Panamanian managers?
4. How could you find out more about Panamanian attitudes toward managerial styles?

✔ CheckPoint

How do cultural differences affect managers of a global workforce?

REVIEW GLOBAL BUSINESS TERMS

Define each of the following terms.

1. managers
2. autocratic managers
3. participative managers
4. free-rein managers

REVIEW GLOBAL BUSINESS CONCEPTS

5. What personal characteristic distinguishes among autocratic, participative, and free-rein managers?

6. What are four culturally influenced dimensions of behavior to which managers should be sensitive?

SOLVE GLOBAL BUSINESS PROBLEMS

"I have been managing the Bristol office of a global corporation for seven years. The office has an international workforce drawn from 18 countries on four continents. Every employee is highly competent in his or her specialty. Consequently, I have learned that I can rely on their judgments to a significant degree. I spend much of my time conferring with employees. Most decisions can be worked out by sharing our viewpoints, discussing the merits of those viewpoints, and selecting the best mutually agreeable viewpoints for implementation. It has been years since I have had to dictate the solutions to my employees."

7. Using a detailed map of the United Kingdom as a guide, describe the location of Bristol, the city in which the British manager works.

8. What is the British manager's prevailing management style?

9. What facts from the narrative support your conclusion about the management style?

THINK CRITICALLY

10. Why do managers often use a combination of autocratic, participative, and free-rein management styles?

11. How can managers increase their sensitivity to cultural differences?

MAKE CONNECTIONS

12. **TECHNOLOGY** How can technology help a manager monitor the work of subordinates?

13. **COMMUNICATIONS** Why is effective business communication considered to be the lifeblood of management?

14. **HISTORY** Why was autocratic management the dominant managerial style in the United States until well into the twentieth century?

15. **CULTURAL STUDIES** Use the Internet to find online cultural resources for international managers.

10-2

GOALS

- Describe the basic components of the process of managing.
- Differentiate between organizational structures based on function, product, and geography.

MANAGEMENT FUNCTIONS AND ORGANIZATION

©Getty Images/PhotoDisc

PROCESS OF MANAGING

The process of managing includes the following major components.

- Planning and decision making
- Organizing, staffing, and communicating
- Motivating and leading
- Controlling

These components are illustrated in Figure 10-2. The exact mix of these components varies depending on the type of managerial job and the people and other resources involved. However, sooner or later managers will be involved with all four broad managerial components.

PLANNING AND DECISION MAKING

Planning and decision making are important components of managing. Planning relates to setting goals or objectives to be attained. Planning is similar to deciding where you want to go. You have to know your destination before you can get there.

Once you decide the goal, you can explore different options or routes that lead to the goal. At various points along the way, you have choices to make. You should weigh the advantages and disadvantages of each alternative and select the best alternative overall. In other words, you should make thoughtful decisions.

THE MANAGERIAL PROCESS IN ACTION

©Getty Images/PhotoDisc

Figure 10-2 The managerial process includes planning and decision making; organizing, staffing, and communicating; motivating and leading; and controlling.

ORGANIZING, STAFFING, AND COMMUNICATING

Organizing, staffing, and communicating are also important components of managing. Organizing involves structuring business operations in logical and meaningful ways. Sometimes organizing relates to how business activities or functions are put together. Sometimes organizing involves assembling the necessary resources in a manner that facilitates the accomplishment of goals.

Staffing is the process of acquiring employees with the necessary knowledge, skills, and attitudes to fill the various positions in the organization. Communicating is interacting with people through verbal and nonverbal means. Communicating is a vital managerial task. An organization cannot function cohesively and reach its goals unless all employees give, receive, and share information in a timely and effective manner.

E-COMMERCE IN ACTION

Virtual Business Plans

Although BizPlanIt markets its online business planning services through its web site, it also provides a variety of free services. One particularly useful free service for managers is the detailed information about creating a virtual business plan.

The BizPlanIt web site has a link to Virtual BizPlan, which provides practical guidance for managers as they develop business plans. It identifies the different sections and what kinds of topics to address in each. It also identifies common errors to avoid when developing business plan sections. By following the guidance that is provided, even managers with limited experience can create sound business plans that will help their organizations prosper in the competitive world of global business.

Think Critically

1. Why is it good business strategy for the managers of BizPlanIt to include free information about business plans at the web site that promotes its services?
2. After viewing the Virtual BizPlan link would you feel comfortable writing a business plan? Why or why not?

▌MOTIVATING AND LEADING

Motivating is creating the desire to achieve. Managers realize that motivation comes from internal and external sources. Internal motivation comes from within the employee. The desire to perform work more efficiently is an example of internal motivation. External motivation comes from outside the employee. A salary increase is an example of external motivation.

Leading is getting employees to voluntarily pursue the goals of the organization. Managers who are effective leaders create a desire within employees to want to achieve what the organization sets out to achieve.

▌CONTROLLING

Controlling is regulating the operations of a business. It involves taking both preventive and corrective actions to keep business activities on track. Controlling helps to ensure that business operations are both efficient and productive. Activities such as verifying, adjusting, and testing seek to maximize output while minimizing input. For example, businesses have the accounting records audited by outsiders periodically as a preventive measure. This verifies the accuracy and truthfulness of the financial records. Some preventive actions that businesses may offer include substance abuse programs for afflicted employees. This helps troubled individuals return to productive status as workers and prevents the company from having to hire and train new employees.

✔ CheckPoint

What are the four major components of managing?

STRUCTURES OF ORGANIZATIONS

WORK AS A GROUP

Identify the ways employees communicate within an organization.

Businesses use various organizational structures to reach their goals. An **organizational chart** is a drawing that shows the structure of an organization. Line and staff are two types of positions. *Line positions* are managerial. Individuals with line positions have authority and responsibility over people and resources. *Staff positions* are nonmanagerial. Individuals with staff positions assist or advise those in line positions.

An organization can be either tall or flat. A tall organization is one that has many levels of management. One manager generally supervises a small number of employees. This results in more levels of managers. A flat organization is one that has few levels of management. Organizations are increasingly becoming flatter with fewer levels of management.

Businesses are commonly organized in one of three ways: by function, by product, or by geography.

ORGANIZATION BY FUNCTION

When a business is organized by function, the departments are determined by what people do. For example, in a sportswear manufacturing company, the function of the manufacturing department is to produce sportswear, the function of the sales department is to sell sportswear, and the function of the accounting department is to keep accurate financial records. Other functional groups might be linked together and given relevant departmental names, too. Figure 10-3 shows part of the organizational chart of a business organized by function.

ORGANIZATION BY FUNCTION

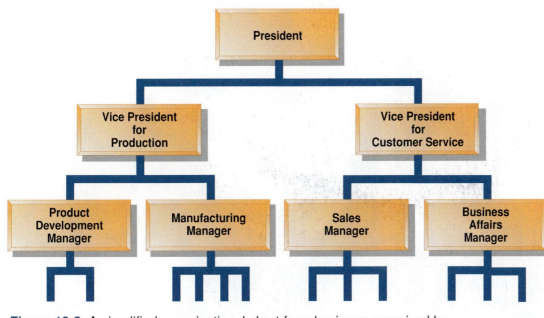

Figure 10-3 A simplified organizational chart for a business organized by function might look something like this.

ORGANIZATION BY PRODUCT

Another way to organize a business is by product. When a business organizes itself in this way, related products are grouped together to form departments. This type of organization is helpful when the product lines are very different. For example, a large manufacturing company that makes airplane parts and small consumer appliances may form two divisions. One division could be for the airplane parts, and it might be called the aviation parts division. Another division could be for the small consumer appliances, and it might be called the consumer small appliance division. Figure 10-4 shows part of the organizational chart of a business organized by product.

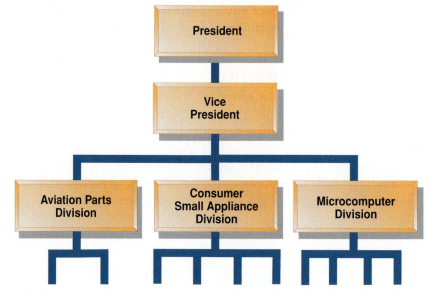

ORGANIZATION BY PRODUCT

President

Vice President

- Aviation Parts Division
- Consumer Small Appliance Division
- Microcomputer Division

Figure 10-4 This is a good example of a simplified organizational chart for a business organized by product.

©Getty Images/PhotoDisc

©Getty Images/PhotoDisc

ORGANIZATION BY GEOGRAPHY

Still another way to organize a business is by geography. When a business chooses this option, it organizes itself on some geographic basis. The geographic basis might be by city, county, state, region, country, or continent. Companies that operate beyond the borders of one country often use geographic organization, as do some domestic companies. For example, a global corporation may have North American, South American, European, African, and Asian divisions. Each division would specialize in business operations in its designated territory. Figure 10-5 shows part of the organizational chart of a business organized by geography.

ORGANIZATION BY GEOGRAPHY

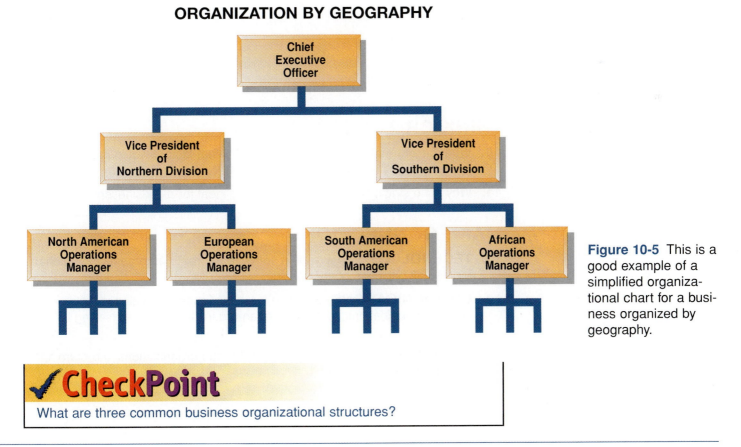

Figure 10-5 This is a good example of a simplified organizational chart for a business organized by geography.

CheckPoint

What are three common business organizational structures?

REVIEW GLOBAL BUSINESS TERMS

Define the following term.

1. organizational chart

REVIEW GLOBAL BUSINESS CONCEPTS

2. How do good managers decide how to achieve goals?

3. What is the difference between a line position and a staff position?

4. What is a tall organization?

SOLVE GLOBAL BUSINESS PROBLEMS

ChemVision Corporation is a research company that develops chemicals, processes, and medicines for various industries. Clients come to ChemVision with a problem to be solved, and ChemVision assembles a team to work on the problem. The company's central management personnel administer the human relations, sales, and accounting functions. Each team is headed by a research scientist. Scientists are recruited to a team based on their reputation, experience, and expertise; and the best-known is usually appointed to head the team. The scientists are personally motivated to make new discoveries to enhance their professional reputations. As a result, however, they each have their own agendas and jealously guard progress in their research. How well is ChemVision succeeding in the following processes of managing?

5. Planning

6. Staffing

7. Communicating

8. Motivating

9. Controlling

THINK CRITICALLY

10. What factors motivate you as a student? What factors would motivate you to perform well as an employee?

11. Why is no single organizational structure ideal for all businesses?

MAKE CONNECTIONS

12. **TECHNOLOGY** Use available software to create an organizational chart for a small business of your choice.

13. **COMMUNICATIONS** Describe a real or fictional situation in which poor communications could prevent an organization from achieving its goals.

14. **TECHNOLOGY** Use the Internet to find the organizational structure for an international business.

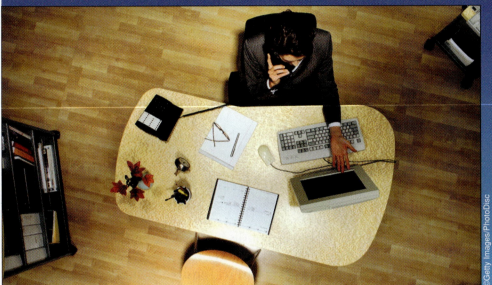

THE CHANGING PROCESS OF MANAGEMENT

10-3

GOALS

- Discuss factors that affect the levels of management in an organization.
- Describe the four stages through which a business passes to reach global status.
- Explain the differences between management today and the way it is expected to be in the future.

©Getty Images/PhotoDisc

LEVELS OF MANAGEMENT

All businesses have managers in charge of operations. The number of managers a business needs, the lines of authority that are established, and the delegation of responsibility all depend on the size of the business and the complexity of its operations.

SPAN OF CONTROL

The **span of control** is the number of employees a manager supervises. For example, a sole proprietorship is a business that has one owner-manager and may have limited operations. The owner-manager oversees and supervises all employees and business activities.

When the volume of business, the complexity of business, or the number of employees grows, one person may no longer be able to manage the business. If a sole proprietor sells half of the business to a partner, then that partner could manage some of the operations. This would reduce the span of control of the original sole proprietor.

As a business continues to expand, more managers are needed. **Front-line managers** are needed to oversee the day-to-day operations in specific departments. The front-line managers may report to a middle manager. **Middle managers** oversee the work and departments of a number of front-line managers. A number of middle managers may report to a senior manager. **Senior managers** oversee the work and departments of a number of middle managers. In a large business, senior managers report to the chief executive officer. The **chief executive officer (CEO)** is the highest manager within a company. Figure 10-6 shows the span of control of various levels of managers within a large organization.

LINES OF AUTHORITY

Regardless of the organizational structure and the number of levels of management, a business must establish clear lines of authority. **Lines of authority** indicate who is responsible to whom and for what. The need for having clear lines of authority grows as the business expands. When a business starts, there may be one owner-manager who is clearly in charge. The owner-manager has the authority or right to make all decisions. As the business expands and other managers are added, lines of authority must be clearly established. Otherwise, chaos results. Managers need to be aware of the specific area for which they are responsible. They also need to have a clear understanding of their relationship to other managers.

DELEGATION OF AUTHORITY AND RESPONSIBILITY

One important decision that managers must make relates to how much authority and responsibility they delegate or transfer to others. If managers retain too much authority and responsibility, they become autocratic. This may cause some employees to be rebellious because they feel powerless. If managers retain too little authority and responsibility, chaos develops. Employees who are not self-directed will have too much independence and more authority and responsibility than they can handle.

Figure 10-6 In this example, the president has a span of control of five, the vice president of marketing has a span of control of four, and the sales manager has a span of control of three.

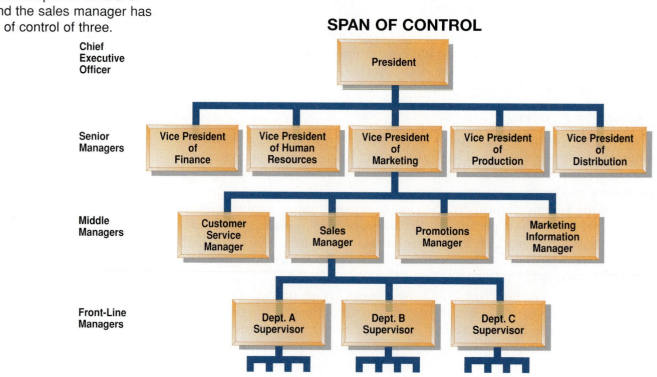

SPAN OF CONTROL

In most circumstances, managers try to balance the authority and responsibility between them and their employees. Participative managers share authority and responsibility with employees. They give employees some degree of freedom to determine and achieve goals with a corresponding degree of accountability for achieving those goals.

The amount of authority and responsibility that is delegated to employees or to organizational units is a reflection of the **degree of centralization** within an organization. If the authority and responsibility are tightly held by the managers and organizational units, then a centralized style of management results throughout the organization. If the authority and responsibility are widely distributed among many employees and organizational units, then a decentralized style of management results. Centralization of authority and responsibility tends to make organizations more autocratic. Decentralization of power and responsibility tends to make organizations more participative. Global organizations must decide how much authority and responsibility to grant to each of their organizational units and managers.

WORK AS A GROUP

Discuss reasons why centralization of authority tends to make organizations more autocratic while decentralization of authority tends to make organizations more participative.

✔ CheckPoint

How are the levels of management related to the span of control, the lines of authority, and the delegation of authority and responsibility?

EVOLUTION OF ORGANIZATIONS AND MANAGEMENT

As a business evolves from a domestic company into a global corporation, unique challenges are encountered. The managerial process must be adapted to meet the particular challenges at each stage. Managing becomes more complex and demanding as the business evolves into a global organization. The evolutionary process and related managerial dimensions of a company can be viewed as a series of stages.

▌ STAGE 1 DOMESTIC COMPANY

The first stage on the way to becoming a global corporation is being a domestic company. A domestic company is one that operates completely within the country of origin. Such a company uses domestic sources to create and sell its products and services. In other words, it acquires materials and sells goods and services in the country of origin. A domestic company has no business dealings with anyone except residents of the country. Consequently, a domestic company is the easiest type to manage. The basic managerial process in the country of origin can be used to resolve most of the challenges of a domestic business.

▌ STAGE 2 EXPORTING COMPANY

As a domestic company grows and becomes successful, it often begins to export, or sell abroad. A company that sells in other countries is known as an exporting company. An exporting company typically relies on its domestic competitive advantages as it expands abroad. Often the managers of an exporting company know little about the markets abroad. Consequently, an exporting company frequently uses independent agents or distributors who understand the markets abroad. This arrangement simplifies the management of the business. Most of the export-related problems are handled by the independent agents or distributors. This lets managers focus their primary attention on domestic operations. This stage allows the company to take advantage of foreign markets while not having to accept full responsibility for operating abroad.

STAGE 3 INTERNATIONAL CORPORATION

An international corporation, also known as a multinational corporation, creates and markets goods and services in both its country of origin and in other countries. The parent or founding company provides the international corporation with an organizational structure and operational strategy.

The local, national, or regional subsidiaries, or companies, of an international organization are usually responsible for decision making and customer service. They make decisions involving production, marketing strategy, sales and service, and the like. Often various subsidiaries of international corporations operate quite independently. An international corporation is like a group of interrelated companies operating in many countries.

The managerial skills needed in an international corporation vary widely. Those who

©Getty Images/PhotoDisc

DOBRISKI ENTERPRISES

Paulina Dobriski, an immigrant from Poland, founded a small business in the United States that manufactures Polish-style foods. Five years ago the products were sold only in the Chicago metropolitan area. Mrs. Dobriski and her family worked diligently at the business, and it has grown every year. Now Dobriski Enterprises exports food products to three countries. Within ten years, Dobriski Enterprises hopes to manufacture and sell food products on five continents. Mrs. Dobriski's children can then manage the subsidiaries

abroad. Within 20 years, Mrs. Dobriski and her family hope to dominate the production and sales of Polish-style food products through worldwide operations Then Paulina Dobriski will have reached her entrepreneurial goal, which is to own and manage her own global corporation.

Think Critically

1. Why did Dobriski Enterprises begin selling its products in the Chicago metropolitan area?
2. If things go as planned, how many years will it take Dobriski Enterprises to become a multinational corporation?
3. What will have to happen if Dobriski Enterprises changes from a multinational corporation to a global corporation?

manage from the parent company need broad managerial skills that cross countries. Managers at the local, national, and regional levels need more specialized skills adapted to their specific assignments.

STAGE 4 GLOBAL CORPORATION

A global corporation is an outgrowth of an international corporation. A global corporation operates so that country boundaries are not an obstacle to operations. It searches for the most efficient combinations of goods and services on a worldwide basis. It markets those goods and services with little or no regard for national boundaries. A global corporation is like a domestic company except that it buys and sells worldwide rather than within the country of origin.

©Getty Images/PhotoDisc

Those who manage in global corporations sometimes need broad managerial skills, since they operate on a worldwide basis. Many decisions require local-, national-, and regional-specific knowledge along with specialized managerial skills.

✔ CheckPoint

What are the stages through which a business passes to attain global status?

MANAGING NOW AND IN THE FUTURE

As business globalization increases, the role of the manager will change. The vision of the manager will shift from the domestic to the global marketplace. While today's managers predict the future based upon the past, tomorrow's managers will need insight into the future.

Managers of the future will not be content to be visionary; they will strive to facilitate the visionary development of others. Managers will shift from functioning alone to functioning as part of a team. While the managers of today enjoy the trust of boards and shareholders, the managers of tomorrow will need the trust of owners, customers, employees, suppliers, and governmental officials. Managers increasingly will meet the needs of the diverse groups to whom they are responsible. Rather than being monolingual and monocultural, as is often the case today, tomorrow's managers will be multilingual and multicultural. They will function like natives outside of their own cultures.

Successful global managers must develop and use global strategic skills. They must skillfully manage transition and change in a culturally diverse world. They must function effectively as team members while coping with changing organizational structures. Global managers will need outstanding communication skills—listening, speaking, reading, and writing skills. They must be able to acquire and transfer knowledge throughout the organization. Successful global managers must quickly adapt to the changing environment. What is your potential to be a manager in the ever changing global marketplace?

REGIONAL PERSPECTIVE

GEOGRAPHY:
VATICAN CITY—HEADQUARTERS OF A WORLDWIDE CHURCH

The world's smallest state, the State of Vatican City (Città del Vaticano), is the headquarters for one of the world's largest multinational organizations, the Roman Catholic Church. This independent state is completely surrounded by Rome, Italy. It consists of the Church of St. Peter (also known as the Vatican Basilica), the Vatican Apostolic Palace (with its world-famous museums and library), various administrative and ecclesiastical buildings, apartments, and the Vatican Gardens. About 109 acres (44 hectares) in size, the State of Vatican City has a population of nearly 1,000 persons who perform special services for the Holy See (the realm, seat of power, authority, and jurisdiction of the pope).

The State of Vatican City has its own symbols of nationhood—constitution, coinage, postal system, seal, and flag. It also has its own radio station and daily newspaper. It exchanges diplomatic representatives with other countries, but they have accreditation to and from the Holy See of the Church, not the State of Vatican City.

Legislative, executive, and judicial power are vested in the pope within Vatican City, but actual internal administration is handled by a governor and other officials. Public order is maintained by a small force of *gendarmes* (or police-soldiers), assisted, when necessary, by the Swiss Guards, the pope's personal regiment of soldiers. Primary judicial power is given to a local tribunal.

Think Critically
1. In what ways is Vatican City like and unlike most other states?
2. In what ways is Vatican City like a multinational corporation?

©Getty Images/PhotoDisc

✔ CheckPoint

How will management tomorrow be different from management today?

REVIEW GLOBAL BUSINESS TERMS

Define each of the following terms.

1. span of control
2. front-line manager
3. middle manager
4. senior manager
5. chief executive officer (CEO)
6. lines of authority
7. degree of centralization

REVIEW GLOBAL BUSINESS CONCEPTS

8. Why is the line of authority important regardless of the span of control?

9. What is degree of centralization, and how does it affect managerial styles?

10. What are the four stages through which a business passes on the way to achieving global status?

11. What is a visionary manager?

SOLVE GLOBAL BUSINESS PROBLEMS

Soltech, Inc., is a company that introduced a software package that manages the human resources function for large companies. The software is based on the U.S. tax structure and uses the English language. It can generate and manage job descriptions, performance appraisals, interns, and salary and benefit administration.

12. What stage is Soltech in now?

13. What stage is Soltech in if it tailors versions of the software for Germany and Japan and opens manufacturing facilities in those countries?

14. What stage is Soltech in if it expands into other kinds of software, with versions in numerous languages, and sells to all countries?

THINK CRITICALLY

15. What would a company do if its span of control at some level became too large to manage?

16. Why do organizations competing in the global marketplace tend to have a limited number of levels of management?

MAKING CONNECTIONS

17. **CULTURAL STUDIES** Choose a product with which you are familiar. Describe how the manufacturer could evolve from a Stage 1 company to a Stage 4 company.

18. **COMMUNICATIONS** Why does having a larger span of control increase the need for better communication within an organization?

CHAPTER SUMMARY

10-1 MANAGERS AND CULTURAL DIFFERENCES

A Managers, who are the people in charge of organizations and their resources, have characteristics and styles that vary.

B Managers must be sensitive to and respect the cultural differences within their businesses.

10-2 MANAGEMENT FUNCTIONS AND ORGANIZATION

A Managers engage in planning and decision making; organizing, staffing, and communicating; motivating and leading; and controlling.

B Organizations can be structured by function, product, or geography.

10-3 THE CHANGING PROCESS OF MANAGEMENT

A The levels of management are influenced by the span of control, lines of authority, and delegation of authority and responsibility.

B The evolution of a business through the domestic company, exporting company, international corporation, and global corporation stages affects its management.

C As globalization continues, the roles of managers will change.

GLOBAL REFOCUS

Read the case at the beginning of this chapter, and answer the following questions.

1. Why do you think the term *virtual corporation* was coined to describe temporary "best-of-everything" businesses?

2. Why do you think that the U.S. film industry has been quick to create virtual corporations.

3. What can managers of other businesses learn from the managers of virtual corporations?

4. Choose a recent U.S. film. Through Internet or library research or direct communication with the production and/or distribution company, investigate how the needed talents were brought together for the project. Determine whether or not the film project was the product of a virtual corporation.

REVIEW GLOBAL BUSINESS TERMS

Match the terms listed with the definitions.

1. Managers who decentralize power and share it with employees.

2. People in charge of organizations and their resources.

3. Managers who oversee the work and departments of a number of front-line managers.

4. Amount of authority and responsibility that is delegated to employees or to organizational units.

5. Managers who oversee the day-to-day operations in specific departments.

6. The highest manager within a company.

7. Managers who centralize power and tell employees what to do.

8. A drawing that shows the structure of an organization.

9. The number of employees a manager supervises.

10. Managers who oversee the work and departments of a number of middle managers.

11. Managers who avoid the use of power.

12. Indicates who is responsible to whom and for what.

a. autocratic managers
b. chief executive officer (CEO)
c. degree of centralization
d. free-rein managers
e. front-line managers
f. lines of authority
g. managers
h. middle managers
i. organizational chart
j. participative managers
k. senior managers
l. span of control

MAKE GLOBAL BUSINESS DECISIONS

13. Why is a participative manager likely to use autocratic and free-rein management on occasion?

14. Devise an analogy between a component of the management process and something that is familiar to you.

15. Draw an organizational chart that depicts the department of your school. What is the span of control for the head of the department?

16. What may the managers of a domestic company not know when their company decides to become an exporting company?

©Getty Images/PhotoDisc

17. Managers in the global environment must become leaders as learners. What does the expression "leaders as learners" mean, and why is it necessary to be a leader as learner in the global marketplace?

GLOBAL CONNECTIONS

18. TECHNOLOGY Describe how using scheduling software could contribute to the controlling process and success of an organization.

19. TECHNOLOGY As a manager, how can technology help you keep track of business operations abroad?

20. CULTURAL STUDIES How does the culture of the United States foster participative management?

21. COMMUNICATIONS How would a memorandum from an autocratic manager to employees about extended breaks differ from one from a free-rein manager?

22. GEOGRAPHY In what region(s) of Europe are most of the countries found that favor family and friendship rather than qualifications when hiring managers?

23. CAREER PLANNING How would you go about locating a book that addresses careers in management?

©Getty Images/PhotoDisc

THE GLOBAL
ENTREPRENEUR
CREATING AN INTERNATIONAL BUSINESS PLAN

IDENTIFYING MANAGEMENT SKILLS AND ORGANIZATIONAL STRUCTURE

Develop a management plan based on the company and country you have been using in this continuing project, or create a new idea for a business in the same or a different country. Make use of previously collected information, and do additional research. This phase of your business plan should include the following components.

1. What skills will managers need to adapt to the social and cultural environment of this country?
2. Describe the management style (autocratic, participatory, or free-reign) most appropriate for this organization.
3. Explain which type of organizational structure (function, product, or geography) would be most appropriate.
4. Which of the organization's activities will be centralized and which will be decentralized?
5. What other management and organizational decisions will need to be adapted for international business operations?

Prepare a written summary or present a short oral report (two or three minutes) of your findings.

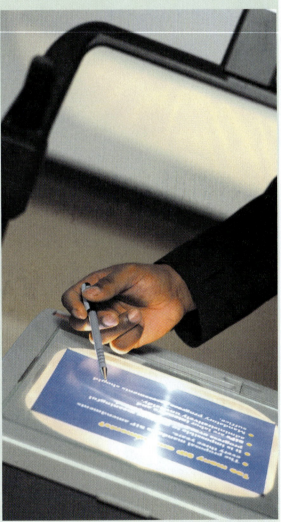
©Getty Images/PhotoDisc

©Getty Images/PhotoDisc

Chapter 11

HUMAN RESOURCES MANAGEMENT

GLOBAL FOCUS

I Want to Go Home

"Sue, we've got to go home! I can't stand living here any longer."

Two months after her transfer to the British office of her employer, Sue Smith (a U.S. citizen) was shocked by the earnestness of her husband's appeal. She replied, "But, Doug, we've been here only a short while. Coming here was a big promotion for me. My career is on the line."

"My sanity is on the line. You go off to work, and I have to stay here and fight the Revolutionary War all over. Everything is a battle. Nothing turns out as it should. Why did the contractor have to plaster over the existing telephone line when this apartment was remodeled? Why should it take four months to get a telephone installed?"

"But, Doug, . . ."

"I had to go to seven different shops to get the things for tonight's meal. Even if I had a car, there's no place to park! This tiny flat is four stories up in a building without an elevator. The refrigerator is so small it's like a toy. It takes two hours to launder four shirts in that washer-dryer. I'm not sure I made the right decision when I gave up my job in the United States. I've had it with this place."

Think Critically

1. Why do you think that Sue is not eager to abandon her international assignment and return to the United States?
2. Why do you think Doug wants to return to the United States immediately?
3. Go to the International Travel Planner section of the Worldwide Classroom web site. Select the Culture Shock guide to learn more about culture shock, reverse culture shock, and traits important to inter-cultural adjustment.

11-1 FOUNDATIONS OF HUMAN RESOURCES MANAGEMENT

GOALS

- Differentiate between host-country nationals, parent-country nationals, and third-country nationals.
- Define the four dominant human resources management approaches.

©Getty Images/PhotoDisc

GLOBAL HUMAN RESOURCE MANAGEMENT

Several factors contribute to the fact that human resources management is somewhat different in the global environment than in the domestic environment. One factor is the differences in worldwide labor markets. Each country has a different mix of workers, labor costs, and companies. Companies can choose the mix of human resources that is best for them. Another factor is differences in worker mobility. Various obstacles make it difficult or impossible to move workers from one country to another. These include physical, economic, legal, and cultural barriers.

Still another factor is managerial practices. Different business subcultures choose to manage their resources, including people, in different ways. When a company operates in more than one country, the problem of conflicting managerial practices increases. Yet another factor is the difference between national and global orientations. Companies aspire toward global approaches. However, getting workers to set aside their national approaches is challenging. A final factor is control. Managing diverse people in faraway places is more difficult than managing employees at home.

WHO MAKES UP THE LABOR MARKET?

Most companies obtain unskilled and semiskilled workers in local markets unless the supply is inadequate. **Host-country nationals**, or *locals,* are natives of the country in which they work. For skilled, technical, and managerial workers, companies have several options. They can sometimes hire these workers locally. In other cases, the companies must choose expatriates. **Expatriates** are people who live and work outside their native countries. Expatriates from the country in which their company is headquartered are called **parent-country nationals**, or *home-country nationals.* Expatriates from countries other than the home country of their company or the host country are called **third-country nationals**.

©Getty Images/PhotoDisc

Each company must balance the advantages and disadvantages of hiring each type of worker. Locals are usually culturally sensitive and easy to find, but they may not have the knowledge and skills needed by the foreign company. Parent-country nationals often have the needed knowledge and skills and sometimes have the desired company orientation, but they often lack the appropriate local language and cultural skills. Companies usually find parent-country nationals more costly to hire than other types of workers. Also, local laws could restrict employment of these parent-country nationals.

Third-country nationals could be more adaptable to local conditions than parent-country nationals. They may speak the local language and be able to make needed changes in culturally sensitive ways. In some cases, they could be more acceptable to locals than parent-country nationals. On the other hand, they may lack the desired company orientation. Regulations may make it difficult to hire them unless locals are unqualified. Selecting the best mix of employees from a variety of nationalities is challenging. Carrying out that mix in the global environment is even more challenging.

✓ CheckPoint

What types of workers make up the global labor market?

FOUR HUMAN RESOURCES MANAGEMENT APPROACHES

A company's approach to human resources management in the global environment is guided by its general approach to human resources management. Most global businesses adopt one of four basic approaches to human resources management. These approaches are ethnocentric, polycentric, regiocentric, and geocentric. The decision depends on several factors, such as governmental regulations and the size, structure, strategy, attitudes, and staffing of the company.

ETHNOCENTRIC APPROACH

The **ethnocentric approach** uses natives of the parent country of a business to fill key positions at home and abroad. This approach can be useful when new technology is being introduced into another country. It is also useful when prior experience is important. Sometimes less developed countries ask that companies transfer expertise and technology by using employees from the parent country to train and develop employees in the host country. The goal is to prepare host country employees to manage the business.

The ethnocentric approach has drawbacks. For example, it deprives local workers of the opportunity to fill key managerial positions. This could lower the morale and the productivity of local workers. Also, natives of the parent country might not be culturally sensitive enough to manage local workers well. These managers could make decisions that hurt the ability of the

Figure 11-1 The ethnocentric approach places natives of the home country of a business in key positions at home *and* abroad.

ETHNOCENTRIC APPROACH

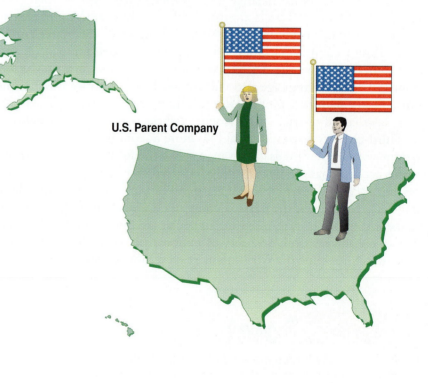

U.S. Parent Company

Mexican Subsidiary

company to operate abroad. Figure 11-1 illustrates the ethnocentric approach to human resources management.

POLYCENTRIC APPROACH

The **polycentric approach** uses natives of the host country to manage operations within their country and parent-country natives to manage at headquarters. In this situation, host country managers rarely advance to corporate headquarters as natives of the parent country are preferred by the company as managers at that level. This approach is advantageous since locals manage in the countries for which they are best prepared. It is also cheaper since locals, who require few, if any, incentives, are readily available and generally less expensive to hire than others. The polycentric approach is helpful in politically sensitive situations because the managers are culturally sensitive locals, not foreigners. Further, the polycentric approach allows for continuity of management.

The polycentric approach has several disadvantages. One disadvantage is the cultural gap between the subsidiary managers and the headquarters managers. If the gap is not bridged, the subsidiaries may function too independently. Another disadvantage is limited opportunities for advancement. Natives of the host countries can usually advance only within their subsidiaries, and parent-country natives can usually advance only within company headquarters. The result is that company decision makers at headquarters have little or no international experience. Nevertheless, their decisions have major effects on the subsidiaries. Figure 11-2 illustrates the polycentric approach to human resources management.

POLYCENTRIC APPROACH

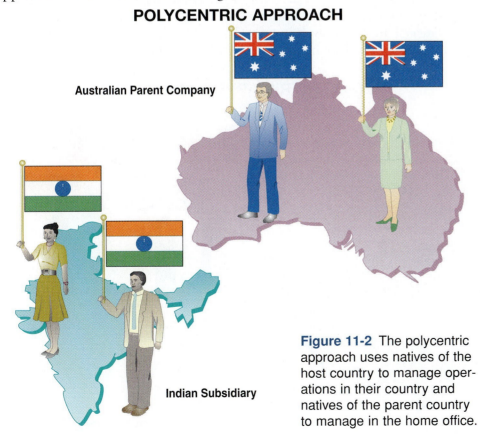

Australian Parent Company

Indian Subsidiary

Figure 11-2 The polycentric approach uses natives of the host country to manage operations in their country and natives of the parent country to manage in the home office.

REGIOCENTRIC APPROACH

The **regiocentric approach** uses managers from various countries within the geographic regions of a business. Although the managers operate relatively independently in the region, they are not normally moved to the company headquarters.

The regiocentric approach is adaptable to fit the company and product strategies. When regional expertise is needed, natives of the region are hired. If product knowledge is crucial, then parent-country nationals,who have ready access to corporate sources of information, can be brought in.

©Getty Images/PhotoDisc

One shortcoming of the regiocentric approach is that managers from the region may not understand the view of the managers at headquarters. Also, corporate headquarters may not employ enough managers with international experience. This could result in poor decisions. Figure 11-3 illustrates the regiocentric approach to human resources management.

Figure 11-3 The regiocentric approach places managers from various countries within geographic regions of a business.

REGIOCENTRIC APPROACH

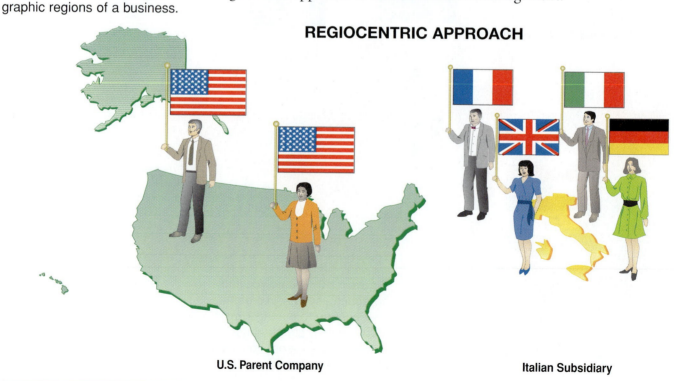

U.S. Parent Company

Italian Subsidiary

GEOCENTRIC APPROACH

The **geocentric approach** uses the best available managers without regard for their countries of origin. The geocentric company should have a worldwide strategy of business integration. The geocentric approach allows the development of international managers and reduces national biases.

On the other hand, the geocentric approach has to deal with the fact that most governments want businesses to hire employees from the host countries. Getting approval for non-natives to work in some countries is difficult, or even impossible. Implementing the geocentric approach is expensive. It requires substantial training and employee development and more relocation costs. It also requires more centralization of human resources management and longer lead times before employees can be transferred because of the complexities of worldwide operations. Figure 11-4 illustrates the geocentric approach to human resources management.

©Getty Images/PhotoDisc

Figure 11-4 The geocentric approach uses the best available managers for a business without regard for their country of origin.

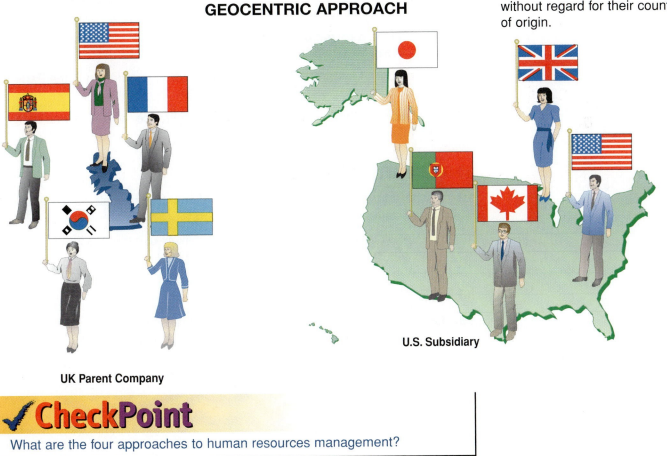

GEOCENTRIC APPROACH

UK Parent Company

U.S. Subsidiary

✓ CheckPoint

What are the four approaches to human resources management?

REVIEW GLOBAL BUSINESS TERMS

Define each of the following terms.

1. host-country nationals
2. expatriates
3. parent-country nationals
4. third-country nationals
5. ethnocentric approach
6. polycentric approach
7. regiocentric approach
8. geocentric approach

REVIEW GLOBAL BUSINESS CONCEPTS

9. Why is human resources management different in the global environment?
10. Which of the four human resources management approaches is usually the least expensive?
11. What are two disadvantages to the polycentric approach to human resources management?

SOLVE GLOBAL BUSINESS PROBLEMS

Xylex Corporation has its home office in Paris, France. Determine whether each of the following Xylex employees is a host-country national, parent-country national, or third-country national.

12. Theresa Ingram, computer programmer, is a French citizen working in the Brussels, Belgium, factory.
13. Julian Moya, a citizen of Mexico, was trained in the Paris office and now works in the Mexico City office.
14. London-born Margaret Harrison is the director of purchasing in the Paris office.
15. Guy Duclos is the national sales manager in France, where he was born and raised.

THINK CRITICALLY

16. In what situations might staffing with third-country nationals be preferable to staffing with parent-country nationals?
17. Why would a truly global corporation most likely use the geocentric approach to human resources management?

MAKE CONNECTIONS

18. **COMMUNICATIONS** Why is fluency in the local language an important consideration when hiring managers for overseas subsidiaries?
19. **LAW** How do the laws of other countries affect the process of selecting employees for international assignments?

SELECTING AND TRAINING STAFF

11-2

GOALS

- Explain how staffing needs are determined.
- Describe how potential employees are recruited.
- Describe three factors to consider when hiring job applicants.

©Getty Images/PhotoDisc

DETERMINING STAFFING NEEDS

A company must assess its staffing needs to compete successfully in the international market. **Employment forecasting** is estimating in advance the types and numbers of employees needed. **Supply analysis** is determining if there are sufficient types and numbers of employees available. Through selection or hiring and reduction or terminating processes, companies balance the demand for and supply of employees.

Once a company assesses its overall staffing needs, managers begin to fill individual jobs. A number of factors must be considered. What will the new employee be assigned to do? What are the qualifications that the employee will need? What is the best combination of technical abilities, personality traits, and environmental factors needed to ensure success?

When these types of questions are answered, specific job data are gathered. This includes information about assigned tasks; performance standards; responsibilities; and knowledge, skill, and experience requirements. From this information, a job description is prepared. A **job description** is a document that includes the job identification, job statement, job duties and responsibilities, and job specifications and requirements.

✓ CheckPoint

How does a company determine its staffing needs?

293

RECRUITING POTENTIAL EMPLOYEES

A company officially announces a job by circulating the job opening announcement and job description through appropriate channels. If someone already working for the company will fill the job, then internal channels will be used. The job information will be sent to all human resources offices within the company. These offices will post the information or notify company employees of the job availability in some other manner.

If someone who currently does not work for the company will fill the job, then different channels will be used. If a decision has been made to hire a parent-country national, then channels within the parent country will be used. If a host-country national will be hired, then channels in the host country will be utilized. If a third-country national will be hired, then channels in other countries that could provide suitable employees will be used.

The type of employee needed could influence the specific types of outlets selected. If an unskilled or semiskilled worker is needed, then a state government employment service or its overseas equivalent might be used. If a skilled, technical, or managerial worker is needed, then public and private outlets might be used. For unusual or high-ranking managerial positions, the company might employ a specialized recruitment firm known as a *headhunter*. Such a firm, sometimes for a substantial fee, locates one or more qualified applicants for the position.

GLOBAL BUSINESS EXAMPLE

IBM USES MODERN-DAY HEADHUNTERS

International Business Machines (IBM) raised corporate eyebrows a few years ago when it used two important headhunters (job placement firms) to find a replacement for John F. Akers, the chief executive officer. The prize assignment went to headhunters Gerald R. Roche, chairman of Heidrick & Struggles, and Thomas J. Neff, president of Spencer Stuart & Associates. Both men have placed many chief executive officers in major companies. IBM purposely chose two headhunters so they could broaden the field of candidates. For their services, Roche and Neff each received an estimated fee of between $400,000 and $500,000—one of the highest on record.

Think Critically

1. Why are job placement firms called corporate headhunters?
2. Why might IBM have been willing to hire two headhunters to secure a new chief executive officer, doubling its recruitment costs in the process?
3. Why do corporate headhunters usually refrain from recruiting employees they place and from hiring employees from a client company for two years?

✓CheckPoint

What factors affect how companies recruit potential employees?

SELECTING QUALIFIED EMPLOYEES

Companies that operate in the global environment use a variety of methods to select the best applicant. The best applicant is the person with the highest potential to meet the job expectations. Most companies use a combination of several selection methods, including careful examination of the applicant's past accomplishments, relevant tests, and interviews. In the process of screening applicants, companies are usually concerned about three major factors. These are competence, adaptability, and personal characteristics.

Competence The factor of competence relates to the ability to perform. Competence has a number of dimensions. One important dimension is technical knowledge. Is the applicant competent in the desired specialty areas? Another dimension is experience. Has the applicant performed similar or related tasks well in the past? For managerial positions, leadership and the ability to manage are important. Can the applicant work with others to accomplish goals? For positions in other countries, cultural awareness and language skills are critical. Does the applicant understand the region or market for which he or she would be responsible? Is the applicant able to communicate fluently in the local language?

Adaptability The factor of adaptability relates to the ability to adjust to different conditions. Possessing a serious interest in international business is necessary. Does the applicant really want to work abroad? The ability to relate to a wide variety of people is important, too. Does the applicant work effectively with diverse groups of people? The ability to empathize with others is needed. Can the applicant relate to the feelings, thoughts, and attitudes of those from other cultures? The appreciation of other managerial styles is also highly desirable. Can the applicant accept alternative managerial styles preferred by locals?

©Getty Images/PhotoDisc

The appreciation of various environmental constraints is needed, too. Does the applicant understand the dynamics of the complex environment in which international business is conducted? The ability of the applicant's family to adjust to another location is particularly important for international assignments. Can the family members cope with the challenges of living abroad?

Personal Characteristics The factor of personal characteristics has many dimensions. The maturity of the employee is one dimension. Is the applicant mature enough given the assignment and the culture in which the assignment will be undertaken? Another dimension is education. Does the applicant have a suitable educational level given the assignment and the location? In special circumstances, gender is a concern. Will the applicant's gender contribute toward or interfere with the ability to be successful in the working environment? In Saudi Arabia, for example, women are not business associates.

The social acceptability of the applicant should also be considered. What is the likelihood that the applicant will fit into the new work environment? Diplomacy is another trait to include. Is the applicant tactful in communicating, especially when unpleasant information is involved? General health is another consideration. Is the applicant healthy enough physically and mentally to withstand the rigors of the work assignment? The stability of the relationships within the family are important, too. Will the family be able to withstand the additional challenges of a new job—perhaps abroad?

As various applicants are screened, one attribute usually stands out. That fact is that no single applicant possesses the perfect combination of competence, adaptability, and personal characteristics. When this happens, the company will have to balance the strengths of the various applicants against their weaknesses. Overall, which applicant best matches the needs of the position? Which applicant has the greatest likelihood of being successful on the job? The answers to such questions result in the selection of the best-qualified individual to fill the job.

©Digital Vision

REGIONAL PERSPECTIVE

HISTORY:
THE MERCHANT-VENTURERS OF BRISTOL

Bristol, United Kingdom, 120 miles west of London, was once one of the world's major seaports. Yet Bristol is not on the coast. Medieval merchant-venturers from Bristol decided to build their docks and warehouses seven miles inland to protect them from pirates. To get to the port, early captains had to sail their ships up the treacherous Avon River, which rises and falls with nearly the highest tides in the world. Getting through the Severn Estuary and up the river to Bristol was tricky business. One major risk for captains and merchant-venturers was getting their ships stuck in the mud during low tides. Even ships berthed at the Bristol docks were in danger of being broken up by tidal surges.

In the early eighteenth century, this problem was solved when merchant-venturers had the Avon River channeled into a new location. This created a floating harbor with a constant water level. However, by then, much of the important transatlantic trade had shifted to other more accessible ports.

Bristol actually became an important port city in the eleventh century, when its merchant-venturers set out for fame and fortune. During the Middle Ages, its merchant-venturers became well known for their trade in wines. During the fifteenth century, the port of Bristol attracted adventuresome sailors bent on discovering new lands and better trading opportunities. For example, John Cabot, who was financed by a wealthy Bristol merchant in 1497, became the first well-documented European explorer to reach the North American mainland. Later, Bristol merchant-venturers helped to develop industry on the continent. They grew rich in the process by trading Virginia tobacco, West Indian sugar and rum, and other goods.

For that time, the merchant-venturers of Bristol were very shrewd. They traded throughout the world, accepting significant risks in return for the possibility of lucrative profits. The merchant-venturers of Bristol were among the first to realize the value of training and developing their workers, not just exploiting their labor. Consequently, as early as medieval times they began to offer instruction that improved the capabilities of their workers. Bristol merchant-venturers also built and supported almshouses that cared for the poor.

Think Critically

1. What was unusual about the seaport of Bristol?
2. How did Bristol merchant-venturers contribute to the economic development of North America?
3. Why do you think the merchant-venturers of Bristol provided employees with training and development?

©Getty Images/PhotoDisc

✓CheckPoint

What are the three major selection factors that most multinational companies use?

Xtra! Study Tools

intlbizxtra.swlearning.com

REVIEW GLOBAL BUSINESS TERMS

Define each of the following terms.

1. employment forecasting

2. supply analysis

3. job description

REVIEW GLOBAL BUSINESS CONCEPTS

4. What process is used to determine staffing needs?

5. How are potential employees recruited?

6. After the screening and interviewing process, how does a company choose the best applicant for a job?

SOLVE GLOBAL BUSINESS PROBLEMS

Mark Evans and Harold Daw are the two finalists for a managerial position in Milan. While Mr. Evans has seven years of management experience at three different sites in one region of the United States, Mr. Daw has seven years of comparable management experience at two sites in different regions. Both are adaptable and want international managerial experience. Mr. Evans speaks fluent Swedish, and Mr. Daw speaks fluent French. Both have similar personal characteristics except that Mr. Evans is divorced and has no children and Mr. Daw has a wife and a teenager who is a junior in high school. Mrs. Daw is currently employed, and the company cannot guarantee that Mrs. Daw can find suitable employment in Italy should her husband be selected for the overseas assignment.

7. Which finalist is better qualified in terms of competence? Why?

8. Which finalist is better qualified in terms of adaptability? Why?

9. Which finalist is better qualified in terms of personal qualifications? Why?

10. Whom would you select for the overseas assignment? Why?

THINK CRITICALLY

11. Why does a company use different methods of recruiting for different jobs?

12. Which of the employee selection factors of competence, adaptability, and personal characteristics is typically the most important one for an international employee? Why?

MAKE CONNECTIONS

13. **TECHNOLOGY** What kinds of technology-related skills do international employees need?

14. **CULTURAL STUDIES** How do family relationships influence the suitability of candidates for international assignments?

MAXIMIZATION OF HUMAN RESOURCES

11-3

GOALS

- Understand the importance of training and development for global employees.
- Identify the common types of training and development for international employees.
- Explain how training and development programs reduce the chance of employee failure.

©Getty Images/PhotoDisc

TRAINING AND DEVELOPMENT ARE CRITICAL

Employees can make or break an international business, just as they can make or break a domestic one. Their daily actions put the life of the company on the line. Consequently, companies need to be sure that all of their employees are well prepared for their work. This includes both lower-level and higher-level employees. Training and developing employees to work at their maximum potential are in the best interest of a company in the long run. Training and development are an investment in the future of the company. The better trained and developed the employees are, the greater the likelihood that the company will be successful.

TRAINING COSTS

Training and developing employees are major expenses for a company. Managers must decide what types of employees in which locations should receive specific types of training and development. These decisions are not easy. Because of limited resources, companies have to balance needs and potential benefits.

Historically many U.S.-based international companies have skimped on training and development. This has contributed to difficulties abroad.

Many of their employees have not been well prepared to compete in the global marketplace. Companies headquartered in other countries often invest extensively in training and development. In fact, some countries have laws that require companies to train and develop their employees. Such employees are often well prepared for work in the highly competitive global marketplace. U.S.-based international companies are realizing the value of providing more extensive training and development.

✓CheckPoint

Why are training and development so important for people working in other countries?

TYPES OF TRAINING AND DEVELOPMENT

Managers working for international companies need a variety of training and development, as illustrated in Figure 11-5.

Job-Related Issues Managers need training in job-related issues. For example, they need to be aware of the current economic, legal, and political environments. They need to be current on relevant governmental policies and regulations. Managers also need to be aware of managerial practices within their areas of responsibility. Current information about the company and its subsidiaries and their operations is needed, too.

Figure 11-5 International managers need job-related training, information about languages and relationships, extensive training in the host-country's culture, and spousal employment counseling.

TRAINING AND DEVELOPMENT

économiques
monnaie

Language and Relationship Issues

In addition, parent-country nationals and their families need training and development relating to relationships. At a minimum, they need to develop survival-skill knowledge in the local language before they are transferred abroad. Ideally, the manager will be fluent in the local language upon arrival or shortly thereafter.

Cross-Cultural Training

Managers and their families need cross-cultural training. They need to understand the various dimensions of the local culture. Also, managers need realistic training about what life is like in the host country. For example, they need to know about the currency. They need to know what foods are available and their approximate costs. They need to understand housing options and prices.

Spousal Employment Counseling

Special counseling may be needed if the manager has a working spouse. Increasingly, both husbands and wives work, and career moves that are beneficial to one may not be beneficial to the other. If only one of the two benefits, is the job change worthwhile? Determining if the spouse can work in the host country is important in many employment decisions. Some governments prohibit the spouses of foreign workers from being employed. What realistic employment options, if any, exist for the spouse in the host country? If the spouse cannot work, can he or she adjust to that fact?

Providing training and development is costly. Nevertheless, companies cannot fail to provide it, especially for parent-country nationals. If parent-country nationals are unsuccessful abroad or if their families cannot adjust to life abroad, the company loses.

GLOBAL BUSINESS EXAMPLE

SOME EUROPEAN EMPLOYERS MUST PROVIDE TRAINING

Employers in some European countries are required to provide training and development for their employees. In France all firms with more than 10 employees must pay a 1.5 percent training levy. Employers are reimbursed from the collected funds for accredited training programs. Individual employees can also use the funds to support training leaves. Regional and industrial employer-union organizations administer the funds. In Spain a similar scheme operates with employee contributions for extra personal training leave.

Think Critically

1. Why would a country require that businesses operating there provide employees with training and development?
2. Why would a country that requires employee training and development exempt certain employers from that regulation?

©Getty Images/PhotoDisc

In effect, a company that provides training and development is like a person who buys insurance. It helps to protect against the risks.

Research suggests that relevant training and development does increase the likelihood of success abroad. Figure 11-6 shows the types of training and development recommended for people who are sent by their companies to work in Japan. For other countries, the recommendations would be similar except that the culture-specific training would change.

©Getty Images/PhotoDisc

SUGGESTED AREAS OF TRAINING AND DEVELOPMENT FOR EMPLOYMENT IN JAPAN

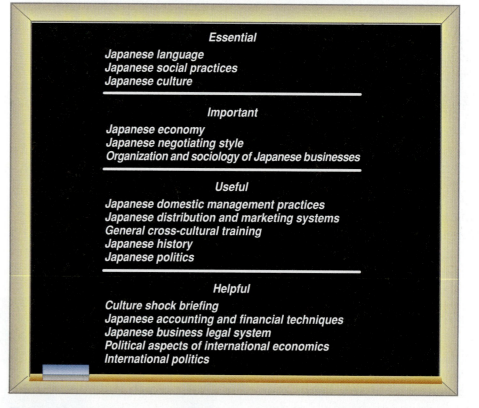

Essential
Japanese language
Japanese social practices
Japanese culture

Important
Japanese economy
Japanese negotiating style
Organization and sociology of Japanese businesses

Useful
Japanese domestic management practices
Japanese distribution and marketing systems
General cross-cultural training
Japanese history
Japanese politics

Helpful
Culture shock briefing
Japanese accounting and financial techniques
Japanese business legal system
Political aspects of international economics
International politics

Figure 11-6 Training and development for work in Japan ranges in importance from essential to helpful.

✓CheckPoint

What are four areas training and development for global employees should address?

TRAINING AND DEVELOPMENT HELP TO PREVENT FAILURE

In spite of the efforts of many companies to provide parent-country nationals with relevant training and development, a number of them are unsuccessful abroad. These employees may return home sooner than expected and be angry and frustrated. They may muddle through the assignment abroad with little or no success. A worker may even leave the company during or at the end of the overseas assignment. The associated monetary and psychological costs of failure are high. Failure hurts both the company and the employee.

WHY GLOBAL EMPLOYEES FAIL

There are several reasons why parent-country nationals fail.

- The employee may be unable to adjust to a different physical and cultural environment.
- The spouse or other family members may be unable to adjust to a different physical and cultural environment.
- The employee's emotional maturity can be seriously strained by an overseas assignment.
- The employee may be unable to work productively.
- The employee may not accept the new responsibilities.
- The employee may lack the motivation to cope with the challenges of working abroad.
- The employee may lack sufficient technical competence.

GLOBAL BUSINESS EXAMPLE

LANGUAGE MATTERS IN FRANCE

If you are going to work or live in France, you should be fluent in the local language. If you don't already speak French, you ought to develop fluency in that language. In many circumstances as an international businessperson, you will need to converse in French. Since the French take great pride in their language, they think others should speak French, too.

The French value their language so much as a tool of communication and as the pinnacle of their culture that they have created the Académie Française to police their language. The Académie Française tries to ensure that businesses and their employees use pure French, not a combination of French and other languages. Nevertheless, some more precise English words are incorporated into French. They are pronounced in the French way so that they don't seem so foreign or corrupting.

Speaking English in France is considered chic within some groups. In many others, however, it is frowned upon. Interestingly, many of the French speak English as a second or third language, although they have a strong preference for their native tongue.

Think Critically
1. If you don't speak French, how could you develop that ability relatively quickly?
2. Conduct an Internet search to discover why French Canadians discount the efforts of the Académie Française. Prepare a summary of your findings.

WORK AS A GROUP

Discuss ways a company could use an employee's international experience when he or she returns from abroad.

REDUCING THE CHANCE OF EMPLOYEE FAILURE

Because an employee's failure in an international assignment is costly to both the employer and the employee, companies need to make plans to reduce the chance of failure. Several areas of training and development before, during, and after the international assignment should be considered.

- Select only successful and satisfied workers for overseas assignments.

- Provide extensive, relevant training and development from before departure, throughout the assignment abroad, and after the return home.

- Make the international assignment part of the long-term employee development process. This effort should benefit both the company and the employee in planned and purposeful ways.

- Provide adequate communication between the company and its employee. The company should know about the employee's overseas experiences.

©Getty Images/PhotoDisc

The employee should know about changes at company headquarters, too.

- Provide a job that uses the employee's international experience when he or she returns to the home country. The knowledge and skills acquired abroad should not be ignored.

- Train company managers, especially those without international experience, to value international experience.

The company should expect returning employees to experience reverse culture shock. However, a supportive training and development program should minimize the readjustment time and difficulty.

✔ CheckPoint

Why should companies make careful efforts to reduce the risk of employee failure on international assignments?

NETBookmark

Many people are fascinated with the idea of working overseas. However, most do not fully understand the amount of preparation necessary in order to be successful. Access intlbizxtra.swlearning.com and click on the link for Chapter 11. Read the Monster.com article entitled "Preparing for an International Career: Developing Needed Global Skills." According to the article, what are the three most important skills that international employers look for in their employees?

intlbizxtra.swlearning.com

REVIEW GLOBAL BUSINESS CONCEPTS

1. Explain why training and development of employees on international assignments is important.

2. Briefly explain four types of training and development that international managers receive.

3. What factors often cause parent-country nationals to fail in their overseas assignments?

SOLVE GLOBAL BUSINESS PROBLEMS

For each of the following cases, determine whether the employee is likely to succeed or fail at an international assignment and explain why.

4. John Deters works in the New York City office but always says he is homesick for his state of Texas. He makes frequent requests for transfers to a Texas branch.

5. Marcia Conners is very ambitious and frequently takes on assignments nobody else wants just to prove her value to the company. Her husband is a freelance graphic designer who says he can do his work from anywhere.

6. Grant Neider is excited about a possible transfer from Chicago to Madrid and is taking Spanish lessons. His 17-year-old daughter is student council president and has the lead role in the spring musical.

7. Tonia Engstrom always orders a cheeseburger in a restaurant because she says she doesn't like to try new things.

THINK CRITICALLY

8. If one of your parents accepted employment as a parent-country national in France, what adjustments would you have to make if you moved there?

9. Why do you think that all recommended training listed in the essential category in Figure 11-6 relates to the general Japanese culture rather than to Japanese business practices?

MAKING CONNECTIONS

10. **CULTURAL STUDIES** Use the library or the Internet to research what foods are eaten regularly in a particular foreign country. How well would you adapt to a similar diet?

11. **CAREER PLANNING** How can you plan your education and work experiences to prepare yourself for work in a foreign country?

12. **TECHNOLOGY** Use the Internet to locate online resources for employee training and development.

11-4 | RETAINING HUMAN RESOURCES

GOALS

- Understand that employee motivation is culturally based.
- Explain the common components of compensation packages for parent-country nationals.
- Appreciate the complexities of evaluating employee performance in an international setting.
- List strategies that help to minimize repatriation problems.

©Getty Images/PhotoDisc

CULTURAL EMPLOYEE MOTIVATION

Managers around the world try to motivate their employees to perform to their fullest potential. While this ideal is commendable, the specific things that contribute to peak performance vary. What motivates a U.S. worker to perform well may have little or no effect elsewhere. Employee motivation is not universal. Instead, it is culturally based and varies from culture to culture.

For example, the U.S. culture values individualism. It also values material possessions. It values taking personal risks to gain personal rewards. Consequently, for most U.S. workers, motivation relates to the personal desire to assume risk in order to gain material rewards.

For many in the United States, money is a major motivator. It is a reward for accepting individual risks and performing well. The more personal responsibility a U.S. worker accepts and handles well, the more money he or she receives. The more money a U.S. worker has, the more material possessions he or she can acquire. Money motivates many in the United States to perform well. Of course, money is not the only motivator. As money allows U.S. workers to fulfill their needs and wants, money becomes less and less a motivator. The possibility of earning $3,000 more motivates a U.S. worker who earns the minimum wage. It will allow him or her to have more creature comforts. However, it does not motivate a U.S. millionaire very much. The millionaire has already used money to fulfill basic needs and wants.

Money cannot buy everything. Some desires must be fulfilled in other ways. Other factors, such as personal recognition and the sense of reaching one's full potential, motivate many U.S. workers more than money does.

Experiences worldwide suggest that U.S. models of motivation work best with U.S. workers in their native country. When U.S.-based international companies try to apply their domestic models of motivation in other countries, the models do not work as well. U.S. models fail to explain motivation elsewhere because what motivates people differs from culture to culture.

For example, publicly praising the individual achievements of a U.S. worker may motivate him or her toward higher achievement. Treating a Japanese employee in the same manner may not motivate him or her. Since the Japanese culture emphasizes group harmony, praising an individual may disrupt the group harmony. It can cause the person singled out to lose face, or to suffer personal embarrassment. In the future, it can cause that person to behave in a way that will not draw attention to himself or herself. In effect, praising a Japanese employee publicly can backfire. Consequently, international managers must use motivation strategies that are culturally acceptable to the employee.

A Question of Ethics

THE COMPANY PICNIC THAT BOMBED

A U.S.-based international company decided it would require a traditional company picnic at each of its sites worldwide since the event was very popular with the employees at headquarters. The first overseas company picnic was held near the location of the Madrid operations. While the U.S. picnic motivated employees and built teamwork at the company headquarters, the Spanish version had the opposite effect. The local workers, Spaniards, were unaccustomed to socializing with those of other ranks. They also felt awkward being served by higher-ranking employees, several of whom were from the United States. They perceived that their class and socialization standards were being violated. To make matters worse, they were coerced into playing the unfamiliar game of baseball, which further alienated them.

Think Critically

1. Was it ethical for headquarters managers to force each company site around the world to have a company picnic and baseball game? Why or why not?
2. What fundamental error did managers at headquarters make?
3. Would it be ethical for the offended Spanish workers to slow down the pace of their work to show their displeasure about the company picnic and baseball game?

✓ **CheckPoint**

How does culture relate to employee motivation?

COMPENSATING EMPLOYEES

Local culturally accepted standards influence employee compensation packages. North American and European international companies tend to reward employees based on the type of work performed and the skills required. In Singapore and Hong Kong, individual performance and skill influence compensation. In Japan, factors of age, seniority, and group or company performance determine compensation. Since compensation standards vary around the world, local laws, employment practices, and employer obligations should guide companies as they design compensation packages.

Cultural Sensitivity International companies motivate employees toward peak performance with culturally sensitive compensation packages. These benefit packages include both cash and noncash items. The mix of employee benefits varies from country to country, but the cash component is typically the largest. Some companies provide discounted products or services to their employees as noncash compensation. In European countries, items such as lunches and transportation are often part of the noncash executive compensation. In less developed and developing countries, basic foodstuff like rice and flour can be part of noncash benefits.

Base Salary Employee compensation packages for parent-country nationals usually are based on several factors. One factor is base salary. For the parent-country national, the base salary at least maintains the customary standard of living of the employee and his or her family while living abroad.

Expatriate Bonus Another factor is an expatriate bonus. Often a company must pay a premium to persuade an employee to work abroad. It provides compensation for adjustment problems and for hardship caused by living and working abroad.

Cost-of-Living Adjustment Another factor is a cost-of-living adjustment. It compensates for the fact that basic living costs vary greatly around the world. Figure 11-7 shows the cost of living in selected locations around the world in comparison to the cost of living in Washington, D.C.

Employee Benefits Finally, fringe benefits often are provided to compensate for the additional expenses of living abroad. They include compensation for having to pay various local taxes and contributions to government insurance programs. They also include relocation expenses, high-risk insurance premiums, and extra educational and medical expenses.

Country	City	Index
Argentina	Buenos Aires	.82
Canada	Toronto	1.08
China	Beijing	1.10
Egypt	Cairo	.85
France	Paris	1.34
India	New Delhi	.93
Japan	Tokyo	1.45
Mexico	Mexico City	1.03
Philippines	Manila	.93
Russia	Moscow	1.10
South Africa	Johannesburg	.85
United Arab Emirates	Abu Dhabi	1.14
United Kingdom	London	1.43
United States	Washington, DC	1.00

Source: Adapted from *Indexes of Living Costs Abroad, 2003*

Figure 11-7 Compensation should take into account the vast differences in the cost of living in cities around the world.

Employee compensation packages for other workers vary worldwide. Typically, they include a base salary that reflects local living costs and some fringe benefits.

✓ CheckPoint

Why do compensation packages vary around the world?

Discuss how employee evaluation practices from the United States might have to be modified for subsidiaries operating in France, Germany, and Italy.

EVALUATING EMPLOYEE PERFORMANCE

Companies that operate internationally must evaluate the performance of their employees. Employee performance, especially for parent-country nationals, is influenced by three factors. These factors are the environment, the task, and the individual's personality.

Business environments differ greatly around the world. Some offer better opportunities for success than others. Job tasks vary, too. Some jobs are more demanding than others. It is more difficult to perform jobs with many challenging tasks. Personality characteristics contribute to the likelihood of success, especially in international assignments. The match between personality types and job demands is important.

The human resources management approach used by the company determines who sets the employee performance standards. For example, with the ethnocentric approach, parent-country nationals primarily set and administer the standards. In contrast, with the polycentric approach, host-country nationals primarily set and administer the standards.

The nature of the employee performance standards varies from job to job. Different jobs require different combinations of competence, adaptability, and personal characteristics. Standards also vary from country to country since different cultures view employee performance in different ways.

Although many companies try to assess the performance of host-country nationals and third-country nationals much like parent-country nationals, it is difficult to do. Even if the evaluation forms are translated into the appropriate languages, misunderstandings can occur. If local evaluation forms are used, can the company headquarters interpret them correctly? Another problem is how employee performance evaluation is perceived in different parts of the world. In some locations, it can be viewed as threatening. It can also be viewed as insulting or as evidence of lack of trust. Finding ways of evaluating employee performance that are both culturally sensitive and meaningful is difficult. Balancing the needs of the employee and the company is indeed a challenge in the global business environment.

✓ CheckPoint

Why is evaluating the performance of international employees so challenging?

ANTICIPATING REPATRIATION

Repatriation is the process a person goes through when returning home and getting settled after having worked abroad. The repatriation period often is a difficult one, filled with many adjustments. It is a challenging time when expatriates experience *reverse culture shock.* They have difficulty becoming reacquainted with their native culture. These major adjustments involve such things as work, finances, and social relationships.

©Getty Images/PhotoDisc

Returning expatriates often experience a sense of isolation. They have grown in different directions while abroad. Because their extended families and friends have not had similar experiences, they seem like strangers.

To minimize the problems when returning home, expatriates need to plan ahead. It is not too early to start, even before leaving on an international assignment. With careful advanced planning, many of the problems of returning employees can be lessened.

Once abroad, they must keep in frequent communication with former colleagues and friends. Expatriates should share new experiences with them and find out what is new in their lives. In addition, they ought to learn to enjoy the benefits of the host culture and its way of life whenever possible.

International employees should also begin exploring new career options at least one year before the end of the assignment abroad. Soon-to-be repatriates should encourage their current employers to find suitable jobs that make use of their recent international experiences. Also, they can explore options abroad and at home with other companies. When returning home, repatriates should be grateful for their adventures abroad. They can view their native culture in another light and appreciate it more than ever before after having experienced firsthand another way of life.

CheckPoint

What can an employee working abroad do to facilitate a smooth transition into his or her native culture?

REVIEW GLOBAL BUSINESS TERMS

Define the following term.

1. repatriation

REVIEW GLOBAL BUSINESS CONCEPTS

2. Motivation is culturally based. Why is the previous statement true?

3. What is typically included in the compensation packages of parent-country nationals?

SOLVE GLOBAL BUSINESS PROBLEMS

Use the cost-of-living index shown in Figure 11-7 to calculate cost-of-living allowances for employees who are living in cities other than Washington, D.C. London is given as an example. (Note: The cost-of-living allowance is usually not reduced when a country's index is less than 1.0.)

	Location	Index	×	Spendable Income	=	Cost-of-Living Allowance
Example:	London	1.43	×	$25,000	=	$35,750
4.	Mexico City	1.03	×	$35,000	=	?
5.	Toronto	1.08	×	$20,000	=	?
6.	Paris	1.34	×	$30,000	=	?
7.	Tokyo	1.45	×	?	=	$79,750

THINK CRITICALLY

8. What factors would cause a German-based international company to pay its employees who live in Tokyo, Japan, more than its employees who live in your hometown?

MAKING CONNECTIONS

9. **TECHNOLOGY** What software could be used to create the cost-of-living allowance for employees assigned to various locations around the world?

10. **CULTURAL STUDIES** How might the collectivist orientation of Sweden influence the compensation package of employees of a Canadian multinational corporation working there?

11. **TECHNOLOGY** Identify a job or career that is available in several different countries. Use the Internet to find the compensation available for that job in different places around the world.

CHAPTER SUMMARY

11-1 FOUNDATIONS OF HUMAN RESOURCES MANAGEMENT

A Human resources management is more complicated in the global environment because of differences in labor markets and managerial practices.

B The four common approaches to human resources management are the ethnocentric, polycentric, regiocentric, and geocentric approaches.

11-2 SELECTING AND TRAINING STAFF

A An international company must carefully determine its staffing needs using employment forecasting and supply analysis.

B Recruiting methods vary depending on the type of employee needed.

C Applicants for most international positions are selected based on their competence, adaptability, and personal characteristics.

11-3 MAXIMIZATION OF HUMAN RESOURCES

A Relevant training and development are critical for success in international business for both employees and companies.

B Training for international positions should include job, language, and relationship issues, cross-cultural training, and spousal job counseling.

C International companies should understand the reasons why employees fail and take steps to reduce the chances of failure.

11-4 RETAINING HUMAN RESOURCES

A Cultural differences can vary the methods of motivating international employees.

B Cultural standards influence employee compensation packages.

C Although subject to cultural variability, the international employee's performance is influenced by three factors: the environment, the task, and the person's personality.

D With proper planning prior to, during, and after an international assignment, repatriation problems can be reduced.

GLOBAL REFOCUS

Read the case at the beginning of this chapter, and answer the following questions.

1. How do you know that the Smiths are encountering culture shock?

2. What stage of culture shock is Doug experiencing? How do you know?

3. What would you tell Sue and Doug to help cope with culture shock?

REVIEW GLOBAL BUSINESS TERMS

Match the terms listed with the definitions.

1. The human resources approach that uses the best available managers without regard for their countries of origin.

2. Expatriates from the country in which their company is headquartered.

3. The human resources approach that uses natives of the parent country of a business to fill key positions at home and abroad.

4. The process of returning home and getting settled after having worked abroad.

5. Natives of the country in which they work.

6. Determining if there are sufficient types and numbers of employees available.

a. employment forecasting

b. ethnocentric approach

c. expatriates

d. geocentric approach

e. host-country nationals

f. job description

g. parent-country nationals

h. polycentric approach

i. regiocentric approach

j. repatriation

k. supply analysis

l. third-country nationals

7. The human resources approach that uses managers from various countries within the geographic regions of a business.

8. Expatriates from countries other than the home country of their company or the host country.

9. People who live and work outside their native countries.

10. A document that includes the job identification, job statement, job duties and responsibilities, and job specifications and requirements.

11. Estimating in advance the types and numbers of employees needed.

12. The human resources approach that uses natives of the host country to manage operations within their country and parent country natives to manage at headquarters.

MAKE GLOBAL BUSINESS DECISIONS

13. Using people, print, and electronic resources, determine if a U.S.-based multinational company should hold an annual company picnic and baseball game for the employees of its Portuguese subsidiary, 75 percent of whom are natives of Portugal. Justify your position.

14. Should a U.S.-based multinational company locate its European division human resources office in London, United Kingdom, or in Paris, France, if the primary considerations are (1) the local cost of living, (2) the central location, (3) the ease of adjustment for parent-country nationals?

15. Using reference resources in a library, identify a multinational company headquartered in a European country of your choice. Find out in which city the company is headquartered. Locate on a map of Europe the country and city in which the headquarters is located. Using the scale on the map, estimate the distance from the city in which the company is headquartered to Brussels, Belgium.

16. Based on your reading of a magazine or journal article about living abroad, would you be a good candidate for an international assignment? Why or why not?

17. If your family relocated in the United Kingdom and enrolled you in what the British call a private comprehensive secondary school, would your family be entitled to an educational adjustment as a part of your father's or mother's employee compensation package? Why or why not?

18. Prepare a list of questions you might ask applicants for managerial positions in major cities throughout Europe.

19. Why might your best friend no longer seem to be your best friend when you return from a lengthy overseas assignment?

GLOBAL CONNECTIONS

20. TECHNOLOGY What types of technology would best facilitate communication between human resources managers at headquarters and at subsidiaries around the world?

21. CULTURAL STUDIES In some developing countries, why would foodstuffs be part of the compensation for local employees?

22. GEOGRAPHY How might the geography and climate of Switzerland influence the cost-of-living allowance for employees working there?

23. HISTORY How did World War II affect the labor supply in Russia?

24. MATHEMATICS What are some of the reasons that the cost of living in London is approximately 43 percent more than the cost of living in Washington, D.C.?

25. COMMUNICATIONS How would the group orientation of South Korea influence how human resources managers recommend motivating host-country employees there?

26. TECHNOLOGY Many major multinational companies have web sites on which they list employment opportunities. Locate such a company using an Internet search, and read the job descriptions for some jobs available in other countries.

27. CAREER PLANNING In preparation for work assignments abroad, what could you do to increase your adaptability to life in other countries?

©Getty Images/PhotoDisc

THE GLOBAL
ENTREPRENEUR
CREATING AN INTERNATIONAL BUSINESS PLAN

HUMAN RESOURCES MANAGEMENT

Plan a human resources strategy for the company and country you have been using in this continuing project, or create a new idea for your business in the same or a different country. Make use of previously collected information, and do additional research. This phase of your business plan should include the following components.

©Getty Images/PhotoDisc

1. Describe the type of human resources management approach (ethnocentric, polycentric, regiocentric, or geocentric) that would be most appropriate for your organization.

2. Describe the actions that would be taken to identify and recruit potential employees.

3. Describe the selection procedures (application process, interview questions) that would be used by your organization.

4. Describe the types of training and development activities that would be appropriate for managers and other employees in this organization.

5. Describe how the organization would motivate employees to improve productivity and plan for retention.

6. Describe the methods that would be used to evaluate employee performance.

Prepare a written summary or present a short oral report (two or three minutes) of your findings.

©Getty Images/PhotoDisc

Chapter 12

INTERNATIONAL CAREER PLANNING

A Global Business Career

Jennifer Yoon is an administrative assistant in San Antonio, Texas, for a multinational company with offices in 16 countries. Her company recently posted a job opening for general manager of the new office in Austria. This position will require knowledge of company operations, financial management, marketing, import-export laws, and Austrian business customs.

Jennifer has not worked full-time in any country other than the United States. However, she has traveled in nine other countries for meetings and short-term work assignments. During her years in school, Jennifer studied global marketing, economic geography, European history, and foreign political systems. While in college, she participated in a work-study program at the Spanish trade office in Washington, D.C.

As Jennifer considers this job in another country, her thoughts go in two directions. "This is the opportunity I have been waiting and training for," she said to a friend. Then Jennifer went on to say, "But what if I can't adapt to the different culture and business activities?"

Think Critically

1. What educational and work experiences have prepared Jennifer Yoon for a position as general manager?
2. What actions should Jennifer take to apply for the general manager position in the Austrian office?
3. Go to the web site for the Trade Information Center of the U.S. Department of Commerce (www.trade.gov/td/tic). Click on Country Information, then on Western Europe. Find the most current commercial guide for Austria.

12-1 SEARCHING FOR YOUR FIRST JOB

GOALS

- Describe the steps of the career planning process.
- List sources of career planning information.
- Identify factors that affect job availability.

©Getty Images/PhotoDisc

CAREER PLANNING

Some people jump out of bed in the morning and can't wait to get to work. Others go to work thinking only about the weekend or an upcoming vacation. What is the difference between these two groups of people? Selection of your life's work could be the most important decision you make.

THE IMPORTANCE OF WORK

Work not only affects income but also influences the amount of leisure time you have, the people with whom you associate, and many other aspects of your life. Career planning activities are likely to continue throughout your life. Changing personal, social, and economic factors affect job satisfaction and available employment positions. Most people who aspire to international careers begin work in some type of business-related job in their own country. After you have job experience within your own country, you may have opportunities to work outside the country. Over time, you will attain your goal of having an international career.

FIVE STEPS IN CAREER PLANNING

In every society, work is necessary. Work makes it possible for people to have food, clothing, housing, and transportation. Besides fulfilling physical needs, work also has social and psychological benefits. Work allows people the opportunity to gain personal satisfaction through interaction with others and to gain recognition for their performance.

The work a person selects can be viewed as either a job or a career. A **job** is an employment position obtained mainly for money. People may work in one or more jobs during their lives without planning for advancement.

In contrast, a **career** is a commitment to a profession that requires continuing education and training and has a clear path for advancement. A person may select a career in health care, information systems, marketing, financial management, exporting, or other areas. Figure 12-1 shows the five activities involved in career planning.

THE CAREER PLANNING PROCESS

Step 1
Determine your personal
goals and abilities

Step 2
Evaluate the job market

Step 3
Identify and apply for
specific job opportunities

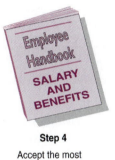
Step 4
Accept the most
desirable job offer

Step 5
Plan for personal
career development

Figure 12-1
Careful planning is required in order to obtain a position that best suits your interests and abilities.

Step 1 Determine Your Personal Goals and Abilities As you plan for a career, start by evaluating your personal situation. Do you like to work with others, or alone? Would you like to work outside or in an office? Do you enjoy working with words or numbers? Determining your personal goals and abilities will help you start the career planning process.

Step 2 Evaluate the Job Market Next, determine what types of jobs are available. You may want to work as a news reporter on television. However, few jobs may be available in that field. Look for career areas in which you can adapt your interests, skills, and knowledge.

Step 3 Identify and Apply for Specific Job Opportunities

The third step of the process involves presenting yourself on paper and in person. After finding organizations with available employment, you will need to communicate your abilities to those responsible for hiring. This communication comes in the form of a resume (or personal data sheet), application letter, and interview. These things help you sell yourself to an employer.

NETBookmark

To learn more about how to choose a career that is right for you, access intlbizxtra.swlearning.com and click on the link for Chapter 12. Read the 10 steps to career planning on the Mapping Your Future web site. Then create a graphic organizer listing your skills and interests on one side and the careers that might match those skills and interests on the other.

intlbizxtra.swlearning.com

Step 4 **Accept the Most Desirable Job Offer** In this step, evaluate the positive and negative aspects of working for various companies. Compare salaries, employee benefits, work situations, and future opportunities in the organization. Remember that the highest-paying job may not be the most enjoyable one or offer advancement in the future.

Step 5 **Plan for Personal Career Development** Finally, workers should continually evaluate their future. As personal goals and employment opportunities change, you may want to obtain further education and training. Technology, economic conditions, or other factors may eliminate certain jobs and force a career change.

Many people work in jobs that are within one country. This is called the *domestic employment market.* Other work opportunities involve international business. For example, a company in Poland may make suits that are sold in Canada. A Japanese bank may have an office in Egypt. As trade among nations expands, the number and types of global careers increase.

✔ CheckPoint

What are the five steps in career planning?

EXPLORING CAREER INFORMATION

Every business and personal decision can be easier to make if you do your homework. Obtaining relevant information helps with all of life's activities. Selecting and planning a career is no different. Career information is available from five main sources.

Library Materials Your school or public library is an excellent starting point for career information. You can obtain books and other publications about selecting a career field, searching for a job, and planning for an interview. These items may be in print or in electronic form.

One very helpful source is the *Occupational Outlook Handbook*, published by the Bureau of Labor Statistics (part of the U.S. Department of Labor). This reference book is revised every two years and provides detailed information about jobs in many career areas. It is also available online at www.bls.gov/oco/. Other helpful career resources include the *Dictionary of Occupational Titles* and the *Occupational Outlook Quarterly.*

Media Occasionally, newspapers publish articles with job search hints and career trends. Television and radio reports about job planning and economic trends can also be useful when selecting a career. For example, news about a company expanding into other nations provides information about the availability of international jobs.

Personal and Business Contacts Every person you meet can help you learn more about work and successful career planning. Friends, relatives, and people in your community all have worked at one time or another. Talking with them about their jobs can be very useful. An **informational interview** is a meeting with another person to gather information about a career or an organization. During an informational interview, you can learn about required skills, job duties, and potential earnings for careers. What questions might you ask a person who works for a multinational company?

E-COMMERCE IN ACTION

Monster

Monster is a leading international career network. It offers a variety of services for job candidates and employers.

Job candidates can post their resumes and access job postings in 20 different countries in Europe, North America, and Asia and the Pacific Rim. Most country-specific information is available in the predominant local language(s). Monster also provides information about job profiles, resumes, interviewing, salaries, networking, diversity, and relocation for job candidates.

Since over 1.6 million job seekers visit Monster network sites each day, Monster can help employers find the right employees to fill their vacancies through the use of screening and hiring tools. Employers can buy job postings and the resumes of the best job candidates from Monster.

Think Critically

1. What advantages does an international recruiting network such as Monster have over a countrywide network?
2. What might create a problem for you in accessing country-specific information?
3. Why do you think an international recruitment web site is typically not used to fill international positions at the highest levels?

In addition, job fairs are held in many large cities. Employers pay for time and space to provide information about available jobs, and some may even interview candidates. Talking with company representatives at job fairs can provide applicants with additional information about companies.

Many career areas also have professional associations. Some will admit student members. The meetings of these professional associations, as well as the journals they publish, can be an additional source of career information and networking.

Community Organizations Most communities have business and civic organizations such as the Chamber of Commerce, Jaycees (Junior Chamber of Commerce), and Rotary Club. Meetings held by these groups can be a source of current business trends. The Chamber of Commerce commonly publishes a directory of its member businesses, many of which may be involved in importing or exporting.

Internet The Internet is increasingly becoming a source of employment information. Many companies have their own web sites that include a list of current job openings and career information. There are also web sites that are job search engines. People can post their resumes, as well as see what jobs have been posted. An Internet search can help locate professional associations relevant to different fields of work. However, some sites may charge a fee to use their services. Some Internet newsgroups are also organized for particular professions and may provide career information.

CheckPoint

What are five sources for career information?

IDENTIFYING CAREER OPPORTUNITIES

Why do some people excel in their chosen careers while others never seem to find satisfying work? The answer to this question involves many things. As you start thinking about your life's work, consider your personal abilities and talents along with what jobs will be available. Trade among nations and technology will eliminate some careers while creating others.

FACTORS AFFECTING CAREER CHOICE

Will your career be one that you enjoy? Will the work involve an activity that will be in demand in the global economy? Career choice is influenced by a variety of factors, as shown in Figure 12-2.

Personal Factors What do you like to do? What do you do well? Answers to these questions can be keys to successful career planning. In addition, when selecting a job, decide how much and what type of education you plan to obtain, what experience you have, and what your personal goals are.

An evaluation of personal interests, experiences, values, and goals is important when selecting the right career. Knowledge of global business activities, geography, foreign cultures, and another language can provide a foundation for an international business career.

Demographic Trends As the population of a society changes, so do the jobs that are available. For example, an increase in the number of working parents in the United States increased the demand for food service and childcare workers. Also, as people live longer, employment in travel services, health care, and retirement facilities expands.

Geographic Influences The location of employment opportunities can change. As economic growth occurs in a geographic region, more jobs are available. However, when economic conditions decline, fewer jobs will exist in that region.

The location of natural resources also influences employment. Areas with seaports and rivers commonly have shipbuilding and shipping industries. Fertile land usually is used for agricultural purposes. Rich mineral deposits lead to mining and related metal-product industries.

Economic Conditions Jobs, like goods and services, are affected by the basic economic principle of supply and demand. For example, as more people want and use home computers, employment in industries

Figure 12-2 The career a person selects is affected by many factors.

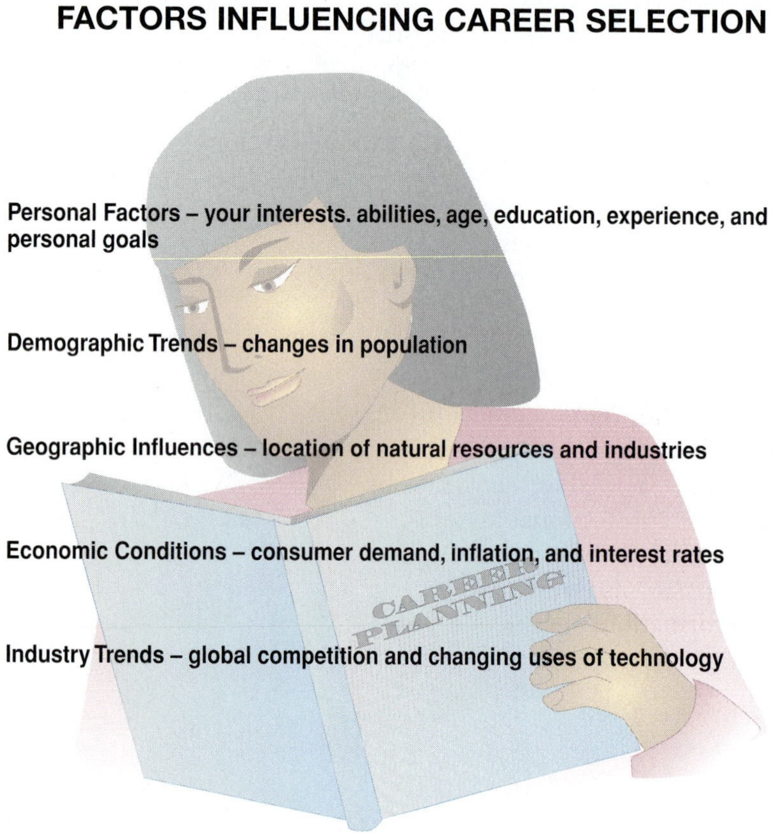

FACTORS INFLUENCING CAREER SELECTION

Personal Factors – your interests. abilities, age, education, experience, and personal goals

Demographic Trends – changes in population

Geographic Influences – location of natural resources and industries

Economic Conditions – consumer demand, inflation, and interest rates

Industry Trends – global competition and changing uses of technology that make, program, and sell these computers increases. Consumer demand in the economy has a strong effect on the job market.

Changing prices affect available jobs. When inflation occurs, people usually reduce spending. Lower consumer demand, once again, causes a decline in the need for products and for the workers who make them.

Changes in the value of the currency of a nation will affect its balance of trade. As the demand for the goods and services of a country increases, employment opportunities in that nation also increase.

Interest rates affect employment opportunities. If companies must pay high rates to borrow for new equipment or to build new factories, fewer businesses will make these capital purchases. As a result, people who build this equipment and these factories will have fewer job opportunities.

Industry Trends Companies have always competed against each other. However, as global business activities expand, foreign competition changes the types of jobs available.

Another business trend affecting jobs is the increased use of technology. Companies with computers in offices, stores, and factories require that employees be able to operate this equipment. In addition, many jobs previously done by people are now handled by computer systems.

SOURCES OF AVAILABLE JOBS

How does a person identify job opportunities? Advertisements are often a place to start looking. Classified ads provide information about some employment positions. Advertisements may help a person find work. However, most jobs are not advertised to the general public. For this reason, personal contacts are an important source of job information. Ask people you know about available jobs where they work. As previously mentioned, an informational interview can be helpful. The people you talk with may be able to tell you what skills are needed, where jobs are located, and whom to contact.

Visit places where you would like to work. While most jobs are not advertised, work opportunities are sometimes posted at a place of business. The extra effort it takes to go to a company can demonstrate a strong desire to work there.

Employment agencies can sometimes be helpful sources of job information. However, be careful of organizations that charge fees and give no guarantees of helping you find a job. State-funded employment services provide information about some available jobs at no charge.

People seeking work may also consider *job creation*. This involves communicating with possible employers the skills you have that could help their companies. For example, a person may be skilled at researching foreign locations. While an owner may have never considered exporting, a new job position could be created in the company to explore possible foreign locations for exporting goods or services.

WORK AS A GROUP

Discuss demographic trends that are affecting career choices today.

✔ CheckPoint

What are five factors that influence the availability of jobs?

REVIEW GLOBAL BUSINESS TERMS

Define each of the following terms.

1. job   **2.** career   **3.** informational interview

REVIEW GLOBAL BUSINESS CONCEPTS

4. How does a job differ from a career?

5. What is the domestic job market?

6. What type of information can be obtained from an informational interview?

7. How can economic conditions affect the availability of jobs?

SOLVE GLOBAL BUSINESS PROBLEMS

Lack of experience is a common problem faced by beginning workers. You are told, "You don't have enough experience." However, to get experience, you need a job.

Work-related experiences can be obtained through part-time or summer jobs. Most schools offer cooperative education or internship programs. Volunteering for community organizations is another method of obtaining work experience. State whether each of the following situations could be relevant experience for a job and why.

8. Supervising youth activities at the community center

9. Writing for the school newspaper

10. Using foreign language skills to translate personal correspondence for foreign visitors

11. Conducting tours of your city for visitors

THINK CRITICALLY

12. Why are you likely to have a part-time or summer job before you have a full-time job?

13. In preparation for an informational interview, gather some questions to ask a person working in international business.

14. Describe international events that could affect the number and types of jobs in a country.

MAKE CONNECTIONS

15. **CULTURAL STUDIES** Why might a multinational company operating in Estonia hire a manager from Finland?

16. **TECHNOLOGY** Find the web site of a large company that includes job postings. Make a list of the jobs, and describe any that have an international component.

APPLYING FOR A JOB

12-2

GOALS

- Describe important elements of a resume.
- Explain successful interview techniques.
- Describe other documents that may be involved in applying for a job.

©Getty Images/PhotoDisc

CREATING A RESUME

"**W**anted: Stock clerk for import company. A knowledge of inventory methods and international business practices required." Someday you may encounter a job advertisement something like this. What actions are necessary for you to obtain this position?

If you find a job that is of interest to you, you must communicate your skills and abilities to your prospective employer. A **resume** is a written summary of a person's education, training, work experience, and other job qualifications. A resume should be prepared on good-quality paper with the best printing or reproduction available in order to make a good first impression. In some cases, the wording on a resume may be changed to tailor the resume for a particular job opportunity.

Figure 12-3 shows a sample resume for a person just out of high school. The sections included on a resume may vary somewhat, but most include the following sections.

Personal Data A resume starts with your name, address, and telephone number. You can include your e-mail address and fax number, too. A person's age (or birth date), marital status, gender, height, and weight should not be listed unless this information is related to specific job qualifications.

Career Objective A brief but precise description of the type of job desired is next. The following sections of your resume support your objective and prove that you are qualified for the job you seek. A career objective also will be communicated in the related application letter.

Education This section includes schools attended, dates of attendance, and fields of study. A listing of courses taken may be appropriate for classes that relate directly to the job for which you are applying.

A SAMPLE RESUME

Terry Connor

1654 Meadow Lane
Central City, Texas 76540-1654
(214) 555-4537

CAREER OBJECTIVE	An inventory clerk position with a business involved in importing or exporting.
EDUCATION	Browne High School Graduated June 2006 International Business Preparation: • French I, II, III • International Business I • Global Marketing • World Geography • Economics • Business Law
EXPERIENCE	Filing Clerk, Jefferson Furniture Co., Allentown, Texas, August 2005 – June 2006 Maintained and retrieved files for all departments. Volunteer, Kenton County Home for the Aged, October 2001 – September 2004 Maintained inventory of supplies.
RELATED ACTIVITIES	Vice President, International Business Club Secretary, Student Council Foreign Missions Program, Student Assistant, Central Baptist Church
HONORS AND AWARDS	Finalist, Martin Foundation Global Business Scholarship Community Service Award, Kenton County Park District Recycling Program
REFERENCES	Furnished upon request.

Figure 12-3 A resume informs employers of the skills and abilities you possess.

Experience This section should include position titles, major job duties, employment dates, and employers' names and addresses for current and past jobs. Community service can be reported like a regular job. Be sure that the description of job duties emphasizes your accomplishments. One good way to do this is to use action-oriented verbs to describe what you did. For example, you would write that you supervised and scheduled two part-time employees.

Related Activities School involvement, hobbies, and other interests directly related to your career can help you get a job. Remember to package these items in terms of how they relate to the desired job.

Honors and Awards A listing of honors and awards can help communicate your ability to do high-quality work.

References People who can report to a prospective employer about your abilities and work experience are **references**. These individuals may be teachers, past employers, community leaders, or adult friends. Be sure to obtain permission from the people you plan to use as references. References are usually not included on the resume. However, you will need to have the names, addresses, telephone numbers, and positions of your references available when prospective employers ask for them.

✔ CheckPoint

What seven sections should most resumes include?

OTHER JOB APPLICATION DOCUMENTS

A resume is possibly the most time-consuming job application document to prepare. However, other documents are also part of the job application process.

DEVELOPING A COVER LETTER

When applying for a job, your resume should be sent with a cover letter, which is sometimes called an application letter. A **cover letter** communicates your interest in a specific employment position. This letter is designed to create enough interest in you that you obtain an interview.

The opening paragraph of a cover letter should get the reader's attention. Express your interest in the job. Communicate why the employer should consider you for the desired position.

The next paragraph (or two) of the letter should highlight specific education, training, and work experiences that qualify you for the position. Remember that employers don't care what you have done in the past. They want to know how your background will help them in the future. You must communicate how your qualifications will contribute to the organization.

The final paragraph should ask for an opportunity to meet in person with your prospective employer. Tell where, when, and how the employer can communicate with you to schedule an interview.

Remember that your cover letter and resume are your tickets to the interview. They represent you to the prospective employer. Be sure that the documents are neat, well organized, and properly prepared. Be sure to proofread the documents carefully to be sure there are no typographical, grammatical, or spelling errors. Many job candidates are disqualified because their application materials are poorly prepared.

COMPLETING AN APPLICATION FORM

Instead of or in addition to a cover letter and resume, a person may be required to complete an application form. This document asks for information similar to the items listed on a resume. An application form should be filled out in a neat and complete manner. When preparing a job application form, be sure you have the needed information available. Before you fill out

WORK AS A GROUP

Select an international job, and discuss what kind of education and experience would be ideal for that job. Repeat with additional jobs as time permits.

EXAMPLE

CROSS-CULTURAL INTERVIEWING

International job interviews can be more challenging than domestic job interviews because of cultural differences. In most cultures, there are certain topics that are unacceptable and should be avoided. Generally speaking, politics and religion are not appropriate topics to discuss. Also, be aware of cultural differences in gestures and body language. The meaning of the "okay" symbol, with the thumb and index finger forming a circle, has a number of meanings around the world, some of which are offensive or obscene. A head nodding up and down usually means yes, but in a few cultures it means no. Pointing with an index finger is sometimes considered impolite or vulgar. Because of such cultural differences, it is critical to know what is acceptable and what is unacceptable before being interviewed for a job abroad. By knowing acceptable cultural standards, you can avoid making embarrassing interview mistakes.

Think Critically

1. Why is interviewing in another culture potentially challenging?
2. What other topics are generally not good ones to discuss during interviews in various countries around the world?

applications, you should prepare a personal data sheet. Your *personal data sheet* is a document that contains all the information you need to complete a job application. An application form is likely to request your social security number; education; work experience; and the names, addresses, and telephone numbers of references.

▌SECURING INTERNATIONAL EMPLOYMENT DOCUMENTS

When traveling, studying, or working in another country, certain documents are usually required. A **passport** is a government document proving the bearer's citizenship in the country that issues it. Passports are issued to citizens of the United States by the Department of State and are valid for ten years. A passport application can be obtained from a post office, a passport agency, or a federal or state court clerk.

A **visa** is a stamp of endorsement issued by a country that allows a passport holder to enter that country. A visa allows a person into a foreign nation for a specified purpose and period of time. Most visas are issued for travel and personal business.

People who plan to work in another country are usually required to obtain a work visa. A **work visa**, also called a work permit, allows a person into a foreign country for the purpose of employment. Some countries limit the number of work visas so their own citizens have more opportunities to fill available jobs.

©Getty Images/PhotoDisc

✔ CheckPoint

What information should a cover letter include?

INTERVIEWING FOR A JOB

"Why should we hire you?" This is a common question that you will probably have to answer when applying for jobs. The process of interviewing for a job requires that you start getting ready well before the interview.

BEFORE YOU INTERVIEW

Prepare for an interview by obtaining additional information about the company. News articles, annual reports, and current and past employees are good sources of company information. Your knowledge of an organization will help you better answer questions about how you can contribute to the company. You will impress the employer favorably if you are already knowledgeable about the company.

Next, prepare questions to ask at the interview. Many interviewers are impressed by the questions a candidate asks. Common questions to ask in an interview include the following.

- What are the main responsibilities of the job?
- What qualities do your most successful employees possess?
- What do people like best about working here?
- What are the opportunities for advancement?

Set up a practice interview. Using a video camera, and have someone ask you sample questions to help you improve your interview skills. Organize your thoughts before answering. Speak clearly and calmly. Provide concise, precise answers. Be confident but not overbearing. Show your enthusiasm for working for the company.

Finally, decide what to wear to the interview and plan to be impeccably groomed. Find out what employees wear to work. Regardless of the dress code of the company, a business suit is usually appropriate for an interview. Avoid trendy and casual styles of clothing. Don't wear too much jewelry. Avoid overpowering colognes or perfumes.

Figure 12-4 Planning answers to these questions can help you prepare for a job interview.

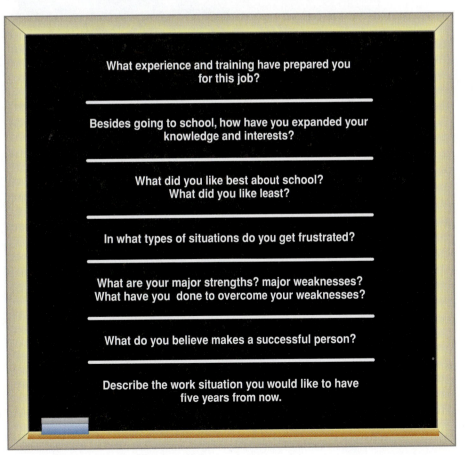

COMMON INTERVIEW QUESTIONS

What experience and training have prepared you for this job?

Besides going to school, how have you expanded your knowledge and interests?

What did you like best about school? What did you like least?

In what types of situations do you get frustrated?

What are your major strengths? major weaknesses? What have you done to overcome your weaknesses?

What do you believe makes a successful person?

Describe the work situation you would like to have five years from now.

WHEN YOU INTERVIEW

Arrive at the interview several minutes before your appointment time. While it may be difficult, try to relax. Remember that you will be asked questions about a topic on which you are the expert—you.

You may first be required to have a **screening interview**, which is an initial meeting to select finalists from the applicant pool for an available position. During the screening interview you will be judged on both the overall impression you create and the answers to a few general questions.

Candidates who pass the screening interview are invited for a **selection interview**. In this meeting, a person is asked a series of in-depth questions designed to help employers select the best person for a job.

AFTER YOU INTERVIEW

While waiting to receive communication from a prospective employer, do two things. First, send a follow-up letter. Use the follow-up letter to resell yourself so that you stand out in a positive way from the others who were interviewed. Let the employer know that you are interested in the discussed position.

Second, evaluate your interview performance. Write down ways you can improve. List questions that you did not expect to be asked and be prepared to answer them in future interviews.

Communication Across Borders

DRESSING UP FOR THE BRITISH

Lee Albright wanted to work for a British-based multinational company. Although she dressed casually for work in Chicago, she decided that for her interview in London, she should dress up. She chose a tailored navy suit with a white blouse, a pearl necklace and earrings, and navy pumps.

Over lunch on the day of her interview, the human resources director said, "Miss Albright, you create a very polished and professional appearance, one that is right for this company. So many people we interview don't seem to realize that their dress communicates much about them. Those who make a smart appearance send a very favorable message about themselves and their employer. Those who are too casual in appearance just aren't accepted here. While I understand that casual business dress is common in the States, we Britons have been slower to accept it. I think we can do business with you, Miss Albright."

Think Critically

1. Why is it generally a good idea to dress more formally rather than less formally for a job interview?
2. Why do you think that British businesspersons tend to dress up for work more than U.S. businesspersons do?
3. What suggests that Miss Albright was hired?

✓ CheckPoint

What are four things that can be done to prepare for a job interview?

REVIEW GLOBAL BUSINESS TERMS

Define each of the following terms.

1. resume
2. references
3. cover letter
4. passport
5. visa
6. work visa
7. screening interview
8. selection interview

REVIEW GLOBAL BUSINESS CONCEPTS

9. Why should a resume be carefully prepared?

10. What is the purpose of a cover letter?

11. How does a passport differ from a visa?

SOLVE GLOBAL BUSINESS PROBLEMS

Answers given to questions in an interview can either clinch a job offer or guarantee that no job will be offered. Indicate whether each of the following statements would be considered positive or negative and why.

12. I enjoy finding solutions to problems.

13. I need to be sure I have vacation time during August for visiting the lake with my friends.

14. I'd like a job where I don't have to take orders from superiors.

15. I enjoy writing, and my teachers have always said that I convey ideas well.

16. What are the opportunities for advancement with your company?

THINK CRITICALLY

17. Why do you think it is important not to mention salary at the beginning of a job interview?

18. How would you dress for an interview for a job working as a construction worker? Explain.

MAKE CONNECTIONS

19. **TECHNOLOGY** Why might you want to include your e-mail address on your resume?

20. **LAW** Why should you not provide prospective employers with your birth date?

21. **CAREER PLANNING** How should you answer questions about your weaknesses?

22. **TECHNOLOGY** Use the Internet to locate resources to help you apply for a job.

12-3 | OBTAINING FUTURE JOBS

GOALS

- Explain why careers can develop and change.
- Explain how to prepare for international careers.

©Getty Images/PhotoDisc

DEVELOPING CAREER OPTIONS

A job is for today, but a career is for a lifetime. Every workday, employees have the opportunity to expand their abilities, knowledge, and career potential. Improving work habits may be achieved by watching others or by creating better ways to do certain tasks.

TRAINING OPPORTUNITIES

Increased technology and changing work activities require employees to learn new skills. Each day on a job can result in new knowledge through informal and formal methods. Informal learning takes place every time people read current materials about their job or the industry in which they work. Talking with others within the company or at other organizations also can help you learn new economic and social trends affecting business.

Formal educational methods include company training programs, seminars, and college courses. Many companies encourage ongoing learning by paying all or part of the tuition costs for education and training that improves job skills.

CAREER ADVANCEMENT

As with every personal and business decision, choices might need to be revised as social and economic factors change. During the first stage of a career, a worker wants to match his or her interests and abilities to a job. However, as a career develops, a person will seek new challenges, increased responsibility, and greater rewards.

CHANGING CAREERS

About 10 million people in the United States change careers each year. Most people will have five to ten different jobs during their working lives. The need to change jobs may come from within. Many people face mental stress or physical illness from their work. When this occurs, a career change is probably appropriate.

External influences also can cause a job change. As companies move and merge, a person's job may be eliminated. Technology can replace the need for certain jobs. For example, many bank tellers have been replaced by automated teller machines.

Numerous factors can cause a person to change jobs. When this occurs, it is necessary to develop a revised career path. Perhaps that revised career path will lead to an international career. Figure 12-5 shows major reasons why young managers would accept or reject work assignments abroad. Does an international career seem right for you?

Common Reasons for Accepting International Work
Cross-cultural experiences and personal growth
Interesting and challenging job
Better financial and other rewards
Career advancement opportunities
A desirable location
A satisfying life

Common Reasons for Rejecting International Work
Undesirable location
Undesirable job and career move
Unacceptable for spouse and family
Inadequate salary and benefits
Unpleasant life abroad
Disruption to home country life

Figure 12-5 There are many reasons why young managers would accept or reject international assignments.

CheckPoint

What causes people to change careers?

PREPARING FOR INTERNATIONAL CAREERS

People can prepare themselves for a variety of international careers by engaging in six actions. You can start these actions as early as high school and continue them throughout your working lifetime.

UNDERSTAND YOURSELF

Before preparing for international careers, you need to understand yourself. You need to understand your own cultural programming that causes you to be the person you are. In other words, you need to know what your beliefs, values, and assumptions are that shape your behaviors. You also need to determine what your employment goals are. Do you truly have the desire to have an international career of some type? Are you really willing to live abroad for a period of time? Are you motivated to use your capabilities and resources to pursue the necessary education and training for international careers? Are you willing and able to obtain firsthand international experiences? Stated another way, do you have what it takes to work in the global economy at home or abroad? Do you think you are well suited for an international career?

WORK AS A GROUP

Discuss the education and training beyond secondary school that a person who aspires to be an international marketing manager needs.

STRENGTHEN YOUR FOUNDATIONAL SKILLS

To prepare for any international career, you need to strengthen your foundational skills. One important foundational skill is cultural understanding. Those who engage in international careers must understand how cultures affect behaviors in the global marketplace. Another critical foundation is communication skills. Communication skills are the backbone that supports and facilitates the transaction of business worldwide. International careers require proficiency in communication with others who may be like or unlike you in a number of ways.

International careers also require possession of analytical skills. These skills include problem-solving and critical-thinking abilities. Since technology is rapidly changing the way in which and the pace at which global business is transacted, technology skills need to be strengthened for international careers. The ability to use appropriate technologies to accomplish work around the world is increasingly important.

Still another group of important foundational skills involves leadership and administration. Careers abroad typically require at least some managerial skills that must be applied in challenging circumstances. Thus, strengthening foundational skills helps to prepare people for international careers. How are your foundational skills developing for a possible career in the global economy?

ENHANCE YOUR LANGUAGE SKILLS

Improving language skills is critical for international careers since you must be able to convey messages to others without confusion. Because English is widely considered to be the language of international business, you need to increase your English language skills. You must be able to convey messages concisely and precisely to both native and nonnative speakers of English.

You also need to develop fluency in one or more foreign languages if you are planning to work abroad. This allows you to access much valuable information that may not be readily available in English. Further, it allows direct communication with those who do not speak English and those who prefer not to speak English. It also shows respect for other cultures. As a result, enhancing language skills helps you prepare for careers around the world. How are your language skills progressing for an international career?

DEVELOP RELEVANT KNOWLEDGE, SKILLS, AND ATTITUDES

Relevant knowledge, skills, and attitudes must be developed in order to be qualified for international careers. Knowledge, skills, and attitudes fall into two broad categories, which are general education and business education.

General Education General education provides a broad background that helps to prepare individuals to function effectively in a global world. A wide variety of subjects fall into this category. Among them are anthropology, English, foreign languages, geography, history, mathematics, politics, psychology, and sociology.

Business Education Business education builds on the foundation of general education and helps prepare you to conduct business around the world. Among its more basic subjects are accounting, business communication, business statistics, economics, finance, human resources, information systems, law, management, marketing, and production and operations management. A more specialized subject is international business. And subjects falling under international business include international business communication, international marketing, international management, and international human resources.

The general education and business education courses together build needed knowledge, skills, and attitudes that are relevant for a wide variety of international careers. How suitable are your skills, knowledge, and attitudes for work abroad?

GAIN INTERNATIONAL EXPERIENCE

Having firsthand international experience contributes to preparation for international careers. But how can relevant international experience be obtained? One way is to travel to other countries. That provides experience in interacting with others who are somewhat different. Another way is to participate in the activities of local organizations that serve diverse ethnic groups. Many community organizations seek volunteers who are willing to devote time and effort to assisting others who can benefit from the offered services. Still another way to get relevant international experience is to participate in a short- or long-term student exchange. This allows participants to spend anywhere from a few weeks to a year living, studying, and sometimes working in another country. Such study-abroad programs are increasingly popular among those who want to experience life in its many forms in another country.

Relevant international experience also can come from hosting overseas visitors. An additional way to gain international experience is through employment in a business with operations abroad. Thus, varied ways exist in which relevant international experience can be obtained. How will you obtain international experience for a career abroad?

NETWORK WITH INTERNATIONAL PROFESSIONALS

Still another way to prepare for international careers is to network with international professionals. This can be done in several ways. One way is to interact with people from other countries who live and work in the immediate area. Often they are eager to share information about their home countries and ways of life. Another approach is to target

GLOBAL BUSINESS EXAMPLE

WHAT IS AN EXPORT-RELATED JOB?

More than 10 million people in the United States have jobs related to the exporting of manufactured goods. In addition, more than 15 million people are employed in nonmanufacturing export industries, including the following.

- trading companies
- business services, including insurance, delivery, information processing, and financial institutions
- transportation
- communication and utilities
- mining and agriculture

In the business services group, for example, a truck driver delivering finished goods from a factory to a port is considered an export-related worker. Other export-related jobs, as defined by the U.S. Department of Commerce, are in factories and offices that do not actually produce exported products. However, these business organizations furnish components, supplies, parts, and administrative services to manufacturing plants that do export products. For example, a steel worker who produces steel used in automobiles made for export has an export-related job.

Think Critically

1. If the U.S. labor force is 136 million, what percent of the United States labor force is employed in export-related jobs?

2. Why does the definition of export-related jobs by the U.S. Department of Commerce include many jobs that are not directly involved in the production of exported products?

3. Under what circumstances, if any, would an accountant be considered to have an export-related job?

companies for which you might like to work sometime in the future. Their employees, especially those in the human resources department, can provide valuable career advice and referrals to other sources of useful information.

Professional organizations are another way to gain access to international professionals. Many times members of professional organizations have lived and worked abroad and are willing to share those experiences with others. Interviews with expatriates who have recently returned from international assignments can also provide valuable information and introductions to other professionals. Thus, those planning international careers can gain valuable insights by networking with professional who have worked abroad. With whom will you network as you prepare for your international career?

After you have adequately prepared yourself for an international career, you can search for the desired types of jobs in the global marketplace. When you do, you can use approaches much like the ones you used for finding jobs in the domestic marketplace. Sooner or later appropriate professional opportunities will become available, and you will be hired. Then you will have achieved your goal of having an international career.

HISTORY: THE BUBONIC PLAGUE

Plagues are the result of widespread disease and poor health care. Between 1347 and 1351, about 75 million Europeans died from the bubonic plague. This reduced the population of Europe by about one-third.

Also known as the Black Death, the bubonic plague is a severe infection in humans and various species of rodents. The disease is spread by fleas that have fed on infected rodents and humans. Once infected, a person's body temperature rises to 40°C (104°F) within a few hours. Left untreated, death occurs for 60 to 90 percent of the victims within a few days. Today certain antibiotics can treat bubonic plague if they are used soon after the symptoms appear.

Plague pneumonia, spread by inhaling infected water droplets, is the most contagious form of the disease. Left untreated, death usually occurs in less than three days.

Today improved sanitation prevents outbreaks of the disease. Modern drugs provide a cure. However, small epidemics of bubonic plague still occur throughout the world, including the United States.

Think Critically
1. What was the approximate population of Europe prior to the plague?
2. Why did most victims of the plague die?
3. What effect did the plague have on the economic development of Europe? Why?
4. Do you think it is possible for a disease to kill a large percentage of the population today?

✓ CheckPoint

What are six ways you can prepare yourself for an international career?

REVIEW GLOBAL BUSINESS CONCEPTS

1. What training opportunities are commonly available to workers who want to improve their skills?

2. How does speaking multiple languages well contribute to a successful international career?

3. How can you gain international experiences without leaving your native country?

SOLVE GLOBAL BUSINESS PROBLEMS

"I've studied three Romance languages: French, Spanish, and Italian. I started with French in high school. I added Spanish while working on my bachelor's degree in finance. I spent my junior year abroad in Madrid, where I studied and worked in a bank. After I graduated, I worked in New York and in Paris. Just prior to being transferred to Rome, I took an intensive four-week course in Italian. Everything was done in Italian, so I quickly picked up that language. Having already studied two related Romance languages helped me progress rapidly in Italian because of the many similarities. It was easier learning three related languages because I could transfer much of what I learned from one language to another. I can now conduct banking business in French, Spanish, Italian, or English as needed. Almost every day I use at least two of the languages I speak."

4. Why did it take the international banker a number of years to master three Romance languages?

5. Why does it make good sense to study languages that are related to each other?

6. Why does an international banker have a competitive advantage if he or she can conduct business in multiple languages?

THINK CRITICALLY

7. What are some jobs that are threatened by technology?

8. How do you know if an international career is right for you?

9. Why are recently returned expatriates an excellent source of information about international careers?

MAKE CONNECTIONS

10. **TECHNOLOGY** How do international employment web sites facilitate international careers?

11. **GEOGRAPHY** How do the Alps contribute to international career opportunities in the travel and hospitality industries?

12. **HISTORY** How did tearing down the Berlin Wall increase international career options?

CHAPTER SUMMARY

12-1 SEARCHING FOR YOUR FIRST JOB

A You can plan your career by determining your personal goals and abilities, evaluating the job market, identifying and applying for specific job opportunities, accepting the most desirable job offer, and planning for personal career development.

B You can explore career information from library materials, media, personal and business contacts, community organizations, and Internet sources.

C Career opportunities are affected by many factors, including personal factors, demographic trends, geographic influences, economic conditions, and industry trends.

12-2 APPLYING FOR A JOB

A A resume should include information such as personal data, career objective, education, experience, related activities, honors and awards, and references.

B A cover letter should get the reader's attention and make the reader want to interview you for a position.

C Prepare for an interview, be early and relaxed for the interview, and send a follow-up letter to resell yourself.

12-3 OBTAINING FUTURE JOBS

A People change jobs for many reasons and need to revise their career paths.

B Prepare for international careers by understanding yourself; strengthening foundational skills; enhancing language skills; developing relevant knowledge, skills, and attitudes; gaining international experience; and networking with international professionals.

Read the case at the beginning of this chapter, and answer the following questions.

1. Why do you think Jennifer Yoon will be able to adjust to the cultural and business differences in Austria?

2. If Jennifer is hired to manage the new Austrian office, how might she develop German language skills?

3. Based on your research about business in Austria, does it have a favorable international business climate? Why or why not?

REVIEW GLOBAL BUSINESS TERMS

Match the terms listed with the definitions.

1. A stamp of endorsement issued by a country that allows a passport holder to enter that country.

2. A written summary of a person's education, training, work experience, and other job qualifications.

3. A meeting where a person is asked a series of in-depth questions designed to help employers select the best person for a job.

4. A commitment to a profession that requires continued education and training and has a clear path for advancement.

5. A document that allows a person into a foreign country for the purpose of employment.

6. A meeting with another person to gather information about a career or an organization.

7. Correspondence that communicates your interest in a specific employment position.

8. An initial meeting to select finalists from the applicant pool for an available position.

9. An employment position obtained mainly for money.

10. A government document proving the bearer's citizenship in the country that issues it.

11. People who can report to a prospective employer about your abilities and work experience.

a. career

b. cover letter

c. informational interview

d. job

e. passport

f. references

g. resume

h. screening interview

i. selection interview

j. visa

k. work visa

MAKE GLOBAL BUSINESS DECISIONS

12. Prepare a poster or bulletin board that shows your top three international business career choices.

13. Conduct library research about the educational background, training requirements, and other information for your top international business career choice.

14. Collect examples of resume formats from career planning books, counselors, and people who have recently applied for and obtained jobs. How are the formats of these documents alike and different? Which format do you think is the most effective one overall? Why?

15. Talk to people who conduct job interviews or who have participated in a job interview. Prepare a report about the common questions asked in an interview and the common mistakes

©Getty Images/PhotoDisc

people make when being interviewed for a job. How can you best make use of what you have learned about interviewing?

16. Design an educational program that will give you the knowledge, skills, and attitudes needed for an international career of your choice.

GLOBAL CONNECTIONS

17. TECHNOLOGY Under what circumstances do you think it would be acceptable to communicate with a prospective employer using e-mail?

18. CULTURAL STUDIES How do study abroad programs develop cultural understanding for international careers?

19. COMMUNICATIONS When applying for an international job in the Netherlands, should you communicate in English or in Dutch? Why?

20. COMMUNICATIONS Why do you think most selection interviews are conducted in person?

21. LITERATURE Find a piece of contemporary literature that has a major character who has a job in international business. What did you learn about that job by reading the selected piece of literature?

22. CAREER PLANNING Create a file of newspaper and magazine articles about an international career that interests you. What have you learned about that career option by gathering and reading the articles?

23. CAREER PLANNING Look at the classified advertising section of your Sunday newspaper. Find three jobs that include an international factor.

©Getty Images/PhotoDisc

THE GLOBAL ENTREPRENEUR

CREATING AN INTERNATIONAL BUSINESS PLAN

PLANNING AN INTERNATIONAL CAREER

Develop a career plan based on the company and country you have been using in this continuing project, or create a new idea for your business in the same or a different country. Make use of previously collected information, and do additional research. This phase of your business plan should include the following components.

1. List types of international jobs available within this multinational organization.

2. List training, skills, and experience commonly required for these international business careers.

3. Describe how social factors, economic conditions, and technology might affect available jobs.

4. Create a fictitious resume for someone applying for a job with this company.

5. List interview questions and tentative answers that might be a part of the application process.

Prepare a written summary or present a short oral report (two or three minutes) of your findings.

©Getty Images/PhotoDisc

©Getty Images/PhotoDisc

Chapter **13**

ORGANIZED LABOR

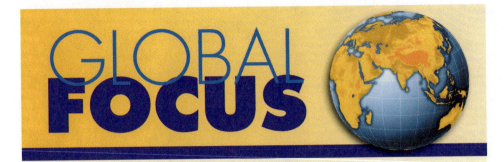

GLOBAL FOCUS

Solidarity in Poland

In the early 1980s, workers in the shipyards of Gdansk, Poland, desired greater economic opportunities and political freedom. The Solidarity labor movement, led by Lech Walesa, organized a strike at the shipyards. This labor action spread to other industries, putting pressure on the Communist government of the country.

In December 1981, in response to the activities of the union, Solidarity was outlawed. Walesa and others were jailed. For the next seven years, the activities of the union moved underground. However, as governments in eastern Europe began their move from Communism to democracy, the Solidarity labor movement again became openly active. Its actions led to the formation of a political party, and in 1989, Solidarity candidates won a majority of the elected seats in the Polish parliament.

One year later Lech Walesa was elected the president of Poland. Walesa was awarded the Nobel Peace Prize in 1983 for his efforts that led to changes in Poland and much of eastern Europe.

Think Critically
1. How did the Solidarity strike at the shipyards set the stage for change in the Polish government?
2. Why do you think Lech Walesa was jailed by the Communist leaders of Poland?
3. Go to the web site of The American Institute of Polish Culture. Click on Poland, Famous Poles, and Lech Walesa to find out what happened to him after he received the Nobel Peace Prize.

13-1

MILESTONES OF THE LABOR MOVEMENT

GOALS

- Describe historical reasons why labor unions were formed and the legal problems they faced.
- Discuss the effects and nature of international labor activities.
- Discuss the history of labor unions and their current status.

©Getty Images/PhotoDisc

FORMATION OF LABOR UNIONS

Unions affect the management of human resources in important ways in the workplace. A **labor union** is an organization of workers whose goal is improving members' working conditions, wages, and benefits. The important principle behind unions is that there is strength in numbers. It is relatively easy to ignore the complaints of one or two employees who are unhappy with some aspect of their jobs. However, it is much more difficult to fire and replace a large organized group of employees.

LABOR UNIONS IN THE UNITED STATES

The members of the early unions in the United States were skilled workers—shoemakers, printers, carpenters, and tailors. Their goal was to protect industry wage rates by preventing other workers who were asking for lower wages from getting hired.

The first large modern unions in the United States were formed during the nineteenth century as a result of the Industrial Revolution. Previously, goods had been made in small quantities and at a fairly slow pace by skilled workers. With the onset of the Industrial Revolution, more goods were produced at a cheaper cost and on a larger scale with the help of machines. Working conditions in factories consisted of long hours of work, unsafe machinery, low wages, few or no benefits, and the use of child labor. In an effort to improve these conditions, workers formed unions.

THE NOBLE ORDER OF THE KNIGHTS OF LABOR

The Noble Order of the Knights of Labor was founded in 1869 as a secret organization by a group of tailors in Philadelphia. Its membership expanded to include both skilled and unskilled workers of all kinds from all over the country. The Knights of Labor supported a broad plan of reform, including the eight-hour workday, abolition of child labor, and public ownership of utilities and railways. The success of a large strike in 1885 against railroads boosted membership in the union significantly. By the late 1880s, membership had reached 800,000.

However, the Noble Order of the Knights of Labor began losing strikes, and violence and chaos marked other strikes. The very diversity of the union prevented a sense of solidarity among its members. Unable to manage the huge union membership, its leaders met with a steady stream of defeats, and members began leaving the organization. By 1900, the Noble Order of the Knights of Labor had virtually disappeared.

Think Critically

1. What factors led to the disappearance of the Noble Order of the Knights of Labor?
2. If it existed today, why would the Noble Order of the Knights of Labor likely be ineffective?

LEGAL STATUS OF THE FIRST UNIONS

Establishing unions in the early years was not easy. U.S. employers formed their own associations to destroy the employees' efforts to organize unions. Management sought the help of the courts, which tended to sympathize with employers rather than with employees.

Unions were described as "criminal conspiracies" whose goal was to hurt trade and commerce. Union members were described as communists, anarchists, and outside agitators by the courts and by management.

A common technique employers used to prevent union activity was to obtain an injunction. An **injunction** is a court order that immediately stops a person or group from carrying out a specific action. Although injunctions were lifted eventually, they stopped union activities and caused the unions to use their time and money to fight legal battles. Union and management conflicts also led to violence and bloodshed. Efforts by management to keep unions in check were matched by the efforts of an ever increasing union membership.

LEGAL STATUS OF UNIONS TODAY

Today U.S. workers have the legal right to join labor unions. The National Labor Relations Act (1935) gave most private-sector workers the right to form unions, bargain with employers, and strike. **Collective bargaining** is negotiation between union workers and their employers on issues of wages, benefits, and working conditions. Since supervisors are considered to be agents of employers, they do not have collective bargaining rights.

The use of injunctions in labor disputes has been limited since 1932. Congress has passed many laws to protect unions and to promote stable labor-management relations. State and local government employees are covered by the various state, county, and city laws. Federal government employees cannot go on strike or negotiate over wages or other money matters.

How was the legal system in the United States used to discourage union activity?

LABOR UNIONS IN OTHER COUNTRIES

In the United States, labor unions developed after laborers already had basic civil rights, such as the right to vote. Labor unions in the United States were mostly concerned with the right to bargain collectively for working conditions. However, unions are not confined to the United States. For example, the close economic relationship between the United States and Canada led to the formation of branches of many U.S. unions in Canada. Typically, these unions represent the workers of U.S. companies operating in Canada. Such unions call themselves international unions. In recent years, Canadian workers have begun to sever their ties with U.S. unions and to establish their own unions.

European labor groups were the vehicle through which workers gained freedom from feudalism, as well as various rights and powers through collective action. There is a strong sense of worker identity in these unions.

Unions in many European countries are major institutions that are often active in national politics. In the United Kingdom, the Labour Party is closely linked with labor unions. Unions provide funds to the party and help in national elections. Historically, when the Labour Party was in power, government policies were more favorable toward unions.

In Germany, unions are organized along industry lines. The unions tend

REGIONAL PERSPECTIVE

HISTORY: UNIONS IN THE UNITED KINGDOM

In the United Kingdom in 1979, the Conservative Party formed a new government under the leadership of Prime Minister Margaret Thatcher. Mrs. Thatcher believed in a free market economy with as little government intervention or involvement as possible. She also thought that labor unions were preventing the United Kingdom from achieving economic success.

When Prime Minister Margaret Thatcher took office, more than half of the workforce were union members who were closely affiliated with the major opposition political party, the Labour Party. In the dozen years that she governed, a series of laws designed to reduce the substantial power and influence of unions in British society were passed.

Many elements of the new laws in Britain were borrowed from the United States, where labor laws are much less open to abuse. Various types of strikes were outlawed, the role of union leaders was reduced, and workers were given the opportunity to stop having a union represent them or to change unions. As a result, union membership in the United Kingdom has fallen

©Peter Turnley/CORBIS

dramatically, and strikes, which were relatively commonplace, occur much less frequently now than in the past.

Think Critically
1. Why did Margaret Thatcher oppose the unions in the United Kingdom?
2. Why was Margaret Thatcher able to radically change the labor laws in the United Kingdom?
3. How do you think the changes in the labor laws benefited the British economy?

to be quite wealthy and to invest their money very carefully in businesses such as banking, insurance, and housing. German unions are also actively involved in the management of businesses. By law, they have representatives on the boards of directors of companies. This policy of having union members serve on the boards of directors is known as **codetermination**.

Japan suffered from much labor unrest in the late 1940s, and the 1950s brought so many strikes that industry output was hampered. Today in Japan, however, the relationship between unions and employers is usually cooperative in nature.

National unions realize that multinational companies sometimes try to escape the unions by transferring production to other countries. Unions perceive this as a threat to the job security of their members. To prevent this, unions have tried to consult with unions in other countries and coordinate their responses to company actions.

Multinational labor activity may increase in the future as the global economy grows in complexity and interdependence. However, national labor unions are divided by differences of opinion. The influence of government and legislation varies significantly from country to country. The level of economic development in a country has a strong effect on the strength and power of a union.

The International Labor Organization is a specialized agency of the United Nations, with headquarters in Geneva, Switzerland. Its primary goal is to improve conditions for workers all over the world. It has been active in establishing minimum standards of working conditions for member-countries to meet.

✓ CheckPoint

What factors affect the strength and power of unions in different countries?

UNIONS PAST AND PRESENT

What is the status of union membership today? Have the economic fluctuations of the last several decades helped or hurt unions and their collective bargaining strength? What effect have the strides in technology had on unionized industries?

EVOLUTION OF THE AFL-CIO

In the United States, labor unions were originally organized along craft lines. Workers with a particular skill formed a local or national union to represent their needs. The American Federation of Labor (AFL), formed in 1886, combined these craft unions to form a huge national labor union, a union of labor unions.

In the 1900s, with the growth of large industries such as automobile, rubber, and steel, some leaders of the AFL pushed to organize the ever increasing number of mass-production workers. Indeed, workers had already begun to form unions not on the basis of their skills, but on the basis of the industry in which they worked. Thus, the workers in the automobile industry organized to form the United Auto Workers Union, and steel industry workers organized to form the United Steel Workers Union.

Leaders of the AFL were divided about whether to allow these unskilled and semiskilled workers into the AFL. This division led to enormous tension in the single largest labor union of the country. Some members of the AFL established the Committee for Industrial Organizations (CIO) in an effort to recruit members from the ranks of industrial workers. (Its name was later changed to the Congress of Industrial Organizations.) The CIO quickly gained millions of members, unionizing workers even where no unions had previously existed. In retaliation, the AFL expelled the unions and their leaders who had organized the CIO. The CIO, with its diverse union membership, became an organization completely separate from the AFL.

In 1955, the AFL and CIO merged to form the AFL-CIO. The **AFL-CIO** is an organization of American unions that uses its size and resources to influence legislation that affects its members. Today most U.S. unions are members of this organization. Figure 13-1 lists some of the major unions that are members of the AFL-CIO and the size of their memberships.

Unions that are strictly craft or strictly industrial are less common today. Most unions have both craft and industrial workers. In addition, unions today have a more diverse membership. Workers in a wide variety of industries and occupations often belong to the same union. Teamster's Union members are a good example of this diversity. They range from truck drivers and chauffeurs to warehouse employees, from service station employees to workers in soft-drink plants, and from dairy workers to airline employees.

MAJOR UNIONS AFFILIATED WITH THE AFL-CIO	
Union	**Members**
National Education Association	2,669,000
International Brotherhood of Teamsters	1,398,000
United Food and Commercial Workers International Union	1,385,000
Service Employees International Union	1,376,000
American Federation of State, County, and Municipal Employees	1,300,000
Laborers' International Union of North America	795,000
American Federation of Teachers	741,000
International Association of Machinists and Aerospace Workers	723,000
International Brotherhood of Electrical Workers	722,000
International Union, United Automobile, Aerospace, and Agricultural Implement Workers of America	702,000
Communications Workers of America	589,000
United Steelworkers of America	589,000
United Brotherhood of Carpenters and Joiners of America	538,000
Source: Adapted from Infoplease almanac.	

Figure 13-1 Most U.S. labor unions are affiliated with the AFL-CIO.

MEMBERSHIP IN UNIONS TODAY

Union membership in the United States is about 14 percent of the total workforce. In the early 1950s, nearly 33 percent of the total workforce was unionized. There are many reasons for this decline in union membership. Manufacturing industries, which traditionally have been union strongholds, have become a smaller part of the economy. Today more jobs are being created in service industries, such as restaurants, banks, and hospitals. Unions have had less experience organizing in service industries. The working conditions in service industries are much different than those in manufacturing industries.

The government has enacted laws that mandate a minimum wage, overtime pay, safe working conditions, and equal employment opportunities for all. Therefore, there is less need to join a union today for collective bargaining with employers.

The decline in union membership is not confined to the United States. Most developed countries with economies and government policies similar to those of the United States have experienced a similar membership decline. Figure 13-2 shows the percentage of the labor force that is active in unions.

WORK AS A GROUP

Discuss the future of unions in the United States.

UNION MEMBERSHIP AS A PERCENTAGE OF THE LABOR FORCE IN 10 COUNTRIES	
Country	**Percentage of Labor Force**
Sweden	90
Denmark	80
Italy	44
Canada	37
Australia	35
United Kingdom	33
Germany	29
Netherlands	25
Japan	24
France	9

Source: World Labour Report 1997-98, International Labour Organization (www.ilo.org)

Figure 13-2 Compared to many other developed countries, the percentage of U.S. workers who belong to a union (14%) is quite small.

✓ **CheckPoint**

Why is union membership declining in many developed countries?

Xtra!
Study Tools
intlbizxtra.swlearning.com

REVIEW GLOBAL BUSINESS TERMS

Define each of the following terms.

1. labor union
2. injunction
3. collective bargaining
4. codetermination
5. AFL-CIO

REVIEW GLOBAL BUSINESS CONCEPTS

6. Explain how the Industrial Revolution created conditions that led to the rise of unions.

7. What is the significance of the National Labor Relations Act of 1935?

8. Why did the American Federation of Labor and the Congress of Industrial Organizations break apart?

SOLVE GLOBAL BUSINESS PROBLEMS

Your restaurant is in a border town and employs workers from each of the two adjacent countries. Your chefs, kitchen helpers, servers, and cashiers have joined a union to negotiate a collective bargaining agreement with you. The agreement will cover wages, working conditions, and other terms of employment. Your goal is to keep the restaurant profitable while meeting the demands of employees.

9. Would you agree to a minimum wage of $10 per hour for all employees? Why or why not?

10. Are you willing to accept the risk of a strike if the employees' demand for at least two weeks of paid vacation for each employee every year is not met? Why or why not?

11. What are your options if the union doesn't take your proposals seriously?

THINK CRITICALLY

12. When you attain your first full-time job, would you consider joining a union? Why or why not?

13. Why has it been very difficult for unions in different countries to cooperate with each other, except to exchange information?

14. Why are federal government and many other public employees (such as police officers and firefighters) not allowed to strike?

MAKE CONNECTIONS

15. **CULTURAL STUDIES** Why might cultures with an individualistic orientation tend to be less tolerant of unions than many other cultures?

16. **LAW** Does codetermination favor the rights of employees over the rights of managers and owners? Why or why not?

UNIONS IN THE WORKPLACE TODAY

13-2

GOALS

- Explain how union representation is achieved.
- Describe methods used to settle labor negotiations.
- Describe how union and management goals are similar.

©Getty Images/PhotoDisc

ACHIEVING UNION REPRESENTATION

The main purpose of a union is to improve the working conditions of its members. Before it can achieve this objective, however, it has to accomplish several steps. First, the union must win the right to represent the workers by a majority vote. Then the workers must individually decide if they want to join the union.

ELECTIONS

Major unions send union organizers to workplaces to convince workers to become union members. Union organizers are trained and experienced in persuading workers to join a union. In other cases, workers may decide on their own that they would like to join a union. When this happens, the workers themselves contact the union.

Unions are always eager to organize workers to increase their membership base. Union members pay membership dues, so more members means more resources for the union. This in turn allows the union to represent union workers more effectively and to persuade new workers to join.

In most cases, the next step is to hold an election. A **union representation election** is held to find out if the workers in a workplace really want to become union members. To win the right to represent workers, the union must get a simple majority of the votes cast. Once the union wins, the employer is required by law to refrain from making arrangements with individual workers. The employer can only negotiate with the union concerning issues such as workers' pay, work hours, benefits, problems, and discipline.

GLOBAL BUSINESS EXAMPLE

THE SAD BUT REAL THING

Coca-Cola is the world's largest soft drink company. It operates in over 200 countries around the world. Although Coke experienced global boom times from the 1980s through the mid-1990s, recent years have been trying for the multinational company.

In an effort to boost global profits, Coca-Cola announced massive layoffs early in 2000. By sacrificing 20 percent of its workforce, about 6,000 employees, Coke hoped to save $300 million a year. It also hoped to give more power to overseas executives.

Usually investors applaud major job cuts and money-saving ways of conducting business. The stock price typically soars in response to bold moves from management. However, Wall Street traders were not favorably impressed, and the stock price quickly fell 13 percent. Investors were wary of the long-term earnings and sales growth for Coca-Cola and concerned about the recent product contamination crisis in Belgium and boycotts in China. Major job and cost reductions weren't enough to redeem the tarnished image of the world's best known brand name, Coca-Cola.
Source: Adapted from "It's the real, sad thing," U.S. News & World Report, February 7, 2000, p. 41.

Think Critically

1. Why do you think Coca-Cola made the highly unusual decision to lay off 20 percent of its employees?
2. What effect do you think the layoffs had on Atlanta, where Coca-Cola is headquartered?
3. Why do you think investors responded unfavorably to the news of massive layoffs at Coca-Cola?

Intense campaigning by both the union and the employer often occurs during the period before the election. The union tries to persuade the workers to vote for the union. The employer tries to dissuade the workers from doing so. To ensure that the election conditions are free and fair, activities such as bribing and threatening workers are forbidden by law.

TYPES OF UNION REPRESENTATION

If the union wins the representation election, it obtains the right to represent all workers, not just those who voted for the union. However, some workers may not want to join the union, and they cannot be forced to join. Because all workers will receive the benefits of union services, the union usually requires that those workers opting not to join still pay a certain fee. This arrangement in which all workers must pay either union dues or a fee is called a **union shop**. It enables the union to obtain resources to perform its functions.

In a **closed shop**, workers are required to join a union before they are hired. Today, closed shops are generally illegal. The other extreme, an open shop, is also very rare. In an **open shop**, workers may choose to join a union or not. If not, they need not pay a fee of any kind. This arrangement is not in the best interest of the union since it may discourage workers from contributing to the union. At the same time, the union has the legal obligation to provide services to the nonmember workers.

✓ CheckPoint

What does a union gain if it wins a representation election?

TOOLS OF LABOR NEGOTIATIONS

©Getty Images/PhotoDisc

Labor and management are required by law to bargain in good faith over issues of wages, hours, and working conditions. However, they may also negotiate over any other issue as long as it is not something illegal. For example, labor and management can negotiate over group health benefits or family leave allowances. Collective bargaining negotiations are often complicated affairs, and it can take several months for employers and union representatives to reach an agreement.

GRIEVANCE PROCEDURE

A grievance procedure is included in most collective bargaining contracts. A **grievance procedure** is the steps that must be followed to resolve a complaint by an employee, the union, or the employer. A discussion of complaints usually begins at the lowest level of management and union officials. If they are unable to settle the matter, the problem then moves to higher levels until the two sides reach an agreement.

ARBITRATION

If the parties can't agree, an arbitrator is needed. An **arbitrator** is an unbiased third party who is called in to resolve problems. The courts have agreed not to overturn or review an arbitrator's decision. Therefore, the decision of the arbitrator is generally final and binding.

While most arbitrators are usually lawyers or university professors, they may be anyone on whom the union and the employer mutually agree. Most arbitrators are members of the American Arbitration Association or the Federal Mediation and Conciliation Service (FMCS). The FMCS also provides services to break deadlocks or mediate disputes that arise when the union and the employer are involved in collective bargaining.

NETBookmark

In India and around the world, child laborers are forming groups and working together to fight for the right to work, a living wage, and better working conditions. Access intlbizxtra.swlearning.com and click on the link for Chapter 13. Read the article entitled "Underage Unions: Child Laborers Speak Up." Then write a paragraph explaining why adult labor groups resist participation by children in labor decisions.

intlbizxtra.swlearning.com

WORK STOPPAGES IN THE UNITED STATES				
Year	Strikes	Workers Involved	Days Involved	Percentage of Working Time Involved
1965	268	999,000	15,140,000	10
1970	381	2,468,000	52,761,000	29
1975	235	965,000	17,563,000	9
1980	187	795,000	20,844,000	9
1985	54	324,000	7,079,000	3
1990	44	185,000	5,926,000	2
1995	31	192,000	5,771,000	2
2000	39	394,000	20,419,000	6

Source: *Statistical Abstract of the United States: 2002*, U.S. Bureau of the Census, Washington, DC, 2003, Table 627.

Figure 13-3 Overall, the number of strikes in the United States has declined during recent decades.

STRIKES

When bargaining with employers, union leaders sometimes threaten strikes to force the employer to make the concessions wanted by union leaders. A **strike** occurs when employees refuse to work to force an employer to agree to certain demands. Part of the dues that members pay usually goes into a strike fund. The union then uses this money to pay striking workers when the need arises.

Some grievance procedures include a *no-strike clause*, which makes it unlawful for workers to go on strike. This allows the company and the union to address a problem when it arises but does not allow interruption of work. Agreeing to a no-strike clause is a big concession on the part of the union. Striking is the most powerful weapon a union has against an employer. In turn, however, the employer agrees to a process to settle any complaints that arise.

Over the years, there has been a decline in strike activity in the United States. Figure 13-3 shows that the number of strikes, the number of workers who actually go on strike, and the total number of workdays lost due to strike have declined.

There are many reasons for this decline in the occurrence of strikes.

- Union membership is decreasing.
- Strikes mean loss of income and benefits, which most workers are not willing to risk.
- Arbitrators help resolve deadlocks before they turn into strikes.
- Employers are better prepared for strikes by learning to operate machines or building up supplies in advance.

WORK AS A GROUP

Discuss the advantages and disadvantages of using arbitration to resolve labor disputes.

- Effectiveness of strikes is reduced by increased automation of manufacturing processes.
- Available workers to defy the strike has increased.
- Workers' fears about losing permanent jobs due to a strike have increased.

Given the general decline in the effectiveness of the strike weapon, unions are resorting to techniques such as pickets, boycotts, and corporate campaigns to put pressure on employers.

✓ CheckPoint

What are three methods used to secure agreement between unions and management?

MANAGEMENT AND LABOR UNIONS

Generally speaking, managers would prefer to work without having to deal with labor unions. Labor unions reduce a manager's freedom to act and to make decisions. Managers must consult with the union on many issues. In addition, unions seek higher wages, better benefits, and improved working conditions for their members. Therefore, the profits of the company are reduced. However, workers who feel secure in their jobs, who believe their wages are fair, and who enjoy safe working conditions are more productive than workers who feel otherwise.

A Question of Ethics

INTERNATIONAL STRIKEBREAKERS

Workers at a brewery near Sydney, Australia, went on strike to demand job security. New Zealand-based multinational company Lion Nathan owned the brewery. Within hours of the beginning of the strike, Lion Nathan hired 50 New Zealanders and flew them to Sydney to take the jobs of the strikers. With unemployment above 10 percent in New Zealand, there were many people willing to cross the Tasman Sea to work. Lion Nathan was able to employ New Zealanders in Australia with ease because treaties between the two countries allowed citizens of one country to work in the other.

The conduct of Lion Nathan con-firmed the worst fears the union in Sydney had about multinational firms. In New Zealand itself, many people criticized the 50 strikebreakers who went to work in Australia. They pointed out that an Australian firm in New Zealand could just as easily employ Australian strikebreakers if New Zealand workers went on strike.

Think Critically

1. If you were a citizen of Australia when the strikebreakers were used, how would you feel? Why?
2. Was it ethical for Lion Nathan to hire New Zealand strikebreakers to work in Australia? Why?
3. Why did many New Zealanders respond negatively to the use of strikebreakers by Lion Nathan?

Employers use many techniques to keep unions out of the workplace. When wages and benefits are good and employees are treated fairly, the workers have no particular need for a union. Workers find unions attractive only when they believe they are being treated unfairly. Many employers resort to illegal activities, such as disciplining union sympathizers or threatening dismissal, to discourage workers from joining a union. In other situations, the employer may prolong the collective bargaining sessions in an attempt to discredit the union in the eyes of its members.

Employers have the right to a **lockout**, which is literally locking employees out of the workplace to force a union to agree to certain demands. A lockout is similar to the workers' right to strike.

WHEN UNIONS AND MANAGEMENT WORK TOGETHER

Unions and employers have often viewed each other more as adversaries than as allies. In recent years, however, there have been an increasing number of cases in which unions and employers have begun to cooperate not only to save jobs, but also to increase productivity. Employers are acknowledging that trained and experienced workers are an asset because they contribute to the efficient operation of the business. Unions, too, realize that their ability to demand better wages and improved working conditions depends on the overall success of the company.

E-COMMERCE IN ACTION

Pinnacle PLC Goes Electronic

In response to aggressive efforts to unionize its operations in several western European countries, the management of Pinnacle PLC decided to change directions. It decided to phase out its luxury goods retail operations in Europe and Asia and to expand its electronic marketing operations over a three-year period.

Managers of Pinnacle PLC decided to transfer its primary operations to Hong Kong for various reasons. Among them were its large English-speaking population, its familiarity with both Western and Eastern business practices, and its manufacturing and shipping capabilities.

During the transition, the managers of Pinnacle PLC realized that major changes in operations would be necessary. They decided to refine and expand the company web site. In conjunction with that, they agreed about the need to find reliable manufacturers, suppliers, and shippers in Southeast Asia. Further, they developed a plan to create a niche market for Pinnacle products with a sustainable competitive advantage. The managers insisted that the emerging electronic operations be fully prepared to cope with the expected volume of web-site activity and the demand for products.

Think Critically

1. Do you think it was ethical for the managers of Pinnacle PLC to move primary operations to Hong Kong to avoid unionization efforts? Why or why not?
2. What suggestions would you offer to managers of Pinnacle PLC to improve the transition plans?

✔ CheckPoint

What are four methods that have been used by management to discourage unionization or influence collective bargaining?

REVIEW GLOBAL BUSINESS TERMS

Define each of the following terms.

1. union representation election
2. union shop
3. closed shop
4. open shop
5. grievance procedure
6. arbitrator
7. strike
8. lockout

Xtra!
Study Tools
intlbizxtra.swlearning.com

REVIEW GLOBAL BUSINESS CONCEPTS

9. What is the process for forming a union in a workplace?

10. What are the reasons for the decline in strike activity?

11. Why is there a trend toward cooperation between employers and unions?

SOLVE GLOBAL BUSINESS PROBLEMS

You are a union organizer trying to persuade the overseas employees of a computer manufacturer to form a union. Because the pay, working conditions, and vacation policy at the plant are well below those at the unionized U.S. plant, you think you can succeed.

12. The overseas employees do seem somewhat dissatisfied. How would you approach them?

13. What would be your top priority that would most benefit these employees in a developing country?

14. How would you respond if the company promises all of its employees a 30 percent raise if they reject the union? Why?

THINK CRITICALLY

15. What reasons might an employer use to persuade workers not to support a union in a representation election?

16. Why do you think other developed countries have a greater percentage of workers who are union members than the United States does?

17. What does an employer gain by having unionized workers?

MAKE CONNECTIONS

18. **TECHNOLOGY** How might technology be used to help persuade employees to form a union?

19. **CULTURAL STUDIES** What aspects of the mainstream U.S. culture discourage union membership?

20. **LAW** Why do you think closed shops are rare in the United States?

21. **TECHNOLOGY** Use the Internet to locate resources that unions have available online.

CHAPTER SUMMARY

13-1 MILESTONES OF THE LABOR MOVEMENT

A Labor unions arose out of the harsh working conditions of the Industrial Revolution to improve members' working conditions, wages, and benefits.

B The AFL and CIO merged to form the largest U.S. organization of unions, the AFL-CIO. Its size and resources make it very powerful.

C Unions in various countries have difficulty cooperating because of differences of opinion, the influence of government and legislation, and the level of economic development.

D Membership in unions is declining in most developed countries because of the increase in service industries versus manufacturing industries and government legislation that is favorable to labor.

13-2 UNIONS IN THE WORKPLACE TODAY

A A workplace becomes unionized when a union wins a representation election.

B Most collective bargaining contracts include a grievance procedure. An arbitrator may be brought in to settle a dispute. A union may use the power of a strike to persuade a company to meet its demands.

C Employers may reduce unionization by offering attractive wages, benefits, and conditions so there is no need for a union. An employer may also illegally discipline or threaten union sympathizers, prolong collective bargaining sessions to discredit a union, or engage in a lockout.

D Unions and employers frequently cooperate as allies today. Unions recognize that a profitable company can afford to offer better wages and conditions, while companies recognize that a satisfied workforce can increase productivity and company success.

GLOBAL REFOCUS

Read the case at the beginning of this chapter, and answer the following questions.

1. What caused the Polish workers to organize and strike?

2. What actions can workers take when they believe their economic and political rights have been violated?

REVIEW GLOBAL BUSINESS TERMS

Match the terms listed with the definitions.

1. An unbiased third party called in to resolve problems whose decision is usually final and binding.

2. A procedure held to find out if the workers in a workplace really want to become union members.

3. A court order that immediately stops a party from carrying out a specific action.

4. A workplace in which workers may choose to join a union or not.

5. A policy of having union members serve on the boards of directors.

6. The steps that must be followed to resolve a complaint by an employee, the union, or the employer.

7. An organization of workers whose goal is improving members' working conditions, wages, and benefits.

8. A workplace in which workers are required to join a union before they are hired.

9. Negotiation between union workers and their employers on issues of wages, benefits, and working conditions.

10. A refusal by employees to work in order to force an employer to agree to certain demands.

11. A workplace in which all workers must pay either union dues or a fee.

12. The closing down of a workplace by an employer to force a union to agree to certain demands.

13. The organization of American unions that uses its size and resources to influence legislation that affects its members.

a. AFL-CIO
b. arbitrator
c. closed shop
d. codetermination
e. collective bargaining
f. grievance procedure
g. injunction
h. labor union
i. lockout
j. open shop
k. strike
l. union representation election
m. union shop

MAKE GLOBAL BUSINESS DECISIONS

14. Identify and contact a union member. Develop a list of questions to ask the person. In your interview, you may wish to ask how the person feels about the union and how the union affects his or her job and workplace.

15. Collect advertisements, pictures, articles, and other information used by unions to persuade consumers to buy union-made products or patronize unionized businesses. What reasons do the advertisements give for supporting those products and businesses? How persuasive are the advertisements? Why?

16. Conduct library research about antiunion activities in the United States in the nineteenth and early twentieth centuries. Develop a list of the most common types of such activities. How do you think these activities affected the development of unions later in the twentieth century?

17. Create, administer, and summarize the findings from a five to ten question survey that determines the attitudes of classmates toward unions.

18. Obtain information about the history of strikes in the United States as well as in other countries for an industry of your choice. Try to explain the differences in strike rates among the countries.

19. Communicate with a union in your community to obtain a copy of a collective bargaining agreement. Review the agreement, and find out how the contract deals with grievances, union dues, seniority, leaves, and strikes. Summarize the information for your class.

20. List reasons why workers in banking, financial services, and real estate are less likely to join a union. What do you think a union could offer that would attract these workers to join?

GLOBAL CONNECTIONS

21. **MATHEMATICS** Create a graph that conveys the data in Figure 13-1.

22. **TECHNOLOGY** Visit the web site of the AFL-CIO (www.aflcio.org), and read about one of the issues presented at the site. Summarize the issue in a short paper.

23. **CULTURAL STUDIES** Research Islamic law to find out what effect, if any, its provisions have on employees. Share your findings with your classmates.

24. **COMMUNICATIONS** Find out how the International Labor Organization, a United Nations agency, communicates with countries around the world to improve the working conditions of laborers.

25. **COMMUNICATIONS** If you want to persuade employees in a high-context culture to unionize, would print or verbal communication be more effective? Why?

26. **HISTORY** Why did a number of early U.S. unions disappear by the beginning of the twentieth century?

27. **HISTORY** Research the contributions of a nationally prominent union leader in a country of your choice, and prepare a related oral report.

28. **CAREER PLANNING** Research the role of unions in a country where you might like to work in the future, and write a summary report.

29. **HISTORY** Use the Internet to identify important events in the history of a labor union or the labor movement.

30. **LAW** Use the Internet to find more information on a law that affects labor unions.

31. **TECHNOLGY** Use the Internet to identify one recent union representation election, the issues in the election and the final out come.

THE GLOBAL
ENTREPRENEUR
CREATING AN INTERNATIONAL BUSINESS PLAN

LABOR-MANAGEMENT RELATIONS

Develop a labor relations plan based on the company and country you have been using in this continuing project, or create a labor plan for a different business or a different country. Make use of previously collected information, and do additional research. This phase of your business plan should include the following components.

1. What is the role of organized labor (unions) in the country?

2. What laws exist to protect workers?

3. What actions are commonly taken by workers to protect their rights?

4. What types of employment positions will be available as a result of your business idea? What are the average wage rates and salary levels for these jobs in that country?

5. What benefits are available to workers in the country?

6. What other issues are of concern to workers in this country?

Prepare a written summary or present a short oral report (two or three minutes) of your findings.

©Getty Images/PhotoDisc

GLOBAL
CROSS-CULTURAL TEAM PROJECT

Manage International Business Operations

Planning, organizing, implementing, and controlling are every manager's responsibilities. While these tasks may seem similar around the world, various social and cultural factors affect them. Participating in a cross-cultural team allows managers to better understand and work with people of differing values and beliefs.

GOAL

To determine the influence of culture on management activities in various regions of the world.

ACTIVITIES

Working in teams, select a geographic region you will represent—Africa, Asia, Europe, Latin America, Middle East, or North America.

1. Information about management activities in various regions may be obtained on the Web, in the library, and by talking to people who have lived in or visited those areas. Your findings will be applied to various duties of managers.
2. Summarize how organizational decisions are commonly made in your region. Are business actions based on the decisions of people at the top of the organization? Or are plans the result of participation by people at various levels in the organization?
3. Explain the process commonly used to select employees. Are family members or friends given preference over others in the hiring process?
4. Research the educational systems and career paths taken by people in various countries in your region. What factors influence a person's choice of training and employment in this region of the world?
5. Describe the activities of organized labor in your region. How influential are labor unions in various countries in this geographic area?
6. **Global Business Decision** An international company needs you to create a promotion policy. Decide if managers for offices around the world should be (a) from the home country of the company, (b) from the country where the office is located, or (c) a qualified person from anywhere in the world. Explain which of these choices your team would select.

TEAM SKILL

Traits of Cross-Cultural Team Members
Desired characteristics of team members vary from region to region. Discuss with your team the traits that might be preferred in each geographic area. How do the desired traits differ from one region to another?

PRESENT

• Prepare a 2- or 3-page summary report of management activities in your geographic region.
• As a team, develop a script and present an in-class dramatization of the management differences in various regions of the world.

Marketing Management Role Play

You are the business administrator of a large U.S. hospital. Technology has improved maintaining files for the thousands of patients who have used your hospital. Your position requires you to make decisions that improve the profitability of the hospital. Record keeping has become increasingly expensive in the United States, making it attractive to look at less expensive international markets for outsourcing the job. Outsourcing involves hiring an independent contractor to perform a business function for a company. India has quickly risen as a leader in technology input and record keeping. Wages for technological record keeping in India are much more reasonable than com-parative wages in the U.S. You have been asked to present to the hospital board of directors the pros and cons of outsourcing record keeping to com-panies in India. You are also asked to make a proposal to keep the record keeping in the U.S. or to outsource it to companies in India.

You have ten minutes to come up with a successful strategy concerning outsourcing. You will be presenting your case to the hospital board of direc-tors. You must decide whether to keep jobs in the U.S. or continue to outsourcing to India. You have five minutes to state your case to the hospital board.

PERFORMANCE INDICATORS EVALUATED

■ Understand the implications that outsourcing to international companies has on the U.S. workforce.
■ Determine strategies for the best financial gains.
■ Explain the role of American workers when jobs are outsourced to other countries.
■ Describe the pros and cons of outsourcing work to companies in other countries.

For more detailed information about performance indicators, go to the DECA web site.

THINK CRITICALLY

1. What is the greatest advantage of outsourcing jobs to companies in India?
2. Why will Americans be concerned about outsourcing of jobs?
3. What political concerns may influence the international outsourcing decision?
4. Carefully outline your management decision for the hospital keeping profit as a high priority.

www.deca.org/publications/HS_Guide/guidetoc.html

UNIT 4

INFORMATION AND PRODUCTION SYSTEMS FOR GLOBAL BUSINESS

REGIONAL PROFILE
AFRICA

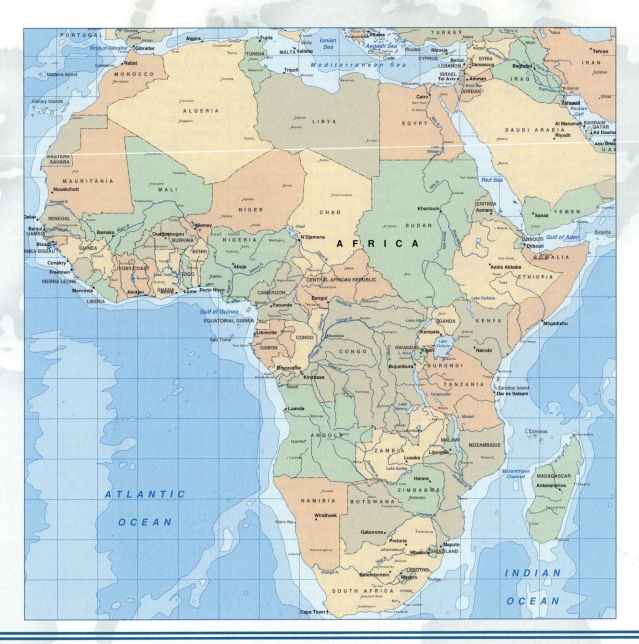

IF YOU WERE THERE

Francis Thuo is a successful businessperson, a member of the Lions Club, and active in the Nairobi Stock Exchange. The view from his office in the International House includes the Hilton Hotel; the Parliament building; and the vast plains in the distance that are home to Kenya's antelope, zebra, and giraffe.

Thuo's view is symbolic of Africa's diverse cultural landscape, which includes modern urban traffic jams as well as nomadic cattle herders. African ethnic groups include Blacks, Arabs, Indians, Asians, Whites, and others. More than 1,000 languages are spoken, and an uncounted number of religions are practiced.

Geography

Africa is almost four times the size of the United States. The continent includes the great highlands in Kenya and Ethiopia and the Great Rift Valley. There are mountains in the north and southeast of Africa. However, the largest mountains stand in the east and are snowcapped—on the equator. Kilimanjaro is the tallest at 19,340 feet.

Much of the interior of Africa is a plateau consisting of rolling hills, deserts, savannas, and rain forests. The Nile, which is the longest river in the world, is in East Africa. The Sahara (Arabic word for *desert*) covers one-fourth of the African continent. The Sahara was once a fertile land that supported a thriving population. However, about 4,000 B.C. the climate changed the Sahara region into a desert. Overfarming, overgrazing, and drought causes the Sahara to expand every year.

©Getty Images/PhotoDisc

Early Civilizations

The earliest African civilizations grew along the Nile River and the Red Sea. At this location, there were Egyptian kingdoms built that date back to 3,100 B.C. To the west, the kingdoms of Ghana and Mali ruled vast territories of sub-Saharan Africa from the fourth to sixteenth centuries A.D. Ghana's position—midway between the salt mines of north Africa and the gold deposits to the south—ensured its hold on a trading empire that spread over 200,000 square miles. Caravans from North Africa carried salt, metal goods, and cloth across the Sahara to Ghana in return for gold, farm produce, and kola nuts from the south.

By the thirteenth century, the kingdom of Mali had taken control of Ghana's empire and expanded it over an even wider area. Mali's city of Timbuktu was a center of learning that attracted scholars from Cairo and Mecca.

European Control

In the 1500s, European immigrants began to arrive, and traders were interested in Africa's gold, diamonds, ivory, and other natural resources. Empires, kingdoms, and tribes continued to rule Africa until the late 1800s. However, the opening of the Suez Canal in 1869 brought a new wave of immigrants. In 1885, fourteen nations agreed to partition the "prize," the land of Africa, and take it away from the native inhabitants. By 1914, France had conquered most of North and West Africa. Britain took control of Egypt and, along with the Germans and the Italians, most of East Africa.

The southern part of the continent was divided among Britain, Portugal, and Germany. King Leopold II of Belgium took the Congo in central Africa as his own private colony. The people became his slaves and through execution and torture, thousands were killed. In 1902, the British defeated the Dutch settlers (Afrikaners) in southern Africa. In 1910, the British created the Union of South Africa, which excluded nonwhites from the political process. Ethiopia and Liberia were the only African nations to retain their independence.

Freedom

Nationalist movements began to appear throughout the continent between the world wars. However, independence for most African nations was not achieved until the late 1950s and early 1960s. A few European nations relinquished control after mass protests and labor strikes. Unfortunately, prolonged guerrilla warfare was usually the real force of liberation in countries such as Algeria, Angola, Mozambique, Guinea-Bissau, Kenya, and Namibia.

Today greater mobility has led many to leave the home village, but family and tribal identity thrive. Independence fostered a renewed sense of pride in African culture. Children are taught tribal and family history.

Religion and Art

Islam has flourished, especially in the north, while European and American churches and schools continue to promote Christianity. Ancient tribal religions are still important, and often they are combined with Christianity. The indigenous African religions believe in one ultimate God along with lesser gods or ancestral spirits who act as intermediaries between God and mortals. This religious system is known as *polytheism*.

African arts are often associated with religion. Music, stories, dance, and carved wooden masks have integral roles in ceremonies that connect humans to their ancestors and the spiritual world. Art also entertains, educates, and stimulates thought. African music is unique for its polyrhythmic structure, with as many as a dozen rhythms all played simultaneously. European painters have been influenced by African artists' expression of the essence of a human or animal subject through sharp angles and exaggerated features. African designs have found their way onto clothing made throughout the world.

©Peter Turnley/CORBIS

The African landscape has often inspired the artist. However, it is a harsh land that, at times, punishes its people. During the 1980s and 1990s, the combination of poor soil, drought, and wars led to the starvation of millions of people in Chad, Ethiopia, Liberia, Mozambique, Sierra Leone, Somalia, Sudan and the Democratic Republic of the Congo (formerly Zaire). The suffering in Ethiopia resulted in the 1985 famine relief concert Live-Aid, which raised funds for food for the hungry. In 1992, images of suffering on Western television helped to pressure the United States into sending a military force to protect relief workers in Somalia.

Apartheid

South Africa's white minority used a government policy called *apartheid* to segregate and to discriminate politically and economically against non-European groups—which included Blacks, Indians, and people of mixed race. However, in 1990, after economic isolation from most of the world, President de Klerk began changing the system of white minority rule when he released Nelson Mandela from prison and lifted the ban on the African National Congress. In 1994, Nelson Mandela was elected president in a peaceful election.

Impediments to Economic Progress

Civil wars, military revolts, and political instability have prevented many African nations from making economic and social progress. Authoritarian systems are more common than democratic institutions; however, peaceful transfers of power have taken place in Botswana, Cameroon, Kenya, Senegal, and Tanzania.

During the 1980s, the African elephant became an endangered species when its population was cut in half as a result of poaching. In 1989, 112 nations agreed on a ban in ivory trade, and some countries began removing tusks to protect the animals. The program was successful, and by 1993, Botswana, Malawi, Namibia, South Africa, and Zimbabwe wanted to restore the trade on a limited basis.

©Getty Images/PhotoDisc

Think Critically

1. Do you think it was a good idea to send soldiers to Somalia to protect relief workers in 1992?
2. Use the library or do Internet research to determine the leadership situation in South African today.
3. Do you think the ivory trade should be resumed? Should African nations be able to do as they wish with their elephants?

COUNTRY PROFILE/AFRICA

Country	Population		GDP		Exports	Imports	Monetary Unit	Inflation	Unemployment	Life Expectancy	Literacy Rate
	thousands	growth rate %	$billions	$ per capita	\$billions			percent	percent	years	percent
Algeria	31,800	1.67	177	5,600	19.5	10.6	Algerian Dinar	3	31	70.54	70
Angola	13,625	3.2	13.3	1,330	7.92	3.04	Kwanza	106	more than half	36.96	42
Benin	6,736	2.65	6.8	1,040	0.392	0.516	*	3.3	NA	51.08	40.9
Botswana	1,785	0.85	12.4	7,800	2.67	2	Pula	8.1	40	32.26	79.8
Burkina Faso	13,002	2.95	12.8	1,040	0.216	0.344	*	3.5	NA	44.46	26.6
Burundi	6,825	3.1	3.7	600	0.049	0.108	Burundi Franc	12	NA	43.2	51.6
Cameroon	16,018	1.83	26.4	1,700	1.74	1.1	*	4.5	30	48.05	79
Cape Verde	463	2.01	0.6	1,700	0.026	0.241	Cape Verdean escudo	3	21	69.83	76.6
Central African Republic	3,865	1.29	4.6	1,300	0.146	0.131	*	3.6	8	41.71	51
Chad	8,598	2.96	8.9	1,030	0.135	212	*	6	NA	48.51	47.5
Comoros	768	2.83	0.242	710	0.011	0.054	Comoran Franc	3.5	20	61.18	56.5

Country	Population		GDP		Exports	Imports	Monetary Unit	Inflation	Unemploy- ment	Life Expectancy	Literacy Rate
	thousands	growth rate %	$billions	$ per capita	\$billions			percent	percent	years	percent
Congo, Democratic Republic of the	55,042	2.88	32	590	0.75	1.02	Congolese Franc	16	NA	48.93	65.5
Congo, Republic of the	2,908	2.57	2.5	900	1.746	0.803	*	4	NA	50.02	83.8
Côte d'Ivoire	16,631	1.62	25.5	1,550	3.95	2.41	*	3.2	13	42.65	50.9
Djibouti	703	1.58	0.586	1,400	0.034	0.205	Djiboutian Franc	2	50	43.13	67.9
Equatorial Guinea	498	2.65	1.04	2,100	0.175	0.292	*	6	30	54.75	85.7
Eritrea	4,141	3.65	3.2	740	0.035	0.471	Nafka	15	NA	53.18	58.6
Ethiopia	70,678	2.46	46	700	0.433	1.63	Birr	4	NA	41.24	42.7
Gabon	1,329	1.79	6.7	5,500	2.5	0.911	*	2.3	21	57.12	63.2
Gambia, The	1,426	2.66	2.5	1,770	0.12	0.207	Dalasi	5.5	NA	54.38	40.1
Ghana	20,922	2.17	39.4	1,980	1.9	2.74	New Cedi	14.5	20	56.53	74.8
Guinea	8,480	1.59	15	1,970	0.731	0.526	Guinean Franc	6	NA	49.54	35.9
Guinea-Bissau	493	2.95	1.2	900	0.049	0.062	*	4	NA	46.97	42.4
Kenya	31,987	1.45	31	1,000	1.89	3.18	Kenyan Shilling	1.9	40	45.22	85.1
Lesotho	1,802	0.14	5.3	2,450	0.279	0.679	Loti	10	45	36.94	84.8
Liberia	3,367	4.05	3.6	1,100	0.055	0.17	Liberian Dollar	15	NA	48.15	57.5
Libya	5,551	1.93	40	7,600	6.76	4	Libyan Dinar	1	30	76.07	82.6
Madagascar	17,404	2.84	14	870	0.068	0.919	Malagasy Franc	7.4	5.9	56.14	68.9
Malawi	12,105	2.01	7	660	0.363	0.639	Malawian Kwacha	27.4	NA	37.98	62.7
Mali	13,007	3	9.2	840	0.562	0.552	*	4.5	14.6	45.43	46.4
Mauritania	2,893	2.98	5	1,800	0.359	0.319	Ouguiya	3	21	51.93	41.7
Mauritius	1,221	0.96	12.9	10,800	1.56	1.95	Mauritarian Rupee	6.4	8.8	71.8	85.6
Morocco	30,566	1.62	112	3,700	7.1	10.2	Moroccan Dirham	3.6	19	70.04	51.7
Mozambique	18,863	1.75	17.5	900	1.71	2.44	Metical	15.2	21	31.3	47.8
Namibia	1,987	1.42	8.1	4,500	1.28	1.45	Namibian Dollar	8	35	42.77	84
Niger	11,972	3.62	8.4	820	0.288	0.306	*	3	NA	42.21	17.6
Nigeria	124,009	2.53	105.9	840	12.9	8.59	Naira	14.2	28	51.01	68
Rwanda	8,387	2.16	7.2	1,000	0.093	0.245	Rwandan Franc	5.5	NA	39.33	70.4
Senegal	10,095	2.39	16.2	1,580	1.03	1.37	*	3	48	56.37	40.2
Seychelles	80	0.88	0.605	7,600	0.215	0.387	Seychelles Rupee	0.5	NA	71.25	58
Sierra Leone	4,971	3.8	2.7	500	0.042	0.168	Leone	1	NA	42.84	31.4
Somalia	9,890	4.17	4.1	550	0.186	0.314	Somali Shilling	NA	NA	47.34	37.8
South Africa	45,026	0.59	412	9,400	31	26	Rand	9.9	37	46.56	86.4
Sudan	33,610	2.17	49.3	1,360	1.7	1.4	Sudanese Dinar	9.2	18.7	57.73	61.1
Swaziland	1,077	0.8	4.6	4,200	0.809	0.882	Lilangeni	11.8	34	39.47	81.6
Tanzania	36,977	1.4	22.1	610	0.666	1.34	Tanzanian Shilling	4.8	NA	44.56	78.2
Togo	4,909	2.34	7.6	1,500	0.362	0.485	*	4	NA	53.43	60.9
Tunisia	9,832	1.07	64.5	6,600	6.61	9	Tunisian Dinar	2.5	15.4	74.4	74.2
Uganda	25,827	3.24	29	1,200	0.452	1.03	Ugandan Shilling	0.1	NA	44.88	69.9
Zambia	10,812	1.16	8.5	870	0.757	0.978	Zambian Kwacha	21	50	35.25	80.6
Zimbabwe	12,891	0.49	28	2,450	1.96	1.8	Zimbabwean Dollar	134.5	70	39.01	90.7

* Communaute Financiere Africaine Franc (CFAF)

Chapter 14

INFORMATION NEEDS FOR GLOBAL BUSINESS ACTIVITIES

GLOBAL FOCUS

ISIS LTD DESIGNS MAJOR INFORMATION SYSTEMS

Isis Information Systems (ISIS), part of the electronics giant Altech, is a prominent South African systems integrator and software development house. It is well known for planning, designing, integrating, and implementing complex information systems for large organizations.

ISIS specializes in governmental, manufacturing, telecommunications, metals, transportation, and banking information systems. It has a reputation for delivering well-designed and fully functional information systems that enhance organizational effectiveness.

For example, ISIS developed a sophisticated production management system at the Toyota Stamping Division in Durban. The system is designed to reduce system maintenance costs, production time, and manufacturing expenses. It provides both workers and managers with timely and relevant information to support operational decision making.

Through its offices in Pretoria and Cape Town, ISIS provides Africa with leading-edge technology and related support servies.

Think Critically

1. Why would it make sense that ISIS is part of an electronics conglomerate?
2. What suggests that ISIS is a major provider of information systems?
3. Go to the web site for ISIS Information Systems to obtain additional information about company operations. Prepare a report of your findings.

14-1 CREATING GLOBAL INFORMATION SYSTEMS

GOALS

- Explain why information is power in the global economy.
- Describe the three major components of global information systems.
- Explain some of the factors to consider when planning and developing global information systems.

©Getty Images/PhotoDisc

INFORMATION IS POWER

Information is the source of power in the global economy. Information technology helps to drive the global marketplace. It also facilitates addressing the many challenges that managers must face when operating in the complex global environment. It is essential in the global economy to have the right information in the right form at the right time. Without such information, businesses are so handicapped that they cannot hope to thrive as they compete against other businesses that do have the valuable information. In fact, organizations with poor information systems struggle to survive in the global world of business.

Strategic Resource Like other valuable business assets, information is an important strategic resource. It allows businesses to position themselves favorably in the international marketplace so they can attain their business goals and objectives.

Competitive Advantage Given enough of the right information, businesses can gain competitive advantages over their competitors. This allows them to function more efficiently and effectively than their competitors and gives them the best possible global business opportunities. By being able to skillfully use information to outmaneuver their challengers, certain multinational businesses enjoy competitive advantages over other businesses with less effective global information systems.

Now that the global economy is a reality, businesses around the world must be able to function effectively 24 hours a day, 365 days a year. To do this, businesses must have highly effective global information systems that deliver appropriate information as needed.

GLOBAL BUSINESS
EXAMPLE

COMPANY EMPLOYEES GETTING WIRED

Employees of multinational companies are getting wired at an increasing rate and at company expense—even at home. Ford Motor Co. is making home computers available for its 350,000 employees to link them to the Internet and other company employees worldwide. The project to electronically empower Ford employees around the globe is estimated to cost $300 million.

The plan is based on the belief that a workforce that is connected is more productive. By increasing the flow of information around historic bottlenecks, decision making can be sped up and improved.

Delta Air Lines is also planning to link 72,000 employees worldwide in a similar manner. If other companies follow the lead of these two companies, ways of conducting business electronically could change significantly.

Source: Adapted from W. Holstein, "Let Them Have PCs: Ford, Delta Get Wired," *U.S. News & World Report*, (February 14, 2000) p. 43.

Think Critically

1. What are the benefits of electronically linking company employees worldwide?
2. What might be some of the challenges of electronically linking company employees worldwide?
3. How might companies benefit by putting computers in employees' homes when many already have computer linkups at work?
4. Do you think that encouraging employees to engage in work from their homes is a desirable practice from the company's perspective? Why or why not? What do you think the employees' perspective is?

▌INFORMATION SYSTEMS IN DOMESTIC BUSINESS

Developing and managing a suitable information system is much easier in a domestic business environment than in an international business environment. In that relatively simple domestic business environment, usually one language dominates. The prevailing culture is relatively similar from location to location. Over time, a well-developed infrastructure develops to support business activities. *Infrastructure* refers to the nation's transportation and communications systems. It is the basic framework of an organization. Usually one primary political entity oversees and regulates business activities. Since only one country on one continent is involved, business is transacted in a limited number of time zones using one currency.

▌INFORMATION SYSTEMS IN INTERNATIONAL BUSINESS

Developing and managing a suitable information system is more challenging in a complex international business environment. So many more variables must be considered and accommodated. For example, a business operating in the global economy must cope with multiple languages. The involved cultures are likely to be significantly different from each other. The countries in which the business operates might all have their own unique forms of government and business regulations. An international business with operations scattered around the globe must function in different countries that are on one or more continents and use various currencies. Figure 14-1 contrasts the major differences between the domestic and international business environments that must be bridged by information systems.

Since the international business environment is more complex than the domestic business environment, it requires a more sophisticated information system. That global information system must adequately reflect all of the variables of the international business environment if it is to provide high-quality information. Creating and refining a powerful global information system is a challenging, time-consuming, and expensive task. Nevertheless, it is an investment that can pay a handsome return in the form of both

Domestic Business Environment	International Business Environment
One dominant language	Multiple languages
One dominant culture	Multiple cultures
Well-developed infrastructure	Multiple infrastructures
One dominant government	Multiple governments
One dominant business regulatory system	Multiple business regulatory systems
One country on one continent	Multiple countries on multiple continents
Limited time zones	Multiple time zones
One currency	Multiple currencies

Source: Adapted from P. C. Deans & M. J. Kane, "Information Systems Management: The Global Perspective," International Dimensions Of Information Systems and Technology (Boston: PWS-Kent Publishing Company, 1992), pp. 1–14.

Figure 14-1 The domestic and international business environments are significantly different and necessitate different types of information systems.

strategic and competitive advantages. Wise multinational organizations develop sophisticated global information systems.

✓ **CheckPoint**

What are two reasons information is so powerful in the global economy?

INFORMATION SYSTEM COMPONENTS

A **global information system** is a computer-based system that provides information about company operations around the world to managers of a multinational organization. A global information system is composed of three basic elements: data inputs, operational components, and system outputs.

DATA INPUTS

Data inputs are those pieces of information that feed the global information system database. These inputs reflect both internal organization inputs and external environment inputs. Components of the internal organization inputs include transaction processing systems, shipping records, a customer database, accounts receivable, inventory records, and the like. Components of the external environment inputs include market research, industry trends, economic trends, competitor trends, and data sharing with business partners.

OPERATIONAL COMPONENTS

Operational components are the parts of an information system that manage the database and system operations. There are five basic types of operational components.

Systems Controls To ensure that the information system functions properly, companies implement controls to regulate the systems. Examples of systems controls include security access, internal operations checks, and system and data integrity checks.

Database Management

To regulate the functioning of the database systems, companies set up database management systems. Examples of database management systems include data files and data dictionaries.

User Interface Systems

To allow access to data and analytical tools, companies typically set up user interface systems. Ideally, user interface systems use **icons**, which are symbols that are meaningful across cultures. Examples of user interface systems include access controls and user interfaces.

Application Systems

To allow inquiry and analysis, applications systems companies will install application systems. These systems address such questions as "What is?" "What has happened in the past?" "Why?" and "What if?" Examples of application systems include regular reports, special reports, statistical analysis, expert systems, and forecasting.

Reporting Systems

Output from reporting systems allows inquiries and analyses to be shared with relevant persons. These analyses can be either in a printed or an electronic format. Examples of reporting systems include text processing, graphical output, and electronic output.

The data inputs and the operational components are the primary components of the global information system that together generate the system outputs, the third component. The relationship among the three components is illustrated in Figure 14-2.

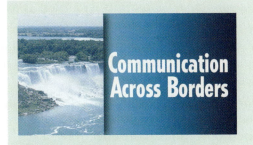

Communication Across Borders

THE EVAPORATING E-MAIL MESSAGE

Jason Pierson was frustrated. He had waited impatiently for 72 hours—three full working days—for a reply to his urgent request for information from the Nairobi, Kenya, office. At midnight local time, he telephoned his Kenyan counterpart.

"Why haven't you responded to my e-mail message? I sent it three days ago. I need the information now."

"What e-mail message are you talking about, sir? I haven't received any e-mails for four days. The last one I got from you was about two weeks ago."

"But I sent it three days ago. It's urgent."

"Mr. Pierson, you've got to realize that Kenya is a developing country. Yes, we have e-mail, but it doesn't always work. The connections to the Internet aren't very good, I'm afraid. Sometimes our power goes out. We have no backup power system. When that happens, we lose everything."

Think Critically

1. Why did Jason Pierson place his call to Nairobi at midnight his time?
2. Why did Jason Pierson expect a prompt response to his e-mail message?
3. What did Jason Pierson fail to understand about the use of e-mail in developing countries?

$$\text{DATA INPUTS} \quad + \quad \boxed{\begin{array}{c}\text{OPERATIONAL}\\\text{COMPONENTS}\end{array}} \quad = \quad \text{SYSTEM OUTPUTS}$$

Figure 14-2 When the data inputs and the operational components of a global information system are combined, they yield the system outputs.

SYSTEM OUTPUTS

System outputs are the various types of data generated from an information system. Managers rely on system outputs as they direct company operations in the global business environment. There are four basic types of application outputs.

- *Product management* outputs data such as sales forecasts and budgets that allow managers to position their products more effectively in the global marketplace.

- *Communication* outputs data such as media plans and impact reports that help global managers to share information more effectively.
- *Sales management* outputs data such as territory design and sales quota planning that help global managers to market their products more effectively around the world.
- *Senior management* outputs data such as financial modeling and strategy simulations that help top-level company managers to direct global business operations more effectively.

✔ CheckPoint

What are the three major components of a global information system?

PLANNING AND DEVELOPING THE SYSTEM

Effective global information systems evolve over time in response to careful planning and developing. Thus, planning and developing the global information system are important activities for multinational organizations.

ROLE OF TOP-LEVEL MANAGERS

Planning for global information systems is an important task for managers. The planning must include top-level managers who are able to envision the global organizational future. Top-level managers should understand the value of an effective global information system and support that system in every way possible. They should also realize that such an information system evolves over time and requires continual maintenance and refinement.

ROLE OF OTHER INFORMATION SYSTEMS MANAGERS

Information technology as well as global business conditions change all of the time. With the input of top-level managers, the information systems management team needs to establish a framework for the desired global information system and also realize that achieving that goal will be a long-term, evolutionary project. As a result, information systems managers must prioritize the competing needs for information and focus their attention on the most critical information needs first. Over time, they can gradually address more and more information needs.

A multinational organization achieves a competitive advantage in the global marketplace by focusing its attention on a global, not domestic, outlook. As information system managers develop and refine the global information system, they must reduce uncertainty while coping with increasingly complex global business operations. They must keep in mind the need for both timely and highly relevant information about operations around the world. While ultimately developing a global information system, they must realize that most of the component systems are developed locally. As the various component systems are integrated, a global information system is gradually built and refined.

REGIONAL PERSPECTIVE

CULTURE: THE TEMPLES OF ABU SIMBEL

The temples of Abu Simbel perpetuate the memory of the Egyptian ruler Ramses II and his wife Nefertari. Nefertari is the only known wife of a pharaoh ever depicted on the face of a temple. The temples were built in ancient times in the middle of the Nubian Desert near the Nile in Upper Egypt, close to the border with Sudan.

©Getty Images/PhotoDisc

With the building of the Aswan High Dam in the 1960s came the realization that the artificial lake it would create might cover these important world heritage sites. The United Nations Educational, Scientific, and Cultural Organization sprang into action to try to save the threatened temples. After much study, a plan was conceived to cut the temples into large blocks and to reconstruct them on nearby higher ground. As the waters of the Nile rose, the cutting and transporting of the stone blocks increased. It was a frantic race against time to save the temples of Abu Simbel.

The funeral complex of Ramses II and Nefertari was reconstructed exactly as it had been, only on higher ground away from the ravages of the rising water. The temples were covered with domes of reinforced concrete to prevent them from being crushed. The domes were then covered with rocks from the temple sites.

Now the waters of the Nile fill the caverns where the temples once stood. The monumental reconstruction effort is so precise that twice a year a ray of sunlight falls on the statues of gods sitting about 200 feet inside the temple of Ramses II, just as it did 2,000 years before. This is called the miracle of the sun. Ramses II and his architectural masterpieces at Abu Simbel continue to exist as they have for centuries.

Think Critically

1. If Abu Simbel is located in southern Egypt, why would this region logically be called Upper Egypt?
2. Why is sunlight falling on the statues inside the temple of Ramses II called the miracle of the sun?
3. Why are the temples at Abu Simbel both ancient and modern masterpieces?

✓ CheckPoint

What are two factors that top-level managers must consider when planning and developing global information systems?

REVIEW GLOBAL BUSINESS TERMS

Define each of the following terms.

1. global information system
2. data inputs
3. operational components
4. icons
5. system outputs

REVIEW GLOBAL BUSINESS CONCEPTS

6. Why is it more difficult to develop and manage an information system in an international business environment than a domestic business environment?

7. What are two examples each of internal organization and external environment inputs?

SOLVE GLOBAL BUSINESS PROBLEMS

Maple Leaf Enterprises, Ltd., is Canadian-based with operations in Canada, the United States, the United Kingdom, South Africa, Australia, and New Zealand. Except for the operations in Canada and the United States, the information that is received at company headquarters in Toronto is not integrated across worldwide operations. Some information from abroad is not compatible with information provided by company operations elsewhere.

8. Does Maple Leaf Enterprises, Ltd., need a global information system? Why or why not?

9. What should top-level company executives do to address the information problems of Maple Leaf Enterprises, Ltd.? Why?

10. How many years would you estimate it will take the company to create and develop an effective global information system? Why?

THINK CRITICALLY

11. Why must a global information system be designed to provide high-quality information 24 hours a day, 365 days a year?

12. Why must global information systems have so many parts and be so complex?

13. Why must top-level company managers, who often don't really understand the workings of global information systems, be directly involved in creating global information systems?

MAKE CONNECTIONS

14. **GEOGRAPHY** What are some geographical features around the world that might create barriers that impede the flow of information within a multinational organization?

15. **CAREER PLANNING** What subjects should you study at the secondary and post-secondary levels if you aspire to be the vice president for global information systems of a multinational organization?

GLOBAL INFORMATION SYSTEMS CHALLENGES

14-2

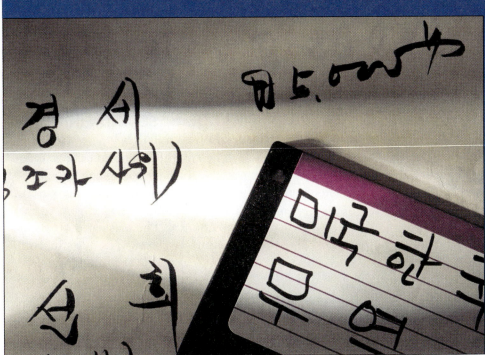

©Getty Images/PhotoDisc

GOALS

- Explain global information challenges arising from cultural and country issues.
- Describe data collection issues related to data sources and data quality.
- Explain how technological issues create challenges to global information systems.

CULTURAL AND COUNTRY ISSUES

One of the major challenges to global information systems involves cultural and country issues. Cultural and country issues usually come from differences involving language, attitudes, the environment, information needs, and degree of control.

LANGUAGE DIFFERENCES

Language differences are an obstacle to the collection and transmission of information. In languages that are not closely related, ideas cannot be simply translated from one language to another. In some cases, no equivalent idea exists in the language of another culture. For example, the idea of depreciation did not exist in the language of the communist Union of Soviet Socialist Republics. Under communism, most resources were controlled by the state, so there was no need to account for the gradual decrease in value of assets through use. Businesses from abroad that established operations there after the collapse of the Soviet Union found that their local employees had difficulty understanding the foreign idea of depreciation. Thus, requests for local depreciation information were typically met with blank stares from most natives of the former Soviet Union. The needed depreciation information was very difficult to get because the locals didn't understand the concept or its importance.

ATTITUDES

Attitudes toward such things as secrecy, authority, and risk taking are reflected in the communication of cultural groups. For example, Japanese workers are programmed by their native culture to respect authority and not disrupt the harmonious relationship of a group. Japanese workers are not likely to openly criticize company managers and policies, even if they are clearly wrong. If Japanese workers bring up sensitive matters, they will do so very discreetly and indirectly, using language that is vague and must be interpreted figuratively, not literally. Only knowledgeable and astute members of other cultures realize that Japanese workers have actually communicated negative information. Thus, obtaining information from various cultures may be difficult.

NETBookmark

The number of Hispanics living in the United States is growing rapidly, and so is the need to communicate with them in business and school. Access intlbizxtra.swlearning.com and click on the link for Chapter 14. Read the Birmingham Business Journal article entitled "Breaking the Language Barrier." What do you see as the major difference between the U.S. and Hispanic cultures?

intlbizxtra.swlearning.com

BUSINESS AND FINANCIAL ENVIRONMENT

The environment also creates potential information challenges. Competition, currency fluctuations, and inflation rates vary from country to country. The taxation systems of countries also vary, as does the control exercised over multinational organizations. These environmental differences create different information needs that can complicate the flow of information.

A Question of Ethics

WHERE DO PERSONAL PRIVACY RIGHTS BEGIN?

Many countries have become increasingly concerned about their citizens privacy rights. They feel uncomfortable that name-linked information is collected, processed, and stored in information systems that are not accurate and carefully controlled.

Some multinational businesses send personal data outside the country of origin to places with less stringent privacy controls. There the personal data is used to make various kinds of decisions. Sometimes the data is used for purposes other than those for

which it was collected. Sometimes it is sold to other businesses.

To limit such abuses, countries such as Sweden require that all private and public organizations register their databases, which are subject to review. Certain types of data about individual citizens cannot be legally sent out of the country.

Think Critically

1. If you applied for a credit card through a bank and later found out the bank had sold personal information about you to a business in another country without your permission, how would you feel? Why?

2. Even if the bank did not break any laws when selling information about you, would its actions be ethical or not? Why?

3. Since freedom is a founding principle in the United States, should the federal government restrict the right to process information about its citizens? Why or why not?

4. Is it ethical for countries to pass legislation to protect the privacy rights of their citizens if in doing so, they violate the rights of multinational businesses to process business information as they desire? Why or why not?

DIFFERING INFORMATION NEEDS

Information needs also vary widely within multinational businesses, creating additional challenges to global information systems. Different organizational levels within far-flung company operations have significantly different information needs. Managers generally prefer to receive their information in terms of the local standard units of information. Thus, information about such matters as planning, budgeting, and accounting will likely have to be processed multiple times in different units. For example, financial statements for managers of subsidiaries in Tunisia will need to be prepared in Tunisian dinars, while those for managers of subsidiaries in Egypt will need to be prepared in Egyptian pounds. Financial statements for managers at the headquarters office in Canada will need to be prepared in Canadian dollars. This increases not only the volume but also the redundancy of information that the global information system must generate to meet the needs of various parts of a multinational business.

DEGREE OF CONTROL

The degree of control that is exercised within a multinational organization also creates challenges to global information systems. A multinational organization must weigh the trade-offs between centralization and decentralization. **Centralization** means that managers at company headquarters make most major decisions. Centralization favors a broad view of corporate strategy when decisions are made. **Decentralization** means that local managers at different company locations around the world make most major decisions. Decentralization favors the effects of local conditions when decisions are made. Different international businesses choose to control their operations in different ways, which influences both the needs for and the types of information that must be generated by global information systems.

WORK AS A GROUP

Debate the pros and cons of centralizing all major decisions relating to a global information system.

✓ CheckPoint

What are five types of cultural and country issues that present challenges to global information systems?

DATA COLLECTION ISSUES

Another of the major challenges to global information systems involves data collection issues. Data collection issues usually come from data sources and/or data quality. The quality of the outputs generated by a global information system is strongly influenced by the adequacy of the data inputs.

SOURCES OF DATA

Data sources present challenges to global information systems. Data sources are either primary sources or secondary sources. **Primary data** are data collected by the user firsthand for a specific purpose. **Secondary data** are data not collected by the user but available for his or her use. Surveys from customers are examples of primary data if they are collected by the same business unit that uses the gathered information. If some other business unit or organization, such as a governmental agency, gathers the survey information, then the gathered information is secondary data.

Generally speaking, users have more faith in the quality of the information they gather themselves (since they know its strengths and weaknesses) than in the information others gather. Nevertheless, it is frequently not feasible or practical for multinational businesses to gather firsthand all of the information they need for their specific purposes. As a result, these businesses must often use secondary data for decision-making purposes. Since managers usually know considerably less about the circumstances under which secondary data is gathered and reported, they accept more risk from using inaccurate information when they rely on secondary data sources.

Managers of multinational organizations often rely on secondary data for information about the business environment in which they operate. Such groups as the United Nations, the home country and host country governments, business and trade associations, and data subscription services often provide data that managers of international businesses use.

QUALITY OF DATA

The quality of the data is a major issue in data collection. The quality relates to the validity, reliability, and comparability of the data.

Data Validity The extent to which the data measures what the user expects it to measure is called **validity**. For example, if both the data gatherer and the data user use identical definitions, then the gathered information will be valid. Some countries and organizations may define things that are measured in different ways. This results in measurements that are not valid from the perspective of users from other countries and organizations.

Data Reliability The consistency of the gathered data is called the **reliability**. For example, if the thing being measured does not change, then repeated measurements using the same data-gathering techniques by various persons will yield the same results again and again. Some countries and organizations may not measure things with the same degree of accuracy as other countries and organizations do. This results in misleading data that may be useful only for propaganda purposes.

Data Comparability The extent to which secondary data from different sources are measured, computed, and reported in the exact same ways is called **comparability**. Some countries and organizations make different assumptions when gathering and reporting data. This results in data that are not exactly comparable. It is important to know the assumptions before deciding whether the information should be used for decision-making purposes.

Multinational businesses must strive to obtain the best quality data possible for use in their global information systems so they can rely with a high degree of certainty on the system outputs. If the input data lack integrity, then it is garbage in and garbage out of the global information system. This makes the system outputs worthless, and managers would be foolish to make decisions based on them.

What are data collection issues related to data sources and data quality?

TECHNOLOGICAL ISSUES

Still another of the major challenges to global information systems involves technological issues. Technological issues come from communication technology problems, host-country requirements, and host-country and international regulations.

COMMUNICATION TECHNOLOGY

Those in charge of a global information system must be concerned about the adequacy of the data collection and transmission from company offices worldwide to company headquarters. If a multinational organization has total control over that process, then technology problems are not usually a major concern. However, some countries require that local technologies be used to process data. Brazil, for example, requires that locally produced computers must be used to process data generated within the country. That equipment may not be compatible with equipment used elsewhere within a multinational organization, which impedes the effectiveness of data transmission.

©Getty Images/PhotoDisc

HOST-COUNTRY REQUIREMENTS

Another type of technology problem can arise from having to transmit data through local systems, which are sometimes under the control of the domestic postal, telephone, or telegraph agency. Some of these systems cannot accommodate high-speed data transmission. Others may not have enough equipment available to support the desired volume of data transmission. Sometimes a multinational business may have to transmit less information out of a country or accept a less rigid time line for transmitting information to company headquarters to work around such problems.

Host country requirements about data transmission can also create technological issues. Countries that regulate data transmission, such as Brazil, effectively impose their equipment requirements on multinational organizations operating there, restricting or eliminating their equipment choices. This complicates the design and operation of the global information system. National requirements that a domestic agency transmit all data moving inside and outside of the country can negatively impact the quality, speed, and availability of information. Such constraints create more challenges to the effective operation of both domestic and global information systems.

HOST-COUNTRY AND INTERNATIONAL REGULATIONS

Host-country and international regulations often relate to technological issues, too. Multinational organizations sometimes experience higher costs for moving data across national borders. Higher costs might be caused by requirements to

GLOBAL BUSINESS EXAMPLE

THE GREAT FIREWALL OF CHINA

The People's Republic of China was once known for its Great Wall. Now it is also known for its great firewall, which attempts to control Web content in and out of the country.

Chinese Internet users and independent analysts continue to report filtering of their browsing, searching, and e-mailing. This suggests that the government is using a more sophisticated approach to controlling electronic communica-tion. Gone are the old days when addresses disapproved by the government were unreachable. Now such sites can be accessed, but some content and functions are not operational. The Internet monitoring and blocking is accomplished through packet filtering. It ensures that every bit and byte meets programmed criteria.

The extent of the government's monitoring is difficult to assess. Tighter Internet restrictions are reported by some. Others experience occasional and geographic restrictions. Still others report problem-free use. While evidence suggests that blocking is highly likely, such things as congestion and routing problems might cause the noted disruptions.

Officials of government agencies involved with the Internet and country security say they know nothing about the claimed blocking.

Source: Adapted from T. Crampton, "China's 'Great Firewall' Limits Internet," *International Herald Tribune*, October 1, 2002 (www.iht.com/articles/72279.html).

Think Critically

1. Why would the Chinese government want to control access to Internet information?
2. Should access to technology be limited, since it could potentially be used to undermine the government?

use local equipment or agencies or by high international communication and data transfer charges. Another reason for the higher costs could be the taxes on the movement of data or the excessive data line charges. Regardless of the source, managers of multinational organizations must carefully weigh the value added by having additional information against the increased costs associated with obtaining that information. Making appropriate trade-offs contributes to having a cost-effective global information system.

Host-country regulations about the types and volume of transmitted information using various technologies is a growing concern for those in charge of global information systems. A number of developed and developing countries are concerned about privacy rights, national security, and national sovereignty issues. Countries such as Austria, France, Germany, Norway, the People's Republic of China, Sweden, the United Kingdom, and the United States have these concerns. Some of these countries already have regulations or are considering regulations about data transfers across their borders. The laws and regulations are different in every country, which complicates the design and operation of a global information system. As countries around the world increasingly recognize the strategic value of market-related information, more laws and regulations governing the flow of information between countries are likely to be created. Such governmental restrictions are sometimes established to protect information, including economic data, that some cultures view as politically sensitive.

✓ CheckPoint

What are three types of technological issues that create challenges to global information systems?

REVIEW GLOBAL BUSINESS TERMS

Define each of the following terms.

1. centralization

2. decentralization

3. primary data

4. secondary data

5. validity

6. reliability

7. comparability

intlbizxtra.swlearning.com

REVIEW GLOBAL BUSINESS CONCEPTS

8. What kinds of business and financial issues create challenges to global information systems?

9. Why is primary data generally more reliable than secondary data?

SOLVE GLOBAL BUSINESS PROBLEMS

Libya is a developing northern African country with most of its population clustered in cities along the Mediterranean Sea. Libya is an Arabic-speaking Moslem country where the will of Allah influences all details of life. Most Libyans do not view technology as positive; in fact, most Libyans have a neutral (at best) or negative view of technology. Their belief that it is either undesirable or impossible to control their environment shapes their way of life.

10. Do typical Libyans view technology and their environment like typical Americans do? What facts support your position?

11. How accepting do you think most Libyans would be of the development of a global information system? Why?

12. How might you make Libyans more receptive to the creation of a global information system that contains information from their country?

THINK CRITICALLY

13. How would having a currency whose value regularly rises and falls by 50 percent present a challenge for a global information system?

14. Why is it often not practical for a multinational organization to gather primary data about the business environment in each of the countries in which it operates?

15. What are some sources of information that are likely to have relatively valid and reliable data a multinational business can rely on?

MAKE CONNECTIONS

16. **TECHNOLOGY** How would having to use the domestic telephone system in a developing country create a likely barrier to the transferring of information to a developed country?

17. **LAW** How do laws that restrict the flow of information out of a country pose a threat to global information systems?

CHAPTER SUMMARY

14-1 CREATING GLOBAL INFORMATION SYSTEMS

A Information is power in the global economy. It serves as a strategic resource and provides a competitive advantage. An information system in an international environment is more challenging to create because there are many more variables to consider than in a domestic environment.

B Data inputs and operational components together yield the system outputs of a global information system. Four basic types of system outputs are product management, communication, sales management, and senior management.

C An effective global information system requires careful system planning and developing with input from senior managers as well as other managers.

14-2 GLOBAL INFORMATION SYSTEMS CHALLENGES

A Cultural and country issues are one type of challenge to global information systems. Issues concerning language, attitudes, and the business and financial environment must all be accommodated.

B Data collection issues also create challenges to global information systems. For use in decision making, data must have validity, reliability, and comparability.

C Technological issues are still another group of challenges to global information systems. Those in charge of global information systems must consider communication technology, the requirements of the host country, and host-country and international regulations.

GLOBAL REFOCUS

Read the case at the beginning of this chapter, and answer the following questions.
1. What are some domestic companies that engage in work similar to what ISIS does?
2. How are businesses in other African countries likely to view the goods and services offered by ISIS? Why?
3. What are some major projects in which ISIS has engaged?

REVIEW GLOBAL BUSINESS TERMS

Match the terms listed with the definitions.

1. The extent to which secondary data from different sources are measured, computed, and reported in the exact same ways.

2. Data not collected by the user but that are available for his or her use.

3. Parts of an information system that manage the database and system operations.

4. A system in which managers at company headquarters make most major decisions.

5. The consistency of gathered data.

6. Data collected by the user firsthand for a specific purpose.

7. A system in which local managers at different company locations around the world make most major decisions.

8. A computer-based system that provides information about company operations around the world to managers of a multinational organization.

9. Symbols that are meaningful across cultures.

10. The extent to which data measures what the user expects it to measure.

11. Various types of data generated from an information system.

12. Pieces of information that feed the global information system database.

a. centralization

b. comparability

c. data inputs

d. decentralization

e. global information system

f. icons

g. operational components

h. primary data

i. reliability

j. secondary data

k. system outputs

l. validity

MAKE GLOBAL BUSINESS DECISIONS

13. How can information be both a strategic resource and a competitive advantage for multinational organizations?

14. How is transacting business in the international environment like transacting business in the domestic environment in spite of the fact that the domestic and international business environments are significantly different?

15. Why is it so important to have accurate data inputs in a global information system?

16. Why must a global information system always be operating?

17. How might attitudes toward risk taking in a culture be reflected in its language and communication practices?

18. Why do local managers usually want the outputs from a global information system in terms of local standard units of information?

19. What are some examples of business-related information from various sources that do not have comparability?

20. Why might the government of a developing country charge a multinational business an excessive amount to transfer data out of the country?

21. How does a company policy of centralization increase the influence of the headquarters staff at the expense of local staff when it comes to global information systems?

22. Why would a country want to specify that only locally manufactured equipment can be used to process data?

GLOBAL CONNECTIONS

23. **MATHEMATICS** The United States does not use the metric system as its national measurement standard. How is this a challenge to creating a global information system?

24. **CAREER PLANNING** How might a statistician contribute to the accuracy of inputs into a global information system?

25. **HISTORY** How might historical events make it more challenging to create a global information system that links business operations in certain countries around the world?

26. **COMMUNICATIONS** Why is two-way communication between upper-level company managers and information systems managers so critical in the process of planning for a global information system?

27. **COMMUNICATIONS** How can the communication practices of countries influence the quality of information in a global information system?

28. **TECHNOLOGY** What might be some practical limitations to using technology to improve a global information system in developing African countries?

29. **GEOGRAPHY** How might having major river systems contribute to the development of global information systems?

30. **LAW** Why might some countries perceive global information systems as threats to their national security?

31. **HISTORY** How was the early recording of business transactions on clay tablets a milestone in the development of global information systems?

©Gianni Dagli/CORBIS

THE GLOBAL ENTREPRENEUR
CREATING AN INTERNATIONAL BUSINESS PLAN

DEVELOPING AN INTERNATIONAL BUSINESS INFORMATION SYSTEM

Information is needed by all organizations to efficiently plan and implement business activities. Develop an information management system based on the company and country you have been using in this continuing project, or create a new idea for your business in the same or a different country. Make use of previously collected information, and do additional research. This phase of your business plan should include the following components.

1. List the major external and internal data sources the company will use.

2. Describe the information needs (types of data and reports) that will be required for the organization to operate?

3. Describe the types of computer network systems that might be useful for obtaining and processing the organization's information.

4. Describe how the cultural, economic, and political environment of the country might affect the organization's information system.

5. Explain how recent new technology might improve or expand the company's information system.

Prepare a written summary or present a short oral report (two or three minutes) of your findings.

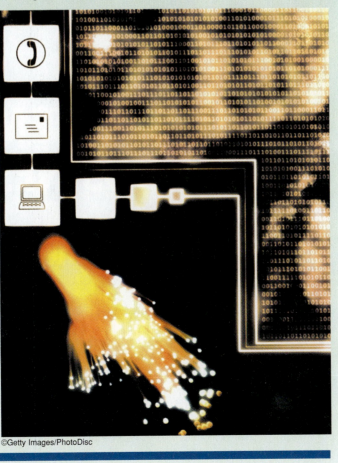

©Getty Images/PhotoDisc

Chapter 15

PRODUCTION SYSTEMS FOR GLOBAL BUSINESS

GLOBAL FOCUS

Mauritania's Riches from the Sea

Have you ever tried an exotic seafood such as octopus or calamari (squid)? These foods—as well as fish, lobster, and shrimp—are important natural resources for Mauritania, a country on Africa's Atlantic coast. The fishing grounds off the coast of Mauritania are rich with lobster, octopus, and a variety of fish.

Mauritania has a population of over 2.7 million. The country has limitations on sources of economic development because about three-fourths of the country is covered by the Sahara Desert. Minerals important to the country's economy include iron ore, gypsum, and copper. Mauritania is a member of the Economic Community of West African States (ECOWAS).

Although always important to its economy, fishing has recently become Mauritania's main source of foreign sales income. Production increased when the Mauritanian government entered into joint ventures with companies from other countries—including Algeria, Iraq, and Romania. These nations also share the profits. Mauritania has benefited from the sophisticated fleets used by its partners, including large trawlers capable of processing, freezing, and transporting fish without entering a port.

Think Critically

1. What natural and human resources provided a foundation for the country's economic development?
2. In the joint fishing ventures between Mauritania and its partners, which resources are contributed by Mauritania and which are provided by the partners?
3. Conduct Web research about Mauritania to obtain additional information about the country's business and economic environment. Prepare a report of your findings.

15-1 | GLOBAL PRODUCTION METHODS

GOALS

- Diagram the basic model for all production processes.
- Summarize methods of operations management.
- Describe the different production methods used in various countries.

THE PRODUCTION PROCESS

The **production process** is the means by which a company changes raw materials into finished goods. For example, diamond miners find rough gems below ground. The stones are cut, polished, and set before they are finally sold as bracelets, necklaces, and rings to consumers around the world.

As the word "process" suggests, the production process is composed of a series of activities. The three major elements of the production process are resources, transformation, and final goods and services. The flow of these elements is shown in Figure 15-1.

FLOW CHART OF PRODUCTION PROCESS

Resources
- Natural
- Human
- Capital

Transformation
- Machines
- Process
- Facility

Goods and Services

Figure 15-1 Organizations transform a combination of resources to produce goods and services that will meet consumer needs.

RESOURCES

Resources are the people and things a company uses to produce a good or service. Resources fall into one of three categories: natural resources, human resources, and capital resources.

Natural Resources Natural resources come from the air, water, or earth. These basic elements can be used to create goods. The fishing banks off the shores of Mauritania and the diamonds of Angola are examples of natural resources. South Africa leads the world in gold mining and production. Approximately 47 percent of the gold mined in the last 100 years has come from South Africa. This precious natural resource is found in the northeastern corner of the country.

Researching a country's natural resources is vital for companies that are choosing a new site for manufacturing and identifying global business opportunities. Many countries are concerned about the depletion of their natural resources since a loss of resources means a loss of economic vitality. Recycling is one way to preserve natural resources.

Human Resources The human resources of a country are its people and their physical and intellectual abilities. A company must research the available labor force for such characteristics as mobility, literacy rate, and culture (including traditions, gender roles, and religious beliefs). For example, India's many English-speaking workers with advanced degrees make that country an important source of labor for the information technology industry.

Capital Resources Capital resources are the funds and materials necessary to produce a good or service. In addition to financial investment, a country's monetary system, tax structure, economic conditions, and availability of materials are all important to take into consideration when discussing the capital resources of a company.

TRANSFORMATION

Transformation is the use of resources to create a good or service. A resource may be transformed by a machine (tractor, sewing machine, or computer), by a process (statistical analysis or teaching), or through a facility (colleges, restaurants, or health clinics). Resources are often transformed through the use of machines and processes. For example, cotton harvested along the lower Nile in Egypt must be cleaned and baled. Machines process the cotton and spin it into yarn and thread. Weaving machines turn the thread into cloth.

GOODS AND SERVICES

The final stage of the production process is the output of the goods and services that have been created by the transformation activities. These goods and services are now ready to enter the market as finished products for the consumer. A fish served at a restaurant is an example of output. Its production process began with a natural resource that was harvested, transported, and prepared (transformed) for a consumer's dining pleasure.

The production process does not end with the output of a product. Consumer response and changes in external factors (such as the economy) affect the process. Feedback from consumers and external influences affects input as the production cycle continues.

WORK AS A GROUP

Work as a group. Select a product commonly used in your community. List the natural, human, and capital resources needed to produce this item.

✔**CheckPoint**

Give examples of the transformation stage of the production process.

METHODS OF OPERATIONS MANAGEMENT

Operations management is the process of designing and managing a production system. The goal of operations management is to produce a good or service at the lowest possible cost while maintaining the highest possible quality.

Forecasting Operations managers use several methods to help them design efficient production systems. Forecasting is the method used to determine how much of a product to produce. Often that decision is based on the company's previous sales. Adjustments are made for changes in consumer demand and the country's economic conditions.

Scheduling Scheduling is the time frame for producing a good or service. Operations managers consider the availability of raw materials, human resources, and facilities needed for production when they create schedules. Recently Toyota offered custom-made cars in just five days—from the time the order was received until the vehicle left the assembly line. Delivery time to the customer wasn't included in the five days. Toyota's 360 key suppliers were linked to the company by computer, creating a virtual assembly line. Parts were loaded onto trucks and delivered in the order of installation.

Inventory Control A method of monitoring the amount of raw materials and completed goods on hand is called **inventory control**. This count, or inventory, gives the operations manager an idea of how much to produce to meet consumer demand. One current method of inventory control is called

---

GLOBAL BUSINESS EXAMPLE

HORIZONTAL AND VERTICAL COMPANIES

Horizontal integration takes place when a company expands its operations in a similar line of business. For example, if a food store company buys another chain of food stores, horizontal integration takes place.

In contrast, *vertical integration* occurs when a company expands into various stages of production and distribution. An auto manufacturer that owns its own glass company or tire manufacturer is referred to as vertically integrated.

Should a company buy the parts it uses in an assembly plant or make the component? This is not an easy question to answer. In recent years, fewer companies have been making needed production parts. Technology has allowed many small companies to specialize in various parts and offer them at a lower cost. In recent years, Sundram Fasteners Ltd., a company in India, was supplying more than 300,000 radiator caps for use in General Motors cars.

Another dimension of vertical integration has been called *value-added* production. This occurs when a company takes a natural resource such as lumber or fresh fruits and processes the item into a finished good such as wood pulp or canned fruit.

Think Critically

1. How would a company decide whether to buy or make a part that would be used in the production process?
2. Select some natural resources. Describe actions companies could take to process these items into more useful goods.

just-in-time (JIT). This method ties a manufacturer closely to a material supplier so that the raw materials are provided only when the production process needs them. This allows a company to respond quickly to changes in the marketplace while keeping only a small amount of inventory in stock. Warehouse costs are low, and the company is not left with unused goods at the end of the year. Goods are produced on an as-needed basis.

What is just-in-time inventory control?

PRODUCTION METHODS AROUND THE WORLD

Production methods refer to the processes used during the transformation stage of production. Production methods can be categorized as manual production, automated production, or computerized production.

MANUAL PRODUCTION SYSTEMS

The **manual production** method involves using human hands and bodies as the means of transforming resources into goods and services. Manual production was the earliest means of production and is still a primary method of production in many parts of the world.

In some cases, as in the South African gold mines, workers perform the labor because machines are unable to do so. In other cases, manual production is considered more valuable than any other form. Handmade quilts, sweaters knitted by hand, and furniture handmade by a master carpenter are rare and more costly than their machine-made counterparts. For many developing countries, manual production is a necessity because of the initial cost of automation.

AUTOMATED PRODUCTION SYSTEMS

In **automated production** systems, machines perform the work. A machine offers some advantages to production. The equipment performs tasks quickly and precisely and does not get bored by repetition. Machines can do some tasks that people cannot do, such as refine oil or make plastic. In some areas of production, machines have replaced workers. Cotton that was once spun by hand is now spun by machine. This shift in production has allowed workers to direct their attention to more complex tasks.

COMPUTERIZED PRODUCTION SYSTEMS

Computerized production systems use computers to control machines and perform work in the production process. The automated factory is designed to use the latest computer technology to increase productivity. Computer-controlled equipment reduces the number of people required for manual labor, but it increases the required number of trained technicians.

Computer-Assisted Manufacturing The method of using computers to run production equipment is called **computer-assisted manufacturing (CAM)**. Examples of CAM equipment are computerized assembly lines, drills, and milling machines. **Computer-aided design (CAD)** uses sophisticated computers that allow a designer to develop a very detailed design and key it to the CAM equipment specifications. CAD increases the creative potential of the designer. Figure 15-2 lists a variety of computer-aided applications that are in use around the globe.

Robotics The name for the technology connected with the design, construction, and operation of robots is called **robotics**. *Robots* are simply computerized output devices that can perform difficult, repetitive, or dangerous work in industrial settings. The use of robotics has dramatically changed the appearance of many manufacturing plants. Robots carry out tasks that once posed risks for humans. Robots also can be programmed to deliver consistently precise work.

In recent years, over 1 million industrial robots were being used in Japan. This number represented over half of the world's total. Recent robotic technology includes an ant-size robot used to inspect and repair pipes in power plants.

Automated Warehouses Similar to the automated factory, the automated warehouse relies on computers, software, and robotics to perform

NETBookmark

Some inventors have developed robots for use in the home. Access intlbizxtra.swlearning.com and click on the link for Chapter 15. After exploring the web site, imagine you had a robot at home. Write a few paragraphs about how your life would be changed. What problems, if any, might you have if a robot did your daily chores?

intlbizxtra.swlearning.com

COMPUTER-AIDED MANUFACTURING APPLICATIONS

Type of Computer-Aided Application	Typical Business
Computer-aided design (CAD)	architectural design, interior decoration, drafting work
Computer-assisted manufacturing (CAM)	airplane manufacturing industry, nuclear plants, defense industry
Computer-aided engineering (CAE)	engineering, scientific research, highway and bridge construction
Computer-integrated manufacturing (CIM)	automobile production, prefabricated housing construction

Figure 15-2 Computerized production methods are in use in both goods-producing industries and service industries.

Communication Across Borders

TURNING A DEAF EAR TOWARD TECHNOLOGY

American Jewelry Machines sent its regional sales representative to Rwanda to call on a jewelry manufacturer there. The sales rep noted that the company was using manual production methods. Reasonably priced machinery sold by the U.S. company could easily automate many steps in the jewelry production process. That would not only increase the amount of jewelry produced but also decrease labor costs, making the company more profitable.

Initially, American Jewelry Machines was puzzled about why the prospering Rwandan company wasn't interested in its machines. Later, it realized that many Rwandans are not eager to embrace technology because they view it skeptically. To them, technology is not very desirable and is difficult to control. Further, it takes jobs away from workers who provide for extended families. Consequently, the Rwandan jewelry manufacturer wasn't seriously interested in communicating with American Jewelry Machines about its labor-saving technology. The company simply turned a deaf ear to the sales rep's efforts.

Think Critically

1. Why do you think the regional sales representative misjudged the interest of the Rwandan company in regards to technology?

2. How did U.S. and Rwandan attitudes about technology set the communication agenda?

stock, inventory, order, and delivery tasks. Computers store large databases of inventory information. As robots disperse merchandise to trucks for delivery, they scan a bar code, and the merchandise is automatically reordered. The repetitive functions of running a warehouse are handled by computers and robots rather than by people. Trained technicians and managers are still necessary to make sure that the warehouse stays in efficient working order.

The warehouses of companies such as Wal-Mart, eToys, Fingerhut, and other online retailers can process as many as 30,000 items an hour. While an Internet retail operation (e-tailer) can be started up fairly easily, delivering products to customers is a more complicated task. Computer programs must be developed to coordinate forklift trucks and other equipment for selecting and packing items for shipping.

Computer-Integrated Manufacturing As production systems evolve, manufacturers will begin to incorporate computer-integrated manufacturing (CIM). In a **computer-integrated manufacturing (CIM)** production system, computers guide the entire manufacturing process. Production is completely controlled by computer integration—from product design through processing, assembling, testing, and packaging. Two elements of a CIM production system are minimum inventories and production based on consumer demand.

Recently Ford Motor Company in Australia used a CIM software package that prepared technical illustrations of more efficient and cost-effective motor vehicles. Another feature of this software was then used to develop manufacturing instructions. In addition to designing and producing the restyled cars at the Australian Ford plant, the operational process also was used to produce vehicles at other Ford plants in Japan, Korea, and China.

✓ CheckPoint

What are the three main types of production methods?

REVIEW GLOBAL BUSINESS TERMS

Define each of the following terms.

1. production process
2. transformation
3. operations management
4. inventory control
5. manual production
6. automated production
7. computerized production
8. computer-assisted manufacturing (CAM)
9. computer-aided design (CAD)
10. robotics
11. computer-integrated manufacturing (CIM)

REVIEW GLOBAL BUSINESS CONCEPTS

12. What are the three main stages of the production process?

13. What is the goal of operations management?

14. What advantages do machines offer in an automated production system?

SOLVE GLOBAL BUSINESS PROBLEMS

For each of the following situations, decide if the company is making use of manual, automated, or computerized production methods.

15. Rather than cutting leather for shoes by hand, a punch press is used.

16. Hand-designed jewelry is created in large cities in Europe and Asia.

17. A chemical company plans to make use of the latest technology for handling substances that could be dangerous to human beings.

18. On an island country, hand-woven baskets are exported.

19. Light-sensitive machines produce computer components in Taiwan.

THINK CRITICALLY

20. What actions can companies and businesses take to avoid depletion of a country's natural resources?

21. How can a country assist workers whose jobs are taken over by machinery or computers?

MAKE CONNECTIONS

22. **CULTURAL STUDIES** Describe how tradition might influence the use of manual production methods in a society.

23. **VISUAL ART** Select a product or service. Prepare a flow chart or other visual presentation showing the production process for that item.

24. **TECHNOLOGY** Use the Internet to research the use of robotics for doing tasks that are dangerous for humans, such as undersea exploration and handling of toxic substances.

EXPANDING PRODUCTIVE ACTIVITIES

15-2

GOALS

- Identify two ways production output is measured.
- Differentiate between producing products and creating services.
- Describe how technology influences office activities.

MEASURING PRODUCTION OUTPUT

The goal of operations management is to produce a good or service at the lowest cost while maintaining the highest quality. To evaluate the production process, operations managers measure production output. Production output is measured in terms of productivity and quality control.

PRODUCTIVITY

Productivity refers to the amount of work that is accomplished in a unit of time. Productivity can sometimes be increased by making a simple change in the work pattern, such as using all of your fingers to keyboard instead of just two. At other times, an increase in productivity requires a capital investment, such as buying a new faster computer to replace an old slower one. Operations managers want to increase productivity to get the most work possible for the cost of production investment.

One approach to productivity is the just-in-time (JIT) system of inventory control. Companies using JIT have a limited product inventory and little time delay in manufacturing.

Another approach to productivity, synchronized manufacturing, evolved from JIT. In **synchronized manufacturing**, the workflow is distributed as needed throughout the production cycle. The company distributes the work to all points of the manufacturing process according to output demands. The

workflow may appear to be unbalanced in this approach. For example in a shirt factory using synchronized manufacturing, the fabric-cutting department may work at 80 percent capacity due to an increase in orders. The packaging and distribution department, on the other hand, may be working at only 40 percent capacity to meet current orders.

QUALITY CONTROL

The second approach to measuring production output depends on quality products. To evaluate the quality of their output, companies use a method called **quality control**, which is the process of measuring goods and services against a product standard. By using a standard for goods and services, companies can compare their products to similar products from all over the world. Many companies employ quality control inspectors to monitor the comparison between products and standards.

Total Quality Control (TQC) The Japanese created an approach to quality control called **total quality control (TQC)**. This approach requires every employee, not just the inspectors, to take responsibility for high-quality production. Many companies have reported an increase not only in their employees' work output but also in the quality of work as a result of TQC. Employees work harder because they see their value to the company's growth.

Working in Teams One method of improving output quality is the quality circle. A **quality circle** consists of a small

©Getty Images/PhotoDisc

GLOBAL BUSINESS
EXAMPLE

YOUR CAR IS FROM WHAT COUNTRY?

Companies with a global perspective obtain production inputs and parts from many areas of the world. In recent years, Ford vehicles produced in Europe had parts from more than 20 countries. The carburetor, clutch, oil pump, and several other parts were manufactured in the United Kingdom. France provided brakes, seat pads, and hose clamps. The exhaust pipes came from Sweden, while the paint and tires came from the Netherlands. Glass and the radio

were produced in Canada with the starter and other parts coming from Japan. Manufacturing facilities in Denmark provided fan belts, while the radiator and air filter came from Spain. The final assembly took place in Halewood, United Kingdom, or Saarlouis, Germany.

Think Critically

1. What factors influence a manufacturer's use of parts from many countries?
2. Go to the web site of Ford Motor Company to obtain additional information about the company's international production facilities.

group of employees who have different jobs within the same company but have the same goal of producing a quality good or service. For example, a quality circle at a manufacturing plant might include the project supervisor, production-line workers, an employee from distribution, and an employee from accounting. This "circle" of employees meets on a regular basis to assess how well the manufacturing process is working. They brainstorm improvements to the production cycle or to the product itself. Because they are from all areas of the plant, they can make informed decisions together. Quality circles make use of a team management style.

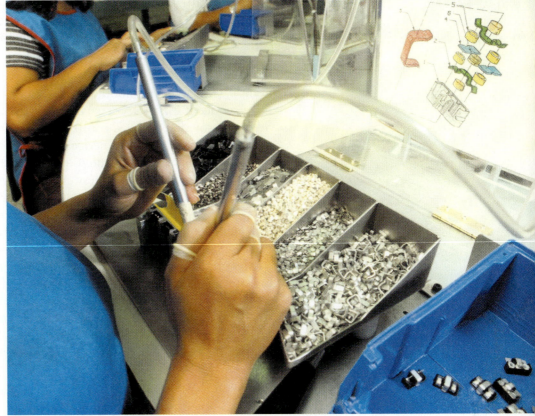
©Getty Images/PhotoDisc

A team approach is often used by businesses for various company projects. A product team might be assigned to redesign a package, to reduce production costs, or to improve consumer convenience. A regional management team may be used to introduce an existing product into new global markets. Or a systems team might be asked to create a process for buying parts around the world at a lower cost.

A *cross-functional team* is one with members from different parts of an organization. This team is likely to include representatives from marketing, finance, information systems, and production. Each team member brings different skills and experiences. Problem solving using cross-functional teams provides solutions that take several points of view into account.

Success in working on teams involves the following skills.

- An ability to work with others who have different experiences and come from different cultural settings
- An enthusiasm to focus on team needs rather than individual accomplishments
- A readiness to cooperate with shared leadership roles
- A competency to participate in group decision making and divide tasks among team members
- A willingness to compromise for the benefit of the team's goals

✓ **CheckPoint**

What is a cross-functional team?

CREATING AND DELIVERING SERVICES

Service industries perform tasks rather than provide goods for consumers. A major portion of U.S. exports involves the sale of these *intangible* items—services. With about 70 percent of GDP in the United States coming from service industries, international trade by service industries is significant. Services provided by U.S. companies comprise over 20 percent of the world's total cross-border sales of services.

Service industries continue to grow while new ones are being created. In recent years, some of the fastest growing service industries include telecommunications businesses (such as Internet service providers and satellite television systems), business training programs, private vocational schools, healthcare facilities, food service companies, entertainment and hospitality businesses, delivery services, and financial and banking services.

Meeting consumer needs is essential when providing a service. Tailored logistics is a strategy for meeting those needs. Companies using **tailored logistics** combine services with a product to better serve consumers. In recent years, McDonald's tested an automated order taker. This machine uses pictures, text, and audio to allow people to order their food and pay without interacting with a person. The system also permits a person to regulate the

E-COMMERCE IN ACTION

Mass Customization

When the automobile was first mass-produced in the early 1900s, Henry Ford would tell potential customers they could have any color car they wanted as long as it was black! Since that time, businesses have continually attempted to meet the individual needs and wants of customers.

Today companies with millions of customers are producing products designed for the individual. Consumers can buy vitamins matched to their needs. CDs are available with selected music tracks. Cosmetics can be mixed to match a person's skin tone. Financial service companies offer investment advice based on a person's income, age, and household situation.

Many online companies are involved in mass customization, providing goods and services uniquely tailored to customer demand. Dell Computer only builds personal computers that have actually been ordered. This approach keeps profit margin up by keeping inventory down.

Mattel allows girls to go online to design a friend for Barbie. They can choose the doll's skin tone, eye color, hair color, clothes, accessories, and name. The doll is delivered with a computer-generated paragraph about its personality.

©Vince Streano/CORBIS

Think Critically

1. Suggest situations in which companies can use technology to create products and services designed for individual needs and wants.
2. Locate a web site that allows customers to order items created for their personal situation.

condiments on a sandwich by touching plus or minus signs on the screen. Workers then deliver the food and any change to the customer. This automated order-taking system has tailored logistics to serve consumers and save costs.

✔ CheckPoint

What are some of the fastest growing service industries?

WORK AS A GROUP

Discuss why the fastest growing service industries are growing so rapidly.

INFORMATION AND OFFICE PRODUCTION

Technology creates continuing improvement in office environment productivity. Improved office productivity can be described as "smaller," "faster," "interactive," "visually enhanced," and "integrated." Office machines are becoming smaller as computer technology moves from desktop to notebook to palm-held devices. Faster and less expensive technology, especially microprocessors, creates computers that process information quicker and with greater flexibility of input and output.

In addition, technological design is focusing on integrated systems. Most information processing installations combine computers with an audio system, a scanner, a DVD or CD-ROM drive, cable television, and the Internet. These systems provide a link between business information providers and other sectors, such as schools and the entertainment market.

Office workers once used telephones, typewriters, and paper and pencils. Today, office systems involve wireless networks of notebook computers along with personal digital assistants (PDAs), laser printers, scanners, fax modems, pagers, cellular phones, CD-ROMs, and other devices. These devices have increased the ability and efficiency of office workers to provide needed information for making local and global business decisions.

©Getty Images/PhotoDisc

©Getty Images/PhotoDisc

REGIONAL PERSPECTIVE

HISTORY: AN AFRICAN-AMERICAN OIL ENTREPRENEUR

Jake Simmons, Jr., was born in 1901 in Oklahoma, the ninth child in an African- and Native-American family of cattle ranchers. Who could have guessed he would become an international tycoon and the most successful African-American in the history of the oil industry?

Two events helped young Simmons to find success. The first was being granted 160 acres of tribal land because of his birthright as a black Creek born prior to 1907. This land provided financial security. The second event was hearing Booker T. Washington speak in 1914. Simmons followed Washington to the Tuskegee Institute in Alabama, where he studied for five years. Washington provided motivation for Simmons to take risks in his struggle to succeed.

When Simmons returned to Oklahoma, he began to broker (act as an agent in) oil leases for black landowners who had previously been cheated. Such work was risky; this was a time in U.S. history when racial segregation was enforced and lynchings were not uncommon. Simmons learned about the oil business from those real estate dealings.

In 1949, he formed the Simmons Royalty Company and began to drill for oil himself. By 1952, Simmons was a rich man, respected in both his community and in the oil business. He expanded his interests into international business when he made his first trip to Africa. He visited Liberia, a country that had just begun to permit rights to its natural resources. Simmons proposed to pay for oil exploration rights by sharing the profits made from his company.

In 1963, he was part of a U.S. trade mission to East Africa, and he became the first African-American to represent a major oil company abroad. As his peers recall, because he was an African-American, Simmons was able to interact with African leaders in a way that other oil executives could not. Contemporaries also describe him as a man of character.

Source: Adapted from Jonathan Greenberg, *Staking a Claim: Jake Simmons, Jr. and the Making of an African-American Oil Dynasty* (New York: Athenaeum), 1990.

Think Critically
1. What actions taken by Jake Simmons could help a person be successful in various life endeavors?
2. Conduct an Internet search for additional information about the economic and social contributions of Jake Simmons, Jr.

✓CheckPoint

What components are commonly included in an integrated information system?

REVIEW GLOBAL BUSINESS TERMS

Define each of the following terms.

1. productivity

2. synchronized manufacturing

3. quality control

4. total quality control (TQC)

5. quality circle

6. tailored logistics

REVIEW GLOBAL BUSINESS CONCEPTS

7. How can production output be measured?

8. How do service industries differ from manufacturing industries in their production processes?

9. How is information processing and office productivity changing?

SOLVE GLOBAL BUSINESS PROBLEMS

Balancing trade with the protection of natural resources is important. In some African countries, trade in tropical timber is restricted. Governments place heavy tariffs on exported finished-wood products. Yet these countries strive to develop their economies. A proposal in Uganda suggested lifting tariffs on finished-wood products such as furniture, since these items have a higher market value than raw timber. African countries could maintain their income levels while harvesting fewer trees.

10. What changes in input and transformation of the production process of timber would occur?

11. Which production method (manual, automated, or computerized) would make the proposal most feasible?

12. Do you think this proposal would enable the African countries to increase their profits from tropical timber? Why or why not?

THINK CRITICALLY

13. List objections that employees might have to working on cross-functional teams.

14. Measuring quality of services is more difficult than measuring manufactured goods. What are some ways in which a business could assess the quality of service provided?

MAKE CONNECTIONS

15. **MATH** Without quality control, small numbers of defective products can result in large business expenses. A manufacturing company produces 1.2 million computer chips a month, costing $7 each. Currently, 1.5 percent of these are defective each month. How much would the company save each month if the rate of defective items could be reduced to 0.6 percent?

16. **ECONOMICS** Why are more personal and business services offered in developed economies than in less-developed economies?

CHAPTER SUMMARY

5-1 GLOBAL PRODUCTION METHODS

A The production process changes raw materials into finished goods and services. The three elements in the production process are resources, transformation, and goods and services.

B The goal of operations management is to produce a good or service at the lowest possible cost while maintaining the highest possible quality. Operations managers use forecasting, scheduling, and inventory control to manage the process.

C The production methods used in global business are manual production, automated production, and computerized production.

15-2 EXPANDING PRODUCTIVE ACTIVITIES

A Production output might be measured in terms of productivity and quality control. Productivity is the amount of work that is accomplished in a unit of time. Quality control measures goods and services produced against a product standard.

B Creating services involves performing tasks that provide value to consumers and businesses. Services are about 70 percent of U.S. GDP and a major portion of global sales.

C Technology influences office activities through improved productivity resulting from faster and more efficient equipment and systems.

GLOBAL **REFOCUS**

Read the Global Focus at the beginning of this chapter, and answer the following questions.

1. Which production systems have been used in Mauritania's production of seafood?

2. How have changes in technology contributed to Mauritania's success in the fishing industry?

REVIEW GLOBAL BUSINESS TERMS

Match the terms listed with the definitions. Some terms may not be used.

1. The means by which a company changes raw materials into finished goods.

2. A method of production in which machines perform the work.

3. The use of resources to create a good or service.

4. The process of designing and managing a production system.

5. A measurement of the amount of work that is accomplished in a unit of time.

6. A method of production using computers to control machines and perform work.

7. The process of measuring goods and services against a product standard.

8. A method of monitoring the amount of raw materials and completed goods on hand.

9. A method of production that involves using peoples' hands and bodies as the means of transforming resources into goods and services.

10. A production system in which computers guide the entire manufacturing process, from product design through processing, assembly, testing, and packaging.

11. A small group of employees who have different jobs within the same company but have the same goal of producing a quality good or service.

12. The technology that designs, constructs, and operates devices that can perform difficult, repetitive, or dangerous work.

a. automated production
b. computer-aided design (CAD)
c. computer-assisted manufacturing (CAM)
d. computer-integrated manufacturing (CIM)
e. computerized production
f. inventory control
g. manual production
h. operations management
i. production process
j. productivity
k. quality circle
l. quality control
m. robotics
n. synchronized manufacturing
o. tailored logistics
p. total quality control (TQC)
q. transformation

MAKE GLOBAL BUSINESS DECISIONS

13. A region's production opportunities are often determined by its natural resources. Which of your state's natural resources have been used to encourage business in your state? Are any of the natural resources unique to your state? If so, what has that meant for production in your state?

14. As a consumer of a particular product, how would you suggest tailoring the product to better serve consumer demands?

15. What effects do you think robotics and computer-integrated manufacturing (CIM) will have on U.S. business during the next two decades?

16. What production methods do you and others use to accomplish daily tasks at home, school, or work? List examples for each method used.

17. What actions might be taken by a company to improve quality?

18. Prepare a list (with job descriptions) of roles that might be assumed by team members working on a project, such as team leader and recorder.

19. How can a person prepare to have the skills necessary for employment in the future as technology changes the types of jobs that are in demand?

20. Describe safety situations and other reasons that a country might continue to use manual production methods rather than automated or computerized ones.

GLOBAL CONNECTIONS

21. **GEOGRAPHY** Identify companies that contribute significantly to your local economy. Are these organizations manufacturing or service business-es? Which resources (natural, human, or capital) may have attracted these companies to your area?

22. **COMMUNICATIONS** Choose a company, and obtain information from library research or the Internet about its production activities. Create a flow chart of the production process of this company. Include the resources used in input, the activities involved in transformation, and the goods and servic-es produced as output.

23. **CULTURAL STUDIES** Describe how cultural differences might affect team project activities of a group of workers from different countries.

24. **SCIENCE** Interview a person who is involved with manufacturing about production processes used in his or her business. What natural resources and scientific principles are used by this organization? What possible health and safety concerns might be encountered in various countries around the world?

25. **MATHEMATICS** Research methods used to measure production output. What numeric standards are used to measure productivity? How is quality control maintained?

26. **CAREER PLANNING** Conduct library research about the technology used in different countries. Prepare a list of computer and technology skills that office workers and other employees should possess for career suc-cess.

27. **GEOGRAPHY** Choose a country. Use the Internet to identify five natural resources the country supplies to the rest of the world.

28. **TECHNOLOGY** Use the Internet to identify companies with operations that have horizontal integration and vertical integration.

29. **TECHNOLOGY** Use the Internet to online resources for computer-assisted manufacturing and computerized production systems.

THE GLOBAL ENTREPRENEUR

CREATING AN INTERNATIONAL BUSINESS PLAN

PLANNING PRODUCTION FOR GLOBAL BUSINESS

Based on the company you have been using in this continuing project or on a new idea for your business, obtain information related to the following elements of production planning.

1. List natural resources needed for this enterprise.
2. Describe the human resources of the organization.
3. List capital resources necessary for providing the good or service.
4. Prepare a visual presentation of the production process. (Describe how manual, automated, or computerized production will be used.)
5. Describe what types of technology the company will use.
6. Describe types of items (parts, supplies, finished goods) will be kept in inventory.
7. Describe factors will be used to measure productivity.
8. Describe actions could be taken to assure quality control.

Prepare a written summary or present a short oral report (two or three minutes) of your findings.

GLOBAL CROSS-CULTURAL TEAM PROJECT

Implement International Business Operations

The information systems and production activities of businesses vary significantly around the world. While these differences are frequently the result of the level of economic development, history and culture may also affect these business operations. Cross-cultural teams, with people from around the world, can add to the efficiency of a company's information processing and manufacturing.

GOAL

To identify regional differences for planning and implementing information systems and manufacturing facilities.

ACTIVITIES

Working in teams, select a geographic region you will represent—Africa, Asia, Europe, Latin America, the Middle East, or North America.

1. To research information processing and manufacturing in your region, consider doing the following: conduct a web search, use library resources, and, if possible, talk to people who have lived or visited that area of the world.
2. Identify the extent to which computers are used in various countries in your region.
3. Explain common information processing procedures used by companies in your geographic region. How does the availability of information improve the efficiency of business activities?
4. Describe common production activities in some countries in your region. What benefits and concerns are associated with these factories?
5. Evaluate how technology is used in production activities for several countries in the region. What are some of the limitations of using technology in this area of the world?
6. **Global Business Decision** Your team has been assigned the task of selecting a location for a production facility. This manufacturing plant will make automobile parts for vehicles assembled in the United Kingdom, United States, Japan, Germany, Mexico, and Brazil. Compare your findings with those of others on your team and decide which region would be the best location for this factory. What factors need to be considered when making this decision?

TEAM SKILL

Cross-Cultural Team Leadership
Leadership has a significant influence on the success of a team. Describe the skills of team leaders valued in your geographic region. Do any of these competencies differ from those of effective team leaders in other regions?

PRESENT

Create a flowchart or other visual presentation to communicate the types of information systems and production facilities found in your geographic region.

Human Resource Management

Successful business people are faced with tough decisions that may involve relocation to another country. Frequently individuals who move up the company ranks are promoted to positions that involve international travel or relocation to another country. While promotion within a country is a strong incentive, moving to another part of the world becomes challenging. All factors must be given careful consideration before an employee agrees to relocate to another country. Your company plans to expand its operations to Mexico. The success of this expansion depends on top managers relocating from the United States to Mexico.

Many of your top managers are hesitant to relocate to Mexico due to cultural, economic, and language concerns. Most of your top managers have young families who attend good schools in the U.S. Some of the managers only speak English.

The human resource department (you) is challenged to develop a compensation package that is attractive enough for managers to relocate to Mexico. Top concerns of the managers include salary, schools, language barriers, economic challenges, moving costs, and quality of life.

PERFORMANCE INDICATORS EVALUATED

- Demonstrate knowledge of human resources management and management concepts.
- Apply critical thinking skills to interpret personnel policies.
- Demonstrate effective oral communication skills.
- Demonstrate understanding of human relations skills
- Discuss compensation, benefits, and incentive programs.

For more detailed information about performance indicators, go to the BPA web site.

THINK CRITICALLY

1. Why is salary not necessarily the top concern for managers you wish to relocate?
2. What five items do you feel are most important to include in the manager compensation package? Why?
3. What will you offer managers who want their young children to attend the best private schools?
4. Outline your compensation package. Make sure to include all benefits and allowances for moving costs and travel to/from the U.S.

www.bpa.org/

UNIT 5

MARKETING IN A GLOBAL ECONOMY

IF YOU WERE THERE

As your four-wheel-drive truck struggles up the bank of yet another river crossing, the mountain village of Bocay is just around the next bend in the narrow road. From here, you will begin the 70-mile canoe trip down the Río de Bocay to the Sumu village.

You see the village stretching along the bank of a muddy river. Its 1,800 people live in two-room boxlike houses along the road. The walls are wood, the roofs are tin, and the floors are dirt. There is no plumbing, but there is talk of having electricity in a few months. A family shares some of its rice and beans with you and offers you a place to sleep on the floor. Your anthropology classes did not prepare you emotionally for this culture that is so different from your own.

The 1,800 Sumus who live in five villages along the Río de Bocay are having a difficult time surviving. Their bamboo huts contain just a few pots and maybe some rice and beans. They wear secondhand clothes from North America. However, the Sumus are in the process of setting up a cooperative business in each village. The Sumu will make crafts from the wood found in the forest, and the villagers will cooperatively sell these products in markets such as Bocay.

Mayan and Incan Empires

The Mayan Empire extended over several areas of Central America between A.D. 250 and A.D. 900. Mayan culture centered around religion and ceremony. Mayan cities contained great temple-pyramids, which attracted large crowds during festivals. The study of astronomy and mathematics was essential to Mayan religion.

Another of the great empires of Latin America was the Incan Empire, whose ruins of Machu Picchu in the Andes Mountains of Peru attract visitors from all over the world. The Incan Empire extended from the northern border of modern Ecuador to central Chile. Its 10-12 million inhabitants enjoyed the benefits of the strong central government in return for helping with the construction of public buildings and roads. The important buildings were plat-

©Getty Images/PhotoDisc

ed in gold. In 1532, the Spanish, led by the conquistador Francisco Pizarro, captured the Incan Emperor Atahuallpa. Atahuallpa was murdered by the Spanish in 1533, leaving the Incan people without a leader.

Colonization

The colonization of Central and South America was based on an economic system known as *mercantilism*—in which a nation's power depended on its accumulation of wealth. Portuguese and Spanish ships carried away great quantities of gold, silver, and other raw materials to the parent countries. In turn, the colonies served as markets for manufactured exports. The Native Americans were forced to work the mines and plantations. Later, when European diseases significantly reduced the Indian population, Africans were enslaved and imported.

During the colonial period (1521-1820), approximately 5,400 Spanish and Portuguese immigrated to Latin America each year. These immigrants developed a society based on their European heritage, but also one that was influenced by cultural aspects of their new environment. They brought Roman Catholicism to the colonies, and it remains the dominant religion today.

Struggle for Independence

In the early 1800s, the nationalist leaders Simón Bolívar, José de San Martin, and Bernardo O'Higgins led wars of independence from Spanish rule. However, the liberal Portuguese King Joâo VI, who fled to Brazil after Napoléon invaded his country, fostered Brazilian independence from Portugal. He then declared the colony's independence as a means to retaining his royal sovereignty.

Traditionally, wealthy landowners, merchants, and the military have controlled Latin American governments since independence. Governments were frequently overthrown by the army in an attempt to gain power or to protect the wealth and power of the ruling class. Those who spoke up for the poor were often assassinated. In 1991 and 1992, coup attempts occurred in Guatemala, Haiti, Venezuela, and Peru.

Geography

The Andes Mountains and their snowcapped peaks extend almost 4,500 miles from Venezuela to the tip of South America, dominating the topography of the western part of the continent.

©Getty Images/PhotoDisc

Inland plains spread from Venezuela south through Brazil, Paraguay, Uruguay, and Argentina. A vast desert region in Peru and Chile is one of the driest areas in the world. Rain forests are common in areas of Central America; the Amazon basin rain forest takes up one-third of South America. The longest river in the Western Hemisphere is the Amazon. It flows 4,000 miles across the continent before pouring its vital nutrients into the ocean, enriching sea life as far away as the Grand Banks of Newfoundland.

Ethnic Groups

The ethnic groups of Central and South America are as diverse as the land. African, Asian, Middle Eastern, European, Native American, Mestizo (Native American-European), and Mulatto (European-African) all live together in this region.

Industries

Farming and mining continue to be the most important industries in Latin America. Coffee, sugar, bananas, wheat, cotton, and cacao are exported. However, the region still has difficulty feeding its people because of a growing population and primitive farming methods. A few countries produce oil and natural gas. Most countries mine mineral resources such as iron, tin, copper, silver, lead, and gold. Brazil ranks in the top ten countries for world gold production.

Economic Growth

Future economic growth will depend on industrial development. Many governments are looking to their sparsely populated interiors for hydroelectric power to run factories and offices. The interiors are also rich in timber and could provide farms for the millions of hungry, landless peasants. Rain forests are essential to the global environment and must be preserved. The wild rivers attract tourists, and the rain forest is home to many indigenous people. The rain forests contain an abundance of animal and plant species, which are possible sources of medicines.

Latin American nations are under pressure to protect the environment at the expense of industrial development. The northern countries continue to consume and pollute. The population of Latin America could double in the next 20 to 25 years, and governments will be hard-pressed to fill basic food, housing, health, and education needs for their people. These social, economic, and health problems are all interrelated, and their solutions might be found by those regional and global problem solvers who comprehend just how interdependent we are.

Think Critically

1. How does having a government consisting of wealthy officials and military personnel affect the citizens of a country?
2. How do North American consumption trends affect the rain forests in Central and South America?
3. Why is industrial development essential for the economic growth of this region?
4. Use the library or do an Internet search to determine how many and what kinds of species are estimated to exist in the Amazon River area. What kinds of medical uses have already been discovered for some of these species?

©Getty Images/PhotoDisc

COUNTRY PROFILE/CENTRAL AND SOUTH AMERICA

Country	Population		GDP		Exports	Imports	Monetary Unit	Inflation	Unemployment	Life Expectancy	Literacy Rate
	thousands	growth rate %	$billions	$ per capita	$billions			percent	percent	years	percent
Antigua and Barbuda	72	0.69	0.67	10,000	0.4	0.46	East Caribbean Dollar	0.4	11	71.31	89
Argentina	38,428	1.17	392	10,200	26.7	20.3	Peso	41	21.5	75.48	97.1
Bahamas, The	295	1.13	5	16,800	0.61	1.77	Bahamian Dollar	1.8	6.9	65.71	95.6
Barbados	270	0.35	4	14,500	0.29	1.03	Barbadian Dollar	-0.6	10	71.84	97.4
Belize	256	2.06	0.83	3,250	0.21	0.4	Belizean Dollar	1.9	9.1	67.36	94.1
Bolivia	8,808	1.89	21.4	2,600	1.29	1.49	Boliviano	2	7.6	64.78	87.2
Brazil	178,470	1.24	1,340	7,400	58.2	57.7	Real	8.3	6.4	71.13	86.4
Chile	15,805	1.23	153	10,000	18.5	16.4	Chilean Peso	2.5	9.2	76.35	96.2
Colombia	44,222	1.59	255	6,300	12.8	12.3	Colombian Peso	6.2	17.4	71.14	92.5
Costa Rica	4,173	1.93	31.9	8,500	4.91	6.12	Costa Rican Colon	9.1	6.3	76.43	96
Cuba	11,300	0.27	25.9	2,300	1.8	4.8	Cuban Peso	7.1	4.1	76.8	97
Dominica	70	0.29	0.26	3,700	0.5	0.13	East Caribbean Dollar	1	23	74.12	94
Dominican Republic	8,745	1.49	50	5,800	5.33	8.78	Dominican Peso	5.3	14.5	67.96	84.7
Ecuador	13,003	1.49	39.6	3,000	4.86	5.33	U.S. Dollar	12.5	7.7	71.89	92.5
El Salvador	6,515	1.55	28.4	4,600	2.9	4.81	U.S. Dollar	3.8	10	70.62	80.2
Grenada	89	-0.26	0.42	4,750	0.85	0.22	East Caribbean Dollar	2.8	12.5	64.52	98
Guatemala	12,347	2.55	48.3	3,700	2.87	5.14	Quetzal	8.1	7.5	65.23	70.6
Guyana	765	0.24	2.5	3,600	0.5	0.54	Guyanese Dollar	4.7	9.1	63.09	98.8
Haiti	8,326	1.32	12	1,700	0.3	0.64	Gourde	11.9	NA	51.61	52.9
Honduras	6,941	2.34	17	2,600	1.93	2.81	Lempira	7.7	28	66.65	76.2
Jamaica	2,651	0.92	9.8	3,700	1.6	3.1	Jamaican Dollar	7	15.4	75.85	87.9
Nicaragua	5,466	2.43	12.3	2,500	0.6	1.63	Gold Cordoba	3.7	24	69.68	67.5
Panama	3,120	1.84	16.9	5,900	5.88	6.71	Balboa	1.1	16	72.32	92.6
Paraguay	5,878	2.37	26.2	4,600	2.41	2.95	Guarani	10.5	18.2	74.4	94
Peru	27,167	1.5	132	4,800	7.11	7.2	Nuevo Sol	0.2	9.4	70.88	90.9
Saint Kitts and Nevis	39	-0.3	0.34	8,700	0.06	0.17	East Caribbean Dollar	1.7	4.5	71.57	97
Saint Lucia	149	0.78	0.7	4,400	0.06	0.31	East Caribbean Dollar	3	16.5	73.08	67
Saint Vincent and the Grenadines	116	0.58	0.34	2,900	0.05	0.14	East Caribbean Dollar	-0.4	22	73.08	96
São Tomé and Príncipe	155	0.8	1.5	3,500	0.01	0.02	Dobra	9	N/A	66.28	79.3
Suriname	436	0.71	1.48	3,500	0.44	0.3	Surinamese Guilder	17	17	69.23	93
Trinidad and Tobago	1,303	0.34	10.6	9,000	2.26	3	Trinidad and Tobago Dollar	4.3	10.8	69.59	98.6
Uruguay	3,415	0.72	31	9,200	2.15	2.92	Peso Uruguayo	14.1	19.4	75.87	98
Venezuela	25,699	1.86	146.2	6,100	26	17.4	Bolivar	31.2	17	73.81	93.4

N/A — Data not available

©Getty Images/PhotoDisc

Chapter 16

GLOBAL MARKETING AND CONSUMER BEHAVIOR

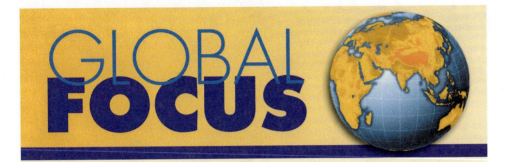

GLOBAL FOCUS

Breakfast in Britain

In recent years, the population growth rate and the demand for packaged food products in the United States have slowed. In addition, fewer people are eating a traditional breakfast of cereal. Instead, people have turned to bagels, cereal bars, toaster pastries, and fast-food breakfast-to-go meals. This sales decline caused cereal producers to look for new markets for their products.

International marketing efforts by cereal companies to sell Kellogg's Rice Krispies, Kellogg's Frosted Flakes, Cheerios, Wheaties, and other cereals to the British and other Europeans are gaining strength. Traditionally, Europeans have eaten less cereal per person than U.S. consumers have. However, these areas were selected because their breakfast habits are similar to those in the United States. General Mills created a joint venture with Nestlé, called Cereal Partners Worldwide, to sell its cereals in Europe, Latin America, the Middle East, and other regions. This agreement allows General Mills to take advantage of the extensive distribution system and a strong global Nestlé brand. The joint venture sells cereal in more than 130 countries.

The Kellogg Company has sold cereal in London since 1924. The company recently modernized and expanded its 22 foreign factories. Kellogg achieves about 35 percent of its sales outside of the United States. While sales are expected to continue, the marketing of cereals in a global marketplace will continue to be a challenge for Tony the Tiger and his buddies.

Think Critically

1. What factors influenced cereal companies to expand their marketing in foreign countries?
2. What problems might a cereal company face when planning to sell its products in a new foreign market?
3. Go to the web site of Kellogg's or General Mills to obtain additional information about international marketing of cereal. Prepare a report of your findings.

16-1 | MARKETING AROUND THE WORLD

GOALS

- Describe the nature of markets.
- Identify trends that influence global marketing opportunities.

©Getty Images/PhotoDisc

INTERNATIONAL MARKETS

Survival for every company depends on creating and delivering items that consumers will buy. Distribution of products and development of consumer awareness are major tasks of marketing. Marketing does not always involve a specific good or service. Places such as Bermuda, Jamaica, Mexico, and Puerto Rico advertise in magazines, on television, and on the Internet to attract visitors. This type of marketing can stimulate tourism and consumer interest in the goods and services of those geographic areas.

One business sells carpeting in one city, while another sells global telecommunications systems throughout the world. Both companies must get the product or service from the producer to the consumer. Customers must first become aware of a product. Then the item must be delivered at a cost acceptable to both the buyer and the seller.

Marketing is the creation and maintenance of satisfying exchange relationships between businesses and their customers. Marketing includes shipping, packaging, pricing, advertising, selling, and many other tasks. **International marketing** involves marketing activities between sellers and buyers in different countries. Japanese automobile manufacturers perform marketing activities in more than 140 countries. Overnight delivery services are also involved in international marketing as they move packages throughout countries and continents.

GLOBAL BUSINESS EXAMPLE

GLOBAL MARKETING OF FAST FOOD

Over the past two decades, fast-food companies have expanded their international marketing activities into several new areas. Burger King, Arby's, Taco Bell, and Wendy's became competitors for McDonald's and KFC in Mexico, Brazil, France, Japan, South Korea, China, and many other countries.

Recently, U.S. fast-food chains had high-speed expansion in China. Pizza Hut increased the use of home delivery in the world's biggest market. McDonald's added 100 more restaurants to bring the number to over 600 in the country.

KFC opened its 1,000th location in China and works to balance its traditional menu with local consumers tastes. The company created "Old Beijing Twister" — a wrap served like Peking Duck, but with fried chicken inside.

Think Critically

1. What difficulties may fast-food companies face when doing business in other countries?
2. Go to the web site of a fast-food company such as McDonald's Burger King, Wendy's, Taco Bell, or KFC to obtain additional information about international business activities.

The main focus of marketing is to define and sell to a specific group. A **market** refers to the likely customers for a good or service in a certain geographic location. A market could be teenagers in France or retired people in Mexico. Markets are commonly divided into two categories—consumer markets and organizational markets.

CONSUMER MARKETS

A **consumer market** consists of individuals and households who are the final users of goods and services. You are part of the consumer market when you buy food, clothing, transportation, health-care, and recreational products. Consumer markets exist in every country of the world. However, buying habits vary because of factors such as climate, culture, political environment, values, tradition, and religious beliefs.

ORGANIZATIONAL MARKETS

Not all goods and services are sold to end users. An **organizational market**, also called a *commercial* market or *business-to-business* (B2B) marketing, consists of buyers who purchase items for resale or additional production. These buyers include manufacturers, stores, schools, hotels, hospitals, and governments. Items commonly purchased in commercial markets are raw materials, machines, machine parts, warehouses, computers, office space, office supplies, and Internet services.

Organizational markets are important to the economy of a country. As nations create more factories and start companies, jobs are created. The income earned by these employees contributes to increased consumer spending, which results in economic expansion.

Describe the two different kinds of markets.

GLOBAL MARKETING OPPORTUNITIES

Most businesses need to develop new markets in order to maintain and expand profits. Quite often new customers are found in other countries. For example, when sales for electronic products leveled off for Asian companies in their home region, these firms expanded to sell to customers in South America and Europe.

Opportunities for international marketing are influenced by five global trends. These trends include expanded communications, technology, changing political situations, increased competition, and changing demographics.

Expanded Communications Computer networks make it possible to communicate quickly with customers all over the world, as shown in Figure 16-1. The Internet, video teleconferencing, fax machines, and other electronic communications allow companies to respond to requests from customers within minutes.

TELECOMMUNICATIONS AND INTERNATIONAL MARKETING

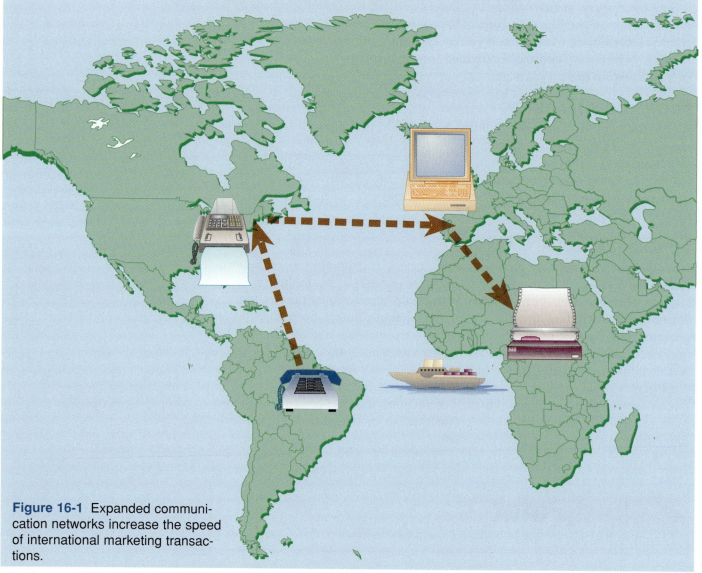

Figure 16-1 Expanded communication networks increase the speed of international marketing transactions.

Technology Automated production systems have made it easier for companies to set up manufacturing plants in other countries. Technology has also improved product distribution. Companies are able to ship goods from one location to destinations around the world within a matter of days or even hours.

Changing Political Situations Countries that desire economic growth are cooperating with new trading partners. Several nations that were formerly governed by communism now have a more cooperative economic attitude toward international business. Many global companies now do business in various eastern European countries in which trade was previously restricted.

Increased Competition As more companies get involved in exporting and foreign investment, business firms look for new markets in other countries. A more competitive environment requires companies to be more creative and more efficient when selling around the world.

Changing Demographics The traits of a country's population (such as birthrate, age distribution, marriage rate, gender distribution, income distribution, education level, and housing situation) are its **demographics**. Demographic trends create different marketing opportunities. A lower birthrate in a country could mean a baby food company must market in other nations or create other types of products.

Identifying business opportunities is the start of the marketing process, as shown in Figure 16-2. When a business finds a new use for its products or finds a new group of customers, an opportunity to expand marketing occurs. The Disney Company, for example, built amusement parks in Japan, France, and Hong Kong. The company saw opportunities for foreign expansion of its entertainment services.

WORK AS A GROUP

Discuss the kinds of product opportunities that would occur if a country advanced rapidly in adding electronic technology for the use of all its citizens.

Figure 16-2 The marketing process can help a company plan and execute its global marketing activities.

THE MARKETING PROCESS

Identify Business Opportunities → Evaluate Potential Demand and Consumer Behavior Patterns → Plan the Marketing Strategy for the Marketing Mix Based on Marketing Research → Carry Out the Marketing Plan

REGIONAL PERSPECTIVE

GEOGRAPHY: THE RAIN FOREST

Rain forests are located in 33 countries in Africa, Asia, and Central and South America. The largest rain forest covers areas in Brazil, French Guiana, Suriname, Guyana, Venezuela, Colombia, Ecuador, Peru, Bolivia, and Chile.

©Getty Images/PhotoDisc

Many common food products originate in rain forests. These include avocados, bananas, black pepper, cashews, chocolate, cinnamon, coconuts, coffee, cola, lemons, oranges, sugarcane, and vanilla.

More than 5 million different plant and animal species live in rain forests. Tens of thousands of other species may still be undiscovered. In the Amazon River region of Brazil, every few miles you will find hundreds of different insects, mammals, birds, reptiles, and amphibians making their homes in trees and other plants. Many plants from these jungles are used to treat various diseases, including cancer. Aspirin was originally made from a tropical willow tree.

In recent years, farmers, loggers, cattle ranchers, and highway builders have used many rain forest areas. Their activities have resulted in a changed environment. Many plants and animals are lost forever. Rain forests are being destroyed at the rate of thousands of square miles a year. Much of the Pacific rain forests in Guatemala, for example, are now used for coffee, cotton, and sugar farming. Attempts are being made to plant over 50 million new trees in that country to improve the ecology.

Throughout the world, environmental groups are working to save the rain forests. Actions recommended for those concerned about the situation include recycling, using reusable containers, and avoiding products that come from destroyed rain forest areas.

Think Critically
1. How do consumers and businesses benefit from rain forests?
2. What actions might be appropriate to preserve the rain forests?
3. Conduct an Internet search for additional information about the benefits provided by rain forests.

✓ CheckPoint

What are five global marketing trends?

REVIEW GLOBAL BUSINESS TERMS

Define each of the following terms.

1. international marketing
2. market
3. consumer market
4. organizational market
5. demographics

REVIEW GLOBAL BUSINESS CONCEPTS

6. What business activities are included in marketing?
7. How do consumer markets and organizational markets differ?
8. What is a global marketing opportunity, and what influences it?

SOLVE GLOBAL BUSINESS PROBLEMS

Determine whether each of the following activities is a marketing activity.

9. Planning a label design for canned tomatoes.
10. Placing a product order form on a web site.
11. Ordering office supplies.
12. Sending a product catalog to a customer.
13. Using overnight delivery services to send a sample to a customer.
14. Processing the payroll for the marketing department.
15. Conducting a survey in a mall about product preferences.

THINK CRITICALLY

16. Explain why money spent on a factory has the potential for greater economic growth than money spent by consumers on video games.
17. Based on this unit's Regional Profile, which three countries have the highest population growth rate? What marketing opportunities are created by a high population growth rate?

MAKE CONNECTIONS

18. **TECHNOLOGY** Describe examples of marketing opportunities that were not possible a few years ago that have been created by technology.
19. **LAW** What types of laws might be encountered in other countries that would restrict marketing activities?

16-2
GOALS

- List the four elements of the marketing mix.
- Describe a marketing plan and its use in global marketing activities.

THE MARKETING MIX AND THE MARKETING PLAN

©Getty Images/PhotoDisc

THE MARKETING MIX

As a company plans and organizes its global marketing activities, several questions must be considered. What will be sold? How much will be charged? How will the item get to the consumer? How will consumers become informed about the product? These questions address the four major elements of the **marketing mix**, which are product, price, distribution, and promotion. Figure 16-3 illustrates examples of each element of the marketing mix. The marketing mix is important whether you are selling clothing in a small community or expanding credit card services throughout South America.

PRODUCT

Before goods are purchased, the items must satisfy a need or want. **Product** refers to a good or service being offered for sale that satisfies consumer demand. The term "product" refers to everything from automobiles and green beans to life insurance and cable television channels. Not all products are offered by businesses. Nonprofit organizations such as museums and symphony orchestras offer educational and cultural experiences as their products.

Many factors, such as culture, weather, and economic conditions, can affect the acceptance of a product or service in a foreign market. For example, instant foods may not sell in cultures where careful preparation of the family meal is important.

THE MARKETING MIX

Product
- Goods
- Services

Price
- Value to consumer
- Production costs

The Marketing Mix

Distribution
- Transportation
- Storage
- Wholesaling
- Retailing

Promotion
- Advertising
- Personal selling
- Publicity
- Sales promotions

Figure 16-3 Businesses coordinate the four elements of the marketing mix to reach their customers.

PRICE

The monetary value of a product agreed upon by a buyer and a seller is the **price**. What if you agree to purchase 100 stereo systems at a price of £53 per stereo from a United Kingdom firm? Do you know how much you are paying? As you know, different nations use different money systems. Prices may be stated in terms of euros, pesos, yen, or other currency.

DISTRIBUTION

Distribution involves the activities needed to physically move and transfer ownership of goods and services from producer to consumer. Transporting, storing, sorting, ordering, and retailing are examples of distribution activities. Distribution activities vary from country to country. For example, some countries do not have refrigeration systems in stores. Therefore, products such as milk are distributed differently than they are in the United States.

WORK AS A GROUP

Select two products, both a good and a service. Discuss how the elements of the marketing mix would vary for the two products. Repeat with other pairs of products as time allows.

PROMOTION

The final component of the marketing mix is promotion. **Promotion** involves the marketing efforts that inform and persuade customers. Different languages and customs influence promotional decisions. Many companies have used inappropriate wording when advertising in another country. For example, a Canadian importer of Turkish clothing translated the labels into French for sale in Quebec. The French language has a different word for turkey the bird and Turkey the country. So a confused translator created labels that read "made in a turkey" instead of "Made in Turkey."

MARKETING OF SERVICES

Demand for health care, financial services, and information systems have increased in recent years. This demand has resulted in expanded marketing opportunities for these and other services. *Consumer services* include those provided by lawyers, doctors, dentists, hairstylists, daycare centers, repair shops, travel agencies, and music teachers. *Commercial services* include advertising, information systems, delivery, maintenance, security, and equipment rental. Services continue to gain importance for companies involved in exporting and international trade.

When a business markets services, it must adapt the marketing mix for a nonphysical item. Many of the advertising and pricing activities used for goods also apply to services. Distribution of services, however, is quite different. The service is most often produced at the time of consumption. For example, a haircut or dental checkup is produced and consumed at one time.

✓ CheckPoint

Name the four major elements of the marketing mix. Give an example of each.

E-COMMERCE IN ACTION

Japanese Convenience Stores Go Online

While Japan trailed other countries in the use of the Internet, consumers in that country were making use of e-commerce through convenience stores. Online shoppers are able to buy a late-night snack of seaweed-covered rice balls with mayonnaise or chocolate chip *mochi* (rice cakes) from their local *combini*—the Japanese name for convenience store.

7-Eleven Japan had an agreement with a software company and other companies to sell programs, videos, books, and other products over the Internet. Japanese consumers can choose from one of the more than 10,000 7-Eleven stores in Japan and have the merchandise delivered to their home.

Think Critically

1. Why might customers buy online?
2. What are the benefits of selling online for convenience stores?
3. Find web sites that allow consumers to buy food online.

THE MARKETING PLAN

A *marketing plan* is a document that describes the marketing activities of an organization. A marketing plan may consist of the seven sections shown in Figure 16-4. Some companies may use different titles or change the number of sections in their marketing plans. However, the elements shown in the illustration and described below should be considered in all marketing plans.

Company Goals The first item of the marketing plan presents what the company wants to accomplish. Some common marketing goals may be "to increase consumer awareness for our new personal computer among Brazilian small business owners," "to reduce selling costs for customers in Japan," or "to increase sales in the South American region."

Description of Customers and Their Needs The second part of the marketing plan describes the company's customers. What are their needs? What types of television programs do they watch? How often do they go to the store? This information helps the company meet consumer needs.

Competitors With whom will you be competing? What are the products offered by the competitor? How are competing products promoted, priced, and distributed?

Economic, Social, Legal, and Technological Trends What trends can be observed? How will the local economic conditions and forecasts affect your business? What social trends, such as an increase in women entering the workforce or an increase in the literacy rate, might affect your strategy? Are there legal trends that will affect your plans, such as environmental or consumer legislation? Will technological changes affect your product?

Financial and Human Resources Every company has limited resources. How will your company's financial and human resources be used to market your product? Are sufficient funds available to fulfill the marketing plan? Are there enough people available to complete the required tasks?

Time Line When will each part of the marketing effort occur? Many companies fail because they launch a product too early or too late. Sometimes promotion efforts build demand for a product that is not ready in time to meet the demand. Other times products are launched too late, and competitors or other products fill the demand, replacing your new product.

THE PARTS OF A MARKETING PLAN

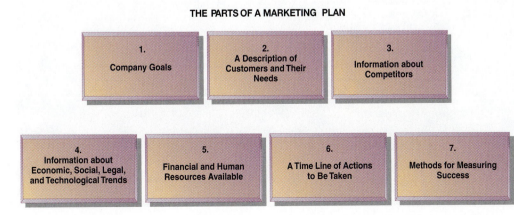

1. Company Goals
2. A Description of Customers and Their Needs
3. Information about Competitors
4. Information about Economic, Social, Legal, and Technological Trends
5. Financial and Human Resources Available
6. A Time Line of Actions to Be Taken
7. Methods for Measuring Success

Figure 16-4 A marketing plan provides a business with details for promoting, selling, and distributing a product or service.

Methods for Measuring Success Measurement of success can be done by comparing financial results with company goals. How many new customers were obtained? How does this compare to the number you wanted to obtain?

ELEMENTS OF AN INTERNATIONAL MARKETING PLAN

A marketing plan with an international emphasis should discuss the following topics.

- How will the geographic, cultural, and political factors influence global marketing activities?
- Can the product (or service) be sold in a standardized form, or will it need to be adapted to local situations?
- Will the people be able to afford the product (or service), or will the price need to be revised for global customers?
- Does the infrastructure of other countries allow for efficient and low-cost distribution?
- Should advertising be similar to or different from the promotions used in other countries?
- Is the use of strategic partnerships, such as joint ventures, appropriate for doing international marketing?

✔ CheckPoint

What are seven common sections of a marketing plan?

REVIEW GLOBAL BUSINESS TERMS

Define each of the following terms.

1. marketing mix
2. product
3. price
4. distribution
5. promotion

REVIEW GLOBAL BUSINESS CONCEPTS

6. Which element of the marketing mix for services differs the most from marketing for goods?

7. How does a marketing plan serve the needs of an organization?

SOLVE GLOBAL BUSINESS PROBLEMS

Describe each component of the marketing mix for the following Latin American business situations. For each: (a) identify the product or service, (b) give one factor that might affect price, (c) describe a possible distribution method, and (d) explain a possible promotion.

8. A forestry company in Chile.
   a. product
   b. price
   c. distribution
   d. promotion

9. A shoe store in Panama.
   a. product
   b. price
   c. distribution
   d. promotion

10. A restaurant in Brazil.
   a. product
   b. price
   c. distribution
   d. promotion

THINK CRITICALLY

11. Choose a product that you buy regularly. Then identify each element of the marketing mix for the item: product description, price, stores at which the product is sold (distribution), and types of advertising and other promotions.

12. Why is it important to include methods for measuring success in a marketing plan?

MAKE CONNECTIONS

13. **CULTURAL STUDIES** Use the Internet or library resources to determine the kinds of food eaten in a foreign country of your choice. Then list five U.S. foods that are not usually eaten in that country.

14. **DEMOGRAPHICS** What are some differences between people who live in rural and urban areas in your country?

16-3 PLANNING GLOBAL MARKETING ACTIVITIES

GOALS

- Explain the international marketing environment.
- Identify factors that influence consumer behavior in different countries.
- Describe the methods used to segment markets and identify a target market.

©Getty Images/PhotoDisc

THE MARKETING ENVIRONMENT

Factors external to companies affect all marketing decisions. As food companies expand into foreign markets, they may have to adapt their recipes to meet the tastes of other cultures. A different seasoning for existing food items may be necessary. Or they may sell foods not usually sold in their home country. All business activities are affected by four elements of the marketing environment, which are geography, economic conditions, social and cultural influences, and political and legal factors.

Geography Climate and terrain can affect the types of products sold and transportation methods used in another country. Cake mixes sold in mountainous areas must be prepared differently than those used in lower elevations.

Economic Conditions High inflation may discourage a company from entering a foreign market. The value of a country's currency usually affects the selling price, consumer demand, and profits on a product.

Social and Cultural Influences Tastes, habits, customs, and religious beliefs must be considered. A Pepsi advertisement in Israel once had a caption referring to "Ten Million Years Before the Choice." This phrasing contradicts the Orthodox Jewish belief that the universe was created about 5,800 years ago.

Political and Legal Factors Local political and legal factors also affect marketing decisions. For example, as political differences resulted in the division of the former Yugoslavia into different countries, companies had to deal with different government regulations in various regions.

✔ CheckPoint

What four factors make up the marketing environment?

CONSUMER BEHAVIOR

Think about why you made a recent purchase. The item may have been something you needed for school. Also, it could have been something that you simply enjoy. Most consumer purchases involve several factors. Multiply this by the many buying decisions made in the world each day, and you can see that consumer behavior is quite complex. The four main factors that influence consumer behavior are shown in Figure 16-5.

PHYSICAL AND EMOTIONAL NEEDS

Every person requires air, water, food, shelter, clothing, and health care. But these basic needs of life can differ for people in different countries. Consumers in industrialized countries demand easy-to-prepare food products, current fashion clothing, and homes with many appliances and comforts. People in less developed economies may have homegrown food, homemade clothing, and modest housing. In both situations, however, physical needs influence consumer decisions.

Figure 16-5 Consumer buying decisions are influenced by many factors.

FACTORS AFFECTING CONSUMER BEHAVIOR

Physical and Emotional Needs

Food, clothing, shelter, health care, transportation, approval of others, personal satisfaction

Geographic and Demographic Factors

Location, climate, population trends, age, gender, income, education

Personality and Psychographic Factors

Attitudes, beliefs, opinions, personality traits, activities, interests

Social and Cultural Factors

Business organizations, community activities, religious or political affiliation, family, friends

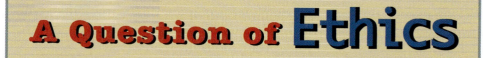

A Question of Ethics

SELLING LUXURY ITEMS IN LESS DEVELOPED ECONOMIES

When a company enters a new market in a developing economy, consumers are attracted to the new products. However, many people in these new markets may not be able to afford the items sold by the multinational company.

A fast-food company or cosmetic distributor may start selling its products in a country with a very low income per household. The availability of these new products can create very high demand. People have been known to wait in line for hours to buy a fast-food meal or another item that costs several days' pay. They are willing to make this sacrifice to obtain an item not previously available.

Think Critically

1. What are potential benefits and drawbacks of selling products in countries with very low levels of income?

2. Use the three guidelines for ethical analysis to examine the above situation.

Another level of consumer needs involves human emotions. People in many cultures want to feel good about themselves and want to be accepted by others. Products may be offered that appeal to these emotional needs. Personal care products, cosmetics, clothing, and even automobiles are presented to appeal to a need for social acceptance and personal satisfaction.

GEOGRAPHIC AND DEMOGRAPHIC FACTORS

Where you live influences buying habits. A person living in a warm area will require different housing and clothing and may prefer different foods than someone living in a cold climate. Another geographic factor influencing consumer buying habits is terrain. Living in mountainous areas requires different types of transportation and consumer products than living in desert regions.

Demographic traits such as your age, gender, and family situation influence how you spend your money. Information on the birthrate, age, marriage, income, education level, and housing situation differ from country to country and have a strong effect on a company's marketing plans. For example, as the people of a nation live longer, older consumers will demand more health, travel, and recreational services.

Data show that people in New Zealand, Canada, the United States, and Australia move more often than people in other countries. This information may help moving companies and relocation services plan business activities. These businesses will find more marketing opportunities in countries with high mobility rates.

©Getty Images/PhotoDisc

PERSONALITY AND PSYCHOGRAPHIC FACTORS

Attitudes are another influence on consumer behavior. Each day our attitudes and beliefs are shaped by experiences and information. These inputs, in turn, create the personality that determines our buying decisions. Personality traits include your attitudes toward risk, change, convenience, and competition. Marketers use this information to attract customers to certain goods and services.

©Getty Images/PhotoDisc

Attempts to better understand personality traits resulted in the study of psychographics. **Psychographics** are buying factors related to lifestyle and psychological influences, such as activities, interests, and opinions. A person's psychographic profile may include hobbies, family activities, work interests, and political and social opinions. As you would probably guess, cultural experiences make the psychographic characteristics of U.S. consumers different from those of consumers in Argentina, India, Morocco, and other countries.

SOCIAL AND CULTURAL FACTORS

How we relate to others is another consumer buying factor. Families, friends, business organizations, community activities, and religious affiliation can affect buying behavior. An understanding of such cultural factors as social structure and religion is critical for international marketing decisions to be successful.

WORK AS A GROUP

Give examples of how various demographic factors and social situations create a need for various goods and services.

NETBookmark

Access intlbizxtra.swlearning.com and click on the link for Chapter 16. Study the "Maslow's Hierarchy of Needs" web page. Consider your own life situation, and then make a ladder chart. Label the chart from top to bottom: Self-Actualization, Esteem, Love, Safety, and Physiological. Write your personal needs under each heading. Write a few paragraphs describing how you or those around you work to meet your needs.

intlbizxtra.swlearning.com

✓ **CheckPoint**

What are the four main factors affecting consumer behavior?

SELECTING A TARGET MARKET

Marketers use consumer buying factors to divide customers into subsets that have similar needs. After segmenting the market, marketers must determine which subgroup to serve.

MARKET SEGMENTS

A **market segment** is a distinct subgroup of customers who share certain personal or behavioral characteristics. High-income individuals, for example, purchase certain items that lower income people would not be able to afford. Market segments can be based on characteristics such as demographics, psychographics, buying behavior, or product benefits, as shown in Figure 16-6.

Social and economic factors cause changes in market segments. In recent years, more women have begun working in Japan. The result was new market segments that demanded more child-care services and convenience foods.

Figure 16-6 Consumer markets are divided into market segments based on personal characteristics, attitudes, activities, and buying preferences.

MARKET SEGMENTATION

Demographics

People of different gender, income, age, and family siltuations require different products. Households with a newborn child will buy diapers or use a diaper service; whereas, single people may be interested in travel services.

Psychographics

Different opinions and attitudes can affect buying; people concerned about nutrition select different food items than other consumers.

Buying Behavior

Actions and shopping preferences differ; some shoppers use mail-order buying, while others go to shopping malls or stores.

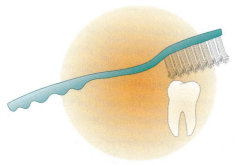

Product Benefits

People require different advantages from their buying choices; some people prefer a toothpaste with good taste, while others want one that fights cavities.

Market segments are commonly given names that describe the attitudes and behaviors of those in the group. *Achievers* may be used to refer to successful, upper income people. *Strivers* could describe young, hard-working people. *Traditionalists* would be the consumers who resist change and prefer the familiar. Since each market segment has different attitudes and buying habits, marketing actions aimed at each group must be different.

Market segments usually differ from country to country. Dividing potential customers into subgroups based on type of employment would not be practical in a nation in which most people work in agricultural jobs.

©Getty Images/PhotoDisc

TARGET MARKET

A **target market** is the particular market segment that a company plans to serve. After identifying the target market, a company attempts to meet the specific needs of those customers. Target markets for international business may be selected on the basis of geography, as shown in Figure 16-7.

A GEOGRAPHIC TARGET MARKET IN CENTRAL AND SOUTH AMERICA

Figure 16-7 A company involved in international marketing commonly may select one or more countries as its target market.

To better understand consumers and to segment and target markets effectively, companies analyze buyer behavior through marketing research. Marketing research may be conducted to determine the television viewing habits of Japanese college students or the potential sales among older consumers of an Italian soft drink in the United States.

GLOBAL BUSINESS EXAMPLE

MARKET SEGMENTS OF THE RUSSIAN CONSUMER

As foreign companies increased their marketing and selling activities in Russia, researchers took a closer look at Russian customers. Five market segments were created to describe the buying habits of Russian consumers based on their attitudes and beliefs.

- *Kuptsi* (or merchants) were found to be practical and to seek value in their buying.
- *Cossacks* were determined to be independent and ambitious status seekers.
- *Students* tended to be passive and idealistic.
- *Business executives* were busy, ambitious, and receptive to products and ideas from industrialized countries.
- *Russian souls* were found to be passive, fearful of new ideas, and followers of others.

This market research information can be used to target the selling of various products and services to the best potential customers.

Think Critically

1. How do companies use market segments for planning their marketing activities?
2. Conduct an Internet search to obtain additional information about market segments.

✔ CheckPoint

What types of consumer characteristics are used to segment markets?

©Getty Images/PhotoDisc

REVIEW GLOBAL BUSINESS TERMS

Define each of the following terms.

1. psychographics

2. market segment

3. target market

REVIEW GLOBAL BUSINESS CONCEPTS

4. What factors affect the marketing environment of a company?

5. What factors influence consumer behavior?

6. What is the difference between demographics and psychographics?

7. What is meant by the target market of a company?

SOLVE GLOBAL BUSINESS PROBLEMS

Find a product made in another country and sold in the United States. Be careful! Some products that appear to have a foreign origin are actually from U.S.-based companies. Based on this product, answer the following questions.

8. What are possible reasons that the company sells its product in the U.S.?

9. What are some difficulties the company may have encountered when introducing the product to U.S. consumers?

10. What economic and social factors may contribute to the success or failure of the product in the United States.

THINK CRITICALLY

11. Give an example of how a person's needs might affect consumer behavior.

12. How does personality influence buying habits?

13. Some people believe that defining and using market segments are unfair since consumers are treated in different manners. Do you agree or disagree with this belief? Why?

MAKE CONNECTIONS

14. **CULTURAL STUDIES** Describe a situation in which the religious beliefs of a society would affect a company's marketing activities.

15. **GEOGRAPHY** How would the climate of a country influence the products commonly bought by consumers in that nation?

16. **TECHNOLOGY** Use the Internet to identify online resources for global marketing activities.

CHAPTER SUMMARY

16-1 MARKETING AROUND THE WORLD

A International marketing involves marketing activities between sellers and buyers in different countries.

B Trends that influence global marketing opportunities include expanded communications, technology, changing political situations, increased competition, and changing demographics.

16-2 THE MARKETING MIX AND THE MARKETING PLAN

A The four elements of the marketing mix are product, price, distribution, and promotion.

B A marketing plan is used to plan, communicate, and implement global marketing activities.

16-3 PLANNING GLOBAL MARKETING ACTIVITIES

A The international marketing environment consists of geographic elements, economic conditions, social and cultural influences, and political and legal factors.

B Consumer behavior is influenced by physical and emotional needs, geographic and demographic factors, personality and psychographic factors, and social and cultural factors.

C Methods used to segment markets include demographics, psychographics, buying behavior, and product benefits.

Read the Global Focus at the beginning of this chapter, and answer the following questions.

1. What actions might a cereal company take when adapting its marketing mix to new customers?

2. As demand for cereal declines in various markets, what actions might be taken by Kellogg's, General Mills, and other cereal companies?

REVIEW GLOBAL BUSINESS TERMS

Match the terms listed with the definitions.

1. The monetary value of a product agreed upon by a buyer and a seller.

2. Buying factors related to lifestyle and psychological influences, such as activities, interests, and opinions.

3. Marketing efforts that inform and persuade customers.

4. Likely customers for a good or service in a certain geographic location.

5. Marketing activities between sellers and buyers in different countries.

6. The activities needed to physically move and transfer ownership of goods and services from producer to consumer.

7. A distinct subgroup of customers who share certain personal or behavioral characteristics.

8. The traits of a country's population, such as birthrate, age distribution, marriage rate, gender distribution, income distribution, educational level, and housing situation.

9. An item (good or service) offered for sale that satisfies consumer demand.

10. Individuals and households who are the final users of goods and services.

11. The four major elements (product, price, distribution, and promotion) of marketing.

12. Buyers who purchase items for resale or additional production.

13. The particular market segment that a company plans to serve.

a. consumer market

b. demographics

c. distribution

d. international marketing

e. market

f. market segment

g. marketing mix

h. organizational market

i. price

j. product

k. promotion

l. psychographics

m. target market

MAKE GLOBAL BUSINESS DECISIONS

14. How does demand for consumer goods and services affect demand in organizational markets?

15. What are some examples of global marketing opportunities created by technology or changing demographics?

16. How would the marketing plan for services or a nonprofit organization differ from the marketing activities for a tangible product?

17. What social and economic factors might affect how a society defines its basic consumer needs?

18. Why do you think many marketing managers believe that demographic information has limited value for defining a company's target market?

19. List some psychographic factors that could affect a person's buying habits.

20. What do you believe to be the most influential social institution in our country that affects buying decisions?

GLOBAL CONNECTIONS

21. **GEOGRAPHY** Research the climate, terrain, waterways, and other geographic conditions of a country. Explain how these factors would affect the marketing activities of a company.

22. **COMMUNICATIONS** Prepare a bulletin board, a poster, or another visual display showing goods and services from other countries that are sold in the United States.

23. **CULTURAL STUDIES** Conduct library research and prepare a two-page written report on the four elements of the marketing mix for a good or service sold in more than one country. Compare the marketing activities in different cultures.

©Getty Images/PhotoDisc

24. **SCIENCE** Select a product that is aimed at different types of customers, such as cereal, toothpaste, or shampoo. Compare the ingredients listed on packages and information in advertisements for two or more variations of the product. Explain how the contents can influence the target market at which the product is aimed.

25. **MATHEMATICS** Survey several friends to determine the factors that affect their buying habits for food, clothing, or another commonly purchased item. Prepare a chart that reports the frequency of stores used, types of items purchased, amounts spent, and influences on buying.

26. **CAREER PLANNING** Prepare a letter of application for a job with an international marketing company. Explain how your global marketing knowledge could be useful to the company. List examples of methods the company might consider to enhance its international marketing plan.

THE GLOBAL ENTREPRENEUR

CREATING AN INTERNATIONAL BUSINESS PLAN

AN INTERNATIONAL MARKETING PLAN

Create a marketing plan for the business idea you have used in previous chapters, or select another business idea. Use the country you have previously researched, or select a different country. Using library and Internet research, obtain information for the following topics.

1. **Company goals:** Clearly state the marketing objectives that the business wants to achieve, including the target country or region.

2. **Description of customers and their needs:** Provide details of the buying behaviors of potential customers.

3. **Information about competitors:** Describe other companies that are aiming their marketing activities at the same customers.

4. **Information about economic, social, legal, and technological trends:** Describe unique factors that will affect the company's marketing activities.

5. **Financial and human resources available:** List estimated operating costs and skills that employees will need to achieve the company's goals.

6. **Time line of actions to be taken:** Estimate the amount of time that will be needed to implement the marketing plan.

7. **Methods for measuring success:** Describe how the company will know if it has achieved its goals.

Prepare a written summary or present a short oral report (two or three minutes) of your findings.

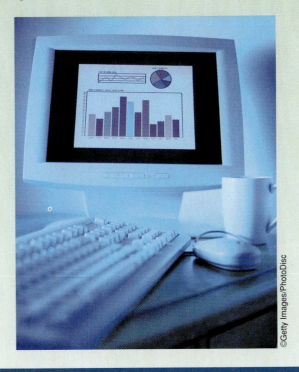

©Getty Images/PhotoDisc

Chapter 17

DEVELOPING GOODS AND SERVICES FOR GLOBAL MARKETS

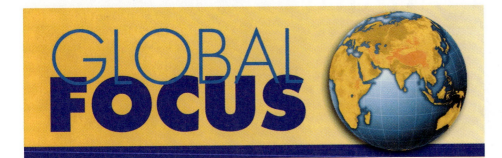

GLOBAL FOCUS

Global Strategy for Barbie

The Barbie doll was introduced in the United States in 1959, and 351,000 were sold at $3 each. Since then, over 1 billion Barbies have been sold. While Mattel is assured of new young U.S. consumers each year, the company also looks to markets in other countries for Barbie sales.

The first Barbie dolls were manufactured in Japan in the late 1950s. In the late 1970s, Mattel started distributing the dolls in Japan by creating a limited joint venture with the Bandai Company. The first Barbies sold in Japan had dark eyes. Later, the company began marketing its blue-eyed Barbie throughout Asia.

When Barbie was introduced in the Czech Republic, she wore traditional Czech clothing of a black vest and red tights under a yellow and black skirt. When first available, more than 1,000 dolls were sold a day. People in Prague stood in line for hours to pay from $5 to $20 for dolls and accessories. The average monthly salary of a skilled worker was about $130.

Today Barbie dolls and related items are sold in over 150 countries. In recent years, about 35 percent of Mattel's sales were outside of the United States. In addition to the company's global success, Mattel is using technology to expand its product line and marketing efforts. Mattel allows girls to go online to design a friend for Barbie. In addition to choosing skin tone, eye color, hair color, clothes, accessories, and name, customers receive a computer-generated paragraph about the doll's "personality."

Think Critically

1. What factors may have influenced Mattel's decision to sell Barbie dolls in other countries?
2. What factors may have influenced Mattel's decision to introduce a different style of Barbie doll in Japan initially?
3. Go to the Mattel web site to obtain additional information about the company's international operations. Prepare a one-page summary of your findings.

17-1 GLOBAL PRODUCT PLANNING

GOALS

- Describe sources of product opportunities for international marketing.
- Identify categories of consumer products and the importance of product lines.
- Explain how services are marketed.

©Getty Images/PhotoDisc

INTERNATIONAL PRODUCT OPPORTUNITIES

Every day you see advertisements for clothing, food, motor vehicles, financial services, Internet sites, and other consumer goods and services. It sometimes seems as though everyone has something to sell. When you apply for a job, you also are selling your talents and abilities. The product offerings of global companies are the foundation of international business and foreign trade.

A *product* is a marketplace offering (good or service) that satisfies a need or want. Marketing's major goal is to satisfy needs that have not been met. This can be accomplished in one of four ways: a new product, an improved product, an existing product with a new use, or an existing product sold in a new market.

New Product An organization's marketing activities may start with a marketplace offering that did not previously exist. For example, Federal Express pioneered overnight delivery services. Now, several companies are involved in this industry.

Improved Product Sometimes a product is on the market for several years, but it may no longer be as popular with consumers. When this happens, a company may introduce variations, such as new flavors of a food product. Also, technology may result in improved versions of an item.

Existing Product with a New Use When a company wants to expand its sales, it may attempt to find new uses for a product that has been on the market for years. Various kitchen storage containers have been adapted to store tools and supplies for a home workshop or office.

Existing Product Sold in a New Market In the late 1970s and early 1980s, when fewer babies were born in the U.S., Johnson Baby Shampoo was advertised as being mild for adults who wanted to shampoo every day. Selling existing products in new markets is a significant part of international business. Soft drinks, fast foods, and hundreds of other products that originated in one country are now sold in the global marketplace.

WORK AS A GROUP

Suggest ways to use an existing product in different ways.

✔ CheckPoint

What are four ways a company can satisfy the consumer's needs that have not been met?

MARKETING PRODUCTS AROUND THE WORLD

Each day people around the world buy and use thousands of different products. A student in Brazil buys a home computer, while a person in Egypt purchases a bottled soft drink.

CONSUMER PRODUCT CATEGORIES

The many items sold in the global market can be classified as convenience goods, shopping goods, or specialty goods, as shown in Figure 17-1.

Convenience Goods You probably buy low-cost items on a regular basis without thinking much about them. **Convenience goods** are inexpensive items that require little shopping effort. Examples include snacks, soft drinks, personal care products, and school supplies. Marketing for convenience goods involves offering an item in many locations. For example, candy bars are sold in food stores, movie theaters, gas stations, and vending machines.

Shopping Goods Some products (such as clothing, furniture, cameras, televisions, and home appliances) are purchased only after consumers take

Figure 17-1 The items bought by people around the world can be classified as convenience goods, shopping goods, or specialty goods.

TYPES OF CONSUMER PRODUCTS

Convenience Goods   **Shopping Goods**

Specialty Goods

some time to compare buying alternatives. **Shopping goods** are products purchased after consumers compare brands and stores. Shopping goods require a marketing effort that communicates differences in price, quality, and features of various brands.

Stores selling shopping goods may offer several brands and models of the same item to prevent a customer from going to another store to compare products. You will commonly see stores and online retailers with many makes and models of video recorders or digital cameras.

Products that are convenience goods in one culture may be shopping goods in another. Toothpaste for U.S. consumers is usually bought quickly without much thought. This same purchase in some South American nations may require comparison shopping and some consideration. Consumers in these countries may not be as familiar with the item, or the toothpaste may be an expensive purchase compared to their income.

Specialty Goods When buying certain products, you would probably take a lot of time and effort. **Specialty goods** are unique products that consumers make a special effort to obtain. Buyers of these items refuse to accept substitutes. Marketing of specialty goods requires high brand recognition. In Europe, for example, various types of designer clothing, jewelry from well-known firms, and customized automobiles would only be available at select stores.

THE PRODUCT LINE

Manufacturing companies and stores usually produce and offer a variety of items. A **product line** is an assortment of closely related products designed to meet the varied needs of target customers. Shoe stores commonly include socks, shoelaces, and shoe polish in their product lines. Procter & Gamble makes different shampoos for people with different wants and needs. There are shampoos for dandruff problems, shampoos for easy-to-manage hair, and shampoos for dry hair.

ORGANIZATIONAL PRODUCTS

Organizational products are items used to produce other goods and services. Companies buy factories, machinery, office equipment, components, and raw materials for their daily business activities.

Most organizational products require less adaptation than do consumer goods before they are

GLOBAL BUSINESS EXAMPLE

A JAPANESE APPROACH FOR PRODUCT DEVELOPMENT

The Kao Corporation of Tokyo is Japan's largest producer of personal care, laundry, and cleaning products. The company also makes cooking oils and chemicals. Kao sells items in over 40 countries in Asia, North America, and Europe and uses five principles when planning new products.

- The new product should be useful to society now and in the future.
- The product should be based on Kao's creative technology.
- The item should be superior, in both cost and performance, to the new products of competitors.
- The new product should be able to survive exhaustive product testing at all stages before going on the market.
- The item should be able to deliver its own message of usefulness and quality at every level of distribution.

Think Critically

1. How could other companies use Kao's product development principles to plan their international marketing activities?
2. Go to Kao's web site to obtain additional information about the company's research and development activities. Write an outline describing your findings.

sold in different countries. This situation arises because cultural factors and personal taste influence production activities less than consumer purchases. For example, the same forklift truck used on a loading dock can be sold in most places around the world. However, laundry detergent might require adaptation due to clothes-washing habits and water hardness.

✓ **CheckPoint**

How do organizational products differ from consumer goods?

CONSUMER SERVICES

A variety of services also are used by organizations. Commercial services may include security systems, information processing, equipment maintenance, and overnight package delivery. How does buying a haircut differ from buying a can of green beans? One is an intangible service, and one is a tangible good.

CHARACTERISTICS OF SERVICES

Services cannot be touched like a physical product. In other words, services are *intangible*. Most purchases are a combination of both tangible and intangible items. While you can touch the reel from which a movie is shown, the movie you have seen becomes a memory that is intangible. Since services are intangible, it is more difficult to judge the quality of these purchases. Common measures of service quality are company reputation, comments from customers, and training qualifications of employees.

Increased use of computers and technology for services contributes to more consistent quality. For example, automatic teller machines, when operating properly, will make fewer errors than humans do.

Services are consumed as they are produced. Mass production of services is often not possible. Each haircut, oil change, or income tax preparation is produced separately. However, businesses are using technology to provide fast, individualized services. Financial companies, for example, offer investment advice based on a person's income, age, and household situation.

Services have no inventory. Empty airline seats, for example, cannot be saved and sold later. They are simply lost revenue opportunities.

TYPES OF SERVICES

Services available to consumers may be viewed in three categories.
1. *Rented-goods services* involve a payment for temporary use of items, such as an automobile, an apartment, a video, or cleaning equipment.
2. *Owned-goods services* are fees for service to the consumer's property, such as auto repair, dry cleaning, or landscaping.
3. *Non-goods services* are personal or professional services for a fee, such as health care, overnight delivery, tax return preparation, real estate sales, legal assistance, and baby-sitting.

Communication Across Borders

COMMUNICATE WITH CUSTOMERS IN THEIR OWN LANGUAGE

When a multinational organization develops a strategy for communicating with customers, selection of the correct language is not good enough. It must also choose the right form of that language to reach the targeted customers successfully.

Every major world language exists in a number of culture-specific forms that vary in terms of some of the language details. The differences often involve pronunciation, word choice, and word meaning. Sometimes they involve spelling and grammar, too. Although such differences are small, they are important in terms of the acceptability of the message. Communications are better received when they are customized to reflect the culturally sanctioned language of a distinct group of customers.

Throughout Latin America, for example, multinational businesses need to do more than use Spanish to communicate with Spanish-speaking customers. They need to use the same form of Spanish as the targeted group of customers. Some of the details of communications with customers in Honduras will be different from those of communications with customers in Colombia and Argentina.

Think Critically

1. Why should speakers of a language receive communications in their own culture-specific form?
2. What other major languages besides Spanish have a number of culture-specific versions that are used for international communication purposes?

MARKETING OF SERVICES

Services require special marketing efforts. Since the consumer must often be where the service is produced, convenience of location is important. Some hospitals have created urgent-care facilities in several locations. Banks may bring their services to customers, such as when a bank sets up a temporary cash machine at a sporting event or concert.

The packaging of services is done through the image created by the business. Furniture, decorations, and even the appearance of employees can create a reputation of quality.

Services are also personalized. Each transaction for a hairstylist, tax accountant, or health-care worker will be slightly different. An organization's ability to meet the individual needs of customers is vital for success.

SERVICES AND INTERNATIONAL TRADE

In recent years, services have played an increasing role for the United States in its foreign trade activities. About 70 percent of GDP in the United States results from service industries. While our nation has a total trade deficit, exported services exceed imported services. Companies in other countries have a strong demand for health care, delivery services, information systems, processing, management consulting, financial services, education and training, hospitality (hotels, food service), and entertainment (movies, television production, and amusement parks).

As in most industrialized countries, services in the United States are becoming a greater economic influence. Today, more people work in service industries than in manufacturing companies.

✔ CheckPoint

What are the three categories of services?

REVIEW GLOBAL BUSINESS TERMS

Define each of the following terms.

1. convenience goods
2. shopping goods
3. specialty goods
4. product line

REVIEW GLOBAL BUSINESS CONCEPTS

5. How can marketing satisfy a need that has not been met?

6. How does a shopping good differ from a specialty good?

7. In what ways are services different from goods?

SOLVE GLOBAL BUSINESS PROBLEMS

For each of the following situations, list a possible problem that could be encountered if a company planned to sell its service in other countries.

8. Childcare centers aimed at households with two working parents.

9. Repair service for home and office computers.

10. Carpet cleaning service for homes and businesses.

11. Trash collection and recycling service.

THINK CRITICALLY

12. Describe an example of how a convenience good in one culture may be a shopping good or specialty good in another society.

13. What tangible factors could be measured to determine the quality of services offered by a company?

14. Choose a service company in your community. Describe attributes that contribute to the company's image.

MAKE CONNECTIONS

15. **TECHNOLOGY** Describe how technology has created new product opportunities for existing goods and services.

16. **TECHNOLOGY** Use the Internet to identify three products that are available around the world. Describe any differences the products might have from country to country.

17. **TECHNOLOGY** Use the Internet to find examples of companies that provide services internationally. What type of services are offered? Are there any differences from country to country?

18. **GEOGRAPHY** Explain how the climate, terrain, and other geographic factors in a country could expand or limit the availability of services.

17-2

GOALS

- Discuss the steps in the new product development process and the marketing research process.
- Describe data collection methods used in international marketing research.

DEVELOPING AND RESEARCHING PRODUCTS

©Getty Images/PhotoDisc

CREATING NEW PRODUCTS

Each year over 25,000 new products are introduced in the United States. However, within a year, about 75 percent of them are no longer on the market. Why do most new products fail? Some say it is because too many new products are introduced into an already saturated marketplace. Others believe it is because of poor planning. Either way, new products are a high risk for companies.

NEW PRODUCTS

Companies introduce new products for two reasons. First, as old products are no longer popular with customers, sales revenue must come from other sources. Second, competitors' actions result in lower sales revenue. New products must match or exceed the marketplace offerings of other companies.

Customer Needs The needs of customers is one of the main sources of new product ideas. For example, "call waiting" was the answer for people who didn't want to miss a phone call while talking to someone else. Caller ID allowed customers to see the telephone number of incoming calls and select which calls to answer. These services were created in direct response to customer needs. Other products developed to fill customer needs include carbon monoxide detectors for in-home use and electronic invisible fences for pet containment.

Technology Technology is another major source of new products. Fax machines, cellular phones, and video games would never have been possible without technological breakthroughs.

NEW PRODUCT DEVELOPMENT PROCESS

Companies use a logical procedure to create successful new products. The new product development process involves the four steps shown in Figure 17-2. This procedure is used to help a business select products that will likely succeed.

NEW PRODUCT DEVELOPMENT PROCESS

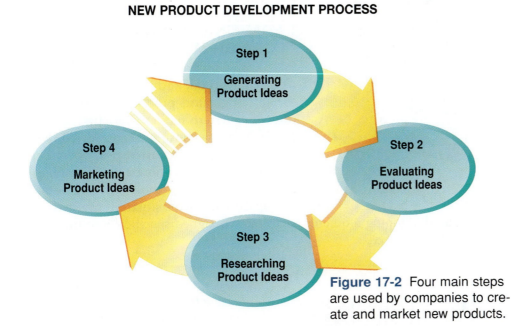

Step 1
Generating Product Ideas

Step 2
Evaluating Product Ideas

Step 3
Researching Product Ideas

Step 4
Marketing Product Ideas

Figure 17-2 Four main steps are used by companies to create and market new products.

Generating Product Ideas
In the first stage, ideas for possible products are based on comments from customers, product ideas other companies have developed, and new technology. At this stage, products planned for international markets are viewed from a global perspective.

Evaluating Product Ideas
Next, ideas are evaluated based on cost, production possibility, and marketplace acceptance. Can the new item be offered to potential customers at an acceptable price? Are the facilities available to produce the item in needed quantities? Can the product be adapted to meet the cultural and economic needs of customers in various countries?

©Getty Images/PhotoDisc

WORK AS A GROUP

Brainstorm a list of possible new products or services that might be developed to sell in other countries.

©Getty Images/PhotoDisc

Researching Product Ideas
In the third stage, research is conducted on the proposed product to measure customer attitudes and potential sales.

Marketing Product Ideas
The final phase of the new product development process involves putting the item on the market. After research shows a strong probability of success, the item is produced, distributed, and sold in one or more countries.

ADAPTING PRODUCTS TO FOREIGN MARKETS

Products will frequently need to be adapted to social, cultural, and political factors. When refrigerators produced by manufacturers in Western nations were first sold in Japan, Japanese consumers considered them too noisy. The motors needed to operate the cooling unit could easily be heard through the very thin walls of most Japanese homes and apartments. This situation resulted in companies developing a quieter refrigerator designed specifically to meet Japanese market needs.

GLOBAL BUSINESS EXAMPLE

COLLECTING MARKETING RESEARCH DATA IN VENEZUELA

How can marketing information be obtained in countries without extensive information systems? While visiting Caracas, a researcher may observe to see what items consumers commonly buy. These observations can help managers decide if a certain product might be successful in Venezuela.

Next, researchers might interview selected business owners about their product line. Owners would answer questions about what items sold well in the past, current consumer tastes, and common complaints from customers.

Finally, talking with government officials can provide details about foreign trade barriers and regulations affecting business in Venezuela. Combining information from these various sources can provide managers with a better understanding of the marketing opportunities in nations with limited research data.

Think Critically

1. What things might be observed in another country that could help a manager plan to do business in that country?
2. When interviewing a person about another country's business environment, what questions might be asked?
3. Conduct an Internet search on international marketing research. Locate a web site that would be useful for companies planning to do business in another country. Write an explanation about what this web site has that would be useful.

THE MARKETING RESEARCH PROCESS

When developing and marketing new products, companies must find out what consumers need, want, and are willing to buy. **Marketing research** is the orderly collection and analysis of data that is used to obtain information about a specific marketing concern. While some companies have investigated consumer buying patterns in over 150 countries, marketing research is done regularly in only about 60 or 70 nations.

Marketing research may be conducted to determine the television viewing habits of Australian college students. Also, a company may measure the potential sales for a Brazilian soft drink company in the United States. Figure 17-3 provides an overview of the marketing research process with an international example.

THE MARKETING RESEARCH PROCESS

Phase 1—Identify Problem

Example

Is there a market demand for microwave popcorn in major cities in South America?

Phase 2—Collect Data

Example

A survey of consumer preferences and buying habits for microwave popcorn in major South American cities is conducted.

Phase 3—Analyze Data

Example

Survey results are tallied to show potential demand for the product.

Phase 4—Report Results

Example

A report is prepared with the survey and recommendations for expansion into selected cities.

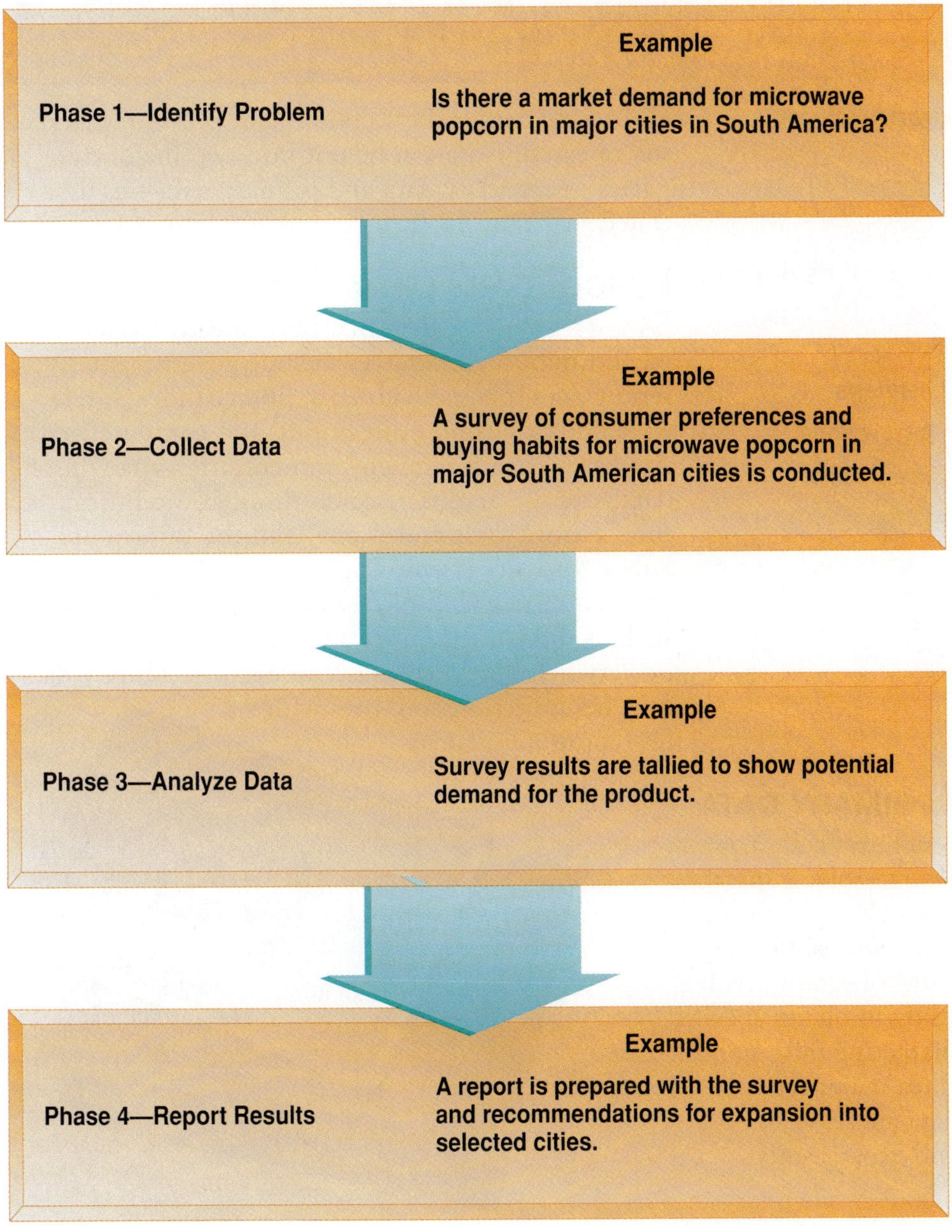

Figure 17-3 The steps of the marketing research process are designed to help a company collect consumer behavior data.

Every research study starts with a research problem. The word "problem" does not necessarily mean that something is wrong—such as declining sales. A research problem provides the basis for studying some aspect of a company's marketing mix. For example, a computer company may conduct a marketing research study to determine the information needs of manufacturing companies in Chile, or a soup company may study consumer taste preferences in Jamaica. In each situation, the business seeks information to better plan and carry out its marketing activities.

CheckPoint

What are the steps of the new product development process?

DATA COLLECTION AND ANALYSIS FOR MARKETING RESEARCH

SOURCES OF MARKETING RESEARCH DATA

Secondary Data Sources

• Government reports
• Business documents
• Indexes
• Reference books
• Computerized databases

Primary Data Sources

• Surveys
• Interviews
• Observations
• Experiments

Figure 17-4 Secondary data and primary data help marketing managers make international business decisions.

Collecting data is the second major phase of marketing research. Data can be put into two major categories—secondary data and primary data—as illustrated in Figure 17-4.

SECONDARY DATA

Secondary data are data that have already been collected and published. Sources include government reports, company documents, library indexes, reference books, business directories, and computerized databases. The federal government offers many useful databases for market research through the Bureau of the Census (www.census.gov) and the Bureau of Labor Statistics (www.bls.gov).

In countries with modern information systems, such as the United States, secondary data sources can be very helpful. In contrast, access to secondary data may be limited in countries with few computer systems.

PRIMARY DATA

Marketers collect *primary data* to solve a specific research problem. In other words, primary data collection involves a study to obtain specific marketing information. The three major types of primary data are surveys, observations, and experiments.

©Getty Images/PhotoDisc

Surveys Companies use surveys to collect data about opinions, behaviors, and knowledge of consumers. Large-scale surveys that collect numeric data, called **quantitative research**, are often used to study consumers. Companies such as ACNielsen conduct market research surveys in various countries. Nielsen Media Research measures television viewing patterns and other media habits.

In many countries, however, collection of quantitative data is difficult. A country with only a few computers makes a Web survey almost impossible and the results questionable. If a nation has a low literacy rate, the use of mail surveys will have little value. These situations require other types of research.

Qualitative research, using open-ended interview questions, allows researchers to obtain comments from consumers about their attitudes and behaviors. An example of qualitative research is the focus group, or group-depth interview. A **focus group** is a directed discussion with 8 to 12 people. This group interview obtains information from focus group members about their opinions and buying habits and what they know about a product, a package, or an advertisement.

Focus groups can offer insight into planned marketing activities. This information, however, is based only on the opinions of a small group of consumers. In addition, focus groups and personal interviews may not be appropriate in cultures in which people do not talk openly to strangers.

©Getty Images/PhotoDisc

Observations What people say they do is often different from what they actually do. Observation is the best way to measure consumer behavior. **Observational research** involves data collection by watching and recording shopping behaviors.

Common observations involve watching shoppers in stores or counting customers during certain hours. Computerized cash registers with scanners allow companies to *observe* the purchases of customers. These data are used to determine the number of employees needed at certain hours and to set prices at a level for maximizing sales.

In some research settings, such as with children, observations are necessary. These young consumers may not be able to express themselves well verbally. However, observational research has a major weakness. It cannot provide information about the attitudes, opinions, or motivations of consumers.

Experiments The most complex type of data collection is the **experiment**, which involves a statistical comparison of two or more very similar situations. For example, a company may introduce a package with a photograph in one city and a package with a drawing in another city. The firm wants to know how the different packages affect consumer preference and sales. Experiments are expensive to conduct and are most helpful in industrialized countries with access to computerized data collection methods.

Experiments also can predict the success of a product before mass distribution. A **test market** is an experimental research study that measures the likely success of a new good or service. Companies often use one or two cities to try out a new item. U.S. companies usually use cities in the United States. Some firms, however, use foreign cities as test markets. KFC tested its grilled chicken in Regina, Saskatchewan, Canada. Carewell Industries, a New Jersey company, first sold its Dentax toothbrush in Malaysia and Singapore.

ANALYZING AND USING RESEARCH DATA

For data to be useful for planning marketing activities, research results must be analyzed after collection. Statistical tests are commonly used with quantitative data. The results help managers make marketing decisions. By knowing which consumers watch certain television programs or read certain magazines, a manager can plan a company's advertising. Information about customer opinions and habits can help plan domestic and international marketing activities.

©Getty Images/PhotoDisc

✔ **CheckPoint**

What are the three main types of primary data collection?

REVIEW GLOBAL BUSINESS TERMS

Define each of the following terms.

1. marketing research   **4.** focus group   **6.** experiment

2. quantitative research   **5.** observational research   **7.** test market

3. qualitative research

Xtra!
Study Tools
intlbizxtra.swlearning.com

REVIEW GLOBAL BUSINESS CONCEPTS

8. What causes a need for new products?

9. What are the sources for new products?

10. What is the difference between secondary data and primary data?

11. What is the purpose of a test market?

SOLVE GLOBAL BUSINESS PROBLEMS

For each of the following research situations, tell which data collection method might be most appropriate.

12. A package food company wants to know the breakfast eating habits in Chile.

13. A manufacturing company wants to determine computer needs of small businesses in Panama.

14. A bank needs information about the satisfaction of checking account customers in Argentina.

15. A company needs information on the number of companies in Guatemala that use refrigerated food-storage areas.

16. A travel company is interested in knowing the attitudes and needs of Brazilians who travel regularly on business.

THINK CRITICALLY

17. Describe a situation in our society that could be the basis for a new product or service that does not currently exist.

18. Explain how the behavior of a shopper in a store might be interpreted differently by different observers.

MAKE CONNECTIONS

19. **TECHNOLOGY** Use software to prepare a flowchart presentation using the steps of the new product development process to show the development of an actual product.

20. **LAW** Why might a government in another country create a law to restrict certain marketing research activities?

17-3 AN INTERNATIONAL PRODUCT STRATEGY

GOALS

- Describe branding and packaging techniques used by global business organizations.
- Explain actions involved in planning a global product strategy.

©Wally McNamee/CORBIS

BRANDING AND PACKAGING

You are probably familiar with the names Coca-Cola, McDonald's, Kodak, and Disney. Millions of people around the world also know these names.

BRANDING AND MARKETING

A **brand** is a name, symbol, or design that identifies a product. This marketing technique helps consumers remember and regularly buy a company's products. Common, well-known brand names (such as Kellogg's, Kraft, Ivory soap, and Crest toothpaste) may appear on several products or on a single product.

Service companies and other organizations also use brands. American Express, UPS, and amazon.com are examples of brands not associated with packaged products.

Brands may need to be revised for foreign sales. For example, Coca-Cola had to change *Diet Coke* to *Coke Light* in Japan. The consumers in Japan did not want to be reminded that it was a diet soft drink.

TYPES OF BRANDS

Brands range from ones known worldwide to those known only in a small region. A *global brand* is used worldwide and is recognized by people in many geographic areas. The Gerber Products Company uses a "super-brand" approach for global marketing activities, with the company's famous name appearing on baby food, child-care products, and children's clothing.

A *national brand* is one that is well known within one country. For example, before expanding to overseas markets, Nike and Frito-Lay were considered national brands.

Regional brands are used on products sold only in one geographic region. Certain snack chips or soft drinks may only be available in a few states or regions of countries.

Stores and producers will sometimes put their own names on products. *Store or manufacturer brands* are used on products sold only at certain stores or distributed through certain sellers. Many drug stores and department stores have a line of health and personal care products with their own names on labels. Store and manufacturer brands are also called *private brands*.

Loblaw Companies, based in Toronto, created the President's Choice label. This upscale, private brand of more than 1,000 food products is exported from Canada to over 20 U.S. states and eight other countries.

Generics are non-name brand, plain wrapper products that can provide a bargain in certain situations. As with store brands, many generics can provide low-cost alternatives for consumers. Certain generics, such as aspirin, bleach, and sugar, are almost exactly the same as higher priced brands.

GLOBAL BUSINESS EXAMPLE

THE WORLD'S MOST FAMOUS BRANDS

Of the world's 20 most valuable brands, 14 are from U.S. companies. These include Coca-Cola, Microsoft, IBM, General Electric, Ford, Disney, McDonald's, Gillette, and Kodak. Some of the most famous brands of companies from other countries are Nokia (Finland), Mercedes and BMW (Germany), Nestlé (Switzerland), and Sony, Honda, and Toyota (Japan).

Think Critically

1. Why are most well-known brands associated with U.S. companies?
2. How might the Internet and other technology influence the best-known brands in the world?

PACKAGING

Have you ever noticed a new product because of the color, design, and shape of its package? Companies spend millions of dollars to get the right package.

NETBookmark

In early times people consumed their food where they found it. They were self-sufficient, only using what they caught or made and using natural materials such as gourds for storage. Today we buy our food and other products in a vast array of packaging. Access intlbizxtra.swlearning.com and click on the link for Chapter 17. After reading the article, construct a timeline that demonstrates the development of packaging.

intlbizxtra.swlearning.com

Create a list of factors that would need to be considered when selling a product or service in another country.

When Diet Coke was introduced, the company tested more than 30 combinations of colors, lettering, and designs for its new soft drink can.

Packaging serves three major purposes for companies and consumers.

1. A package protects the product from spoilage or damage during shipping and storage.
2. A package attempts to capture the attention of both new and regular users of the product.
3. The package should make the product easy to use. Easy-to-pour containers and resealable packages add to consumer convenience.

In recent years, packaging has increased in importance as a result of environmental concerns. Many companies now offer packages that are either reusable, refillable, or recyclable.

In some countries, certain packaging regulations influence marketing activities. Food labeling laws in the United States require that certain ingredient and nutrition information be presented in a clear format. While Coca Cola uses the English version of its name in many countries, Korea and Thailand require the name be presented in the national languages of those countries.

✓ CheckPoint

How does a global brand differ from a national brand?

PLANNING A GLOBAL PRODUCT STRATEGY

Every company must make decisions about what it will sell. These choices are influenced by the popularity of its product offerings and the ability of the business to serve consumer needs throughout the world.

THE PRODUCT LIFE CYCLE

The stages a good or service goes through from the time it is introduced until it is taken off the market is the **product life cycle (PLC)**. As you get older, you act differently and have different needs. The same thing is true for products. After a company's product has been on the market for awhile, the company will change its marketing approach. The PLC has four stages, as shown in Figure 17-5.

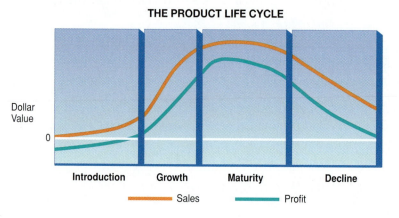

THE PRODUCT LIFE CYCLE

Figure 17-5 All goods and services go through steps as they increase and decrease in popularity.

E-COMMERCE IN ACTION

E-Brands

You will usually see Kellogg's, Campbell's, Kraft, Green Giant, Crest, Colgate, and Tide when shopping in stores. However, you will not see eBay, Dell, or amazon.com in stores. These are examples of online brands, or e-brands.

Establishing a brand identity on the Internet is a concern for companies. Advertisers with "real-world" brands developed using television are worried that they will be left out if they don't create a presence on the Web. For companies that are web-based, creating a recognized brand name is even more important.

Think Critically

1. Prepare a list of traditional brands and web brands. Survey other students to determine which brands are the best known.
2. Locate a web site of a company with a famous brand. Describe how the company is using the Internet for expanding brand awareness.

Introduction The first stage of the product life cycle is *introduction*, when the product is new and few competitors exist. Marketing activities should emphasize creation of awareness of the item among potential customers. Sales are low, and a profit has not been realized.

Growth Next, the *growth* stage of the PLC finds increasing sales and profits starting. New competitors with similar or substitute products enter the market.

Maturity Then in the *maturity* stage, sales start to level off as the market is saturated, more competitors appear, and new products compete for the dollars of consumers.

Decline Finally, in the *decline* stage, sales and profits start to decrease. The company must decide whether to attempt to revive the product or stop production of it.

Competition and technology determine the speed at which a product moves through the product life cycle. Years ago, radios and televisions would take years to move through the PLC, as new models and features were rarely introduced. Today movement through the product life cycle is measured in months for electronic equipment such as video players, computers, and cellular phones.

©Getty Images/PhotoDisc

GLOBAL PRODUCT DECISIONS

A major marketing decision that many companies must make involves whether to keep its products the same or adapt them to foreign customers. A **global product** is a standardized item offered in the same form in all countries in which it is sold. Common examples of global products are cameras, film, and many home appliances. Food products are usually difficult to market as global products because of differences in tastes. Unilever, however, sells tea, ice cream, and pasta in nearly identical forms worldwide.

In contrast to a global product, an **international product** is customized or adapted to the culture, tastes, and social trends of a country. As a result of different laws and customs, health and personal care products must be adapted to different settings. Food companies often add different seasonings to products sold in various cultures.

CEASING FOREIGN MARKET ACTIVITIES

Can you think of a product, such as a breakfast cereal based on a cartoon character, that is no longer on the market? As the character declined in popularity, sales of the product probably declined also.

When sales of an item continue to decline, a company will probably decide to stop making and selling it. Gerber no longer operates daycare services and has eliminated its toy and furniture divisions. Such decisions allow the company to concentrate on more profitable products.

REGIONAL PERSPECTIVE

CULTURE: THE GAUCHOS OF ARGENTINA

©Kit Houghton Photography/CORBIS

Cattle production is one of the major industries of Argentina. A *gaucho*, similar to a U.S. cowboy, helps to make beef and related products available for consumers in South America and around the world.

Between 1600 and 1750, early settlers in Argentina hunted wild cattle and horses for the hides. These were used to make clothing and other products. Over the next 100 years, herds of cattle were raised in the estancia system—large ranches in the fertile plains of the Pampas region of east and central Argentina that were worked by gauchos. Also during this time, the fat and salted meat of the cattle were processed, which made new products available to Argentinean consumers. This period was followed by the creation of far-reaching sheep ranches between 1830 and 1900.

Today gauchos continue to contribute to the economic production of Argentina—as the country is one of the world's largest producers of livestock. Nearly 60 percent of Argentina's land is used for grazing and agriculture.

Think Critically
1. What factors may influence the future working environment of gauchos?
2. Conduct a web search for additional information about gauchos. Write a short summary of your findings.

What is the product life cycle?

REVIEW GLOBAL BUSINESS TERMS

Define each of the following terms.

1. brand

2. product life cycle (PLC)

3. global product

4. international product

intlbizxtra.swlearning.com

REVIEW GLOBAL BUSINESS CONCEPTS

5. What purpose does packaging serve?

6. What are the stages of the product life cycle?

7. How does a global product differ from an international product?

SOLVE GLOBAL BUSINESS PROBLEMS

Most packaged products sold in the United States and almost all products in other countries use the metric system for weights and liquid measurements. The following is an approximate reference for converting to metric measurements.

When you know:	Multiply by:	To find:
ounces (oz)	28.35	grams (g)
pounds (lb)	0.45	kilograms (kg)
pints (pt)	0.47	liters (l)
quarts (qt)	0.95	liters (l)
gallons (gal)	3.79	liters (l)

8. A 14-ounce package of spaghetti would weigh about _____ grams.

9. Six pounds of cheese would weigh about _____ kilograms.

10. Eight pints of fruit juice is equal to about _____ liters.

11. Three quart bottles of soft drinks contain about _____ liters.

12. Estimate how many gallons are equal to 12 liters. Then check your answer with a calculator. How accurate was your estimate?

THINK CRITICALLY

13. Locate examples of famous brands not associated with packaged products.

14. Explain why different advertising would be needed in different stages of the product life cycle.

15. Why do companies often take legal action against others who try to use the same brand name?

MAKE CONNECTIONS

16. TECHNOLOGY What types of technology have improved packaging for consumers and the environment?

17. CULTURAL STUDIES How might a nation's customs or traditions affect the brand names used in a country?

CHAPTER SUMMARY

17-1 GLOBAL PRODUCT PLANNING

A The sources of product opportunities for international marketing are new products, improved products, new uses for existing products, and existing products in new markets.

B The categories of consumer products are convenience goods, shopping goods, and specialty goods. A product line provides an assortment of items available for sale to varied target markets.

C Services are marketed with an emphasis on personalization, as they are usually produced as they are consumed.

17-2 DEVELOPING AND RESEARCHING PRODUCTS

A The steps in the new product development process are (1) generating product ideas, (2) evaluating product ideas, (3) researching product ideas, and (4) marketing product ideas. The steps in the marketing research process are (1) identify problem, (2) collect data, (3) analyze data, and (4) report results.

B Data collection methods used in international marketing research include secondary data and primary data (surveys, observations, and experiments).

17-3 AN INTERNATIONAL PRODUCT STRATEGY

A Brands used by companies are names, symbols, or designs that identify a product or service. Packaging is used to protect the product, to capture the attention of customers, and to make the product easy to use.

B A global product strategy involves decisions about whether to offer a standardized version or an adapted version of a good or service.

GLOBAL REFOCUS

Read the Global Focus at the beginning of this chapter, and answer the following questions.

1. In what ways does Mattel use both a global product approach and an international product approach?

2. How might Mattel use technology and joint ventures for continued success of its international operations?

REVIEW GLOBAL BUSINESS TERMS

Match the terms listed with the definitions.

1. Data collected by watching and recording shopping behaviors.

2. Large-scale surveys used to collect numeric data that are often used to study consumers.

3. Products purchased after consumers compare brands and stores.

4. A standardized item that is offered in the same form in all countries in which it is sold.

5. An assortment of closely related products designed to meet the varied needs of target customers.

6. A directed discussion with 8 to 12 people.

7. The stages a good or service goes through from the time it is introduced until it is taken off the market.

8. Inexpensive items that require little shopping effort.

9. A customized product adapted to the culture, tastes, and social trends of a country.

a. brand
b. convenience goods
c. experiment
d. focus group
e. global product
f. international product
g. marketing research
h. observational research
i. product life cycle (PLC)
j. product line
k. qualitative research
l. quantitative research
m. shopping goods
n. speciality goods
o. test market

10. The type of data collection that involves a statistical comparison of two or more very similar situations.

11. Open-ended interview questions that allow researchers to obtain comments from consumers about their attitudes and behaviors.

12. The name, symbol, or design that identifies a product.

13. Unique products that consumers make a special effort to obtain.

14. An experimental research study that measures the likely success of a new product or service.

15. The orderly collection and analysis of data that is used to obtain specific marketing information.

MAKE GLOBAL BUSINESS DECISIONS

16. Why do stores and online retailers have larger product lines than in the past?

17. Name some services that have increased in importance for our economy in recent years.

18. List some ideas that could be the basis for new products in our society.

19. Create some examples of topics for international marketing research studies that would be interesting to investigate.

20. When may qualitative research be preferred to quantitative research for a marketing research study?

21. What makes certain brands popular and easy to remember?

22. Does packaging cost too much for certain products? Find examples of products with packaging that could be made less expensive.

23. Why do some items go through the stages of the product life cycle faster than others?

24. Create a list of products that may be sold anywhere in the world without major changes being made. What determines whether an item is a global product or an international product?

GLOBAL CONNECTIONS

25. **GEOGRAPHY** Describe geographic factors that might influence whether a company could sell its product as it is in other countries or if they would have to adapt it.

26. **COMMUNICATIONS** Conduct a survey of the products people buy without extensive comparison shopping. How important is place of purchase, price, and brand for these items?

27. **HISTORY** Talk to older people about products that are no longer on the market. What factors might have influenced the decline of these items?

28. **CULTURAL STUDIES** Collect advertisements, labels, and packages from products made in other countries. How would you describe the marketing approach for these items?

29. **RESEARCH** Find examples of secondary data in the library and on the Internet that could help a company with its international marketing activities. Describe how the information could be of value for preparing a global marketing plan.

30. **VISUAL ART** Prepare a poster or bulletin board display with examples of products or services in the various stages of the product life cycle. Suggest marketing activities that would be appropriate for one item in each stage of the cycle.

31. **CAREER PLANNING** Select a good or service. Describe the jobs that would be required to make the product available to consumers in another country.

32. **TECHNOLOGY** Use the Internet to locate online resources for data collection and analysis. Prepare a description of each of the resources you find.

THE GLOBAL
ENTREPRENEUR
CREATING AN INTERNATIONAL BUSINESS PLAN

PRODUCT PLANNING FOR INTERNATIONAL MARKETING

Develop a marketing strategy based on the company and country you have been using in this continuing project, or create a new idea for your business in the same or a different country. Make use of previously collected information, and do additional research. This phase of your business plan should include the following components.

1. A description of the product (good or service), including characteristics and benefits of the item.
2. A description of the target market. Who would be the main buyers and users of the product? What are their demographic characteristics? What are their social attitudes and cultural behaviors?
3. A description of how the product might need to be adapted to accommodate social, cultural, or legal differences.
4. A description of what research activities could the company do to better understand its potential customers and the marketplace.
5. A description of branding and packaging ideas that could be used for this item.

Prepare a written summary or present a short oral report (two or three minutes) to communicate your main findings.

©Getty Images/PhotoDisc

©Getty Images/PhotoDisc

Chapter 18

GLOBAL PRICING AND DISTRIBUTION STRATEGIES

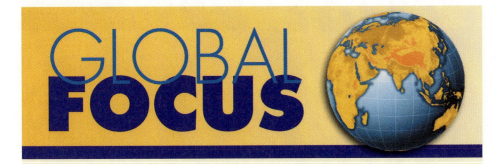

GLOBAL FOCUS

Toys "R" Us in Japan

In 1984, after becoming the largest U.S. toy seller, Toys "R" Us started its international expansion into Canada, Europe, Hong Kong, and Singapore. The company was then attracted by the over $6 billion annual toy sales market in Japan. However, Toys "R" Us faced several barriers when entering the world's second-largest toy market.

Japan's Large-Scale Retail Store Law attempted to protect smaller businesses. For any store larger than 5,382 square feet (approximately 500 square meters), owners had to obtain approval from government agencies to build the facility. This process could take as long as ten years. Pressure from U.S. trade representatives and price-conscious Japanese consumers reduced the time needed for Toys "R" Us to gain approval for a store. The first Toys "R" Us store in Japan was 44,000 square feet and stocked nearly 15,000 products.

Toys "R" Us buys items in large quantities, which allows the company to sell at discounted prices. Instead of buying through wholesalers, Toys "R" Us attempts to deal directly with manufacturers. In the beginning, many toy producers hesitated to participate since they did not want to upset their long-term relationships with wholesalers and retailers.

For Toys "R" Us stores to gain acceptance among business people and consumers in Japan, McDonald's Company of Japan purchased 20 percent of the Toys "R" Us stores in that country. Both enterprises have similar target markets—families with children—resulting in many cooperative selling efforts.

Today, even though Toys "R" Us has over 500 stores outside the United States in 29 countries, the company faces strong competition. Wal-Mart and other discount retailers have expanded their market share of the retail toy market. Online selling by eToys.com and others has also put competitive pressure on Toys "R" Us.

Think Critically

1. What factors may have affected the decision of Toys "R" Us to first expand into Canada, Europe, Hong Kong, and Singapore?
2. How did the Large-Scale Retail Store Law in Japan protect small stores?
3. Go to the web site of Toys "R" Us to obtain additional information about the company's international operations and online selling activities.

18-1 | INTERNATIONAL PRICING ACTIVITIES

GOALS

- Identify the factors that must be considered by businesses when setting prices.
- Describe pricing methods used by businesses.
- Discuss some pricing factors that are unique to global markets.

©Getty Images/PhotoDisc

PRICE PLANNING FOR INTERNATIONAL MARKETING

As a part of its marketing plan, every business must decide what amount to charge and how to get goods and services to customers. Factors such as export costs, values of foreign currencies, and the availability of transportation systems influence pricing and distribution for international marketing.

Price is the monetary value of a good or service. Everything has a price. Interest is the price paid on loans. Fare is the price paid for airline transportation. Fees are the prices paid for medical and legal services. The three main factors that influence the price a company charges for goods and services are costs, consumer demand, and competition, as shown in Figure 18-1.

FACTORS AFFECTING PRICE

Figure 18-1 Costs, consumer demand, and competition are the main factors that influence the price of goods and services.

Costs   Consumer Demand   Competition

COSTS

A company cannot sell an item for less than it costs the company to make or for the company to buy. Production and other operating costs must be covered by the price of an item. Besides incurring ordinary business expenses, organizations involved in international marketing will incur other costs, such as the following.

1. The cost of modifying a product to meet cultural or legal restrictions
2. Tariffs and other taxes that must be paid when selling to customers in another country
3. Fees to acquire export or import licenses
4. Expenses for the preparation of export documents
5. Changes in the exchange rate for a nation's currency
6. Transportation costs due to selling to buyers at a greater distance

CONSUMER DEMAND

When prices are high, consumers tend to buy less of an item than when prices are low. The basics of demand operate in all buying situations. Lower incomes, higher prices, and needs for other items result in reduced demand for a good or service. The economic conditions, cultural preferences, and legal restrictions in a foreign market also are likely to affect potential demand and the price that is charged.

©Getty Images/PhotoDisc

COMPETITION

If many companies are selling an identical or similar product, consumers have more choices than if only one company or a few companies were selling the item. Competition tends to keep prices lower. For example, if many stores in Bogota are selling similar products, consumers will purchase at the store with the lowest price. This competition will force companies to offer special prices or promotions to attract customers. When a company starts marketing their goods and services in another country, it faces competition from domestic companies in that country and from other exporting companies around the world.

CheckPoint

What factors affect consumer demand?

WORK AS A GROUP

List the costs associated with producing various products and services. Tell how these costs would affect the price charged for these items.

PRICING METHODS

International marketing managers use a variety of methods to determine appropriate prices. Markup pricing, new product pricing, psychological pricing, and discount pricing can be effective price determination methods.

MARKUP PRICING

Many prices are based on the cost that the store paid for an item plus an amount to cover the expenses and add profit. **Markup** is an amount added to the cost of a product to determine the selling price. The markup includes operating costs and a profit on the item.

Markups are commonly stated in percentages. For example, a company may use a 40 percent markup on its products. For an item that costs $50, this would result in a $70 selling price. To determine the selling price, multiply the cost by the markup percentage; then add this result to the cost.

Markup	=	Percentage	×	Cost
	=	0.40	×	$50
	=	$20		
Selling Price	=	**Cost**	+	**Markup**
	=	$50	+	$20
	=	$70		

Competition affects markup, like many other marketing decisions. Products in competitive markets with constant demand, such as food products, tend to have low markups. In contrast, products with inconsistent demand—such as high-fashion clothing items and jewelry—will usually have higher markups to cover the carrying costs of these items.

NEW PRODUCT PRICING

When a company decides to sell a new product, managers face the problem of deciding what price to charge. The pricing strategy used for a new product is affected by the product image desired, the amount of competition, and sales goals. Three commonly used methods for pricing new products are competitive pricing, skim pricing, and penetration pricing.

Competitive Pricing If the new product has competition already on the market, a company may decide to sell its new product at a comparable price. Certain products and services always seem to be priced about the same at all selling locations. Gasoline, pizza, and basic groceries tend to have competitive prices in a given geographic area. Any price differences can usually be attributed to special services or special product features.

Skim Pricing When a new product is introduced, managers may decide to charge as much as possible. This approach, called **skim pricing**, sets a relatively high introductory price. Skim pricing attempts to attract buyers who are not concerned with price while also quickly covering the research and development costs of the new product. This approach was used when video recorders and personal computers were first introduced.

With skim pricing, a company faces two potential problems. First, the high price may quickly attract competitors to the market. Second, the company faces the risk of setting the price too high and selling very few items.

SKIPPY IN HUNGARY

Peanut butter is not as popular in other countries as it is in the United States and Canada. In an attempt to expand sales of Skippy peanut butter, Skippy's parent company, Bestfoods, obtained assistance from Dove Frucht, a trading company in Budapest, Hungary.

Most young Hungarians liked the taste of the product. Parents, however, had concerns. The $4 price for a 12-ounce jar was quite expensive for consumers in that country. The average monthly wage in Hungary is about $150. The company only had a limited number of Hungarian households that could afford the product.

Bestfoods (a part of Unilever) distributes its products in over 130 countries, with about 60 percent of its sales coming from international markets. Some of the company's other well-known products are Knorr soup, Thomas' English muffins, Hellmann's salad dressings, and Boboli pizza crusts.

Think Critically

1. What factors affected the pricing for Skippy peanut butter in Hungary?
2. Go to the web site of Bestfoods and Unilever to obtain additional information about the company's international operations. Write a brief description of your findings.

Penetration Pricing In contrast to skim pricing, **penetration pricing** is the setting of a relatively low introductory price for a new product. This approach attempts to gain strong acceptance in the market. This low-pricing strategy can help a company take sales from competitors as the law of demand suggests people will buy more at lower prices than at higher prices. Penetration pricing can be effective when competing against established companies in other countries and when selling in nations with low economic development.

PSYCHOLOGICAL PRICING

In an attempt to persuade consumers to purchase a product or service, companies may use pricing to create an image. For example, certain prices can communicate that an item for sale is a bargain. Or another item may be priced to portray an image of high quality. Common psychological pricing approaches include promotional pricing, odd-even pricing, prestige pricing, and price lining.

Promotional Pricing Advertised specials are a common marketing activity, especially in supermarkets and discount stores. Special-event low prices may be offered as "back-to-school" or "end-of-the-season" sales. A **loss leader**, which is a very low-priced item used to attract customers to a store, is used with the hope that shoppers will make other purchases while shopping for low-priced items. In a grocery store, milk is generally a loss leader.

Odd-Even Pricing Have you ever noticed that many items are priced at 59¢, $1.79, $8.95, and $79.99? Over the years, U.S. companies have found that prices ending in 5 or 9 (odd numbers) present a bargain image. A price ending in an even number or rounded to the nearest dollar amount, such as $175 or $49.50, generally gives an impression of quality. Bargain-oriented restaurants will price meals at $6.95 and $8.99, while quality-conscious restaurants may use $17.50 and $22. This strategy may vary by country. For example, in Japan, the numbers 4 and 9 are considered unlucky.

Prestige Pricing Extensive research has revealed that people believe a higher priced item is better quality than the exact same item at a lower price. French manufacturers such as Yves Saint Laurent, Limoges, and Christofle set prices to project an image of status, influence, and power.

Price Lining To make shopping easier for customers and salesclerks, a store may offer all merchandise in a category at the same price. All suits offered by a store may be sold at $150, $225, and $300. Music CDs may be sold for $8.99, $11.99, and $14.99. Each price category includes a variety of items from which customers in that can choose.

©Getty Images/PhotoDisc

DISCOUNT PRICING

Price reductions are one of the most common actions taken by companies to attract and keep customers. Four common types of discounts are seasonal, cash, quantity, and trade.

Seasonal Discounts At various times of the year, companies may reduce prices to sell the remaining items in stock. Seasonal discounts in the United States include price reductions of summer clothing in August and reductions on Christmas cards and decorations the day after Christmas. In Santiago, Chile, during late July and August, the end-of-winter sales feature discounts on coats and other heavy clothing.

Cash Discounts Companies may reduce the price charged for items to encourage customers to pay their bills quickly. For example, customers may be offered a 2 percent discount if their bill is paid within ten days. If a customer decides not to take advantage of the discount, the full invoice amount is due within 30 days. This discount is expressed as 2/10, net/30.

Quantity Discounts To encourage customers to purchase more of an item, businesses may offer a quantity discount. For example, a garden shop may sell bags of potting soil using the following pricing schedule.

1 to 4 bags	$2.79 per bag
5 to 9 bags	$2.39 per bag
10 or more bags	$2.09 per bag

Trade Discounts Manufacturers commonly sell to distributors and stores based on a percentage of the *list price*, also called the *suggested retail price*. An electronics producer, for example, may sell televisions to stores at a 50 percent trade discount. In other words, a television that sells to consumers for $450 would cost stores $225.

✓ CheckPoint
Why are cash discounts offered?

PRICING IN GLOBAL MARKETS

Managers setting prices for domestic markets are aware of competitors' prices, consumer demand, and currency values. However, when businesses are setting prices for trade across borders, the process is not as easy, and information may not be readily available.

The recession in the United States in the early 1980s had little effect on demand for Mercedes-Benz automobiles. However, the economic downturn in 1991 was a different story for the German auto manufacturer. Because of a weak dollar (compared with the deutsche mark) and a newly imposed U.S. luxury tax, sales of Mercedes dropped 24 percent in the United States.

Fluctuations in exchange rates for currencies can result in receiving less money than expected. One way to minimize the effect of fluctuating currency rates is to set prices high enough to cover these changes. *Countertrade,* which is the direct exchange of products or services between companies in different countries, can also minimize this risk.

Sometimes a company may intentionally set prices extremely low for foreign trade. **Dumping** is the practice of selling exported products at a lower price than what is asked in the company's home country. While this can benefit consumers, others will suffer. The lower price drives out competition, causing workers to lose jobs.

Businesses often pressure governments to prevent dumping. Countries may adopt *antidumping laws* or *antidumping tariffs.* These trade barriers prohibit importers from selling products at artificially low prices.

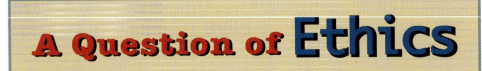

A Question of Ethics

DUMPING

For twenty years, Smith Corona Corporation charged Brother Industries, Limited, of Japan with dumping. Brother was accused of hurting U.S. competitors by unfairly selling portable word processors at exceptionally low prices in the United States. Although Smith Corona obtained several legal rulings in its favor from the International Trade Commission, the practice continued.

More recently, fish producers in Maine protested that Chile was driving down the market price of salmon by selling at below-production cost. This action was believed to be an unfair trade practice. In contrast, several supermarket chains and restaurants believed the salmon was beneficial to their companies and consumers. The supporters of the Chilean fish industry contended that the lower-cost boneless salmon fillet was the result of investments in new processing equipment. They argued that this was a different product than was being produced by U.S. fishing companies.

While dumping may benefit consumers and the country selling the low-cost product, others are harmed. The country receiving the products can find that the lower price drives out competition, causing workers to lose jobs. Prices might become inflated once competition is driven out of the market.

Think Critically

1. Use the three guidelines for ethical analysis to examine the above situation. Are the fish producers in Chile acting ethically?
2. What actions might be appropriate for a country that is victimized by dumping?

CheckPoint

How can losses from currency fluctuations be minimized?

REVIEW GLOBAL BUSINESS TERMS

Define each of the following terms.

1. markup

2. skim pricing

3. penetration pricing

4. loss leader

5. dumping

REVIEW GLOBAL BUSINESS CONCEPTS

6. What are the three main factors that affect the price of a product?

7. What does a markup include beyond the cost of manufacturing or buying the product to be sold?

8. What are the advantages and disadvantages of dumping?

SOLVE GLOBAL BUSINESS PROBLEMS

For each of the following situations, calculate the requested markup, discount, cost, or price.

9. A Japanese clothing store marks up its prices 70 percent. What would be the selling price for a jacket that cost the store 8,000 yen?

10. A British company offers a 3 percent discount on a £600 purchase paid within 10 days. What is the amount of the purchase if the customer pays within 10 days?

11. A Brazilian store sells blank videocassettes for 6.3BRL each if less than five are purchased or 5.8BRL each if five or more are purchased. What would be the cost of six tapes?

12. A Mexican appliance manufacturer sells to retailers with a trade discount of 35 percent. If a washing machine has a list price of Mex$900 (pesos), what would be the cost of the item to a store?

THINK CRITICALLY

13. Assume a can of vegetables sells for $1. Estimate the amount for each of the following business costs: (a) product ingredients, (b) processing, (c) package and label, (d) advertising, (e) warehouse storage, (f) transportation, and (g) store profit.

14. Do antidumping laws promote or deter free trade?

MAKE CONNECTIONS

15. **TECHNOLOGY** Compare prices for products sold in local stores and through online shopping web sites. Do the items cost more or less online? How do shipping charges, taxes, and delivery time affect online shopping?

16. **MATHEMATICS** Collect advertisements with examples of odd and even prices used at different stores. What types of retailers use this pricing method most often?

GLOBAL DISTRIBUTION ACTIVITIES

18-2

GOALS

- Contrast direct and indirect channels of distribution.
- Describe the activities of agents, whole-salers, and retailers.
- Explain the role played by global intermediaries.

©Getty Images/PhotoDisc

DISTRIBUTION CHANNELS

For a product to be useful, it must be transported from the producer to the user. A **distribution channel** is the path taken by a good or service to get from the producer to the final user.

When would a company sell directly to the user of a product, and when would a business use wholesalers and retailers? How products are distributed is influenced by the type of product and consumers involved. For example, a small company that wants to distribute its products in many stores probably will use a distribution channel with many retailers. Figure 18-2 on the next page shows the common distribution channels used.

In a **direct distribution channel**, producers sell goods or services directly to the final user. Some examples of direct distribution (Channel A) include farmers selling produce at a roadside stand, sales representatives for a cosmetic company calling on consumers in their homes, and publishing companies selling their books through a web site.

More common than direct distribution is the use of agents, wholesalers, and retailers. An **indirect distribution channel** occurs when goods or services are sold with the use of one or more intermediaries between the producer and the consumer. Channel B is a common distribution method for automobiles and other motor vehicles. Channel C is used to distribute packaged food products and other items sold in supermarkets and discount stores.

COMMON DISTRIBUTION CHANNELS

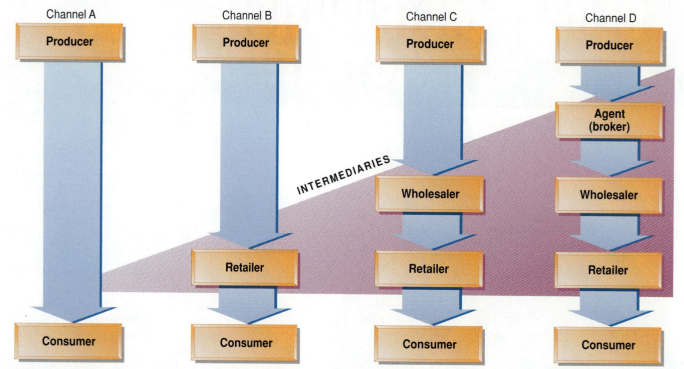

Figure 18-2 Products can be distributed to final consumers through various channels of distribution.

Finally, Channel D may be used for foreign trade in which an import-export agent is involved.

✓ CheckPoint

What is the difference between a direct distribution channel and an indirect distribution channel?

DISTRIBUTION CHANNEL MEMBERS

Several parties are usually involved when selling goods across borders. An **intermediary** is any person or organization in the distribution channel that moves goods and services from the producer to the consumer. The most common intermediaries are agents, wholesalers, and retailers.

AGENTS

An **agent**, also referred to as a *broker*, brings together buyers and sellers but does not take ownership of the products. International agents serve export companies by being knowledgeable about global markets and international trade barriers.

WHOLESALERS

A **wholesaler** is a business that buys large quantities of an item and resells them to a retailer. Wholesalers do not usually sell directly to final users of a product. Wholesalers have five main functions: providing information, processing orders, storing and transporting, financing and taking possession, and promoting. These functions are further described in Figure 18-3.

The film, equipment, and photographic supplies made by Kodak are available in almost every country. The company's headquarters in Rochester, New York, maintains close contact with sellers to determine demand for its products throughout the world. Factories are kept informed of needed inventory so sufficient merchandise is produced. Kodak's Distribution Division coordinates these efforts to ensure that distribution centers have the product when it is needed.

Many people believe that eliminating wholesalers would reduce marketing costs. While wholesalers may be eliminated, the duties performed cannot be eliminated. Transporting, storing, and ordering must still be done. Either the manufacturer or the retailer must perform these duties, which would probably be less efficient than leaving the functions with wholesalers who specialize in those tasks.

FUNCTIONS OF WHOLESALERS

PROVIDING INFORMATION: Communicating between manufacturers and retailers

PROCESSING ORDERS: Providing needed products for retailers to sell

STORING AND TRANSPORTATION: Maintaining warehouses and shipping capabilities

FINANCING AND TAKING POSSESSION: Accepting ownership of finished goods and extending credit to customers

PROMOTING: Advertising and selling to retailers and helping retailers promote to their consumers

Figure 18-3 Wholesalers perform important functions that assist with international marketing activities.

RETAILERS

A **retailer** is a store or another business that sells directly to the final user. Each day hundreds of millions of shoppers make purchases from retailing businesses. In Cairo, Egypt, many people buy needed goods at an open market, while in Paris, most people make their purchases at small shops or large retail stores. Retailers attempt to serve customers in five main ways. These ways include product selection, convenience, product quality, sales staff assistance, and special services. These functions are further described in Figure 18-4.

SERVICES PROVIDED BY RETAILERS

A VARIETY OF STYLES TO CHOOSE FROM FOR EVERYONE!

PRODUCT SELECTION: Variety of sizes, styles, and brands

CONVENIENCE: Location, hours of operation, parking availability, and ease of making purchases

PRODUCT QUALITY: Product excellence and reputation

SALES STAFF ASSISTANCE: Information about product features, uses, and store policies

SPECIAL SERVICES: Delivery, ease of exchanging or returning items, and special sales

Figure 18-4 Retailers provide a variety of services to attract customers.

©Getty Images/PhotoDisc

Retailers in the United States may be viewed in six major categories, which are convenience stores, general merchandise stores, specialty stores, direct sellers, online retailers, and automatic vending.

Convenience Stores A family needs milk and bread, or a student needs a report cover for school. These buying situations may result in consumers shopping at the stores closest to their homes. Convenience stores are usually located near the homes of potential customers or have gas stations. Easy parking, easy-to-find items, and fast service are common among convenience stores.

General Merchandise Retailers Some retailers offer a larger variety of product types and offer more service than convenience stores. General merchandise retailers include supermarkets, department stores, discount stores, warehouse club stores, and outlet stores.

In recent years, several major retailing companies have created superstores, also called *hypermarkets*. These giant one-stop-shopping facilities offer a wide variety of grocery items and department-store merchandise. While the typical supermarket has about 40,000 to 50,000 square feet, superstores may have 200,000 square feet or more. The first hypermarket was started in France in 1963. Today these superstores are likely to include a bakery, a restaurant, a pharmacy, and banking facilities.

GLOBAL BUSINESS EXAMPLE

COKE VS. PEPSI AT THE BERLIN WALL

When the Berlin Wall fell in 1989, many businesses were ready to enter the previously closed East German market. Pepsi presented dramatic television commercials celebrating the end of the cold war. While Pepsi sales grew, the company continued to ship products from existing bottling plants in western European locations.

Coca-Cola used a different distribution strategy. Coca-Cola invested $400 million to buy five bottling plants, 13 distribution centers, 370 trucks, 900 cars and vans, 170 forklifts, and 20,000 vending machines. This commitment to distribution in eastern Europe by Coca-Cola resulted in the company's outselling Pepsi in the German market by the early 1990s.

Think Critically

1. How do the costs and risks differ for the distribution strategies used by Coca-Cola and Pepsi?
2. Go to the web sites of Coca-Cola and Pepsi to obtain information about the international operations of these companies. Write a brief description of your findings.

Specialty Stores Shoes, furniture, clothing, sporting goods, computer software, and baked goods are commonly sold in stores that specialize in a limited product line. Specialty stores offer a variety of styles and brands of an item along with knowledgeable sales personnel.

In recent years, very large specialty stores have grown in market power. These specialty superstores offer low prices and a very extensive product line. Examples of these retailers include OfficeMax, Home Depot, Best Buy, and PETsMART.

Direct Sellers Mail order, telephone contacts, door-to-door marketing, and e-mail messages are called *direct selling*. This retailing method involves direct contact between the seller and the buyer. Personal care products, home appliances, books, and financial services are commonly sold through in-home parties, sales demonstrations, and seminars.

Direct selling varies in success from country to country. In cultures where personal contacts are important when doing business, direct selling thrives. In other societies, direct selling may have limited success.

Online Retailers The Internet is changing the way people shop. A person can view products, prices, and other information from hundreds of retailers without leaving home. While mail order and television home-shopping channels paved the way for this process, the World Wide Web takes electronic retailing to new levels. Online retailers include both existing companies including Wal-Mart, OfficeMax, and The Gap, as well as Web-only sellers such as eBay and amazon.com.

©Getty Images/PhotoDisc

Product demonstrations, customized products, and other features make online buying very popular. While consumers continue to have concerns about online shopping, improved security systems and privacy regulations are reducing those anxieties. Online retailing is expected to have strong growth for many years.

Automatic Vending Vending machines have been used for years for the purchase of soft drinks, snacks, and newspapers. Recent technology has expanded vending machine use to sell books, videos, computer time, clothing, and cooked-to-order foods. Automatic teller machines (ATMs), a type of vending machine, provide a variety of financial services, including depositing money, obtaining foreign currency, purchasing train or airline tickets, and selecting investments.

WORK AS A GROUP

Prepare a list of retailers in your community. Explain how these businesses are involved in the global economy.

▌INTERNATIONAL RETAILING ACTIVITIES

©Getty Images/PhotoDisc

Fast-food and snack-food companies that sell pizza, hamburgers, fried chicken, yogurt, and ice cream take to the road in many countries. Vehicles converted into minirestaurants allow companies to serve customers at temporary locations. Popular locations for these rolling restaurants are sporting events, amusement parks, community fairs, concerts, and zoos. Banks and other financial institutions also use a similar distribution approach with *ATMobiles* (portable cash machines).

Sidewalk merchants and street vendors in Mexico City are being joined by U.S. discount stores. After the Mexican government reduced import restrictions, Sam's Club, a division of Wal-Mart, opened in a vacant factory and started to sell clothing, appliances, personal care products, and packaged and frozen foods in that country. Mexican consumers were attracted to the quality, spare parts, service, and warranties offered by these retailers. Wal-Mart has also entered the European market with stores in Britain, Germany, France, and several other countries.

Communication Across Borders

FLEXIBLE SCHEDULING—BRAZILIAN STYLE

Scheduling delays of 15 to 45 minutes are common throughout Latin America. There, punctuality may actually be disruptive because others aren't necessarily ready to meet.

To work around the problem, Brazilian businesspersons try to schedule appointments in their own offices so they can work while waiting for others to arrive. Sometimes they take additional work with them to another person's office, where they work while they wait for that person to return to the office. Appointments for meals and drinks also typically begin in offices, where waiting time can be put to good use.

Think Critically

1. Why might a U.S. businessperson plan to arrive slightly late for a meeting with a Brazilian businessperson?
2. How does the Brazilian system of scheduling appointments promote personal productivity?

✔ CheckPoint

How do agents, wholesalers, and retailers differ?

GLOBAL INTERMEDIARIES

The distribution channels used for international trade are often different from those used for domestic trade. Common international intermediaries include export management companies, export trading companies, freight forwarders, and customs brokers.

Export Management Company

An **export management company (EMC)** provides complete distribution services for businesses that desire to sell in foreign markets. EMCs make it easier to sell in other countries since they have immediate access to established buyers. Most EMCs are small firms that specialize in specific products or in a certain foreign market. EMCs provide exporters with reliable global distribution channels.

Export Trading Company

An **export trading company (ETC)** is a full-service global distribution intermediary. An ETC buys and sells products, conducts market research, and distributes goods abroad. An export trading company may also be involved in banking, financing, and production activities. Japanese trading companies, called *sogo shoshas*, have been in operation since the late 1800s. Today these companies handle more than half of Japan's imports and exports.

©Getty Images/PhotoDisc

Freight Forwarder A **freight forwarder** ships goods to customers in other countries. Like a travel agent for cargo, these companies get an exporter's merchandise to the required destination. Often a freight forwarder will accumulate several small export shipments and combine them into one larger shipment in order to get lower freight rates.

Customs Broker A **customs broker**, also called a *custom house broker*, is an intermediary that specializes in moving goods through the customs process. This process involves inspection of imported products and payment of duties. Customs brokers are licensed in countries in which they work and must know the import rules and fees.

What services are provided by a freight forwarder?

REVIEW GLOBAL BUSINESS TERMS

Define each of the following terms.

1. distribution channel
2. direct distribution channel
3. indirect distribution channel
4. intermediary
5. agent
6. wholesaler
7. retailer
8. export management company (EMC)
9. export trading company (ETC)
10. freight forwarder
11. customs broker

REVIEW GLOBAL BUSINESS CONCEPTS

12. What are three common intermediaries in the distribution channel?
13. What are examples of direct selling?
14. What services does an export trading company provide?

SOLVE GLOBAL BUSINESS PROBLEMS

For each of the following international business situations, tell which global intermediary (export management company, export trading company, freight forwarder, or customs broker) would be involved.

15. A clothing company needs assistance with import rules and fees.
16. A company must have 17,000 shirts transported to Africa.
17. A manufacturer of lights for home use wants to use the services of a distributor with established buyers in Southeast Asia.
18. A packaged food business needs a global distribution intermediary to research, package, and ship its products to Central America.

THINK CRITICALLY

19. Some businesspeople believe that eliminating agents and wholesalers reduces their operating expenses. Discuss the opportunity costs associated with eliminating intermediaries.
20. As an importer of clothing, would you rather have your products sold by a general merchandise retailer or a specialty store? Why?

MAKE CONNECTIONS

21. **TECHNOLOGY** Select an item not commonly sold online. Sketch or describe a web site that might be used to sell this good or service.
22. **STATISTICS** List the names of all retailers you and your family have used in the past 30 days and the number of visits. Categorize the retailers by type, such as convenience store, online retailer, or automatic vending. Create a frequency chart of the results.

MOVING GOODS AROUND THE WORLD

18-3

©Getty Images/PhotoDisc

GOALS

- Summarize the shipping requirements for international distribution.
- Compare transportation modes available to international distributors.

PREPARING FOR SHIPPING

As exports are prepared for international distribution, goods must be packed and labeled, and various documents may be required.

PACKING AND LABELING

When an item is prepared for international shipping, it should be packed to meet the following criteria.

- avoid breakage
- maintain the lowest possible weight and volume
- provide moisture-proof surroundings
- minimize theft

Shipments going by land or sea require strong containers. In contrast, air shipments do not require such heavy packing. Shippers recommend that exporters avoid mention of brand names or contents on the package. This reduces the potential for theft.

The shipping label for exported goods should include

(a) name and address of the shipper
(b) country of origin
(c) container's weight
(d) size of the container
(e) number of packages per container
(f) destination
(g) labels for hazardous material

UNIVERSAL PACKING SYMBOLS

Figure 18-5 Universal package symbols communicate important information that can be understood around the world.

Universally recognized symbols are commonly used on containers to inform package handlers of warnings and contents, as shown in Figure 18-5.

DOCUMENTATION

Various export forms are normally required when shipping merchandise to other countries. These documents include the bill of lading, certificate of origin, export declaration, destination control statement, and insurance certificate.

Bill of Lading A *bill of lading* is a contract between the exporter and the transporter. This form describes the weight, number, and value of goods along with the names and addresses of the seller and buyer. A bill of lading serves as a receipt for the exported items.

Certificate of Origin A *certificate of origin* documents the country in which the goods being shipped were produced. This document may be required to determine the amount of any import tax.

Export Declaration An *export declaration* is required by the U.S. Department of Commerce for shipments with a value of more than $500. This form lists the same information that is on the bill of lading along with the name of the carrier and the exporting vessel.

Destination Control Statement A *destination control statement* verifies the country to which goods are being shipped. This document notifies the carrier and all other handlers that the shipment may only go to certain destinations.

Insurance Certificate An *insurance certificate* explains the amount of insurance coverage for fire, theft, water, or other damage that may happen to goods in shipment. This certificate also lists the names of the insurance company and the exporter.

✔CheckPoint

What is the purpose of a certificate of origin?

TRANSPORTATION IN THE GLOBAL MARKET

A critical ingredient of distribution is the shipping and delivery of a product. For a package of Wrigley's Doublemint gum to get to customers in some areas of China, several transportation modes may be required. These could include a trip by truck or train, a rusting freighter, a tricycle cart, or a bicycle.

Physical distribution refers to the process of transporting, storing, and handling goods in transit between the producer and consumer. As shown in Figure 18-6, the physical movement of goods sold in the global economy is usually done in one of five ways.

Motor Carrier The trucking industry is a vital distribution link in almost every country. Motor carriers can quickly and consistently deliver large and small shipments to just about anywhere. Trucks are commonly used for shipping food products, clothing, furniture, lumber, plastic products, and machinery.

©Getty Images/PhotoDisc

NAFTA has created some difficulties for trucking companies transporting goods between Canada, Mexico, and the United States. Some Canadian trucks that were not loaded properly resulted in accidents and injuries on U.S. highways. U.S. trucking companies have faced long delays at the Mexican border

NETBookmark

Although it is called the Silk Road, this desert trading route in Asia was used to transport many other things, from gold and ivory to exotic animals, plants, glass, and religion. Access intlbizxtra.swlearning.com and click on the link for Chapter 18. Read the article and make a graphic organizer that charts all the ways that the Silk Road influenced trade and other aspects of society.

intlbizxtra.swlearning.com

WORK AS A GROUP

Have some students name products for shipping. Have others explain which transportation mode would be most appropriate.

TRANSPORTATION MODES FOR INTERNATIONAL MARKETING

Figure 18-6 International marketers use a variety of transportation modes to move goods and services from the producer to the consumer.

when the smaller, older highways could not handle the many vehicles wanting to enter the country.

Railroad Within the United States and many other countries, railroads continue to be a major transportation mode. The products most commonly shipped by rail are automobiles, grain, chemicals, coal, lumber, iron, and steel.

To add flexibility to rail shipping services, truck trailers and containers are transported on flat cars across country. Once near the destination, motor carriers make the local deliveries. These *piggyback* operations combine the long-haul capability of railroads with the door-to-door delivery of trucking.

Waterway Inland water carriers, such as barges, can efficiently transport bulky commodities. Oceangoing ships are slower than other transportation modes. However, they are very cost effective for shipping items overseas. These container-carrying vessels allow exporters to transport items such as coal, steel, lumber, grain, oil, and sand.

GLOBAL BUSINESS EXAMPLE

AVON IN THE AMAZON

In the Amazon region of Brazil, Avon sells its cosmetics with the use of company representatives who travel by canoe or in an animal-powered cart. In Brazil, about 400,000 beauty consultants sell Avon products. That number is twice the size of the country's army.

Avon uses direct selling when doing business in more than 130 countries. However with the low-income consumers in the Amazon region, adaptation of marketing is necessary. Payments, for example, may be unusual. Instead of money, a chicken or homemade flour may be exchanged for cologne, lipstick, and other beauty items.

This marketing career can provide an economic opportunity for people in the region. One representative in the Amazon region, a retired teacher, used to make about $110 a month at her previous job. Today she makes about seven to eight times as much selling lipstick and other Avon products to female Indian consumers.

Orders for cosmetics are processed through a computer system at regional offices around Brazil. The products are then shipped as far as 2,500 miles from Avon's production facilities in Sao Paulo, Brazil, to customers in the Amazon region.

Think Critically

1. What factors influenced Avon to adapt its distribution strategy in Brazil?
2. Go the Avon web site to obtain additional information about the company's product line and distribution methods. Write a paragraph about your findings.

Containerization is the process of packing cargo in large standardized containers for efficient shipping and handling. Before this process, cargo was handled manually using crates, pallets, and forklifts. Damage to cargo and delays were common. Containerization is used when shipping from major deepwater ports, such as those in Elizabeth, New Jersey, and Oakland, California. Other new containerization developments have also made it possible to transport fresh fruits and vegetables in refrigerated compartments from Chile to Japan.

Pipeline More than 200,000 miles of pipelines are in operation in the United States alone. Pipelines provide a dependable, low-cost method for transporting natural gas and oil products. The limitation of this transportation method is speed. Liquids travel at a speed of only three or four miles per hour. In addition, few products can be transported by this method, and international pipelines can only be used when a geographic link exists between two countries.

Air Carrier The use of air transportation for international business activities continues to expand. As global demand for products increases, companies use the quick service offered by air carriers. Items commonly shipped by air include high-priced specialty products, specialized equipment parts, and perishable items (such as fresh flowers).

©Getty Images/PhotoDisc

Intermodal Movements Companies frequently use more than one mode of transportation when shipping to other countries. *Intermodal movements* refer to the transfer of freight involving various modes of transportation. Containers used today can easily be transferred from a ship or plane to a train or truck.

REGIONAL PERSPECTIVE

HISTORY: THE PANAMA CANAL

The Panama Canal shortens water travel between the Atlantic and Pacific Oceans by 7,000 miles (11,270 kilometers). This 51.2-mile waterway connects the Caribbean Sea with the Pacific Ocean at the Isthmus of Panama, the neck of land connecting North and South America.

The idea of a canal connecting the Atlantic and Pacific Oceans was first considered in the sixteenth century. In 1534, Charles V of Spain ordered a survey for a possible canal route across Panama. A French company finally started the project in 1881. However, work ceased after eight years due to the treacherous terrain and diseases such as malaria and yellow fever. Nearly 20,000 workers died during the attempted construction. After Panama gained

©Getty Images/PhotoDisc

its independence from Colombia in 1903, work started again on the canal. Construction was completed in 1914 at a cost of $336 million.

Six pairs of locks raise or lower a ship to the next water level along the length of the Panama Canal. The trip takes between seven and eight hours with more than 12,000 ships traveling through the canal each year. In 1999, the possession of the Panama Canal was transferred from the United States to Panama after 85 years.

Think Critically
1. What are the international trade benefits of the Panama Canal?
2. Conduct an Internet search for information about the current activities of the Panama Canal. Write a description of your findings.

✔ CheckPoint
What activities are involved with physical distribution?

REVIEW GLOBAL BUSINESS CONCEPTS

1. What documents are commonly required when shipping goods to other countries?

2. What are the five main transportation systems used for shipping goods?

3. When would a business use intermodal movements?

SOLVE GLOBAL BUSINESS PROBLEMS

Suggest an appropriate transportation method for the following international marketing situations.

4. A company in Argentina is shipping oil to other countries in South America.

5. A British company is shipping machines for use in factories in various African countries.

6. A company in Hawaii is shipping fresh flowers to Japan and California.

7. A mining company is shipping iron ore to steel factories within the same country.

THINK CRITICALLY

8. How might shipping labels be improved to assist businesses and to contribute to the safety of workers?

9. What actions could be taken to make border crossings of shipped goods more efficient?

10. Describe how a company would balance the tradeoff between cost and speed when selecting a shipping method.

MAKE CONNECTIONS

11. **COMMUNICATIONS** Prepare a map display that shows the trade route that would be used for transporting various products from one region of the world to another.

12. **SCIENCE** Research containerization and pipeline methods to determine how these transportation modes have improved international distribution.

13. **GEOGRAPHY** Describe how intermodal transportation could solve distribution problems created by the terrain and geographic conditions in a country.

14. **LAW** Why would a country have laws to prevent the shipping of various types of products into that nation?

15. **TECHNOLOGY** Use the Internet to locate online resources for transporting goods around the world.

16. **TECHNOLOGY** Use the Internet to find examples of some of the documentation needed to ship products around the world.

17. **TECHNOLOGY** Visit the web sites of three different companies that transport products internationally.

Xtra! Quiz Prep

intlbizxtra.swlearning.com

CHAPTER SUMMARY

18-1 INTERNATIONAL PRICING ACTIVITIES

A Businesses need to consider costs, consumer demand, and competition when setting prices for international markets.

B The common pricing methods used by businesses include markup pricing; new product pricing, which includes competitive pricing, skim pricing, and penetration pricing; psychological pricing; and discount pricing.

C Pricing factors that are unique to global markets include changing currency values and unfair actions, such as dumping.

18-2 GLOBAL DISTRIBUTION ACTIVITIES

A Direct channels of distribution involve selling goods or services directly to the final user. Indirect channels of distribution involve the use of intermediaries: agents, wholesalers, and retailers.

B Agents, wholesalers, and retailers are distribution channel members who provide services to move goods and services from the producer to the consumer.

C Global intermediaries include export management companies, export trading companies, freight forwarders, and customs brokers.

18-3 MOVING GOODS AROUND THE WORLD

A Shipping requirements for international distribution require proper packaging and labeling along with necessary documents. These may include a bill of lading, certificate of origin, export declaration, destination control statement, and insurance certificate.

B The main transportation modes available to international distributors are motor carrier, railroad, waterway, pipeline, and air carrier.

GLOBAL REFOCUS

Read the Global Focus at the beginning of this chapter, and answer the following questions.

1. Do you think the entrance of Toys "R" Us into the Japanese market served the best interests of Japanese consumers and workers?

2. How do you think increased competition and online selling will affect prices for toys in Japan?

REVIEW GLOBAL BUSINESS TERMS

Match the terms listed with the definitions.

1. When goods or services are distributed with the use of one or more intermediaries between the producer and the consumer.

2. Setting a relatively low introductory price for a new product.

3. A very low-priced item used to attract customers to a store.

4. A full-service global distribution intermediary.

5. An amount added to the cost of a product to determine the selling price.

6. The path taken by a good or service to get from the producer to the final user.

7. A business that buys large quantities of an item and resells them to a retailer.

8. A company that provides complete distribution services for businesses that desire to sell in foreign markets.

9. Setting a relatively high introductory price for a new product.

10. A person or an organization in the distribution channel that moves goods and services from the producer to the consumer.

11. A business that ships goods to customers in other countries.

a. agent

b. customs broker

c. direct distribution channel

d. distribution channel

e. dumping

f. export management company (EMC)

g. export trading company (ETC)

h. freight forwarder

i. indirect distribution channel

j. intermediary

k. loss leader

l. markup

m. penetration pricing

n. retailer

o. skim pricing

p. wholesaler

12. When goods or services are sold directly from the producer to the final user of the item.

13. The practice of selling exported products at a lower price than that asked in the company's home country.

14. An intermediary that specializes in moving goods through the customs process.

15. A store or another business that sells directly to the final user.

16. An intermediary that brings together buyers and sellers but does not take ownership of the products.

MAKE GLOBAL BUSINESS DECISIONS

17. Companies involved in international marketing usually encounter higher operating costs than do domestic marketers. What benefits are associated with global marketing?

18. What types of products have a high percentage markup?

19. Give examples of discounts used by stores to attract customers.

20. How can dumping have a negative effect on a nation's economy?

21. Explain how wholesaling serves the needs of consumers throughout the world.

22. Describe how different types of retailers in your community attract different types of customers.

23. How might the success of retailers in different countries be affected by cultural, economic, and political factors?

GLOBAL CONNECTIONS

24. GEOGRAPHY Research the economic importance of various crucial waterways—Panama Canal, Suez Canal, Strait of Gibraltar, Strait of Hormuz, and Strait of Malacca.

25. COMMUNICATIONS Prepare a list of common goods, and ask people of various ages for their best guess at the price of each item. Which consumers are most knowledgeable about prices?

26. TECHNOLOGY Conduct library and Internet research about online retailing. What types of electronic shopping systems and cyberstores are expected to increase in popularity over the next few years?

27. CULTURAL STUDIES Talk to someone who has visited or lived in another country. Obtain information about the types of stores and informal retailing (street vendors, pushcarts, open-air markets) that exist in that country.

28. VISUAL ARTS Prepare a bulletin board, a poster, or another visual display showing how various products are shipped within and between countries.

29. MATHEMATICS Estimate the markup of various food products, articles of clothing, and other items. Talk with a retail store manager or employee to obtain information about (a) the wholesale cost of the products they sell and (b) the operating expenses that influence the final selling price.

30. CAREER PLANNING If you were the manager of a distribution center that shipped products to over 50 different countries, what types of workers would you need to hire? What skills would you need to have to be a global distribution manager?

©Getty Images/PhotoDisc

THE GLOBAL
ENTREPRENEUR

CREATING AN INTERNATIONAL BUSINESS PLAN

CREATING AN INTERNATIONAL PRICING AND DISTRIBUTION PLAN

Create a pricing and distribution strategy for the business idea you have used in previous chapters, or select another business idea. Use the country you have previously researched, or select a different country. Using library and Internet research, obtain information for the following topics.

1. How do operating costs and competition affect the prices charged by the company? Prepare a list of the company's production costs and other expenses.
2. List the factors that affect the demand for the company's goods and services in different countries.
3. Describe the distribution channel that might be used to get the company's goods or services to consumers.
4. Describe the types of retail stores used to sell the company's goods or services.
5. Describe the types of shipping methods that would be used by the company to get its products to foreign markets.

Prepare a written summary or present a short oral report (two or three minutes) of your findings.

©Getty Images/PhotoDisc

Chapter 19

GLOBAL PROMOTIONAL STRATEGIES

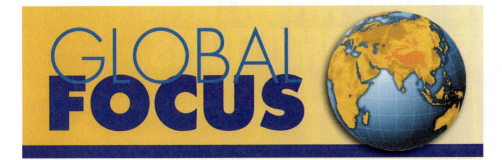

UNILEVER: AN ADVERTISING GIANT

Unilever sells products known around the world. The company owns brands such as Lipton tea, Breyers ice cream, Promise margarine, Dove soap, Wisk detergent, and Close-up toothpaste. Unilever is the largest advertiser in many countries, including India, Austria, Britain, Greece, Italy, the Netherlands, Turkey, Argentina, Brazil, and Chile.

Despite its success in many nations, Unilever has had to take a back seat to Procter & Gamble in the United States and a few other markets. In the early 1990s, Unilever introduced Omo laundry detergent in the Persian Gulf in an effort to take away some of Procter & Gamble's control in that region. Omo was adapted for use in washing machines from the formula used in Egypt, where most people wash clothes by hand.

Instead of running its operations from London, the company created Unilever Arabia to administer marketing, research, sales, and advertising activities. This division of the company also expanded its product offerings in the Persian Gulf by selling Vaseline petroleum jelly, Vaseline Intensive Care lotion, and Lux soap.

In recent years, Unilever has more than 1,000 brands. Many of those are known around the world, while others are leaders in local markets. Every day, 150 million people around the world purchase a product with a Unilever brand.

Think Critically

1. How did competition influence the actions of Unilever in the Persian Gulf?
2. How might a reduction in the number of brands strengthen the marketing efforts of Unilever?
3. Go to the Unilever's web site to obtain additional information about recent actions of the company. Prepare a report of your findings.

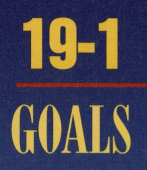

19-1
GOALS

- Diagram the elements of the communication process.
- Describe the elements of the promotional mix.

GLOBAL COMMUNICATIONS AND PROMOTIONS

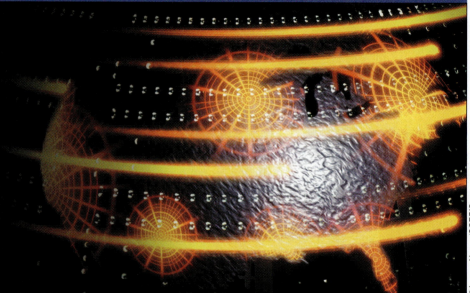

©Jeremy Horner/CORBIS

THE COMMUNICATION PROCESS

Every business needs to communicate with potential buyers. A company's ability to inform and persuade consumers with promotional efforts is a basic business activity.

Each day the average person sends and receives thousands of communications. Many of these messages involve television commercials, online promotions, magazine advertisements, and other marketing promotions.

Have you ever said something to someone and the other person didn't hear you? Or have you ever said one thing and a listener interpreted it to mean something completely different from what you intended? In the communication process, the message is sent from a *source* (the sender) to the *audience* (the receiver). You may be the source, and a friend may be the audience. In marketing, a company is commonly the source, and consumers are the audience.

The source puts the message in a form that hopefully the audience will understand. This is known as *encoding*. The message travels to the audience over a *medium*—such as a television, a telephone, a magazine, the Internet or a salesperson talking in a store. *Decoding* is the process in which the audience makes meaning of the message.

THE COMMUNICATION PROCESS

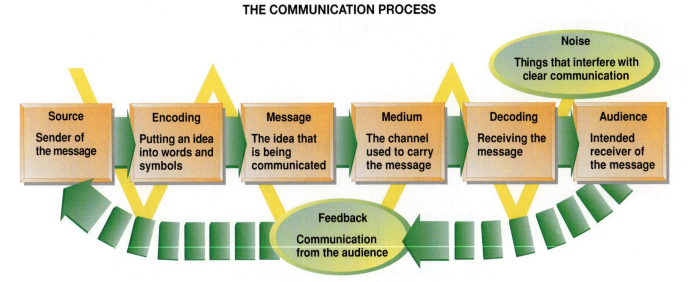

Source	Encoding	Message	Medium	Decoding	Audience
Sender of the message	Putting an idea into words and symbols	The idea that is being communicated	The channel used to carry the message	Receiving the message	Intended receiver of the message

Noise
Things that interfere with clear communication

Feedback
Communication from the audience

Figure 19-1 The communication process is the system used to send and receive marketing messages.

While communication may seem easy, *noise* can disrupt the process. Noise refers to anything that interferes with the communication process. Types of noise that can obstruct international business communication include language differences, varied cultural meanings for words and gestures, and the setting in which communication takes place.

Finally, *feedback* is communication from the audience back to the sender. A common example of consumer feedback is the availability of toll-free numbers that allow people to ask questions, obtain information, and make complaints. These toll-free telephone numbers often appear on packages and in advertisements. Or you can obtain the telephone numbers of companies that have these lines by calling 1-800-555-1212. E-mail and web sites also allow consumers to offer feedback to companies.

The communication process is summarized in Figure 19-1.

✓ CheckPoint

What kinds of noise can obstruct international business communications?

Suggest ways companies could encourage customers to visit their web sites.

INTERNATIONAL PROMOTIONAL ACTIVITIES

Communication is the basis of promotional activities. Companies attempt to convey product information to potential customers. *Promotion* involves marketing efforts that inform, remind, and persuade customers.

FOUR MAIN PROMOTIONAL ACTIVITIES

The four main promotional activities available to companies are advertising, personal selling, publicity, and sales promotion. Examples of these activities are illustrated in Figure 19-2.

Advertising Any form of paid, nonpersonal sales communication is **advertising**. Advertising is also called *mass selling* since many people are addressed at one time. Millions of people may see a television commercial, or thousands may see an advertisement in a magazine or on a web site.

Personal Selling In contrast to the nonpersonal mass selling used in advertising, **personal selling** is direct communication between sellers and potential customers. This may happen in a face-to-face setting, over the telephone, or with personalized e-mail messages. Personal selling can provide the opportunity for immediate feedback directly from the customer to the sales representative.

Publicity Business organizations benefit from favorable news coverage about their products and business activities. **Publicity** is any form of unpaid promotion, such as newspaper articles or television news coverage.

Sales Promotion The final element of promotion includes a variety of activities. **Sales promotion** comprises all of the promotional activities other than advertising, personal selling, and publicity. Sales promotions include coupons, contests, free samples, and in-store displays.

PROMOTIONAL ACTIVITIES

Advertising

Personal Selling

Publicity

Sales Promotion

Figure 19-2 Multinational companies use promotional activities to inform, remind, and persuade potential customers.

THE INTERNATIONAL PROMOTIONAL MIX

A **promotional mix** is the combination of advertising, personal selling, publicity, and sales promotion used by an organization. Which of the four promotional elements should be used most often? Managers must consider a nation's cultural, legal, and economic environments when answering this question.

Cultural factors will influence the promotional mix for international marketers. Radio is very popular in Mexico, and advertising is usually a major component of the promotional mix in that country. In nations with poorly developed postal systems, mail advertising would not be as effective as personal selling or sales promotions.

Marketers also must choose between aiming promotions at end-users of an item or at distributors. **Pull promotions** are marketing efforts directed at the final users of an item. In this promotional approach, companies want consumers to "pull" the product through the distribution channel by demanding the item at stores. Pull promotions include television commercials, advertisements in consumer magazines, coupons, and other selling efforts aimed at consumers.

In contrast to pull promotions, **push promotions** are marketing efforts directed at members of the distribution channel. These promotional activities attempt to get wholesalers and retailers to "push" a product to their customers. Push promotions may include discounts to retailers, special in-store displays, or contests for salespeople.

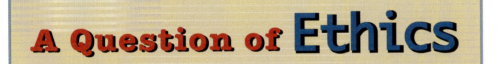

A Question of Ethics

Several years ago, the province of Quebec banned television commercials aimed at children. However, English-speaking residents of the Canadian province can view ads for toys, cereals, and snacks on television programs broadcast from Ontario or the United States.

In Europe, several countries also place limits on advertising aimed at young consumers. Norway and Austria prohibit commercials before, during, and after children's television programs. Toy ads are banned in Greece.

Those who favor these restrictions point out that in Britain, the average child sees nearly 18,000 ads a year. In the United States, that number is about 25,000. Supporters of these laws also believe children are not able to carefully process the many messages received from commercials. In contrast, businesses believe these restrictions violate free-speech rights.

Think Critically

Use the three guidelines for ethical analysis to examine the above situation. Is advertising aimed at young consumers appropriate, or should children be protected from communication that they may not completely understand?

CheckPoint

How does advertising differ from personal selling?

REVIEW GLOBAL BUSINESS TERMS

Define each of the following terms.

1. advertising
2. personal selling
3. publicity
4. sales promotion
5. promotional mix
6. pull promotions
7. push promotions

REVIEW GLOBAL BUSINESS CONCEPTS

8. What are the elements of the communication process used in marketing?
9. What are the four promotional activities?

SOLVE GLOBAL BUSINESS PROBLEMS

For each of the following situations, decide which element of the promotional mix is being used.

10. A sales representative from Norway goes to a customer's place of business to describe a new product.

11. A Belgian company sponsors an environmental cleanup and sends press releases to the media announcing it.

12. A South African company provides special display racks to retailers who carry its products.

13. A Greek company hires college students to distribute samples of its new product at the town square during lunch hour.

14. A Chilean company sponsors a television situation comedy and includes three commercials for each broadcast.

15. A Japanese company signs a contract with a web site to include a banner on the site announcing a new product.

THINK CRITICALLY

16. Describe situations when push promotions may be more appropriate than pull promotions.

17. How does deceptive and false advertising reduce competition and hurt consumers?

MAKE CONNECTIONS

18. **TECHNOLOGY** Go to an Internet web site that sells merchandise from many companies. Write a description about how the merchandise of a particular company is promoted on that web site.

19. **COMMUNICATIONS** Select a newspaper or magazine advertisement. Describe how the language used in the advertisement promotes the product.

PLANNING GLOBAL ADVERTISING

GOALS

- Explain the activities involved in planning advertising for global markets.
- Explain the advantages of using an advertising agency.

©Nik Wheeler/CORBIS

ADVERTISING PLANNING PROCESS

Several years ago, during the Winter Olympics, the Coca-Cola Company broadcast television commercials in 12 languages—with a potential of being seen by 3.8 billion viewers in over 130 countries. Since soft drinks are not significantly affected by cultural differences, Coca-Cola was able to use the same basic commercial in every country. However, this is not always possible. Multinational companies often adapt advertising to fit social and political differences. The four steps involved in planning advertising are shown in Figure 19-3.

STEP 1 ANALYZE TARGET MARKET

The advertising process starts by identifying potential users of a good or service. This *target market* should be defined in terms of geographic area, demographic characteristics, customer needs, buying habits, and media usage. For example, young male consumers in Brazil will require a different advertising message than older female shoppers in France.

THE ADVERTISING PLANNING PROCESS

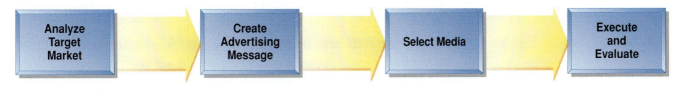

Figure 19-3 Multinational companies must plan advertising effectively to reach consumers in different countries.

STEP 2 CREATE ADVERTISING MESSAGE

The traits of a target market influence the advertising message a company uses. For example, jeans in Brazil are sold with an emphasis on fashion. However, in Australia, customers are more concerned about product benefits, such as quality and price. An advertising message should accomplish one of the following goals.

- Get the customer's attention.
- Increase interest in the good or service.
- Improve a company's image in the minds of consumers.
- Boost the potential of a customer's desire to buy.
- Motivate customers into action.

Companies use some common advertising techniques to create unique messages for specific target markets. These techniques are explained in Figure 19-4.

If customers for a product are similar from one nation to another, a company may use a common advertising message. **Standardized advertising** is the use of one promotional approach in all geographic regions. For example, Tony the Tiger promotes Kellogg's Frosted Flakes in more than 50 countries.

In contrast, cultural factors and social customs may require a company to adapt advertising messages in different nations. **Localized advertising** is the use of promotions that are customized for various target markets. Yogurt, for example, is promoted as a breakfast food in some countries, as a lunch item in other nations, and as a snack in still others. Because of social customs, a multinational company must customize its yogurt advertisements in different societies.

Figure 19-4 Advertisers use a variety of techniques to communicate with consumers.

COMMON ADVERTISING TECHNIQUES

PRODUCT QUALITY ADS present the quality, brand, price, or features of a product.

COMPARATIVE ADS contrast the features of competing brands.

EMOTIONAL ADS attempt to obtain a response from consumers by appealing to feelings or needs and desires, such as fear, guilt, love, beauty, pleasure, convenience, safety, power, status, or security.

HUMOROUS ADS use comedy to draw attention to a product or service.

LIFESTYLE ADS present a product or service in a situation to which people can relate, such as at home, at work, or in recreational settings.

ENDORSEMENT ADS make use of famous or ordinary people as spokespersons for a product, service, or company. These are also called testimonial advertising.

STEP 3 SELECT MEDIA

Marketers must decide what media to use to deliver the advertising message. The major advertising media include newspaper, television, radio, magazine, direct mail, outdoor, and Internet.

The availability of advertising media varies considerably among the nations of the world. For example, Turkey has over 300 newspapers with varied political positions, while other countries have less than 20. In the past, advertising in movie theaters was important in countries with limited commercial television, such as India and Nigeria.

Newspaper Advertising Most people do not realize that a very significant portion of advertising dollars is spent on advertising in newspapers. In addition to store ads throughout the newspaper, think too about the classified ads in which thousands of people pay to promote jobs and garage sales, as well as used cars and pets for sale. Many of these classified ads are moving to the Internet as newspapers use a combination of print and electronic editions of their publications.

With expanded international business, some newspapers have created regional editions for different geographic areas. *The Wall Street Journal,* for example, has Latin American, European, and Asian editions.

Television Advertising   Television commercials can have a strong effect on potential customers. Nonetheless, some nations limit the time available for television advertising. However, expansion of cable and satellite television systems makes it easier for advertisers. Channels such as CNN, ESPN, and MTV are available to billions of viewers.

Radio Advertising   Radio advertising can be adapted to changing marketplace needs faster than most other media. Radio is frequently more available than other communication methods. Nations with few television sets or with people who can't read are likely to make greater use of radio.

Magazine Advertising   Magazines, like newspapers, encourage international advertising by creating regional editions. *Business Week* has specific editions for Europe, Asia, and Latin America. *National Geographic* also covers these regions along with separate editions for Africa and the Middle East. *Reader's Digest* publishes over 45 different editions in 19 languages with more than 100 million readers around the world.

Direct Mail   Each day hundreds of millions of ads and catalogs fill the mailboxes of the world. Technology fosters increased use and reduced costs of direct mail advertising. **Database marketing** is the use of computerized information systems to identify customers with specific demographic traits and buying habits. With a database, direct mail marketers can target potential customers to receive appropriate advertisements. For example, families in a database who have computers in their homes might receive mailings selling software for children to learn a foreign language.

Outdoor Advertising   Billboards and transit ads on buses and trains are common in most countries. The use of this advertising medium, however, is usually limited to high-traffic and urban areas. In recent years creativity and technology have expanded outdoor advertising to include mechanical characters and three-dimensional displays.

Internet Advertising   The World Wide Web has created a new way for advertisers to communicate with existing and potential customers. Companies have their own web sites on which they promote their products. Some companies use banner ads on other web sites. And some companies use a variation on direct mail by sending e-mail messages to target customers to promote product offerings. This electronic media has the potential visual impact of television along with the flexibility of radio and

WORK AS A GROUP

Describe advertisements and television commercials. Determine what features of the product made it something you wanted to purchase.

NET Bookmark

In 1957, a market researcher named James M. Vicary conducted a six-week test in a New Jersey movie theater. He claimed that the results of the test proved that subliminal stimuli were an effective means of advertising. Even though Vicary's methods have been discredited, many companies still use subliminal messages. Access intlbizxtra.swlearning.com and click on the link for Chapter 19. Do you think that advertisers should use subliminal messages? Why or why not?

intlbizxtra.swlearning.com

E-COMMERCE IN ACTION

Banners, Buttons, and E-Mail Blasts

"Click Here to Speed Up Your Web Searches." "Low-Rate Credit Cards." "Win a Free Vacation."

These phases are just a few of the many promotions taking online advertising to new levels of creativity—and irritation. *Banners* are interactive advertisements across the tops or bottoms of search engine pages and other web sites. *Buttons* are the smaller "click here" areas that attempt to get Internet users to visit another section of a web site. Banners and buttons are designed to get users to take action—such as requesting additional information or making an online purchase.

The *e-mail blast* is another online promotion. This technique involves sending promotional messages to many potential customers. People may be reminded of special offers or new products.

Customers continue to have concerns about online security and privacy. However, promotional efforts in cyberspace will expand to attract both new and repeat buyers.

Think Critically

1. What types of promotions, which were not available in the past, have the Internet made possible?
2. Locate a web site with examples of online promotions. What are the potential benefits and drawbacks of this type of advertising?

direct mail. As the Internet evolves, companies are trying to decide how best to take advantage of this type of media.

STEP 4 EXECUTE AND EVALUATE

Once advertising is planned, it must be executed. The advertising plan should include a schedule for the ideal launch time of the campaign. For example, a new line of winter clothing would be advertised at the beginning of (or a little before) the winter season. The advertis-

©Jeremy Horner/CORBIS

ing effort would not be as effective if launched halfway through the selling season. In addition, most advertising must consider the lead times involved in executing the program. Magazine advertising, for example, may have to be planned a month or more in advance of the publication of the advertisement.

After the advertising is executed, it should also be evaluated for effectiveness. Surveys may be conducted to test product awareness, and sales figures should be analyzed to determine whether the advertising caused an increase in sales. Information from the evaluation is then used to plan more effective advertising in the future.

✓ CheckPoint

What are the four steps in the advertising planning process?

USING AN ADVERTISING AGENCY

Some companies have their own advertising department to do promotional activities. However, most multinational companies use the services of an advertising agency. An **advertising agency** is a company that specializes in planning and implementing advertisements. Companies use advertising agencies to benefit from the agencies' experience in promoting different kinds of products and services in varied markets. A multinational company would choose an agency with broad experience in global markets to be assured of effective global promotions.

Most of the large advertising agencies in the world are located in the United States, Tokyo, and Europe. These organizations usually have the following four main divisions.

1. The research department studies the target market and measures the effectiveness of advertisements.
2. The creative department develops the message and the artistic features to deliver the message.
3. The media department selects where and when the advertising will be presented.
4. Account services is the link between the agency and the client (the company selling the product).

✓ CheckPoint

Why would a company use an advertising agency?

©Getty Images/PhotoDisc

REVIEW GLOBAL BUSINESS TERMS

Define each of the following terms.

1. standardized advertising
2. localized advertising
3. database marketing
4. advertising agency

REVIEW GLOBAL BUSINESS CONCEPTS

5. What goals should an advertising message accomplish?
6. What are the seven main media used by advertisers?
7. What are the main divisions of an advertising agency?

SOLVE GLOBAL BUSINESS PROBLEMS

For each of the following international business situations, decide if the company should take a standardized or localized advertising approach.

8. Selling cameras and film in Africa, Asia, and Australia.
9. Promoting computers among small business owners in 140 countries.
10. Advertising soaps and personal care products in various regions of the world.
11. Promoting a juice drink with different flavors for different cultures.
12. Selling different colored clothing styles in South America and Asia.

THINK CRITICALLY

13. How does each division of an advertising agency correlate with the four steps in the advertising planning department?

MAKE CONNECTIONS

14. **TECHNOLOGY** Select an example of advertising on a web site. Describe the message, identify the intended audience, and evaluate the effectiveness of this promotion.

15. **LAW** What actions might a government take to prevent deceptive and false advertising?

©Brand X Pictures

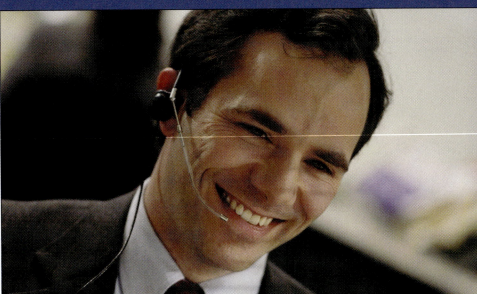

GLOBAL SELLING AND SALES PROMOTIONS

19-3

GOALS

- Summarize the personal selling process used in international business.

- Discuss the use of public relations and sales promotion by multinational companies.

©Getty Images/PhotoDisc

PERSONAL SELLING

Consumers encounter salespeople in stores, on the phone, at their doors, and at their places of work. Personal selling is direct communication between sellers and potential customers.

PERSONAL SELLING ACTIVITIES

Personal selling involves activities to promote and sell goods and services. These duties include locating customers, taking orders, processing orders, providing information, and offering customer assistance.

In the past, most personal selling took place in face-to-face settings. Today, however, telemarketing has increased in importance. **Telemarketing** involves the selling of products during telephone calls to prospective customers. Personal selling over the telephone allows businesses to contact potential customers quickly and at a low cost. This selling method is most commonly used for insurance, investments, credit cards, magazine subscriptions, books, videos, personal care products, and home improvements.

THE PERSONAL SELLING PROCESS

The ability to plan and execute a sales presentation is important in many career fields. The personal selling process may be viewed in five steps.

Step 1 Identify Customers In step 1 of the personal selling process, potential customers are identified. Names of prospects may come

Figure 19-5 Personal selling involves the ability to plan and make a sales presentation.

THE PERSONAL SELLING PROCESS

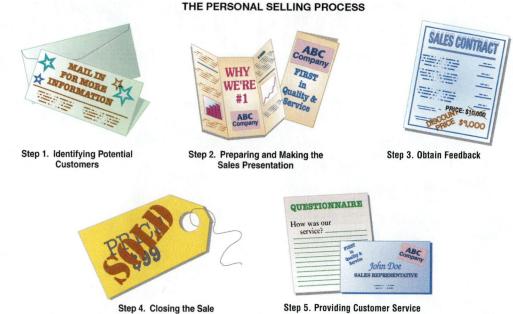

Step 1. Identifying Potential Customers

Step 2. Preparing and Making the Sales Presentation

Step 3. Obtain Feedback

Step 4. Closing the Sale

Step 5. Providing Customer Service

©Getty Images/PhotoDisc

from computer databases, current customer lists, telephone calls, referrals from employees, mail-in coupons, and many other sources.

This first step, *prospecting*, is the foundation of successful personal selling. Qualified prospects are usually identified based on age, income, occupation, or interests. A company selling golf equipment would contact people who regularly participate in that sport.

Step 2 Prepare a Presentation Step 2 of the personal selling process involves preparing and making the sales presentation. In this stage, a creative and effective product description and demonstration must be prepared. The sales presentation should highlight a product's main features, positive traits, and marketplace acceptance. For instance, one hotel chain demonstrated its room features to potential customers by presenting a simulated room inside a truck trailer.

In the sales presentation, specific information is provided to address the needs and wants of customers. For example, some automobile buyers are interested in the performance of a vehicle, while others identify style as the most desired product attribute.

Step 3 Obtain Feedback The third phase of the personal selling process involves obtaining feedback. A salesperson is looking for objections, or opposition, to the product. Awareness of objections allows the salesperson to provide additional information to overcome perceived negative aspects of the product.

Objections may be addressed either by clarifying some aspect of the sales presentation or by changing the conditions of the sale. For example, if a customer likes everything about a product except the color and style, a reduced price may eliminate these objections.

Step 4 Close the Sale Once major objections are overcome, the closing of the sale should occur. In step 4, the salesperson asks the customer to commit to the purchase. Questions such as the following are commonly used to close a sale.

- Is this the style you were thinking about buying?
- If we can deliver it in three days, would you be interested?
- Would you like the item in blue?
- If we include the extended warranty, would that meet your needs?

Favorable responses to questions of this type can result in the completion of the sale.

Step 5 Provide Customer Service Finally, personal selling should not end when the sale is closed. Customer needs continue with operating instructions, repairs, and additional products. Customer service efforts by companies have increased in importance in recent years. Research studies reveal that keeping existing customers is less expensive than finding new ones. As a result, businesses work to communicate regularly with their customers.

Relationship marketing attempts to create a long-term, mutually beneficial buyer-seller relationship. Examples of these efforts include following up with customers to ensure satisfaction, sending notices of special sales and reduced prices, and creating frequent-buyer programs to earn bonus gifts or special services.

PERSONAL SELLING IN INTERNATIONAL MARKETS

Global managers need salespeople with product knowledge who are able to work in the social and cultural context of a country. International companies have three choices when selecting sales staff members—expatriates, local nationals, and third-country nationals.

Expatriates are employees living and working in a country other than their home nation. Multinational companies use expatriates when the available number of host country salespeople is limited. Expatriate salespeople are probably familiar with their companies and products. However, they may not be acquainted with a nation's culture and social customs. For example, getting right down to business may be accepted in some societies. In other

---

GLOBAL BUSINESS EXAMPLE

COLGATE'S PROMOTIONAL EFFORTS IN THAILAND

To become the largest selling toothpaste in Thailand, Colgate-Palmolive used a variety of promotional activities for its Colgate toothpaste. First, the company used the *Nok Lae* Children in its television commercials. This popular singing group was well known among young consumers and families and emphasized Thai heritage in the advertising.

After the commercials attracted much attention for Colgate, the company distributed printed information about proper dental hygiene. Colgate then made drinking cups, notebooks, posters, and audiocassettes highlighting both the singing group and the company's product. This led to the creation of the Colgate New Generation Kid's Club, whose members received a free dental checkups, bumper stickers, buttons, and other items.

Think Critically

1. What are the social and economic benefits of Colgate's action in Thailand?
2. Go to the web site of Colgate to obtain additional information about the company's international activities.

cultures, business associates are expected to get to know each other on a personal level before conducting business.

As the demand for international business employees increases, companies must expand the pool of workers. Organizations are using more people from within the targeted country to sell products and services in that country. *Local nationals* are employees based in their home country. Because local nationals are familiar with the culture, their training usually emphasizes product knowledge.

A third source of international salespeople involves those with a broad global viewpoint. *Third-country nationals* are citizens of one country employed by a company from another country who work in a third country. These salespeople frequently are able to speak several languages and possess a highly developed sense of cultural sensitivity. An example of a third-country national would be a German working in Chile for an Italian company.

Sales managers and other executives of Samsung, South Korea's largest company, attend a month-long training camp before starting an assignment in another country. This culturally sensitive instruction covers language, eating habits, leisure activities, clothing styles, and cultural values. The program has helped Samsung managers, who work in more than 50 countries, avoid social blunders.

✔ CheckPoint

How do salespeople overcome customer objections?

OTHER INTERNATIONAL PROMOTIONAL ACTIVITIES

Advertising and personal selling are a large portion of an organization's promotional efforts. However, other types of promotions address various marketing objectives.

PUBLIC RELATIONS

Companies are continually concerned about communicating a favorable public image. Companies can gain publicity with press releases, company newsletters, and sponsorship of sporting and entertainment events. A company may take actions such as the following to improve or keep its image.

©Getty Images/PhotoDisc

- Hewlett-Packard Company donated computers to the University of Prague, in the Czech Republic.
- H. J. Heinz funded infant nutrition studies in China and Thailand.
- DuPont sent water-jug filters to African nations to remove dangerous impurities from drinking water.

GLOBAL SALES PROMOTIONS

As noted earlier, sales promotions comprise all promotional activities other than advertising, personal selling, and publicity. These communication efforts attract attention and stimulate demand for a company's products.

Coupons Over 300 billion coupons are distributed each year in the United States. The use of money-off coupons is also expanding around the world. Over 6 billion coupons are distributed each year in the United Kingdom. In Italy and Spain, most coupons are right on the package rather than distributed through newspapers, magazines, or the mail. In Belgium, door-to-door distribution is most common. The use of coupons as a promotion was just legalized in Denmark in recent years.

Premiums For more than 50 years, consumers have bought Cracker Jack, looking forward to the toy surprise inside. Food packages commonly include sports cards, toys, or other items to attract buyers. Many fast-food restaurants offer children's toys with a purchase.

Contests and Sweepstakes "You may already be a winner" is a common promotional slogan. Everything from a free bottle of ketchup to trips around the world are offered as prizes when companies want to attract attention to their products. Many contests are used to create a database of customer information.

Contests can result in problems, however. Pepsi-Cola used a contest promotion to attract attention to its soft drink in Chile. The results were not what the company expected. Chileans could win from $14 to $30,000 depending on the amount next to the prize number under the bottle cap. Pepsi expected to award 40 prizes over an eight-week period. However, when 688 was announced as the winning number instead of the planned 588, more than 100 people demanded prizes. Many of the people who thought they were winners had already started spending their prize money. Two brothers who came to claim $17,000 did not have money for the 40-mile trip home. Pepsi and its advertising agency eventually worked out an arrangement with all the winners. Contests may be highly regulated in some countries.

©Getty Images/PhotoDisc

Point-of-Purchase Promotions
The use of in-store advertising continues to increase. Electronic exhibits, television monitors, and display screens on shopping carts attempt to influence customers to select a product or brand at the point of purchase.

Specialty Advertising Look around home or school, and you will see the names of organizations almost everywhere. You will see pens, key chains, calendars, notepads, briefcases, ice-cream scoops, drinking cups, towels, T-shirts, baseball caps, and golf balls with advertising messages. These promotional items keep a company's name and products in the eyes and minds of consumers.

REGIONAL PERSPECTIVE

CULTURE: PROMOTIONAL EFFORTS EXPAND SOCCER'S POPULARITY

By almost all estimates, soccer is the most popular sport in the world. Each year, more than 20 million organized soccer matches are played. Major tournaments are held on three continents. The European Cup is the goal of European soccer players. In South America, teams compete for the Liberator's Cup. The Cup of Nations and the Cup of Champion Clubs are the ambition of African nations. In 2002, nearly 2 billion television viewers watched the World Cup Final.

©Getty Images/PhotoDisc

In most countries, the game is referred to as *football*. Soccer was introduced to the United States in the late 1800s. However, it was not until 1959 that the National Collegiate Athletic Association (NCAA) recognized it as an official collegiate sport. Today more than 15 million athletes in the United States under the age of 19 are involved in organized soccer programs.

The global popularity of soccer continues to expand. In the mid-1990s, Japan started its first professional soccer league. Companies such as Mitsubishi, Mazda, Nissan, Toyota, Ford Japan, WordPerfect Japan, and Coca-Cola Japan sponsored teams. Promotional efforts are expected to result in extensive ticket sales for games. Television advertising, soccer magazine subscriptions, and sales of products featuring players and team logos are a major promotional feature of Japanese soccer activities.

Think Critically
1. How do advertising and other promotions contribute to the growth in popularity of soccer?
2. Conduct an Internet search for additional information about efforts to promote soccer in various countries.

✓ CheckPoint

What are five common types of sales promotions used by companies?

REVIEW GLOBAL BUSINESS TERMS

Define each of the following terms.

1. telemarketing

2. relationship marketing

REVIEW GLOBAL BUSINESS CONCEPTS

3. What duties are involved in personal selling?

4. What are the five steps of the personal selling process?

5. How do salespeople who are expatriates differ from local nationals?

6. What are common sales promotions used by companies?

SOLVE GLOBAL BUSINESS PROBLEMS

What qualifications would a salesperson look for in prospective customers when selling the following items?

7. Vacation homes in the Caribbean.

8. Computer software for teaching children at home in Peru.

9. Men's and women's business suits in Thailand.

10. Investment plans for retirement funds in Scotland.

11. Health-club memberships in Egypt.

THINK CRITICALLY

12. Explain how frequent-buyer programs can benefit both companies and customers.

13. Create a promotional contest that could be used in many countries without having to make major changes to the procedures.

MAKE CONNECTIONS

14. **TECHNOLOGY** How can the Internet be used in the personal selling process?

15. **CULTURAL STUDIES** Describe differences in personal selling activities that might be necessary when doing business in various countries.

16. **GEOGRAPHY** What are possible limitations of Internet promotions in some countries?

©Getty Images/PhotoDisc

CHAPTER SUMMARY

19-1 GLOBAL COMMUNICATIONS AND PROMOTIONS

A The elements of the communication process include the source, encoding, a message, a medium, decoding, an audience noise, and feedback.

B The elements of the promotional mix are advertising, personal selling, publicity, and sales promotion.

19-2 PLANNING GLOBAL ADVERTISING

A Planning advertising for global markets involves analyzing the target market, creating a message, selecting media, and executing and evaluating.

B Many companies use advertising agencies because they have experience in promoting different kinds of products and services in different markets. Advertising agencies usually have four divisions: research, creative, media, and account services.

19-3 GLOBAL SELLING AND SALES PROMOTIONS

A The personal selling process for international business involves identifying potential customers, preparing and making the sales presentation, obtaining feedback, closing the sale, and providing customer service.

B Public relations involves communicating a favorable public image with the use of press releases, newsletters, and sponsorship of events. Sales promotion by multinational companies may involve coupons, premiums, contests and sweepstakes, point-of-purchase promotions, and specialty advertising.

GLOBAL REFOCUS

Read the Global Focus at the beginning of this chapter, and answer the following questions.

1. What promotional efforts have contributed to the success of Unilever in global markets?

2. How might Unilever use technology to address new competitive pressures in global markets?

REVIEW GLOBAL BUSINESS TERMS

Match the terms listed with the definitions.

1. Direct communication between sellers and potential customers.

2. Promotional efforts directed at the final users of an item.

3. Promotional activities other than advertising, personal selling, and publicity.

4. A company that specializes in planning and implementing advertisements.

5. Any form of paid, nonpersonal sales communication.

6. An attempt to create a long-term, mutually beneficial buyer-seller relationship.

7. The use of one promotional approach in all geographic regions.

8. The use of computerized information systems to identify customers with specific demographic traits and buying habits.

a. advertising

b. advertising agency

c. database marketing

d. localized advertising

e. personal selling

f. promotional mix

g. publicity

h. pull promotions

i. push promotions

j. relationship marketing

k. sales promotion

l. standardized advertising

m. telemarketing

9. Any form of unpaid promotion, such as newspaper articles or television news coverage.

10. Promotional efforts directed at members of the distribution channel.

11. The combination of advertising, personal selling, publicity, and sales promotion used by an organization.

12. The use of promotions that are customized for various target markets.

13. The selling of products during telephone calls to prospective customers.

MAKE GLOBAL BUSINESS DECISIONS

14. List examples of noise that can reduce the effectiveness of communication in your classroom, in your home, and in stores.

15. Describe marketing situations in other nations in which sales promotions or publicity would be used more effectively than advertising or personal selling.

©Getty Images/PhotoDisc

16. Why would a company use push promotions instead of pull promotions?

17. Describe examples of advertisements that use the endorsement method.

18. Name some products that could be best promoted using standardized advertising. What types of products would require localized advertising?

19. What advantages could third-country nationals have over expatriates and local nationals when applying for a sales manager position with a multinational company?

20. How important is publicity to the success of a company?

21. List examples of specialty advertising you see in your home, school, and community.

GLOBAL CONNECTIONS

22. GEOGRAPHY Collect advertisements that reflect different areas of the world. Explain how these images are used by the company to promote its product or service.

23. COMMUNICATIONS Create an idea for a product or service demonstration that allows the potential customer to see, hear, or touch some aspect of the item.

24. CULTURAL STUDIES Analyze television commercials with the sound off to determine how much of the information presented is visual.

25. TECHNOLOGY Conduct an Internet search or library research about the availability of television, radio, newspaper, and the Internet in selected countries. Choose nations in different geographic regions and with different levels of economic development.

26. COMMUNICATIONS Describe possible differences in consumer reactions to television commercials and online advertisements.

27. CAREER PLANNING Find an advertisement from a company that sells its goods or services around the world. Prepare a poster or bulletin board display that identifies the various careers involved in planning and executing the ad.

28. CAREER PLANNING Talk to a person who works in personal selling. What skills are important for success in this career field?

©Getty Images/PhotoDisc

THE GLOBAL
ENTREPRENEUR
CREATING AN INTERNATIONAL BUSINESS PLAN

CREATING A GLOBAL PROMOTIONAL MIX

Develop a promotional plan based on the company and country you have been using in this continuing project, or create a new idea for your business in the same or a different country. Make use of previously collected information, and do additional research. This phase of your business plan should include the following components.

1. A description of the product's target market
2. Examples of advertisements that would be appropriate for the company
3. An explanation of the different advertising media used by the company
4. Examples of Internet promotions that might be used by the company
5. A description of personal selling activities that the company could use to promote its good or service
6. An explanation of how publicity could help the company or product's image
7. Types of sales promotions that would be most appropriate for this situation.

Prepare a written summary or present a short oral report (two or three minutes) of your findings.

©Getty Images/PhotoDisc

GLOBAL CROSS-CULTURAL TEAM PROJECT

Plan International Marketing Activities

Decisions regarding products, pricing, promotion, and distribution may be some of the most difficult international business activities. Marketing is commonly influenced by the cultural values and social trends in a country. The use of cross-cultural teams can help an organization better adapt its marketing plans to the consumers in diverse societies.

GOAL

To analyze influences on marketing activities in a region of the world.

ACTIVITIES

Working in teams of 3 to 6 students, select a geographic region you will represent—Africa, Asia, Europe, Latin America, the Middle East, or North America.

1. To obtain marketing information from countries in your region, try to talk to people who have lived in or visited the area. View products, packages, labels, and advertising from the region. Some of these items may be available in local stores or online. Finally, library sources can be of value.
2. Identify products unique to your geographic region. What factors influence the demand for these goods and services?
3. List examples of customs, traditions, and cultural behavior that affect consumer buying in this region.
4. Research pricing activities in the region. What influences the amount people are willing and able to pay for various items? To what extent are prices negotiated for various purchases?
5. Describe the common promotional activities in your region. How do these compare with advertising and sales promotions in other areas of the world?
6. **Global Business Decision** Your team has been selected to advise an international organization that plans to distribute low-cost clothing in various regions of the world. What types of transportation modes would be most effective in your region? How would the distribution costs in your region compare with those in other geographic areas? What other factors would need to be considered?

TEAM SKILL

Resolving Cross-Cultural Team Conflict
Differences of opinion are inevitable in almost every team situation. What are some common areas of team conflict that might arise in your region? How are conflicts commonly resolved in that geographic area?

PRESENT

Create a display, using product samples, labels, packages, ads, foreign currency, and other items, to communicate marketing activities in your region.

Emerging Business Issues

Emerging Business Issues is a team event that involves 2-3 members. Interdependence in a global economy has both positive and negative implications. International trade has increased sales for agricultural products, technology, and automobiles. International trade involves a system of give/take between trade partners.

Political unrest, economic conditions, cultural differences, and trade barriers influence international trade. NAFTA (North American Free Trade Agreement) was passed with the intention of strengthening international trade among North American countries. This policy has received praise from proponents and criticism from opponents.

During election years much attention is given to international trade. Issues range from outsourcing of jobs to financial benefits of expanded markets. NAFTA is an agreement that has positive and negative arguments. You are assigned to research the NAFTA agreement to determine the pros or cons for the agreement. Your presentation should be so thorough that the audience will make a choice to defend/oppose the NAFTA agreement. The best presentation should include facts to support your position. Your presentation must include facts that support the position you draw.

Your assignment requires you to conduct research about NAFTA. Be prepared to list the pros and cons of this policy. Use 4" by 6" note cards to record your findings about NAFTA.

Your team will draw either "pros" or "cons" fifteen minutes before your presentation. The team has fifteen minutes to put together the final 5-minute presentation. After the 5-minute presentation, team members must be prepared for five minutes of questions from the judges or audience.

PERFORMANCE INDICATORS EVALUATED

- Explain the "pros" or "cons" of NAFTA with facts gathered from research.
- Define NAFTA.
- Present information in a logical manner.
- Respond appropriately to follow-up questions.

For more detailed information about performance indicators, go to the FBLA web site.

THINK CRITICALLY

1. What is NAFTA?
2. List three "pros" for NAFTA.
3. List three "cons" for NAFTA.
4. How does NAFTA influence the economies of participating countries?

www.fbla-pbl.org/

IF YOU WERE THERE

Zainab is a young Iraqi woman who is studying to be an archaeologist at a university in Baghdad. During both the 1980–1988 war with Iran and the war with the 28-nation coalition after Iraq invaded Kuwait, Zainab feared for the safety of the ancient ruins. Her recent visit to the site of the Mesopotamian capital of Babylon calmed her fears of large-scale damage to the ruins. The famous Ishtar gate, the remains of the tower of Babel, and the remains of Nebuchadnezzar II's palace had not been damaged.

Zainab's study of history has made her deeply aware of this land between the Tigris and Euphrates Rivers. Known as Mesopotamia, this area allowed farmers to produce a surplus of food as early as 4000 B.C. About 500 years later, Sumerians moved into the area and established 12 city-states. The Sumerians invented cuneiform (a type of writing), the wagon wheel, the 12-month calendar, and the metal plow.

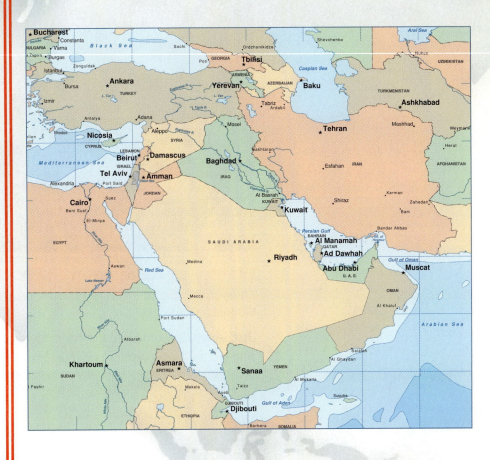

Geography

The area known as the Middle East includes countries on three continents. The Near East consists of a few additional countries that have cultures similar to the Middle East countries, primarily because of the predominance of the Islamic religion. The Middle East is bordered by several bodies of water, including the Mediterranean Sea, the Black Sea, the Caspian Sea, the Red Sea, the Persian Gulf, the Arabian Sea, and the Indian Ocean. It is home to about 262 million people; holds almost 60 percent of the world's supply of oil; and is the site of continuous political, ethnic, and religious conflicts.

Status of Women

Zainab knows that in some nations of the Middle East, the conditions under which women live are extremely restrictive when compared to those in Europe and the United States. They must cover their heads and faces, they may not drive a car, and they may not vote. However, Zainab is aware that women in Iraq have enjoyed greater rights since the revolution of 1958. In several Middle East countries, women continue their struggle to achieve equality of rights.

©Getty Images/PhotoDisc

History of Religion in the Middle East

Three major monotheistic religions—Judaism, Christianity, and Islam—began in the Middle East.

Judaism According to the Torah, Judaism can be traced back to Abraham, who led the Hebrews from the Mesopotamian city of Ur west to the land of

©Getty Images/PhotoDisc

Canaan. The Hebrews believe that God made a covenant with Abraham. In return for their faithfulness to God, they would be protected and made a great nation. The Hebrews migrated to Egypt, where they lived for many years before being enslaved by the pharaohs. In the twelfth century B.C., Moses led the Hebrews in an exodus from Egypt into the Sinai Desert, where they believe that God renewed the covenant and gave them the Ten Commandments. At this time, they became Jews, or "God's chosen." Eventually they returned to Canaan and established the kingdom of Israel with its capital at Jerusalem.

Christianity By the time Jesus was born, the Roman Empire had control over much of the Middle East. The Jews were treated poorly by the Romans, and many of them looked forward to a savior who would restore their kingdom. According to the Bible, about 26 to 30 A.D., Jesus preached a new message to the Jews in Palestine. He told them to love one another just as they love themselves. His followers believed he was the long-awaited messiah, or savior, while others thought he was an imposter and accused him of blasphemy. The Romans believed that Jesus might cause civil strife or even political rebellion. He was arrested as a troublemaker and crucified. After his death, his followers said that he had risen from the dead and called him the Son of God. Those who believed this to be true called themselves Christians, and they began spreading Jesus' teachings and their beliefs throughout the world.

Islam Zainab, like the majority of the people of the Middle East, is a Muslim. Muslims are followers of the religion of Islam. According to the Islamic holy book, the Koran, the Islamic religion was founded on the Arabian Peninsula in

©Getty Images/PhotoDisc

622 A.D. The nation of Saudi Arabia accounts for most of the peninsula today; however, when Islam was founded, the area consisted of many separate Arab tribes. The city of Mecca was a center of trade and pagan worship, and it is where the founder of Islam, the prophet Muhammad, claimed God first spoke to him and revealed the Koran.

Beginning in 613 A.D., Muhammad began preaching that there was just one God, Allah, and people had to worship and obey him or else they would be punished. He also said that Allah's followers were equal and that the rich must help the poor. Many among the poor welcomed his message, but the merchants of Makkah forced him to flee in 622. This year of Hijrah, or emigration, is considered the first year of the Islamic calendar. Muhammad found success in the city of Medina,

©Getty Images/PhotoDisc

where he was given authority in religious and political matters. Thus began the Islamic state that was based on a system similar to that of the Islamic Republic of Iran. In 630 A.D., Muhammad defeated the Meccans in battle and took control of their city.

After Muhammad's death, Caliphs, or successors, were elected to lead the political-religious community and to spread the teachings of Islam. The Caliphs sent armies to the Byzantine and Persian empires to bring converts and wealth to the growing empire. By 750 A.D., the Islamic Empire stretched from the Indus River in Asia across North Africa and into most of Spain.

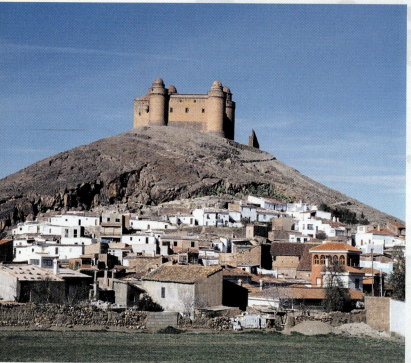

©Getty Images/PhotoDisc

Post-World War II Era

Following World War II, the complex geopolitical forces that operated in the Middle East involved the conflicted interests of the Soviet Union and the United States. Since the creation of the Jewish state of Israel in 1948, the ongoing wars between the Arabs and the Israelis were the most obvious problem. Israel received billions of dollars from the United States in foreign aid, and the Soviet Union supplied weapons and advisers to some Arab countries. Other sources of great interest to outsiders are the region's strategic waterways and the abundant oil supplies in the Persian Gulf region.

Economics of the Middle East

The Persian Gulf countries continue to enjoy the benefits of their oil industries, but many countries in the Middle East are not so fortunate. Most economies, with the exception of Israel and Turkey, do not have strong industrial bases. The region suffers from an inadequate base of skilled and professional labor, insufficient transportation facilities, religious and ethnic conflicts, and the absence of a reliable supply of fresh water.

In political developments, by 1993, the Israeli government had agreed to a peace plan with the Palestine Liberation Organization (PLO).

©Getty Images/PhotoDisc

In return, some Arab countries began to acknowledge Israel's right to exist. Despite this positive development, the situation in the region continues to be volatile. Zainab is hopeful for peace in a land that has experienced both widespread suffering and great enlightenment since the beginning of recorded Western history.

Think Critically

1. The Islamic religion has rules of daily living for its followers, as well as rules for behavior, dress, and food. How does this affect companies that wish to do business in the Middle East?
2. How does the inadequate base of skilled and professional labor affect the economies of countries in the Near and Middle East?
3. Use the library or do an Internet search to determine which Middle East countries produce the most oil. How do the per capita incomes of these countries compare to the other countries in the Near and Middle East?

COUNTRY PROFILE/NEAR AND MIDDLE EAST

Country	Population		GDP		Exports	Imports	Monetary Unit	Inflation	Unemployment	Life Expectancy	Literacy Rate
	thousands	growth rate	$billions	$ per capita	$billions			percent	percent	years	percent
Afghanistan	23,987	3.88	21	800	1.2	1.3	Afghani	N/A	N/A	46.97	36
Armenia	3,061	-0.45	11.2	3,350	0.35	0.77	Dram	1.1	20	66.68	98.6
Azerbaijan	8,370	0.89	27	3,300	2.08	1.47	Manat	2.6	1.2	63.16	97
Bahrain	724	2.17	8.4	13,000	5.55	4.01	Dinar	0.5	15	73.72	89.1
Cyprus	802	0.76	9.1	15,000	1	3.53	Pound	2.8	3.3-5.6	77.27	97.6
Egypt	71,931	1.99	258	3,700	7.03	13.7	Pound	4.3	12	70.41	57.7
Georgia	5,126	-0.92	15	3,100	0.46	0.97	Lari	5.2	17	64.76	99
Iran	68,920	1.24	456	7,000	28.4	15.2	Rial	15.3	16.3	69.35	79.4
Iraq	25,175	2.68	59	2,500	15.8	11	Dinar	70	N/A	67.81	40.4
Israel	6,433	2.02	122	19,000	27.7	30.9	New Shekel	5.7	10.4	79.02	95.4
Jordan	5,473	2.66	22.8	4,300	2.3	4.3	Dinar	3.3	16	77.88	91.3
Kazakhstan	15,433	-0.36	98.1	5,900	9.1	8.3	Tenge	6	8.8	63.48	98.4
Kuwait	2,521	3.46	30.9	15,100	16.2	6.93	Dinar	2	7	76.65	83.5
Kyrgyzstan	5,138	1.4	13.5	2,800	0.48	0.44	Som	2.1	7.2	63.66	97
Lebanon	3,653	1.56	18.8	5,200	0.7	6.6	Pound	3.5	18	72.07	87.4
Oman	2,851	2.93	21.5	8,200	11.1	5.31	Rial	-0.5	N/A	72.58	75.8
Qatar	610	1.54	16.3	21,200	11	3.5	Riyal	1.9	2.7	73.14	82.5
Saudi Arabia	24,217	2.92	241	10,600	73	28.6	Riyal	1	25	68.73	78.8
Syria	17,800	2.38	54.2	3,200	5.15	3.7	Pound	0.9	20	69.39	76.9
Tajikistan	6,245	0.86	7.5	1,140	0.64	0.7	Somoni	12	40	64.37	99.4
Turkey	71,325	1.42	468	7,000	34.4	38.9	Lira	45.2	10.8	71.8	86.5
Turkmenistan	4,867	1.54	21.5	4,700	0.77	1.01	Manat	5	N/A	61.19	98
United Arab Emirates	2,995	1.94	51	21,100	47.6	28.6	Dirham	2.8	N/A	74.75	77.9
Yemen	20,010	3.52	14.8	820	4.09	2.48	Rial	12.2	30	60.97	50.2

N/A = Data not available

Chapter 20

GLOBAL FINANCIAL ACTIVITIES

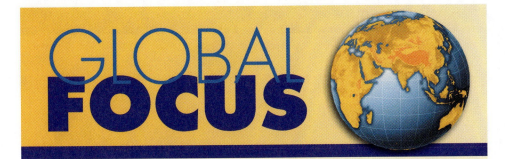

GLOBAL FOCUS

KOOR INDUSTRIES, LTD.

Koor Industries, based in Tel Aviv, is a diversified company involved in telecommunications, building supplies, metals, chemicals, food processing, tourism, and foreign trade. The company is a significant part of Israel's economy, at one time accounting for nearly 10 percent of the country's industrial output.

From its creation, the primary goal of Koor Industries was to provide employment. The company was never very profitable, and when economic conditions declined, the situation went from fair to poor. Sales revenue and profits declined, and Koor was unable to pay off loans when they were due.

In order to pay off debt, the company started to cut costs by closing factories and cutting staff. These cost reductions resulted in a 50 percent smaller workforce at Koor Industries.

When Koor faced bankruptcy, the Israeli government approved an IS275 million ($100 million) loan guarantee to help Koor out of its financial difficulties. In addition, the company decided to sell part ownership in some of its subsidiaries. The company is listed on both the Tel Aviv and New York Stock Exchanges. Obtaining funds by issuing stock also helped the company reduce its level of debt and improve its overall financial situation.

Think Critically

1. How did the cost reduction activities of Koor Industries affect the company?

2. What problems can occur during poor economic times for a company with high levels of debt?

3. Go to the web site of Koor Industries to obtain information regarding the company's current operations.

20-1 FINANCING GLOBAL BUSINESS OPERATIONS

GOALS

- Describe the flow of funds for international businesses.
- Identify types of global financial institutions.

©Getty Images/PhotoDisc

INTERNATIONAL FLOW OF FUNDS

A global clothing manufacturer plans to update its equipment. A computer company plans to expand into Egypt, Saudi Arabia, Israel, Turkey, and Iran. These plans, like every international business activity, require funding. International financing activities are necessary for a company to operate in the global business market.

In your daily life, you are probably aware of the fact that you and your family must have money coming in to cover living expenses (the money going out). The same is true for businesses. Financial operations involve two major activities—the receipt of money and the payment of money.

SOURCES OF FUNDS

Every company must have money to operate. Employees must be paid, operating expenses are incurred, and equipment must be purchased. Organizations have two main sources of funds, these are equity and debt.

Equity Capital The owners of a business are the initial source of financial resources. **Equity capital** consists of funds provided by a company's owners. Equity capital comes from several sources, including investments from owners, reinvested profits, sale of stock, and liquidation of company assets. The stock market is a major source of equity capital funds in the global economy.

Debt Capital When a company has limited equity capital sources, it must turn to outsiders. **Debt capital** involves funds obtained by borrowing.

Bank loans, bonds, and mortgages are examples of debt. The bond market is the main source of international debt capital.

The use of debt has advantages. First, debt allows a company to expand when equity funds are not available. Second, debt has tax benefits. The interest on loans is a business expense. Like other business expenses, interest payments reduce a company's net income and lower the amount paid in taxes. Third, debt doesn't affect the control of a company. Lenders do not have ownership in a company.

Despite advantages, debt also has risks. If a company cannot make its interest payments on what is borrowed or is unable to repay a loan, creditors may take control of the company.

Companies that have most of their sales during one part of the year often borrow money. For example, a company that manufactures summer clothing will have most of its sales concentrated in late winter and spring. Borrowing may be necessary in the summer, fall, and early winter months. The loans are then repaid during the main selling season as the company receives money.

Nations as well as individuals and businesses use debt. During the Persian Gulf War in the early 1990s, tourism to Egypt declined and Suez Canal receipts fell, which resulted in a lower national income for the country. Egypt had to borrow from financial institutions and other countries.

WORK AS A GROUP

List reasons why a company may borrow money.

USES OF FUNDS

The daily operations of a business also involve making payments for various business costs and other expenses. Current expenses and long-term costs are the two main uses of funds, as shown in Figure 20-1.

Current Expenses Current expenses include rent, materials, wages and salaries, utilities, repairs, advertising, supplies, and other items that keep a business operating from day to day. These expenses usually cover a period of one month to one year.

Long-Term Costs Some business costs cover longer periods of time. For example, a new building, heavy machinery, or a computer system will probably be paid for and used over several years. These long-term costs, also called *capital projects*, are necessary for companies to produce, store, and deliver goods and services.

FLOW OF FUNDS

Sources of Funds	Uses of Funds
• Equity capital	• Current expenses
• Debt capital	• Long-term costs

Figure 20-1 Every organization has money coming in and going out.

CheckPoint

What is the difference between current expenses and capital projects?

GLOBAL FINANCIAL INSTITUTIONS

Each day millions of financial transactions occur. These business activities use cash, checks, letters of credit, credit cards, countertrade, and other financial services. The different kinds of institutions illustrated in Figure 20-2 serve the financial needs of consumers and businesses.

Figure 20-2 Several financial institutions exist to serve the needs of consumers and businesses when they make financial transactions.

GLOBAL FINANCIAL INSTITUTIONS

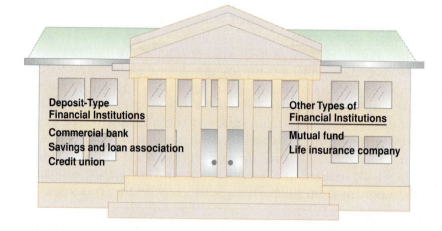

Deposit-Type Financial Institutions

Commercial bank
Savings and loan association
Credit union

Other Types of Financial Institutions

Mutual fund
Life insurance company

▌ DEPOSIT-TYPE FINANCIAL INSTITUTIONS

Most consumers are familiar with companies that are in business to receive money for deposit and then make that money available for personal and business purchases. These organizations are called *deposit-type* financial institutions.

Commercial Banks The financial institution with the most international business visibility is the commercial bank. A **commercial bank** is a business organized to accept deposits and to make loans. Traditionally, commercial banks offer the widest range of services of any financial institution. The main services offered by commercial banks are shown in Figure 20-3.

FINANCIAL SERVICES OF COMMERCIAL BANKS

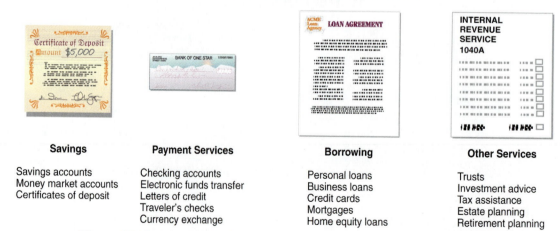

Savings	Payment Services	Borrowing	Other Services
Savings accounts	Checking accounts	Personal loans	Trusts
Money market accounts	Electronic funds transfer	Business loans	Investment advice
Certificates of deposit	Letters of credit	Credit cards	Tax assistance
	Traveler's checks	Mortgages	Estate planning
	Currency exchange	Home equity loans	Retirement planning

Figure 20-3 Commercial banks offer a wide range of services to meet the needs of consumers and businesses.

Services provided by banks differ throughout the world. In the United States, stock investments are usually made using a stockbroker or an online investment service. In contrast, traditionally, most British stock purchases are made through banks.

In recent years, the largest commercial banks in the world were based in Japan, France, Britain, Germany, Switzerland, China, and the Netherlands. Large commercial banks based in the United States include Citigroup, JP Morgan, Chase, Bank of America, Wells Fargo, and Bank One.

Savings and Loan Associations A **savings and loan association** traditionally specialized in savings accounts and home mortgages. As laws regulating financial institutions changed, savings and loan associations expanded the services they offered. Today these organizations provide checking accounts, auto loans, financial planning advice, and electronic banking.

In the United Kingdom, a financial institution comparable to the savings and loan association is the *Building Society*. As the name implies, this financial institution actively provides funds to finance buildings for businesses and home purchases by individuals.

Credit Unions *Cooperatives* are businesses owned by their members and operated for their benefit. A **credit union** is a nonprofit financial cooperative. Credit unions were originally organized based on various groups in society, such as places of employment, religious organizations, and community organizations. The consumer services offered by credit unions are comparable to most commercial banks.

Because of their nonprofit status, most credit unions offer slightly higher rates on savings and slightly lower rates for loans than do other financial institutions. Since most credit unions are community based, these organizations commonly provide more personalized service than do other financial institutions.

The World Council of Credit Unions reports that over 115 million people around the world are credit union members. Credit unions operate in nearly

GLOBAL BUSINESS EXAMPLE

THE TECHIMAN WOMEN'S MARKET CREDIT UNION

Most days for the market women of Techiman begin at sunup and continue until after sundown. The women sell multicolored fabrics and produce dried cassava (a starchy root), soup, furniture, and clothing. As many as 10,000 customers come to the Techiman market in Ghana on a Thursday or Friday.

The vendors in this market need money for stall fees, supplies, school fees, and day care. Before the creation of the Techiman Women's Market Credit Union, moneylenders were the main source of borrowed funds and charged as much as 50–60 percent interest. Now the more than 200 credit union members can borrow at 18 percent interest.

Think Critically

1. What services are commonly offered by credit unions?
2. Go to the web site of the World Council of Credit Unions to obtain current information about this organization. Write a summary of your findings.

80 countries, including Kenya, Ethiopia, Nigeria, Botswana, India, Singapore, Australia, New Zealand, Fiji, and most countries in Central and South America.

OTHER TYPES OF FINANCIAL INSTITUTIONS

The financial needs of consumers and businesses are also served by organizations that specialize in specific financial services.

Mutual Fund How would you like to be able to own stock in hundreds of companies while only investing a small amount of money? That's what is possible when you purchase shares in a mutual fund. A **mutual fund** is an investment company that manages a pool of funds from many investors.

A major benefit of a mutual fund is *diversification*. By pooling money from many investors, a mutual fund manager is able to invest in many types of stocks and/or bonds. This spreads out the risk for the investors and reduces the danger of losing all of one's money.

Over 8,000 different mutual funds exist in the United States. More than 90 million U.S. citizens own mutual funds. Mutual funds are available to meet a variety of investment goals. For example, someone who desires current earnings from investments selects an income fund. A *balanced fund* is designed to have an appropriate proportion of stocks and bonds, depending on current market conditions.

Global mutual funds allow investors to own the stock of companies in many countries. This method of international investing eliminates the high brokerage commissions and currency conversion fees of individual investments. Global mutual funds help reduce the risk of lost profits due to changes in exchange rates.

Other types of international mutual funds include regional funds. For example, a Latin American fund invests in companies with long-term growth in Central and South America. A Pacific fund would invest in companies in that region.

Life Insurance Company People throughout the world buy life

©Getty Images/PhotoDisc

insurance policies to protect family members and others from financial difficulties when a person dies. Insurance companies invest the money received from insurance premiums. Life insurance companies commonly lend these funds to large corporations and invest in commercial real estate. These actions make capital available to companies.

E-COMMERCE IN ACTION

Cyber Banks

Traditional banks face new competition from financial institutions operating online. Many Web banks usually require little or no minimum balance on checking accounts. Some Internet banks may pay higher interest on amounts in your checking account. While ATMs might not be readily available from some Web banks, these online financial companies usually offer banking and customer service over the telephone. Traditional banks have also expanded their financial services to offer services online.

Online banking also makes it possible to provide financial services to remote areas. In rural India, "virtual" banking is provided by ICICI with the use of the Internet and cellular telephone service.

When considering whether to use Internet banking services, consumers should to compare interest rates and costs of both online banks and traditional financial institutions. In addition, online customers should investigate the security systems and privacy policies of the Internet banks.

Think Critically

1. What actions should consumers take when considering whether to use online banking services?
2. Visit the web site of an online bank to obtain information about the services offered and the cost of these services. Make a list of these services and costs.

✓CheckPoint

What are examples of deposit-type financial institutions?

©Leif Skoogfors/CORBIS

REVIEW GLOBAL BUSINESS TERMS

Define each of the following terms.

1. equity capital
2. debt capital
3. commercial bank
4. savings and loan association
5. credit union
6. mutual fund

REVIEW GLOBAL BUSINESS CONCEPTS

7. How does equity capital differ from debt capital?
8. What are examples of current expenses encountered by most businesses?
9. What are the main financial institutions that specialize in specific financial services?
10. How do credit unions serve their members?
11. How does a mutual fund reduce financial risk?

SOLVE GLOBAL BUSINESS PROBLEMS

For each of the following situations, indicate if the company would make use of debt or equity funding.

12. A Mexican company will obtain funds from additional owners.
13. A company in Thailand plans to issue bonds to finance a new factory.
14. A company in Kenya is borrowing from a bank.
15. A Brazilian company is using a mortgage to finance the purchase of real estate.
16. A Belgian company is issuing additional shares of stock.

THINK CRITICALLY

17. How do higher interest rates increase the risk of using debt?
18. What factors influence the value of a mutual fund?

MAKE CONNECTIONS

19. **TECHNOLOGY** Locate a web site for a bank, a credit union, or another financial institution that provides services to consumers online. Describe the services available.
20. **HISTORY** Research events that changed the role of savings and loan associations in the United States during the 1980s.
21. **LAW** Conduct research to compare equity capital or debt capital as a legally binding obligation for a company.

GLOBAL FINANCIAL MARKETS

GOALS

- Describe how and where stocks are bought and sold.
- Describe factors that affect stock prices.

©Leif Skoogfors/CORBIS

GLOBAL STOCK MARKETS

International companies may borrow from financial institutions; however, they also raise funds by selling stock. Stock represents a share of ownership in an organization. Stockholders are the owners of a corporation who elect the board of directors. The board hires the officers who run the company.

MAJOR STOCK EXCHANGES

A **stock exchange** is a location where stocks are bought and sold. The New York Stock Exchange (NYSE) is the largest in the world. The stock of many multinational companies based in other countries (such as British Airways,

MAJOR COMPANIES TRADED ON SELECTED GLOBAL STOCK EXCHANGES

London

British Aerospace,
British Petroleum,
Rolls-Royce, Tesco,
Unilever

Tokyo

Canon, Fuji, Mazda,
Konica Minolta,
Nippon Steel, Sony

Euronext
(Amsterdam, Brussels,
Paris alliance)

Bic, Carrefour, Danone,
Euro Disney,
Michelin, Renault

Figure 20-4 Stock exchanges provide a location where shares of stock are bought and sold.

Nestlé, Royal Dutch/Shell, and Sony Corporation) is bought and sold on the New York Stock Exchange.

In addition to the NYSE, there are other major stock exchanges around the world, including Euronext (Paris, Amsterdam, and Brussels), Bombay, Copenhagen, Dusseldorf, Istanbul, London, Milan, Rio de Janeiro, Seoul, Stockholm, Taiwan, Tel Aviv, Toronto, and Zurich. Figure 20-4 on the preceding page shows some of these stock exchanges.

In total, more than 170 stock exchanges are in operation around the world. These include several in the African countries of Botswana, Ghana, Ivory Coast, Kenya, Namibia, Nigeria, Zambia, and Zimbabwe. Many of these stock markets started very small, with stock of less than 20 companies traded.

THE STOCK MARKET IN ACTION

Every hour of the day, investors buy and sell stocks. On the trading floor of the stock exchange and through computer systems, representatives of buyers and sellers interact to determine the prices of shares of stock. Figure 20-5 summarizes the main steps involved in a stock transaction.

The purchase of stock through a stock exchange commonly involves a stockbroker. A **stockbroker** is a person who buys and sells stocks and other investments for customers. *Full-service brokers* also provide information about current stock market trends and other types of investments.

To save money on transaction fees, investors have other choices. *Discount brokers* provide less service than a full-service broker and does not provide as much information and investment research assistance. *Online trading services*, such as E*trade and Ameritrade, offer investors low-cost commission fees.

Figure 20-5 Stocks are bought and sold at a stock exchange or online with prices determined by supply and demand.

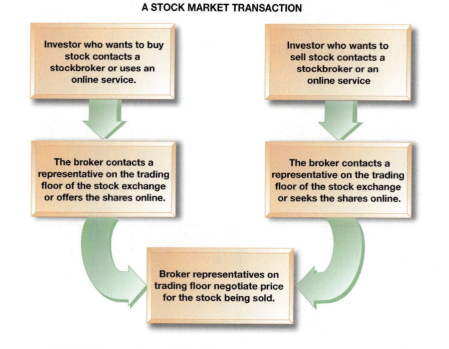

A STOCK MARKET TRANSACTION

Investor who wants to buy stock contacts a stockbroker or uses an online service.

Investor who wants to sell stock contacts a stockbroker or an online service

The broker contacts a representative on the trading floor of the stock exchange or offers the shares online.

The broker contacts a representative on the trading floor of the stock exchange or seeks the shares online.

Broker representatives on trading floor negotiate price for the stock being sold.

NETBookmark

Many people let fear of the stock market keep them from investing in it. Access intlbizxtra.swlearning.com and click on the link for Chapter 20. Navigate through the web site. When you think you understand how the stock market works, click on the simulation link and then the STOCKQUEST link to experience the stock market without the risks. What companies did you choose to invest in? Do you have more confidence to invest?

intlbizxtra.swlearning.com

Completely *computerized* stock trading stock exchanges, without trading floor representatives, are common today. These high-speed, low-cost automated systems are used by most major stock exchanges in Europe and Canada. Some of the world's largest screen-based systems for buying and selling global stocks are based in Europe. Computerized stock trading allows a broker in London to buy and sell stocks of multinational companies listed on stock exchanges in Bombay, Istanbul, Rio de Janeiro, Seoul, or Taiwan anytime, day or night.

GLOBAL BUSINESS EXAMPLE

THE PRAGUE STOCK EXCHANGE

On January 1, 1993, Czechoslovakia split into two separate countries—the Czech Republic and the Republic of Slovakia. As the countries moved from a central-planned economy under communist rule to a free-market economy, citizens were allowed to invest in stocks.

The Prague Stock Exchange (in the Czech Republic) started transactions in 1993 with only seven stocks. Within a few years, over 1,000 companies were offered to investors. Most of these enterprises were previously government-controlled busi-nesses that had been privatized. Some of the most popular stocks are companies in the hotel and glass manufacturing industries. The low inflation, low unemployment, low foreign debt, and high political stability of the 1990s created an economic environment that attracted many investors to make use of the Prague Stock Exchange.

Think Critically

1. What political and economic factors influenced the development of the Prague Stock Exchange?
2. Conduct an Internet search for web sites of foreign stock exchanges. Obtain information about current activities of a stock exchange in another country. Write a paragraph about your findings.

✓ CheckPoint

What are the differences between full-service brokers, discount brokers, and online trading services?

WORK AS A GROUP

Create news headlines that could cause stock prices to rise. Then create news headlines that could cause stock prices to decline.

STOCK MARKET PRICE INFORMATION

Stock prices are affected by many factors. The main influence on stock prices is demand for ownership in a company based on its current and future profitability. If people believe a company is a good investment, demand will cause the stock price to rise. In contrast, as fewer investors buy the stock of a company, its stock price will decline. In addition, economic conditions, the political situation, and social trends can influence stock prices.

After an agreement on price is reached, this information becomes public. Each day millions of stocks are bought and sold. Information about current stock prices, dividends, volume, and past prices are reported online and in newspapers. Figure 20-6 presents a sample of the stock market information reported every day.

REPORTING STOCK INFORMATION

NYSE 52 WEEKS		Stock	Sym.	Divd.	Yld %.	PE	Vol. 100s	High	Low	Close	Net Chg.
High	Low										
1	2	3	4	5	6	7	8	9	10	11	12
56^{50}	38^{25}	AmExpress	AXP	0.32	0.7	26	17226	49^{94}	48^{69}	49^{06}	$+^{25}$
43^{88}	23^{38}	Disney	DIS	0.21	0.5	85	33186	40^{25}	39^{25}	38^{88}	—
94^{63}	59^{75}	GenMotor	GM	2.00	2.8	8	74061	73	69^{81}	70^{44}	-1^{69}
49^{56}	29^{81}	McDonalds	MCD	0.2	0.5	27	31280	37^{94}	37^{19}	37^{75}	$+^{44}$
70^{25}	38^{88}	WalMart	WMT	0.24	0.4	41	39684	55	53^{13}	53^{88}	-1^{13}

Column	Explanation
1	Reports the highest price paid for one share of the stock over the past year.
2	Reports the lowest price paid for one share of the stock over the past year.
3	Lists the abbreviated name of the corporation.
4	Identifies the symbol used to report stock prices for the corporations in column 3.
5	Reports the dividends paid per share during the past 12 months.
6	Represents the yield percentage, which is the dividend divided by the current price of the stock.
7	Identifies the price-earnings ratio, which is computed by dividing the current price per share by the company's earnings (profits) per share over the last 12 months.
8	Reports the number of shares traded during the day, based on hundreds of shares.
9	States the highest price paid for one share on the trading day.
10	States the lowest price paid for one share on the trading day.
11	Reports the price paid for a share in the last stock purchase of the day.
12	Represents the difference between the price paid for the last share bought this day and the price for the last share bought on the previous trading day.

Figure 20-6 Current stock prices and other information on stock market activities are reported each business day in newspapers and online.

What is the main influence on stock prices?

REVIEW GLOBAL BUSINESS TERMS

Define each of the following terms.

1. stock exchange

2. stockbroker

REVIEW GLOBAL BUSINESS CONCEPTS

3. What is a stock exchange?

4. What services does a stockbroker provide?

5. What factors affect daily stock prices?

SOLVE GLOBAL BUSINESS PROBLEMS

For each of the following news items, tell what types of companies might be affected and how (higher or lower stock prices).

6. A country announces strict regulations to protect the environment.

7. A new food-processing system keeps foods fresh without refrigeration for several weeks.

8. Families are spending more time at home rather than going out for food and entertainment.

9. Scientists discover a device that makes an electric car more practical.

THINK CRITICALLY

10. What are the risks of buying and selling stocks online?

11. Describe how changes in economic conditions (lower interest rates or higher consumer spending) might affect stock prices.

MAKE CONNECTIONS

12. **TECHNOLOGY** Go to a web site that provides stock information to obtain the current price of shares for a company of interest to you.

13. **MATH** Refer to Figure 20-6 to answer the following questions.
   a. What was the highest price paid for a share of McDonald's stock during the past year?

   b. How many shares of WalMart were traded on this business day?

   c. What was the highest price paid for a share of Disney stock on this trading day?

   d. What was the closing price of General Motor's stock on the previous trading day?

   e. If a company pays an annual dividend of $2 per share and the stock sells for $50 a share, what is the yield percentage?

20-3 | INTERNATIONAL FINANCIAL MARKETS

GOALS

- Describe the different kinds of bonds and how investors earn money from bonds.
- Describe the role of other global financial markets.

©Getty Images/PhotoDisc

THE BOND MARKET

A *bond* is a certificate representing money borrowed by a company or another organization to be repaid over a long period of time. The bond market helps organizations raise debt capital.

CORPORATE BONDS

A **corporate bond** is a debt certificate issued by a multinational company or another corporate enterprise. Most corporate bonds in the United States are sold in amounts of $1,000. This amount is called the *face value,* or *maturity value.*

The interest rate on a bond is important to investors. For example, a 10 percent bond would pay $100 a year in interest, calculated as follows.

Face Value × Interest Rate × Time in Years = Interest
$1,000 × 0.10 × 1 = $100

The *rate of return* on a bond is calculated by dividing the income from the investment by the cost of the investment. For example, if annual income from a $1,000 bond is $72, the annual rate of return is 7.2 percent, as calculated below.

Annual Income ÷ Cost of Investment = Annual Rate of Return
$72 ÷ $1,000 = 0.072, or 7.2%

GLOBAL BUSINESS EXAMPLE

ARE ALL JUNK BONDS GARBAGE?

Risky bonds are sometimes referred to as *junk bonds.* This investment can be attractive to people seeking a high return. Remember, however, high risk is associated with junk bonds. During the 1980s, junk bonds had average returns of nearly 14 percent. During that same period, several companies filed for bankruptcy with bondholders receiving nothing.

The debt of many companies in less developed foreign countries may be rated as "junk bonds." This label results from economic and political uncertainty in their nations. As foreign companies attempt economic expansion, they will issue bonds to fund business activities. While many of these investments are risky, some will provide a high return for those willing to take a chance.

Think Critically

1. Why do some investors purchase high-risk bonds?
2. Conduct an Internet search to obtain additional information about investing in high-risk bonds. What guidelines should an investor follow for this type of investment?

Bond investors should also consider the *maturity date.* This is the point in time when the loan will be repaid. A 20-year bond, for example, means an investor will earn interest each year for 20 years. Then at the end of the 20 years, the investor will be repaid the face value. Remember, when a company issues bonds, it is borrowing money that must be repaid.

GOVERNMENT BONDS

Governments also issue bonds for example, the federal government of the United States sells treasury bonds to obtain needed funds for its operations. State and local governments in the United States also borrow by issuing municipal bonds.

Federal Government Bonds The U.S. government sells bonds to finance the national debt and to pay operating expenses. Two common debt instruments of the federal government are available to investors.

- Treasury bills (T-bills) are short-term borrowing instruments with maturities ranging from 91 days to 1 year.
- Treasury notes (T-notes) are intermediate-length borrowing instruments with maturities from 1 to 10 years.

U.S. savings bonds are another type of federal government debt instrument. Individuals who want to save for the future commonly purchase these bonds. U.S. savings bonds are purchased at one-half of their face value (e.g., a $100 bond costs $50). The time it takes for a savings bond to grow to the maturity value will vary depending on the current interest rate paid by the U.S. Treasury Department.

In recent years, earnings on U.S. savings bonds were not taxed if the funds were used to pay tuition and fees at a college, university, or qualified technical school. For a quick update on U.S. savings bonds rates and other information, call 1-800-US BONDS, or go to www.savingsbonds.gov.

WORK AS A GROUP

Describe a situation in which investing in government bonds could be an appropriate investment decision.

State and Local Government Bonds A **municipal bond** is a debt certificate issued by a state or local government agency. Since most countries organize their government structures differently from the United States, municipal bonds are not common in other nations.

The major benefit of municipal bonds for U.S. investors is that the interest earned is excluded from federal income taxes. Such income, not subject to tax, is called **tax-exempt income**. Other types of investments, such as certain types of retirement accounts, earn **tax-deferred income**, which is income that will be taxed at a later date.

REGIONAL PERSPECTIVE

HISTORY: JERUSALEM

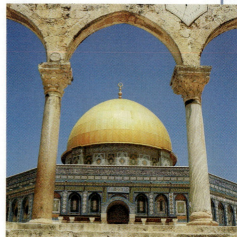

©Getty Images/Digital Vision

No city in the history of the world has more religious significance than Jerusalem. Located between Israel and the West Bank, this walled city has a deep heritage of Christianity, Judaism, and Islam.

For nearly 3,000 years, Jerusalem has seen conflict and controversy. The United Nations Partition Plan declared it an international city in 1947. However, a year later, West Jerusalem was occupied by Israel. After the Six-Day War in 1967, Israel took greater control of the city.

Although Jerusalem has served as Israel's capital since 1950, most countries maintain their embassies in Tel Aviv. Recently, only three countries (Costa Rica, El Salvador, and the United States) recognized Jerusalem as Israel's capital. The city has four main sectors: Jewish, Christian, Armenian, and Muslim.

The Palestinians in East Jerusalem continue to face uncertainty with various proposals offered. Some contend that the city should be ruled by an international administration. Others suggest that Israel keep the Jewish quarter and that the other areas be transferred to a new Palestinian state.

Today, Jerusalem is home to more than 400,000 Jews, over 200,000 Muslims, and about 20,000 Christians. The city is a blend of ancient and modern buildings and activities in a very diverse setting of ethnic, religious, and socioeconomic groups.

Think Critically
1. What historic aspects of Jerusalem are likely to affect current business activities?
2. Conduct an Internet search to obtain additional historic and religious background on Jerusalem.

How do investors earn money from bonds?

OTHER FINANCIAL MARKETS

In addition to stock and bond markets, other financial markets exist to serve companies involved in global business.

THE OVER-THE-COUNTER MARKET

Large companies that meet financial requirements of a stock exchange and are traded regularly are called *listed stocks*. In contrast, stocks of new and small companies are traded through a system of computers, fax machines, and telephones. The **over-the-counter (OTC) market** is a network of stock-brokers who buy and sell stocks not listed on a stock exchange.

The National Association of Securities Dealers Automated Quotations (NASDAQ) is the major computerized trading system for OTC stocks in the United States. In recent years, other OTC markets have developed. The Unlisted Securities Market is the over-the-counter market for fast-growing companies in England. In Germany, the Neuer Markt trades the stocks of emerging companies in the European Union.

FOREIGN EXCHANGE MARKET

The foreign exchange market involves the buying and selling of currencies needed to pay for goods and services bought from companies in other countries. A **Eurodollar** is a U.S. dollar deposited in a bank outside of the United States and used in the money markets of Europe. *Eurodollars* should not be confused with the *euro*, which is the official currency of the European Union.

The term "Eurocurrency" has come to mean any money deposited in a bank outside the country of its origin and used in the money markets of Europe. These funds are used to make payments among countries for foreign trade.

FUTURES MARKET

Farmers want to get a fair price for their grain. Food companies want to avoid paying high prices for grain that will be used to make breakfast cereals and other products. By agreeing to a price now for delivery in the future (usually three or six months from now), a farmer is protected from receiving a lower price for grain. The food company is protected from higher costs.

©Getty Images/PhotoDisc

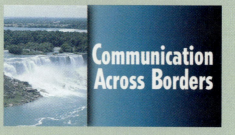

Communication Across Borders

THE CHAMELEON-LIKE SAUDI ARABIAN FINANCIERS

Like chameleons, Saudi Arabian financiers often change their appearance to reflect their surroundings. In other words, they typically try to blend in with the prevailing dress of their current location. At home, they typically wear traditional Saudi business dress. It consists of a long flowing white robe called a *thobe* and a headcloth called a *ghutra*. Abroad, unless they are in another Arab country, they often wear traditional Western business dress. It consists of a dark suit, a white shirt, and a conservatively colored tie. Occasionally, however, they may choose to dress in the traditional Saudi manner while engaging in business outside of their region. When this happens, Saudi Arabian financiers are trying to stand out from their surroundings.

Think Critically

1. Why is traditional Saudi business dress different from traditional Western business dress?

2. Why might Saudi Arabian financiers choose to wear the traditional business dress of their country within the Middle East?

The **futures market** allows investors and others to buy or sell contracts on the future prices of commodities, metals, and financial instruments. Futures markets involve contracts on corn, oats, soybeans, wheat, cattle, cocoa, sugar, oil, natural gas, gold, silver, treasury bonds, and currencies—yen, pound, euro, and Eurodollars.

©David Turnley/CORBIS

✓ CheckPoint

What are the functions of the OTC, foreign exchange, and futures markets?

REVIEW GLOBAL BUSINESS TERMS

Define each of the following terms.

1. corporate bond
2. municipal bond
3. tax-exempt income
4. tax-deferred income
5. over-the-counter (OTC) market
6. Eurodollar
7. futures market

intlbizxtra.swlearning.com

REVIEW GLOBAL BUSINESS CONCEPTS

8. How is the rate of return on a bond computed?
9. What are three common debt instruments used by the federal government of the United States?
10. What types of stocks are commonly traded on the over-the-counter (OTC) market?

SOLVE GLOBAL BUSINESS PROBLEMS

For the following corporate bond situations, calculate the amounts requested.

11. Earnings for three years of a $1,000 bond with a 7 percent interest rate.
12. Earnings for five years of a $1,000 bond with a 5.65 percent interest rate.
13. Annual rate of return from the purchase of ten $1,000 bonds with a total annual income of $860.
14. Maturity value of a $1,000 bond with a 10 percent interest rate, maturing in 6 years.

THINK CRITICALLY

15 How do changes in interest rates affect the market value of bonds?
16. What are the benefits of the futures market?

MAKE CONNECTIONS

17. **TECHNOLOGY** Conduct an Internet search to find web sites for stock exchanges in other countries.
18. **GEOGRAPHY** Create a chart showing the current market value of the natural resources of various countries, such as oil, wheat, corn, and soybeans.
19. **TECHNOLOGY** Use the Internet to locate online resources for international financial markets.
20. **CURRENT EVENTS** Use the Internet to identify three recent events around the world that had a significant effect on international financial markets.

20-4

GOALS

- Describe the two major goals of investors.
- Analyze international investment opportunities.
- Identify major sources of investment information.

ANALYZING INTERNATIONAL INVESTMENTS

©Getty Images/PhotoDisc

INVESTMENT GOALS

Changing currency rates, environmental concerns, and political instability are typical in the international business environment. Just as companies attempt to make the right global business decisions, individuals want to make investments that will achieve their personal financial goals.

The long-term financial security of a person or family results from an ability to save and invest for the future. *Saving* is the storage of money for future use. In contrast, *investing* involves putting money to work in a business venture. The risks associated with investing are higher than the risks associated with saving. However, the potential returns from investing are also greater. Investing has two common goals, which are current income and long-term growth.

CURRENT INCOME

Some people depend on investment income for current living expenses. Retired people and others may need investments that provide income. These earnings may be in the form of dividends (from stocks), interest (from bonds), or rent (from real estate).

LONG-TERM GROWTH

In contrast to current income, many people invest for long-term financial security. They want funds for retirement or for their children's college education. Investors who desire long-term growth of their funds will choose investments that they hope will increase in value over time.

The earnings obtained over the long term can provide substantial wealth. A **capital gain** is the profit made from the resale of investments—such as stocks, bonds, or real estate. For example, land purchased in 1998 for $12,000 and sold in 2005 for $31,000 represents a capital gain of $19,000.

The growth in value of an investment can be projected with the use of future value calculations. Future value involves computations for determining the expected worth of an investment in the future.

REACHING YOUR INVESTMENT GOALS

Current Income
- Stocks paying dividends
- Savings certificates
- Corporate bonds
- Rental property

Long-Term Growth
- Growth stocks
- Raw land
- Gold, silver
- Coins, stamps
- Art, antiques

Figure 20-7 People with different investment goals select different types of investments.

The following example shows how future value is calculated. The n represents the number of years the investment will be earning the yield. The future value of $1,000 invested at 7 percent for two years would be calculated as follows.

Amount Invested $\times$ (1 + Annual Rate Earned)^n = Future Value
$1,000 $\times$ 1.07^2 = $1,144.90

Figure 20-7 lists some of the common investments used to meet the two main investment goals of current income and long-term growth.

✓CheckPoint

What is the difference between the two major goals of investing?

GLOBAL INVESTMENT OPPORTUNITIES

Should a person invest in a gold mine in South America, real estate in the Middle East, or a computer company in Nevada? When planning to invest, people must identify potential investments and evaluate those investment opportunities.

IDENTIFYING POTENTIAL INVESTMENTS

Successful investments can result from a variety of business activities around the world. For example, as the demand for health care increases because of illness or an aging population, companies involved in medications, medical supplies, and hospital equipment may become more profitable.

News stories can be used to identify investment opportunities, as shown in Figure 20-8. When you hear a news report, ask yourself what types of companies might be affected by this news. Next, decide what type of investment would be appropriate. Investors may buy stock in the company or even start their own company. Finally, investors must select an action to take—buy, sell, or keep holding certain investments.

Figure 20-8 Local, national, and world news provide information about investment opportunities every day.

FINDING INVESTMENT OPPORTUNITIES

1. Monitor news reports.

2. Determine industry and specific companies affected.

3. Select investment type and action (buy, sell, or hold).

Heinz Hockmann of Commerz International Capital Management, Frankfurt, Germany, recommends that when investing, to select a country before choosing specific companies. A nation's economic conditions and political environment strongly influence business success. Companies in the same industry (automobiles, chemicals, or electrical equipment) tend to perform differently depending on the country. For example, auto stocks in Britain may decline during a period in which German auto stocks rise.

EVALUATING INVESTMENT OPPORTUNITIES

Consider four major factors when choosing between various investments. These factors are rate of return, liquidity, taxes, and safety.

Rate of Return The annual earnings for an investment are measured by the annual *rate of return,* or *yield.* This rate is the percentage of the investment cost that is earned in a year.

For example, an investment that costs $5,000 and produces an annual income of $450 has an annual rate of return of 9 percent, calculated as follows.

Annual Income ÷ Cost of Investment = Rate of Return
$450 ÷ $5,000 = 0.09, or 9%

Liquidity Many people want to be able to obtain and use their money quickly. **Liquidity** refers to the ability to easily convert an asset into cash without a loss in value. Certain types of assets are highly liquid, such as stocks, bonds, and mutual funds. These investments have a continuing market of buyers and sellers.

In contrast, real estate, rare coins, and other collectibles have low liquidity. These assets may be difficult to sell quickly. Buyers for these investments are not always available.

A trade-off between liquidity and rate of return is common for investments. In general, assets with high liquidity have a lower return over time. Low liquidity can give you a higher rate of return over the long run.

Taxes The amount earned on an investment is frequently affected by taxes. If an investor has to pay taxes on earnings, that lowers the annual rate of return. A *tax-exempt* investment earns income that is not subject to tax. In contrast, a *tax-deferred* investment earns income that will be taxed at a later date.

Safety When making an investment, people expect their money to be available in the future. Most people want investments that minimize their chance of losing money. Generally, the higher the return expected, the higher the risk involved.

✓ CheckPoint

What four factors are usually considered before making an investment?

INVESTMENT INFORMATION SOURCES

Wise investing, as with any business decision, requires reliable, up-to-date information. The main sources of investment information are the news media, the Internet, financial experts, and investment information services.

News Media Business periodicals and the business section of the daily newspaper provide a readily available source of investment news. Many investors find *The Wall Street Journal, Financial Times, Business Week, Fortune, Forbes,* and *The Economist* helpful. In addition to domestic and international business, economic, and financial news, these publications feature articles on companies and product trends. Cable television channels such as CNN Financial and CNBC also provide news and data about financial markets and investment opportunities.

Internet The Internet and the World Wide Web are very important sources for investment information. The periodicals mentioned above all have web sites with news, articles, and financial data. Also, hundreds of other web sites are available to assist investors with researching, selecting, and monitoring their stocks, bonds, mutual funds, and

©Getty Images/PhotoDisc

WORK AS A GROUP

Prepare a list of factors to consider when buying an international mutual fund.

other investments. Some of the most useful investment web sites are those maintained by *Money* magazine, Motley Fool, and Yahoo Finance.

Financial Experts A stockbroker advises customers and sells investments. Other financial experts who provide investment recommendations and assist with purchases are bankers, personal financial planners, insurance agents, and real estate brokers.

EXAMPLE

ONLINE INVESTING

Today people with a computer and online access can be their own stockbrokers. Online investing is made possible through the web sites of companies such as E*trade and Ameritrade. Instead of calling a broker, investors select and purchase stocks and other investments through a web site.

The lower operating costs of online stock brokerage firms have pushed transaction fees down. A stock trade that previously had a commission of about $100 can now be done online for as low as $5.

Traditional brokers are also offering online investment services. For example, Merrill Lynch, the largest U.S. stockbroker, offers Internet-based investment services in Australia, the United Kingdom, Japan, and several other countries.

Think Critically

1. How do online stockbrokers affect competition and prices in that industry?
2. Go to the web site of a traditional broker or an online broker to obtain information on the services offered to investors. Write a list of the services found.

Before acting on the advice of any investment advisor, wise investors take the following additional precautions.

- Research the investment and company using several sources.
- Talk to others who have this type of investment.
- Contact state and federal government agencies for information about the investment and the seller of the investment.
- Compare costs of the investment broker with others who provide this service.

Each year U.S. citizens lose more than $5 billion on phony investments. Common investment scams in recent years included fake low-cost stocks, wireless cable television partnerships, Internet services, and paging licenses.

Investment Information Services Information on the current performance and the future of stocks and bonds is published in *Value Line*, *Moody's Investors Service*, and *Standard & Poor's Reports*. These investment services provide financial data, current stock prices, recent company developments, and recommendations for buying and selling. Investors can find these information sources at libraries or through the organizations' web sites.

✓ CheckPoint

Who are some of the financial experts that can provide assistance with your investment decisions?

REVIEW GLOBAL BUSINESS TERMS

Define each of the following terms.

1. capital gain

2. liquidity

REVIEW GLOBAL BUSINESS CONCEPTS

3. What are two common goals of investing?

4. What is the rate of return of an investment?

5. What are common sources of investment information?

SOLVE GLOBAL BUSINESS PROBLEMS

Calculate the future value of the following investments.

6. The expected value of a stock in three years that grows at 4 percent a year and has a current value of £100.

7. The future value of land in five years that costs Cr$3,000 today with an expected growth rate of 7 percent per year.

8. The future value of an antique automobile after eight years, with a current value of $12,000 and an expected growth rate of 6 percent per year.

©Getty Images/PhotoDisc

THINK CRITICALLY

9. Describe a situation in which a person would be investing for income. Next, describe a situation in which a person would invest for long-term growth.

10. How would a person decide if a web site were a reliable source of investment information?

MAKE CONNECTIONS

11. **TECHNOLOGY** Locate a web site that offers investment information and assistance. What types of investments might be wise choices based on the information offered on this web site?

12. **MATHEMATICS** What is the annual rate of return for these situations?
  a. A share of stock in a company in Singapore costs $40 and has an annual dividend of $4.
  b. A South African government bond costing $1,000 earns $65 interest a year.
  c. An oil investment in the Middle East costs $20,000 and pays an annual income of $4,400.

CHAPTER SUMMARY

20-1 FINANCING GLOBAL BUSINESS OPERATIONS

A The flow of funds for international businesses involves sources of funds (based on equity and debt) and uses of funds (for current expenses and long-term costs).

B Global financial institutions include commercial banks, savings and loan associations, credit unions, mutual funds, and life insurance companies.

20-2 GLOBAL FINANCIAL MARKETS

A The activities of global stock markets include providing a location or computer system for the buying and selling of shares of ownership in corporations. Stock market transactions involve negotiations between broker representatives or online negotiations to agree on a price settlement between the buyer and seller of a stock.

B Stock prices are affected by demand based on a company's expected current and future profitability. Economic conditions, the political situation, and social concerns can also affect demand for a stock.

20-3 INTERNATIONAL FINANCIAL MARKETS

A The purpose of the bond market is to provide a place where the debt instruments of companies and governments are bought and sold. Investors earn interest on bonds.

B Other global financial markets include the over-the-counter (OTC) market, the foreign exchange market, and the futures market.

20-4 ANALYZING INTERNATIONAL INVESTMENTS

A The two major goals of investors are current income and long-term growth.

B The analysis of international investments involves identifying potential opportunities in other countries. The rate of return, liquidity, tax situation, and safety of the investment should also be considered.

C The major sources of investment information are the news media, the Internet, financial experts, and investment information services.

GLOBAL REFOCUS

Read the Global Focus at the beginning of this chapter, and answer the following questions.

1. To what extent should the government assist major companies when they face financial difficulties?

2. What actions would you suggest for Koor to strengthen its financial situation for the future?

REVIEW GLOBAL BUSINESS TERMS

Match the terms listed with the definitions.

1. A financial institution that traditionally specialized in savings accounts and home mortgages.

2. Funds obtained by borrowing.

3. Income that will be taxed at a later date.

4. An investment company that manages a pool of funds from many investors.

5. A network of stockbrokers who buy and sell stocks not listed on a stock exchange.

6. Funds provided by a company's owners.

7. Income not subject to tax.

8. The ability to easily convert an asset into cash without a loss in value.

9. A debt certificate issued by a state or local government agency.

10. A business organized to accept deposits and to make loans.

11. A location where stocks are bought and sold.

12. A market that allows investors and others to buy or sell contracts on the future prices of commodities, metals, and financial instruments.

13. A U.S. dollar deposited in a bank outside of the United States and used in the money markets of Europe.

14. The profit made from the resale of investments—such as stocks, bonds, or real estate.

15. A debt certificate issued by a multinational company or another corporate enterprise.

16. A person who buys and sells stocks and other investments for customers.

17. A nonprofit financial cooperative.

a. capital gain

b. commercial bank

c. corporate bond

d. credit union

e. debt capital

f. equity capital

g. Eurodollar

h. futures market

i. liquidity

j. municipal bond

k. mutual fund

l. over-the-counter (OTC) market

m. savings and loan association

n. stockbroker

o. stock exchange

p. tax-deferred income

q. tax-exempt income

MAKE GLOBAL BUSINESS DECISIONS

18. Explain why a company uses debt. Also tell why a company might avoid using debt to finance its operations.

19. Would your needs as a consumer be better served by a large international bank or a small local bank?

20. How does a mutual fund provide small investors with opportunities they might not have otherwise?

21. Why are many international companies traded on the New York Stock Exchange (NYSE) as well as on stock exchanges in their home countries?

22. Why do some people use an online stockbroker instead of a full-service broker?

23. What happens when there is no buyer for shares of stock that someone wants to sell?

24. Which type of investment, stocks or bonds, involves more risk for an investor? Why?

25. How does the futures market serve the needs of many groups of people in a country?

GLOBAL CONNECTIONS

26. **GEOGRAPHY** Describe how the climate, terrain, waterways, and natural resources of a country could affect the investments in that nation.

27. **COMMUNICATIONS** Survey people who use different types of financial institutions. Obtain information about their reasons for doing business with a certain bank, savings and loan association, credit union, or another financial institution.

28. **CULTURAL STUDIES** Talk to people from different countries about their attitudes toward investing. Compare your findings about what types of investments people prefer.

29. **MATHEMATICS** Select a company, and chart the changing price of its stock. Prepare a graph showing the closing price of a share over a three-week period. Conduct library research to locate news about the company and economic conditions. Prepare a short report explaining how this news has affected the company's stock price.

30. **RESEARCH** Locate bond prices in *The Wall Street Journal* or the business section of a daily newspaper. Report to the class about the information included in the daily bond report.

31. **TECHNOLOGY** Prepare a list comparing the features presented on different web sites that provide investment information.

32. **CAREER PLANNING** Collect articles and other information about financial institutions in other countries. How do the jobs with these companies differ from finance jobs in the United States?

©Getty Images/PhotoDisc

THE GLOBAL
ENTREPRENEUR
CREATING AN INTERNATIONAL BUSINESS PLAN

INTERNATIONAL FINANCIAL ACTIVITIES

Conduct research on global financial activities based on the company and country you have been using in this continuing project, or create a new idea for your business in the same or a different country. Make use of previously collected information, and do additional research. This phase of your business plan should answer the following questions.

1. To what extent does the company use debt to finance its business activities?

2. What long-term projects is the company currently planning or implementing?

3. If the company is a major corporation, on what stock exchange is the company's stock traded? What is the current price of a share of the company's stock?

4. What recent economic, social, and political factors could affect the company's stock price?

5. What is the current interest rate paid on the company's bonds?

Prepare a written summary or present a short oral report (two or three minutes) of your findings.

©Getty Images/PhotoDisc

559

Chapter 21

MANAGING INTERNATIONAL BUSINESS RISK

GLOBAL FOCUS

Lloyd's of London

The world's most famous insurance organization began in Edward Lloyd's coffeehouse in London. In 1688, ship owners and merchants bought marine insurance from Lloyd's to cover the risks of sending goods to other countries. In the late 1800s, Lloyd's of London expanded into nonmarine insurance.

Over the years, this association of insurance underwriters has insured some unusual assets—the legs of Hollywood dancers, the voices of singers (such as Frank Sinatra and Bruce Springsteen), and the athletic ability of sport stars. Other unusual coverage provided by Lloyd's have included the following.

- Insurance policies providing protection against crocodile attack in northern Australia.
- Employers buying protection against staff members winning the British national lottery and not returning to work.
- Insurance coverage against death or injury caused by a piece of a disintegrating satellite falling from the sky.

Lloyd's of London is different from other insurance companies. This insurance society consists of investors called *Names,* who pool their money to cover possible financial risks. The Names profit when insurance claims are less than income. However, when a disaster occurs, the Names have to be prepared to pay for the financial losses from the disaster.

In recent years, Lloyd's has experienced lower profits due to natural disasters, environmental problems, and changing tax laws in Britain. These events have resulted in changes in the organization. Nonetheless, some traditions continue. In Lloyd's headquarters is the bell from the *Lutine,* which shipwrecked in 1857. The bell tolls once for good news, twice for bad news.

Think Critically

1. How does Lloyd's of London serve the needs of global business organizations?
2. What factors have reduced profits for Lloyd's?
3. Go to the web site of Lloyd's of London to obtain information on the history and current operations of the organization. Prepare a one-page summary of your findings.

21-1 GLOBAL RISK MANAGEMENT

GOALS

- Describe the types of risks related to international business activities.
- Discuss the risk management process.

©Getty Images/PhotoDisc

INTERNATIONAL BUSINESS RISKS

Whenever a company implements a business decision, risk is involved. The organization faces the risks of consumers not buying its product or a supplier not delivering materials on time. **Risk** is the uncertainty of an event or outcome. Every company faces potential risks—from employee theft to natural disasters. Companies and individuals must manage risk.

If all business ventures were sure things, life would be a lot simpler. However, in reality, every business activity has some risk. A war may destroy a factory in another country, or a company may go bankrupt and not be able to repay its debts. The three common risks faced by companies involved in international business are political risk, social risk, and economic risk, as shown in Figure 21-1.

POLITICAL RISK

Would a company be safer doing business in a democratic country with a newly formed government or in an autocratic nation that has been ruled by the same dictator for ten years? Political risk is difficult to evaluate. Government instability and political uncertainty are risks global companies must monitor constantly. Political control may change hands during civil unrest or a revolution. The new government may not allow certain companies to continue to operate in the country.

Business regulations vary from country to country. Regulations on business might be very tight in one nation, while great freedom is allowed elsewhere. Food packages in one country may require extensive nutritional

TYPES OF INTERNATIONAL BUSINESS RISKS

Political Risk

- Government instability
- Change in business regulations
- New trade barriers

Social Risk

- Religious beliefs
- Values
- Family-work relationships

Economic Risk

- Consumer spending patterns
- Inflation
- Exchange rate fluctuations

Figure 21-1 Companies involved in international business activities face different risks.

information. However, another market may not have any laws regulating food labeling.

Trade barriers also pose a potential political risk. Tariffs, antidumping laws, import quotas, and currency exchange controls are examples of political actions taken to limit imported goods.

SOCIAL RISK

As you know, business is conducted differently in different parts of the world. Social and cultural factors such as religious beliefs, values, and family-business ties affect the risk faced by multinational companies.

Companies doing business in other countries must respect the religious beliefs of people in those nations. Failure to do so is likely to result in an unsuccessful endeavor even if all other business actions are appropriate. In a similar manner, companies that stress individualism would face greater risk when doing business in nations that emphasize collectivism.

The connection between family and business is very important in some cultures and less important in others. In most areas of Central and South America, much of southern Europe, and most of Asia, northern Africa, and the Middle East, family business ties are strong. Companies must work within this cultural environment to minimize business risk.

©Getty Images/PhotoDisc

GLOBAL BUSINESS EXAMPLE

PRACTICING FOR UNEXPECTED EVENTS

Royal Dutch/Shell is one of the world's largest petroleum and natural gas companies. The company is a joint venture between Royal Dutch Petroleum (60 percent ownership) and Shell Transport and Trading (40 percent ownership). It has business activities in more than 130 countries and operates about 50,000 gas stations.

Shell continually encounters fluctuating oil prices, environmental concerns, and uncertainty in supplier nations. When the Persian Gulf War started in the early 1990s, Shell was no longer able to obtain oil from Kuwait and Iraq. How can a company prepare for these types of risks? Royal Dutch/Shell prepares by simulating disasters.

A couple of times a year, oil shipments are unexpectedly interrupted. Then employees must put backup plans into operation. Therefore, during the Gulf War, the company had already arranged to locate and ship oil from alternative sites.

Think Critically

1. Why do companies conduct disaster drills?
2. Go to the web site of Royal Dutch/Shell to obtain additional information about the risks faced by the company around the world. Write a report of your findings.

ECONOMIC RISK

Economic conditions have ups and downs. The demand for a company's goods and services varies based on the income of consumers, interest rates, and levels of employment. When fewer people are working, less money is available for consumer spending.

When a company receives one dollar today, it hopes to be able to buy something worth one dollar in the future. However, if *inflation* erodes the buying power of a currency, the monetary unit will not have as much purchasing power in the future.

Companies that do business in other countries face the risk of receiving payment in a currency that may have less value than expected. With exchange rates changing daily, financial managers must make sure that the payment received is appropriate after the currency conversion.

MONITORING GLOBAL BUSINESS RISK

Change is the only constant in all aspects of business. Reading current materials, talking with residents, and watching economic data are ways to note changes in a country's business environment. Awareness of factors such as political stability, religious influences, and fluctuating interest rates can help a manager predict changes in business risk. An ability to anticipate and act early can reduce risk and lessen the chances of poor business decisions.

✔ CheckPoint

What are the three main categories of risk faced by multinational companies?

THE RISK MANAGEMENT PROCESS

Multinational companies will face many business risks. Figure 21-2 shows four steps commonly taken to manage these international business risks. These are identify potential risks, evaluate risks, select a risk management method, and implement the risk management program.

THE RISK MANAGEMENT PROCESS

Step 4

Implement the risk management program

Step 3

Select a risk management method

Step 2

Evaluate risks

Step 1

Identify potential risks

Figure 21-2 Companies manage risk by following a step-by-step approach.

WORK AS A GROUP

Using an international business situation, prepare an example for each step of the risk management process shown in Figure 21-2.

STEP 1 IDENTIFY POTENTIAL RISKS

In the first step of the risk management process, managers list the factors that might affect a company's operations. Government policies, currency values, and local customs are some examples of risk-causing elements. Managers can use current reports, field interviews, and other data sources to uncover conditions that increase uncertainty.

STEP 2 EVALUATE RISKS

In this step, managers analyze the potential effect of risks on a company. Will a change in government mean higher costs to cover new environmental regulations? Or could the change in government result in the company facing new trade barriers when doing business in that nation? Managers must decide how and to what extent the risks will influence sales and profits.

Be aware that a factor in the international business environment can affect different companies in different ways. A weak economy may hurt a company selling entertainment products. However, the same poor economic conditions may benefit a company selling low-cost clothing.

STEP 3 SELECT A RISK MANAGEMENT METHOD

Next, managers must decide how to handle the identified risks. The four methods used to manage risk—risk avoidance, risk reduction, risk assumption, and risk sharing—are shown in Figure 21-3.

Figure 21-3 Companies manage risks in four main ways.

RISK MANAGEMENT METHODS

Risk Avoidance

Risk Reduction

Risk Assumption

Risk Sharing

Risk Avoidance Certain risks can be avoided. A company avoids the risks related to international business by only selling products in its home country. However, this approach to risk management is not always practical. A business limits its potential for expansion by selling only in its domestic market or in markets in safe geographic regions.

Risk Reduction The risk of an event may be reduced by taking precautionary actions. For example, businesses use security systems and sprinklers to reduce the risk of theft and fire. Multinational companies can reduce business risks by selling products that have been successful in other countries.

Risk Assumption Sometimes a company takes responsibility for losses from certain risks. For example, a business may set aside funds for fire damage that may occur to its factories. This action, called **self-insurance**, involves setting aside money to cover a potential financial loss. A company with many stores or factories in different locations may save money by using self-insurance.

Risk Sharing Sharing risks among many companies that face similar risks is a common practice. Insurance is often purchased for financial protection from property losses, motor vehicle accidents, and other business activities.

STEP 4 IMPLEMENT THE RISK MANAGEMENT PROGRAM

Finally, managers must execute the risk management plan. This phase involves both taking relevant action and measuring the success of the action. Various factors in the business environment and within the company may change an organization's risk management course in the future.

©Getty Images/PhotoDisc

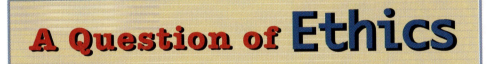

A Question of Ethics

UNREPORTED BUSINESS ACTIVITIES

In most countries, an *underground* economy exists. This phrase, sometimes called the *black market*, refers to business activities outside the formal economy. Underground economy transactions are not reported to government agencies.

In some regions of developing countries, over half of the construction work and other business activities are "off the books"—never reported for paying sales and income taxes. These unreported business transactions could benefit the people of a country. Jobs are created, and people earn income for paying living expenses.

However, the underground economy also has a negative impact. Since sales revenue and incomes are not reported, governments do not collect taxes. Money is not available to pay for public services such as education, police protection, road construction, and trash collection.

Think Critically
Use the three guidelines for ethical analysis to examine the above situation. How does the underground economy affect businesses, consumers, and society?

CheckPoint
What are the steps of the risk management process?

REVIEW GLOBAL BUSINESS TERMS

Define each of the following terms.

1. risk

2. self-insurance

REVIEW GLOBAL BUSINESS CONCEPTS

3. What are examples of social risks?

4. How can managers monitor international business risk?

5. What are the four methods used to manage risk?

6. What is self-insurance? Give an example.

SOLVE GLOBAL BUSINESS PROBLEMS

For each of the following situations, describe actions that the organization might take to manage its business risk.

7. Stealing by employees and customers.

8. Changes in the value of foreign currencies.

9. Actions of global competitors.

10. Changing clothing styles.

11. Political instability in a foreign country.

THINK CRITICALLY

12. What are some examples of government regulations that create global business risks?

13. Describe a risk-reduction action that a company could use.

14. What are some actions you take each day to avoid and reduce risks in your life?

MAKE CONNECTIONS

15. **TECHNOLOGY** Explain how changing technology could increase and decrease risks for a global company.

16. **CULTURAL STUDIES** Describe differences in customs, traditions, and language that could create a social risk for a company operating in another country.

17. **TECHNOLOGY** Use the Internet to identify online resources for risk management.

18. **CURRENT EVENTS** Use the Internet to find a recent event that poses a risk to international business. Identify the type of risk and describe a plan for managing this risk.

INTERNATIONAL INSURANCE

21-2

GOALS

- Explain the basic elements of insurance coverage.
- Describe elements of an insurance policy.

©Getty Images/PhotoDisc

INSURING AGAINST RISKS

Insurance is planned protection for sharing economic losses among many people. Insurance is commonly purchased to reduce or eliminate the financial loss due to risks. A company's place of business is usually covered by property insurance. When driving a car, a traveling salesperson probably has automobile insurance. Most everyone reading this book uses insurance as a method for managing risk.

Insurance is an agreement between one party, called the *insured*, and an insurance company, the *insurer*. A **stock insurance company** is owned by stockholders and is operated for profit. A **mutual insurance company** is owned by its policyholders. This type of organization returns any surplus to policyholders after claims and operating expenses are paid.

INSURABLE INTEREST

A basic requirement of insurance is the presence of an *insurable interest*, something of value that may be lost or destroyed. For example, equipment owned by a company represents an insurable interest. In the case of life insurance, the insurable interest is the financial loss caused by someone's death.

INSURABLE RISK

Another basic requirement of insurance is the presence of an *insurable risk*. An insurable risk is a risk that has the following elements.

- Common to many people—The risk must be one that is faced by many people or businesses. This allows many people with the same risk to share the cost with the few who actually suffer a financial loss due to the risk.

GLOBAL BUSINESS EXAMPLE

AIG IN CHINA

Small business owners in Shanghai are the newest customers of American International Group (AIG), one of the first insurance companies to sell directly to Chinese citizens. The People's Insurance Company of China, a state-owned monopoly, fought to keep AIG out of the country. However, political leaders ruled in favor of AIG. As this business relationship proves to be satisfactory for both sides, the Chinese market is opening for other service companies. Accountants, airlines, banks, freight forwarders, and stockbrokers are hoping to sell in a country with one-fifth of the world's population.

Doing business in more than 130 countries, AIG is one of the world's largest insurance enterprises. The company is involved in property, casualty, auto, life, and worker's compensation insurance. Other business activities of AIG include financial services, currency hedging, and aircraft leasing.

Think Critically

1. What political factors create difficulties when a company attempts to compete in another country against domestic businesses?
2. Go to the web site of AIG to obtain current information about the company's global business activities. Write a report on your findings.

- Definite—The risk must be something that can be documented. The destruction of a building by fire or the death of a person is something that can be documented.
- Not excessive in magnitude—An insurance company would not be able to cover the cost of replacing all homes it insures at one time. Recent hurricanes in Florida caused such extensive damage that some insurance companies can no longer afford to do business in that state.
- Not trivial—Insurance on small items would not be worth the time, effort, and expense necessary to provide coverage.
- Able to be calculated—The insurer must be able to calculate the probability that the risk will occur. This allows the insurer to plan what amount to charge for insurance.

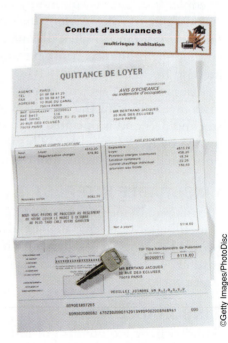

©Getty Images/PhotoDisc

✓ CheckPoint

What are the elements of an insurable risk?

INSURANCE POLICY ELEMENTS

WORK AS A GROUP

Describe actions a company could take when comparing the coverages and costs of insurance.

An **insurance policy** is the legal agreement between an insurance company and the insured. This contract states the conditions of protection. Figure 21-4 shows the major elements of an insurance policy.

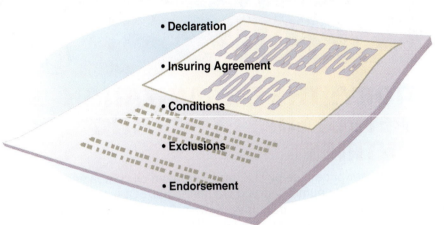

THE ELEMENTS OF AN INSURANCE POLICY

- Declaration
- Insuring Agreement
- Conditions
- Exclusions
- Endorsement

Figure 21-4 An insurance policy is the contract between an insurance company and the insured.

Declaration The *declaration* states what is covered and lists the amount of coverage. For example, the declaration for a multinational company's insurance would describe the enterprise's factories in different countries and at what amount they were covered.

Insuring Agreement The *insuring agreement* explains the coverages of the insurance policy. A company's insurance policy may cover fire and theft losses for property up to a set amount, such as $14 million—the amount of the coverage.

Conditions The *conditions* of an insurance policy provide information about the cost of insurance, called the **premium**. Also listed are any deductibles. A **deductible** is the portion of an insurance claim paid by the insured. A company with a $1,000 deductible, for example, may incur $4,500 of wind damage to a building. In this situation, the insurance company would pay $3,500. The first $1,000 of the claim is paid by the insured. Deductibles reduce the cost of insurance premiums.

Exclusions Property or risks not covered by an insurance policy are called *exclusions*. For example, many insurance policies do not cover property losses resulting from war. Why do you think insurance companies exclude financial loss due to war from policies?

Endorsement An **endorsement** is a certificate that adds to or changes the coverage of an insurance policy. For example, if a company sells a factory, an endorsement would delete the building from its insurance coverage.

©Getty Images/PhotoDisc

Exports should be insured against loss or damage that could occur while in transit. An *insurance certificate* provides evidence of insurance to protect goods from loss or damage while in transit. Sales terms determine if the importer or the exporter pays insurance costs.

REGIONAL PERSPECTIVE

HISTORY: THE ORGANIZATION OF PETROLEUM EXPORTING COUNTRIES

To prevent further price cuts by U.S. and European oil companies, the Organization of Petroleum Exporting Countries (OPEC) was created in 1960. The original members were Iran, Iraq, Kuwait, Saudi Arabia, and Venezuela. Today OPEC has 11 members, including the countries of Algeria, Indonesia, and Nigeria that, like Venezuela, are from outside the Persian Gulf region.

During its first decade, OPEC was concerned mostly with maintaining stable world oil prices. However, by 1970, as the world price for oil dropped (supply exceeded demand), OPEC worked to raise oil prices by reducing production levels. During 1973–74, petroleum prices rose by 400 percent. This was followed by a four-year period of stable prices.

The OPEC countries accounted for 66 percent of the world's petroleum supply in 1979. Ten years later their share dropped to 34 percent. In 1993, increased production, especially by Kuwait after the Gulf War of 1991, resulted in a higher supply and lower worldwide oil prices.

Think Critically

1. What factors influence the world market price of oil?
2. Go to the OPEC web site for additional information about the current activities of the organization. Write a paragraph about your findings.

©Getty Images/PhotoDisc

✓ CheckPoint

What are the main elements of an insurance policy?

REVIEW GLOBAL BUSINESS TERMS

Define each of the following terms.

1. insurance
2. stock insurance company
3. mutual insurance company
4. insurance policy
5. premium
6. deductible
7. endorsement

Xtra!
Study Tools
intlbizxtra.swlearning.com

REVIEW GLOBAL BUSINESS CONCEPTS

8. How does a stock insurance company differ from a mutual insurance company?

9. What is an insurable interest?

10. What is the purpose of an endorsement?

SOLVE GLOBAL BUSINESS PROBLEMS

For each of the following items, name the insurance policy element that is involved.

11. "For all claims, the insured party will pay the first $2,000 of damages."

12. "This policy provides coverage for damage to the factory at 1765 Industrial Drive."

13. "As of June 3, 2001, this policy no longer covers damages as a result of civil riots in foreign countries."

14. "This coverage has a cost of $5,600 for the period of August 7, 2001, to August 6, 2002."

15. "This policy does not cover damage resulting from hurricanes or acts of war."

THINK CRITICALLY

16. What are the benefits of a mutual insurance company?

17. How does a deductible reduce insurance costs for the insurance company and the policyholder?

MAKE CONNECTIONS

18. **MATHEMATICS** If a company has insurance coverage with a $5,000 deductible and encounters a claim for $6,200, how much would the insurance company pay?

19. **LAW** Obtain a sample of an insurance policy to observe the elements of this contract.

21-3 REDUCING GLOBAL RISKS

GOALS

- Identify the major types of insurance coverages for international business activities.
- Describe strategies that multinational companies use to reduce risk.

©Getty Images/PhotoDisc

GLOBAL INSURANCE COVERAGES

Companies involved in international business can share certain risks by using insurance. Commonly used coverages of multinational companies are marine insurance, property insurance, coverage for political risk through the Overseas Private Investment Corporation, and credit risk insurance.

MARINE INSURANCE

Overseas transporters usually assume no responsibility for the merchandise they carry unless the loss is caused by their carelessness. Marine insurance provides protection from loss during shipment of products. This insurance has two types of coverage.

Ocean marine insurance protects goods during shipment overseas or while temporarily in port. In contrast, **inland marine insurance** covers the risk of shipping goods on inland waterways, railroad lines, truck lines, and airlines. Marine insurance is usually sold in three forms with varied coverages.

1. *Basic coverage* provides protection from hazards such as sea damage, fires, jettisons, explosions, and hurricanes.
2. *Broad coverage* includes basic coverage plus theft, pilferage, nondelivery, breakage, and leakage.
3. *All-risk coverage* consists of any physical loss or damage due to an external cause, excluding risks associated with war.

As expected, an all-risk policy is the most expensive of the three types since the most coverage is provided. Also be aware that some losses are not covered by all-risk policies. Items not covered include improper packing, damage caused by natural properties of a product (such as rusting of steel), and loss caused by delay (such as a labor strike).

The amount charged for marine insurance is affected by a variety of factors. Premium factors include the value of the goods, the destination, the age of the ship, the storage location (on deck or under deck), the packaging, and the size of the shipment (volume discounts are common).

NETBookmark

In maritime law, the "law of finds" traditionally means whoever discovers a shipwreck is entitled to claim it and anything it holds. Access intlbizxtra.swlearning.com and click on the link for Chapter 21. After reading the article, write a few paragraphs explaining who you think should own shipwrecks. Do you agree with the "law of finds"? Why or why not?

intlbizxtra.swlearning.com

PROPERTY INSURANCE

Crimes such as burglary, theft, and arson disturb business activities throughout the world. Companies face three main risks as property owners.

1. Loss of real property
2. Loss of personal property
3. Financial responsibility for injuries or damage

Loss of Real Property *Real property* refers to structures permanently attached to land, such as factories, stores, garages, and office buildings. A company's building and land represent a significant financial investment. Property insurance provides protection for damage or loss of real property. Buildings and structures are insured for loss or damage from fire, lightning, wind, hail, explosion, smoke, vandalism, and crashes of aircraft and motor vehicles.

Loss of Personal Property *Personal property* refers to property not attached to the land. Loss or damage of office furniture, machinery, equipment, and supplies also can be covered by property insurance.

Financial Responsibility for Injuries or Damage *Liability* is legal responsibility for the financial cost of someone else's losses or injuries. Customers, company guests, employees, and others may be injured while on the premises of a business. Or a company representative may accidentally damage the property of others. When any of these occur, the company may be responsible for the financial loss that results from the incident.

Quite often legal responsibility is the result of *negligence*, or failure to take ordinary or reasonable care. An employer may also be held financially responsible for the actions of an employee. Liability insurance protects a company from financial losses due to the actions of its employees.

©Getty Images/PhotoDisc

THE OVERSEAS PRIVATE INVESTMENT CORPORATION

To encourage investment in less developed countries, the U.S. government created the Overseas Private Investment Corporation (OPIC). This agency protects U.S. companies from various hazards. OPIC protects 150 developing nations and emerging markets from financial losses, which may be the result of the three major types of risk.

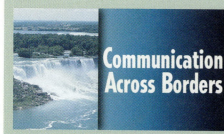

NOT ALL LANGUAGES ARE EQUAL FOR BUSINESS PURPOSES

Businesses can increase their international risks by using certain languages. For example, Hebrew is not a particularly good language for international business purposes. It is a holy language that evolved primarily for religious purposes, not for common speech purposes, including the accomplishment of business.

As the dominant language of only one small country, Israel, Hebrew is not widely known by businesspersons around the world. Very few opportunities for learning Hebrew exist in most countries. Further, finding knowledgeable establishments that can accurately print documents in Hebrew is very difficult in many locations outside of Israel. Thus, a multinational organization that chooses Hebrew as its only business language will likely expose itself to greater communication risks than one that chooses a more common language of international business.

Think Critically

1. How does a multinational organization increase its risks by choosing Hebrew as its only business language?
2. If Hebrew is determined to be too risky as the official business language for an Israeli multinational organization, what other language(s) should be considered? Why?

1. Inconvertibility—This is an inability to convert foreign currency into U.S. dollars. Most refusals by a host government to convert a currency to dollars are covered under this insurance program.
2. Expropriation—This refers to the seizure of assets by a host government. OPIC provides protection against the loss of control of an investment in a country where political actions by host governments may result.
3. Political unrest—This includes financial losses of assets and property resulting from war, revolution, or civil conflicts.

A U.S. company is eligible for OPIC coverage if U.S. citizens own 50 percent or more of the corporation. A foreign corporation may be eligible for the program if U.S. citizens own at least 95 percent of the company.

CREDIT RISK INSURANCE

One hazard of conducting business in other countries is not receiving payment. **Credit risk insurance** provides coverage for loss from nonpayment of delivered goods. This protection helps reduce the risk of international business activities.

Credit risk insurance is available through the Foreign Credit Insurance Association (FCIA), a private association that insures U.S. exporters. FCIA enables exporters to extend credit to overseas buyers.

Credit insurance covers 100 percent of losses due to political reasons, such as war, asset seizure, and currency inconvertibility. This insurance covers up to 95 percent of commercial losses, such as nonpayment due to insolvency or default.

About 200 banks in the United States have purchased master policies from FCIA and can insure loans made to U.S. exporters. Banks typically charge about 1 percent of the amount insured for the coverage.

What are the three main risks faced by property owners?

RISK REDUCTION FOR GLOBAL BUSINESS

Risk is something every company will face in every business situation. However, management experts recommend the four strategies shown in Figure 21-5 to help reduce international business risk.

MULTINATIONAL RISK REDUCTION STRATEGIES

Figure 21-5 Companies can reduce international business risk by taking certain actions.

Conduct Business in Many Countries. When a company depends on a variety of nations for its sales and profits, it will not be greatly affected by turmoil in one of its markets. U.S. companies doing business in Cuba when Castro gained power in 1959 lost some of their business assets. Fortunately, most of these multinational companies also were operating in many other nations.

Diversify Product Offerings Just as a company should operate in several nations, it should not be dependent on only one or a few products.

By having a varied portfolio of goods and services, an organization reduces its risk when consumers no longer desire one product. By seeking new uses for products and by creating new products, a company reduces its international business risk.

Involve Local Ownership Local ownership of multinational firms usually is viewed favorably by local governments. A company that is completely owned by citizens of another country faces the greatest risks. A host nation feels threatened when people who may have different political and social beliefs control its economic existence. Joint ventures with local private partners are frequently less risky.

Employ Local Management Hiring local managers allows a company to maintain a good working relationship with the host government. Administrators who are native to a country or region understand local customs and cultural norms. A comfortable working relationship will be more likely when local managers are employed.

GLOBAL BUSINESS EXAMPLE

THE RUSSIAN INSURANCE INDUSTRY

When the former Soviet Union evolved from communism to capitalism, many insurance companies were started. Russia's first insurance law, effective January, 1993, allowed an applicant to become a licensed insurance seller with only 2 million rubles in capital—about $1,100. This allowed many inexperienced entrepreneurs to enter the market.

Foreign ownership of Russian insurance companies is restricted to 49 percent. One company, Giva, received financial support from RBS Holding, a communications and food service firm from Bloomfield Hills, Michigan. In 1993, Giva earned 80 million rubles (about $65,000) on over one billion rubles ($820,000) in insurance premiums.

Vera (Russian for "trust") is an insurance company that has the Christian Russian Bank as one of its largest shareholders. Vera specializes in insuring the real estate of the Russian Orthodox Church. The company also provides insurance coverage for the church's art and other priceless treasures made from gold and diamonds.

More recently, Nakhodka Re offers a variety of coverages, including liability, property, motor vehicle, aircraft, cargo, and fishing vessel crew insurance. The company also works with overseas insurance brokers to assist businesses shipping goods to and within Russia and other eastern European countries.

Think Critically

1. How did changes in the Russian political and economic environment affect the insurance business in that country?
2. Conduct an Internet search to obtain current information about insurance activities in Russia and other eastern European countries. Write an outline of your findings.

✔ CheckPoint

How does doing business in several countries reduce risk for a global company?

REVIEW GLOBAL BUSINESS TERMS

Define each of the following terms.

1. ocean marine insurance

2. inland marine insurance

3. credit risk insurance

intlbizxtra.swlearning.com

REVIEW GLOBAL BUSINESS CONCEPTS

4. What are the three forms of marine insurance?

5. How does real property differ from personal property?

6. What is the purpose of the Overseas Private Investment Corporation?

7. What is the purpose of credit risk insurance?

8. How can companies reduce risks associated with international business activities?

SOLVE GLOBAL BUSINESS PROBLEMS

For each of the following business situations, indicate the type of insurance that would cover the financial loss.

9. Goods shipped overseas and stolen while in port in southern Europe.

10. Fire damage to a factory in South America.

11. Nonpayment for a shipment of clothing to eastern Europe.

12. Goods damaged while shipped by railroad in Asia.

13. Accidental injury to guests from another company visiting a factory in Africa.

THINK CRITICALLY

14. What risks are associated with shipping goods by railroad, truck, and airplane?

15. What problems might a company encounter when involving local ownership or employing local management?

MAKE CONNECTIONS

16. **TECHNOLOGY** Go to the web site of the Overseas Private Investment Corporation to obtain information on the current activities of this organization. Write a paragraph summarizing your findings.

17. **GEOGRAPHY** Create a map showing countries with similar climates in which a company could sell its products.

16. **TECHNOLOGY** Use the Internet to locate online business insurance resources.

CHAPTER SUMMARY

21-1 GLOBAL RISK MANAGEMENT

A Companies involved in international business commonly face political, social, and economic risks.

B The risk management process involves (1) identifying potential risks, (2) evaluating risks, (3) selecting a risk management method, and (4) implementing the risk management program.

21-2 INTERNATIONAL INSURANCE

A The basic elements of insurance coverage involve (1) an insurable interest—something of value and (2) an insurable risk—an event common to many people that is definite, not excessive in magnitude, not trivial, and able to be calculated.

B The elements of an insurance policy include the declaration, the insuring agreement, the conditions, the exclusions, and any endorsements.

21-3 REDUCING GLOBAL RISKS

A The major types of insurance for international business are marine insurance, property insurance, the Overseas Private Investment Corporation coverage, and credit risk insurance.

B Strategies that multinational companies use to reduce risk include conducting business in many countries, diversifying product offerings, involving local ownership, and employing local management.

GLOBAL REFOCUS

Read the Global Focus at the beginning of this chapter, and answer the following questions.

1. What are the similarities and differences between Lloyd's and other insurance companies?

2. What actions might Lloyd's take to expand its operations around the world?

REVIEW GLOBAL BUSINESS TERMS

Match the terms listed with the definitions.

1. The portion of an insurance claim paid by the insured.

2. Coverage for loss from nonpayment of delivered goods.

3. An insurance company owned by stockholders and operated for profit.

4. Setting aside money to cover a potential financial loss.

5. The uncertainty of an event or outcome.

6. Protection from loss while goods are being shipped overseas or while temporarily in port.

7. Planned protection for sharing economic losses among many people.

   a. credit risk insurance
   b. deductible
   c. endorsement
   d. inland marine insurance
   e. insurance
   f. insurance policy
   g. mutual insurance company
   h. ocean marine insurance
   i. premium
   j. risk
   k. self-insurance
   l. stock insurance company

8. A certificate that adds to or changes the coverage of an insurance policy.

9. The cost of insurance.

10. An insurance company owned by its policyholders.

11. Protection from a loss while shipping goods on inland waterways, railroad lines, truck lines, and airlines.

12. The legal agreement between an insurance company and the insured.

MAKE GLOBAL BUSINESS DECISIONS

13. Name some risks exporters could face that might not be present when a company sells within its own country.

14. Describe ways you could reduce risks in your home and at your school.

15. Speculative risks include such things as starting a new business or introducing a new product. These cannot be covered by insurance. Why will

©Getty Images/PhotoDisc

insurance companies not cover speculative risks? List other examples of speculative risks.

16. Explain why deductibles reduce the premium paid for insurance.

17. An exporter might not make a marine insurance claim, even if it is valid. Many small claims can increase the cost of insurance in the future. Why might an exporter decide not to make a claim?

18. Most people who own or operate a business consider liability insurance coverage vital. Why?

19. You are the regional manager for a multinational company in Saudi Arabia that manufactures and distributes plastic products. What actions would you take to reduce risk for your company?

GLOBAL CONNECTIONS

©Getty Images/PhotoDisc

20. GEOGRAPHY Prepare a map that indicates some of the countries that have had political unrest or military conflicts in recent years. Explain how companies could reduce risks in these countries.

21. COMMUNICATIONS Talk to someone with homeowner's or renter's insurance. Report to the class about the types of risks that are covered by property insurance.

22. HISTORY Conduct library or Internet research about marine insurance. Prepare a report that explains risks and hazards of this international business insurance.

23. CULTURAL STUDIES Interview a person who has lived or worked in another country. Obtain information about differences in customs, traditions, and language that could create business risks.

24. VISUAL ART Prepare a poster illustrating methods that companies could use to reduce business risk.

25. MATHEMATICS Contact several insurance agents to obtain information about the cost of property or liability insurance. Prepare a graph that shows differences in costs and coverages.

26. CAREER PLANNING Interview a person who works in an insurance career. What training and skills are required for jobs in the insurance industry?

THE GLOBAL
ENTREPRENEUR
CREATING AN INTERNATIONAL BUSINESS PLAN

GLOBAL RISK MANAGEMENT

Conduct research on global business risks and insurance based on the company and country you have been using in this continuing project, or create a new idea for your business in the same or a different country. Make use of previously collected information, and do additional research. This phase of your business plan should answer the following questions.

1. What are the company's main international business risks?
2. Is self-insurance practical for the company?
3. For what situations might the company make use of marine insurance?
4. What types of property does the company own that need to be insured?
5. Why might liability coverage be important to the company?
6. What types of insurance might the company provide as an employee benefit for its workers?

Prepare a written summary or present a short oral report (two or three minutes) of your findings.

©Getty Images/PhotoDisc

GLOBAL CROSS-CULTURAL TEAM PROJECT

Finance International Business Operations

Obtaining loans, attracting investors, and evaluating international business risk are some of the financial aspects of global operations. As companies expand into various geographic regions, cross-cultural teams allow financial managers to better understand various influences on their decisions.

GOAL

To identify differences in finance activities in various regions of the world.

ACTIVITIES

Working in teams, select a geographic region you will represent—Africa, Asia, Europe, Latin America, the Middle East, or North America.

1. International finance topics may be researched in current articles, library materials, and Web searches. Also, if possible, have a discussion with people who have lived or visited your region of the world.
2. Research attitudes toward the use of credit in your region. How do tradition, religion, and culture affect borrowing?
3. List common financial institutions that operate in your geographic region. What services do they provide for businesses?
4. Identify common investments people make in the region. To what extent are stocks, bonds, mutual funds, real estate, and other investments used to achieve financial goals?
5. Describe the major political, social, and economic risks faced by companies doing business in this region. What actions might be taken to reduce or eliminate these risks?
6. **Global Business Decision** An international company has asked your team for advice to finance the expansion of business operations around the world. How might the use of debt be viewed in different regions? What additional financing alternatives might be taken?

TEAM SKILL

Measuring the Success of Cross-Cultural Teams
The completion of a team project includes evaluating the level of achievement. Measures of success vary among geographic regions. Describe possible items that might be used to measure the success of a team in your region. Compare your list with those of other members of your team.

PRESENT

Plan and present a debate among your team members to compare the risks associated with doing business in various geographic areas. Discuss the types of risks and actions that might be taken to reduce or eliminate these risks.

Multimedia Presentation

WinningEdge FBLA-ΦBΛ

The global economy depends upon international trade. When a business decides to conduct international trade or to locate in another country, important information must be researched. Good international business decisions depend upon understanding the major economic, political, and demographic issues of other countries where international trade will take place. The best research will convince decision makers to conduct trade with other countries. Also a well-planned presentation will convince other countries of the value to accepting a new multinational company. You are challenged to prepare a presentation to convince the audience to conduct business in another country. Your presentation will be evaluated on content and possible results.

Choose a country that conducts international trade with the United States. Prepare a multi-media presentation that covers demographics, political system, currency, education, culture, economic system, and customs for the country.

This presentation will prepare business leaders who have been promoted to positions in companies located in your chosen country. The presentation should give strategies to make seamless adjustments to a new country. The presentation should include a wide array of features, including transitions, sound effects, music, and other enhancements.

PERFORMANCE INDICATORS EVALUATED

- Define the demographics, political system, currency, education, culture, economic system, and customs for the country.
- Explain how transfer employees can make smooth transitions to jobs located in the new country.
- Use solid examples to describe all aspects of the country.
- Incorporate a wide array of multimedia functions to enhance the presentation.

For more detailed information about performance indicators, go to the FBLA web site.

THINK CRITICALLY

1. Outline information about the demographics, political system, currency, education, culture, economic system, and customs for your chosen country.
2. List three tips for an individual who has been promoted to a position in the new country.
3. What customs should the business leader understand about the country? Why?

www.fbla-pbl.org/

WORLD POLITICAL MAP

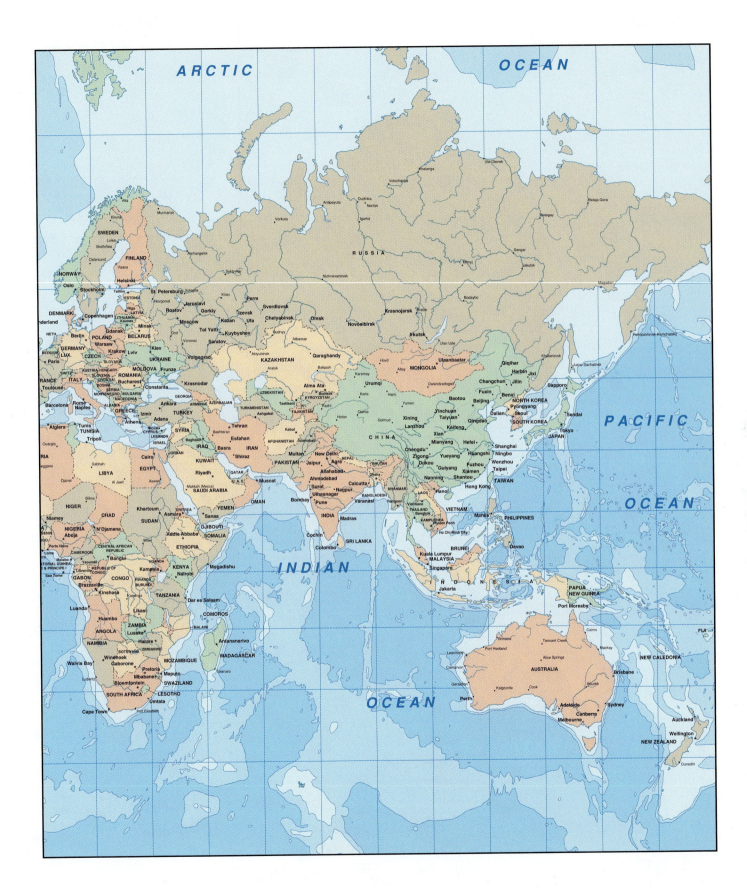

NORTH AMERICA

ASIA-PACIFIC RIM

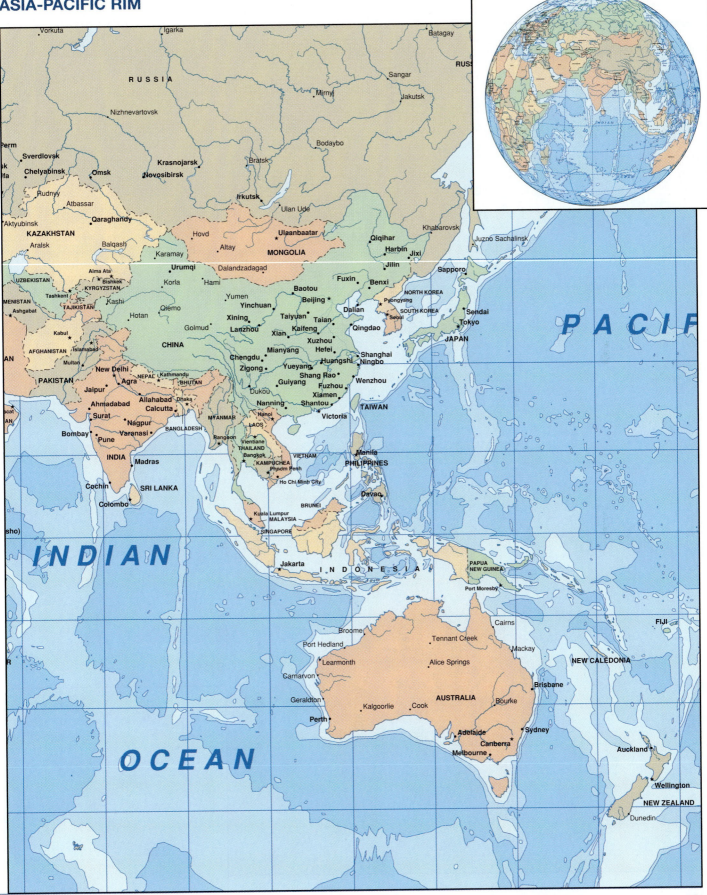

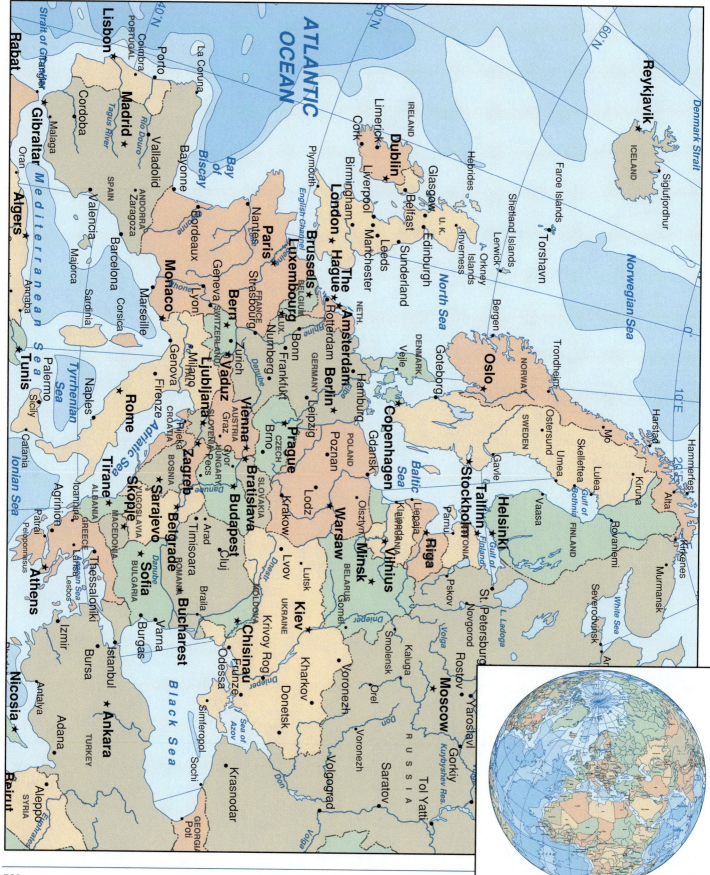

AFRICA

CENTRAL AND SOUTH AMERICA

ATLANTIC OCEAN

exico City
JAMAICA
DOM. REP.
BELIZE
HAITI
HONDURAS
GUATEMALA
EL SALVADOR
NICARAGUA
PANAMA
COSTA RICA
Caracas
VENEZUELA
Georgetown
Bogota
GUYANA
Paramaribo
FRENCH GUIANA
COLOMBIA
SURINAME
ECUADOR
Quito
Manaus
Belem
Fortaleza
Talara
Sao Goncalo
PERU
Porto Velho
Cachimbo
Recife
Trujillo
BRAZIL
Barreiras
Lima
Salvador
Cuiaba
Brasilia
La Paz
Goiania
BOLIVIA
Sucre
Belo Horizonte
Campinas
PARAGUAY
Rio De Janeiro
Antofagasta
Curitiba
Sao Paulo
Asuncion
CHILE
Porto Alegre
ARGENTINA
Rosario
URUGUAY
Santiago
Buenos Aires
Montevideo
Concepcion
Neuquen
Valdivia

Comodoro Rivadavia

FALKLAND ISLANDS
Port Stanley
SOUTH GEORGIA ISLAND

NEAR AND MIDDLE EAST

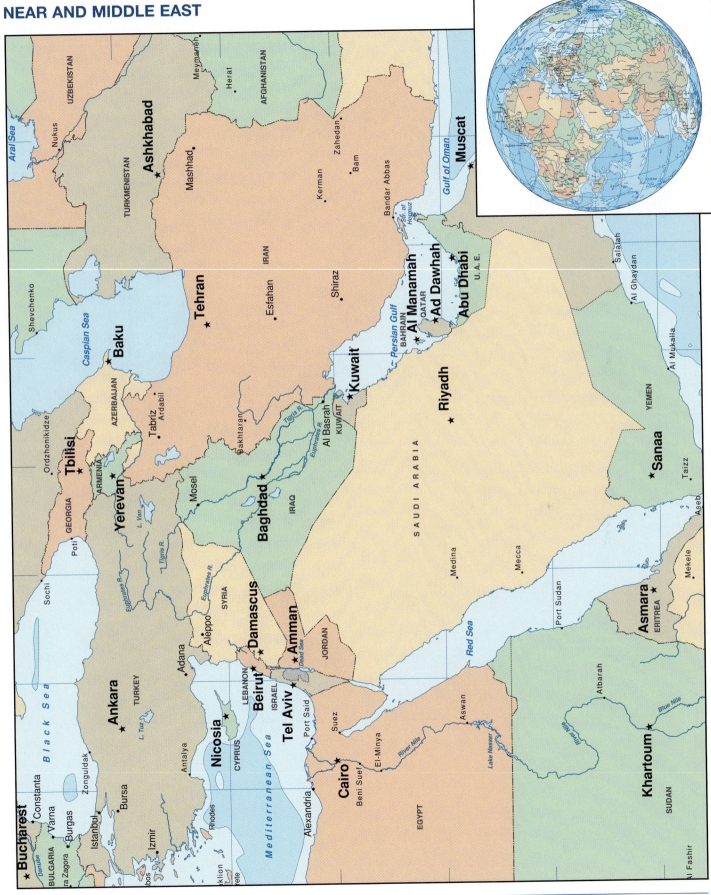

WORLD TIME ZONES

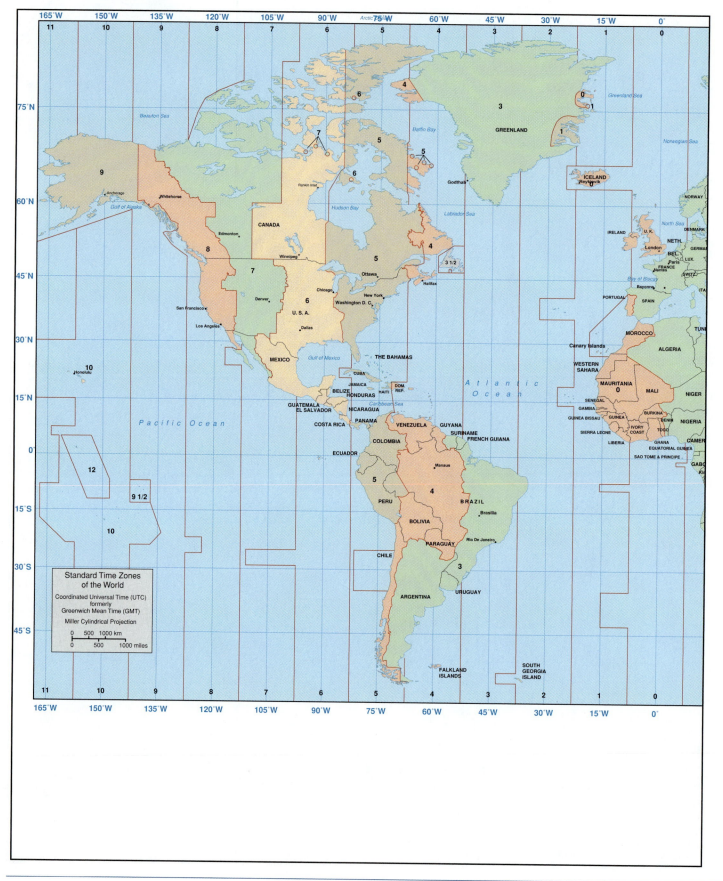

Standard Time Zones
of the World

Coordinated Universal Time (UTC)
formerly
Greenwich Mean Time (GMT)

Miller Cylindrical Projection

0   500   1000 km
0   500   1000 miles

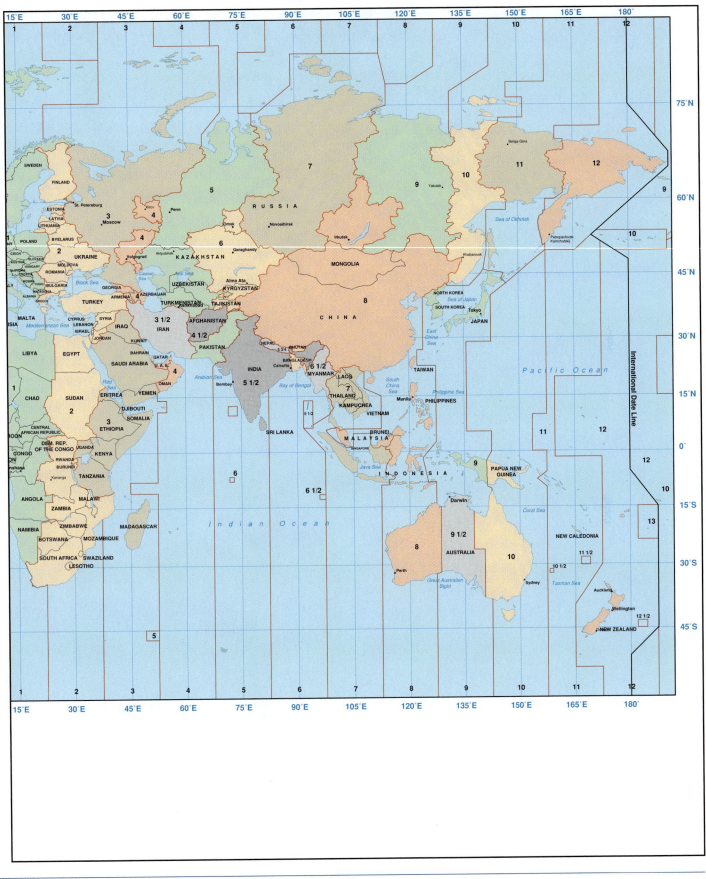

WORLD TERRAINS

ARCTIC OCEAN

Leptev Sea

Kara Sea

Barents Sea

Siberia

Sea

Baltic
Sea

North
Sea

Ural Mts.

Sea of
Okhotsk

EUROPE

Alps

Black Sea

Caucasus

Caspian Sea

Aral Sea

ASIA

Gobi Desert

L. Baykal

Sea of
Japan

Mediterranean Sea

Red Sea

Plateau of
Tibet

Himalaya

Yellow
Sea

East
China
Sea

PACIFIC

hara Desert

Arabian Sea

Bay
of
Bengal

South
China
Sea

AFRICA

INDIAN

OCEAN

Kalahari
Desert

AUSTRALIA

Victoria
Desert

OCEAN

Great Australian
Bight

Tasman Sea

GLOSSARY

A

absolute advantage 2-5 a situation that exists when a country can produce a good or service at a lower cost than other countries

account payable 7-3 amount owed to a supplier

account receivable 7-3 amount owed by a customer to a company that sells on credit

advertising 19-1 any form of paid, nonpersonal sales communication

advertising agency 19-2 a company that specializes in planning and implementing advertisements

AFL-CIO 13-1 an organization of American unions that uses its size and resources to influence legislation that affects its members

agent or broker 18-2 an intermediary that brings together buyers and sellers but does not take ownership of the products

arbitration 8-3 a method of conflict resolution that uses a neutral third party to make a binding decision

arbitrator 13-2 an unbiased third party called in to resolve problems whose decision is usually final and binding

autocratic managers 10-1 managers who centralize power and tell employees what to do

automated production 15-1 the production system in which machines perform the work

B

balance of payments 6-3 the total flow of money coming into a country minus the total flow going out

balance of trade 2-5 the difference between a country's exports and imports

balance sheet 9-3 the document that reports a company's assets, liabilities, and owner's equity

barter 7-1 the direct exchange of goods and services for other goods and services

bill of exchange 7-3 a written order by an exporter to an importer to make payment

bill of lading 6-2 a document stating the agreement between the exporter and the transportation company

body language 3-3 a type of nonverbal communication where meaning is conveyed by facial expressions, upper and lower body movements, and gestures

bond 7-3 a certificate representing money borrowed by a company over a long period of time

boycott 4-2 absolute restriction on the import of certain products from certain countries

brand 17-3 a name, symbol, or design that identifies a product

breakeven point 9-3 the number of units a business must sell to make a profit of zero

budget 9-3 a financial tool that estimates a company's funds and its plan for spending those funds

business plan 9-2 a guide used to start and operate a business

C

capital gain 20-4 the profit made from the resale of investments such as stocks, bonds, or real estate

capital project 7-3 an expensive, long-term financial activity

capitalism 2-3 the political and economic environment where a market economy exists

career 12-1 a commitment to a profession that requires continuing education and training and has a clear path for advancement

cash flow 9-3 the inflow and outflow of cash

centralization 14-2 information system in which most major decisions are made by managers at company headquarters

certificate of origin 6-2 a document that states the name of the country in which the shipped goods were produced

charter 5-1 the document granted by the state or federal government that allows a company to organize as a corporation

chief executive officer (CEO) 10-3 the highest manager within a company

civil law 8-1 a complete set of rules enacted as a single written system or code

class system 3-2 a means of dividing the members of a cultural group into various levels

closed shop 13-2 a workplace in which workers are required to join a union before they are hired

codetermination 13-1 a policy of having union members serve on the boards of directors

collective bargaining 13-1 negotiations between union workers and their employers on issues of wages, benefits, and working conditions

collectivism 3-4 the belief that the group is more important than the individual

command economy 2-3 the situation where the government or a central-planning committee regulates the amount, distribution, and price of everything produced

commercial bank 20-1 business organized to accept deposits and to make loans

commercial invoice 7-3 a certificate prepared by the exporter that provides a description of the merchandise and the terms of the sale

common law 8-1 a legal system that relies on the accumulation of decisions made in prior cases

common market 4-3 an agreement among countries that eliminates trade barriers, encourages investment, and allows workers to move freely across borders

communism 2-3 the political and economic environment where the government owns all the productive resources of the economy and a single party controls the government

comparability 14-2 the extent to which secondary data from different sources are measured, computed, and reported in the exact same ways

comparative advantage 2-5 a situation that exists when a country specializes in the production of a good or service at which it is relatively more efficient

computer-aided design (CAD) 15-1 using sophisticated computers that allow a designer to develop a very detailed design and key it to the CAM equipment specifications

computer-assisted manufacturing (CAM) 15-1 using computers to run production equipment

computer-integrated manufacturing (CIM) 15-1 using computers to guide the entire manufacturing process, from product design through processing, assembly, testing, and packaging

computerized production 15-1 using computers to control machines and perform work

consumer market 16-1 individuals and households who are the final users of goods and services

consumer price index (CPI) 2-5 the monthly United States federal government report on inflation

contexting 3-3 the level of how direct or indirect communication is

contract 8-2 a legally enforceable agreement between two or more persons either to do or not to do a certain thing or things

convenience goods 17-1 inexpensive items that require little shopping effort

cooperative 5-2 a business owned by its members and operated for their benefit

copyright 8-2 a legal right that protects the original works of authors, music composers, playwrights, artists, and publishers

corporate bond 20-3 a debt certificate issued by a multinational company or other corporate enterprise

corporation 5-1 a business that operates as a legal entity separate from any of the owners

cost and freight (C&F) 6-2 the price includes the cost of the goods and freight, but the buyer must pay for insurance separately

cost, insurance, and freight (CIF) 6-2 the cost of the goods, insurance, and freight are included in the price quoted

cost-push inflation 2-2 the situation when the expenses of a business increase

countertrade 6-3 the exchange of products or services among companies in different countries with the possibility of some currency exchange

cover letter 12-2 communicates your interest in a specific employment position

credit risk insurance 21-3 coverage for loss from nonpayment for delivered goods

credit terms 7-3 conditions of a sale on account including the time required for payment

credit union 20-1 a nonprofit, financial cooperative

cultural baggage 3-1 the idea that you carry your beliefs, values, and assumptions with you at all times

culture 1-2, 3-1 the accepted behaviors, customs, and values of a society or a system of learned, shared, unifying, and interrelated beliefs, values, and assumptions

culture shock 3-4 a normal reaction to all of the differences of another culture

currency future 7-2 a contract a person or company buys that allows the buyer the option to purchase a foreign currency sometime in the future at today's rate

customs broker 18-2 an intermediary that specializes in moving goods through the customs process

customs official 6-1 government employee authorized to collect the duties levied on imports

D

data inputs 14-1 pieces of information that feed the global information system database

database marketing 19-2 the use of computerized information systems to identify customers with specific demographic traits and buying habits

debt capital 20-1 funds obtained by borrowing

debt funds 9-3 business funds obtained by borrowing

decentralization 14-2 information system in which most major decisions are made by local managers at different company locations around the world

deductible 21-2 the portion of an insurance claim paid by the insured

degree of centralization 10-3 the amount of authority and responsibility that is delegated to employees or to an organizational unit

demand 2-2 the relationship between the amount of a good or service that consumers are willing and able to purchase and the price

demand-pull inflation 2-2 the situation when demand exceeds supply

democracy 4-1 a political system in which all people take part in making the rules that govern them

demographics 16-1 the traits of a country's population, such as birthrate, age distribution, marriage rate, gender distribution, education level, and housing situation

developing country 2-4 a country evolving from less developed to industrialized

direct barter 6-3 the exchange of goods and services between two parties with no money involved

direct distribution channel 18-2 producers sell goods and services directly to the final user

direct exporting 5-3 a company that actively seeks and conducts exporting

distribution 16-2 the activities needed to physically move and transfer ownership of goods and services from producer to consumer

distribution channel 18-2 the path taken by a good or service to get from the producer to the final user

dividends 5-1 a share of corporate earnings paid to stockholders

domestic business 1-1 making, buying, and selling goods and services within a country

dumping 18-1 the practice of selling exported products at a lower price than that asked in the company's home country

duty 4-2 a tax placed on products that are traded internationally

E

economic community 6-3 an organization of countries that bond together to allow a free flow of products

economic nationalism 4-2 a policy of restricting foreign ownership of local companies and hindering foreign imports

economic system 2-3 the method a country uses to answer the basic economic questions

economics 2-1 the study of how people choose to use limited resources to satisfy their unlimited needs and wants

electronic funds transfer (EFT) 7-3 a method of moving payments through banking computer systems

employment forecasting 11-2 estimating in advance the types and numbers of employees needed

endorsement 21-2 a certificate that adds to or changes the coverage of an insurance policy

entrepreneur 9-1 a risk taker who operates a business

equity capital 20-1 funds provided by a company's owners

equity funds 9-3 business funds obtained from the owners of the business

ethnocentric approach 11-1 the human resources approach that uses natives of the parent country of a business to fill key positions at home and abroad

ethnocentrism 3-4 the belief that one's culture is better than other cultures

Eurodollar 20-3 a U.S. dollar deposited in a bank outside of the United States and used in the money markets of Europe

exchange controls 7-2 government restrictions to regulate the amount and value of a nation's currency

exchange rate 7-1 the amount of currency of one country that can be traded for one unit of the currency of another country

expatriates 11-1 people who live and work outside their native countries

experiment 17-2 a type of data collection that involves a statistical comparison of two or more very similar situations

export management company (EMC) 18-2 a company that provides complete distribution services for businesses that desire to sell in foreign markets

export trading company (ETC) 18-2 a full-service global distribution intermediary

exports 1-2 products sold in other countries

expropriation 4-2 when a government takes control and ownership of foreign-based assets and companies

extended family 3-2 a group that consists of the parents, children, and other relatives living together

F

factors of production 2-3 the three types of resources used to produce goods and services

fixed costs 9-3 expenses that do not change as the level of production changes

floating exchange rates 7-2 system in which currency values are based on supply and demand

focus groups 17-2 a directed discussion with 8 to 12 people

foreign debt 2-5 the amount a country owes to other countries

foreign direct investment (FDI) 5-3 the purchase of land or other resources in a foreign country

foreign exchange 7-1 the process of converting the currency of one country into the currency of another country

foreign exchange market 7-2 the network of banks and other financial institutions that buy and sell different currencies

foreign exchange rate 2-5 the value of one country's money in relation to the value of the money of another country

franchise 5-3 the right to use a company name or business process in a specific way

free on board (FOB) 6-2 terms of sale that mean the selling price of the product includes the cost of loading the exported goods into transport vessels at the specified place

free-rein managers 10-1 managers who avoid the use of power

free-trade agreement 4-3 an arrangement between countries that eliminates duties and trade barriers on products traded among themselves

free-trade zone 4-3 a designated area where products can be imported duty-free

freight forwarder 6-2 a company that arranges to ship goods to customers in other countries

front-line managers 10-3 managers who oversee the day-to-day operations in specific departments

futures market 20-3 a market that allows investors and others to buy or sell contracts on the future price of commodities, metals, and financial instruments

G

geocentric approach 11-1 the human resources approach that uses the best available managers without regard for their countries of origin

global dependency 1-1 a condition that exists when items consumers need and want are created in other countries

global information system 14-1 a computer-based system that provides information about company operations around the world to managers of a multinational organization

global product 17-3 standardized item offered in the same form in all countries in which it is sold

grievance procedure 13-2 the steps that must be followed to resolve a complaint by an employee, the union, or the employer

gross domestic product (GDP) 2-5 a measure of the output of a country within its borders, including items produced with foreign resources

gross national product (GNP) 2-5 a measure of the total value of all goods and services produced by the resources of a country

gross profit 9-3 the difference between the cost of an item for a business and the price for which the business can sell that item

H

hard currency 7-2 a monetary unit that is freely converted into other currencies

home country 4-1 the country in which a multinational enterprise is headquartered

host country 4-1 the country in which a multinational enterprise is a guest

I

icons 14-1 symbols that are meaningful across cultures

imports 1-2 products bought from businesses in other countries

income statement 9-3 a document that summarizes a company's revenue from sales and its expenses over a period of time

indirect distribution channel 18-2 goods or services are sold with the use of one or more intermediaries between the producer and the consumer

indirect exporting 5-3 the selling of a company's products in a foreign market without any special activity for that purpose

individualism 3-4 the belief in the individual and his or her ability to function relatively independently

industrialized country 2-4 a country with strong business activity that is usually the result of advanced technology and a highly educated population

industry 6-4 a group of companies in the same type of business

inflation 2-2 an increase in the average prices of goods and services in a country

informational interview 12-1 a meeting with another person to gather information about a career or organization

infrastructure 2-4 a nation's transportation, communication, and utility systems

injunction 13-1 a court order that immediately stops a party from carrying out a specific action

inland marine insurance 21-3 protection from loss while shipping goods on inland waterways, railroad lines, truck lines, and airlines

insurance 21-2 planned protection for sharing economic losses among many people

insurance certificate 7-3 a certificate explaining the amount of insurance coverage for fire, theft, water, or other damage that may occur to goods in shipment

insurance policy 21-2 the legal agreement between an insurance company and the insured

intellectual property 8-2 the technical knowledge or creative work that an individual or company has developed

interest rate 7-1 the cost of using someone else's money

intermediary 18-2 any person or organization in the distribution channel that moves goods and services from the producer to the consumer

international business 1-1 all business activities needed to create, ship, and sell goods and services across national borders

International Court of Justice 8-3 a court that settles disputes between nations when both nations request that it do so and also advises the United Nations on matters of international law

international marketing 16-1 marketing activities among sellers and buyers in different countries

International Monetary Fund (IMF) 7-2 an agency that helps to promote economic cooperation by maintaining an orderly system of world trade and exchange rates

international product 17-3 a customized product adapted to the culture, tastes, and social trends of a country

inventory control 15-1 monitoring the amount of raw materials and completed goods on hand

J

job 12-1 an employment position obtained mainly for money

job description 11-2 a document that includes the job identification, job statement, job duties and responsibilities, and job specifications and requirements

joint venture 5-3 an agreement between two or more companies to share a business project

L

labor union 13-1 an organization of workers whose goals are improving members' working conditions, wages, and benefits

less-developed country (LDC) 2-4 a country with little economic wealth and an emphasis on agriculture or mining

letter of credit 7-3 a financial document issued by a bank for an importer in which the bank guarantees payment

liability 8-1 a broad legal term referring to almost every kind of responsibility, duty, or obligation

licensing 5-3 selling the right to use some intangible property for a fee or royalty

limited liability 5-1 the situation in which a business owner is only responsible for the debts of the business up to the amount invested

lines of authority 10-3 indicate who is responsible for whom and for what in an organization

liquidity 20-4 the ability to easily convert an asset into cash without a loss in value

litigation 8-3 a lawsuit brought about to enforce the rights of a person or an organization or to seek a remedy to the violation of their rights

localized advertising 19-2 the use of promotions that are customized for various target markets

locals or host-country nationals 11-1 natives of the country in which they work

lockout 13-2 the closing down of a workplace by an employer to force a union to agree to certain demands

loss leader 18-1 a very low-priced item used to attract customers to a store

M

management contract 5-3 a situation in which a company sells only its management skills in another country

managers 10-1 the people in charge of organizations and their resources

manual production 15-1 using human hands and bodies as the means of transforming resources into goods and services

market 16-1 the likely customers for a good or service in a certain geographic location

market economy 2-3 the situation where individual companies and consumers make the decisions about what, how, and for whom items will be produced

market price 2-2 the point at which supply and demand cross

market segment 16-3 a distinct subgroup of customers who share certain personal or behavioral characteristics

marketing 9-2 the business activities necessary to get goods and services from the producer to the consumer

marketing mix 16-2 the four major marketing elements of product, price, distribution, and promotion C265

marketing plan 9-2 a document that details the marketing activities of an organization

marketing research 17-2 the orderly collection and analysis of data in order to obtain information about a specific marketing concern

markup 18-1 the amount added to the cost of a product to determine the selling price

mediation 8-3 a dispute resolution method that makes use of a neutral third party

middle managers 10-3 managers who oversee the work and departments of a number of front-line managers

mixed economy 2-3 the situation with a blend between government involvement in business and private ownership

money 7-1 anything people will accept for the exchange of goods and services

monopolistic competition 6-4 a market situation with many sellers, each with a slightly different product

monopoly 6-4 a situation in which one seller controls the entire market for a product or service

most-favored nation (MFN) status 4-3 designation given to certain countries that allows their products to be imported into the granting country under the lowest customs duty rate

multinational company or corporation (MNC) 5-2 an organization that conducts business in several countries

municipal bond 20-3 a debt certificate issued by a state or local government agency

municipal corporation 5-2 an incorporated town or city organized to provide services for citizens rather than to make a profit

mutual fund 20-1 an investment company that manages a pool of funds from many investors

mutual insurance company 21-2 an insurance company owned by its policyholders

N

negligence 8-1 the failure of a responsible party to follow standards of due care

net income or profit 5-1 the difference between money taken in and expenses

nonprofit organization 5-2 groups created to provide a service and not concerned with making a profit

nonverbal communication 3-3 communication that does not involve the use of words

nuclear family 3-2 a group that consists of a parent or parents and unmarried children living at home

O

observational research 17-2 data collected by watching and recording shopping behaviors

ocean marine insurance 21-3 protection from loss while goods are being shipped overseas and while temporarily in port

oligopoly 6-4 control of an industry by a few large companies

open shop 13-2 a workplace in which workers may choose to join the union or not

operational components 14-1 the parts of an information system that manage the database and system operations

operations management 15-1 the process of designing and managing a production system

opportunity cost 2-1 the most attractive alternative given up when a choice is made

organizational chart 10-2 a drawing that shows the structure of an organization

organizational market 16-1 buyers who purchase items for resale or additional production

over-the-counter (OTC) market 20-3 a network of stockbrokers who buy and sell stocks not listed on a stock exchange

P

parent-country nationals or home-country nationals 11-1 expatriates from the country in which their company is headquartered

participative managers 10-1 managers who decentralize power and share it with employees

partnership 5-1 a business that is owned by two or more people, but is not incorporated

passport 12-2 a government document proving the bearer's citizenship in the country that issues it

patent 8-2 the grant of an exclusive right of an inventor to make, sell, and use a product or process

penetration pricing 18-1 setting a relatively low introductory price for a new product

personal selling 19-1 direct communication between sellers and potential customers

political risk 4-2 condition where government actions or political policies could change at any time so foreign companies could be adversely affected

political system 4-1 the means by which people in a society make the rules by which they live

polycentric approach 11-1 the human resources approach that uses natives of the host country to manage operations within their country and parent-country natives to manage at headquarters

premium 21-2 the cost of insurance

price 16-2 the monetary value of a product agreed upon by a buyer and a seller

primary data 14-2 data collected by the user firsthand for a specific purpose

privatization 2-3 the process of changing an industry from publicly to privately owned

product 16-2 an item (good or service) being offered for sale that satisfies consumer demand

product liability 8-1 specific responsibilities that both manufacturers and sellers have for the safety of their products

product life cycle (PLC) 17-3 the stages a good or service goes through from the time it is introduced until it is taken off the market

product line 17-1 an assortment of closely related products designed to meet the varied needs of target customers

production process 15-1 the means by which a company changes raw materials into finished goods

productivity 15-2 the amount of work that is accomplished in a unit of time

promissory note 7-3 a document that states a promise to pay a set amount by a certain date

promotion 16-2 the marketing efforts that inform and persuade customers

promotional mix 19-1 the combination of advertising, personal selling, publicity, and sales promotion used by an organization

property 8-2 everything that can be owned

property rights 8-2 exclusive rights to possess and use property and its profits, to exclude everyone else from interfering with it, and to dispose of it in any legal way

protectionism 4-2 a government policy of protecting local or domestic industries from foreign competition

psychographics 16-3 buying factors related to lifestyle and psychological influences, such as activities, interests, and opinions

publicity 19-1 any form of unpaid promotion

pull promotions 19-1 marketing efforts directed at the final users of an item

pure competition 6-4 a market situation with many sellers, each offering the same product

push promotions 19-1 marketing efforts directed at members of the distribution channel

Q

qualitative research 17-2 using open-ended interview questions to obtain comments from consumers about their attitudes and behaviors

quality circle 15-2 a small group of employees who have different jobs within the same company but have the same goal of producing a quality good or service

quality control 15-2 process of measuring goods and services against a product standard

quantitative research 17-2 large-scale surveys that collect numeric data used to study consumers

quota 4-2 a limit on the total number, quantity, or monetary amount of a product that can be imported from a given country

R

references 12-2 people who can report to a prospective employer about your abilities and work experience

regiocentric approach 11-1 the human resources approach the uses managers from various countries within the geographic regions of a business

relationship marketing 19-3 an attempt to create a long-term, mutually beneficial buyer-seller relationship

reliability 14-2 the consistency of the gathered data

repatriation 11-4 the process a person goes through when returning home and getting settled after having worked abroad

resume 12-2 a written summary of a person's education, training, work experience, and other job qualifications

retailer 18-2 a store or other business that sells directly to the final user

risk 21-1 the uncertainty of an event or outcome

robotics 15-1 the technology connected with the design, construction, and operation of robots

robots 15-1 computerized output devices that can perform difficult, repetitive, or dangerous work in industrial settings

S

sales promotion 19-1 marketing activities other than advertising, personal selling, and publicity

savings and loan association 20-1 a financial institution that traditionally specialized in savings accounts and home mortgages

scarcity 2-1 the limited resources available to satisfy the unlimited needs and wants of people

screening interview 12-2 an initial meeting to select finalists from the applicant pool for an available position

secondary data 14-2 data not collected by the user but that are available for his or her use

selection interview 12-2 a meeting where a person is asked a series of in-depth questions designed to help employers select the best person for the job

self-insurance 21-1 setting aside money to cover a potential financial loss

senior managers 10-3 managers who oversee the work and departments of a number of middle managers

shopping goods 17-1 products purchased after consumers compare brands and stores

skim pricing 18-1 setting a relatively high introductory price for a new product

small business 9-1 an independently owned and operated business that does not dominate an industry

social responsibility 4-1 the process when people function as good citizens who are sensitive to their surroundings

socialism 2-3 the political and economic system with most basic industries owned and operated by government with the government controlled by the people as a whole

soft currency 7-2 a currency that is not easy to exchange for other currencies

sole proprietorship 5-1 a business owned by one person

span of control 10-3 the number of employees that a manager supervises

specialty goods 17-1 unique products that consumers make a special effort to obtain

standardized advertising 19-2 the use of one promotional approach in all geographic regions

statutes 8-1 laws that have been enacted by a body of lawmakers

stock certificate 5-1 a document that represents ownership in a corporation

stock exchange 20-2 a location where stocks are bought and sold

stock insurance company 21-2 an insurance company owned by stockholders and operated for profit

stockbroker 20-2 a person who buys and sells stocks and other investments for customers

stockholders or shareholders 5-1 the owners of a corporation

strict liability 8-1 imposes responsibility on a manufacturer or seller for intentionally causing injury to another

strike 13-2 a refusal by employees to work in order to force an employer to agree to certain demands

subculture 3-1 a subset or part of a larger culture

supply 2-2 the relationship between the amount of a good or service that businesses are willing and able to make available and the price

supply analysis 11-2 determining if there are sufficient types and numbers of employees available

synchronized manufacturing 15-2 system where the workflow is distributed as needed throughout the production cycle

system outputs 14-1 the various types of data generated from an information system

T

tailored logistics 15-2 the system where services are combined with a product to better serve the consumers

target market 16-3 the particular market segment that a company plans to serve

tax holiday 4-3 situation where a corporation does not pay corporate income taxes to a foreign government if it invests in their country

tax-deferred income 20-3 income that will be taxed at a later date

tax-exempt income 20-3 income not subject to tax

telecommuting 9-1 using a computer and other technology to work at home instead of in a company office or factory

telemarketing 19-3 the selling of products during telephone calls to prospective customers

test market 17-2 an experimental research study that measures the likely success of a new good or service

third-country nationals 11-1 expatriates from countries other than the home country of their company or the host country

total quality control (TQC) 15-2 a work approach that requires every employee to take responsibility for high-quality production

totalitarian system 4-1 a government system in which political control is held by one person or a small group of people

trade barriers 1-2 restrictions that reduce free trade among countries

trade credit 7-3 buying or selling on account

trade deficit 6-3 the total amount a country owes to other countries as a result of importing more goods and services than the country is exporting

trade embargo 4-2 a sanction imposed by a country against another country that stops all import-export trade with that country

trademark 8-2 a distinctive name, symbol, word, picture, or combination of these that is used by a business to identify its services or products

transformation 15-1 the use of resources to create a good or service

U

union representation election 13-2 a procedure held to find out if the workers in a workplace really want to become union members

union shop 13-2 a workplace in which all workers must pay either union dues or a fee

unlimited liability 5-1 the situation in which a business owner's personal assets can be used to pay any debts of the business that are unpaid

V

validity 14-2 the extent to which the data measures what the user expects it to measure

value-added tax (VAT) 4-2 a tax assessed on the increase in value of goods from each stage of production to final consumption

variable costs 9-3 business expenses that change in proportion to the level of production

visa 12-2 a stamp of endorsement issued by a country that allows a passport holder to enter that country

W

wholesaler 18-2 a business that buys large quantities of an item and resells them to a retailer

wholly-owned subsidiary 5-3 an independent company owned by a parent company

work visa (work permit) 12-2 a document that allows a person into a foreign country for the purpose of employment

World Bank 7-2 a bank whose major function is to provide economic assistance to less-developed countries

INDEX